MW01026997

THE AMERICAN BOY'S BOOK OF SPORTS AND GAMES

THE
AMERICAN BOY'S BOOK
OF SPORTS AND GAMES

A Practical Guide to
Indoor and Outdoor Amusements

THE LYONS PRESS

Originally published in 1864 by Dick & Fitzgerald

First Lyons Press edition September 2000

Printed In Canada

Designed by White, Herrick, Wier, and Harvey; engraved by N. Orr.

10 9 8 7 6 5 4 3 2 1

The Library of Congress Catalog-in-Publication Data
is available on file.

STRENGTH, courage, and a wholesome spirit of emulation, are among the best characteristics of all really great nations; and the presence of these noble attributes in the Man depends largely upon his training as a Boy.

Though the pursuit of simple and healthy amusements may not actually *make* heroes, it may certainly cultivate and develop all the heroic elements that may be inherent.

For this reason, as well as for many others, of less vital importance, perhaps, it is believed that a complete Manual of Games and Pastimes for American Boys will now be found especially acceptable. There have been several excellent works of a similar nature published heretofore, but none of the national character in which the present volume has been conceived and executed.

While the Games of other nations are fully represented here, our

American method of playing them has been strictly adhered to in every case where it differs from the foreign way; and many purely national amusements, unknown abroad, such as Base-ball, etc., have been accorded a prominent place.

Gymnastics, as the parent of all out-door exercises, are minutely explained, so that the student of physical culture may become expert without the aid of any teacher besides this book. Among other branches of the science, the healthful and graceful art of Skating, which, through the increase of our parks and skating-ponds, is annually doubling its popularity, has not been forgotten. The same may be said of Fencing,—an accomplishment that must become universal among our young men as the military prestige of America increases. The importance of Riding, Driving, Fishing, and other manly sports, has also been duly recognized; and in these departments much valuable information is given concerning horses, dogs, pets, and fish in their proper seasons, etc.

Nor have the less exciting, though more refining occupations of in-door life been neglected in these pages. Directions for the preparation of Aquaria, the study of Experimental Chemistry, Parlor Magic, etc., combining recreation with instruction; and a host of amusing games and devices, well adapted to relieve the tedium of the long wet days, when open-air exercise is impracticable, are here given in detail, with much more matter of a kind to fascinate and delight the youth of America.

In a word, it has been the aim of the Publishers to produce, in the handsomest style, the most complete and perfect book for Boys that has ever been issued from the press.

The Illustrations with which the work abounds are in many instances from original designs, by WHITE, HERRICK, WIER, HARVEY, and other celebrated American and English artists. These have been engraved in Mr. N. ORR'S most felicitous manner, and leave nothing to be desired in the way of artistic beauty, finish, or correctness.

The letter-press is edited by a Gentleman of acknowledged literary ability, who has not forgotten that he too was once a Boy, and who, on the contrary, retains the warmest sympathy with the heart and feelings of the young.

It is but just to add, that we are indebted to the compilers of the "BOY'S OWN BOOK," "EVERY BOY'S BOOK," and the "BOY'S HANDY BOOK OF GAMES," for sundry extracts, descriptions, and hints, of which we have made use in the preparation of this volume.

CONTENTS.

PART I.

THE PLAY-GROUND; OR OUT-DOOR GAMES.

PART II.

ATHLETIC AND GRACEFUL RECREATIONS.

PART III.

AMUSEMENTS WITH PETS.

PART IV.

PLAY-ROOM GAMES FOR RAINY DAYS.

PART V.

EVENING AMUSEMENTS.

PART VI.

MECHANICAL AND MISCELLANEOUS AMUSEMENTS.

PART I

The Play-Ground:

OR,

OUT-DOOR GAMES WITH AND WITHOUT TOYS.

INCLUDING

GAMES OF ACTIVITY AND SPEED—GAMES WITH TOYS:
MARBLES, TOPS, HOOPS, KITES, ARCHERY, ETC.:
WITH CRICKET, CROQUET, BASE-BALL, AND
NUMEROUS OTHER BALL GAMES.

PLAYGROUND

GAMES

White

OUT-DOOR PLAYS AND GAMES

WITHOUT TOYS.

HOP-SCOTCH.

THIS is a game played by hopping on one foot and kicking an oyster-shell or small flat stone from one compartment to the other, without halting the lifted foot, except in one case, to the ground, and without suffering the shell to rest on any of the lines. A diagram is first drawn similar to the subjoined. It consists of thirteen compartments, twelve being numbered, and the last one having a large P, standing for plum-pudding. In commencing the game, the players take their stand at the place marked by a star, and "quoit" for innings. He who can go nearest to the P, plays first.

Method of Playing.—The winner begins by throwing his shell into No. 1; he then hops into the space, and kicks the shell out to the star *; he next throws the shell into No. 2, kicks it from 2 to No. 1, and thence out. He then throws it into No. 3, kicks it from 3 to 2, from 2 to 1, and out. He next throws it into No. 4, kicks it from 4 to 3, from 3 to 2, from 2 to 1, and out; and so he proceeds till he has passed the cross and comes to No. 7, when he is permitted to rest himself, by standing with one foot in No. 6 and the other in No. 7; but he must resume hopping before he kicks the shell home. He then passes through the beds 8, 9, 10, and 11, as he did those of 1, 2, 3, 4, 5, &c., and so on, till he gets to P, when he may rest, and placing his shell on the P, he is required, while standing on one foot, to kick it with such force as to send it through all the other beds to * at one kick. If one player throws his shell into the wrong compartment, or when he is kicking it out, he loses his innings, as he does also if the shell or his foot at any time rests on a line, or if he kicks his shell out of the diagram.

I SPY

Is a good game for the play-ground or the field. The players separate into two parties; one party must hide their eyes in a chosen base or *home* (and no peeping allowed), while the rest seek out the best hiding-places they can find. One of the hiding party waits until his companions are hidden, and then ensconces himself in some nook, crying "Whoop" as he does so, as a signal to the opposing party that they may sally forth. The object of the hidden ones is to rush out suddenly, and touch one of the opposing party, before they can retreat to the shelter of the "*home*." On the other hand, if one of the seekers can detect the lurking-place of any foe, he gives the alarm by crying—"I spy Jones!" or "I spy Robinson!" whereupon the said Jones or Robinson must come out and try to touch one of the retreating crew, who scour away home at his appearance. Every one thus touched counts *one* toward the side of the player who touched him. When all that are of one side have come out of their concealment, the opposite party take their turn at hiding; and the side which manages to touch most of the enemy's men, wins the game.

BASTE THE BEAR.

AN INSTRUMENT OF TORTURE.

The boys who are to play at this game begin by twisting their handkerchiefs into the form of whips, with a knot at the end—a thing which most boys can do uncommonly well. A boy is then fixed upon to act "Bear." He crouches down, holding a cord in his hands, while another boy, who represents his master, seizes the opposite end. The boys try to hit the bear with their pocket handkerchiefs, while the master's aim is to touch one of them, without letting go the rope, or overbalancing the bear, who, from his squatting position, is easily overturned by a jerk of the rope. The first boy touched takes the bear's place, while the late bear becomes bear-leader, and the leader joins the assailants.   This is a capital game, requiring the three qualities we like to see developed by all boys—temper, ability, and endurance.   Care must be taken, however, that the handkerchiefs are not knotted too tightly, and that the assailants are forbearing with the bear, whose position would otherwise become unbearable.

PITCH-STONE.

This game is played by two boys, each of whom takes a smooth, round pebble.   One player then throws his pebble about twenty feet before him, and the next tries to strike it with his stone, each time of striking counting as one.   If the two pebbles are near enough for the player to place one upon the other with his hand, he is at perfect liberty to do so, and it will count one for him.   It is easy enough to play at this game when the pebbles are at some distance apart; but when they lie near each other, it is very difficult to take a good aim, and yet send one's own pebble beyond the reach of the adversary's aim.   Two four-pound cannon-balls are the best objects to pitch, as they roll evenly, and do not split, as pebbles always do when they get a hard knock.   The game is ten, and whoever gets ten first, wins the game.

AMERICANS AND ENGLISH.

This is a very merry old game, and one of the simplest kind.   Two captains are named, who choose their men alternately, until all the players are divided into two equal parties.   A line is chalked or scratched on the ground, and all the players take hold of each other as represented in the engraving.   The object of each party is, by dint of judicious pulling, to draw their adversaries over the line.   This is not a mere matter of strength.   It depends in a great measure upon the skill of the leaders, who show their skill by letting their respective followers know, by a secret sign, when they are suddenly to slacken their hold, and when to give a long pull, and a strong pull, and a pull altogether.   We have seen, assisted, and led this game, hundreds of times, and never failed to find it productive of very great amusement. The game is not to be considered as won, unless the entire side has been dragged over the line.

FOX.

One player is termed Fox, and is furnished with a den, where none of the players may molest him. The other players arm themselves with twisted or knotted handkerchiefs (the ends tied in knots), and range themselves round the den waiting for the appearance of the Fox. When the Fox is ready he calls out, "Twice five is ten." The next answers, "Fox, Fox, come out of your den!" Thereupon, the Fox, being also armed with a knotted handkerchief, hops out. When he is fairly out, the other players attack him with their handkerchiefs, while he endeavors to strike one of them without putting down his other foot. If he does so, he has to run back as fast as he can, without the power of striking the other players, who baste him the whole way. If, however, he succeeds in striking one without losing his balance, the one so struck becomes Fox; and, as he has both feet down, is accordingly basted to his den.

COCK-FIGHTING.

This game, which is productive of fun, is a trial of skill between two players. It is also called "trussing." The players are made to sit down on the ground, and draw their legs up, clasping the hands together below the knees. A stick is then passed under the knees, and over the elbows of each player, as shown in the cut; and then the two players, being placed face to face, try to overbalance each other, by pushing with the points of their toes. Of course, the hands may not be unclasped; and when a combatant rolls over, he lies quite helpless, until set up again by the spectators, or by his backers. The cock who overturns his adversary twice out of three times is considered to have won the fight.

HOPPING ON THE BOTTLE.

Various games are in vogue among boys, in which hopping on one foot is the principal object. Among these is one which not only assists in strengthening the limbs, but also teaches the performers the useful art of balancing themselves upon a movable substance. A wooden bottle, a round wooden log, or something of that description, is laid upon the ground, a mark is made at a certain distance, and the players have to hop from the mark upon the bottle, and retain their possession while they count a number agreed upon. In the olden times of Greece, this was considered an exercise of sufficient importance to give it a place at the public games. The performers in this case had to hop upon inflated leather bags, carefully greased, and of course, by their inevitable upsettings and floundering, caused great amusement to the spectators. The sports took place on the Dionysia, or festivals of Bacchus, when the vintage was gathered in, and the victor was appropriately rewarded with a cask of wine.

PRISONER'S BASE.

This is a capital game. It is a war in miniature, with attack, retreat, stratagems, bold sallies, with defeat and imprisonment for the vanquished, and honor and credit for the victors. The various incidents of this game, its exciting character, and the scope it affords for the display of activity, readiness, and ingenuity, give "Prisoner's Base" an undoubted right to the first place among play-ground games, not requiring toys. It is played in the following manner:

The players should be about sixteen to twenty in number. They are divided into two parties, the men being chosen alternately by two leaders or captains, so as to make the forces as equal as possible. Two bases are then marked out side by side, one for each party, and two prisons or smaller bases opposite the first, at about twenty yards distance—the prison belonging to base No. 1 being opposite to base No. 2 (see diagram), and *vice versa*. A player now

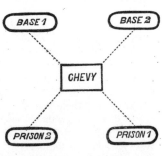

runs out from base No. 1, to the space between the bases and the prisons, and standing still, cries out, "Chevy, chevy chase, once, twice, thrice," which is considered as a challenge to the opposite party in base No. 2; one of whom, accordingly, runs out to try and touch the challenger before he can get back to his own base. If he can succeed in this, then must the person thus touched go to the prison belonging to his base, and there remain until he is rescued by one of his own party sallying forth, and touching the prisoner, if he can manage to get to him without being himself touched by one of the opposite party. If, however, "chevy chase" gets back untouched to his own home, the pursuer in his turn is followed by another from the enemy's camp, and is liable to be touched. Thus, any player may sally forth and pursue any other of the opposite party *who has left* the base before him, with the intent to touch him before he can get back to his own base; and every one so touched must go to prison, until he is released by one of his own side getting to his prison and touching him. The two leaders, who of course are the best runners, should not quit their bases except in cases of emergency, as much depends upon their generalship. When several prisoners are in prison together, they may take hold of hands; and the last only need keep his foot in the prison, the rest stretching out in a diagonal line toward their own base. This shortens the distance the rescuer has to run to release one of them. No one who quits the base for the rescue of one prisoner may attempt to rescue another, until he has first returned to his base. When all the prisoners on both sides are released, the game begins again, by a "chevy" being given in their turn by the party last challenged; and it is seldom such a challenge passes without one or more prisoners being the result. The side which manages to send all its adversaries to prison, so that none remain to rescue them, wins the game.

There is a variety of this game in which no prisoner can be rescued; once touched, he is shut out of the game, which concludes when all on one side have been thus excluded. This way of playing at "Prisoner's Base" is, of course, more expeditious than the ordinary method; but far less amusing to those players who happen to get shut out early in the campaign, and have to walk about doing nothing until the contest is decided.

KING SENIO.

This sport, the name of which is probably a corruption of "King Cæsar," . is rather a romp than a game, but it affords capital fun in cold weather. Two lines are drawn, at about seven or eight yards' distance from each other, on the ground. The players range themselves behind these lines, leaving the intermediate space clear. One of them, called the "king," stands in the vacant space. The object of the players is to run from one base to another, across this space, without being arrested by the king, who, on his part, must try to hold any one of them, while he taps him on the head, and repeats the following formula:

> "One, two, three, I crown thee;
> Now thou art in Senio's fee."

The player thus captured becomes one of the king's men, and must assist in capturing his former comrades, in their expeditions from base to base. They, on their part, may *hop* some way out of a base, and *hop* back again, on the approach of danger; but if they *run* out, or put both feet to the ground, they may not return, but must run to the opposite base, be the risk what it may. When more than half the players have been captured, a rush is sometimes made by the stronger party into the bases, to capture the remainder *en masse*, as ships in war-time used to be taken by boarding; at any rate, the game must end sooner or later in the triumph of the king, whose power goes on increasing with every fresh capture; for when a man has once been taken, there is no way of redeeming him.

KING OF THE CASTLE.

The accompanying engraving will explain what this game is like. One of the players posts himself on "ground of vantage," and the rest try to pull him down from his elevated position. Sometimes the players divide into two parties, one for attack, and the other for defence, and a good deal of fun, not unmingled with tearing of jackets, is generally the result. In this sport, which is rather a rough one, boys should be particularly careful to "fight fairly," and to keep their tempers, though they may lose the game. Fair pulls and fair pushes only, are allowed in this game; the players must not take hold of any part of the clothes of the king, and must confine their grasps to the hand, the leg, or the arm. The player who succeeds in dethroning the king, takes his place, and is subjected to the like attacks.

SIMON SAYS.

This, if well managed, is a very comical game. The players are arranged as in Drill Sergeant, the player who enacts Simon standing in front. He and all the other players clench their fists, keeping the thumb pointed upward. No player is to obey his commands unless prefaced with the words, "Simon says." Simon is himself subjected to the same rules. The game commences by Simon commanding,—"Simon says, *turn down:*" on which he turns his thumbs downward, followed by the other players. He then says, "Simon says, *turn up,*" and brings his hands back again. Or, he may say, "Simon says, wig-wag," when the whole party follow his example and twiddle their thumbs. When he has done so several times, and thinks that the players are off their guard, he merely gives the word, "Turn up," or "Turn down," or "Wig-wag," without moving his hands. Some one, if not all, is sure to obey the command, and is subject to a forfeit. Simon is also subject to a forfeit, if he tells his companions to turn down while the thumbs are already down, or *vice versa*. With a sharp player enacting Simon, the game is very spirited.

SPANISH FLY.

The first boy out, by counting, sets a back as in playing "Leap-Frog," sideways, and the others follow. Then they all leap back; and then over him in the second position of leap-frog. In this last leap, the leader leaves his cap on the boy's back, and the others must jump over without displacing the cap, until the last, who must take it with him as he leaps. If either fail to do this, the failing boy sets a back for the rest, instead of the first boy out. This game may be varied by depositing a handkerchief rolled in a ball, or by "knuckling," that is, going over with the hands clenched; or by "slapping," that is, placing one hand on the boy's back, and hitting him when going over; or in many other amusing ways. But whoever fails to do what he attempts, goes down, and becomes "back," instead of the other, who takes his place among the leapers.

FOLLOW MY LEADER.

The name of this game sufficiently indicates its nature. A quick, clever lad is chosen as "leader," and the other players have to follow him wherever he goes, to take any leap he chooses, to clamber up any steep place he has climbed; in fact, they must never desert him. The game may be made very amusing, if the leader have wit enough to set his followers such tasks as they can just manage to accomplish by dint of great exertion;—for instance, we have heard of a leader who made some of his followers, they being somewhat of the fat type of boys, crawl through the very narrow windows of an out-house, at the imminent risk of sticking in the middle, in their zeal to stick to their leader. The sailors on board ship often play at this game when they are "turned up," on a fine afternoon, to "skylark" or enjoy themselves; and Captain Marryat tells a tale of an impudent fellow of a sailor leader, who, after leading his followers a wild-goose chase all over the ship, ran off to the galley-fire, and blacked his face with the soot. All the men had to do the same thing; and as they followed their leader, shouting and laughing, he led them to the end of the mainyard, and dropped off *into the sea.* Of course it was a point of honor to follow him, and sailors are not the men to hang back in such a case; but some of them, who could not swim, were nearly drowned. The sailor was called before the captain to be reprimanded; and touching his hat very respectfully, excused himself on the ground that the men were all so dirty, he thought a little washing would do them good—whereupon the captain laughed, and said no more about the matter.

MOUNT HORSE.

This game is best played by four boys of a side; one party being the Horses, and the other the Riders. The party to be Horses are determined by tossing up, and they arrange themselves in the following manner: No. 1 stands erect with his face to the wall; No. 2 places his head against the back of No. 1, and bends his back. No. 3 does the same at the back of No. 2, and No. 4 the same at the back of No. 3. The Riders now make their leaps. The first, making a run, must endeavor to leap over Nos. 4 and 3, to the back of No. 2, and the second rider to leap over No. 4, to No. 3; the last leaping on the back of No. 4. When thus seated, it is the province of the Horses to wriggle off the Riders, or to make their feet touch the ground, without falling themselves. They must not, in wriggling, touch the ground with any part of their bodies but their feet; and if they can succeed in making the Riders touch or fall off, they become Riders; and those who touch or fall, the Horses. The leader of the Riders has no Horse to mount, the other leader standing against the wall. So he stands off, and counts twenty, or repeats the words, "Jump, little nag-tail, one, two, three," three times, adding, at the last time, "Off, off, off!" If the Riders can keep their seats while this is being done, or if any Horse gives way under the weight of the Rider, and comes to the ground, the Riders have another go. But if either of the Horses can wriggle off or throw his Rider, without himself touching the ground, except by his feet, then the Riders become Horses, and the Horses Riders. This play in England is called "Little Nag-tail." Before jumping on, the first Rider always cries out, "Warning!" or "Boot and Saddle!"

TOM TIDDLER'S GROUND.

This is a very favorite game with little boys, and may be considered as a modification of King Senio. A large base is formed by drawing a line across the play-ground, and one boy, called "Tom Tiddler," takes his station within it, while the others run in, crying out, "Here am I on Tom Tiddler's ground, picking up gold and silver." If Tom Tiddler can touch any boy while he is on his ground, the boy so touched takes his place as the guardian of the imaginary gold and silver.

TAG.

This game may be played by any number of boys. One of the players being chosen as Tag, it is his business to run about in all directions after the other players, till he can touch one, who immediately becomes Tag in his turn. Sometimes when the game is played it is held as a law that Tag shall have no power over those boys who can touch iron or wood. The players then, when out of breath, rush to the nearest iron or wood they can find, to render themselves secure. Cross-tag is sometimes played, in which, whenever another player runs between Tag and the pursued, Tag must immediately leave the one he is after to follow him. But this rather confuses, and spoils the game.

MY GRANDMOTHER'S CLOCK.

In this amusing sport the players join hands, and extend their arms to their full extent. One of the outside players remains stationary, and the others run round him as fast as they can, which proceeding is called "winding the clock." In this manner the straight line becomes a confused spiral, and all the players get huddled together in a most laughable manner. The winding of the clock usually leads to such disorder that it is next to impossible to unwind it without breaking the line of boys.

BUCK, BUCK, HOW MANY HORNS DO I HOLD UP?

This is a very good game for three boys. The first is called the Buck, the second the Frog, and the third the Umpire. The boy who plays the Buck is blindfolded, and gives a back with his head down, on some wall or paling in front of him, and his hands on his knees. The Frog now leaps on his back, and the Umpire stands at his side: the Frog now holds up one, two, three, five, or any number of fingers, and cries, "Buck, Buck, how many horns do I hold up?" The Buck then endeavors to guess the right number; if he succeeds, the Frog then becomes Buck, and in turn jumps on his back. The Umpire determines whether Buck has guessed the numbers rightly or not.

BATTLE FOR THE BANNER.

This game is to be played from a mound, the same as in the engraving of King of the Castle, and it may consist of any number of players. Each party selects a Captain, and having done this, divide themselves into Attackers and Defenders. The defending party provide themselves with a small flag, which is fixed on a staff on the top of the mound, and then arrange themselves on its side and at its base, so as to defend it from the attacks of their opponents, who advance toward the hillock, and endeavor to throw down those that oppose them. Those that are so thrown on either side, are called "dead men," and must lie quiet till the game is finished, which is concluded either when all the attacking party are dead, or the banner is carried off by one of them. The player who carries off the banner is called the Knight, and is chosen Captain for the next game.

BULL IN THE RING.

This active, merry, noisy game can be played by any number of boys, and commences by their joining hands and forming a ring, having inclosed some boy in the middle, who is the Bull. It is the Bull's part to make a rush, break through the ring, and escape, and the part of the boys who form the ring to hold their hands so fast together that he cannot break their hold. Before making a rush the Bull must cry "Boo," to give warning, so

that the boys may grasp their hands more tightly. The whole ring generally replies to the Bull's challenge by crying "Boo" all together, and a
pretty noise they make. When the Bull breaks through the ring, he is
pursued until captured, and the boy who seizes him first is "Bull" when
they return. A good "Bull" will lead them a pretty dance, clearing fences
and ditches, and if he gets back and touches some mark agreed upon, near
to where he broke through the ring, he is "Bull" again.

DRAWING THE OVEN.

Several boys seat themselves in a row, clasping each other round the
waist, thus representing a batch of loaves. Two other players then approach, representing the baker's men, who have to detach the players from
each other's hold. To attain this object, they grasp the wrists of the second
boy, and endeavor to pull him away from the boy in front of him. If they
succeed, they pass to the third, and so on until they have drawn the entire
batch. As sometimes an obstinate loaf sticks so tight to its companion, that
it is not torn away without bringing with it a handful of jacket or other part
of the clothing, the game ought not to be played by any but little boys.

KNOCK-'EM DOWN,

Is made by scooping a hole in the ground, and placing in it an upright stick;
on the top of it is placed a stone, or similar substance.
The player then retires to a distance, and flings at the stone
with clubs or balls, the latter being preferable. If the
stone falls into the hole, the player only counts one toward
game, but if it falls outside the hole, he counts two. This
is a capital game for the sea-side, and can be played upon
the sands. This is similar to a game called Baton, which
is played in this wise:

A stick is fixed in a kind of cup or hole, about six inches
over, in a loose moist soil, and the players consist of the
Keeper and Throwers. The Keeper places on the top of
the stick some article, such as an apple or orange, and the
Throwers endeavor to knock it off, by throwing at it short thick sticks, or
batons; whoever succeeds in doing this claims the prize, whenever it falls
without the hole. The Thrower will soon find, in his play, that to hit the
stick is of little importance, as from the perpendicular line of gravity which
the apple or orange will take in its descent, it is almost certain to fall in the
hole. The aim, therefore, should be to strike the object from the stick.

THE DRILL SERGEANT.

This is a game something like Follow my Leader. It consists of the
Drill Sergeant and his Squad. The Drill Sergeant places himself in a central
spot, and arranges his Squad before him in a line. He then commences
another guard here with various odd gestures, which all the Squad are bound

to imitate. He moves his head, arms, legs, hands, feet, in various directions, sometimes sneezes, coughs, weeps, laughs, and bellows, all of which the Squad are to imitate. Sometimes this is a most amusing scene, and provokes great laughter. Those who are observed to laugh, however, are immediately ordered to stand out of the line, and when half the number of players are so put out, the others are allowed to ride them three times round the play-ground, while the Drill Sergeant with a knotted handkerchief accelerates their motions.

WARNING.

This is an excellent game for cold weather. It may be played by any number of boys. In playing it "loose bounds" are made near a wall or fence, about four feet wide and twelve long. One of the boys is selected, who is called the Cock, who takes his place within the bounds; the other players are called the Chickens, who distribute themselves in various parts of the play-ground. The Cock now clasps his hands together, and cries, "Warning once, warning twice, and warning three times over; a bushel of wheat, and a bushel of rye, when the Cock crows, out jump I." He then, keeping his hands still clasped before him, runs after the other players; when he touches one, he and the player so touched immediately make for the bounds; the other players immediately try to capture them before they get there; if they succeed, they are privileged to get upon their backs and ride them home. The Cock and his Chick now come out of the bounds hand-in-hand, and try to touch some other of the players; the moment they do this they break hands, and they and the player now touched run to the bounds as before, while the other players try to overtake them, so as to secure the ride. The three now come from the bounds in the same manner, capture or touch a boy, and return. If, while trying to touch the other boys, the players when sallying from the grounds break hands before they touch any one, they may immediately be ridden, if they can be caught before they reach the bounds. Sometimes when three players have been touched the Cock is allowed to join the out party, but this is of no advantage in playing the game.

DUCK ON THE ROCK, OR DUCK-STONE.

This capital game requires at least three players, but its interest is considerably increased when there are six or eight. A large stone, called "the mammy," having a tolerably flat top, is placed on the ground, and "home" is marked off about twelve feet from it. Each player being provided with a stone about double the size of a base-ball, the game is commenced by pinking for "Duck"—that is, by all standing at the home and throwing their stones or ducks in succession at the mammy. The player whose duck falls or rolls farthest from it becomes Duck, and must place his stone on the top of the mammy. The other players are allowed to take up their ducks and go to the home unmolested, while Duck is placing his stone down; they then throw their ducks, one after the other, at it, and endeavor to knock it off the mammy. Duck must replace his stone whenever it is knocked off, and the throwers must pick up their ducks and endeavor to run home while he is so engaged. Should the duck remain on after four or five have thrown at it, the stones must rest where they fell, until some player more skilful than the others knocks off the duck, and so gives the throwers a chance of getting home. If Duck can touch one of the throwers as he is running home with his duck in his hand, the one so touched becomes Duck. When the duck is knocked off by any player, it must be instantly replaced, as Duck cannot touch any one while it is off the mammy. When a thrower's duck falls and lies before the mammy, Duck may touch him if he can, even before he picks up his duck. When Duck succeeds in touching a thrower, he must run to the mammy and quickly remove his duck; if he has time, he should tap the mammy twice with his duck, and call out, "Feign double-duck!" as he may then walk home without fear of being touched by the boy whom he has just made Duck. Should all the players have thrown without being able to knock the duck off, it is frequently proposed by some of them to Duck to take either a "heeler," a "sling," or a "jump" toward home, in order that they may have a chance of reaching it. Duck may refuse or assent to these proposals at his option. The "heeler" is performed by the player kicking his duck backward toward home; the "sling" by placing the duck on the middle of the right foot, and slinging it as far in the direction of home as possible; and the "jump" by placing the duck between the feet, and holding it in that manner while a jump is taken, the jumper letting the stone go as he alights, so that it may roll forward. If the duck is so far from home that one sling, jump, or heeler will not suffice, two or more of each may be taken, provided of course that Duck allows them. If the player does not get his duck home in the number of slings, jumps, or heelers, agreed on, he becomes Duck. Duck-stone is one of the liveliest of winter games, but we must caution our readers against playing roughly or carelessly at it, as they may through negligence do one another much harm, on account of the weight of the stones and the force with which they must be thrown.

LEAP-FROG.

This game is very simple. It consists of any number of players; but from six to eight is the most convenient number. Having by agreement or lots determined who shall give the first "back," one player so selected places himself in position, with his head inclined and his shoulders elevated, and his hands resting on his knees, at ten yards' distance from the other players; one of whom immediately runs and leaps over him—having made his leap, he sets a back at the same distance forward from the boy over whom he has just leaped. The third boy leaps over the first and second boys, and sets a "back" beyond the second; and the fourth boy leaps over the first, second, and third, and sets a "back" beyond the third, and so on till all the players are out. The game may continue for any length of time, and generally lasts till the players are tired; but the proper rule should be that all who do not go clean over should be out. Those who "make backs" should stand perfectly stiff and firm; and those who "make leaps" should not rest in their flight heavily upon the shoulders of their playmates, so as to throw them down, which is not fair play. The backs may be sideways (1), which is the first position, or with the back to the frogs (2), which is the second position. But no boy should "fudge," as it is termed, that is, stoop suddenly, as the other touches him. If he should do such a vile trick, there is danger that the boy will fall suddenly to the ground, and put out his arm, or shoulder, or otherwise injure himself.

2

FLY THE GARTER.

One boy selected by chance gives a back as in Spanish Fly. The player who gives the back must stand sideways, with one foot a little forward, near a line which has previously been drawn on the ground. This line is called the " garter." The other players have not only to vault over his back, but must alight with their heels beyond the garter or line. Any one failing to do this has to take the place of the lad who has hitherto given the back to the rest, and the game begins anew. Supposing all to have *flown* satisfactorily, the back-giver takes a jump backward from his position and offers himself again to the rest. These must now start from beyond the garter, give one spring, and then clear the back. Failing to do this, places are changed. Any one stepping on the garter, taking more than one jump, or failing to clear the back satisfactorily, must take his comrade's place, and present his back to the rest; and so the game commences *de novo*.

SEE-SAW.

A stout plank is laid over a log or low fence, and nicely balanced if the players are of the same weight; but if one is heavier than the other, the end on which he intends to sit should be the shortest. Two players then take their seats on the plank, one at each end, while a third stations himself on the middle of it, as represented in the illustration; the name of this player is in some places Jack-o'-both-sides, and in others Pudding. As the players by turns make slight springs from their toes, they are each alternately elevated and depressed, and it is the duty of Pudding to assist these movements by bearing all his weight on the foot, on the highest end of the plank, beyond the centre of the tree or wall on which it rests; this will be best understood by referring to the illustration; thus, A is the trunk of a tree, across it a plank is laid, on which two players, B, C, take their seats; D is "Pudding;" it will be seen that his left foot is beyond the centre of the trunk A, on the highest end of the board, and consequently his weight being added to that of B will depress that end of the plank, and the end on which C sits must, of course, rise; Pudding then bears on his right foot, and C in turn descends; and thus the game continues during pleasure, Pudding bearing alternately on each side.

CLIMBING TREES.

In climbing trees both the hands and feet are to be used, but the climber should never forget that it is to the hands that he has to trust. He should carefully look upward and select the branches for his hands, and the knobs and other excrescences of the trees for his feet. He should also mark the best openings for the advance of his body. He should also be particularly cautious in laying hold of withered branches, or those that have suffered decay at their junction with the body of the tree, in consequence of the growth of moss, or through the effects of wet. In descending, he should be more cautious than in ascending, and hold fast by his hands. He should rarely slide down by a branch to the ground, as distances are very ill calculated from the branches of a tree.

HOP, STEP, AND JUMP.

Make a mark on the ground at a place called the "starting point." At ten yards' distance from this make another, called the "spring." Then let the players arrange themselves at the starting point, and in succession run to the second mark called the spring. From the spring make first a *hop* on one leg, from this make a long *step*, and from the step a long *jump*. Those who go over the greatest space of ground are of course the victors.

SNOW-BALLS.

Every boy has played at snow-balls, from the time that his little fingers were first able to grasp and mould a handful of snow. Elderly gentlemen know to their cost how apt the youthful friend is to hurl very hard snow-balls, which appear to pick out the tenderest parts of his person, generally contriving to lodge just at the juncture of the chin and the comforter, or coming with a deafening squash in the very centre of his ear. Even the dread policeman does not always escape; and when he turns round, indignant at the temporary loss of his hat, he cannot recognize his assailant in the boy who is calmly whistling, as he saunters along, with both his hands in his pockets. The prudent schoolmaster will also not venture too near the playground, unless he has provided himself with an umbrella.

THE SNOW FORT.

To make a snow fort, wooden spades may be used, if the snow is loose; when, however, it cakes, heavier implements are necessary, as the weight and resistance of the blocks would soon destroy a wooden shovel. A snowball may be brought to almost any size, by first kneading a small one with the hands, for the nucleus, and then rolling it over and over, when it will gain size in its progress, until at last it can only be moved by employing the leverage of long poles. To make a snow fort, the foundations should at first be marked out, either in a square or circular form, and then clear out the snow from within, piling it upon the line of boundary to form the wall. A similar process goes on from without, and thus a good stout wall is soon produced, which must be considerably broader at the base than at the top. The size of the construction, and the plan, must necessarily depend upon the number of boys engaged in rearing it, and the supply of material in the form of snow. In a castle of ambitious construction, there should be a parapet, raised above the wall, on the top of which latter the defenders stand, to ward off the attacks of the besieging party. Loopholes should also be pierced, through which the smaller boys, hidden in the interior, harass the approaching enemy with snowballs. The height of the fort, exclusive of the parapet, should not exceed six feet, or seven at the most; and care must be taken, in piercing the loopholes, to strengthen the surrounding parts, or the attacking party may find a breach most conveniently made, through which they can enter the fortress, to the discomfiture of the defenders. The snow-balls used for the bombardment and defence must not be made too hard or too large, and all the military operations should be conducted with that good humor and love of fair play for which American boys are in general famous.

SNOW GIANT.

This is made in the same way as the snow fort, that is, by rolling large snow-balls to the place where the giant is to be erected, and then piled up and carved into form. He is not considered completed until two coals are inserted for eyes, and until he is further decorated with a pipe and an old hat. When he is quite finished, the juvenile sculptors retire to a distance, and with snow-balls endeavor to knock down their giant, with as much zest as they exhibited in building him. If a snow giant is well made, he will last until the leaves are out, the sun having but little power on so large a mass of hard snow.

COASTING.

What better sport is there than coasting down hill! Take your sled on a clear, winter day—start from the top of a long slippery hill—and—away you go—sliding, rushing along—faster and faster—your very blood dancing in your veins—now jumping over this knoll, and then over that—bouncing away to the bottom of the hill. What if your feet are cold, and your fingers too? Off of your sled quick, and trudge back again—the exercise will warm you ready for another start.

Well do I remember a good time I had years ago. It was two days before Christmas—there was a heavy fall of snow, and all of us boys, and some of the girls too, were rejoicing over the capital fun we should have as soon as it stopped snowing.

In the afternoon as we left school, one of our number, who was always prophesying about the weather, said, "See! how red it is in the west! and look, the wind is in the north—it will stop snowing before morning, and will be cold enough." "What sport we will have then!" said another who stood by; "I will have my 'Gen. Jackson,' ready to run a race with any of you!"

And sure enough, the next morning it was clear and cold, and half an hour before school we boys were at work, clearing away the snow, and making a good path on the hill just back of the school-house; before we had finished, however, the bell rang, and with red cheeks and cold fingers we rushed into the school-house out of breath.

As it was the day before Christmas, we were dismissed early in the afternoon. Once out of school, there was a rush for sleds; and boys and girls, all of us were ready for a start. We found our hill one glare of ice, with deep snow banks on both sides; we soon found out how this came. One of the boys asked permission to "go out" during the morning exercises, and had taken the opportunity to draw several buckets of water, and pour it upon the track we had opened.

Soon we were at it, "Gen. Jackson" taking the lead, followed by several larger combatants. I was ready with my long sled, seated in front steering, with two of the girls behind; all were cheering, laughing, and shouting, "out of the way, or I'll run over you!" Gen. Jackson did keep ahead; but some said, he did not start fair. We were soon back again for another start—one of our number, more adventurous than the rest, took his sled in his hands, ran a short distance, and then threw himself at full length on the seat, using his feet behind for steering when half way down the hill, and at full speed; suddenly his sled turned, and away he went head first into the snow bank, nothing left but his feet, kicking furiously in the air; he soon found his way out, with a red face and clothes covered with snow. We all laughed heartily, which so vexed him, that he left the hill and was not seen again that day; but I was as unfortunate, for soon after, when near the bottom of the hill, with my sleigh load of girls, over we went, I into a bed of snow, they here, there, and everywhere; and what a time, sleds whizzing past—boys hallooing, girls crying—all in confusion. We soon found that we were all safe, no one hurt, and all was forgotten in the excitement.

THREAD THE NEEDLE.

This game can be played by any number of boys, who must all join hands; the game is begun by the outside players at each end of the line holding the following dialogue: "How many miles to Babylon?" "Threescore and ten." "Can I get there by candle-light?" "Yes, and back again." "Then open the gates without more ado, and let the king and his men pass through." The player and the one next to him at the end of the line opposite the last speaker then elevate their joined hands as high as they can, to allow the speaker to run under, and the whole line follow him, still holding hands. This should be done, if possible, without breaking the line by letting the hands go, and is styled "threading the needle." When all the boys have passed through, the same conversation begins again, excepting that the respondent in his turn becomes the inquirer, and runs between the opposite players, the others following as before.

MODES OF PRECEDENCE.

It is usual to toss up coppers between two leaders as to who shall have first choice of men, or who shall have first "innings" or "go" at a game. In games where one has to first give "back," as in leap-frog, or go out first, as in "tag," one player repeats a jingle, touching each player in succession, as a word, or letter comes out. Whoever he touches at the last word goes out. There are a great many of these jingling rhymes. The following are some of the best known:—

> One-ery, two-ery, hickory Han,
> Phillisy, follisy, Nicholas John;
> Spinkum, spankum, winkum, wankum,
> Twiddlum, twaddlum, twenty-one.
>   O–U–T, out,
>   With a white dish-clout—out!

Heater, beater, Peter mine,
Hey Betty Martin, tiptoe fine,
Higgledy-piggledy, up the spout,
Tip him, turn him round about,
    One, two, three;
    Out goes he!

Eena, deena, dina, dust,
Cattla, weena, wina, wust,
Spin, spon, must be done,
Twiddlum, twaddlum, twenty-one;
    O–U–T—spells out,
    With the old dish-clout—
    Out, boys, out!

Aila, maila, tip-tee tee;
Dila, dila, dominee;
Oka, poka, dominoka,
    High prong tusk;
One flew east, and one flew west,
And one flew over the cuckoo's nest.

We will here close our department of *Out-door games without toys.* We have given our juvenile friends a host of amusing games to choose from, and we might have added many others, such as *Pot* and *Puss wants a corner,* but our readers will agree with us that such childish games should not be included among the sports of sturdy American boys, being at best only fit to amuse very little boys, and therefore to be considered as mere

" CHILD'S PLAY."

OUT-DOOR PLAYS AND GAMES

WITH TOYS.

MARBLES.

THE old-fashioned marbles were made by the attrition of pieces of stone against each other in a kind of mill, and were far better than many of those now in use, which are made of porcelain. When we were young the painted marbles, now a deal in vogue, were called "Chinese," and were not valued so much as others. They are generally too smooth to shoot well. Marbles then, and still are wherever marbles is much played, divided into common marbles and "alleys." Of these last a "red alley" is equal to two common marbles, a "black alley" equal to three, and a "white alley" to four. Very large marbles called "tomtrollers," are sometimes, but not often used—never in the ring games; and the very small marbles, called "peewees," are only fit for children with very small hands.

There are three ways of shooting a marble. 1, *Trolling*, which consists in projecting the marble so that it rolls along the ground, until it strikes the marble at which it is aimed; 2, *Hoisting*, where the marble is shot from at or above the level of the knee, while the party stands; and *Knuckling down*, where the player shoots with the middle knuckle of his fore-finger touching the ground, but makes his marble describe a curve in the air on its way to the ring. A boy has to be a good player, a "dabster," as they say, to knuckle down well.

2*

HOW TO HOLD YOUR MARBLE.

To shoot a marble properly, it must be held between the tip of the fore-finger and the first joint of the thumb, resting on the bend of the second finger, and propelled forward by suddenly forcing up the thumb-nail. Some boys place it between the bend of the first finger and the thumb-joint. This is called "shooting cunnethumb," and not only subjects those who do it to the ridicule of their associates, but tires the thumb very much.

Marbles is a game played in different ways. We play it in the United States different somewhat from the English, and in different parts of this country various games prevail.

The old-fashioned

LONG TAW,

Which merely consists in shooting at each other's alleys in turn, the one who hits his opponent's alley taking it as his prize, is very little played.

NINE-HOLES

Is another game not much used. A board, with nine little arches, each just large enough to admit a marble, is held by one party, while another shoots his alley at one of the holes. The shooter pays one marble for the privilege of a shot. If his marble goes through a hole, he gets the number of marbles written above that—the holes being numbered as in the cut.

TEETOTUM

Is a game of marbles. A teetotum, with figures on its sides, is set spinning, and shot at. If it be hit and knocked over while spinning, the lucky shooter gets the number of marbles set down on the upper side of the teetotum.

BOUNCE-EYE

Is an English game requiring no skill. Each player puts his marble in a ring, and then each in turn drops a marble on the pile. All they thus knock out they take. If a player's marble stays in the ring, it is lost and goes to the general stock.

THE PILE GAME

Is similar, but requires better players. Three
marbles are placed in the ring, and one set on top.
The shooters get all they knock out, but forfeit their
alley if they miss.

BOUNCE ABOUT, OR BOUNCE ALONG,

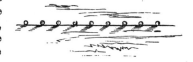

Is played with tomtrollers, and instead of shoot-
ing the marbles with finger and thumb, they are thrown by hand, and he
who hits the other's bounce being winner.

PICKING CHERRIES

(In England " Picking Plums") is
played by laying the marbles of the
players in a row, instead of a ring,
and shooting at them under the same
rules of gain and loss as in the
" Pile game."

DIE-SHOT

Is an English game. We have never seen it played
here. A marble is rubbed nearly square—at least enough
to stand firmly, and to have a flat upper surface. On
this last part an ivory die is placed. The player is to
strike the marble so that the die will fall off, paying first
one marble for his shot. If he succeeds, whatever number is uppermost on the die indicates the number of
marbles he is to receive.

THE POT GAME

Is played by making three holes, or "pots," in the ground,
about four feet apart. To determine who shoots first, one boy
takes a marble and places his hands behind his back. He then
shows his closed fists to one of the others, who guesses which
hand holds the marble. If he guesses right, the other boy goes
last, and the successful one tries with another. If he succeeds
with him, he tries another, and so on. If he fails he·is next to
last, and the one who guessed right goes before him, and takes
his place to try. For instance : four boys are to play. John
Smith takes a marble, and puts it in one hand behind his back.
He then shows both fists to Peter Brown, and asks which hand
has the marble. Peter Brown touches the right hand. The hands are

opened, and the marble is found to be in the left hand. Peter Brown is the last to play. John Smith now tries Andrew Jones. Andrew guesses the right hand, and it is found there. Now John Smith is next to last, and Andrew Jones tries Alfred Williams. Alfred guesses the left hand, and the marble was in the right hand. Consequently he falls back; and the players shoot in the following order: 1. Andrew Jones. 2. Alfred Williams. 3. John Smith. 4. Peter Brown. Andrew now knuckles down at a line six feet from the first hole, and shoots. If his marble gets into the hole, he shoots from there to the second; and if he gets into that, then into the third, and wins a marble from each of the others. If he misses, he puts his alley, or another instead, into the first hole; and Alfred takes his turn. So it goes in succession. If the player who wins the first hole chooses, he can make each of his opponents in turn put down their alleys for him to shoot at. If he hits them they are his. If he misses, the one whose alley he aimed at may shoot at his alley. If that be hit, he is out of the game, and his alley gone.

Another method of playing this game is as follows: Make three holes in the ground at about a yard and a half distance from each other. Then make a mark at a yard and a half distance from the first hole. The first player *knuckles down* at the mark and shoots his marble into the first hole if he can. If he succeed, he then takes a span toward the second hole, and shoots his marble again toward that hole, and so on. If he does not succeed, the next player tries his luck with his own marble, and if he enters the hole and his adversary's marble is near it, he may either try to knock the former player's marble away with his own or try to enter the second hole. If he succeed, he goes on again to the next, taking a span toward it as the former did, and throughout the whole game, having the privilege of knocking his adversary's marble away if he can, whenever he has first entered a hole; and when he has knocked it away, he continues from the place his marble goes to. If he miss either the marble or the hole, the first player goes on again, or if there be a third player he takes his turn in like manner, and whoever plays may, if he can, knock away all other marbles that surround either of the holes, thus rendering it more difficult for the next player to get in his marble. Whoever first gets his marble into the ninth hole wins the game. The ninth hole is reckoned thus: First, 1, 2, 3, 2, 1, 2, 3, 2, 1. So that he goes up and down the three holes twice. The loser must pay to him whatever they agree to play for. Sometimes the loser puts his knuckles on the ground at a certain distance, and allows the winner to shoot his marble at them from that distance, then from wherever the marble goes to.

TIPSHARES, OR HANDERS,

Is played by two or more players. To play it, a hole, of the diameter of three inches, is first made on a smooth or level piece of ground, and a line is marked at about seven feet from it. Each boy puts down two, three, or four marbles, as may be agreed upon, and then the whole party bowl for their throws, by retiring to three times the distance already marked from the hole, and bowling one marble to it; the order of throws being determined by the nearness that each boy's marble approaches the hole. When this is settled, the first thrower takes all the marbles in his hand, and throws them in a cluster toward the hole. If an even number falls in, such as 2, 4, 6, 8, 10, he wins all; but if an odd number falls in, he loses all, and the next player throws. Sometimes it happens that the game is so soon finished, that the other players have not a chance of a throw. When this happens, those thrown out have first innings in the next game, which restores the equilibrium of chances. This game is sometimes played by giving to the thrower all the marbles he can put into the hole, while the other players take the remainder.

SPANS AND SNOPS

Consists of one boy laying down his marble, and, giving a distance, his antagonist shoots at it; if he misses, the first boy shoots at the alley of the second, till one is struck, which the striker claims. He also gets it, if he can span the space between the two marbles, so that his thumb will rest on one and his forefinger on the other. Failing to do this, his companion shoots with his marble at that of his adversary, and thus the game goes on, a marble being paid each time a span or a snop occurs.

CONQUEROR

Is played in some places. A piece of hard ground, and free from stones, is chosen for the spot. The first player lays his marble on the ground, and the second throws his own at it with all his force, and endeavors to break it. If he succeeds, his marble counts one, and the vanquished player lays down another marble. If two players have marbles that have already vanquished others, the "Conqueror" counts all the conquered of the other party in addition to his own. For example, suppose A, being conqueror of twenty, breaks B, also a conqueror of twenty, A counts forty-one, i. e., twenty of its own, twenty for the vanquished belonging to B, and one for B itself.

FORTIFICATIONS

May be called an elaborate version of "picking cherries." The marbles are not merely ranged along a line, but disposed on a diagram, as in the illustration, and the players try to shoot them out of the limits of the fortification, not being allowed to consider a marble as won until it is quite clear of the outworks. If the taw of the attacking person remains within the fortress,

it is considered as a prisoner of war, and must remain where it is, until shot out by another player, whose booty it becomes, according to the laws and regulations of war. This "fortification" game is much played in France, and is supposed to have been recently introduced here by some young Americans, on their return to their native country, after a residence in a French college at Paris.

KNOCK OUT, OR LAG OUT,

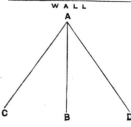

Is played by knocking marbles against a wall, or perpendicular board set up for the purpose; and the skill displayed in it depends upon the player's attention to what is called in mechanics the resolution of forces. For instance, if an object be struck against the wall at A from the mark at B, it will return again to B in a straight line; if it be sent from C to A, it will, instead of returning to C, pass off aslant to D, and its course will form the angle C D; the angle of incidence being equal to the angle of reflection.

The game is played by any number of players; the first player throws his marble against the wall, so that it may rebound and fall about a yard distant from it; the other players then, in succession, throw their marbles against the wall, in such a way as to cause them to strike any of those already lagged out, and the marble struck is considered won by the owner of the marble that strikes it, in addition to which, the winner has another throw.   When only two boys play, each successively throws out till one of the "laggers" is struck, and he who strikes takes up all.

This game may also be played by spanning the marbles, as in *Spans and Snops.*

THE RING GAME, OR RING TAW,

As they call it in England, is the great game of marbles.   The English mode is as follows: Two rings are drawn upon the ground, a small one six inches in diameter, enclosed by a larger one, six feet in diameter.   Into the small ring each player puts a marble, called "shot."   The players then proceed to any part of the large ring, and from thence, as an offing, shoot at the marbles in the centre. If a player knocks a marble out of the ring he wins it, and he is entitled to shoot again before his companions can have a shot. When all the players have shot their marbles, they shoot from the places at which their marbles rested at the last shot.   If the

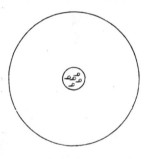

shooter's marble remain in the small circle, he is out, and has to drop a marble in the ring, and he must put in besides all the marbles he had previously won in that game.   It is a rule, also, that, when one player shoots at and strikes another's marble, the one so struck is considered dead, and its owner must give up to the striker of the taw all the marbles he may have previously won during the game.   The game is concluded when all the marbles are shot out of the ring, or all the players' marbles are killed.

In this country it is played that way in some few places.   In others it is varied.   The general way is as follows:—Instead of the outer ring, a line six feet off is drawn, and called the base.   (See illustration at beginning of marbles.)   From this the players knuckle down, unless some one prefers to hoist, when he must call out, "hoistings."   Each player puts one alley in the ring.   If the first shooter knocks any or all the marbles out they are his, and he shoots on until the ring is cleared, or he misses.   If his alley remains inside of the ring, it is "fat," that is, he loses it, and is out of the game, unless it remains after shooting out the last marble.   After any one misses, the next one may, if he chooses, shoot at the alley of the other, and if he hits it, the other is killed, and is out of the game, and his alley gone.

The player who has just killed one of his antagonists may then go to base, and shoot at the ring. If, however, he kills all his antagonists, he takes the ring marbles without shooting at them. And when any one is killed, he gives to the victor all the marbles he has won during the game, whether he got them from the ring or by killing his antagonist. If his opponent's marble has got in a hole or behind any obstacle, he may cry "puts," which will give him a right to place it in an eligible position, at the same distance, or may cry "clearance," and then remove any thing from between him and the marble. But if his antagonist cries "fen puts," or "fen clearance," before he cries "puts" or "clearance," he must shoot as it lies. And he must shoot from where his marble lies always. In some places, however, if he cries "roundings," before his antagonist cries "fen roundings," he can go around to some more eligible point at the same distance, and shoot from thence.

Another way, in vogue in some parts of the West: a ring is made, and one marble placed in the centre, and the others at points on the edge of the circle. The player may either hoist, troll, or knuckle down, as suits him. If he knocks out the centre marble at the first shot, it counts him one. If he hits one of the others he shoots on, till he has hit all, or misses. If he clears the ring it counts one, or if he kills all his antagonists it counts one. The players who follow the first may neglect the ring and follow him to shoot at his alley, and he do the same with them. Whoever counts three first wins the game.

In all these games the players "lag" for first shot. That is, they troll from base to a marble placed in the centre of the ring, and whoever gets nearest, shoots first. Whoever wins a game always shoots first in the next game.

Remember that a "taw" and "marble" are the same; but in this country the word "taw" is rarely used. Strictly speaking, it only applies to the marble a player shoots with.

" MARBLES ARE OUT."

TOPS.

Tops are very good toys—that is to say, the peg-top and whip-top. The humming-top we have always looked upon rather slightingly, as unfit for any but very little boys; for there is no skill required in its use, nor does it afford healthy exercise, or teach a boy that lesson which even in the playground he may always be advantageously learning—namely, the right way of using his wits. Peg-tops are made of various kinds of wood, beech and box being the chief. Tops of box-wood, or "boxers," as they are usually called, are much the best for all purposes, from their superior strength; and, as they are more expensive than tops made of other woods, they are generally provided with the best pegs. Every boy knows that there are two ways of spinning a peg-top—namely, *underhand* and *overhand*. The former method consists in holding the top, with the string wound round it, in the hand, with the peg downwards; and it is spun by suddenly dropping the

top, and drawing away the string with a jerk, or snatch, as it falls. This is undoubtedly the easiest way of spinning; but it is justly decried by schoolboys as a girlish and shuffling proceeding, and totally inferior in every way to the honest *overhanded* method of holding the top tightly in the hand with the peg upward, the end of the string being secured by a loop round the little finger, or a button between the third and fourth fingers, and then bringing the top down, by a bold circular movement of the arm over the head, with a force which will make it spin three times as long as by the *underhand* method. We should advise our friends in this, as in every other more important affair in life, to eschew all underhand proceedings.

WHIP-TOP

Is played by first whirling the top into motion, by turning it sharply with both hands, and then, by flogging it till its motion becomes very rapid. When two persons play Whip-top, the object should be for each to whip his top to a certain goal, he who reaches it first being the victor. Another play is for each whipper to flog his top, so that it strikes and knocks down that of his adversary; this play is called "encoun-

WHIP-TOP.

ters," as the other is denominated "racing." The best kind of thongs are those made of pliable eel-skins, and they should be used carefully, particularly in "races" and "encounters," so that the whippers may not cut each other's eyes out.

PEG-TOP.

There are many kinds of Peg-tops, and they also vary in shape, some being much rounder than others. Those are the best which are shaped like that represented in the cut. There is also great variety as regards the shape and size of the peg, which in some tops is short and thick, in others, long and tapering. Again, tops are made of different kinds of wood, some being made of beech, others of elm, some of sycamore, and others of box-wood. Some of the very best tops are made of lignum-vitæ, with long, handsome pegs. A box-wood or

PEG-TOP.

white beech top is a very good one.

In winding the top, lay one end of the string, commencing at *a*, down to the base of the peg, *b*, and then, commencing at the peg, wind it round and in the grooves, until you come to the upper part, keeping the other end of the string in your hand as you throw.

PEG IN THE RING.

This game may be played by any number of boys. A ring, about a yard in diameter, is first marked on the ground, and another ring, surrounding the first, and at a yard's distance from it, is also marked. The players must stand on this ring, and from it throw their tops. One player begins by throwing his top spinning into the ring, and while it is there spinning, the other players are at liberty to peg at it as quickly as they can. If none of them hit it until it ceases spinning, and if it rolls out of the ring, the owner is allowed to take it up, and having wound it, to peg at the others which may be still spinning in the circle. Should any of the tops, when they cease spinning, fall within the ring, they are considered dead, and are placed in the centre of the circle for the others to peg at. The player who succeeds in striking any of the tops out of the circle claims those so struck out. In some places, each player may ransom his top with a marble.

If a player does not cast his top within the ring, or attempts to take it out before it is down, or fails in spinning when he throws, in either case it is considered "dead," and must be placed in the centre of the ring for the others to peg at. There is no order in this game ; the object of the player being either to split the top of his companions, and thereby gain the peg as his trophy, or to restore them to their owners, by striking them sufficiently hard to drive them without the boundaries of the circle. Sometimes half a dozen dead tops are driven out of the ring by one cast, without any of them being damaged, and, indeed, if they be made of good box it is but rarely that they split.

Sleeping tops are exposed to much danger in the play, for they offer a fair mark to the "pegger," and often get split, when the "peg" is taken by the splitter as his trophy. Long-pegged tops are the best for the game, for as they must lie more upon their sides after their fall, and before the spinning entirely ceases, they are the more likely to spin out of the ring.

There is a way of making the top spring out of the ring directly it has touched the ground. Only long-pegged tops will execute this feat. It is done by drawing the hand sharply toward the body just as the top leaves the string. When the manœuvre is well executed, the top will drive any opponent that it strikes entirely out of the ring, while it does not remain within the dangerous circle itself for more than a few seconds.

CHIPSTONE.

This game is played by two boys in the following manner : Two lines, about six feet apart, are marked upon the ground, which ought to be smooth and hard. Some small stones are then procured and placed midway between the lines ; they should not be larger than a small bean, and the black and polished ones are the most sought after. The tops are now set up spinning on the ground, and the players, being each provided with a small wooden spoon, dexterously introduce them under the pegs of the spinning-tops, and then, with the top still spinning in the spoon, throw the point of the peg against the stone, so as to chip it out of bounds ; he who does this the soonest being the victor. While the top continues to spin he may take it up with the spoon as many times as he can, and when it spins out he must again wind up, pursuing the same plan until he "chips out."

HUMMING-TOPS

Are made hollow, having at their crown a peg, round which is wound a string; this, being pulled through a kind of fork, gives motion to the top, and sets it spinning; the fork and the string being left in the spinner's hand. In spinning the top, care should be taken in winding the string firmly and evenly on the peg, and when it is pulled out, neither too much nor too little force should be used, and a firm and steady hand should be employed, while the top should be held in a perpendicular position. The string should be drawn with a steadily increasing force, or the top will not hum properly.

HUMMING-TOP.

"TOPS ARE IN."

KITES.

KITE-FLYING is fine fun, if you have a good kite, plenty of string, and a day neither too windy nor too calm. In this country, kites are raised by boys only, but in China everybody flies his kite at the proper period; and it looks queerly to a traveller in that country to see old men with big spectacles on their noses, each seeing if his kite will soar higher than his neighbor's.

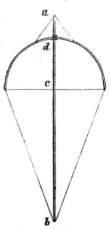

The old-fashioned bow-kite is still made by some boys. It looks well enough, but does not fly so well as the three-sticked kite. An upright, thin stick—say twenty inches long, is taken. A piece of whalebone, fifteen inches long, is bent into a bow, the string of which would be ten inches in length. The whalebone, while straight, is notched in the centre, and fastened by winding thread to the straight stick, at d, which is two inches from the top end. It is then brought down, and the string, five inches from one extremity, is wound twice around the stick, at c, which is thirteen inches from the bottom. It is then carried over, and fastened to the other end of the bow, just five inches from the centre. A string is now fastened to one end of the bow, and brought down over the lower end of the stick (b), which should have a notch to hold it, and carried up to the other end of the bow, where it is secured. At two inches from d, on the bow, a small string is fastened and carried over the top of the stick to a corresponding distance on the opposite side where it is fastened. The frame is made, and you have only to cover it with paper in the manner which we will describe, when treating about the square kite, and when dry, make a hole on each side of the stick, five inches from the top, and again five inches from the bottom, for the belly-band, and you have your kite. The bob-tail is fastened in the same way, by a string passed through near the bottom.

The size of the kite may be varied, but the proportions given should be preserved. That is, if the kite be fifteen inches long, the distance from the bow to the top should be one and a half inches, from the bow-string to the bottom nine and three-quarters, and the length of the bow-string, seven and a half inches, and so for any other length of stick.

1

2

The best kite is that made in the shape of a square (Fig. 1), with the two upper corners cut off—a six-sided figure. The skeleton of this is made of three sticks, tied together as represented in the cut. These are notched at their extremities, and through the notches a thread is laid, and brought around the sides of the figure, so as to give stability to the position of the sticks, and firmness to the kite after it is made. Having made the frame, it is laid upon paper (Fig. 2), which is cut to about an inch wider than the line of the figure, with notches at the corners, as represented by the figure.

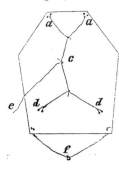

That part of the paper outside of the thread is covered with good boiled paste, the pasted part turned over the edge, and the kite set up to dry. As soon as it is dried thoroughly, the belly-band, which is constructed differently from that of the bow-kite, is put on. Holes are pierced at $d\,d$ in the paper, and a thread put through, and tied. The other end of the loop is fastened in the same way at d, on the opposite side. A similar loop is made at $a\,a$. The belly-band is tied to and between these two loops, in such a manner that it will not slip, and the kite-string (e), attached in about the centre of this at *c*. Holes are made at the lower corners and a loop attached, for the purpose of suspending the bob-tail, at *f*.

The tail of the kite may be made of one piece of paper, or cloth, a long band or strip, enough to balance the kite, and keep it from being "top-heavy;" but not too long, or it will prevent it from rising well. The bob-tail is the best kind, however. This is made by rolling up slips of paper, cut about three inches wide, or wider, according to the size of the kite, into a bob *d*, inserting them in a slip-loop (*a b*), on the tail-string, about three inches apart, as at *c*, using enough to balance the kite properly.

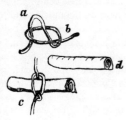

Unless there be a nice breeze stirring, the kite-flyer need not expect to have much sport, as nothing can be more vexatious than attempting to fly a kite when there is not sufficient wind for the purpose. To raise the kite, the flyer will require the aid of another boy. The owner of the kite having unwound a considerable length of string, now turns his face toward the wind and prepares for a run, while his assistant holds the kite by its lower extremity, as high as he can from the ground. At a given signal the assistant lets the kite go, and if all circumstances be favorable it will soar upward with great rapidity. With a well-constructed kite in a good breeze, the flyer need not trouble himself to run very fast nor very far, as his kite will soon find its balance and float quite steadily on the wind. The kite-flyer should be careful not to let out string too fast. When a kite pitches it is a sign that it is lop-sided, or that its tail is not long enough.

If the kite be very large, it may be raised at night, with a lantern appended to the tail. In that case, muslin is used instead of paper, to withstand the dew. A lantern may be made by hollowing out a mock-orange, or small gourd, and placing the stump of a candle in it, impaled on a sharp nail, driven in the bottom of the gourd. The string should be as thin as the kite will bear, or it will "belly" too much. On the other hand, if too thin, it is liable to be broken by the pressure of the wind on the kite. Boys sometimes send up messengers to their kites. To do this, cut a thin piece of pasteboard or stiff paper in a circular form, with a hole in the centre about the size of a dime; put the string of the kite through the hole, and the messenger will gradually and gracefully ascend, until it reaches the kite. The messenger should be about three inches in diameter.

HOOPS.

THE proper and legitimate hoop should be made of a stout ashen lath, round on the outside and flat on the inside, and should be well fastened at its point of juncture; it should be in height so as to reach midway between the youngster's elbow and shoulder, so that he may not have to stoop while striking it. The stick should be about sixteen inches long and made of tough ash; and in bowling the hoop the bowler should strike it vigorously in the centre, and in a direction horizontal with the ground. Such hoop exercise is exceedingly good, and a good run with such a hoop will warm the youth in the very coldest weather. Nothing can be more objectionable than are modern iron hoops; they are exceedingly dangerous to by-passers,

and many are the shins that have been broken, and not a few old men have been thrown down and killed by them. The practice of running them with a crooked piece of iron is also foolish, for it defeats the end of the hoop, which is to give exercise to the arm, while running gives it to the legs. The game called "encounters" can be well played with wooden hoops, but not with iron ones. It consists of two players driving their hoops against each other from long distances, the victor being he who beats the other hoop down. Sometimes a string is extended across the diameter of the hoop, and another at right angles with this, while some pieces of tin are tied loosely in the centre, to jingle as the hoop is driven.

HOOP RACE.

Any number of boys can join in this exciting sport, but they ought all to be provided with hoops as nearly equal in size as possible. At a given signal, the players all start together, and each endeavors to reach the winning-post (which may be any distant object) before his companions. He who arrives at the winning-post last is generally received with groans, hisses, and other vocal signs of disapprobation.

TURNPIKE.

Five or six boys can play at this game though only one hoop is required. Chance decides which of the players shall first take the hoop. The other players become turnpike-keepers. Each turnpike is formed of two bricks or stones, placed on the ground, and separated by about three fingers' breadth. These turnpikes are fixed at regular distances, and their number is regulated by the number of keepers. When all is ready, the first player starts his hoop, and endeavors to drive it through all the turnpikes; should he succeed in this, he turns the hoop, drives it back again, and retains it until it touches one of the turnpikes, the keeper of which now becomes hoopdriver. When a player touches the hoop with his hand, or allows it to fall, he must deliver it up to the nearest turnpike-keeper. Each keeper must stand on that side of his turnpike which is toward the right hand of the hoop-driver, and it therefore follows that he must alter his position when the hoop-driver returns. Should a keeper stand on his wrong side, the driver need not send the hoop through his turnpike. When the players are numerous, there may be two or more hoops driven at once.

THE POP-GUN.

The best pop-guns are made of a strong straight piece of elder, and should be about six inches long. The pith of this should be pierced out by an iron ramrod fitting the hole; and when the inside is thoroughly smooth by rubbing the rod up and down, it is ready for use. The pellets are made with  moistened tow—brown paper is a nasty thing to put into the mouth, and we shall never advise the use of it. When the pellet is prepared, it should be laid over the mouth of the gun in such a quantity as to require squeezing and plugging in. The first pellet should be driven through the gun to its other end; the second pellet is to be driven in, in a similar manner to the first, and then, as it is forced through the gun, the air between the pellets being incompressible beyond a certain point, forces out the lower pellet with a loud "pop;" hence the term "pop-gun," which has been applied to them. Pop-guns are not a very healthy exercise; the pressing of the rammer against the pit of the stomach frequently leading to derangement of that organ. To prevent this, the lad who plays at pop-gun should have a small round board slung over his neck by a string hanging as low as the pit of his stomach, against which he should press the handle of his ramrod when he fires off his pop-gun.

3

THE BLOW-GUN.

This is merely a long and perfectly straight tin or brass tube, through which pellets of putty are driven by the breath. Great accuracy is sometimes attained with this instrument. We knew a young naturalist who shot all the birds he stuffed with a blow-gun, bringing down a yellow-hammer or tom-tit with it, at twenty yards, as surely as with a rifle. For firing at a mark it is capital.

THE SLING.

The art of slinging, or casting of stones with a sling, is of very high antiquity. We see it represented on the Nimroud monuments, and the feat of David, in killing Goliath, is familiar to every one. In the earliest times there were bands of slingers, and probably whole regiments of them, and there is little doubt that the art of slinging was earlier than that of archery.

 In country districts, slinging of stones is a common sport; and the sling so used consists simply of a piece of leather cut into the annexad form, to which are affixed two cords, one having a loop. In using it, the leather is suffered to hang from the string downward ; the slinger places his little finger in the loop, and holds the other end in his hand, and then putting the stone in the hole of the sling at A, which prevents its falling, whirls the whole round for three or four times, to obtain a strong centrifugal force, and, suddenly letting go of that part of the sling held in his hand, the stone flies forward with inconceivable rapidity, making a twanging sound in the ear as it flies. Slinging is a very good exercise for imparting strength to the arm, but young slingers should be very careful where they send their stones, or they may do much damage.

 If any of our readers may wish to construct a better kind of sling, they may do it in the following manner:—Get a currier to cut a piece of very strong buckskin leather in this shape, the centre being cut into bars. Two long strips of the same leather are then cut of this shape,

two cuts being made along them so as to leave three leather cords. These are plaited together, and the flat ends firmly sewn to the centre piece. The shape will then be this,

A sling made on this principle will carry a stone of a pound weight. The

loop and point should be whipped with silk. The accuracy that can be obtained with such a weapon is astonishing, only the missiles should always be leaden bullets of the same weight—two or three ounces being the best average weight.

THE BOOMERANG.

This instrument is a curved piece of wood, flat on one side, and slightly rounded on the other. It is used by the natives of New South Wales, who can throw it so dexterously as to kill a man behind a tree, where he may have fled for safety. It should be held horizontally in throwing it, and cast by bringing the arm backward, and after making a variety of curves it will come back again to the person who sent it. If skilfully thrown, it may be made to go in almost any direction the thrower pleases. We do not recommend its use, however, as with an unskilful person it is very apt to come back on his own head, or hit some one standing near him.

QUOITS

A very ancient and deservedly popular game. It strengthens the arms of the player, opens the chest, and is altogether a most healthful, desirable exercise. The necessary implements consist of a number of iron rings, called *quoits,* and two iron pins, called *hobs;* these are to be obtained from almost every dealer in hardware. The game is played on a piece of level grass or turf. The two hobs are driven into the ground at a distance of sixteen or twenty yards from each other, leaving only a few inches out of the ground. There are either two players, or three playing against each other, or four playing two on each side, and throwing alternately. The players being armed with an equal number of quoits, each steps out in turn beside one of the hobs, and aims his quoits, one by one, at the other hob; his object being to throw the ring over the hob, that the quoit may form a circle round it. This, however, requires very great skill, and is rarely achieved; the next object, therefore, is to bring the quoits as near as possible to the hob. When the first player has thrown all his quoits, the second takes his turn; and when all his ammunition is expended, they walk to the second hob to compare notes. Suppose A has three quoits nearer than any of B's—he counts three points toward the game. If one of his is nearest, and then one of B's comes next, A can count only one, however much nearer his other quoits may be to the hob than the rest of B's. The nearer proximity of one quoit of B's bars all the advantages of position attained by the rest of A's. Standing at the

second hob, they cast their quoits toward the first, and thus the game continues until one or other of the players has gained the requisite number of
points to constitute him the victor. If a quoit completely encircles the hob
it counts ten points.

HOOK 'EM SNIFFEY.

This is a capital amusement, although it cannot boast of a very
euphonious name. All the *rigging*
required for *Hook 'em Sniffey*, is a
high post with an arm to it (the same
as the sign-post to a country inn), or
a tolerably high tree with one long
branch extending from it at a right
angle, a stout piece of twine from
ten to fifteen feet in length, and an
iron ring three or four inches in
diameter. In addition to these, it
is necessary to have
an iron hook which
should be driven in
the post at a suffi-
cient height from the
ground to permit the
ring to catch upon it
when swung from the
hand of the player

Fig. 1.

(see Fig. 1). The game is to try and
get the ring on the hook by standing
off at some distance from the latter,
and swinging the former *beyond it.*
Each boy is entitled to the same number of *swings*, and he who hooks the
ring the greatest number of times, wins the game. A pleasant variation to
this game may be had as follows:

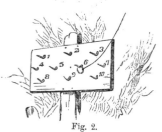

Fig. 2.

Instead of the *single* hook, substitute
a board with several hooks (say ten),
and number each from one to ten; then
fasten the board firmly to the tree or
post, at the proper height from the
ground (see Fig. 2), and all is ready to
begin the game. The boy who is skilful enough to swing the ring so that it
catches on a hook, scores as much as
the hook is numbered. Each player
has an equal number of swings, and he who scores the greatest number is

declared the victor. As at every thing else, it requires practice to become an adept at *Hook 'em Sniffey.* In our happy boyhood days we derived much pleasure from this innocent sport.

RED, WHITE, AND BLUE.

The title of this game is taken from three colored dice, which are placed upon pillars stationed at any distance from the starting point agreed upon by the players on commencing the game. Each player has three balls, which he throws at the pillars, and scores so many toward the game, according to the number the dice, when overthrown, may turn up.

THE SUCKER.

Cut a circular piece of stout leather; bore a hole through its centre; and pass a string, with a knot to prevent the end from escaping, through this hole. Soak the leather well in water before you use it; when thoroughly soaked, place the leather on a stone, and press it down with your foot, by which you exhaust or press out the air from between the leather and the stone; then holding the string, you may, by the pressure of the external air on your leather sucker, raise a considerable weight. If the sucker could act with full effect, every square inch of its surface would support about the weight of fourteen pounds. The feet of the common house-fly are provided with minute natural suckers, by aid of which the insect is enabled to run up a smooth pane of glass and walk along the ceiling.

SKIP; OR RING THE NAIL.

This game, although very simple, is very amusing. The apparatus necessary is, first, a board about eighteen inches square, with a knife or *large* nail
driven in the centre, and sixteen *smaller* nails driven in around it in regular
order; secondly, seventeen rings made of stout iron wire about two inches
in diameter. The board is placed on the ground, and the boy who plays
first takes the rings. The players then stand twenty feet from the board,

or such distance as may have been agreed upon, and pitch the rings at it the
same as in the game of quoits. Each boy tries to pitch the rings so that
they will encircle the nails, or the knife if possible, and the most skilful
pitcher wins the game. Each ring that encircles a nail counts five; if a
player is fortunate enough to ring the knife, he counts twenty The game
may be played at any number of points the players choose.

CAT AND MOUSE.

This sport, which is of French origin, is for two players only. Each
should be blindfolded, and then tied to either end of a long string, to be secured by a loose knot in the middle to a post, so that the players are enabled
to move about with facility. He who takes the part of the "mouse" scrapes
two pieces of wood (one notched) together, so as to make a grating noise,
which attracts the other player, or the "cat;" and he immediately strives
to catch his prey, by following the noise; the "mouse," at the same time,
struggling to escape being caught.

ARCHERY.

THE modern practice of archery is confined, in civilized nations, to mere amusement—and a very graceful and excellent one it is. To consider it properly, we must begin with the several implements.

THE CROSS BOW.

The Cross Bow was formerly used as a weapon of war, and the bow itself being made of a strong steel spring, it required the assistance of mechanical power to bend it; but the cross

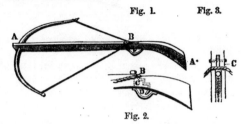

Fig. 1.   Fig. 3.

Fig. 2.

bow we recommend to our readers is not of quite so formidable a nature. The stock of the bow (A A⁎, Fig. 1) is formed something like the stock of a musket, to the extremity of this the bow is fixed; from A to B a semicircular groove is formed, in which the arrow or the bullet is placed; at B there is a step in the wood, as shown more plainly in Fig. 2, over this step the string of the bow is drawn, and there it remains until it is raised by means of the trigger. This last is constructed in various ways; in the plan represented in the engraving, the lock, if we may so call it, is formed of two pieces of brass, or hard wood; these are let into the stock, which is pierced for that purpose, as shown at C, Fig. 3; their shape is indicated by the dotted lines at C and D, Fig. 2: a pin is driven through the stock, and also through each of these pieces, so as to form two axles on which they can work. The effect of this arrangement is as follows: when the finger draws back the trigger D, its upper portion presses against the lower half of the lever C, and the upper part of that lever is consequently forced against the string of the bow, which is thus raised above the step, and being drawn forcibly forward by the bow, it carries with it the ball or the arrow.

THE BOW.

The Bow may be made of the yew-tree, laburnum, thorn, or acacia, and is generally formed of two pieces of wood joined together, the back piece being of a different wood to the front, and the grain reversed. It is of great importance to secure a good bow. We would not, therefore, advise the young archer to make one, but to buy one at a good toy shop, where they may be had at all prices. Upon making a purchase, he should examine the bow well, to observe whether it be well set in all its parts, of an elegant cut or shape, and free from flaws, knots, or cracks. He should look well at the ends, and to those points on which the bow-string is fixed, which ought to be tipped with horn. The proper length of a bow for a youth is about five feet. The flat or outward part of a bow is called its back, and the inward part its belly; and in stringing it the young archer should be particularly careful to keep the belly inward, or the bow will break.

THE STRING.

The string of the bow should be made of hemp, and whipped with sewing silk at that part of it which receives the arrow, marked C in the annexed plan. The thickness of the string should depend upon the length of the bow, and should never be too thin for its powers, as the snapping of a string sometimes causes the snapping of the bow. The young archer should never use a string in the least out of order, and should avoid cat-gut strings especially. A bow five feet long, when bent, should have a string about five inches from the centre. This will be a guide in stringing the bow. The young archer should take great pride in the care of his bow, especially of the string, and look carefully, after every day's shooting, at the "whipping" of the string, and at the wearing points, repairing the least defect. He ought also to place his bow in an oil-skin case, lined with baize; and when put away for the season it should be well rubbed with oil, and polished. He should also have always two or three spare strings in readiness, in case the one in use may fly.

THE ARROWS.

Arrows are generally made of some white wood, such as ash, deal, or the wood of the orbele poplar, and are sometimes varnished. They are both blunt and sharp. The sharp ones are for target shooting, the blunt ones principally for roving; they also vary as regards length, some being long and some short. In purchasing them, the principal thing to be attended to is, that they are perfectly straight, well made, and that the plumes are securely fitted. There should be three on each arrow; one, which is of a darker color than the rest, is called the cock-plume, and in shooting should be placed uppermost. The length and weight of the arrows should be in proportion to the size of the bow. The nicks of the arrows should be cased with horn, and they should fit the string exactly.

STRINGING THE BOW.

The young archer must be very careful in performing this feat, or he will fail in the attempt; to do so safely, he must take the bow in his right hand

by the handle, the flat part toward him; then let his arm rest against his
side, then put the lower end of the bow against the inside of his right foot,
bring his left foot forward, and place the centre of the left wrist on the
upper level of the bow below the loop of the string, the fore-finger knuckle
on one edge of the bow, and the top of the thumb upon the other; then up
with the bow and loop it.   This feat, however, can be best learned by seeing another expert person perform it.   In unstringing the bow, the short
horn should be placed on the ground against the right foot, the middle of
the bow grasped in the right hand, and the left wrist placed on the upper
horn, so that the fore-finger may unloop the string when the bow is brought
down, as in the manner of stringing it.

HOW TO DRAW THE BOW.

POSITION IN SHOOTING LONG BOW.   POSITION IN SHOOTING CROSS BOW.

The directions for drawing the bow, or rather the arrow, are as
follows: The archer having placed himself opposite to the target,
with his face a little inclined to the right, should swing himself slightly
round, so that his eye and the target are in an exact line.   He should stand
quite upright, his left foot slightly in advance.   Holding the bow horizontally
in his left hand, he should draw an arrow from his pouch and carry it under
the string and over the left side of the bow.   The fore-finger of the left
hand now holds the arrow secure on the wooden part of the bow at its centre, while the right hand fixes the nick of the arrow on the string, where it
is held fast between the first and second fingers, the cock-feather being
uppermost.   The forefinger of the left hand may now be removed from the
arrow, and the centre of the bow grasped tightly.   The bow is now raised
gradually by the left hand, at the same time that the string is pulled by the
right; and when the arrow is drawn about two-thirds of its length, the neck

3*

of it should be brought close to the right ear and the aim should be taken. The aim should be taken quickly, and the string loosened freely from the fingers with a peculiar touch, which no books can teach, and which nothing but experience and skill can give. In long shots the right hand must be lowered, and the arrow sent so as to form a greater curve in its flight. The archer should look at his *mark*, not at his shaft, and when he has shot should retreat to the leftward, and take his position behind the person with whom he is shooting.

The following apparatus will be required by the young archer:

A Shield.—This is a broad leather guard, buckled round the inside of the left arm, between the elbow and wrist. Its use is that the string may strike against it when the arrow is discharged. The sharp *twang* of the bow-string against the unprotected arm or wrist will frequently produce such bruises as to prevent the practice of archery for some time afterward.

A Glove, or rather finger-stalls for three fingers of the right hand, will be found almost indispensable. This prevents the fingers from being blistered from the friction of the string and arrow.

A Belt and Pouch.—These are buckled round the waist. The belt is made of various designs, generally of leather, with a pouch to receive the pile of the arrows. The pouch is worn on the right side; the tassel and grease-box being fixed on the left side.

A Quiver, which is generally made of japanned tin, is used to preserve the arrows from damp, &c.; also for keeping the reserve arrows in, as only three are used when shooting in company. It is only worn when roving.

Targets are made of different sizes, varying from one foot to four feet three inches, consisting of five circles. The centre, *gold*, counts nine; *red*, seven; *inner white* or *blue*, five; *black*, three; and the *outer white*, one. There should always be a pair of targets in the field, to save time and trouble. The distance for target-shooting varies. Some gentlemen shoot at sixty yards; others at eighty to one hundred yards. Ladies generally fifty and sixty yards. The young archer should practise at a short distance, and lengthen it as he progresses, commencing at twenty yards, till he is able to hit the smallest mark, which will prove he has attained command over his bow.

A graceful attitude is always requisite in shooting, which the inexperienced archer would scarcely suppose of consequence. The position (or standing), holding, nocking, drawing, and loosing are the points which require great study.

Roving is the most amusing of the various styles of shooting. A party go across country, selecting any object as a mark, at which they shoot with blunt arrows. He whose arrow is nearest to the mark is the winner.

Flight-shooting is practised to determine who can shoot furthest. Strength in drawing the bow, rather than skill, is here called into play. Care should be taken, or in your ardor to excel you may snap your bow.

Clout-shooting is shooting at a piece of pasteboard or paper stuck in a stick and placed in the ground. In the good old days of archery, we hear of archers who could split in twain a willow wand, peeled, and stuck upright in the earth as a mark; but in these degenerate times we require something more tangible.

GENERAL HINTS FOR ARCHERS.

1. In commencing archery never begin with a stiff bow, but select one adapted to your strength, and change this for a stronger from time to time.

2. Never shoot with another person's bow.

3. Never put an arrow in the string when any one stands between you and the target, or you may shoot out an eye.

4. Never talk, jibe, or jest at the time of shooting.

5. Always study to take a graceful attitude in shooting, or in moving about the field.

6. Never draw a bow near another person; as, should it snap, the danger will be greater to him than yourself.

7. Never let your bow-string get untwisted or ravelled by neglect.

8. Never exhibit impatience at the tardy efforts of your compeers, or chagrin at your own failures.

9. Never shoot alone if you can help it, as it leads to negligence and indifference.

10. Take care that the arrows are kept dry; otherwise they will twist and warp, the feathers will fall off, and they will soon be utterly useless.

11. Always walk *behind* the rest of the party, if you have to change your position during the shooting; and when you have shot, always go off to the left, so that your neighbor may step into your place readily, and take his turn. It is scarcely necessary to caution all young archers to refrain from crossing between the target and the shooters, at any time while archery practice is going on.

THE SWING.

Let no one despise this exercise. If any one can stand a twenty feet swing for half an hour, the sea may toss its worst, for he will come off unscathed. Now, we do not mean to say that merely sitting on a board and getting swung by some one else is any great object: far from it. But there are some very graceful exercises to be managed on the swing. Here are some :

1. The way to get into the swing is as follows: Take one rope in each hand, just above the seat; walk backward until the ropes are freely stretched. Now run sharply forward, letting the hands glide up the ropes as far as possible, and the instant that you feel a

Fig. 1.

check, grasp the rope tightly, and spring into the seat standing. When there, work easily up by alternately bending and straightening the knees. (See Fig. 1.)

2. When in good swing, slip the feet off the seat (which should not be more than four inches wide); let the hands slide down the ropes, and come down sitting. To recover the standing position, reach upward with the hands as high as possible, and draw yourself upward as the swing is going forward, when the seat will place itself exactly under your feet.

3. Now for some feats.

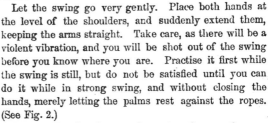

Let the swing go very gently. Place both hands at the level of the shoulders, and suddenly extend them, keeping the arms straight. Take care, as there will be a violent vibration, and you will be shot out of the swing before you know where you are. Practise it first while the swing is still, but do not be satisfied until you can do it while in strong swing, and without closing the hands, merely letting the palms rest against the ropes. (See Fig. 2.)

Swing still. Stand up on the seat, and grasp the rope with the hands as low as possible, without bending the body or the knees. Now lean forward, making your hands the pivot, and do not be astonished at finding your heels in the air,

Fig. 2.

and your head downward. To recover yourself, the body must be bent a little. (See Fig. 3.)

An old proverb says:—" A good beginning makes a good ending," and the sports of youth are no exception to this rule.

The following will teach our young friends

Fig. 3.

how to come gracefully from the swing.

To make a telling exit from the swing, two ways may be adopted. First way : Get the swing into a firm, steady movement, sit down, and bring both hands inside the ropes; and just as the swing has passed its centre, strike the seat away with the hands and you will shoot forward several yards. Take care to come down on the toes, and to lean well backward as you leave

the swing, as the impetus will bring you upright as you touch the ground. (See Fig. 4.)

The second method is, to seat yourself in the same manner, and as the swing crosses its centre backward, lean well forward and strike away the seat. You will then be hurled backward, and if your balance is good, will come to the ground in a very elegant attitude. Be sure to lean well for-

Fig. 4.

ward, cross the feet, clasp the hands, and come down on the toes. (See Fig. 5.)

Great care must be taken to lean well backward if you shoot out forward, and well forward if you shoot backward, or in the one case you will come with your nose on the ground, and in the other you will find the back of your head rather damaged. So practise with gentle swings at first, and then increase. We have often done it with the swing at full speed, and in one instance we shot so far forward that the spot was marked by a row of iron nails driven into the ground.

Fig. 5.

FIRE-BALLOONS.

The best shape for balloons of all kinds, whether large or small, is that of a globe; the lower end of the globe being somewhat opened out into a tube for air-balloons, and widened out still more or else a portion of the globe cut off, for fire-balloons. In the one case to admit the gas, in the other to allow of the fire burning beneath, without setting fire to the paper of which the balloon is made.

The best material for making a fire-balloon is common sheets of tissue paper; the length of the paper is equal to half round the balloon, supposing it to be a perfect globe; therefore supposing you want a balloon three feet in diameter when complete, the sheets of paper to make it of should be 4½ feet long, but as the lower end of the balloon is to be open, the paper will of course be shorter, so that sheets of paper four feet long would make a balloon of the above size and allow an opening below of one foot across. The length of the paper being determined, you must then decide upon the number of sections or gores which it is to have, and this should be twelve in the least; or in a large balloon there should be a much greater number, the width of each of these papers, if there are twelve of them, must be a twelfth of the circumference, which will make about 9½ inches for each, but they must be cut ten inches in the widest part because of folding over and forming the seams. The particular shape of each section is like a part of an orange-peel, cut out from the fruit, of the following shape A.

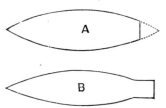

A piece at one end being supposed to be cut off. An improvement, however, is made when the sections are cut as in Fig. B, because the mouth is more open. To cut these sections of a very accurate form requires great care, and a table of decimals is often given to show the accurate length of the cross measurement of different parts, but this is not by any means' necessary for common purposes. It is quite sufficient if the sides be formed by a pair of compasses, one point of them being fixed in the distance, the other point touching the paper at the two ends and in the middle. If one of the papers, or still better if a stiffer piece of paper of full size be doubled in two down the middle, the outer mark may be made by one stroke of the compasses, and the various sections may then be easily cut out by this one pattern.

When the gores are all ready, paste about a quarter of an inch of the edge of one of them, and stick a second to it, carefully and smoothly all along the edge; this it will be difficult to do without assistance; the easiest method is to paste the edge of one section on a flat table and then to transfer it to the edge of a flat hoop of about equal circumference as the balloon; holding it there, take the second section, put it right at one end, and continue it along the hoop to the other end, when the two edges will fit each other as beautifully and cleanly as possible. When stuck together, put them aside to dry, and stick together two other sections, and so on till the whole are joined in twos. When dry join in like manner two of these, till all are joined in fours, let them dry, and join two fours, and when dry the third four, the last joint of which should be done when all the rest are dry, and by the hand without the hoop. As the sections will not be strong enough at the top, a small star of paper is to be pasted over the upper end of all the sections, a small piece of rag about the size of a half-dollar piece is put within side, and pasted down, and then let a string be drawn through the rag at the top to hold the balloon by. Next procure a light hoop which may be rather larger than the opening left at the bottom, and furnish it with two wires across, a smaller hoop and that of wire or else a wire basket being in the middle. Put the hoop in its place and paste the edges of the paper around it, then fasten by wire a piece of sponge to the centre of the hoop or basket, and the balloon will be complete. When it is to be fired, some spirits of wine is to be poured over the sponge, taking care that none of it shall touch the paper, then taking hold of the top of the balloon, move it three or four times up and down in the air, in order partly to inflate it, and thus remove the paper from around the spirit. Then very carefully light the spirits, holding the balloon up from the ground. Let it ascend till you have hold of the hoop, now let it become well inflated by the hot air, and when ready, let it gently fly away. Of course you will always regard the direction of the wind, and the position of the objects around. If the balloon is to be used in damp weather it had better be varnished, cotton and hemp are not so good as sponge to pour the spirits of wine upon, because they are apt to throw out sparks. Spirits of turpentine is not so good, because the heat is less than spirits of wine, it produces a great deal of smoke and its flame is larger, and therefore more apt to set fire to the balloon.

PARACHUTES.

These are easily made by cutting a piece of paper in a circular form, and placing threads round the edges, which may be made to converge to a point at which a cork may be placed as a balance. They ascend by the air getting under them, and are frequently blown to a great distance.

And here we conclude our list of minor out-door games and sports. Of course, many have been necessarily omitted for want of space; and many of the games here chronicled will be known to our young readers in a different form to that here described. But we have endeavored, in every case, to give the most popular, and at the same time the most simple, form of each sport; and think that, with the explanations and hints here afforded, no set of boys need ever be at a loss for the means of amusing themselves in the playground. We will now proceed to give the more difficult games, and those suited to older boys, such as foot-ball, cricket, base-ball, shinny, golf, racket, and kindred sports.

EXCELSIOR.

BALL GAMES.

CRICKET.

THIS is essentially an English game as base-ball is American, but it meets with some favor in this country, and seems to be gaining ground. It is played with single or double wicket—the latter the true game, though the principles of the game are the same in both cases. We will first consider double wicket. The number of players is twenty-two, divided into two sides of eleven each, though when the players on one side are acknowledged to be very superior, they sometimes allow their opponents to have more. One of these sides is in, and the other out, until all the players of the *in* side, except one, have been put *out* as batsmen, one after the other, by the fall of the wickets they defend, or by being *caught out* by one of the other side. The bowler is the chief personage of the *out* side, and the two batsmen are the only ones of the *in* side employed. The ten other players disperse themselves through the field in certain stations which we shall presently indicate; and here are the names of a side:

1. The bowler.
2. The wicket-keeper.
3. The long stop.
4. The point.
5. The cover point.
6. The long slip.
7. The short slip.
8. Middle wicket.
9. Long field—on side.
10. Long field—off side.
11. Leg.

The bowler, having dispersed his men through the field, has to bowl at the wicket of one of the batsmen, who, on his side, defends it, and at the same time strives to make "runs." When the ball has been struck from the bat, the batsman, if he sees a chance, must run and change places with his companion at the other wicket before the ball can be thrown up by the fielders. If he gets to the other wicket in safety, this counts as *one* run. He may sometimes make as many as five runs off a single hit; but this is about the maximum. Twos and threes are more common. The register of these runs is kept by the umpires, and each man has his runs scored against his name. The side that makes most running in two innings wins.

We will now describe the preliminary proceedings at a game of cricket, and explain the different technical terms employed. The laws or rules of the game we shall give literally according to the code laid down by the Marylebone Club, now universally looked upon as the great and chief authority in these matters, in the United States and England.

We will suppose a party of cricketers turning out for an afternoon's sport. Some carry bats, two have cricket balls, and several others bear the stumps of which the wickets are constructed. They come to the place where the wickets are to be set up, or "pitched." It is a level field, and the space between the wickets, in particular, is flat as a billiard-table. Now the bowlers advance, and under their direction the wickets are set up. The distance between the wickets, for full-grown players, is twenty-two yards; where the players are young, it is advisable somewhat to decrease the distance. The distance between the stumps must be a little less than the diameter of the cricket ball, so that the ball cannot pass between the stumps without touching them, and knocking off the bails or little bits of wood placed across the top of the stumps. The companions of the bowler are now dispersed about the field, in various positions, according to the rules we shall describe. They all labor for the same object, namely, to stop the ball when it is struck by the batsman, to catch it (if possible) before it reaches the ground after being delivered from the bat (in which case the batsman is considered *caught out,* and his innings is over), and to throw the ball up, when they have stopped it, to the bowler or wicket-keeper as quickly as possible. The bowler's desire is to knock down the batsman's wicket, while the batsman's province is to defend his wicket by striking away the ball as it is bowled toward him. Beyond this, he has to judge what balls it will be safe for him to strike hard at, and what balls he must content himself with *blocking,* or striking down; for on the number of runs he obtains will depend the share he contributes to the success of his side.

BATS, BALLS, AND STUMPS.

The bat must not exceed thirty-eight inches in length, nor be more than four inches and a quarter in the widest part. Bats are chiefly made of willow, and bound tightly round the handle with waxed twine, to afford the strikers a firm grasp, and to prevent concussion.   The weight of a full-sized bat should not exceed two pounds and a half.   The blade should be about twenty-one inches long, and four inches wide at the shoulder, gradually extending to four inches and a quarter at the tip.   It should likewise increase in thickness from the shoulder to the tip, to produce a greater momentum in striking.   The face should be perfectly smooth, slightly curved from the middle to the sidès; and the back should be more acutely rounded than the

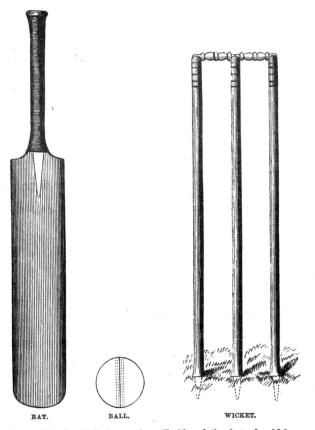

BAT.   BALL.   WICKET.

face.   For a right-handed player, the off side of the bat should be square at the tip, and the near side rounded, to prevent the ball from rising when tipped or blocked; and for a left-handed player, this should be reversed.   In making choice of a bat, never select one that is too heavy to use comfortably, with a handle that feels at all too thick when grasped, as it will be very likely to cramp the hands; but give the preference to one rather stout at the bottom of the handle or shoulder, as they are invariably the strongest.

The ball must not weigh more than five ounces and three-quarters, nor less than five ounces and a half. Its circumference must not exceed nine inches and a quarter; and it should be made of four pieces of leather sewn together so as to form two perfect hemispheres. At the beginning of each innings, when playing a match, either side is entitled to call for a new ball. When the game is over, the ball should be well greased, to preserve the stitches from rotting, and the leather from becoming rough.

The stumps must be sufficiently long to leave twenty-seven inches out of the ground. They should be made either of lance-wood or ash, bound with brass wire or strong twine, and grooved on the top, to hold the bails, each of which should be four inches long.

THE UMPIRES.

The umpires are to be appointed, one by each party, to settle all disputes that may arise in the course of the game. As their decisions are final, two persons should be selected who are distinguished for impartial judgment, and knowledge of the laws. They take their stations, one at each wicket; the umpire at the striker's wicket should stand rather behind it; at the on side, so as not to be in the way of the players; his duty is chiefly to decide whether the batsman is fairly stumped out, or not. The umpire at the bowler's wicket should place himself in a direct line behind it, to see that the bowler delivers the ball fairly, and that the batsman does not stop it when delivered straight, with any part of his dress or person before the wicket. He is likewise to be first appealed to in all questions respecting catches before wicket. The umpires in all cases should pitch fair wickets, and the parties toss up for the choice of innings. The umpires should change wickets after each party has had one innings.

THE SCORERS.

Two scorers are to be chosen, one by each side, to mark the game. They should be placed in a line with cover-point, at some distance out in the field, so as not to be in the way of the players. Each party's score is to be kept separate. Every striker's runs are to be marked separately to his name each innings; and when he is out, it must be described as bowled, caught, etc., etc., as the case may be, and the name of the person attached by whom he was put out.

All overthrows and lost balls are to be scored to the striker; and the wide balls, no balls, and byes, that occur during an innings, are each to be placed in a separate line, and cast up with the runs of the strikers when the innings is finished.

THE GROUND.

The ground selected for the game should be extensive, and as level as possible, that the progress of the ball may not be impeded. To preserve it in good condition, it will be occasionally requisite to have it rolled and watered; and if the grass can be mowed, or eaten off close by sheep, it will be found advantageous.

PITCHING THE WICKETS.

The Wickets must be pitched by the umpires, directly opposite to each other, at the distance of twenty-two yards for men, but may be varied (with the size and weight of the bat, ball, etc.) according to the strength of juvenile players. The stumps should be placed close enough to each other to prevent the ball passing through, without either striking them down, or knocking the bails off. When two matches are played by the same parties, it is usual to allow the party leaving home the privilege of pitching the first wicket within thirty yards of a spot fixed upon by their opponents.

RUN!

POPPING, BOWLING, AND RETURN CREASES.

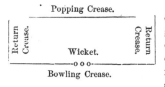

Each wicket is set up on a line, six feet eight inches in length, drawn on the ground. This line is called the bowling crease. At each end of the bowling crease two lines are carried forward at right angles to the bowling crease. These are the return creases; and in front of the wicket, parallel to the bowling crease, at a distance of four feet, runs another line, called the *popping crease*. Within this popping crease the batsman who runs from one wicket to another after the ball has been struck, must ground his bat; for until he does so, he is not home, and can be put out. The batsman must remain within this popping crease until the ball has been delivered by the bowler. The bowler must have one foot within the bounds of the bowling and return creases when he delivers the ball.

STATIONING THE MEN.

It is the bowler's business to place the men in their different stations, which is usually done according to a certain established plan. It rests with the bowler, however, to alter or modify the position of the men, and to increase or decrease the distance at which they stand from the wickets, according to the peculiarities of the play of the batsmen at the wickets. With extraordinarily hard hitters it becomes advisable to increase the distance, that the ball may not be sent skimming far away over the heads of the industrious players who are "fagging out." Where the batsman has a knack of striking the ball up high into the air, it is often well to post some player of quick eye and nimble fingers where he may have a chance of a good catch; and other changes will be made which the bowler's experience will naturally suggest.

The accompanying figure will best explain the positions of the men on the field. When six balls have been bowled at one wicket, *over* is cried, and all the players change their places to corresponding positions on the opposite side of the field to that on which they stood; for now the bowling will be from the opposite wicket. We have now to offer a few remarks to

† Long Stop.

† Long.
Slip.　† Short　† Wicket　† Leg.
　　Slip.　Keeper.
　　　Wicket.
　　　• • •

† Point.　　† Batsman.　　† UMPIRE.

† Cover.

† Middle Wicket.

　　　† Batsman.
† UMPIRE.　• • •　† Bowler.
　　Wicket.

† Long Field "off."
　　　† Long Field "on."

corresponding positions on the opposite side of the field to that on which they stood; for now the bowling will be from the opposite wicket. We have now to offer a few remarks to

THE BOWLER.

He is the most important personage in the eleven, for the time being; for it is to his prowess that the opposing batsmen are to succumb; and it falls

to him to baffle the prowess and perseverance of the batsman opposed to
him, by judicious management, patience, and skill, to put his adversaries
successively *hors de combat.* Nothing will compensate, in a match, for unskilful or careless bowling, if the batsmen on the other side are quick to
take advantage of the opportunities afforded them by their adversaries.
Two or three of the best players on each side generally divide the bowling
between them; the captain or leader of the eleven exercising his judgment
in appointing different bowlers to attack various batsmen. And this is
important, for matches have been won or lost by the way in which the
bowlers and batsmen have been pitted against each other. There are three
chief varieties in bowling, viz.: fast and slow underhand, and overhand,
which last is necessarily fast. Variety of balls, and deception to the eye
of the striker, are the great objects of every good bowler; and for this purpose a peculiar twist, or bias, is given, which is intended to make the ball,
after it touches the ground, take a different course to what is expected by the
striker. In mechanics, the angle of reflection is the same as the angle of
incidence; but at cricket the bias often prevents this, and the ball which is
expected to go clear of the wicket will often turn in to it, almost round the
bat, and take the stumps when least expected. The ball is held by the tips
of the fingers, but no description will serve to teach the mode of producing
this bias, and the young bowler must learn it by imitating the actions of a
practical master of the art, and if possible, a professed bowler. As to the
various methods of bowling, it is very difficult to pronounce an opinion, or
to give a preference, for the great professors of the art are themselves
divided in opinion on the subject. As a rule, however, it may be unhesita-
tingly said that the swift round-hand bowling is the most dangerous and
destructive to wickets in general; it is, however, the most difficult to manage, and should be well practised in private before being attempted in a
match; for, if the balls go wide, all the swiftness in the world will be of no
avail. In under-hand bowling, the wrist is kept *beneath* the arm, with the
knuckles downward. The ball must be pitched in nearer to the wicket than
in round-hand bowling, for it is generally slower than the round-hand
method, and a long, slow pitch, aimed well at the centre stump, will considerably puzzle the batsman. The bowler may deliver the ball from the right
or left side of the wicket at which he stands; and the batsman at that
wicket must stand as the bowler requires. It is usual to take a short run,
and then to deliver the ball—this increases the momentum; but too long a
run is not advisable, as it disturbs the aim.
    The bowler may not deliver the ball with the arm extended straight from
the body, nor with the back part of the hand uppermost. Changes in the
mode of bowling are perplexing to nervous and unpractised batsmen; it is
therefore desirable that the bowler should be an adept in the round-hand as
well as the under-hand style, and be able to alternate the swift style with
the slow.

THE BATSMAN.

He must stand in a firm, steady attitude, with the bat held perpendicularly, the lower end just over the "block-hole," a small hole in the popping crease, just in front of the centre stump. Then his *bat* must be before the wicket, but no part of his body may be there. He must stand fairly beside it. (See Fig. 1, page 82.) The right foot must be put down firmly just within the popping crease, and upon this foot nearly all the weight of the body must rest, that the batsman may turn in any direction to hit out at the ball. In running, take care to keep the bat out of the way of the other batsmen; and hold it in a sloping direction before you, that you may ground it quickly within the popping crease at the very earliest moment. Half a

OUT! A BAD GUARD.

second of time saved in doing this may save your wicket. On first going in, it is best to block a few balls, before attempting to strike out at any. Defer this display of your skill till your hand has got properly in by a few minutes' practice. Keep the left shoulder well up, and forward. Slope the bat-handle slightly forward, when expecting the word "play." Do not sacrifice neatness and precision to an overweening wish to be considered a hard hitter, or you may chance to carry out your bat with the fatal cypher 0 against your name in the list, to represent your score.

Now for a few words respecting the other players; and then we will give the laws or rules established for double and for single wicket.

THE WICKET-KEEPER

Should be one of the sharpest players on the side to which he belongs, for, next to the bowler's, his is the most important post. His first duty is to stop the ball when the bowler has bowled, and the batsman missed it; and, consequently, the first great art in wicket-keeping consists in judging how the ball will bound after it has been pitched toward the wicket. The wicket-keeper stands a yard or two behind the wicket, and, with his wrists close together, catches at the ball as it bounces upward; and if he does this quickly and well, he may, two or three times in the course of a match, como in for a chance of *stumping out* an incautious batsman, who is standing off his ground, by knocking down his wicket for him; but to do this, the wicket-keeper must be entirely behind the wicket, and with no part of his body projecting over it, or the batsman will not be out. To the wicket-keeper the ball is generally thrown up, while the batsmen are running, and thus it will be seen that the chance of putting one of them out depends greatly on his quickness, and on his faculty of catching quickly and securely.

SHORT SLIP AND LONG SLIP.

These two functionaries stand to the right of the wicket-keeper. A slight tip of the ball by the batsman will often send it in these directions, with a good chance of a catch. They must, therefore, be always on the alert, as a ball passing them generally tells toward the score of the opposite party, by adding several runs to their account. Long slip generally gets more of the running, and short slip more of the catching to do; therefore, these two fielders should be posted with regard to their qualifications in these respects. If the wicket-keeper quits his post to run after a ball, short slip must run in and stand at the wicket ready to have the ball thrown up to him, and to stump out the batsman, resigning his post at the wicket-keeper's return.

LEG

Stands on the left, or "on" side of the batsman at the wicket—some yards off. A "leg hit" is one in which the ball is struck sideways by the batsman, in a line with the popping crease, and it is a ball of this kind that "leg" has to stop, or catch, and from this he takes his name, and not, as a wag once facetiously suggested, because it is his duty to stop the ball with his legs if he can't do so with his hands, rather than let the other side get runs, by allowing it to go by him. Nevertheless, he ought to stop it somehow—with his head, if he cannot otherwise! It is also "leg's" duty to stop and throw up balls thrown up toward him by outlying fielders.

LONG FIELD "OFF" AND LONG FIELD "ON"

Are posted a little distance behind the bowler's wicket, and are to run after and throw up those skimming balls which are the delight of batsmen, and the bane of energetic bowlers. They must be quick, active players, able to get over ground quickly in trying circumstances; and their arms should be strong, to enable them to throw the ball well "home," when they have stopped it.

MIDDLE WICKET

Stands on the "off" or right side of the batsman. It will be seen by the diagram that he is placed not quite midway between the wickets, but rather nearer to the bowler's. This is because balls struck in a peculiar way by the batsman often pitch just to the point where he is posted, giving him a chance of a catch, of which he ought to be always ready to avail himself. His post is the next in importance after that of the wicket-keeper.

COVER

Stands not far from middle wicket, but nearer to the striker's wicket. His duties are similar to those of middle wicket, but his post is less important, as, in the ordinary course of cricketing events, he gets fewer chances. It will be seen that the field is more closely watched on the "off" than on the "on" side. This is because, in ordinary playing, the batsman is far more likely to hit the ball in an "off" than in an "on" direction.

POINT

Stands not far from the striker's wicket on the "off" side, and stops the balls hit almost sideways from the wicket on his side. He has likewise to see that he misses no chance of a catch from a ball blocked by the batsman. A good catcher, with a very quick eye and hand, should be placed at this post.

LONG STOP

Stands behind the wicket-keeper, and has to stop all the balls the latter allows to pass. Of course, he must be posted nearer to or farther from the wicket, according as the bowling is fast or slow.

It is general, moreover, to appoint two umpires, one for each side, who take up their positions near the wickets, and to whom every question that may arise during the match is to be referred. Their decision is to be accounted final, and no good cricketer would think of appealing from it, however much it may be at variance with his own opinion. It is the umpire's duty also to see that the rules are properly observed, and that every thing is carried on in good cricketing style. If the bowler, for example, raises his hand above the shoulder in delivering the ball, it is for the umpire nearest him to call "no ball." If the batsmen, in running, fail to ground their bats properly within the popping creases, it is his duty to disallow the run. He also decides when a ball, passing the striker at undue distance, is to be considered as "wide."

4

It is as well to arrange beforehand the turns in which the batsmen are to go in on each side for their innings. Care should, however, be taken not to put any player of extraordinary merit too near the bottom of the list, or it may happen that all his comrades' wickets being put down, he may have to carry out his bat, for want of a companion to stand at the opposite wicket, and thus his side will lose part of the score he might be reasonably expected to make. On the other hand, it is only courteous to see that the player who has been obliged to go out for want of a companion, in the first innings of the match, should go in earlier in the list in the second, so that one, at least, of his innings may be complete.

THE RULES OF THE GAME OF CRICKET.

The following Rules have been taken from those issued in a modified form by the Marylebone Club. Some alterations, which were thought necessary, have been made, and the forty-seven rules of the club have become forty-nine; not by the addition of new rules but by the subdivision of one into two in two instances.

1. The *Ball* must not weigh less than five ounces and a half, nor more than five ounces and three-quarters. It must measure not less than nine inches, nor more than nine inches and one-quarter in circumference.

2. The *Bat* must not exceed four inches and one-quarter in the widest part; it must not be more than thirty-eight inches in length.

3. The *Stumps* must be three in number, twenty-seven inches out of the ground; the bails eight inches in length; the stumps of sufficient thickness to prevent the ball from passing through.

4. The *Bowling Crease* must be in a line with the stumps; six feet eight inches in length, the stumps in the centre, with a return crease at each end toward the bowler at right angles.

5. The *Popping Crease* must be four feet from the wicket, and paralleled to it; unlimited in length, but not shorter than the bowling crease.

6. The *Wickets* must be pitched opposite to each other, at the distance of twenty-two yards.

7. It shall not be lawful for either party during a match, without the consent of the other, to alter the ground by rolling, watering, covering, mowing, or beating, except at the commencement of each innings, when the ground may be swept and rolled; such request to be made to one of the umpires within one minute after the conclusion of the former innings. This rule does not prevent the striker from beating the ground with his bat near to the spot where he stands during the innings, nor the bowler from filling up holes with sawdust, &c., when the ground is wet.

8. After rain the wickets may be changed with the consent of both parties.

9. The *Bowler* shall deliver the ball with one foot on the ground behind the bowling crease, and within the return crease, and shall bowl four balls each over.

10. The ball must be bowled, not thrown or jerked, and the hand must not be above the shoulder in delivery; and whenever the bowler shall so closely infringe on this rule as to make it difficult for the umpire to judge whether the ball has been delivered within the true intent and meaning of this rule or not, the umpire shall call "no ball."

11. He may require the striker at the wicket from which he is bowling to stand on that side of it he may direct.

12. If the bowler shall toss the ball over the striker's head, or bowl it so wide that in the opinion of the umpire it shall not be fairly within the reach of the batsman, he shall adjudge one run to the parties receiving the innings, either with or without an appeal, which shall be put down to the score of wide balls; such ball shall not be reckoned as one of the four balls; but if the batsman shall by any means bring himself within reach of the ball, the run shall not be adjudged.

13. If the bowler deliver a "no ball," or a "wide ball," the striker shall be allowed as many runs as he can get, and he shall not be put out except by running out. In the event of no run being obtained by any other means, then one run shall be added to the score of "no balls" or "wide balls," as the case may be. All runs obtained for "wide balls" to be scored to "wide balls." The names of the bowlers who bowl "wide balls" or "no balls," in future to be placed on the score, to show the parties by whom either score is made.

14. At the beginning of each innings the umpire shall call "play." From that time to the end of each innings no trial ball shall be allowed to any bowler.

15. The *Striker is out* if either of the bails be bowled off, or if a stump be bowled out of the ground.

16. Or, if the ball from the stroke of the bat or hand, but not the wrist, be held before it touch the ground, although it be hugged to the body of the catcher.

17. Or, if in striking, or at any other time while the ball shall be in play, both his feet shall be over the popping crease, and his wicket put down, except his bat be grounded within it.

18. Or, if in striking at the ball he hit down his wicket.

19. Or, if under pretence of running, or otherwise, either of the strikers prevent a ball from being caught, the striker of the ball is out.

20. Or, if the ball be struck and he wilfully strike it again.

21. Or, if in running the wicket be struck down by a throw, or by the hand or arm (with ball in hand), before his bat (in hand) or some part of his person be grounded over the popping crease. But if both the bails be off, a stump must be struck out of the ground.

22. Or, if any part of the striker's dress knock down the wicket.

23. Or, if the striker touch or take up the ball while in play, unless at the request of the opposite party.

24. Or, if with any part of his person he stop the ball, which, in the opinion of the umpire at the bowler's wicket, shall have been pitched in a straight line from it to the striker's wicket, and would have hit it.

25. If the players have crossed each other, he that runs for the wicket which is put down is out.

26. A ball being caught, no run shall be reckoned.

27. A striker being run out, that run which he and his partner were attempting shall not be reckoned.

28. If a lost ball be called, the striker shall be allowed six runs; but if more than six shall have been run before "lost ball" shall have been called, then the striker shall have all which have been run.

29. After the ball shall have been finally settled in the wicket-keeper's or bowler's hand, or shall have passed through the hands of the wicket-keeper for the bowler to resume bowling, it shall be considered dead; but when the bowler is about to deliver the ball, if the striker at his wicket go outside the popping crease before such actual delivery, the said bowler may put him out, unless (with reference to the 21st law) his bat in hand, or some part of his person, be within the popping crease.

30. If the striker be hurt, he may retire from his wicket, and return to it at any time during that innings.

31. If the striker be hurt, some other person may stand out for him, but not go in.

32. No substitute in the field shall be allowed to bowl, keep wicket, stand at the point, cover the point, or stop behind in any case.

33. If any fieldsman stop the ball with his hat, the ball shall be considered dead, and the opposite party shall add five runs to their score; if any be run, they shall have five in all.

34. The ball having been hit, the striker may guard his wicket with his bat, or with any part of his body except his hands; that the 23d law may not be disobeyed.

35. The wicket-keeper shall not take the ball for the purpose of stumping, until it has passed the wicket; he shall not move till the ball be out of the bowler's hand; he shall not by any noise incommode the striker; and if any part of his person be over or before the wicket, although the ball hit it, the striker[3] shall not be out.

36. The umpires are sole judges of fair or unfair play; and all disputes shall be determined by them, each at his own wicket; but in case of a catch which the umpire at the wicket bowled from cannot see sufficiently to decide upon, he may apply to the other umpire, whose opinion shall be conclusive.

37. The umpires in all matches shall pitch fair wickets, and the parties shall toss up for the choice of innings. The umpires shall change wickets after each party has had one innings.

38. They shall allow two minutes for each striker to come in, and ten

minutes between each innings. When the umpires shall call "play," the party refusing to play shall lose the match.

39. They are not to order a striker out unless appealed to by the adversaries.

40. But if any one of the bowler's feet be not on the ground behind the bowling crease, and within the return crease when he shall deliver the ball, the umpire at his wicket, unasked, must call "no ball."

41. If either of the strikers run a short run, the umpire must call "one short."

42. No umpire shall be allowed to bet.

43. No umpire is to be changed during a match, unless with the consent of both parties, except in case of a violation of the 42d law; then either party may dismiss the transgressor.

44. After the delivery of four balls, the umpire must call "over," but not until the ball shall be finally settled in the wicket-keeper's or bowler's hand; the ball shall then be considered dead; nevertheless, if an idea be entertained that either of the strikers is out, a question may be put previously to, but not after, the delivery of the next ball.

45. The umpire must take especial care to call "no ball" instantly upon delivery; "wide ball" as soon as ever it shall pass the striker.

46. The players who go in second shall follow their innings, if they have obtained one hundred runs less than their antagonists.

47. When one of the strikers shall have been put out, the use of the bat shall not be allowed to any person, until the next striker shall come in.

48. At the beginning of each innings, either party may call for a new ball.

49. No bowler shall be allowed to change wickets more than once during the innings.

It is usual for wicket-keeper and bowler to come provided with thick leather gauntlets, to protect the hands; the wicket-keeper especially, who has to stop the bowler's swift balls, will find his gauntlets any thing but useless appendages. Pads for the legs are also worn, and will save a good deal of bruising. Light flannel suits, like those worn by pupils practising gymnastics, are best for cricketing. Shoes with spiked soles, to prevent the players from slipping on the smooth turf are also used.

SINGLE WICKET.

The game of Single Wicket is a substitute for the more legitimate Double Wicket game, when the number of players will not suffice to play in the regular match fashion. The batsman has a stump set in the ground, to which he must run, and then back to his popping crease, as there is, of course, no companion to run with him. The wicket-keeper is generally dispensed with altogether; so that three or four scouts, with the bowler and batsman, are enough to play the game. When the players are very few, they sometimes play "all against each other"—each one taking the bat in turn, and playing to get runs on his own account; he who scores most during two innings being considered the victor. Hits behind wicket do not count, when there are less than five players on a side. As single wicket is frequently played for practice, it is well to let each man change his position as often as convenient, that they may learn something of each separate operation of the cricket-field; the bowler of one innings being the long-stop of the next, the *point* of the third, &c. And here we must be allowed to give our young readers a very emphatic caution to avoid the bane of the cricketer, namely, carelessness in practice. He should always go into the field determined to do his very best, and to play as if he were playing a match, and as if the favorable issue of a day's efforts depended on him alone. Those who follow this game as a mere amusement, without zeal, perseverance, or determination, will not only never excel, but can hardly hope to avoid the ridicule of their more skilful companions. Especially is this caution against carelessness required in the matter of bowling. To obtain a correct method, the distance of the bowler from the wicket against which he bowls should always be the same. If you bowl from different distances at different times, the pitch will always vary; and precision in delivering the ball—the great object of all bowling—will never be obtained.

No match can be considered as decided until it is completely played out, however great the preponderance of runs on one side may be. The side neglecting to finish the match is considered to have lost it.

The following are the laws of Single Wicket:—

1. When there shall be less than five players on a side, bounds shall be placed twenty-two yards each in a line from the off and leg stump.

2. The ball must be hit before the bounds, to entitle the striker to a run; which run cannot be obtained unless he touch the bowling stump or crease in a line with his bat or some part of his person, or go beyond them; returning to the popping crease, as at a double wicket, according to the 21st law.

3. When the striker shall hit the ball, one of his feet must be on the ground and behind the popping crease, otherwise the umpire shall call "no hit."

4. When there shall be less than five players on a side, neither byes nor overthrows shall be allowed, nor shall the striker be caught out behind the wicket, or stumped out.

5. The fieldsman must return the ball so that it shall cross the play between the wicket and the bowling stump, or between the bowling stump and the bounds; the striker may run till the ball be so returned.

6. After the striker shall have made one run, if he start again he must touch the bowling stump and turn before the ball shall cross the play, to entitle him to another.

7. The striker shall be entitled to three runs for lost ball, and the same number for ball stopped with hat, with reference to the 27th and 33d laws of Double Wicket.

8. When there shall be more than five players on a side, there shall be no bounds. All hits, byes, and overthrows shall then be allowed.

9. The bowler is subject to the same laws as at Double Wicket.

10. No more than one minute shall be allowed between each ball.

When Single Wicket is played without sides, the first innings is tossed for; and when out, the striker takes the bowler's place, then that of the wicket-keeper, then fieldsman to the left of the bowler, and so on in succession, according to the number engaged.

GENERAL INSTRUCTIONS.

Hints upon Dress.—Eschew hats of every description. If made of straw they are apt to blow off and strike the wicket, or to baulk you in hitting or catching. Woollen caps, made with peaks to shelter the eyes, are preferable, being not only light and cool to the head, but absorbing the perspiration. As loose shirt-sleeves sometimes stop the ball in their folds, from whence it may be shaken on to the wicket, an elastic cotton or merino flannel shirt will be found the most convenient garment. If you incline to a flannel jacket you will find it of most service when fielding, or to slip on after leaving your wicket with such a score as may have induced copious perspiration. Encase your nether limbs in trousers of well shrunk flannel, with an India-rubber belt passed through loops sewn upon the waistband. Avoid braces, which unquestionably impede a cricketer's movements, whether he be striking, bowling, or fielding. Tie a cotton handkerchief round your neck, in preference even to the silk of Delhi, and this, with merino or thin worsted socks, and well spiked shoes, will complete your toilet. If the bowling be very swift, there is no objection to your donning India-rubber gloves, or, adopting paddings for the better preservation of your shins; and should you, perchance, get a bruise or two, remember the very best remedy is to rub with sweet oil until your arm aches.

Bowling and Wicket-keeping.—In bowling, an ounce of practice is worth a ton of theory. The bowler must learn by observation the weak stump of the batsman (as a commander reconnoitres the weak point of a fortress), and lay siege to it accordingly. As a general rule, the leg-stump is the most vulnerable, though balls pitched rather wide of the direct line to the off-stump, are puzzling to batsmen not well up in the hit known as "*the cut.*" In reaching out at them, the batsman is very apt to strike *under* the ball, and cause a catch. Upon the bowler's judgment must depend the variation of his delivery from swift to slow, and *vice versa*. Where a style of round bowling is attained, accompanied by considerable bias, or twist, in the progress of the ball, after grounding, the batsman has no easy task in defending his wicket. But in adopting round bowling, eschew, by all means, the reprehensible practice of *throwing;*—remember the ball must be delivered with the hand below, and not above the shoulder. When practising, commence with moderate force of delivery, which is easily increased in velocity after you have acquired the art of grounding the ball a proper length. The bias is imparted to the ball by forcibly inverting the wrist in the delivery, and at the same time imparting with the little finger an impulsive twist, by which the ball, according to the natural motion of bodies, acquires a circular rotation, combined with a lateral progression. In playing a match, there should be at least four good bowlers, to allow of a change at each wicket, if necessary.

The whole attention of the player should not be devoted either to bowling or batting, but be equally divided with fielding; for good fielding is a very important item in playing a match, and equally so is good wicket-keeping. Hence, the wicket-keeper is required to possess ready judgment, keenness of sight, and agility of limb. Like Putnam, he should not know *fear*, with reference to the velocity of the coming ball. He should continually watch the positions of the fieldsmen, changing the same by signals, that advantage may be taken of the batsman's weak points. It is also his duty to maintain silence, and prevent confusion during the game.

How to defend your Wicket.—The bifold task of the batsman consists in stopping some balls and hitting others. It is the proper discrimination of which to do that marks the practised player. Batsmen who adopt a slashing style of play, are apt to place too great a reliance upon mere physical force,

which they wrongly look upon as the source of success. Any one can slash away with impunity at a ball coming tolerably wide of the stumps; but our young reader doubtless well knows that, just *without* his reach, there is a spot upon which all straightly delivered balls that happen to ground are difficult to treat, and not merely dangerous, but frequently prove "trimmers." There is but an instant of time in which you must decide whether you will step forward and meet the ball, or receive it with the home block (see Engraving). If you adopt the former plan, most likely the bowler will drop his succeeding balls gradually shorter, until you leave your ground, and (as the natural consequence of missing one of them) your wicket. Remember, if you should decide upon stepping in, and afterward change your mind, you cannot recover yourself sufficiently in time to take the ball on the back play. Now the advantage of stopping these dangerous "length balls" by the home-block on the back play is, that the sight you thus get of the ball, by waiting its arrival, is much better than when the eye is directed forward in opposition to the advancing projectile. Therefore keep on your ground, and smother these balls by the home block, rather than risk your wicket by stepping in to hit them.

Now it must be understood that these observations apply only to balls grounding *without* the batsman's reach. When the bowler delivers the ball a few inches over the spot noted as "dangerous," it must be met by forward play (see Engraving). If the length at which it rises be sufficient for you to do so, lounge well out at it, and make, if possible, your brace of runs by this description of hit, generally known to cricketers as the "forward drive." If, on the contrary, the ball grounds and rises sharply, and your sphere of action is so limited, that in striking at the ball you can hardly fail to strike your stumps at the same time, then smother it by the forward block. Generally speaking, forward play is the safest against swift bowling that comes within your reach, as the rapidity of the delivery, when the ball is met by back play, often sends it off into the Point's hands. While alluding to one chance of the batsman's being caught out, he may as well be reminded not to "spoon" the ball up into the air in his forward play. This he will avoid by not elevating the left elbow too much. The following

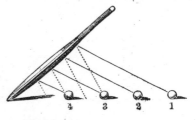

diagram shows the angles at which the ball will rise to the bat, and rebound from it, according to the length of the bowler's delivery. No. 1 is the most difficult to dispose of, for if the batsman lounges out incorrectly, the ball may chance to rise just high enough to pass over the shoulder of the bat. No. 2 may be treated, as previously described, by "forward play." Nos. 3 and 4 deserve the hardest hitting your strength can bestow— a regular forward drive.

The following cuts represent the different positions of the batsman in defending his wicket:

No. 1 shows him in position ready for the ball, after the delivery of which the bat is raised into some one or other of the following positions, or even into a still greater variety. No. 2 shows an advance of the left leg, to reach a wide ball on the "off side." No. 3 is the attitude in the "leg hit." No. 4 is the advance of the right leg for an "off ball." No. 5 shows what is

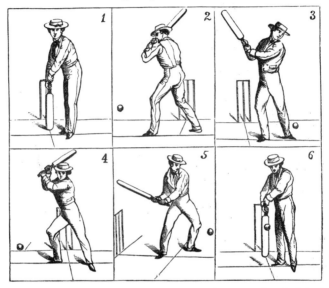

called "the drive;" and No. 6, "the draw." The grand principle is to avoid hitting at all balls coming straight at the wicket, which must be stopped or "blocked," as it is termed, instead; and to hit only at those which are going wide of the stumps, and always with a full bat.

AN UNEXPECTED HIT.

BASE-BALL.

THIS game, which is Rounders, or Town Ball, reduced to a system, and governed by scientific rules, is a graceful and invigorating pastime, and bids fair to become to this country what cricket is to England—the national game. We give the rules and principles of the game, as played by grown players, remarking that boys should reduce the distances there set down about one-sixth.

THE GROUND.

A base-ball ground should be level and free from irregularities; turfy, if possible, but, if gravelly, then the ground around the bases should be turfed, to prevent injury in falling, and the field should be about four hundred feet broad and six hundred feet long. The home base should be seventy feet from the head of the field. The bases should be made of wood, and a ring screwed in each, and they should be set flush with the ground.

In laying off your ground, fix first the point of your home base, then measure from that, down the field, one hundred and twenty-seven feet four inches, and there set your second base. Attach a cord one hundred and eighty feet long, with a knot in the middle, to the rings of the home and second base. By taking the knot in the hand, and stretching the cord as far as you can on the right, you will get the point of the first base; and then, by carrying it over to the left in the same way, you will get the third base. On a line from, and distant from the home forty-five feet toward the second base, is the pitcher's point. The foul-ball posts are placed on a line with the home and first, and home and third base, at least one hundred feet from the bases; and should be painted, and high enough from the ground to be seen by the umpire.

BASES AND PITCHER'S POINT.

The bases are made of canvas, or some heavy stuff, and filled with cotton or hair; are about fourteen by seventeen inches, and fastened to the base-blocks with strips of harness-leather. Four quoits, nine inches across, *flat side up*, and painted white, show the pitcher's point, and the home base, and have iron spikes at the bottom, to keep them from being shifted. A piece of plank, set edgewise, six feet long, two inches wide, and eight inches deep, and the edge above ground enough to catch the umpire's eye, makes the line of the pitcher's position.

BAT AND BALL.

The form and shape of the bat and ball are regulated by the rules. For ordinary use ash is the best material; but those who like a heavy bat will take hickory, and for a light bat, English willow is preferable.

THE STRIKER.

BATTING.

There are different styles. Each player chooses what best suits him. Some give a blow like a woodman, grasping the handle with the left hand, and sliding the right toward it; some take the bat near the middle, with both hands; others seize the handle with both hands, and give a swinging hit. Whichever mode you adopt, plant yourself firmly on the ground, with your left foot on the striker's position, and while you meet the ball with a quick stroke, do not hit so hard as to lose your balance. If your foot is off the position, and a ball comes perpendicularly to the ground, it will not be a foul ball.

THE GAME.

There are nine players on a side—one side having the bat, and the other the field. The fielders are as follows: Catcher, Pitcher, first, second, and third Basemen; Short Stop, and Right, Left, and Centre Fieldsman. By looking at the diagram you will see the relative positions. Whoever wins the toss at the outset, can either bat or field first. The batsman takes his position at the home base, on a line drawn through its centre, parallel to one

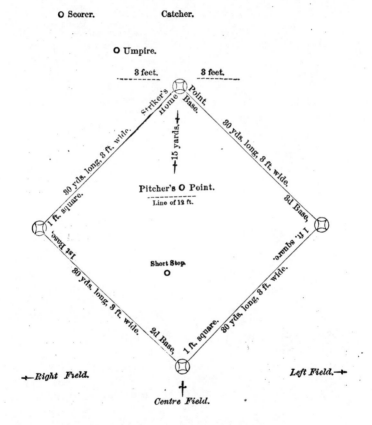

DIAGRAM OF A BASE-BALL FIELD.

extending from the first to the third base, and extending three feet on each side of it. As soon as he hits the ball he starts for the first base, and is succeeded by the other batsmen in turn. When three of these are put out, the fielders take their turns at the bat, and play their innings; and so on, to the close of the game, which consists of nine innings on a side. If the batsman, after touching successively the first, second, and third bases, reach the home base, untouched by the ball in his adversary's hands, he is entitled to score one run; and if he hits the ball so far as to make the four bases before it is returned, he makes a home run. If the game be interrupted or stopped before each side have played five innings, it is drawn. The rest of the game will be found by a reference to the rules.

FIELD POSITIONS.

Catcher.—His business is to catch or stop all balls pitched or thrown to the home base, to catch all tips and foul balls, throw the ball swiftly and

THE CATCHER.

unerringly to the bases, and keep a watch over the whole field. When a player has made the first base, the catcher gets nearer the striker, so as to take the ball from the pitcher before it bounds; and so soon as the ball is delivered, and the player runs from first to second base, he takes the ball before bounding, and delivers it swiftly to the second base, in time to cut off the player before he gets to that base. When the catcher sees several fielders running to catch a ball, he should name the one he thinks surest to take it, when the others should not strive to catch the ball on the fly, but only, in case of its being missed, take it on the bound.

Short Stop.—His duty is to stop all balls that come within his reach, and pass them to whatever base the striker is aiming at. When necessary, he covers the third base, and backs up the second and third bases, when the ball is thrown in from the field. He must be ready to take foul balls on the bound, when missed on the fly by the pitcher, or third baseman.

Pitcher.—His position is behind a line, four yards long, drawn at right angles from the home to the opposite base, at the distance of forty-five feet from the home. He should be chosen for his good fielding, and swift and accurate delivery of the ball, which he must pitch, and not throw. The ball must be delivered as near as he can to the home base, to the striker, and high enough to prevent its bounding at or before the base. He should keep his eye out to the bases, and when he sees the players endeavoring to run to the bases, should deliver an accurate and swift ball to the basemen.

He should be able to pitch the ball quickly and evenly, and give it at the same time that bias, or twist, which is best to baffle the batsman's blow, and yet is a fair ball at the striker. He should catch, too, if a player endeavors to make the home base while he is pitching, and follow his ball to the home, where he will take it from the catcher.

Left Field.—As half, or may be more, of the balls hit are sent in his direction, he should be a sure catcher, as well as a good thrower and runner.

Centre Field.—Right Field.— These require the same qualities as the other field; but as few balls go to him, it is usual to put the poorest player in the last named position.

Batsman.—He must not get over three feet from either side of the line drawn through the centre of the home base, and

THE PITCHER.

wait the coming of a proper ball; but when a fair ball comes he should strike. When he has hit the ball he should drop, not throw his bat, and make for the first base; for if it be a foul ball the umpire will declare it at once, and he can easily return. The rules, if studied, will speak further of him and his duties.

First Base.—He should take a position a little below his base, and inside the line of the foul-ball post, to catch balls he would otherwise miss. The moment the ball is struck, and does not come near him, he must get back to his base, and with one foot on it, be ready to receive the ball from any fielder; because the striker may be put out at the first base without being touched by the ball, provided the baseman, with ball in hand, touches the base before the striker gets there. The moment he has held the ball, he should either send it to the pitcher, or to any other base that players are trying to make.

Second Base.—He should play generally to the left and a little back of his base, though he should be guided in it by the customary play of the striker. When the striker reaches the first base, he should return to his base, prepared to receive the ball from the catcher, and be ready to put out the striker by touching him with the ball. On no base, except the first, can the striker be put out by the baseman holding the ball, except when balls are caught on the fly, or are foul, when the player, in returning to the base he has left, may be put out, as at the first base.

THE BASE-TENDER.

Third Base.—The same general rules will apply here as to the second base, in regard to practice.

ON FIELDING.

The fielders should always be able to throw the ball to base from long field; and whenever they stop the ball, they should return it *at once*, either to the pitcher, or to the baseman needing it. Let each start the moment the ball is struck, so as to take it, if possible, on the fly, and not on the bound. It is easier to take a ball by running forward than backward. You may be deceived by a ball being hit high to long field, and think it will come farther than it will—a ball describing a more sudden curve in its descent than ascent. Practice and a keen eye must strengthen the fielder's judgment on this point.

THE UMPIRE AND SCORER.

The Umpire.—The position of the umpire is not altogether desirable, for he must displease some one with his decision. But he should not merely be impartial, nevertheless, but strict, in enforcing the rules of the game, and prompt in his decision, giving an opinion in general according to the first impression on his mind, which, in ninety-nine cases out of a hundred, he will find correct. If the point is doubtful, the rule is to decide in favor of the ball. He should call a foul ball instantly; and call out "one strike," and so on through to "three strike," whenever a player persists in refusing fair balls. He must keep his eyes about him, see that the pitcher does not jerk the ball, or have one foot before his position, or in any other way violate the rules; and see that the batsman is on his line. If the striker is off his line, and the ball therefore fall behind the base when struck, the umpire will declare it a fair ball. His position is to the right of, and between the striker and catcher, in a line between the third and home base, unless the striker is left-handed, when he takes the opposite side. If either side try to prolong the game, in order that night may stop it, let him decide it by the last fair innings, or make it a draw. Let him remember that a bound is when it has struck the ground but once, though it may have struck against a tree or other stationary object before.

The Scorer.—His duty is very plain. He is the clerk of the game, to set down every thing as it is; and therefore he should know the game thoroughly in every point.

The following are the rules adopted by the National Association of Base-Ball Players, with the latest amendments :

RULES AND REGULATIONS

Adopted by the National Association of Base-Ball Players, held in New York, December 9, 1863.

SEC. 1. The ball must weigh not less than five and one-half nor more than five and three-fourths ounces, avoirdupois. It must measure not less than nine and one-half, nor more than nine and three-fourths inches in circumference. It must be composed of India-rubber, and yarn, and covered with leather, and, in all match games, shall be furnished by the challenging club, and become the property of the winning club as a trophy of victory.

SEC. 2. The bat must be round, and must not exceed two and a half inches in diameter in the thickest part. It must be made of wood, and may be of any length to suit the striker.

SEC. 3. The bases must be four in number, placed at equal distances from each other, and securely fastened upon the four corners of a square, whose sides are respectively thirty yards. They must be so constructed as to be distinctly seen by the umpire, and must cover a space equal to one square foot of surface. The first, second, and third bases shall be canvas bags, painted white, and filled with sand or saw-dust; the home base and pitcher's point to be each marked by a flat circular iron plate, painted or enamelled white.

SEC. 4. The base from which the ball is struck shall be designated the home base, and must be directly opposite to the second base; the first base must always be that upon the right-hand, and the third base that upon the left-hand side of the striker, when occupying his position at the home base. *And in all match games, a line connecting the home and first base and the home and third base, shall be marked by the use of chalk, or other suitable material, so as to be distinctly seen by the umpire.*

SEC. 5. The pitcher's position shall be designated by two lines, four yards in length, drawn at right angles to a line from home to second base, having their centres upon that line at two fixed iron plates, placed at points fifteen and sixteen yards distant from the home base. The pitcher must stand within the lines, and must deliver the ball as near as possible over the centre of the home base, and for the striker.

SEC. 6. Should the pitcher repeatedly fail to deliver to the striker fair balls, for the apparent purpose of delaying the game, or for any other cause, the umpire, after warning him, shall call one ball, and if the pitcher persists in such action, two and three balls; when three balls shall have been called, the striker shall be entitled to the first base; and should any base be occupied at that time, each player occupying them shall be entitled to one base without being put out.

SEC. 7. The ball must be pitched, not jerked or thrown to the bat; and whenever the pitcher draws back his hand, or moves with the apparent purpose or pretension to deliver the ball, he shall so deliver it, and must have neither foot in advance of the front line or off the ground at the time of delivering the ball; and if he fails in either of these particulars, then it shall be declared a balk.

SEC. 8. When a balk is made by the pitcher, every player running the bases is entitled to one base, without being put out.

SEC. 9. If the ball, from a stroke of the bat, *first touches the ground, the person of a player, or any other object,* behind the range of home and the first base, or home and the third base, it shall be termed foul, and must be so declared by the umpire, unasked. If the ball first touches the ground, either upon, or in front of the range of those bases, it shall be considered fair.

SEC. 10. A player making the home base, shall be entitled to score one run.

SEC. 11. If three balls are struck at, and missed, and the last one is not caught, either flying or upon the first bound, it shall be considered fair, and the striker must attempt to make his run.

SEC. 12. The striker is out if a foul ball is caught, either before touching the ground, or upon the first bound.

SEC. 13. Or, if three balls are struck at and missed, and the last is caught, either before touching the ground, or upon the first bound;

SEC. 14. Or if a fair ball is struck, and the ball is caught either without having touched the ground, or upon the first bound;

SEC. 15. Or, if a fair ball is struck, and the ball is held by an adversary on first base, before the striker touches that base.

SEC. 16. Any player running the bases is out, if at any time he is touched by the ball while in play in the hands of an adversary, without some part of his person being on the base.

SEC. 17. No ace or base can be made upon a foul ball; such a ball shall be considered dead, and not in play until it shall first have been settled in the hands of the pitcher. In such cases players running bases shall return to them, and may be put out in so returning in the same manner as the striker when running to the first base.

SEC. 18. No ace nor base can be made when a fair ball has been caught without having touched the ground; such a ball shall be considered alive and in play. In such case players running bases shall return to them, and may be put out in so returning, in the same manner as the striker when running to first base; but players, when balls are so caught, may run their bases immediately after the ball has been settled in the hands of the player catching it.

SEC. 19. The striker must stand on a line drawn through the centre of the home base, not exceeding in length three feet from either side thereof, and parallel with the line occupied by the pitcher. He shall be considered the striker until he has made the first base. Players must strike in regular rotation, and, after the first innings is played, the turn commences with the player who stands on the list next to the one who lost the third hand.

SEC. 20. Players must make their bases in the order of striking; and when a fair ball is struck, and not caught flying (or on the first bound), the first base must be vacated, as also the second and third bases, if they are occupied at the same time. Players may be put out on any base, under these circumstances, in the same manner as the striker when running to the first base.

SEC. 21. Players running bases must touch them; and, so far as possible, keep upon the direct line between them; and must touch them in the following order: first, second, third, and home; and if returning must reverse this order; and should any player run three feet out of this line, for the purpose of avoiding the ball in the hands of an adversary, he shall be declared out.

SEC. 22. Any player, who shall intentionally prevent an adversary from catching or fielding the ball, shall be declared out.

SEC. 23. If the player is prevented from making a base, by the intentional obstruction of an adversary, he shall be entitled to that base, and not be put out.

SEC. 24. If an adversary stops the ball with his hat or cap, or takes it from the hands of a party not engaged in the game, no player can be put out unless the ball shall first have been settled in the hands of the pitcher.

SEC. 25. If a ball, from the stroke of a bat, is held under any other circumstances than as enumerated in Section 24, and without having touched the ground more than once, the striker is out.

SEC. 26. If two hands are already out, no player running home at the time a ball is struck, can make an ace if the striker is put out.

SEC. 27. An innings must be concluded at the time the third hand is put out.

SEC. 28. The game shall consist of nine innings to each side, when, should the number of runs be equal, the play shall be continued until a majority of runs, upon an equal number of innings, shall be declared, which shall conclude the game.

SEC. 29. In playing all matches, nine players from each club shall constitute a full field, and they must have been regular members of the club which they represent, and of no other club, for thirty days prior to the match. No change or substitution shall be made after the game has been commenced, unless for reason of illness or injury. Position of players and choice of innings shall be determined by captains previously appointed for that purpose by the respective clubs.

SEC. 30. The umpire shall take care that the regulations respecting balls, bats, bases, and the pitcher's and striker's positions, are strictly observed. He shall keep a record of the game in a book prepared for the purpose; he shall be the judge of fair and unfair play, and shall determine all disputes and differences which may occur during the game; he shall take especial care to declare all foul balls and balks, immediately upon their occurrence, unasked, and in a distinct and audible manner. *He shall, in every instance, before leaving the ground, declare the winning club, and shall record his decision in the score books of the two clubs.*

SEC. 31. In all matches the umpire shall be selected by the captains of the respective sides, and shall perform all the duties enumerated in Section 30, except recording the game, which shall be done by two scorers, one of whom shall be appointed by each of the contending clubs.

SEC. 32. No person engaged in a match, either as umpire, scorer, or player, shall be, either directly or indirectly, interested in any bet upon the game. Neither umpire, scorer, nor player shall be changed during a match, unless with the consent of both parties (except for a violation of this law), except as provided in Section 29, and then the umpire may dismiss any transgressors.

SEC. 33. The umpire in any match shall determine when play shall be suspended; and if the game cannot be concluded, it shall be decided by the last even innings, provided five innings have been played, and the party having the greatest number of runs shall be declared the winner.

SEC. 34. Clubs may adopt such rules respecting balls knocked beyond or outside of the bounds of the field, as the circumstances of the ground may demand; and these rules shall govern all matches played upon the ground, provided that they are distinctly made known to every player and umpire, previous to the commencement of the game.

SEC. 35. No person shall be permitted to approach or to speak with the umpire, scorers, or players, or in any manner to interrupt or interfere during the progress of the game, unless by special request of the umpire.

SEC. 36. No person shall be permitted to act as umpire or scorer in any match, unless he shall be a member of a Base-Ball Club governed by these rules.

SEC. 37. Whenever a match shall have been determined upon between two clubs, play shall be called at the exact hour appointed; and should either party fail to produce their players within fifteen minutes thereafter, the party so failing shall admit a defeat.

SEC. 38. No person who shall be in arrears to any other club, or who shall at any time receive compensation for his services as player, shall be competent to play in any match.

SEC. 39. Should a striker stand at the bat without striking at good balls repeatedly pitched to him, for the apparent purpose of delaying the game, or of giving advantage to a player, the umpire, after warning him, shall call one strike, and if he persists in such action, two and three strikes. When three strikes are called, he shall be subject to the same rules as if he had struck at three fair balls.

SEC. 40. Every match hereafter made shall be declared by a single game, unless otherwise mutually agreed upon by the contesting clubs.

CROQUET.

THIS game (pronounced cro-kay') is of French origin, and has been only recently introduced into this country. As it is an out-door game, requiring some skill, and giving a variety of exercise, without being too fatiguing, it is likely to become popular; and we will give its details in full.

Croquet can be played only on a level piece of ground; but a good Croquet-ground should be close turf—the grass cut short, the moss killed out, and the ground well rolled. The area required is not large—about sixty by ninety feet. If it be for a permanent Croquet-ground, there should be a shallow ditch around it, to prevent the balls from straying. Of this rectangle laid out for the course of the ball, the lower part is the base, or foot, the opposite end the head, while the sides are respectively the right and left flanks. In the centre of the foot is the spot from whence the play begins, and here the starting-stake is set; and in the centre of the head is the turning-stake. There are ten bridges, with a span of twelve inches, made of iron wire, and stuck in the ground, leaving six to eight inches above ground. The stakes are of wood, two feet in length, and having eight rings of different colors, running down in this way: black, yellow, red, white, blue, orange, brown, green. It is from the starting-stake, through the bridges, touching the turning-stake, and from the other flank, back to the spot, that the balls are driven, by a mallet in the hands of the player. The course of the ball will be seen by an examination of the diagram.

The balls are made of wood, are turned to be ten inches in circumference, of beech, willow, or plane tree, eight in number, and painted to correspond to the rings on the starting-stake. This allows one to each player, though when four play they can either use four, or play two each. The mallet has a head with a diameter of two and one-third inches, and a length of four, a cylinder, slightly hollow in the middle, and having the ends slightly convex. The shank of the mallet is slender, tapering toward the head, about nine-tenths of an inch in diameter at the butt, and two feet and a half long. The shank should be of well-seasoned hickory—the head of dogwood, heart-hickory, or box—the latter preferable.

The distance from the starting-stake should be about ten feet from the base, and the turning-stake should have the same distance from the head.

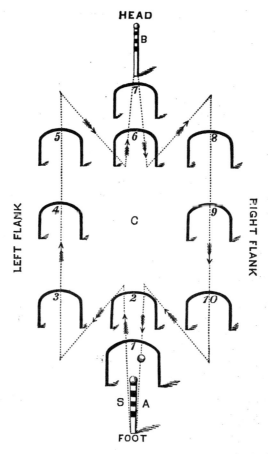

A, The Starting-stake.   B, The Turning-stake.   C, The Centre.   S, The Spot.
1, 2, Lower Central Bridges.   3, 4, 5, Left Flank Bridges.
6, 7, Upper Central Bridges.   8, 9, 10, Right Flank Bridges.
The dotted lines and arrows indicate the course of a ball in making the grand round of the game.

The bridges or hoops should be set—No. 1, ten feet from the starting-stake; No. 2, ten feet farther on in a direct line toward the head; Nos. 6 and 7 should be twenty and ten feet from the turning-stake. The distance between Nos. 2 and 6 is according to the length of the ground. No. 3 and No. 10 should be on a line at right angles with Nos. 1, 2, 6, and 7, and in line with 2; and No. 5 and No. 8 in a like position with No. 6. Midway between 3 and 5, and 8 and 10, the two remaining bridges are set. The precise space of the spot is one mallet's length behind bridge No. 1.

In beginning the game, a match is made—four or two on a side, according to the number of players—under two chiefs. In order to determine first choice of allies, the chiefs drive a ball through the first bridge, and the one who comes nearest to the starting-stake with the first blow has the choice. They then choose alternately. When it is made up they take the balls in rotation, beginning with the color on top of the starting-stake, and going down, and play with those.

Whatever be the number of players, the object of each is to make the *grand round* and *strike out* against the starting-stake—by the accomplishment of which feat, the "victory" is obtained.

The *course* of the ball in making the grand round is, first, from the spot, through bridges 1 and 2 *upward;* then to the left flank in front of 3; thence through 3, 4, and 5; thence back to the line of the centre in front of 6; thence through 6 and 7, making the *half-round.*

The stake is next *tolled;* after which the ball runs back through 7 and 6, *downward,* or in a direction contrary to its previous course.

Having re-run 7 and 6, it crosses over to front of the right flank bridges—their front being the reverse to that of those on the left. It then *runs* 8, 9, and 10, *downward;* crosses again to the centre line above 2; and re-runs 2 and 1 toward the starting stake.

It has thus completed the *grand round;* and being once more placed upon the *spot,* has the option—either of *striking out,* or continuing the play, with the privileges of the *Rover.*

As the victory is not declared till *all* the friends of a side are struck out, the act of *striking out* is usually delayed by each, until the last of that side has completed the grand round. The striking out of any individual ball—while any of its *friends* are still far back in the game—is a serious loss, instead of a gain, to the *side* to which it belongs: more especially since the *rover* is endowed with certain privileges, which render him either a valuable friend, or a formidable enemy.

Under certain circumstances it is not impossible to make the grand round in a *single tour* of play; but the individual who can accomplish this feat, may be regarded as a "crack croquet player." An ordinary player will take a dozen—perhaps a score—of tours to return to the starting-stake; and even a good "hand" at croquet, will usually require a considerable number, to enable him to accomplish the desired end.

A ball in going its round meets with two distinct classes of interruptions—

one voluntary, the other unavoidable. Of the former kind, there is the diverging from its course to attack an *enemy*, by roquet and croquet, and *spoil* the latter's position; or, by the same means to *help on a friend*. A ball may also voluntarily diverge from its course to *place itself near* a friend, so that the latter, when its tour comes on, may by roquing upon it, make position.

The *involuntary* obstructions to the course of a ball are of various kinds: attempting the bridges, and failing to attain them; passing without *running* them; crossing at the *corners*, without the possibility of *turning* them; being roqued or croqued out of position; played out of its proper tour, and duly challenged; attempting to make a roquet, and failing in the attempt; or permitted to "flinch" from under the foot of its player while in the act of croquet;—any of these contingencies will obstruct a ball on its *round*.

Croquet is somewhat like billiards, the mallet taking the place of the cue. The strokes and advantages can be best gleaned from the technical terms of the game, and from the rules, which follow:—

TERMS USED IN CROQUET.

Arena.—The space enclosed within the boundaries of the croquet-ground.

Attacking.—Playing at an enemy's ball, for the purpose of *spoiling* it.

Back of a Bridge.—The side reverse to the *front*.

Blow.—The stroke of the mallet.

Booby.—A ball that has attempted to run the first bridge, and either *rues* or *overruns* it.

Bridged Ball.—A ball that has run the first bridge.

Centre.—The central part of the arena.

Central Bridges.—Those in a line between the two stakes. They are *upper* and *lower*.

Chiefs.—The players selected to marshal the sides.

Climbing on the Scape-Goat.—Roquing a ball into a better position for the player: so that the roquing ball may get in front of its own proper bridge, or obtain some other advantage of position.

Concussion.—The displacement of a ball by another—driven against it by roquet, croquet, ricochet or roquet-croquet; and not hit directly, either by the mallet or the playing ball.

Corners.—The points of passage, between the lines of flank and central bridges.

Course.—The direction taken by the ball on its round.

Croquet.—The title of the game.

Croqueterie.—The implements, viz. :—*Balls, bridges, mallets,* and *stakes*.

Croquing.—A ball, having made roquet on another, is taken up, and placed in contact with the ball on which it has roqued. The player sets foot upon the former; presses firmly, so as to hold it in place; and, with a blow of the mallet, drives the roqued ball in whatever direction may be desired.

Dead Ball.—A *rover* struck against the starting-stake, and therefore struck out of the game.

Double-Point.—Two points made by the same blow of the mallet.

Enemy.—An adversary.

Flank Bridges.—Those upon the flanks—also denominated *right* and *left.*

Flanks.—The sides of the rectangle—or of whatever figure they have been chosen for the croquet-ground. They are *right* and *left.*

Flinch.—When the ball in the act of "croquet," at the blow of the mallet, glides from under the foot of the player.

Fluke.—When a point is made not due to the skill of the player.

Foot.—That part of the arena contiguous to the starting-stake.

Friend.—A partner in the game.

Front of a Bridge is that side, from which the player must proceed, in passing through or *running* it.

Grand Round.—The "grand round" consists in duly running all the bridges—the central ones in both directions—tolling the turning-stake in its proper time, and returning to the *spot*—whence the player may either *strike out* or continue the play.

Half Round.—Having reached the point, where the turning-stake is to be tolled.

Head.—That part of the arena contiguous to the turning-stake.

Helping a Friend.—Roquing, or croquing a friend's ball into position; causing it to run a bridge, toll the turning-stake; or otherwise forwarding it on its round.

Leading Ball.—The ball played first from the spot.

Making Position.—Making roquet, or ricochet, on a ball already in position.

Marshalling the Sides.—Making the match.

Nursing.—Croquing a ball—either a friend or an enemy—through, or around, its own proper bridge; then running the bridge; roquing and croquing the same ball again; and so proceeding on the round.

Oblique Bridge.—A bridge, the plane of whose arch is not perpendicular to the horizon, or to the *course* of play.

Overrunning a Bridge.—When a ball, struck by the mallet, rolls past and not through, the bridge at which it has been played, it is said to *overrun* it.

Point.—Making a success, viz.:—a *point* in the game.

Position.—A ball is *in position*, when it lies in *front* of its proper bridge, with a possibility of running it by a single blow of the mallet; and *out of position*, when the contrary is the case.

Proper Bridge.—That which the player intends to pass through, is his, or her, *proper* bridge for the time.

Push.—When the player presses the ball forward with the mallet, instead of giving it a *blow.*

Re-Roquet.—To roquet the same ball twice, without any intervening action of the play.

5

Ricochet.—A ball making roquet on two or more balls, by the same blow of the mallet.

Roquet-Croquet, or Croquet sans Pied.—A ball having made roquet, is taken up; placed contiguous to the roqued ball; and, without being held under the foot, is struck by the mallet, and driven—as also the roqued ball—in the direction desired.

Roquet.—A ball makes "roquet" when, proceeding from a blow of the mallet, it comes in contact with another ball.

Rover.—A ball that has made the grand round.

Rueing a Bridge.—When a ball, struck by the mallet, fails to reach the bridge at which it has been played, it is said to *rue* it.

Running a Bridge.—When a ball has been driven through the arch of its *proper* bridge, either by a blow of the mallet, by roquet, croquet, ricochet, concussion, or roquet-croquet, it is said to *run* that bridge.

Side.—A set of partners, or *friends.*

Spoiling an Enemy.—Striking an enemy's ball out of position, by roquet, croquet, ricochet, concussion, or roquet-croquet, and so retarding it on its round.

Spot.—The point from which the play commences.

Starting-Stake.—The stake from which the play proceeds—placed proximate to the *spot,* at the lower end of the *arena.*

Striking for First Choice.—The chiefs "strike" for first choice of *friends,* by playing a ball at the starting-stake, from between the piers of bridge No. 1; whoever places the ball nearest to the stake has the choice.

Striking Out.—A ball struck against the *starting*-stake by mallet, roquet, ricochet, concussion, croquet, or roquet-croquet, after having run *all* the bridges—the central ones in both directions—and tolled the turning-stake, is *struck out;* that is, out of the game.

Tolling the Stake.—A ball struck *against the turning-stake* by mallet, roquet, ricochet, concussion, croquet, or roquet-croquet, at its *proper* time,—that is, after having run the *central* and *left flank* bridges *upward,*— is said to *toll* or *pay toll* to the stake.

Tour of Play.—Is the turn given to each player. It *continues* so long as a point is made, and *terminates* with a failure.

Turning a Corner.—Proceeding from the flank to the central bridges, or *vice versa;* and *running* one or more of both in the same *tour* of play.

Turning-Stake.—The stake set opposite to the starting-stake, and near the upper end of the arena.

" *Up the Country.*"—A ball croqued beyond the boundaries is sent to "Hong Kong," or "up the country." The owner, with an indifferent grace, stands gazing after it; and the journey, required to bring it back within the arena, is usually performed with an air of the most profound melancholy—not unmingled with chagrin.

Victory.—When all of a side succeed in *striking out.*

RULES FOR THE GAME OF CROQUET.

1. One of each side plays alternately.

2. The ball must be struck or pushed by the end of the mallet only. In starting, the balls to be placed not more than twelve inches from the post.

3 The bridge or hoop must on no account ever be moved to afford the player any convenience in playing.

4. Going through a hoop gives a fresh move.

5. To count, the ball must be quite through the hoop, but going through one backward counts for nothing.

6. To count, the hoops must be passed in proper succession.

7. Playing out of turn loses the move.

8. To get a roquet, the player must hit the ball he wishes to roquet with his own; in so doing, he may play his ball with sufficient force to move the hit ball into another position. He then places his ball close on any side of the hit ball, taking care, in so doing, not to move the latter.

9. The left foot is placed on the player's own ball, which he then hits with his mallet.

10. When making the roquet, the player's ball must not move from its position, if moved, the balls must be replaced for another trial, three trials being allowed.

11. After the player has passed through a hoop, he is entitled to another stroke; or after having roqued another ball.

12. The player can only roquet the same ball once, until he again passes through the hoop.

13. A ball half through a hoop is considered altogether through.

14. If a player misses a hoop, he must return to the side of it that he played from, either through or around the hoop, as most convenient.

15. A ball must not be lifted from the ground, if in the way of another player. If the ball of one player strike that of another which is not available for a roquet, both balls remain to wherever sent; but if the ball be hit, and available for a roquet, it must be roqued.

16. If the roqued ball be moved ever so little, the players remaining stationary, it is a roquet.

17. No player can roquet or be roqued until he has been through the first hoop.

18. A roquet entitles the player to roquet another ball, or make a move.

19. The player cannot roquet the same ball twice in the same move. He can push it on by hitting it with his own, or, going through a hoop, can again roquet that ball.

20. You can roquet friend or foe—helping your friend, or sending your foe to a distant part of the ground.

21. At any stage of the game the player may go where he pleases to roquet balls.

22. When a ball is hit, it must be roqued.

23. After hitting the lower stick, the ball may be placed in a favorable position, alongside the stick, to go through the proper hoop; but if moved, a roquet cannot be played until the ball has been through a hoop.

24. When the player, having gone through all the hoops, hits the winning stick, he is out; but it is not obligatory to hit it when first reached, the player may return as a "rover," to roquet friend or foe.

25. Going through a hoop does not give a "rover" an additional move, as they have all been previously passed through; he gets other moves by roquing balls.

26. He cannot roquet the same ball again until his turn comes round; but he can roquet other balls.

27. A ball that has not been through the first hoop cannot roquet; but it can be roqued.

28. If a ball that has not passed through the first hoop be sent behind the stick at the starting-point, it can be brought up to the starting-point and start afresh.

29. On striking the second stick, the player has the option of either leaving his ball to wherever it may have glided, or of bringing it back to the stick.

30. When intending to roquet another ball, the player must strike his own ball with as much force as he pleases, in order to drive the ball about to be roqued into an unfavorable or favorable position. The player's ball must always be the one moved in roquing.

31. If, in roquing, the player's ball slips from under his foot when he strikes it, it must be brought back to the place he struck it from.

32. If you hit a ball, and from it glance off through a hoop, you must return to croquet the ball, and are not considered through the hoop. In like manner, if you croquet a ball, and, glancing off from it, hit the post, you have hit the ball, but are not considered to have hit the post.

33. When you croquet a ball, and from it hit another, you must croquet the one hit first, and then the second; but if an intermediate ball be nearer the player than either of them already hit, he must not attempt to croquet it until the others have been disposed of.

34. At the upper post you may not take your ball up after hitting the post, but must proceed from the place to where the ball rebounds.

35. Those balls which roll out of the ground remain where they roll to, until their turn for play comes, and then they are placed on the ground twice the length of the head of the mallet from the edge.

36. Players must identify their balls when called upon to do so, and state also (if asked) which is their next hoop.

37. If, in croquing, you move your adversary's or partner's ball, though you do not hit your own, a fresh stroke may be taken.

38. It is not lawful to follow your ball when striking. If this happens, the striker shall take his ball up, and play again from the point he hit from.

39. A person on each side may be selected to direct the play, but no assistance to be given by holding bats or otherwise.

40. To win, the winning stick must be hit by all on one side.

There are several modifications of this now fashionable game, but the above rules will be found to be the most conducive to the amusement of the players.

FOOT-BALL.

THE players are divided into two parties, equal in number, and each party has to defend one of two goals, or homes (see Diagram), into which the other tries to kick the Foot-ball. The party who gains two out of three "goals" is generally considered to have won the game. The lines C D, drawn at right angles to the goal-lines A B, are called "touch-lines;" when the ball is kicked behind these, it is said to be "in touch," and a player brings it forward to the line, flinging it to his players, who wait at the edge for it. "Place-kick" is when the ball is put on the ground and kicked from where it lies. "Punting" is when the ball is dropped from the hands and kicked before it reaches the ground. In a *drop*, the ball is dropped and kicked at the moment it touches the ground. *A free kick*, is the privilege of kicking the ball, without obstruction, in such manner as the kicker may think fit. *A fair catch*, is when the ball is caught, after it has touched

the person of an adversary, or has been kicked, knocked on, or thrown by an adversary, and before it has touched the ground, or one of the side catching it; but if the ball is kicked from out of touch, or from behind goal-line, a fair catch cannot be made. *Hacking*, is kicking an adversary on the front of the leg, below the knee. *Charging*, is attacking an adversary with the shoulder, chest, or body, without using the hands or legs. *Knocking on*, is when a player strikes or propels the ball with hands, arms, or body, without kicking or throwing it. *Holding* includes the obstruction of a player by the hand, or any part of the arm below the elbow. The goals are placed eighty or one hundred yards apart, and are generally marked by stakes being driven in the ground.

The ball should be an ox-bladder, inflated with air and covered with leather. In order to dispose of the players to the best advantage, the best man should stand in front, and goal-keepers should remain at their stations, to prevent the ball passing through, and not leave them, except when their assistance seems absolutely necessary. After each game, the players change sides; by which means any advantages of wind, sun, or sloping ground are neutralized.

THE LAWS OF FOOT-BALL, AS PLAYED AT RUGBY.

1. Kick off from middle must be a place-kick.

2. Kick out must not be from more than twenty-five yards out of goal.

3. Fair catch is a catch direct from the foot, or a knock on from the HAND of the opposite side.

4. Charging is fair, in case of a place-kick, as soon as the ball has touched the ground; in case of a kick from a catch, as soon as the player offers to kick, but he may always draw back, unless he has actually touched the ball with his foot.

5. *Off Side.*—A player is off his side when the ball has been kicked, or thrown, or knocked on, or is being run with by any one of his own side behind him.

6. A player entering a scrummage on the wrong side is OFF his side.

7. A player is OFF his side when a player on his own side has kicked the ball from behind him, and then run before him.

8. *On Side.*—A player is on his side when the ball has been kicked, thrown, or knocked on, or run with (five yards), or when it has touched the body of any player on the opposite side before him, *i. e.*, in advance of him.

9. A player being off his side is to consider himself as out of the game, and is not to touch the ball in any case whatever (either in or out of touch); or in any way to interrupt the play, and is, of course, incapable of holding the ball.

10. Knocking on, as distinguished from throwing on, is altogether disallowed, under any circumstances whatsoever. In case of this rule being broken, a catch from such a knock on shall be equivalent to a fair catch.

11. A catch from a throw on is not a *fair* catch.

12. If, however, the ball be hit by the arm, and not by the hand, the catch from such a knock on shall not be considered equivalent to a fair catch.

13. It is not lawful to take the ball off the ground, except in touch, for *any* purpose whatsoever.

14. It is not lawful to take up the ball when *rolling*, as distinguished from *bounding*.

15. In a scrummage succeeding a maul, it is not lawful to touch the ball with the hand, except in the event of a fair catch.

16. First of his side, is the player nearest the ball *on his side*.

17. Running in is allowed to any player on his side, provided he does *not take the ball off the ground*, or through touch.

18. *Running In.*—If, in case of a run in, the ball be held in a maul, it shall be lawful for a player on the same side to take it from the runner in, provided he has entered the maul behind the runner in.

19. No player out of a maul may be held, or pulled over, unless he is himself holding the ball.

20. Though it is lawful to hold any player in a maul, this holding does not include attempts to throttle or strangle, which are totally opposed to all the principles of the game.

21. That any player obtaining a ball in a maul, do put it down as soon as possible, when outside the twenty-five yard posts at either end.

22. No player may be hacked and held at the same time.

23. Hacking with the heel is unfair.

24. Hacking above or on the knee is unfair.

25. No one wearing projecting nails, iron plates, or gutta percha on the soles or heels of his boots or shoes, shall be allowed to play.

26. *Trial at Goal.*—A ball touched between the goal-posts may be brought up to either of them, but not between.

27. The ball, when punted, must be within, and when caught, without the line of goal.

28. The ball must be place-kicked, and not dropped; and if it touch two hands the try will be lost.

29. A goal may be dropped by any player, *on his side*, if the ball has not been touched down in goal.

30. It shall be a goal if the ball go over the bar (whether it touch or no), without having touched the dress or person of any player; but no player may stand on the goal-bar to interrupt it going over.

31. No goal may be kicked from touch.

32. *Touch.*—A ball in touch is dead; consequently the first player, on his side, must, in any case, touch it down, bring it to the edge of touch, and throw it straight out, but may take it himself if he can.

33. No player may stop the ball with any thing but his own person.

SHINNY.

THIS is called "Hockey" in England, "Shinty" in Scotland, and "Bandy," or "Hurley," in Ireland. It is played with a stout leather-covered ball, of the same size as that used for cricket, and sticks, shaped like a Golf-stick, but not so heavy at the turn. There are two sets of players, each of which have their own base. One on each side is selected as a "mounter." He

places the ball at his base, and "mounts" it by driving it as far as he can with a blow of his shinny-stick toward the opposite base. Those on his side strive to help it along; those on the opposite side, to beat it back. If it be sent "home" to the opposite side, it counts one to the mounter's party.

SHINNY STICK.

If it be driven back it counts one to the others. Every man must "shinny on his own side," that is, must drive the ball forward toward the opposite home. The party who drive it toward their opponent's home get the next mount.

RULES OF SHINNY.

1. The number of players at the medium game are eleven on a side—one mounter and ten shinniers. Short Shinny has seven on a side—Long Shinny, sixteen. The distance between the bases—the "home" of one party is the base of the other—is two hundred and twenty feet; and the distance between the stations, from the base to the first station, and from the last station to the home, is twenty feet. In Short and Long Shinny, the entire distance is shortened or lengthened in proportion to the players; and the distance between the stations may be altered by consent.

2. The play is for the best two in three games, or three in five. The number scored in a game is twenty-one. A ball sent home counts one. A ball returned to base by the opposite side, before it reaches the fifth station, counts one; before it reaches the ninth, two; and after it has passed the tenth, three. A ball sent home, in one blow, by the mounter, counts, in the short game, four; in the medium game, five; and in the long game, six. A ball returned home by being struck in the air, after having got by the mounter's blow past the sixth station, counts seven. All fouls count five against the party making them.

3. One on each side is placed at a station; and there is one baseman, who cannot advance to play beyond the first station from the base, and it is his duty to mount the ball and direct the game for his side.

4. Each player must "shinny on his own side;" that is, strike the ball in the right direction. If he do not, he may be told to; and should he refuse, it is counted against his side as a foul. Striking a player with a shinny-stick, if it show evidence of intention, is a foul. Tripping up an adverse player, placing the foot on the ball, kicking it, or snatching it up, is foul.

5. If the ball be shinnied or mounted so as to fall in an inaccessible place, the player first reaching it, and crying "Poods," has a right of placing it for a blow. For that purpose he must throw it to some spot in the line between the bases, not less than two nor more than twelve feet from his own person. If he do otherwise, it is a foul.

6. The markers, one from each side, with an umpire, are to be placed at a point equidistant from the bases, where they can command a view of the field; and here they count by tally. In case of their dispute, the umpire's decision is final.

7. The ball should be made of yarn, tightly wound upon an inch thickness of caoutchouc, covered with well-sewed calfskin, and be three inches in diameter The length, weight, and form of the shinny-stick is optional with each player.

8. Ten feet in the rear of its own base, the bunting of each side should be displayed. To prevent confusion, and to render easier the duties of markers and umpire, each side should wear shirts and caps of the same colors as they display in their bunting.

9. A ball once passing a home, or crossing its line, cannot be knocked back by the opposite party; but must be regularly mounted by the baseman, for the commencement of a new round.

10. At the beginning of each round, the shinniers must resume the stations allotted them at the commencement of the game, unless the basemen allow or order them to change for other stations.

Shinny is one of the best of ball-games, and should not be marred by any unnecessary roughness on the part of the players. Our young friends should remember that the absence of good-nature and fairness will spoil any game, however good it may be.

5*

HAND-BALL, OR FIVES.

It is impossible to play at this excellent game unless there be a high wall, free from abutments, and a smooth dry ground before it. When this can

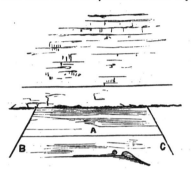

be procured, a line is drawn on the wall, about 38 inches from the ground; another line is drawn on the ground, about ten feet from the wall, A; and two others are drawn on each side as boundaries, B C. The instruments used in the play are a ball of india-rubber and a racket-bat, that is, a bat having a parchment cover in its broadest part. It has a long handle, and an oval bowl, covered with wire. The ball is hard, rebounding, small, and white. The game may be played by any number of persons, but is usually played by four boys, two on each side, who toss up for innings. The method of play is as follows: The game may be played either single-

handed or with partners. When it is played with partners, the players toss up for innings. The first player takes the ball, and, making it rebound from the ground, strikes it against the wall with his bat *above the line on the wall,* and so that it may fall *without the line on the ground.* The other then strikes it, and the players continue to hit it against the wall, either before it comes to the ground or at the first bounce, until one of them missing it, or driving it out

of bounds, or beneath the wall-line, loses or goes out. Of course the ball may fall anywhere within the side boundaries, after being once struck up by the player who is in. The game is usually fifteen, but is sometimes extended to twenty-five. Fives was originally played with the hand, instead of a racket, and in the fourteenth century was called Hand-Tennis, in England, and in France, Palm Play. This game is most frequently played in this country with the hand, and is usually known here as Hand-Ball.

RACKETS.

This game falls within a boy's province to play, and consequently within the province of a writer of a "Boy's Book" to describe. It is very like the play-ground game of fives; the employment of the racket, a kind of large battledore, consisting of a frame with a catgut or gutta percha netting strained within it, instead of parchment, constituting the chief difference. The racket ball is a very small white one, looking like a very well-made little tennis ball, such as all boys have played with and appreciated. The game is, strictly speaking, played in a space prepared for the purpose; the only real requisites, however, are a high wall and a sufficient area of level ground in front of the said wall, that the ball may rebound freely, and the players have sufficient scope for using their rackets. In former times, this and other similar ball-games were played with the open hand, the ball being struck up against the wall exactly as in the game of "fives." Then a glove was used, lined with tough leather, to deaden the blow of the ball on the hand. Then the players took to binding cords and tendons round their hands, to make the ball fly with greater force; and thus gradually the racket came to be made.

The way of playing the game is as follows:—Three feet and a half from the ground, at E, a white chalk line must be drawn along the wall against

which the ball is to be struck. Any stroke which sends the ball below this
line does not count Along the ground, in front of the wall, and parallel

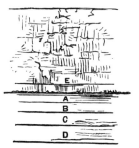

with the wall, four lines are drawn, forming
Bases A, B, C, and D. The two former of these
are called the in-hand, the two latter the out-
hand bases. The players are either two or
four in number ; if four, two play in partner-
ship, and either strikes as the ball comes
nearest to him, a stroke from either player
reckoning for or against his side. We will
suppose two competitors on the racket ground.
One of them has to guard Bases A and B, and is
called the *in-hand* player; the other has Bases
C and D, and is called the *out-hand* player.
Each stands in one of his own bases. The one on whom the lot falls to begin strikes the ball against the wall. We will suppose the in-hand player
beginning the game. He must strike the ball so that, rebounding from the
wall, it falls into one of the *out-hand bases.* If he fail to do this, if the ball
strikes the wall below the chalked line, or falls into one of his own bases, or
goes over the wall, his adversary counts *one.* If, on the other hand, the
ball, rebounding from the wall, comes to the earth in an out-hand base, the
out-hand player must strike it back against the wall at the rebound, in such a
manner that it shall bound off into an in-hand base; and thus the players go
on, each striking the ball in turn against the wall and into his adversary's
ground, until one of them fails to strike it, or strikes it under the line, or
over the wall, or into one of his own bases, when the other counts *one.* And
so the game continues, until one player or one side has gained a certain
number of notches, and is declared the winner. The number of notches to a
game is usually fixed at fifteen. Some players practise *volleying ;* that is, they
strike the ball with the racket before it reaches the ground, without waiting
for the rebound. This is perplexing to the adversary, as the ball comes into
his ground before he expects it. But on various grounds the practice is objectionable.

TENNIS.

This famous game, which was once so fashionable in Europe, is scarcely
ever played—nevertheless, we feel it to be our duty to allude to it, as some
of our young readers may be curious to know why those hard white balls
which they use for Rackets and other ball games, are called "Tennis balls."
Tennis is played with a racket, generally in a covered building called a Tennis
court, but instead of striking the ball against a wall, it is struck over a central net, on each side of which the players stand. The rules and penalties
of the game are very similar to those of "Rackets," but are too elaborate to
be here inserted.

GOLF.

Golf is played with a club and ball. The club is from three to four feet
long, according to the height and length of arm of the player. It is curved
and massive towards the end, to give strength and weight. This knob is
formed for strength from some very tough wood, as beech, and as it curves
and proceeds upwards, is planed off, so as to adapt itself to the handle,

to which it is partly glued and tightly corded down. A want of due attention to these particulars in the making of it will render the head liable to
split and fly off, by either a very hard or indirect stroke. The
face of the club is further secured by a piece of hard bone,
and occasionally of ivory, at least half an inch thick. It is
also loaded with from four to six ounces of lead, according to
the will of the player. The handle is usually bound with
cord, list, or velvet, at the pleasure of the owner. It is, however, to be remembered, that the form of the club, the materials of which it is made, and the numbers taken to the
golfing ground, vary considerably, according to the circumstances and habits of the players, the attendant cad or
caddie having usually many varieties, to suit every peculiarity
under which the ball may be placed; for in many clubs it can
never be touched by the hand until holed.

The Golf ball is about the size of an egg, and is made very
hard. It is composed of stout leather, which, having been
previously soaked in boiling water, allows of its being first very
firmly sewed, and then turned inside out, leaving a small opening only, by which it is very forcibly stuffed with feathers. The leather

being yet wet, it contracts into a ball of the dimensions stated, but never gets circular as that used in the game of cricket: it is afterwards painted over with several coats of white paint, in doing which, it is requisite that the lead used should be very pure and exceedingly well ground down, as well as that each coat laid on should be perfectly dry and hard before another is applied.

The game is played by two or more persons, so that there be an equal number on each side; but only two balls are used, one belonging to each party.

In regular matches, attendants, called "*caddies*," accompany the players with clubs of various sizes, shapes, and weights, called *pullers*. These are used when the balls lie near holes, and especial tact and skill are required to drive them into these holes; also, when the balls are in *hazards*, or positions of difficulty from the nature of the ground, and require to be raised or dealt with in a particular way. There are six kinds of clubs: the *common club*, used when the ball lies on the ground; the *scrape* and *half-scrape*, to extricate the ball from long grass; the *spoon*, to get the ball out of a hollow; the *heavy iron club*, to hit it out from among stones and mud; the *light iron club*, to knock the ball from shingly or sandy ground. The number of holes is not limited, but may be adapted to the peculiarities and capacity of the ground. A greater number than four may play; but where there are too many, confusion is likely to occur. At the beginning of each game, the ball is to be struck with all the force of the striker toward the first hole; afterward, when it gets near the hole, the strokes must be dealt judiciously and with tact, for now not strength, but accuracy, insures the victory. To insure a wider range for the ball at starting, it is struck not from the level ground, but from a slight elevation, made of earth or turf, and called a *tee*. When four players play a match—1 and 2 against 3 and 4—each party having a ball, the striking must be in this order: 1 plays, first striking off his own ball; then 3, the first player of the opposite side, strikes his; if he does not drive his ball as far as 1 did his, then 4, the partner of 3, strikes their ball to overtake, and, if possible, to pass that of their antagonists. This is called "one more;" and then 2 strikes his partner's ball, which is called playing "the like," or equal of the other side. Sometimes it may happen that two, three, or even four strokes must be played by one party to bring their ball to a level with the other: then the score will be one to two, one to three, or one to four, as the case may be. If the balls are nearly equal, the players strike alternately.

TOWN-BALL.

This is the game called "Rounders," in England, and is undoubtedly the origin of the popular game of Base-ball. It is played as follows: The players divide into two sides—about eight on each side is the best number. One side has first innings, and must assemble in the circle called "home," while the players on the *out* side are distributed over the ground to watch for the ball, or "fag out," with the exception of one, who acts as feeder, and whose position is indicated in the diagram. The first player on the *in* side takes up a little hand-bat, and the feeder pitches the ball toward him. The batsman strikes at the ball. If he misses it, or tips it behind the home, or if it is caught off his bat by any of the scouts, he is out, and the next player takes his place. If he succeeds in hitting the ball he at once flings down his bat, and runs off toward base No. 1, while the outsiders try to pick up the ball, and hit him with it, before he can get to the shelter of the base. If he can manage it, he may run to the second,

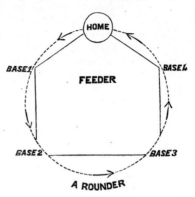

or even the third base: and sometimes such a good hit is given to the ball, that he is enabled to run all round, from one base to another, and get home, before it is flung at him; and this feat is called a rounder, and counts one. However, suppose him only to have got to base No. 1, when the ball is thrown up, he must stay there until the feeder has it in his hands again to feed for the second player, who has now taken up the bat in the home. As soon as the feeder begins to feed, the player at any base may make a bolt for the next. The feeder knows this, and therefore sometimes makes a feint of throwing the ball to the batsman, while he really retains it in his hand, to have a shy at the incautious player, who leaves his ground; for when a base is once quitted, there is no returning thither. The player must run on to the next, and stand his chance of getting put *out* by the way.

Sometimes it will occur that there is a player at each base; but it is a rule that none may let a companion pass him. Thus, if A, the first player, has got to base 3, and B is at base 2, when C, the third player, starts from home, after hitting the ball, C may not pass B or A, but A, at every risk, must keep on running, so as to be ahead of B and C. The player who arrives safe home takes his position at the end of the line, and begins *de novo*, when his turn comes round. When all the players on one side, excepting two, have been put out, it is competent for the best player of the two, with his friend's leave, to demand *two fair balls for the rounder*. This arrangement is carried out in the following way: The less skilful player retiring altogether, the other stations himself in the "home," bat in hand, and the feeder begins feeding him. The batsman need not strike at any feed unless he likes, as he is to have two "fair" or favorable balls; but if he strikes at the ball, and misses, or does not send it far enough to warrant him in running, this counts as one of his two balls. At the second hit, he must, *nolens volens*, drop the bat, and start off at full speed; for his task is to accomplish a "rounder," and get home again, without being hit by the ball. If he accomplish this, his whole side goes in again; if he fails, they are out. When some of the players on one side are out, and the remainder in different bases, so that the home is left empty, if even for a moment, the feeder, or any scout who can get the ball, may run into the home with it, or pitch it in, and then the other side is out; but if the ball misses the home, it counts one against the side who throws it. The side that counts most in rounders wins the match.

BALL-STOCK.

Ball-Stock, or as it is rendered in English, Ball-Stick, is, as its name would indicate, a German game. In the method of playing, it is very similar to Town Ball. The players are divided into two parties, as nearly equal in point of numbers and skill as possible. The bases are then marked out, as in the annexed figure, the principal ones being at A B, and C D, with the intermediate one at F; the distance is, of course, at the option of the players. They then toss up for innings, the in-party occupying the base, or home, A B, and the out-party stationing themselves in various parts of the ground, as in Town-Ball, or Cricket, reserving one boy as feeder, who should stand at 1, and another at 3, to toss back the rejected balls and "tips." The feeder, it is almost unnecessary to say, should be an active, clever player, and particularly clever in catching, the success of the party mainly depending on him. Having arranged these preliminaries, the feeder commences by tossing the ball gently toward the striker, who stands at 2, making it fall as near the end of the bat as possible, so as to allow good scope for the hitter's aim. Should the latter, after having got a pitch to his satisfaction, succeed in striking a good blow, he makes the best of his way to the base, C D, taking care to touch at the "resving-base," E F. On the contrary, should the ball be only tipped, or struck but a short distance, or stopped by one of the lookers-out, he should run to the "resting-base," and remain there till another of his party be more fortunate, and then take his opportunity. It sometimes happens that half a dozen or more are detained at the "resting-base" at one time, all looking forward to a successful hit to relieve them; the runners must be cautious not to quit this base too hastily, for when they have once left they cannot return, but must proceed; if struck with the ball while running from one base to another, they are out, and must remain inactive spectators of the game till the rest are so too. In the same way, when at the lower base, C D, they must watch their opportunity to return to the home, where they again take their turns with the bat, in rotation, in the order in which they arrive. Thus the game continues till all of the in-party are either caught or struck out, or fail in hitting the ball, three offers being the number allowed, as in Town-Ball. It is necessary that a good player be stationed at 4, that being, next to feeder, the most important post. Care should be taken to strike the ball as low as possible, to avoid giving "catchers." A looker-out should not throw at a boy running, unless he is sure of his mark, but should rather throw up the ball to the "feeder," or down to the one who stands at 4, as circumstances require, as they cannot fail to intercept the boy's arrival at the base where they are stationed.

TRAP, BAT, AND BALL.

In England, this game is considered to rank next to Cricket, but it is not played much in this country. The ball being much smaller than a cricket-ball, it is more difficult to catch; indeed, to stand before the balls of a good player requires great quickness of sight. The half-round bat is now seldom used, except by very young players; that in general use is flat, about one inch thick, and is called "spoon-shaped."

The trap is an instrument used to elevate the ball for the batsman. It is made in the form of a shoe, the heel part being hollowed out for the reception of the ball. (*See Illustration.*) In fixing it, it is best to sink the heel a little in the ground. The following are the laws of the game: Two boundaries are formed, equally placed, and at a great distance, on each side of the trap, between which it is necessary the ball should pass when struck by the batsman; if it fall outside either of them he is out. In playing the scientific game, besides the side boundaries, a line or tape should be stretched across the ground, several feet high, and twenty feet in front of the trap; over this line the batsman must send his ball or he is out; but this mode of playing is seldom adopted by juvenile players. The game is played by any number, either singly or by choosing sides. The innings are tossed up for, and the player, who is to commence, places the ball in the spoon of the trap, touches the trigger with the bat, and, as the ball hops from the trap, strikes it as far as he can. One of the other players endeavors to catch it; if he does so before it reaches the ground, or if the striker miss the ball when he aims at it, or hits the trigger more than twice without striking the ball, or makes "an offer" (the trigger to be touched but once), he is out, and the next in order, which must previously be agreed on, takes his place. Should the ball be fairly struck, and not caught, as we have stated, the out-player, into whose hands it comes, bowls it, from the place where he picks it up, at the trap, which if he hit, the striker is out. If he miss it, the striker counts one toward the game, which may be any number decided on. There is also a practice in some places, when the bowler has sent in the ball, of the striker's guessing the number of bat's lengths it is from the trap; if he guess within the real number, he reckons that number toward his game; but if he guess more than there really are, he loses his innings. It is not necessary to make the game in one inning.

In playing, do not touch the trigger too forcibly, but sufficiently so as to rise the ball about a foot and a half from the trap, and catch it in your hand once or twice, instead of striking, before you call "play." This will enable you to judge better where you should stand, so as to strike the ball with greater force, and to observe in which direction you should send it, with the least chance of its being caught.

NINE-HOLES.

Dig near a wall nine holes, of about six inches in diameter, and three deep. Let each player have one of these, according to his number, which must be determined by lot. At about six yards from the holes draw a line, and from this, as a fielding-place, one player pitches the ball into one of the holes. The boy to whom this hole is assigned immediately runs to it, while all the other players run off in different directions. The player snatches the ball from the hole, and throws it at one of the "runners;" and if he hits him, the one so hit becomes "pitcher," and the one that struck him marks one. Should he not hit him, the player who throws the ball loses a point, and bowls. The player who misses his aim at throwing the ball at his partners a second time, becomes a "tenner." If he loses the third hit, he is a "fifteener;" if the fourth, he stands out, and can play no more. When all the players are thus out, the last player remaining in wins the game, and he can compel each of the losers to stand, with their hands open, against the wall, for him to throw at, and give what is called the "brandy ball." If the ball be a soft one, this conclusion of the game is all very well; but if a hard ball be used, it ought to be omitted, or the "brandy" may be too strong.

HAT-BALL.

The players put their hats or caps on the ground, close to the wall, in such a manner that a ball can be easily pitched into them. A line being marked on the ground, about fifteen feet from the wall, one of the players takes his station at it, and begins the game by throwing the ball into one of the caps. As soon as he does this all the boys run away, excepting he into whose cap the ball is thrown, who immediately runs to take it out, and endeavors to strike one of the fugitives by throwing the ball at him; if he can do so, the one struck has a small stone, called "an egg," placed in his cap, and has to take his turn at pitching the ball. Should the thrower fail to hit one of the boys as they are running away, an "egg" is put into his cap, and he has to pitch the ball into the caps again. If a player fails to throw the ball into a cap, he earns an "egg," but continues throwing until he succeeds. When a player gets three "eggs" in his cap, he is out. When all the players but one have been struck out, he is considered the winner, and the punishment of the losers then commences; one of them standing near the wall bounces the ball at it with all his force, and next stands with his back to the wall, stretching out his right arm, and placing the back of his hand quite close to the wall, while the winner, standing where the ball fell, takes aim, and throws the ball at the said loser's hand three times; each of the losers likewise receives the same punishment from him. In some places it is usual, when one boy gets out, for him to bounce the ball against the wall, and all the other players, standing at the spot where the ball first touched the ground, to have their three balls at his back,

as he stands with his face to the wall. Should the ball in rebounding swerve either to the right or left, a line must be drawn from the spot where it falls, to a place directly in a straight line from the boy at the wall; thus, suppose A is the boy who has just bounced the ball, which instead of going direct to B, has deviated from the straight line A B to C, a line should be drawn from C to B, and the winner should stand at the latter.

CATCH-BALL.

This is very simple play. The ball is thrown into the air by one player, the others standing round him. He calls out the name of the player for whom the ball is thrown. If it be caught by the player so called, before the ball reaches the ground twice, he scores a point; if any of the other players catch it, they score a point, and the other loses one.

RING-BALL.

This is a game which requires great skill to play properly. A short post is inserted in the ground, a large ring is fastened to the top of the post; the ring is placed upright, and turns upon a swivel, so that if any thing strikes against the sides of the ring, it turns round. This ring and post is a fixture. The players have then a large ball, made of light wood, and about six inches in diameter or eighteen inches round. The players either play in two parties, or else all against each other; a large circle is marked on the ground, having the ring for the centre, and the player that is first, goes in, holding the ball in his right hand, bowls or pitches it at the movable ring. If he is lucky enough to pitch it through the ring, he counts one; if not, one of the other party goes on, and tries his luck; but if the first is successful, he goes on again and again, as long as the ball completely passes the ring, counting one each time. So, also, when the other party gets the ball, they go on as long as they can; and when there are several players, he who loses a ball is out of the game till all the others have had their turn. The parties play for a certain number, as thirty or fifty, and whoever gains that number first has the game. At opposite sides of the circle upon the ground, and which ought to be about five yards from the post, there are two marks made, one for each party, and it is from these marks that the ball must be pitched. The lower part of the ring should not be above three or four inches from the ground, and the size of the ring should be such that the ball can easily pass through it, but not with much space to spare, so that if the ball is six inches in diameter, six and a half will be quite enough for the ring. The difficulty in playing is this, that if the ball strikes the side of the ring, instead of passing through it, the ring will turn round, and then instead of presenting a flat face to the next player, he will perhaps have it sideways to him, when it will be almost impossible for him to pass it through. Sometimes the players agree to stand at any part of the circle they please, which makes the game much easier.

LAWN BILLIARDS.

This very pretty game is easily played, and will accommodate any number of players, from ten to twenty.

The apparatus consists, firstly, of a number of differently colored wooden balls; secondly, cues, in wooden handles about five feet long, with a ring at their extremity; thirdly, of an iron ring just large enough to permit the balls to pass through, and which revolves on a pivot.

In playing the game, the sharp point of the ring is stuck into the ground, so as only to allow the ring to be visible. Care must be taken to ascertain that, when thus fixed, the ring can spin freely on the pivot. The players now withdraw to a spot about sixteen paces from the ring, and the first player pushes his ball with the cue, so as to make it pass through the ring. If he succeeds, he counts one towards his game, and gets another stroke. If he misses, he loses one, and the next player proceeds. When all have played at the ring, they are at liberty either to play at each other, or at the ring, and if they can "carom," i. e., strike another player's ball and then pass through the ring, they count two. As the game proceeds it becomes very exciting, as the good player will often manage to drive his opponent into such a position that the edge only of the ring is presented to him; and whenever he himself is in such a case, he will contrive to give his ball a peculiar twist that strikes the ring aside as it touches, and enables the ball to pass through. The game is thirty-one points.

TEN-PINS.

This game in England is played out of doors, on smooth turf, which is known as the bowling green. In this country it is played on long, smooth

platforms, called "alleys," at the end of which the pins are set up, on a frame, in a triangular arrangement, with the point of the triangle toward the player, as in the diagram.

At the end of the alley there is a padded cushion to diminish the force with which the ball is sent down the alley. Each player in the match game has three balls to roll. If by hitting the centre and foremost pin by a winding motion of the ball, he knocks down all of the pins, it is called a ten-strike, and he counts ten on the game, with two more balls to roll. The pins are set up again, and if he can do it twice more, he will get thirty; but this is rarely done. As many pins as he knocks down, however, in the three rolls are put to his count. Sometimes the whole ten pins are knocked down in two rolls, when the player has a "spare ball," and the pins are set up for his last ball, and whatever he knocks down is added to his former count. A bad player may roll his three balls down the alley, and not hit more than three or four, or it may be no pins.

TIP CAT.

Tip Cat, although not strictly a Ball game, ought to be noticed here. It is a dangerous game, and should be played with great caution on the part of the players. It is a game well known in England, but is seldom played in this country. It is played with a club resembling a ruler. Its name is derived from a piece of wood called a "Cat," of about six inches in length, and an inch and a half or two inches in diameter, diminished from the middle to both the ends, being of the shape of a spindle or double cone; by this contri-

vance the places of trap and the ball are at once supplied, for when the
cat is laid upon the ground, the player with his stick tips it at one end by a
smart stroke, which causes it to rise in the air with a rotary motion, high
enough for him to strike it as it falls, in the same manner as he would a ball.

There are various methods of playing the game of Cat. The first is exceedingly simple, and consists in making a large ring upon the ground, in
the middle of which the striker takes his station. His business is to beat

the Cat over the ring; if he fails in so doing he is out, and another player
takes his place; if he is successful, he judges with his eye the distance
the Cat is driven from the centre of the ring, and calls for a number at pleasure to be scored for the game; if the number demanded be found upon
measurement to exceed the same number of lengths of the club, he is out—
on the contrary, if it does not, he obtains his call.

The second method of playing Cat is to make four, six, or eight holes in
the ground, in a circular direction, and as nearly as possible at equal distances from each other, and at every hole is placed a player with his club.
One of the opposite party, who stands in the field, tosses the cat to the batsman who is nearest to him, and every time the bat is struck, the players
are obliged to change their situations, and run once from one hole to another
in succession. If the cat be driven to any very great distance, they continue
to run in the same order, and claim a score of one toward the game every
time they quit one hole and run to another. But if the cat be stopped by
their opponents and thrown across between any two of the holes before the
player who has quitted one of them can reach the other, he is out.

SKITTLES.

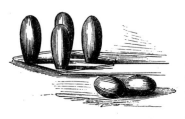

Skittles is played in a manner
somewhat similar to ten-pins, but the
number of pins is only four. These
are very large, and are arranged
on a square frame-work, so as to present one of the angles to the player.
The bowl used for playing this game
is of the shape of a cheese, and is
usually made of lignum vitæ, as being very heavy and hard wood.
The game requires more bodily strength than ten-pins, as the bowl must be
thrown upon the skittles, and not rolled up to them.

The best play is to throw the bowl with a round-handed swing of the arm, so as to strike the nearest skittle at the right of its upper third. The ball then springs to the second skittle, and from this generally twists to the third, while the fourth skittle is sent down by the roll of the one first struck. It is very difficult to make this throw successfully, and many players prefer driving down the first and third skittles with a straightforward shoot, and then making their second ball spring across from the second to the fourth. This latter stroke appears very difficult, but is soon learned; the great point being to throw the bowl high, so that it may drop as perpendicularly as possible on the left of the upper third of the second skittle. In the long run, the constant repetition of this practice will overbalance occasional brilliancy of play. The game is not played in this country, except in a few places.

DUTCH PINS.

This game is nothing more than a modification of ten-pins; the pins being lower, and the centre one bearing the name of king, and a crown upon its head. The great point in this game is to strike the king out of the board without knocking down any of the subjects. If this can be done, the game is won. In all other cases the king counts for no more than any of his subjects. It will be observed that nine pins only are used.

BOWLS.

This is a thoroughly English game. Indeed, we do not remember ever having seen it played in America. However, it is capital sport, and one that will tend to develop the muscles. We therefore give it as a novelty to American boys.

In former days kings of England did not disdain to play at bowls; and in the improvements made by bluff King Harry VIII., at the palace at Whitehall, "divers fair tennice-courts and bowling alleys" are particularly mentioned. The game has been traced back to the thirteenth century, to the times of King John and Henry III.; how long before those days it existed, there are no means of ascertaining.

Songs and poems, too, were written and recited in praise of bowling. here is a piece of one, as a specimen:

> " Perferment, like a game at boules,
>   To feede our hope hath divers play:
> Heere quick it runns, there soft it roules;
>   The betters make and shew the way
> On upper ground : so great allies
>   Doe many *cast* on their desire;

Some are thrust, and forc'd to rise,
  When those are stopt that would aspire.
*   *   *   *   *   *

" Some get by *knocks*, and so advance
  Their fortune by a boysterous aime :
And some, who have the sweetest chance,
  Their en'mies *hit*, and win the game.
The fairest *casts* are those that owe
  No thanks to fortune's giddy sway ;
Such honest men good *bowlers* are,
  Whose own true *bias cutts* the way "

Bowling-greens are simply perfectly level tracts of smooth turf; but a very good game may be played on a selected spot on a common or field where the grass is short, and the ground tolerably level. A small bowl, perfectly round, and called the *jack*, is placed on the ground. The bowlers, each armed with two balls, which are numbered, to distinguish them from each other, take up their positions at a certain distance from the jack, and each in turn bowls toward it, he whose ball comes nearest counting *one*. When there are more than two players, sides are formed; the balls being played alternately, and the side one of whose balls comes nearest counting one point. The number of points which must be made to win the game varies, but is generally fixed at twenty. When only two play, they may stand side by side to deliver their bowls; when there are several on a side, the usual plan is to bowl from opposite ends of the green, the jack being placed in the middle. The balls for bowling are not exactly spherical, but are flattened slightly at two ends, making the ball a spheroid, like the earth. If, after both sides have delivered their balls, two of one side are nearer than any balls of the other side, the side whose balls are nearest to the jack counts *two :* if more balls are nearer than any of their opponents', they count a higher number in proportion. The art in bowling consists in knocking away the opponents' balls from their position near the jack, or in carrying off the jack itself from among the opponents' balls, and in bowling nearer than any other without disturbing ball or jack

A CONVENTION OF BALLS.

PART II.

Athletic and Graceful Recreations:

INCLUDING

GYMNASTICS, SKATING, SWIMMING, ROWING, SAILING,

HORSEMANSHIP, RIDING, DRIVING, ANGLING,

FENCING, AND BROADSWORD.

ATHLETIC SPORTS

GYMNASTICS.

GYMNASTIC exercises may be begun by a boy of about eight years of age, or may be commenced at any age; but, in all cases, he should begin gently, and proceed gradually, without any abrupt transitions. They should be commenced before breakfast in the morning, or before dinner or supper; but never immediately after meals; and the pupil should be very careful, after becoming heated by exercises, of draughts or cold, and especially refrain from lying on the damp ground, or from standing without his coat or other garments; and rigidly guard against the dangerous practice of drinking cold water, which, in many instances, has been known to produce immediate death.

A proper practice of, and mastery over, the feats of Gymnastics, serve to develop the muscles, and are preparatory to the proper performance of all athletic sports and exercises. What we propose to show, are feats as may be performed by any lad, without expensive apparatus, and without a teacher; and which will be amusing as well as healthy to the performer. These are preliminary to other and more pleasing exercises; for fencing, rowing, riding, etc., are gymnastic feats of a more advanced kind. We shall commence with Marching, and so advance through the whole round.

MARCHING.

It is not necessary to say any thing about the ordinary mode of walking, which should be easy, free, and natural; or about the Indian lope, which is used in fast walking, the body being thrown forward, and the strides long; but the principles of the military step should be explained, as a good preparation for gymnastic exercises.

The boys should choose a captain, who should be a rather bright fellow, and he must study out thoroughly the following, so as to be able to drill the rest, who act as his company. He should first teach them the position and facings, and then the principles of the step. In giving out the words of command, he should pronounce the first word, or words, if there are two or more, slowly, by way of caution, and the last word quick and sharp. The moment the boys hear the first word they should get ready, and then execute the command when the second word comes. If the command consists of one word only, the last syllable is the part to be obeyed, and the first the caution.

The Position.—At the word of command, "Atten—*tion!*" which should be pronounced with the last syllable accented, every boy will stand in this way:

His heels on the same line, and touching each other.

The feet turned out equally, so as to make a shape like a broad letter V.

The knees straight, but not stiff.

The body erect, but inclining a little forward.

The shoulders square.

The arms hanging naturally.

The elbows near the body.

The palm of the hand turned a little to the front, with the little finger resting on the seam of the pantaloons.

The head erect and square to the front, but not stiff nor constrained.

The eyes looking straight to the front, and at a spot on the ground about fifteen paces off.

Each boy will place himself so that he can touch the left side of his right-hand neighbor, without jostling him, by raising his elbow slightly, take the position given, and wait for the next word of command.

The captain will now give the word, "Eyes—*right!*" At the word *right,* each boy will turn his head gently and quickly, so as to bring the inner corner of the left eye on a line with the centre of his breast, so as to look down the line of boys on that side. But he must not move his body or his shoulders. The head must turn, as it were, on a pivot.

At the word "*Front!*" the head will be brought back to its former position.

At the word, "Eyes—*left!*" the head will be turned to the left, in the same manner as was previously done to the right.

At the word "*Front!*" the head will take its former position.

At the word "*Rest!*" each boy may stand in any easy way he likes, but will not step out of his place. Whenever the word "Attention!" is given, he will take the position before taught.

The Facings.—The next thing is the facing to the right and left. At the word "Right—*face!*" each boy will raise the right foot slightly, turn on the left heel, raising the toes a little, and then replace the right heel by the side of the left, on the same line. This will bring the boy in a position at right angles to the right, with the way he stood before.

At the word "Left—*face!*" he will raise the left foot slightly, turn on the right heel, raising the toes a little, and replace the left heel by the side of the right, on the same line. This will place him on the left, at right angles with his former position.

To turn completely around, the word is, "About—*face!*" At the word *about*, each boy will turn on the left heel, bring the left toe to the front, carry the right foot to the rear, without turning it, the hollow of that foot opposite to, and about three inches from, the left heel, the feet at right angles with each other. At the word *face*, he will turn on both heels raise the toes a little, extend the hams, face to the rear, and, at the same time, bring the right heel by the side of the left. He must take care, at the same time, to keep his body as square as possible, these motions being done with the feet.

The Step.—Having learned the position and facings, each boy will now exercise the step. To do this the captain will give the word, " Forward—common time—*March!*" At the word "*Forward!*" each boy will throw the weight of the body on the right leg, without bending the left knee. At the word "*March!*" he will carry his *left* foot smartly forward to the length of this step,* the sole near the ground, the ham extended, the toe a little depressed, and slightly turned out, the knee also slightly turned out; he will, at the same time, throw the weight of the body forward, and plant flat the left foot, without jarring or shocking the leg, precisely at the distance where it finds itself from the right when the weight of the body is brought forward, the whole of which will now rest on the advanced left foot. The right foot will next be brought forward in the same manner, without striking one leg against the other, or turning the shoulders, and with the face kept to the front. This will be repeated until the word " Halt!" At the word " *Halt!*" the foot in front will be put to the ground, and the other foot brought up to it, and there remain.

To practise this properly, the boy who acts as captain should either cry "one," as the left foot is set down, and "two," as the right foot is brought to the ground; or use the words "left! right!" in the same manner, thus marking the time.

Common time is ninety steps to the minute; the time of the quick step is one hundred and ten to the minute. The captain can learn this cadence

---

* In a man this would be twenty-eight inches, from heel to heel; and it is proportionately less for boys.

by counting with a watch before him, and the other boys will get it by practice.

The quick step is executed in the same way as the step in common time; but the time is not named in the command. The word is "Forward—March!" and when it is given without the time being mentioned, it will always be the quick step.

The double-quick step is faster, and is, in fact, a slow run, in the time of one hundred and sixty-five steps to the minute. Before commencing this, the boys will be taught the principles of the step by being exercised in marking time, which is a funny but necessary proceeding.

The word is "Double-quick step—*March!*" At the word "Double-quick step!" each boy will raise his hands to a level with his hips, the hands closed, the nails toward the body, the elbows in the rear. At the word "March!" he will raise to the front his *left* leg, so bent as to give the knee the greatest elevation, the part of the leg between the knee and the instep being kept perpendicular, the toe depressed; he will then replace the foot in its former position, and execute the same movement with his right leg, and so on, alternately, *without moving forward*, until the word "*Halt!*" when he will bring the foot which is raised by the side of the other, drop his hands by his sides, and resume the position he would take at the word "Attention!"

When the captain has practised the boys for some time in marking time in this way, he will set them to execute the step itself. The word is "Forward—Double-quick—*March!*" At the word "*Forward!*" each boy will throw his weight on the right leg. At the word "*Double-quick!*" he will place his body just as he would do at the command "Double-quick—Step," in marking time. At the word "March!" he will carry forward the left foot, the leg slightly bent, the knee somewhat raised; will plant his left foot, the toe first, at the quick-step distance;* and then do the same with the right foot, throwing the weight of the body on the foot that is down, and giving the arms a slight natural motion. This will be done alternately until the word "Halt!" when the boy will stop in the same manner set down for the other steps.

In executing these manœuvres the line of boys should be taught to dress —that is, to align itself, or keep itself straight. To do this properly, the captain will number the boys, from right to left, and each boy will learn to know his number. He will then place No. 1 and No. 2 on the right, two paces in front of the line of boys, and, having put them in a perfect line, just so close that they can touch each other's elbow, without opening their own, but not so close that they jostle each other. He will now call out, "Number Three!" At the word, No. 3 will march forward two paces in quick time, shortening the last pace so as *to be about six inches behind the line.* He will move up by steps of two or three inches, quickly and steadily, until he

---

* This, in a full-grown man, would be thirty-three inches.

reaches the side of No. 2, and, with his *eyes* to the right, without removing his shoulders from their square position, will see that he is in exact line, and at the same time that he can touch slightly the elbow of No. 2. Then No. 4 will go through the same movement at the word, and so on. When this has been practised for some time, the boys will be able to align themselves easily at the word of command. This, if the boys are desired to dress toward the right, is "Right—Dress!" If toward the left, is "Left—Dress!" As soon as the rank is aligned, the captain gives the word, "Front!" when the head and eyes are brought square forward again.

If the boys are marching in quick, or double-quick time, and they want to face about, without halting, the word is, "Right about—March!" At the word "*March!*" which must be given at the instant the *left* foot is coming to the ground, each boy will bring this foot to the ground, and by turning on it, face the other way. Then he will put down his right foot, and step off, left foot forward, in the new direction.

It is necessary to particularly remember—1. That where there is no time mentioned between the word *Forward* and *March*, the quick step is always to be used.

2. That the order for marking time in the double-quick may be distinguished from the order to march in the same step in this way—it has no "*forward*" before it, and the cautionary word is "Double-quick step," instead of "Double-quick." Thus, to mark time, the word is "Double-quick *step*—March!" while to march in the same time, the word is "*Forward*—Double-quick—March!"

3. The command "About face!" is to turn each boy to the opposite face, when he is at a halt; and the command "Right about!" when he is marching.

RUNNING.

In running, you go through the same motions as the double-quick step in marching, but you increase the swiftness of your motion accordingly.

LIMB EXERCISES.

Independently of the walking and running, there are exercises of the arms and legs which are worthy attention; and may either follow or precede the learning of the step.

The boys are to be brought by their captain to the attitude of "Attention."

First Arm Exercise.—At the word *one*, throw out the palm to a line with the body, and raise the arms slowly, without bending the elbows, till they are horizontal with the shoulder, and the boys stand in the form of the letter T, the palm of the hand pointing downward; at the word *two*, bring the arms down sharply into the first position. (*See Illustration.*) Remember that all the boys must be taught to keep exact time in their exercises—and the word of command must help them to this—the word *one* being given slowly, and *two* sharply. Thus: oo-nn-ne, *two*, oo-nn-ne, *two*, and let each exercise be repeated till the boys learn to do it all together, smartly and well.

Second Arm Exercise.—At the word *one*, bend the right elbow, without moving the upper part of the arm, and bring the fist up in front of the shoulder, with the knuckles toward the shoulder; at the word *two*, drop the arm to the former position. Repeat—one, two; one, two; the same exercise with the left arm; the same with both arms. (See Fig. 1.)

Third Arm Exercise.—At the word *one*, raise the right arm as in the last exercise; at *two*, bring it straight up beside the head (fist doubled); *three*, return to the same position as at *one; four*, drop arm to position of attention. Repeat—one, two, three, four; one, two, three, four; same exercise with left arm; same with both arms. (See Fig. 2.)

Fourth Arm Exercise.—At the word *one*, raise the right arm as in the second exercise; *two*, stretch it out horizontally *in front* of you, as if striking a blow (knuckles upward); *one*, arm as in second exercise; *two*, strike out again. Repeat— one, two; the same with left arm; the same with

FIRST POSITION—ATTENTION! both arms.

Fig. 1.   Fig. 2.   Fig. 3.

Fifth Arm Exercise.—Same as the fourth, but at the word *two* turn the arm in stretching it out so that in the horizontal position the knuckles are downward. Repeat with left arm; then with both. (See Fig. 3.)

Sixth Arm Exercise.—At the word *one* double the right arm as in the third exercise; at *two* bring it straight up above the head, (fist doubled;) *three*, extend it outwards from *the side* so as to form a right angle with the body; at *four* bring the arm back to the position of *one*, striking the right lung. Repeat—one, two, three, four; one, two, three, four; same with left arm, same with both. (See Fig. 4.)

Seventh Arm Exercise.—At the word *one* raise the arm slowly forward (keeping it quite stiff till it has described half a circle and is raised above the head; at *two* complete the circle by bringing it down backward, letting the fist be as far be-

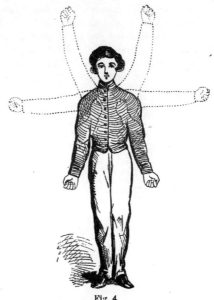

Fig. 4.

hind the body as possible, till the hand returns to the first position. Repeat this, increasing the rapidity of the movement, as the exercise becomes more familiar, but always keeping perfect time to the word of command; the same with the left hand, and with both hands.

Eighth Arm Exercise.—The same as the seventh, but begin the circle by moving the arms backward from the body, and bring them forward in the descending half of the circle, thus reversing the movement.

A variety of other exercises may be undertaken, all tending to give strength and suppleness to the arms; but the foreging, if perfectly under-stood, will be found sufficient for the purpose.

LEG EXERCISES.

First Leg Exercise.—At the word *one*, advance the left foot, keeping the knee straight, and the point of the foot a little outward, and just touching the ground; the whole of the weight of the body being balanced on the right leg; at the word *two*, draw the left leg rapidly behind the other, and repeat the exercise several times. Then go through the same with the right leg.

6*

Second Leg Exercise.—This exercise consists in lifting each leg alternately as high as possible, the body being kept perfectly straight and steady. In all these exercises care must be taken that the boys move exactly in time.

Flexion of the Lower Extremities.—This is an important exercise, and should be executed with particular care. Bring the tops of the feet nearer together than in the usual position, and place your hands on your hips, the thumbs in the front and the fore fingers behind. Then bend the legs, keeping the body perfectly erect and the knees together. At first this bending

must be only partial, but as the movement is repeated, the pupil should bend lower and lower each time, until he can assume the position shown in the engraving, and resume an erect posture, standing on the top of his toes, without moving his feet further. The head and body must be kept perfectly erect during the whole time.

JUMPING.

There are several ways of jumping, the principal being upward, downward, and the long leap. These should be well studied in sport, as circumstances may arise in after life in which it becomes necessary to practise them in earnest.

The Long or Horizontal Leap.—To execute this leap, the boy, without a run, must bring his feet close together, then bend his legs slightly, throwing his arms forward, with the hands closed, at the height of the shoulders. This bending of the knees must be repeated two or three times, as by this means an impetus is acquired, similar to the "accumulation of power" obtained by swinging a stone round the head with a sling two or three times

before discharging it. When the requisite impulse is obtained, he must press the soles of the feet hard against the ground, and by a sudden and vigorous spring, extending his arms and his legs at once, he launches himself forward, alighting, as far on as possible, on the tips of his toes. Care must be taken to bend the legs the moment the feet touch the ground after the leap, as this deadens the shock caused by the sudden weight of the body thrown on the feet, and the weight of the spring. In this, as in all kinds of leaping, it is advisable to begin with short distances, taking care to leap neatly and gracefully, gradually extending the distance as proficiency is attained. By attempting too much at first, the learner will only expose himself to disappointment, besides getting into a slovenly way of leaping, and running the risk of a sprained ankle.

The Downward Leap.—This is a very useful exercise; and as it presents

THE DOWNWARD LEAP.   THE UPWARD LEAP.

some difficulties, it should be practised sedulously at gradually increasing heights. It is, moreover, a gymnastic operation which many have involuntarily to perform in some emergencies of actual life. The number of people annually mutilated, or even killed, by jumping down from heights, in cases of fire and similar calamities, is lamentable; and yet the majority of these might have escaped unhurt, if they had only known how to set about the undertaking. Like poor little Prince Arthur, in Shakspeare's play of " King John," they have been compelled to say:—

> " The wall is high, and yet I will leap down;
> Kind ground, be merciful, and hurt me not."

Whereas, had they known how to leap, they need not have been at the mercy of the "kind ground" at all. Proceed in the following manner:

Having mounted to the height from which you are to leap down, stand with your feet together, the toes pointed forward, not outward. Close your fists at your sides, and raise yourself gradually on tiptoe, bending the knees, and raising your hands as you do so (see Illustration); on bending for the third time, drop gently off the elevation (carefully avoiding any thing like a spring), and as you descend through the air, straighten the body, throwing the arms upward as much as possible. Directly the points of your toes touch the ground, bend the knees forward, to break the impetus of your fall. Take care to increase the height from which you leap very gradually, and never attempt a deeper jump till you are quite perfect in the previous ones.

The Upward Leap.—Bring the feet close together. Close the fists, raising them above the head, and bend the knees two or three times, to get an impulse. Jump suddenly from the ball of the foot (the heel not touching the ground), and as you rise, bring the hands rapidly down to your sides, as this will give you an additional impulse upward. Here, too, the distance of your leaps must be increased very gradually, as the effect of missing your *tip*, as it is called, may be painful and unpleasant.

Running Leap.—For a horizontal leap, with a run, the boy should start at a brisk pace, increasing as he nears the point from which he is to spring; on reaching which, he must jump forward, without a moment's pause, so as to lose none of the impulse of his run. On rising to his leap, let him press the balls of his feet strongly against the ground, throwing his fists forward horizontally in the direction of his leap. On touching the ground after the leap, the knees must be bent and the body thrown backward. The same rules apply to the upward leap, except that here the fists must be thrown not forward, but upward, as the body rises.

Two points are to be particularly observed in jumping *with a run.* The first is to bound from the ground with as much force, and the second, to alight upon it with as little force as possible. If the leaper comes down upon his heels, the whole body receives a very unpleasant shock, in which the brain partakes, and violent headache is frequently the consequence. If he comes down flat-footed, and his shoes happen to be a little short, or too flexible, he will *stump* his toes in a very painful fashion.   The right way is to come down upon the ball of the foot, with both toes and heels raised, and then to bring down the heels as the legs are straightened after the jump. In a horizontal leap, the jumper sometimes finds himself thrown unpleasantly forward.   This is because he has not leaped high enough off the ground, but has skimmed along it like one of the stones used in "Ducks and Drakes."   But "Duck and Drake" practice in leaping is a very painful affair, frequently accompanied by "bumps" on prominent parts of the face, and bruises on the hands.

POLE LEAPING.

The pole should be made of some tough, hard wood, not liable to snap, and adapted to the height and strength of the boy, and to the length of the leaps he is to undertake.

The boy should begin with a short pole, and practise leaping without a run.   Rest one end of the pole on the ground, holding it by both hands, placed near each other, a little above the head.   Then spring up evenly on both feet, managing the arms so that the elbows are bent when the body passes the pole.   Push yourself forward as far as possible, leaning all your weight on the pole, and continue this practice, gradually increasing the distance of your leaps.

For a horizontal leap, with a run, stand at some distance from the space you wish to clear. Hold the pole with the right hand above your head, thumb upward, and with the left hand at the height of the thigh, thumb downward.   Then start with a run, keeping the lower end of the pole in front of you.   On reaching the edge of the ditch, or space which you wish to jump, stick the end of the pole into the earth, and by a sudden and powerful spring, raise the body, leaning the weight on the arms as you rise, making a half turn as you clear the space, and alight on the balls of the feet, on the other side, bending the knees to break the force of the descent.   The longer the distance you have to leap, the nearer the top must you grasp the pole, the distance between your hands and the lower end of the pole being in fact the radius of a half-circle, of which your feet, in leaping, describe the circumference.

Low walls and fences may be jumped by means of the leaping pole.

Here it becomes necessary to lift the feet high as you rise, so as to clear the wall, and as you descend bring the upper hand smartly down, so as to jerk the lower end of the leaping pole upward, that it may clear the wall.

DUMB-BELLS

Fig. 1.

Fig 2.

Fig. 3.

Are excellent for opening the chest and developing the muscles of the arms; but care must be taken not to put too heavy a pair into the hands of a novice. In ancient times they were used by the Greeks and Romans in their gymnastic evolutions. The first exercise consists in raising the dumb-bells alternately to the height of the shoulder, the hands of the boy being brought steadily up, straight before him; all appearance of jerking or effort must be avoided. The movements of dumb-bell exercises are generally pretty much like those in arm exercise; but they are more efficacious, inasmuch as the weight of the dumb-bells develops the muscular powers of the arms and opens the chest. The motions must not, however, be continued too long without rest, as the work is rather heavy. We give the following two exercises, which, together with the motions described in the hand and arm exercises, already given, will be amply sufficient for the young gymnast.

First Exercise.—Take the position of Fig. 1, incline the body forward, throwing the arms upward behind the back, as in Fig. 2; resume position of Fig. 1. Repeat this four times. Take the position of Fig. 1, throw the chest and arms backward as in Fig. 3; resume position of Fig. 1. Repeat four times. Then perform the combined exercises four times. *These motions should not be performed rapidly.*

Second Exercise.—Take the position of Fig. 4, stand *erect*, head inclined a *little* back, with the arms extended full length in front, and the bells held horizontally, with the thumbs together. At the command *one*, bend the body a little forward, and bring the arms directly to the rear, as represented by the dotted lines in Fig. 4, turning the bells completely over, and still keeping the thumbs together in making the motion. At the command *two*, bring the bells to first position. Repeat this rapidly several times.

THE INDIAN CLUB.

This branch of gymnastics is one we strongly recommend to boys. In using the clubs the chest is expanded, greater freedom is given in the use of the arms, the muscles of the legs and arms as well as those of the whole

Fig. 4.

body are brought into full use, the wrist is strengthened, the grasp of the hand is made firmer, the circulation of the blood is regulated, and the health in general is greatly improved. If their use is persevered in, they will render the person who practises with them *ambidextrous*—that is to say, he will be able to use his left arm almost as well as his right in hurling,

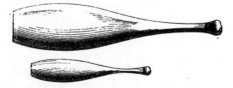

flinging stones, lifting weights, and similar operations. The young gymnast must be careful, and use light clubs at the outset, remembering that if he persevere, he may soon achieve the skill and strength necessary to wield heavy ones with ease. The clubs vary in length, ranging from eighteen to thirty inches. The shape mostly used is shown in the foregoing illustration.

The illustration represents the largest and smallest sizes; there should be at least six sizes between these two, making eight different sizes in all.

As these clubs increase in length they increase in diameter (at the bottom) also.

Two clubs must be made of each size, and each fellow in size should be as nearly as possible of the same weight as the other. They are usually made of hard wood, to withstand any accidental blow, for it will frequently

Fig. 1.

happen that they will be brought in contact one against the other, especially by beginners. Again, it is for their weight that they are used; were it not for that, the using of them would not have the required effect.

First Exercise.—Hold the smallest club in the right hand, and with the motion of the wrist only, give a circular motion to the club; as from left to right, from right to left, from front to back, from back to front, as near as possible. The arm must be kept straight down at the side. Repeat the exercise with the left hand.

Second Exercise.—Repeat the above exercise with the arm bent at the elbow, but the forearm must be kept perfectly still.

Third Exercise.—Hold a small club in either hand, and repeat the above exercise, allowing both the clubs to revolve the same way.

Fourth Exercise.—The same exercise as last, but causing the clubs to revolve in opposite directions, thus: let the left hand club go from left to right, whilst the right hand one goes from right to left, or *vice versâ.*

Fifth Exercise.—Repeat the same exercise with the arms extended in front, at the sides, or straight over the head.

Sixth Exercise.—Repeat the last exercises, allowing the arm to be bent at the elbow.

Seventh Exercise.—Repeat the last exercises with the elbow as the centre of the described circle instead of the wrist, placing the arm in the several relative positions. (See Fig. 1.)

Eighth Exercise.—Exercise the arms in any of the foregoing exercises, with a large and small club at the same time, and one arm doing the same exercise as the other, or different.

Ninth Exercise.—Lift the club to the shoulder, first with the right arm, then with the left, then both arms together. Then the clubs must be whirled slowly round the head (see Fig. 2), each arm being used alternately, and the foot of the club depressed toward the shoulder as the club passes round the head. The motions must be made slowly at first, and gradually increase in rapidity as the pupil becomes proficient.

Fig. 2.

Tenth Exercise.—The same exercise with two clubs, and both arms to revolve in the same, or in different directions.

Eleventh Exercise.—Hold a club in either or both hands, with the arm bent at the elbow. Let the club lean on the shoulder first, then as low as possible, and with the motion of the wrist only, carry the club out straight with the forearm. This should be done as if a blow were intended to be given.

Twelfth Exercise.—Hold as large a club as possible, with the arm or arms extended in front or at the sides.

Thirteenth Exercise.—Whilst holding out a club with one hand, achieve any of the aforementioned exercises with the other.

Fourteenth Exercise.—Hold any of the clubs (the larger the better) in either or both hands, bring the hands up suddenly under the arm-pits, and drop them again as quickly as possible.

Fifteenth Exercise.—Bring the hands up under the arm-pits, and extend them suddenly in front or at the sides with the clubs upright.

Sixteenth Exercise.—Repeat the above exercises successively. The hands may be brought up under the arm-pits or to the shoulders, as most conve. nient, before proceeding with the next.

In performing the last three exercises, the elbows must be kept as high and as far back as possible.

Seventeenth Exercise.—Hold a club in each hand with the arms extended at the sides, the hands to be kept as high as the shoulders, and the sides of the clubs, and if possible the hands, made to meet behind.

Eighteenth Exercise.—Achieve any of the foregoing exercises whilst standing on one leg.

Nineteenth Exercise.—Aim at any imaginary object with either of the largest size clubs, allowing the blow to be given as if to descend on a man's head, and when the club shall have reached that imaginary point, it is to be brought to a sudden standstill, as if something had impeded its progress, and there held for a short time. This exercise should be done both in front and at the sides.

Twentieth Exercise.—Repeat the above exercise with a club in each hand, the blows to be given both at the same time in front or at the sides, or with one in front and one at the side.

PARALLEL BARS—OUT-DOORS.

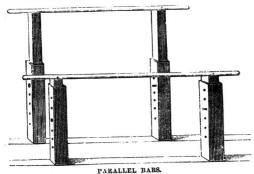

PARALLEL BARS.

If the apparatus be intended for the open air, four posts must be fixed in the ground, perpendicular on the inside, eighteen or twenty inches apart at the ends, and about five feet six inches apart lengthways, which will give the form of a parallelogram. These posts should be about three feet six inches* above the ground, and made of fir poles, as near the same size as possible.

The bars should be of elm, and free from knots, and should extend about a foot beyond the posts at each end, which will make them seven feet six inches long. They should not be perfectly round, but slightly flattened on both sides, and about two inches and a half in the longest diameter.

There should be a kind of shoulder in those parts of the bars which rest on the posts, which will give additional strength to the bars. The ends should be slightly rounded, to fit the hollow of the hand.

* Four feet would not be too high.

If this apparatus be erected in a building, we should recommend the posts to be made so as to allow the bars to be lifted higher, if required, and according to the height of the gymnast, or the height required to perform the feat.

Let the case for each post be made to allow a two-inch square pillar to slide up and down inside it, thus:

The case should be made of wood, from three-quarters of an inch to one inch in thickness, according to the strength of the wood used.

Holes (represented by the dotted lines) must be bored through both pillar and post, into which an iron pin is put to keep the bar at the required height.

These holes are to be made in the direction of the bars, about four inches apart, and six in number, counting from the top. All four pillars must be alike in every respect. The bars and posts should be neatly mortised together, and, for further security, a wooden peg should be used instead of an iron one.

1.—TO GET ON THE BARS.

Stand between the bars, with the hands hanging close to the sides, spring up, place a hand on either bar, and keep yourself suspended.

Another Method.—When the bars are about level with the top of the learner's hips, the hands must be placed on each bar, and the legs lifted from the ground, which will cause the whole weight of the body to be upon the arms; the head will now be thrown a little forward.

All that is requisite for the learner to do now is to straighten his arms, thereby raising his body into an upright position. (See Fig. 1.)

This requires great strength in the wrists as well as in the arms, and cannot be performed but by one who has strength in those parts.

Practise this exercise with the fingers on the inside of the bars, as well as on the outside.

2.—WALKING.

Suspend yourself, as in No. 1, at the end of the bars, and move

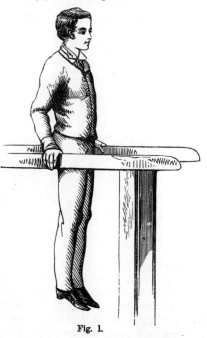

Fig. 1.

the hands alternately along them, which must be done without bringing the shoulders out of their place, or hasty and irregular steps being made, the body or legs twisted about, or any like irregularity.

When the opposite end has been reached, the walk must be repeated backward to the point of starting.

This will be a little tedious at first, but after a little practice it will be quite easy.

This exercise must be repeated with the fingers on the inside of the bars. The arms must be kept perfectly straight, or you are liable to fall.

3.—HOPPING.

This exercise tries the strength of the wrists very much, and to perform it the learner must mount between the bars as in the last, and instead of moving the hands alternately, they are to be moved both at the same time; the legs are to be kept perfectly straight.

Short steps should at first be taken, and increased in length gradually, as soon as the learner can do it with ease.

4.—SWINGING.

In order to get a perfect freedom in the arms and wrists, the swing is an exercise to be practised.

While suspended between the bars, the learner must swing the legs and

Fig. 2.

body to and fro; very little at first, until he can with safety increase it. The legs must be kept close together and straight.

In increasing the swing, the legs must be made to do their utmost both in the forward and backward swing, and in either case the feet must be carried as high as the head, the higher the better. (See Fig. 2.)

In the backward swing the body will be parallel with the bars. (See Fig. 3.)

5.—JUMPING.

This exercise is similar to the last, but in order to do it the learner must get his body into a good swing, the jump being made between the swing.

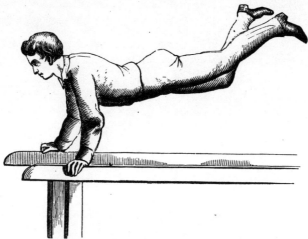

Fig. 3.

Owing to the variety of exercises to be achieved in this, we have, for the purpose of its being the better understood, divided it into parts.

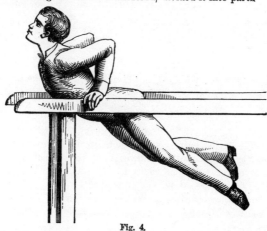

Fig. 4.

First.—During the swing, advance the arms alternately, one in the forward and the other in the backward swing.

Second.—Advance one arm alternately in the forward swing only.

Third.—Advance one arm alternately in the backward swing only.

Fourth.—Advance both arms at once in the forward swing only, as in Fig. 2.

Fifth.—Advance both arms at once in the backward swing only, as in Fig. 3.

Sixth.—Advance the arms in either the forward or backward swing.

These exercises will be found to make the arms ache, but this will soon wear off after a few times practising.

Keeping one leg (or both) up will make the exercise more difficult, yet this should be also practised.

6.—THE LONG LEAP.

Great strength is required in this exercise. It is performed by swinging the body at one end of the bars, and, with a sudden spring, jump to the

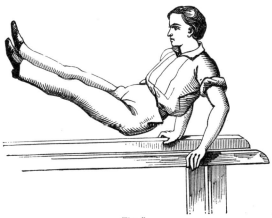

Fig. 5.

other end (or as far as you can), which must be done in the forward swing, and, in alighting on the bars again, let the arms be bent, as in Fig. 4. The position of the body in the forward spring is given in Fig. 5.

7.—THE LONG RUN.

When the body has been swung as high as possible, and in the backward swing (see Fig. 3), make as many alternate movements of the hands along the bars as you can before you allow your legs to fall.

This must be repeated to the end of the bars.

This exercise may also be done with the body in the forward swing, but this is much more difficult; yet it is to be overcome by practice.

8.—THE KICK, OR SPUR.

While swinging, as described in No. 4, draw up either leg alternately, and send it out again with all your force; or bring up both legs at once, but it must be done in the back swing, and when the legs are high above the bars, or you are likely to feel the effects of your own kick.

The sudden motion of the legs is likely to throw the body a little out of its balance, yet, grasping the bars firmly will prevent it, after a little practice.

9.—To Bring the Legs Over.

Swing between the bars, and, with a gradual motion, throw both legs over the right-hand bar.

Fig 6.

With a sudden spring, bring the legs between the bars again, and throw them over the left bar. (See Fig. 6.)

The hands must grasp the bars firmly in this and the next exercise.

10.—To Rise and Fall Below the Bars, or the Letter L.

Sit on the ground, grasp the bars with the hands on the outside, and pull yourself up gradually until the shoulders are level with the bars; then as gradually lower yourself, still keeping yourself in the same position, namely, the feet elevated and the legs straight, as in Fig. 7. It should be repeated two or three times.

Difficult at first, but soon achieved by practice.

This exercise may be done in No. 1, when the legs are to be gradually raised until level with the bars. The knees are to be kept perfectly straight.

11.—To Rise and Sink Down above the Bars.

Mount between the bars as in No. 1, grasp them firmly, and lower the body gradually by bending the arms until you assume the position shown in

Fig. 8, but without allowing your feet to touch the ground, then gradually raise yourself by trying to straighten your arms; this will put the whole strength of your muscles to their utmost.

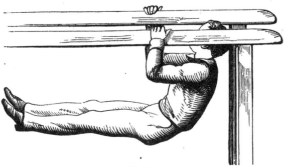

Fig. 7.

Do not allow your body or legs to move or turn about, but take it easily, and after a few times trying you will become perfect master of it.

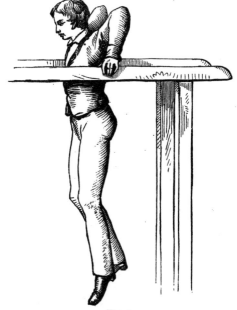

Fig. 8.

12.—THE JANUS.

Mount between the bars in the middle, and throw a leg over each in front of your hands.

Grasp the bars firmly, and, with a spring, bring the legs between the

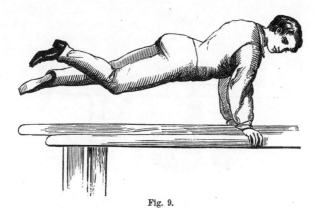

Fig. 9.

bars, and carry them behind you, but in so doing cross the legs, as in Fig. 9, and in giving the body a slight twist, allow them to rest on the bars, when the right leg will be on the left-hand bar, and the left leg on the right-

Fig. 10.

hand bar. (See Fig. 10.) Do not always turn your body the same way, or let the same leg be always uppermost in crossing them.

This exercise should be repeated five or six times successively.

7

13.—THE BARBER'S CURL.

Stand between the bars, and sink down until the head be below the bars. Grasp the bars with the hands and straighten the knees into a sitting posture, thereby forming the letter L (Fig. 7).

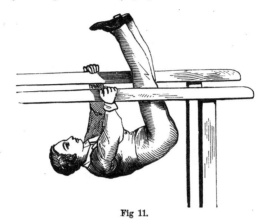

Fig 11.

Now bring the legs gradually over between the arms (Fig. 11), till they perform a circle, or until they come nearly down to the ground (Fig. 12),

Fig. 12.

and after staying in that position for a short time, bring them back again quite as slowly as you brought them over.

The knees must be kept straight during the performance of this exercise, likewise the feet kept off the ground.

Difficult to beginners, and makes the arms ache, but it is nevertheless easily performed after a little practice.

Do not give it up in despair if unable to do it the first, or even the second time trying, for this is a very pleasing exercise, and tends greatly to strengthen the muscles of the arms, and likewise causes the grasp to be much firmer.

14.—THE TURNOVER.

Sit astride the bars as across a saddle, stretch your hands in front, fall forward, drop between the bars with a quick motion, and grasp the bars behind you, which will cause you to release your hold with your legs (see Fig. 13), and by bringing them together directly they are free of the bars, they will drop between them, when you may alight on the ground.

Fig. 13.

Try it slowly at first, so as to understand the mode of catching hold of the bars, and do not attempt to let go the bars with your legs until your hands have a firm hold, or when sure of not making a false aim at them.

Gradually increase the quickness of the motion until you can achieve it without any pause, for it is necessary to do it quickly in order to do it properly.

15.—THE FORWARD SOMERSAULT.

This feat is generally performed at the end of No. 2, or any other exercise which brings you to the end of the bars. It gives a very brilliant finish to any of those exercises, and is not so difficult as may at first appear.

When you reach the ends of the bars with your hands firmly grasping the ends, as shown in Fig. 14, lean a little forward and bring the body into an upright position, with the legs bent over the head, and in so doing bend the arms, which will cause the shoulders to come between the bars, bring the legs over, and when you find yourself nearly overbalanced, give a slight spring

Fig. 14.

with the wrists, and let go your hold of the bars, when you will alight on your feet, but keep the toes pointed towards the ground.

To beginners a slight swing will enable him to carry over his legs a little better, but in so doing the swing must not be too strong, or his head is very likely to go much farther than is required, and may cause him to measure his length on the ground.

Do not mind if, in endeavoring to keep yourself on your feet after reaching the ground, you fall forward or backward (the latter happens if you let go your hold too soon), for after you have accomplished it at least five or six times, you will be more eager to go on to other and more difficult exercises.

16.—THE SPANISH FLY.

This feat is a very brilliant finish when the gymnast is at the end of the bars: it is not so difficult as at first appears.

Fig. 15.

When at the end of the bars, place the hands over the ends, swing to and fro twice, making the back swing last, which must be made much higher than the bars, then open the legs, carry them over both bars, and by letting go your hold, alight on the ground. (See Fig. 15.)

In flying over the ends of the bars, let the body lean well forward, assisted with a slight spring of the hands, which will give you greater courage to let go, likewise a better and easier method of bringing your legs together again without knocking them.

The greater the impetus used in swinging, the greater will be the success of achieving the feat.

17.—To Stand on the Bars.

Place your hands on either bar, spring with your toes, and throw the right leg over. Bring the other leg up and hitch the toe under the bar (see Fig. 16), lean the body forward, with the arms extended in front to balance yourself, then bring the other (right) foot on the bar, as close as possible to

Fig. 16.

the body, and by means of the toe under the bar, with which you are to steady yourself, raise your body up so as to stand on the right leg. Do not unhitch the toe until you are firmly standing on the bent leg.

Now gradually lower yourself again, taking care how you slide the toe along under the bar, and likewise to maintain a good balance.

THE HORIZONTAL BAR.

For Out-doors.—Three posts, one lower than the other two, are to be fixed in the ground about six feet apart, and a bar to be fixed in either two of them, as in the annexed cut.

The bars, if made of wood, to be about a quarter of an inch more

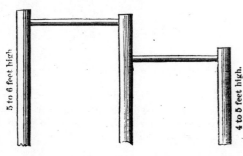

in diameter than the parallel bars, as greater strength is required in some of the exercises, during the performance of which the bar is very much bent.

If these bars be made of iron, they should be much smaller, and should not be used if rusty, but first rubbed with a piece of coarse sand-paper, otherwise the clothes will suffer. We prefer the wooden bar for several reasons, and therefore recommend it.

For In-doors.—Two posts, about eight inches square, are to be so fixed as to withstand any amount of work on the bar without being loosened in the ground.

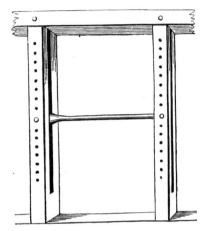

Previous to their being fixed, a groove about six feet long should be cut through each post to about eighteen inches from the ground.

About twelve or fourteen holes should be bored through the post within the length of the groove for an iron pin to pass through, to keep the bar at the required height.

The bar may be of the same length and size as required for the out-door, but it should have a small shoulder at each end, in order to rest firmly against each post, thus:

HORIZONTAL BAR.

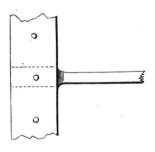

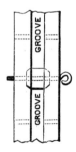

The bar may then be lifted to any height required.

18.—TO HANG ON THE BAR.

Jump up and lay hold of the bar with both hands, let the thumbs be on the same side of the bar as the fingers, and likewise the knuckles as far upward as possible.

Grasp the bar firmly without any fear of not being able to retain your hold for a long time, and alternately take away the right and left hands.

Suspend yourself as long as convenient, but do not overtire yourself, and in dropping from the bar be careful to alight on the toes.

19.—WALKING.

Grasp the bar as in the last, and move the hands alternately along the bar, beginning with short and even steps, increase their length until able to take them with ease, and when capable of so doing, place one hand on either side of the bar, and proceed as above, but the hands must now advance one before the other, and in returning walk backwards.

Keep the legs straight and the toes pointing to the ground, and do not move them about in performing this exercise.

20.—JUMPING.

This exercise is performed in the same manner as the last, but the hands must move both at the same time instead of alternately.

The legs may be bent a little, to assist the learner in making the spring.

21.—SWINGING.

Hang by the hands about the middle of the bar, move the legs and body to and fro as if on a common swing, and after a little practice you will find your body rise level with the bar. (See Fig. 17.)

Fig. 17.

Do not be afraid of swinging too high, as many feats, to be hereafter mentioned, depend greatly on the neatness of the swing.

Swing to and fro at least a dozen times, not more, and in leaving the bar do so in the forward swing, and when your feet are rising to a level with your face, when you must let go your hold, and with a motion of the body alight on the toes.

This is a very neat way to leave the bar, and the farther the gymnast can alight on his feet from the bar, the greater will be his after success, and the more graceful will his performance appear.

Above all, avoid jerking the legs in swinging.

22.—TO RISE AND FALL.

This exercise is very similar to No. 10, but this sometimes receives the name of breasting the bar; it is, nevertheless, nothing more than the pulling up of the body as high as the arms will allow.

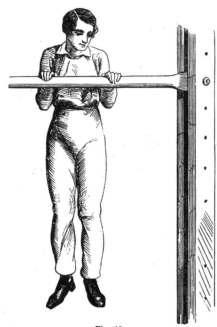

Hang on the bar, and gradually pull yourself up until your breast is as high as the bar, then steadily lower yourself again. (See Fig. 18.)

Repeat this five or six times at least, and if not able to succeed in doing it the first time of trying, do not despair, for on this exercise likewise depends the being able to accomplish many others, as it tends greatly to strengthen the muscles of the arms and the wrists.

23.—THE LETTER L.

This exercise only differs from the last in one respect, that instead of the legs being allowed to hang straight, they are brought to a right

Fig. 18.

angle with the body, thereby forming the letter L, and in this position raise the body as in the last exercise. (See Fig. 7.)

This will seem more difficult to the learner than No. 10, partly owing to the difference in the position of the body; but practice will soon overcome that difficulty.

24.—THE PANCAKE.

Proceed as described in No. 21, and when the body has swung nearly as high as the bar, let go your hands, and after bringing them smartly together (see Fig. 19), renew your hold on the bar, and continue to swing. Persevere in doing it until able to do it with ease and perfection; the former only to be obtained by constant practice, while the latter consists in the smartness with which the hands are brought together.

The farther the gymnast springs from the bar, the greater the effect.

Fig. 19.

This exercise should be repeated three times before allowing the feet to touch the ground.   It is a difficult exercise to beginners, but very soon overcome.

The bar should be about two feet above the head of the gymnast, when standing on the ground.

25.—To Turn a Pancake.

Proceed as described in No. 21, and every time the body is in the forward swing (when the back will be toward the ground), give a smart turn, letting go the bar and grasping it again quickly, before the body has time to descend.

After a little practice, the body should be turned every time, thereby preventing it from descending in the backward swing, consequently the gymnast has the opportunity of seeing which way he goes.

The gymnast will find that he will improve in this exercise every time he practises it.

26.—To Bring the Body Through.

Hang on the bar as before described, and with a gradual motion bring the legs up toward the bar, bend the knees, pass them between the arms under the bar, and allow the legs to pass through, together with the body,

7*

which must fall as low as the arms will allow; when the body, arms, and legs ought to be nearly in a line with each other. (See Fig. 20.)

After remaining in that position for a short time, return through the arms again, without allowing the hands to loose their hold, or the feet to touch the ground.

It will be found very difficult for beginners to return; until able to do so,

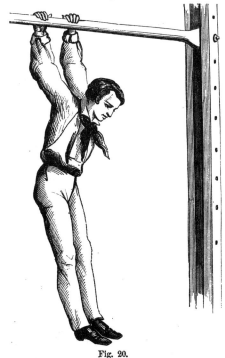

release the hands and fall to the ground; but after a little practice, especially with a little assistance at first, it will become very much easier than it would at first appear.

27.—THE EVERLASTING TWIST.

This is an excellent exercise, and one we strongly recommend, as in performing it the gymnast must, if he have not yet done so, suspend himself by one hand, thereby testing the strength of each wrist.

Proceed as last described, but in lieu of bringing the body again through the arms, let go one hand, when the body will swerve completely round, grasp the bar again, and repeat the exercise as often as convenient. If it be done six times without stopping, and always letting go the same hand, it will ap-

Fig. 20.

pear as if the arm was being twisted completely round.

We have always found the above give the greatest satisfaction, and we should therefore recommend its constant practice and attention.

Do not always use the same hand.

28.—TO HANG BY THE LEGS.

Bring the legs through as described in No. 26, and throw the legs over the bar instead of allowing them to fall toward the ground. Rest them as shown in Fig. 21, bending them over the bar as far and as firm as possible, let go the hands and allow them to hang loosely.

After remaining in that position as long as convenient, bring the arms up, and by drawing the body up a little, grasp the bar again and allow your body, after having unhitched your legs, to fall as in No. 26, and drop to the ground, taking care to alight on the toes.

Another method will be described in a future exercise, as it will be necessary to achieve one or two exercises to bring the body above the bar in order to sit on it.

29.—CIRCLING THE BAR.

This, to a beginner, is a difficult and annoying exercise. Difficult because he is very likely to be a long time before he be able to do it to perfection; annoying because his shins are sure to suffer if he does not go over the bar as he intended. Yet when once accomplished, no exercise will be found more easy.

Hang on the bar and proceed with No. 26, but carry the legs above the bar, instead of under, and by pulling the body up with the arms, and a slight motion of the wrist, carry the legs completely over the bar, and in going over they will act as a sort of balance to your body, and with the assistance of your arms, the body will be brought into the required position.

As a means of enabling a young gymnast to circle the bar sooner than by the method just described, only let him fix the bar about as high

Fig. 21.

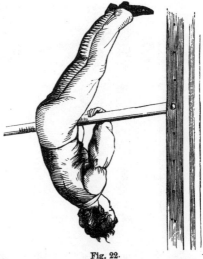

Fig. 22.

as his chin, when, after having placed his hands·on the bar, and with a step
forward, he might give his legs that impetus upward, which will carry him
over the bar quickly as possible, but in so doing the legs must be

Fig. 23.

straightened (see Fig. 22), and carried over the bar by the simultaneous
motion of the arms, especially the wrists.   This will, in a very short time,

Fig. 24.

enable him to do it as first described, when the bar should be raised high
enough to cause the gymnast to jump in order to reach it.

30.—THE LEVER.

This exercise requires great strength in the muscles of the arms, and is only to be achieved by practice, and with a determination to succeed.

Go through the arms as in No. 26, keep the legs perfectly straight with the body, and gradually lower them until level with the ground as in Fig. 23. After remaining in that position a short time, either drop to the ground, or carry the body back again through the arms; the latter should be preferred.

31.—THE SUSPENDER.

This exercise is meant to test the strength of the grasping of the bar with one leg.

Stand under the bar and grasp it with both hands, one on either side, and with a sudden spring throw the right leg over the bar toward the left; then place the toes of the left foot under the bar, as in Fig. 24; let go the hands, and allow your body to lower itself as much as possible, remaining in that position as long as convenient.

The hands may either hang loosely, as in Fig. 24, or be folded across the chest.

Repeat the exercise by reversing the position of the legs.

The leg under the bar must be kept perfectly straight.

THE SUSPENDED BAR, OR TRAPEZE.

This is preferable to what is generally termed the "triangle," for two reasons: first, the ropes need not be but one-half the length; second, the gymnast can perform a greater number of the horizontal bar feats with the suspended bar than with the triangle. It is constructed thus,—two ropes are suspended from the ceiling or roof of the building, by means of crooks, each rope to have a loop at each end, cased with iron, to prevent its wearing away.

A bar of tough wood, about twenty-eight inches long, is hung on to the ropes by means of crooks fixed to the ends of the bar, thus:

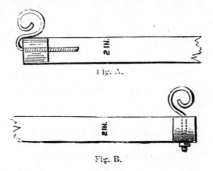

Fig. A.

Fig. B.

The crook in Fig. A is screwed *into* the end, and the wood is kept from splitting by an iron ring or cap, represented by the shaded part.

The crook in Fig. B is screwed *through* the cap and bar, and kept in its place by an iron nut.

An extra iron ring should be fixed in the lower end of each rope, to enable the bar to be hitched on the more readily, the ring to be about the size of the crook.

The ropes should not be less than five-eighths of an inch in diameter, and six feet six inches long.

32.—THE TURN.

Place the left hand on the bar, with the fingers backward, and the thumb in front of the bar, close to the left-hand rope, which must be grasped with

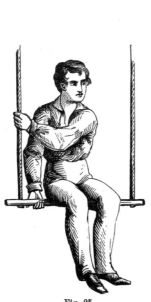

Fig. 25.

Fig. 26.

the right hand about the height of the shoulder, then carry your body round the left-hand rope, and by lifting your legs over the bar resume your position on it.

Do the same with the right-hand rope, only let the left hand be uppermost. (See Fig. 25.)

The rope must be grasped as shown above.

33.—To Stand on the Bar.

First sit on the bar, grasp the ropes as high as possible, and with a gradual motion, similar to No. 10, pull yourself up until you can place your feet on the bar; then place the hands a little higher, to ease yourself, or proceed with the next exercise.

34.—To Stand at Ease.

Turn your back against one of the ropes, with your feet on the bar, but the toes turned out (see Fig. 26), and when perfectly steady, fold the arms across the chest.

Do this against either rope, and do not always keep the same foot in front.

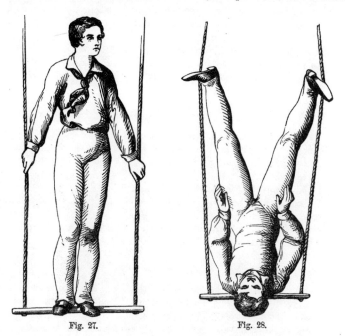

Fig. 27.   Fig. 28.

The feet may be placed as in Fig. 26, or the front foot may be slided forward, so as to rest the hollow of it against the bottom of the rope, and the other laid across it, as when sitting in a chair a person stretches out his legs for ease and comfort.

35.—The Overthrow.

Stand on the bar and grasp the ropes firmly, as shown in Fig. 27, which shows that the knuckles are in front, and the thumbs downward, the elbows may be a little up, but the hands should be as high as the hips; then, by leaning forward and lifting your feet off the bar, allow yourself to turn quite over, when you may either alight on the bar in the sitting posture, or place your feet on the bar again; the latter you will be able to do if your hands be high enough before you turn over.

This exercise may be reversed, and the best description or idea how it should be done will be to advise the learner to notice the position of his arms and hands after he has accomplished the above exercise, and reverse the motion of the body on turning over.

36.—To Stand on the Head.

Grasp the ropes about a foot above the bar, after having first knelt on it; then, with a motion similar to the last, throw your legs upward, open them and place them against the ropes to steady yourself, then lower the body, and place the head on the bar.

After a little practice the young gymnast will be able to let go his hold of the ropes and fold his arms across his chest, or in any other position; but he must be very careful how he does it the first time.

The hands should be placed as shown in Fig. 27.

37.—The Rest.

This exercise is very similar to the above.

Sit on the bar, grasp the ropes, slide down until the bar touches the back of the neck, and in so doing, throw the legs up and rest the feet against the ropes. (See Fig. 28.)

The body must be bent a little at the hips.

The hands may be folded across the chest, or placed as shown in Fig. 28.

Care must be taken in this as well as the last, for a slip might cause you to repent of not having paid sufficient attention to the advice given.

38.—The Swing.

In swinging with the suspended bar, the ropes are sure to sway to and fro, and in thus swinging, the force required must be given at the right time, otherwise the ropes might check you.

It would give additional beauty to this exercise if the young gymnast were to perform any other exercise during the swaying of the bar, as Nos. 22, 26, or 29, or any other that he might select.

The leg-swing must be made while hanging by the legs, as in No. 28, when the arms must be well used to accomplish the exercise, to give satisfaction.

Do not omit to keep your feet well toward the ground in the leg-swing, after having once set yourself in motion.

39.—THE CATCH.

Sit on the bar without holding, and, in throwing yourself back, open the legs wide, and turn the toes outward, when they will hitch around the rope, as shown in Fig. 29.   After remaining in that position for a short time, pull the body up and grasp the bar, when you can easily unhitch the feet.

40.—THE LEAP.

After achieving No. 38, and when you think yourself high enough from the ground, let go the bar and alight on it, either in the forward or backward swing, but let the toes bear the weight of the body on alighting, and not the heels.

This should be practised with a slight swing at first, as the position of the body is not the same on alighting with the forward as with the backward swing.   After a little practice, the gymnast may try how far he can leap from the bar.   The higher the swing, the farther will be the leap.

THE SUSPENDED ROPES.

This rope is supposed to be about six feet six inches long.   The top loop-hole is protected by an iron ring, similar to those with the bar just mentioned.   The middle loop is formed by tying the rope as represented, the bottom of the loop to be about three feet from the lower loop, which ought to be bound with some kind of metal,* both to protect

Fig. 29.

the hands from rubbing against the ropes, and to keep the loop always in the same shape; otherwise, when the hands are in them, and the whole weight of the body off the ground, they will be very much squeezed, owing to the ropes not retaining their proper position.

The top and bottom loops should be spliced to the required size.   The lower loop to be about eight inches long, and about five inches in diameter near the bottom, which will give, very nearly, the shape of the battledore.

The ropes are to be the same size required for the bar.

* Brass is mostly used, and is not liable to rust.

A few knots may be tied in these ropes to facilitate the climbing of them; but this should be done after the rope has been well stretched, or at least sufficient room should be left between any knots previously tied for an additional one, in case the rope should be at any time too low.

Many parties prefer these ropes joined at the top, and in many gymnasiums this is found very useful; the rings on the top are firmly bound in with tar-core, after which each single rope is bound round a few times to prevent the rings from slipping out of their places.

The knots and loops in both ropes must correspond, and the middle loops must, if possible, hang outward when the ropes are suspended, and not hang between them, or the feet are liable to be caught in them whilst performing an exercise requiring the feet in the air.

41.—SIMPLICITY.

Grasp the bow ends of the ropes, one in each hand, throw the legs up as quickly as possible, something similar to No. 13, only much quicker, and on the feet falling to the ground, let go the ropes and alight on the ground.

Difficult as it may appear to beginners, there is not one more simple when accomplished.

The quicker this exercise is done, the more likely is the gymnast to succeed, and after trying it a few times he will be able to alight on his feet in safety.

42.—THE BARBER'S CURL.

This exercise is described in No. 13; but instead of grasping the bar, the loops must be grasped (see Fig. 30), and in doing it the ropes must be perfectly steady, and not allowed to sway to and fro.

43.—THE EVERLASTING CURL.

This exercise differs from the other two just mentioned, insomuch that the feet *must* not touch the ground, and ere that can be allowed the gymnast will have to undergo a very severe punishment, which we shall not here attempt to describe, but will leave him to proceed as in the last, and on the feet coming down, spread the arms a little, when he will find that his arms will seem to come out of their sockets; but heed it not, for this exercise when done three or four times without stopping, will give extra freeness in the use of the arms, and likewise give greater satisfaction to any one who may see it done.

In doing this exercise, say three or four times without stopping, the feet are not to touch the ground under any pretence whatever, and when able to do it without feeling the least unpleasant sensation, we will leave the

young gymnast to judge of the injuries or
benefits obtained by the practising of it.

44.—ANOTHER METHOD.

Proceed as last described, but allow the
feet to touch the ground, and spring very
slightly every time you carry up the legs.

This should be repeated both backward
and forward as often as possible; it will
make you very giddy, but will soon wear
off after reversing the motion of the body.

The ropes must not be let go until the
exercise be finished, but allowed to twist
up as many times as the gymnast goes
round.

Fig. 30.

45.—THE LIFT.

Grasp the ropes and throw the legs up
as before, but in so doing, straighten
them and keep them upright. Keep your
body down, and do not let it be bent, nor
the feet touch the ropes. (See Fig. 31.)

When in this position, pull yourself up
as far as possible, and let your body fall
suddenly, still keeping the legs and body
in the same position.

This is a good exercise, and tends to
make the gymnast keep a firm hold of the
ropes.

46.—THE LEVER.

This exercise is described in No. 30, the
only difference being in the position of
the hands.

47.—THE TWIST.

This is a very difficult exercise both to
achieve and to describe.

Hang by the hands and throw the legs
over; but before allowing them to fall too
far, give the body a twist so as to bring
the back (the nearer the middle of the
back the better) against the arm toward
which you turn, and in so doing, let go
the other rope, and keep yourself suspended as long as agreeable. (See Fig. 32.)

Fig. 31.

The legs and disengaged arm must be kept extended as far as possible.

and the body must incline a little backward, for it to rest on the arm more securely.

Great practice is required before a beginner might be able to accomplish the difficult part of this exercise, as it not only tries the strength of the muscles of the arm, but the twist given at the shoulder, and the difficulty

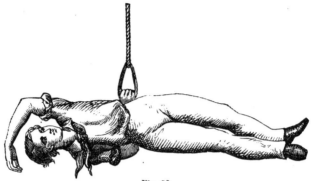

Fig. 32.

found in balancing the body evenly, causes many to abandon the exercise as *impossible*. But when a young gymnast has once achieved it, he will feel a pride in doing it before those who before deemed it *impossible*.

48.—The Letter L.

This exercise is described in No. 10, the hands here grasping the loops instead of the bars.

49.—The Stretch.

After rising as high as possible, as in the last exercise, bring one hand to the front and stretch the other out (see Fig. 33): the loop in the front must be grasped firmly, whilst the other is kept in the required position by the open hand, as seen below, the fingers being extended, and the whole strain falling on the hollow of the hand.

This should be done with both hands. The legs should be kept perfectly straight, or they may be made use of as if ascending a flight of stairs, the slower the better.

50.—The Change.

Proceed as last described, and after bringing one hand in front, let go the other, and keep yourself suspended for a short time; then grasp the other loop and do the same with that one, changing as often as convenient.

This is a very clever and amusing exercise, and one which should be persevered in.

51.—To Mount between the Ropes.

This is another very trying exercise, but, like No. 46, the shoulders will reap the full benefit.

Rise between the ropes as in No. 49, and with a sudden turn of the arms (one at a time at first) bring the elbows uppermost (see Fig. 34), when you may gradually straighten them by raising the body.

This exercise should be persevered in until achieved, as it will enable the gymnast to be the better able to do the next.

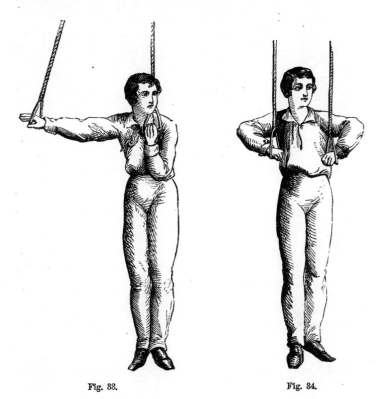

Fig. 33.   Fig. 34.

52.—THE TURN-OVER.

Whilst mounted between the ropes as in the last, but previous to straightening them, this exercise must be done.

Lean forward, throw the legs (backward) over the head, allowing them to fall to the ground, still retaining your hold of the ropes.

After a little practice, let go the ropes on alighting on the ground, but be careful how you do it at first.

This is a difficult exercise, but perseverance will soon overcome the difficulty.

53.—To Climb the Rope.

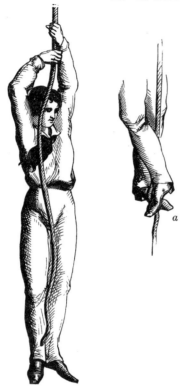

Fig. 35.

We have introduced this exercise here, as it will be required sometimes to reach the cross-piece at the top, in lieu of doing either of the other exercises.

There are two ways of climbing the rope.

First.—Grasp the rope with both hands, and move them alternately one above the other, and in order to support yourself whilst so doing, the feet must be used by pressing the rope between them, as shown at *a*, Fig. 35, where the feet are crossed and the rope is pressed by the top foot against the under one.

Second.—Grasp the rope with both hands, and without the aid of your feet move your hands alternately one above the other, but in so doing the gymnast will have to make use of the rise and fall exercise with one hand only, whilst he raises the other.

These climbing exercises should be practised on a rope free from knots, and not too small.

On descending the rope, do so by reversing the motion of the feet and hands, or the hands only. Do not let the rope slip through your hands, as the friction caused by so doing will be sure to rub the skin off, and perhaps cut the flesh to the bone.

54.—The Spring.

This exercise is somewhat similar to that described in No. 41, but it will be found a little more difficult at first to perform.

Grasp the ropes as in No. 41, and in bringing the legs over open them so as to pass one on either side of the ropes, which must be brought closer together (see Fig. 36), then, when nearly over, let go the ropes and alight on the ground.

Do this exercise also with one rope only, when both hands must be in the same rope.

This is a very clever feat, but it must be done quickly to succeed.

55.—THE JERK.

Grasp the ropes, one in either hand, and throw the right leg over the right arm (as in Fig. 37), or the left leg over the left arm, letting the other leg hang loosely in front. Now with a sudden jerk, and at the same time extend the disengaged arm a little, throw the body forward with as great an impetus as possible, when you will turn completely over, and in so doing you must not let go your hold, neither must the leg slip off the arm.

This is a very difficult exercise, and requires great nerve and practice for it.

56.—THE DESCENT.

This exercise must be done on a single rope, and the higher it is fixed from the ground the better. It should be at least

Fig. 36.

from fifteen to twenty feet long, and a 56 lb. weight should be attached to the lower end of it, which should be about a foot from the ground.

Fig. 37.

Climb the rope as far as you can, and let it hang in front of you,  and come down between the legs. Bring the right leg round the rope, and hitch the foot around it again; and having so done, bring the right arm in front of the rope (as in Fig. 38), when you may descend very gradually, according to the strain put against the rope by the leg around it.

The other leg must hang loosely.

To give this feat a greater effect, the weight should be twirled round; this will cause you also to turn round as you descend.

The hands, whilst descending, should be placed in as graceful an attitude as possible.

57.—THE REVOLVER.

Grasp the ropes, one in each hand, throw the legs up and hitch one (right) foot in one of the loops, (the right), and in so

Fig. 38.

doing, let go your hold of the loop in which you hitch your foot, and grasp the other rope with that hand (the right), carrying the other (left) leg over, and allow it to hang down.

Take care on carrying the leg over as just described, that the (right) foot does not slip out of the loop.

Now with both hands grasping the one rope, and one foot in the other, pull yourself up by moving the hands alternately, and when up a sufficient height, place the other foot (left) in the spare loop, and grasp a rope with each hand.

Cross the feet one over the other, to keep them together, and pass the arms to the front, grasping the ropes, as above shown, about the height of the hips, lean forward, throwing your feet up slightly behind, and you will turn completely over.

THE GIANT STRIDE

Consists of a pole, with a swivel at the summit, to which several ropes of equal length are attached, with small cross-sticks at their extremities. The boys take hold of the cross-stick or handle with one hand, grasping the rope with the other (see Illustration), and starting together, commence running round the pole, leaning the chief weight of the body on the hands, and only letting the tips of the toes touch the ground at intervals. Care must be taken to keep time, so that no runner trips up the companion in front of him, as this will disorder the whole economy of the exercise. After a time, a great velocity will be attained, and a mere occasional touch of the toes on the ground will be sufficient to carry the players round and round the course, literally with giant strides. Care must be taken that the boys vary the direction in which they run. In all gymnastic exercises they should be taught to depend upon the right leg and left leg, and

right arm and left arm equally; and a habit of running in one direction with the giant stride, say from right to left, would give the right arm and right leg too much work, and develop them at the expense of the left limbs.

THE LADDER.

The first use of the ladder exercises in gymnastics is to give confidence to the boy, and to teach him to depend on his power of balancing himself, in mounting or descending, without the aid of his hands. To do this, keep the knees a little bent, and hold the hands slightly forward in front of the chest, as shown in the illustration. Keep the body always in the same position, fixing the eye upon one point—for instance, the fourth rung of the ladder above the lower foot—and take care that the eye moves upward in the same ratio with the feet, always keeping four rungs above the step on which the lower foot is resting. Observe the same rules in descending the ladder.

8

To mount the ladder by the hands, stand underneath it and grasp the sides of the ladder, above your head, and work the hands alternately upward, slightly drawing up the body by the elbows, keeping the feet quite still. Work your way downward in the same manner. To mount with the hands by the steps, stand under the ladder, grasping the highest rung you can reach with both hands; then raising yourself by the elbows, grasp at the next rung, and so work your way up till you get to the highest. Descend in the same manner.

STILTS

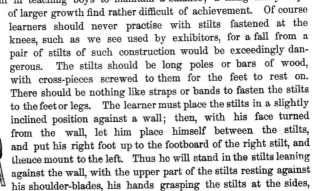

Are useful in teaching boys to maintain a balance; a thing many boys of larger growth find rather difficult of achievement. Of course learners should never practise with stilts fastened at the knees, such as we see used by exhibitors, for a fall from a pair of stilts of such construction would be exceedingly dangerous. The stilts should be long poles or bars of wood, with cross-pieces screwed to them for the feet to rest on. There should be nothing like straps or bands to fasten the stilts to the feet or legs. The learner must place the stilts in a slightly inclined position against a wall; then, with his face turned from the wall, let him place himself between the stilts, and put his right foot up to the footboard of the right stilt, and thence mount to the left. Thus he will stand in the stilts leaning against the wall, with the upper part of the stilts resting against his shoulder-blades, his hands grasping the stilts at the sides, and his chest thrown well forward. Then let him set off and try to walk.

TRICKS AND FEATS OF GYMNASTICS.

The Book.—Fix an old book between the toes of the feet, and, by a jerk, throw it over the head.

The Chalk Line.—Draw a line with chalk on the floor; against this place the toes of both feet; then kneel down and rise up again without leaving the line, or using the hands.

Stepping Through.—Take a small piece of cane about a foot long, and holding it between the hands, leap through it. Afterward take a tobacco-pipe, and perform the same feat without breaking; after this, join the hands together, and leap through them, which is not very difficult of accomplishment.

Armless.—Lying upon the back with the arms across the chest, the attempt must be made to rise on the feet again.

Hop Against the Wall.—Stand with one toe close against the wall, about two feet from the ground, and turn the other over it, without removing the toe from the wall.

Stoop if You Can.—One boy having placed his heels against the wall, another must place near his toes a dime, and tell him he may have it if he can pick it up. This he will find to be impossible for him to do while his heels touch the wall, as there is no room for his back to balance the other parts of his body.

The Spring from the Wall.—Placing yourself at a proper distance from the wall with your face opposite to it, throw yourself forward until you support yourself by one hand. Then spring back into your former position. Begin this feat at a short distance from the wall, and increase the distance by degrees. The "athlete" will, in a short time, be able to stand at nearly the length of his body from the wall. This feat is sometimes called the palm spring, but the palm has really nothing to do with it. The thumb spring is similar, but dangerous, and many have sprained their thumbs in attempting it.

The Long Reach.—This is a somewhat difficult feat, and requires great caution in its performance. A line is chalked on the floor, at which the toes must be placed, and from which they are not to remove. The left hand is then to be thrown forward in a long reach until the body descends upon it, without any part touching the floor in its descent; the right hand is now to be stretched out as far forward as possible, and with a piece of chalk a mark is made on the floor at its fullest extent, the body being sustained by the left hand during the operation. The boy should now recover the upright position on his legs,

by springing back from the left hand without touching the floor in any way. The length reached, and the perfection with which the body recovers itself, distinguishes the winner of the game.

The Stooping Stretch.—In this feat a line is drawn on the floor, at which the outer edge of the left foot is placed, and behind this, at a short distance, the right heel. Taking a piece of chalk in the left hand, the youngster passes it between the legs, and under the bend of the left knee, chalking the floor with it as far forward as

he can. He then recovers his position without moving his feet from the line at which they had been fixed.

The Chair Feat.—Place three chairs in the situation indicated in the cut, and lie down upon them, the head resting on one, the heels upon another, and the lower part of the body on the third or mid-

dle chair, which should be much lighter than the others. Then. by stiffening the body and limbs, and throwing up the chest into a state of rigidity, it will not be difficult for a boy to remove the middle chair, and to pass it quite over on the other side of him.

The Poker Feat.—Take a common poker and hold it the lower end downward, in the manner shown in the cut, *i. e.*, by the fingers, thumb, and ball of the palm. Then, by the mere motion of the fingers and thumb, and the fulcrum of the palm, work the poker upward till you raise it through the whole length to that part of it which goes into the fire. This trick depends mainly upon the strength of the muscles of the hand and fingers, combined with a certain knack to be acquired by practice.

The Stick Feat, or from Hand to Mouth.—Take a piece of stick of the length of the fore-arm, measuring from the elbow to the end of the middle finger. Hold it in the hand horizontally before you, the knuckles being down and the nails upward, and the elbow being on a line with the hand. Then raise the left end of the stick from the breast to the mouth, without any other movement of the hand than the arm at the wrist. This is a difficult feat, but may be easily acquired by practice.

THE STICK FEAT.

SKATING.

Skating is deservedly popular. To become a graceful and accomplished skater requires practice, after a study of the principles involved. These things are preliminary to success: The skate to be properly made and securely fastened; and the skater to get rid of fear.

Skates may be had in variety—some with high irons and some with low; some with narrow and some with broad irons; some with the bottom of the irons ground at right angles with the sides, and some with a groove running lengthways through the bottom of the iron.

For beginners a rather low iron is best, and squarely ground. Indeed, the grooved are apt to fill with ice, or "ball" in the groove; and the young skater, instead of "cutting High Dutch," will be cut by a fall.

In fastening the skates, those are to be preferred with three straps, one of which comes around the toes, one around the instep, and one from just below the heel to a spot above the instep. Three small spikes, to fit in corresponding holes in the boot-heel, should be in the heel of the skate. The iron should be at right angles with the surface of the wood, and the holes in the strap should be at a short distance from each other, so as to avoid looseness in the strapping, on the one side, and undue pressure on the foot, on the other.

THE START.

We will suppose the novice's skates have been fastened on for him, and he stands on his feet, on a well-selected piece of ice, neither so smooth as to increase the difficulty he will find in keeping his feet, nor so rough as to trip him up. As soon as he stands upright, he should start at once. Inclining his body a little forward toward the right leg, he slides forward, with his whole weight on the right foot, which must be slightly turned outward,

Fig. 1.

his other foot being slightly raised off the ice, and kept behind the right. (*See Illustration.*) He then brings the left foot forward, in its turn, and slides a yard or two on that foot, and so on alternately. He may, at first, make use of his hands to maintain his balance, raising or depressing them, with the fingers turned upward. He should, however, aim at skating, after a short time, entirely without the use of his arms, which look much better hanging carelessly by the side, than flung wildly about in wind-mill fashion. Some learners make use of a stick at first starting. This we think a bad plan. It is better, at first, to have

STARTING OFF.

STOPPING.

the support of a companion, who can skate (Fig. 1), and, by degrees, he may leave you to your own exertions. The learner should proceed patiently, and with caution, at first, and be content to increase his speed gradually with his knowledge; the opposite extreme, however, must also be avoided, for no one ever becomes a good skater who is afraid of a fall. When the inside edge movement has once been learned, the skater will find that his progress is greatly hastened by a push given to the ice with the left skate, as he starts with the right foot, and *vice versâ;* but, above all things, let him thoroughly understand "inside edge," and be confident of his own powers, before he begins practising the feats we will now describe. But first the skater must be taught

HOW TO STOP.

Bring the second foot down upon the ice, and glide forward, with both feet pointed in front of you, and parallel to each other, like the irons of a sledge. Bend the body forward, and throw all the weight upon the heels of the skates. Those who wear the skates with rounded heels cannot, of course, stop in this way, as the rounded irons, instead of sticking into the ice, would trip their wearer up; he puts the second foot to the ground, at right angles with the other, pointed entirely sideways, which immediately stops his career.

HOW TO PERFORM THE VARIOUS EVOLUTIONS.

Before the skater attempts to cut figures and other devices, he must be able to skate on the outside edge of the skate, to skate backward, and to turn round. The *outside edge* implies what it is by its name; when acquired, it sends you exactly in opposite directions, on both sides, to what the *inside edge* does. In explanation: Suppose that you are skating on the *right* foot, it is easy to turn to the left, but not so to the right, to effect which you must use the *outside* edge, by striking out upon it either foot, inclining, at the same time, the skate, the leg, the body, and the head toward whichever side you are skating, holding the other foot raised up behind, and rounding the arms. The most difficult forward movement is the cross outside edge, which is done by passing one leg across the other, and striking out with the foot as it comes down on the ice. As the foot on which you first rested disengages itself (which it will do as you proceed) from the crossed-leg position, throw that leg over the other, and, by continuing this, you will soon learn to sweep round on either side with ease. This is called the Mercury figure.

The salute in a right line is not easy of execution. Having first struck out, you must place the feet in a horizontal line, elevating and rounding the arms. Continue the movement as long as you can, or think fit to do so. This attitude, though difficult, is frequently practised by good skaters.

The salute in a curved line is much easier. Having started, you put your feet in the position you would adopt to describe the salute in a right line (see Fig. 2), only less horizontally. The head and body must be upright, the arms rounded, the hands placed on the haunches; in this position you describe a circle. You then draw yourself up, the knees having become slightly bent, and, raising the right or left foot, prepare for another evolution; as either striking out straight forward, or toward one side.

To describe circles and curves will be found the most graceful and useful of evolutions. To describe a curve on the outside edge forward, fix on some

Fig. 2.   Fig. 3.

point as a centre, and take a run proportioned to the number of curves you propose describing. Strike out on the outward edge, turning in a curve round the centre fixed upon. Your eyes must look toward the shoulder opposite that which directs the general movement of the side on which you turn. The hips must be kept in, and the leg on which you are propelled bent slightly at the knee-joint; the opposite leg must also be bent, and thrown backward, to modify, by its weight and position, the impulse forward, and to insure your equilibrium.

To describe a curve, or circle, on the inside edge forward, you must select a small piece of cork, or any other light body, as a centre, take a sufficient run, and strike out on the inward edge. Your head and body must be in the position described for outward curves, only the leg on which you skate must not be bent. The opposite leg should be almost stiff, and the foot about eighteen inches distant from the one you rest upon. (See Fig. 4.) Curves on the inside edge are terminated by stopping in the usual manner; but if you desire to *pirouette*, or turn round, you throw the foot on which you do not skate over that on which you do, and, from the impulse given to your body, in order to describe the curve, you spin round on the middle of the skate, as on a pivot. After having done this a few times, you bring down the foot you are not revolving on, and proceed to other evolutions.

To skate backward, you must incline the head and body slightly forward, in order not to lose the centre of gravity. Strike out behind on each foot alternately, and raise the heel of the skate slightly up from the ice; by this operation each foot will describe an arc or segment of a circle. Should you feel to be losing your equilibrium, bring both skates together upon the ice.

This evolution is performed sometimes on one foot, sometimes on the other, and occasionally on both together, by the help of a slight motion of the hips.

Retrograde or backward curves differ from ordinary curves by their direction only; and at first sight appear difficult, because a person cannot

Fig. 4.

move backward with the same facility that he can go forward. When, however, you are used to this manner of skating, it will appear natural and tolerably easy of execution. The backward curve is of equal importance with the ordinary curve on the outside edge, and constitutes the base of all retrograde or backward figures. In this evolution the position of the arms and head is not the same as for the ordinary curve on the outside edge. When executing the outward retrograde curve, your face must be turned toward the left shoulder. The backward curve may be extended to circles, spiral rings, as shown by Figs. 5 and 6, and be finally concluded by the *pirouette*.

The oblique stop is the most proper to adopt when you are skating backward. In order to perform it, when engaged in a retrograde

Fig. 5.

movement, you bring down on the ice in an oblique and transverse position the skate on which you are not resting, stiffening at the same time the leg you thus bring down. The effect of this manœuvre is prompt and certain, and the only variation it admits of is, that it can be performed on either foot.

8*

Fig. 6.

To turn round, bring either heel behind the other, and you turn as a matter of course.

By carefully attending to the above directions, with practice, you will be able to cut the numerical figures, or any device that you may wish. The figure 8 is the best practice, and is described by completing the circle on the outside edge forward. This is performed by crossing the legs, and striking from the outside instead of the inside edge. To cross the legs, the skater, as he draws to the close of the stroke on his right leg, must throw the left quite across it, which will cause him to press hard on the outside of the right skate, from which he must immediately strike, throwing back the left arm and looking simultaneously over the left shoulder, so as to bring him well up on the outside edge of the left skate. The 8 is formed by completing a perfect circle, in the manner described, on each leg, before changing the foot. The figure 3, which is performed on the inside edge backwards, may next be practised.

No pains should be spared upon this figure, as it is a most elegant one, and is, besides, the key to all figures. When the 3 is once mastered, other figures become quite easy. The mode of doing it is this: Start on the right foot as if going to make an 8, but do it as gently as possible. But, instead of swinging the left foot round so as to make a circle, *let it remain at least a foot behind the right foot.* The consequence

of doing so is, that when three-fourths of the circle are completed, the off-foot gives a curious sway to the body, and the skater spins round on his right foot, changing at the same time from the outside to the inside edge, and cuts the second half of the 3 backwards. When the skater can do this easily with the right foot, he should practise it with the left; and when he can cut the 3 with equal ease with either foot, he should cut two together, as seen in the drawing. Let the reader here refer to the drawing, while we trace the skater through it. He begins with the left hand 3, starting with his left foot on the outside edge; when he gets to the twist of the 3 he spins round, and finishes the figure (still with the left foot) *on the inside edge backward.* His right foot is now at liberty to pass to the top of the right hand 3, which he cuts in like manner. Especial care must be taken to keep the knees straight, and to preserve a graceful carriage of the body. If the skater should be so far off his balance as to find any difficulty in spinning round, he will gain his object by throwing his weight a very little toward the toe of the skate. The reason why the skater curves round in this twist is, that the steel of the skate has a curved form ; and when for a moment the body is quite upright, the whole skate spins round on its centre, as on a pivot.

GENERAL DIRECTIONS TO BE FOLLOWED BY PERSONS LEARNING TO SKATE.

1. Let your dress fit closely, but at the same time be of sufficient ease to insure freedom of motion. Neither skirts to coats nor full trousers should be worn.

•2. Let flannel be worn next the skin by the delicate, and an extra undergarment by the robust. Let the chest be well defended against the cold. A piece of brown paper laid between the waistcoat and shirt is one of the best chest protectors.

3. Be careful in venturing upon the ice, unless it be sufficiently strong to bear the weight of the number that flock to it; and watch for the increase of numbers, that you may retire before danger ensues.

4. Avoid rough and very smooth ice, and look carefully out for obstructions thereon; such as small twigs of trees, stones, or "hobbles;" as well as for rotten ice, cracks where the ice has risen higher on one side than the other, or holes. Should you suddenly come upon rotten ice, do not stop, but pass over it as rapidly as possible. Should you fall down upon it, roll lengthwise toward the firmer part, without attempting to stand or walk upon it.

5. Should the skater fall into a hole, he should extend his pole or stick across it, and hold on to it till assistance arrives; should he have no stick, he may extend his arms horizontally across the edges of the ice, till a rope can be thrown to him.

6. After an unlucky immersion in the water, the unfortunate skater should immediately take off his skates, and, if able, run home as quickly as he can.

He should then pull off all his wet clothes, take a tablespoonful of brandy in a glass of hot water, rub himself thoroughly with dry towels, and go to bed.

SLIDING.

SLIDING is performed by taking a short run (gradually increasing the speed as you approach the slide), and simultaneously jumping on the left foot, and striking out forward with the right. You maintain your balance by varying the position of the arms, which are raised upward and slightly curved, the nails of both hands pointing toward the head.

In accomplishing a long slide, when the impetus you have first acquired fails to carry you the entire length, it may be revived by slightly stooping, and then quickly raising your body, at the same time lounging forward with the right arm as in fencing.

SWIMMING.

IT is astonishing how many persons are ignorant of this useful and neces-sary accomplishment. An American, who has more of the travelling mania than the native of any other country, should, by all means, be master of it; as he runs a risk of sudden immersion in water during his wanderings, and, should he be no swimmer, stands a great chance of being drowned.

A horse, or a dog—indeed, most animals—will swim when thrown into the water; and, among savages, children are taught to swim at a very early age. An Indian who could not swim would be a wonder to his tribe. Among civilized men, however, the proportion of those who swim to those who do not, appears to be less than one-half. And yet the art of swimming is easy to learn—a little confidence and care only being required.

In the essential part of swimming, *i. e.*, in the art of keeping the head above the water, there is literally no skill at all. Confidence in the sustain-ing power of the water is the only secret; and if the novice will only dare to trust in the water, and will remember three simple rules, he cannot pos-sibly sink below the surface. These are the golden rules of swimming:

RULE 1.—KEEP THE HANDS AND FEET WELL BELOW THE SURFACE, AND IMMERSE THE WHOLE BODY UP TO THE CHIN.

The reasons for this rule are simple, and are based upon common sense. Every one, with the least smattering of physical science, knows that the flotation of various bodies is exactly in proportion to the quantity of water displaced. No man can stand upright upon the water, because the amount of water displaced by the soles of the feet would not counteract the weight of the body. And, it will be seen, by the simple carrying out of this principle, that exactly in proportion to the immersion of the body is it sustained by the water.

All practical swimmers know that when a man swims with his whole head and part of his shoulders out of the water, he cannot endure for any length of time, because the force that ought to be used in propulsion is wasted upon sustaining the body.

Every inch of the body that is raised above the surface becomes a dead weight, pressing the body under water and calling for great exertion on the part of the swimmer. Many persons, when they fall into the water, plunge about and try to lift themselves out of it, acting as if they were attempting to kneel upon its surface. This action is instinctive, and is one of those where instinct is inferior to reason. In point of fact, ninety-nine out of every hundred who perish in the water, drown themselves as effectually as if they had tied a heavy weight round their necks.

The weight of the head, breast, and arms of a human being is, on the average, about forty pounds; and when a drowning person lifts those portions of the body above the surface, he practically acts as if he fastened a forty-pound weight upon his head.

Every one who has attained some knowledge of swimming, and tries to perform the feat of holding one leg out of the water, is made practically aware of this fact.

RULE 2.—HOLLOW THE SPINE AND THROW THE BACK OF THE HEAD UPON THE SHOULDERS.

Like all the rules in swimming, this is founded upon common sense.

Bulk for bulk, the body of an ordinary human being is about the same as that of the water. There are, however, two exceptional portions—namely, the head, which is somewhat heavier, and the chest, which is much lighter. Any one will, therefore, see that it is most essential to support the former upon the latter, as well as to make the water support both as much as possible.

By hollowing the spine and throwing the back of the head upon the shoulders, the heavy, solid mass of the brain is supported by the air-filled lungs, and the eyes and nostrils are kept above the surface. As to the mouth, that may be above or below the surface, for, if the lips be kept firmly closed, and respiration conducted through the nostrils, no water can enter.

The chief object in hollowing the back is, that it aids the swimmer in keeping his nostrils out of the water. No viler habit can be found than that of rounding the back, and there is none which is so difficult to eradicate.

RULE 3.—MOVE THE LIMBS QUIETLY.

A good swimmer is at once distinguished by the ease and quietude of all his movements. The arms and legs are flung out to their fullest extent, sweep round in the water equably, and are drawn up for another stroke, without the least hurry. The bad swimmer, on the contrary, never waits long enough to make a full stroke, but gives short and hurried jerks with his arms and legs, never extending them more than half their length.

The *slow stroke* is the very essence of good swimming. Of course, we are not speaking of racing, when the strokes are necessarily quick and powerful, but merely of the method of obtaining a good and enduring style. Try how far you can go at each stroke, and do not draw back the limbs until the force of the stroke is all but exhausted. At first you will appear to make but little progress; but the endurance of the long, slow stroke is surprising, and its speed by no means contemptible.

Dr. Franklin, himself an expert swimmer, recommends that at first a familiarity with the buoyant power of water should be gained; and to acquire this, he directs the learner, after advancing into the water breast high, to turn round, so as to bring his face to the shore: he is then to let an egg fall in the water, which, being white will be seen at the bottom. His object must now be by diving down with his eyes open, to reach and bring up the egg. He will easily perceive that there is no danger in this experiment, as the water gets shallower of course towards the shore, and because whenever he likes, by depressing his feet he can raise his head again above water.

The thing that will most strike beginners will be the great difficulty they experience in forcing themselves through the water to reach the egg, in consequence of the great resistance the water itself offers to their progress: and this is indeed the practical lesson derivable from the experiment; for the learner becomes aware of the very great sustaining or supporting power of water, and hence has confidence. This sustaining power of water is shown under many circumstances: thus, a stone which on land requires two men to remove it, might in water be easily carried by one. A man might walk without harm on broken glass in deep water, because his weight is supported by the water. This knowledge of fluid support constitutes the groundwork of all efforts in swimming, or in self-preservation from drowning.

Dr. Arnot, in allusion to this subject, says that many persons are drowned who might be saved, for the following reasons:—

1. From their believing that their constant exertions are necessary to preserve the body from sinking, and their hence assuming the position of a swimmer, with the face downward, in which the whole head must be kept out of the water, in order to enable them to breathe; whereas, when lying on the back, only the face need be above the water.

2. From the groundless fear that water entering by the ears may drown as if it entered by the mouth or nose, and their employing exertions to prevent this.

3. The keeping of the hands above water, already alluded to.

4. Neglecting to take the opportunity of the intervals of the waves passing over the head, to renew the air in their chest by an inspiration.

5. Their not knowing the importance of keeping the chest as full of air as possible, which has nearly the same effect as tying a bladder full of air around the neck would have.

But although floating in water is sufficient to preserve from immediate danger, this will not alone enable us to swim. To swim, does not mean simply to float, but to progress; and progression by this means depends, like the flight of birds, upon the law in mechanics of every action being followed by a corresponding reaction, but in an opposite direction; and thus, as the reaction of the air compressed by the downward action of the bird's wing, causes it to mount aloft in proportion to the force it communicates by that motion; so, the backward stroke communicated by the simultaneous movement of the hands and feet of the swimmer, causes his forward progress in the water. When once familiarized with the support derived from the water itself, he soon learns to make the stroke correctly, especially if aided and supported by some more experienced friend,—a far better assistant than corks and bladders.

PLACES AND TIMES FOR BATHING AND SWIMMING.

It is presumed that most young lads who go to bathe will take the opportunity of learning to swim. In crowded cities there are but few places in which the youngster can learn the art: but in the country there are many rivers, ponds, canals, or lakes, where both bathing and swimming may be indulged in without annoyance. The best kind of place for bathing is on a shelving gravelly shore, on which the water gradually deepens, and where no awkward sweep of current may take the bather off his legs. The spot should also be free from holes, weeds, and hard stones; and a muddy bottom is to be avoided by all means. Should the banks of such a spot be shaded by a few trees, and should there be close by an open space for a run on the grass after the bathe, so much the better; and the young learner will then have the chief inducement to venture the sudden dip or headlong plunge.

The best time of the day for bathing or swimming is either before breakfast, between the hours of six and eight in the summer-time, or between eleven and twelve in the forenoon. Delicate persons should not bathe early in the morning; and it would be always well to munch a biscuit before early bathing at all times. No one should ever think of entering the water on a full stomach, or immediately after dinner, and never when over-heated and exhausted by fatigue. He should also avoid entering it when cold, or with a headache. Before bathing, it is best to take a moderate walk of about a mile, and while the system is in a glow, to undress quickly and plunge in. It is bad to walk until you get hot, then to sit down and cool, and afterward to enter the water; many have lost their lives by this. It is also very wrong to enter the water during rain, as the clothes are often wetted or damp, which gives the bather cold.

ENTERING THE WATER.

Having stripped the body, the bather should select the best place on the bank for going down to the stream; and then proceeding cautiously but quickly, wade up to his breasts, turn his head to the shore and dip. He then technically, as the boys say, gets his pinch over. Should he not be man enough to proceed in this way, he should, as soon as he gets his feet wet, splash some water over his head, and go into the water more gradually, and try the rapid rush and dip when he gets bolder. He must not attempt to swim or strike out till he can master the feat of going into the water up to his armpits, and till he feels himself confident and void of timidity.

AIDS TO SWIMMING.

Many aids have been used for the benefit of young swimmers: corks and bladders fastened under the arms are the common ones; but they offer dangerous temptations for bathers to go out of their depth, and then should cramp, cold, or any other accident occur, the event may be fatal. Besides, these aids often slip about from one place to the other. We remember, in our younger days, of the "corks" slipping to the hips, and seeing a young friend, now an old man, suspended in the water with his head downward;

while collapsing of bladders and of air-jackets is by no means uncommon. The plank may be serviceable to enable the beginner to throw out his legs and feet. A piece of wood, a yard in length, two feet in breadth, and about two inches in thickness, will be found best adapted for the purpose. When the pupil can support himself without the aid of corks, &c., the plank being thrown into the water, he should grasp one end of it with both hands, and striking out his legs, push it on before him; but if he let go the plank, he will probably be left to sink.

The best aid to a young swimmer is a judicious friend, himself a good swimmer, who will hold up his head, when he strikes off, by the "tip of the finger to the tip of the chin," and who at the same time will show him how to strike off, and how to manage his hands and feet. It is not a bad plan to put out a spar from a boat, to which a rope is attached, which the young learner may make use of by affixing it to a belt round his body under his arms, which will afford him support while he learns to strike his legs in the water. The rope may also be held in the hand of a friend, by the side of the boat, and the learner may strike off hands and feet as the boat proceeds. The plank is a dangerous aid, from its tendency to slip about, and to take

the swimmer out of his depth, and although it has many advantages, is very unsafe. The safest plan of all is, as we have before stated, for the learner to advance gradually up to his arm-pits in the water, and then turning about, to strike slowly out toward the shore, taking care to keep his legs well up from the bottom. Rigid perseverance in this course will in a very short time enable the youngster to feel himself afloat, and moving at "all fours,"—a delight equal to that experienced by the child who first feels that he can walk from chair to chair.

STRIKING OFF AND SWIMMING.

In striking off, the learner, having turned himself to the shore, as before recommended, should fall toward the water gently, keeping his head and neck perfectly upright, his breast advancing forward, his chest inflated;

then, withdrawing the legs from the bottom, and stretching them out, strike the arms forward in unison with the legs. The back can scarcely be too much hollowed, or the head too much thrown back, as those who do otherwise will swim with their feet too near the surface, instead of allowing them to be about a foot and a half deep in the water. The hands should be placed just in front of the breast, the fingers pointing forward and kept close together, with the thumbs to the edge of the fore-fingers: the hands must be made rather concave on the inside, though not so much as to diminish the size. In the stroke of the hands, they should be carried forward to the utmost extent, taking care that they do not touch the surface of the water; they should next be swept to the side, at a distance from, but as low as, the hips; and should then be drawn up again, by bringing the arms toward the side, bending the elbows upward and the wrists downward, so as to let the hands hang down while the arms are raising them to the first attitude.

PLUNGING AND DIVING.

There are two kinds of plunging; that belonging to shallow, and that belonging to deep water. In shallow-water plunging, the learner should fling himself as far forward as possible into the stream at a very oblique angle; and when he touches the water, he should raise his head, keep his back hollow, and stretch his hands forward. In the deep-water plunge, his body is to descend at a greater angle; his arms are to be stretched out, his hands closed and pointed, and his body bent, so that his nose almost touches his toes.

Diving is one of the greatest amusements connected with swimming. There are many kinds; the two most common and easiest and necessary modes of going below the surface, are:

1. The feet-foremost jump.
2. The head-foremost jump.

In the first, the legs, arms and head are to be kept perfectly rigid and stiff. The pupil must not allow fear, or the strange sensation felt in the bowels in leaping from considerable heights, to induce him to spread the arms or legs, or to bend his body.

In the second mode, or head-foremost plunge—which is the safest mode for persons who are heavily built about the chest and shoulders, if they have to enter the water from heights,—the head is drawn down upon the chest, the arms stretched forward and hands closed to a point; and as soon as the swimmer feels that he has left the bank, his knees, which till then were bent, are to be stiffened. The diver must avoid striking on the belly —the general consequence of fear; and turning over so as to come down on his back or side—the consequence of pushing with the feet. When he has gone as deep as he wishes, the arms are to be raised and pressed downward.

HOW TO MANAGE THE LEGS.

The legs, which should be moved alternately with the hands, must be drawn up with the knees inward, and the soles of the feet inclined outward; and they should then be thrown backward, as widely apart from each other as possible. These motions of the hands and legs may be practised out of the water; and whilst exercising the legs, which can only be done one at a time, the learner may rest one hand on the back of a chair to steady himself, while he moves the opposite leg. When in the water, the learner must take care to draw in his breath at the instant that his hands, descending to his hips, cause his head to rise above the surface of the water; and he should exhale his breath at the moment his body is propelled forward through the action of the legs. If he does not attend precisely to these rules, he must invariably have a downward motion, and as the boys say, swim furthest where it is deepest.

SWIMMING UNDER WATER.

When under the water, the swimmer may either move in the usual way, or keep his hands stretched before him, which will enable him to cut the water more easily, and greatly relieve his chest. If he observes that he approaches too near the surface of the water, he must press the palms of his hands upward. If he wishes to dive to the bottom, he must turn the palms of his hands upward, striking with them repeatedly and rapidly whilst the feet are reposing; and when he has obtained a perpendicular position, he should stretch out his hands like feelers, and make the usual movement with his feet, then he will descend with great rapidity to the bottom. It is well to accustom the eyes to open themselves under the water, at least in those beds of water that admit the light, as it will enable the swimmer to ascertain the depth of water he is in.

SWIMMING ON THE SIDE.

In this, the body is turned either on the left or right side, while the feet perform their usual motions. The *arm from under* the shoulder stretches itself out quickly, at the same time that the feet are striking. The other arm strikes at the same time with the impelling of the feet. The hand of the latter arm begins its stroke on a level with the head. While the hand is again brought forward in a flat position, and the feet are contracted, the stretched-out hand is, while working, drawn back toward the breast, but not so much impelling as sustaining. As swimming on the side presents to the water a smaller surface than on the waist, when rapidity is required, the former is often preferable to the latter.

SWIMMING ON THE BACK WITHOUT EMPLOYING THE FEET.

This is twofold: 1. *In the direction of the feet.* The body is placed in a horizontal position, the feet are stretched out stiffly, and the heels and toes are kept in contact; then the body is to be somewhat curved at the seat, the hands are to be stretched flatly forward over the body, and, slowly striking in small circles, the loins are somewhat drawn up at each stroke. 2. *In the direction of the head.* The body is placed horizontally, but somewhat curved in the seat, the head in its natural position, the arms are kept close to the body, with the elbows inclined inward, and the hands describe small circles from the back to the front, at about a foot and a half from the hips. These modes serve to exercise and strengthen the arms in an extraordinary degree without in the least fatiguing the breast.

FLOATING.

The body is laid horizontally on the back, the head is bent backward as much as possible, the arms are stretched out over the head in the direction

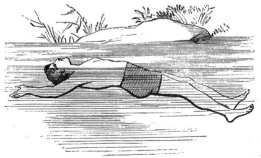

of the body, the feet are left to their natural position; if they sink, the loins must be kept as low as possible. In this position, the person, which is

specifically lighter than water, remains, and may float at pleasure. The
lungs should be kept inflated, that the breast may be distended, and the circumference of the body augmented.   In order not to sink while in the act of
taking breath, which the greater specific weight of the body would effect,
the breath must be quickly expelled, and as quickly drawn in again, and
then retained as long as possible; for, as the back is in a flat position, the
sinking, on account of the resistance of the water, does not take place so
rapidly but the quick respiration will restore the equilibrium before the
water reaches the nose.

TREADING WATER.

This is a perpendicular position of the swimmer, and is of great use to
enable him to save a person from drowning.   It is in general thought to be
extremely difficult, but it is very easy.   There are two ways of performing
the action: in the first the hands are compressed against the hips, and the

feet describe their usual circle; the other mode consists in not contracting
both legs at the same time, but one after the other, so that while the one remains contracted the other describes a circle.   In this mode, however, the
legs must not be stretched out, but the thighs are placed in a distended position, and curved as if in a half-sitting posture.

THE FLING.

The swimmer lays himself flat upon his waist, draws his feet as close as
possible under the body, stretches his hands forward, and, with both feet
and hands beating the water violently at the same time, raises himself out
of the water.   In this manner one may succeed in throwing one's self out of
the water as high as the hips.   This exercise is very useful, for saving one's
self by catching a rope or any other object that hangs from above the surface of the water, or from any perpendicular height.

SWIMMING ON THE BACK.

In this the swimmer turns upon his back in the water by the combined motion of the arm and leg, and extending his body, his head being in a line with it, so that the back and upper part of the head may be immersed, while the face and breast are out of the water. The hands should be placed on the thighs straight down, and the legs moved as in forward swimming, tak-

ing care that the knees do not rise above the surface in striking them out. Sometimes the hands are used after the motion of a wing or fan, by which a slight progression is also made at the same time that the surface of the body is well lifted out of the water.

THRUSTING.

In the thrust the swimmer lies horizontally upon his waist, and makes the common motions in swimming. He then simply stretches one arm for-

ward, as in swimming on the side, but remains lying upon the waist, and, in a widely-described circle, he carries the other hand, which is working under the breast, toward the hip. As soon as the arm has completed this motion, it is lifted from the water in a stretched position, and thrown forward in the greatest horizontal level, and is then sunk, with the hand flat, into the water; while the swimmer thus stretches forth the arm, he, with the other hand stretched as wide as possible, describes a small circle, in order to sustain the body; after this he brings his hand in a largely described circle rapidly to the hip, lifts the arm out of the water, and *thrusts* it forward. During the describing of the larger circle the feet make their movements. To make the thrust beautifully, a considerable degree of practice is required. This mode of swimming is useful where a great degree of rapidity is required for a short distance.

THE DOUBLE THRUST.

In the performance of this the arm is thrust forward, backward, and again forward, without dipping into the water; in the mean time, the stretched forth arm describes two circles before it begins the larger one.

TO SWIM LIKE A DOG.

In this motion each hand and foot is used alternately, as a dog uses them when swimming, as the term implies. The hands are alternately drawn toward the chin in a compressed form, and then expanded and slightly hollowed, with fingers close, and, as they strike the water, the feet are likewise drawn toward the belly, and struck backward with a kind of kick. This mode of swimming is of use to relieve the swimmer, from time to time, when going a distance.

THE MILL.

The swimmer lays himself on his back, and contracts himself so that the knees are brought almost to the chin, and while one of the hands keeps the equilibrium by describing circles, the other continues working. Thus the body is kept turning round more or less rapidly.

THE WHEEL BACKWARD AND FORWARD.

In the *forward wheel* the hands are put as far backward as possible, and so pressed against the water that the head is impelled under the surface, and the feet, by a pressure of the hands in a contrary direction, are rapidly flung above the head, which in this manner is rapidly brought again to the surface.

In the *backward wheel* the swimmer lies upon his back, he contracts himself, the hands, stretched forward as far as possible, describe rapidly small circles, the feet rise, and as the point of equilibrium has been brought as near as possible to the feet, the head sinks and the feet are thrown over.

TO SWIM WITH ONE HAND.

The learner, to do this, swims on one side, keeps his feet somewhat deeply *sunk*, while the arm, which in the mean time ought to work, is kept quiet—and might even be taken out of the water. It is a good practice of strength to carry, first under and then over the water, a weight of four or eight pounds.

HAND OVER HAND SWIMMING.

In this process the right hand is lifted out of the water from behind, swung forward through the air with a kind of circular sweep, to the extent of its reach forward, then dropped into the water edgeways, and immediately turned—with the palm a little hollowed—downward, the body being at the same time thrown a little on one side, and the right leg struck out backward to its full extent. The hand descends toward the thigh, and then passes upward through the water in a kind of curve toward the surface. The left hand and leg perform a similar movement alternately with the right, and the measure of progression attained by these combined similar movements is very considerable.

BALANCING.

When the swimmer has obtained ease and confidence in the water, he will find many things easy which before he deemed impossible. Balancing is one of these. To perform it, he has only, when out of his depth, to fall gently back, with his chin elevated to a line passing exactly through the centre of his body, from the chin to the toes, then, folding his arms and remaining perfectly motionless, he may suspend himself perpendicularly: but if he should extend his arms backward, and pass them gradually beyond his head, his toes, tips of his knees, abdomen, and part of his chest, with the whole of his face, will appear, and he will be balanced and float horizontally without the slightest motion

THE CRAMP.

The cramp generally proceeds from acidity of the bowels, arising from a bad state of the stomach, or from the effects of the cold water on the muscular system. Some persons are very subject to it on slight occasions, and such persons will do well never to go out of their depth. But should a tolerable swimmer be seized with the cramp, he should not be frightened, but the moment the cramp is felt in the foot or leg, strike out that foot or leg, with the heel elongated, and the toes drawn upward toward the shin-bone, never minding any little pain it may occasion, as he need not fear breaking a bone, muscle or tendon. Should this not succeed, he should throw himself on his back, and float quietly, and paddle himself gently to the shore. He may also swim with his hands, like a dog, and practise any of the motions of the upper part of the body for keeping his head above water till assistance arrives.

SAVING FROM DANGER.

Above all things, the good swimmer should be anxious to save life, and to rescue those who are in danger, *without himself becoming the victim, as it often happens.* The following rules are highly important to be observed: The swimmer must avoid approaching the drowning person in front, in order that he may not be grasped by him; for whatever a drowning person seizes, he holds with convulsive force, and it is no easy matter to get disentangled from his grasp; therefore, he should seize him from behind, and let go of him immediately if the other turns toward him. His best way is to impel him before him to the shore, or to draw him behind; if the space to be passed be too great, he should seize him by the foot and drag him, turning him on his back. If the drowning person should seize him, there is no alternative for the swimmer than to drop him at once to the bottom of the water, and there to wrestle with his antagonist; the drowning man, by a kind of instinct to regain the surface, when drawn down to the bottom, usually quits his prey, particularly if the diver attacks him there with all his power.

For two swimmers the labor is easier, because they can mutually relieve each other. If the drowning person has still some presence of mind remaining, they will then seize him, one under *one arm, and the other under the other,* and without any great effort in treading water, bring him along, with his head above water, while they enjoin him to keep himself stretched out and as much as possible without motion.

SPORTS AND FEATS IN SWIMMING.

1. *The Float.*—In this sport one swimmer lays himself horizontally on the back, with the feet stretched out, the hands pressed close to the body, and the head raised forward. The other swimmer takes hold of him by the extremity of the feet, and, swimming with one hand, impels him forward. The first remains motionless.

2. *The Plank.*—One swimmer lays himself horizontally, as before, another lays hold of him with both his hands, immediately above the ankle, and pulls him obliquely into the water, while he extends himself and impels himself forward; thus both the swimmers drop rapidly the one over the other.

3. *The Pickaback Spring.*—One swimmer treads the water, the other swims near him behind, places his hands upon the shoulders of the first, and presses him down. He then leaves his hold, and puts his feet upon his shoulders, and, flinging himself out of the water, pushes the first toward the bottom. Now he treads water, and the first performs the part of the second, and so on.

4. *The Shove.*—Two swimmers place themselves horizontally on their backs, the legs are strongly extended, and the soles of the feet bear against each other; each impels forward with all his power, and he who succeeds in pushing back the other is the conqueror.

5. *The Wrestle.*—Two swimmers place themselves opposite to each other, tread water, and hold their right hands in the air; the question is, who shall first force his opponent under the water by pressure. Only the head of the adversary is to be touched, and that only by pressure.

9

THE PRUSSIAN SYSTEM OF PFUEL.

The best of all methods for teaching swimming is that originally introduced by General Pfuel into the Prussian swimming-schools. By this method a person may be made a very good swimmer in a very short time.

The apparatus for teaching consists of a hempen girdle five inches in width, of a rope from five to six fathoms in length, of a pole eight feet long, and a horizontal rail fixed about three and a half feet above the platform, on which the teacher stands, to rest the pole on.

The depth of the water in the place chosen for swimming should, if possible, be not less than eight feet, and the clearest and calmest water selected.

The swimming-girdle, about five inches wide, is now placed round the pupil's breast, so that its upper edge rests on the chest, without getting tight. The teacher takes the rope, which is fastened to the ring of the girdle, in his hand, and directs the pupil to leap into the water, keeping the legs straight and close together, and the arms close to the body, and, what is very important, to breathe out through the nose as soon as his head rises above the water, instead of breathing in first, as every man naturally does after a suspension of breath. The object of this is to prevent the water from getting into the throat, which produces an unpleasant feeling of choking and headache. This expiration soon becomes natural to the swimmer.

The pupil is next invited to leap. He is drawn up immediately by the rope, pulled to the ladder, and allowed to gain confidence gradually. The rope is now fastened by a noose to the end of the pole, the other end of it being kept in the hand of the teacher; the pole is rested on the horizontal rail, and the pupil stretches himself horizontally on the water, where he remains, supported by the pole. Next the arms are extended stiffly forward, the hands clasped, the chin touches the water; the legs are also stiffly stretched out, the heels being together, the feet turned out, and the toes drawn up. This horizontal position is important, and must be executed correctly. No limb is permitted to be relaxed.

The movement of the limbs is now taught; that of the legs is taught first. The teacher first says, loudly and slowly, "One;" when the legs are slowly drawn under the body; at the same time the knees are separated to the greatest possible distance, the spine is bent downward, and the toes kept outward. The teacher then says briskly, "Two;" upon which the legs are stiffly stretched out, with a moderate degree of quickness, while the heels are separated, and the legs describe the widest possible angle, the toes being contracted and kept outward. The teacher then says quickly, "Three;" upon which the legs, with the knees held stiffly, are quickly brought together, and thus the original position is again obtained.

The point at which the motions "two" and "three" join are the most important, because it is the object to receive as large and compact a wedge of water between the legs as possible; so that when the legs are brought together their action upon this wedge may urge the body forward. In ordinary cases of swimming, the hands are not used to propel, but merely to assist in keeping on the surface. By degrees, therefore, "two" and "three" are counted in quick succession, and the pupil is taught to extend the legs as widely as possible. After some time, what was done under the heads "two" and "three" is done when "two" is called out. When the teacher sees that the pupil is able to propel himself with ease, which he frequently acquires the power of doing in the first lesson, and that he performs the motions already mentioned with regularity, he teaches the motions of the hands, which must not be allowed to sink, as they are much disposed to do while the motion of the legs is practised.

The motion of the hands consists of two parts. When the teacher says "One," the hands, which were held with the palms together, are opened, laid horizontally an inch or two under water, and the arms are extended till they form an angle of 90°; then the elbow is bent, and the hands are brought up to the chin, having described an arc downward and upward; the lower part of the thumb touches the chin, the palms being together. When the teacher says "Two," the arms are quickly stretched forward, and thus the original horizontal position is regained. The legs remain stiffly extended during the motion of the hands. If the motion of the hands is correctly done, the legs and arms are moved together; so that while the teacher says "One," the pupil performs the first motion of the hands and legs; when he says "Two," the second and third motions of the feet, and the second of the hands.

As soon as the teacher perceives that the pupil begins to support himself, he slackens the rope a little, and instantly straightens it if the pupil is about to sink. When the pupil can swim about ten strokes in succession, he is released from the pole, but not from the rope. When he can swim about 50 strokes, he is released from the rope too; but the teacher remains near him with a long pole until he can swim 150 strokes in succession, so that should he sink, the pole is immediately held out to him. After this he may swim in the area of the school, under the eye of the teacher, until he proves that he can swim half-an-hour in succession, so that should he sink, the pole may be held out to him; he is then considered fit to be left to himself.

BOATING.

IT would be an interesting study to trace the origin of vessels intended for conveying people on the water, commencing with Noah's Ark, the first on record, and coming down through the galleys of the Romans, and the vessels of the Vikings, to the improved ships of the present time. But this would take a great deal of time, and our young readers who are looking after specific information, would doubtless prefer us to get at once to the subject in hand.

OF BOATS.

A *Boat* is properly a vessel propelled by oars. In a more extensive sense the word is applied to other small vessels, which differ in construction and name, according to the services in which they are employed. Thus they are light or strong, sharp or flat-bottomed, open or decked, according as they are intended for swiftness or burden, deep or shallow water, &c.

The *Barge* is a long, light, narrow boat, employed in harbors, and unfit for sea. The *Long Boat* is the largest boat belonging to a ship, generally furnished with two sails, and is employed for cruising short distances, bringing the cargo and bales on board, &c.

The *Launch* is more flat-bottomed than the long boat, which it has generally superseded. The *Pinnace* resembles the barge, but is smaller. The *Cutters* of a ship are broader and deeper than the barge or pinnace, and are employed in carrying light articles, single passengers, &c., on board.

Yawls are used for similar purposes to the barge and pinnace. A *Gig* is a long, narrow boat, used for expedition, and rowed with six or eight oars. The *Jolly Boat* is smaller than a yawl, and is used for going on shore. A merchant ship seldom has more than two boats—a long boat and a yawl.

A *Wherry* is a light, sharp boat, used in a river or harbor for transporting passengers. A *Punt* is a flat-bottomed boat, chiefly used for fishing on a fresh-water river. A *Skiff* is a small sharp-nosed boat, used in rivers. A *Dingy* is a very small stiff boat used by yachts. A *Yacht* is a pleasure sailing-boat. A *Lugger* is a boat furnished with sails of a peculiar cut. A *Funny*, called in the West a *skiff*, is a little boat with her bow and stern nearly alike. When the bow and stern are both square, this is called a *Scow*. A *Bateau* and *Punt* are the same. A *Canoe* is a long, narrow boat hollowed out of the trunk of a tree. It is sometimes made by stretching birch bark on light ribs of tough and flexible wood. In the West the Mandan tribes of Indians used one covered with skins and nearly round. This was also used by the ancient Britons, and called a *Coracle*. An improved barge is used in New York harbor, where it is known as the Whitehall Boat. For races and regattas, a skeleton boat is built, long and narrow, with outriggers upon which the rowlocks are set.

THE COMPONENT PARTS OF BOATS.

Rowing boats consist of the bows (1); the stem, or entrance (2); the stern (8), where are the rudder and the lines for steering; the rowlocks (3), for giving purchase to the oars; and the thwarts, or seats (4). At the bottom are the foot-boards (5), which are easily removed, in order to bail out any

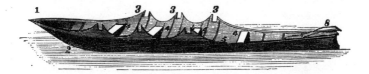

water which may leak into the boat. Besides these parts there is a board placed across the boat for the feet of the rower, called a stretcher. The whole boat is composed of one or more planks, called streaks, nailed upon a light oak framework, called the timbers, or ribs; and the upper streak, upon which the rowlocks are placed, is called the wale-streak. Boats with two rowlocks opposite each other are called sculling boats, and are propelled by a pair of light oars called sculls, the art being called "sculling." When a boat is fitted with a pair of rowlocks not opposite each other, it is called a pair-oared boat. If with two in the middle opposite each other, and two others, one before and the other behind, but not opposite each other, it is called a *randan.* When a boat has four rowlocks, none of which are opposite one another, it is called a four-oared boat, and so on up to ten oars, which is the utmost limit in common use for any kind of boat but the pleasure barge, which sometimes has twenty-four oars. The rowlock nearest the bow is called the bow rowlock, or No. 1; the next No. 2, and so on; and the oars used in them receive the same number, the one nearest the stern being called the "stroke oar." The rowlocks in river and sea boats are somewhat different in shape though identical in principle, both consisting of a square space of about the breadth of a man's hand, and both lying on the wale-streak; but in river boats being generally bounded before and behind by a flat piece of oak or ash called, respectively, the thowl-pin and stopper; whilst in sea boats they are merely common round wooden pins dropped into holes made in the wale-streak, but still receiving the same names. The thowl-pin is for the purpose of pulling the oar against, whilst the stopper prevents the oar from slipping forward when the rower is pushing it in that direction after the stroke.

THE OARS AND SCULLS.

A scull is a small oar used with one hand, and requiring a pair, as in the case of oars, one being placed in the rowlock on each side the boat, and the pair being used by one person with his right and left hands. Oars are used by both hands, and a pair-oared boat consequently requires two oarsmen; a four-oared boat four, and so on. Both sculls and oars consist of the same

parts, except that the handle of the *oar* is made long enough for both hands, as at *a*. In every case there is a rounded handle, *a b*, a loom, square in form, and extending from the handle to the button, or about one-third of the length of the oar; and beyond the button is the blade, which is first nearly round, and then gradually widens, until it assumes the form best adapted for laying hold of the water, which is now found to be broad rather than long, as was formerly thought to be desirable. The button is a piece of leather nailed on to prevent the oar from slipping through the rowlock, but only used in river rowing, as it is not adapted for the rough work which is often met with in sea rowing.

BOATING TERMS.

WEATHER OAR.

BOW OAR, the *starboard* upright oar towards the bow of the boat.

STROKE OAR, the oar rowed by the strokesman.

STROKESMAN, the *sternmost* man of the rowers.

STROKESIDE, the port or right side.

BOWMAN, the man nearest the bow of the boat.

COCKSWAIN, the man who steers the boat.

THOWL-PINS, the pins which sometimes are used for the rowlocks.

HEADFAST, sometimes called the *painter*. A rope fixed forward to fasten the boat after landing.

TO UNSHIP THE SCULLS, simply means to take them out of the rowlocks.

ROWED OFF; when this direction is given by the cockswain, all the oars are laid in with their blades forward.

IN BOW; at this phrase, the bowman gets the boat-hook ready to clear away for the shore.

SEA ROWING.

This is necessarily less elegant than river rowing, because of the rough nature of the element on which the exercise is pursued. The oar must be held firmly in the hands, the inside hand being placed at b, and the outside at a, and both hands grasping the oar between the thumbs and fingers. The whole art consists in the crew moving backward and forward together, called "swinging," and laying hold of the water as well as they can, taking care to avoid pulling in the air with great force when there is a trough or interval between two waves, and on the other hand equally avoiding a heavy wave, which has a tendency to dash the oar out of the hand. All this requires practice in the rowers, and also in the steersman, called the cockswain, who should watch for the high waves, and warn his men when a heavy one is coming. He should also take care to cross the roll of the sea as much as possible, so as to avoid being struck on the side of the boat called "the counter," which would either swamp her or else knock the oars out of the rowlocks. In this kind of rowing, the "feathering" of the oar, to be presently described, is not attempted, on account of the roughness of the water, but it merely is pulled steadily, but strongly, backward, and is then pushed forward in the rowlocks.

RIVER ROWING.

The art of river rowing is capable of a high degree of elegance, and few sights are more pleasing to a lover of graceful forms than that of a crew of fine lads, or young men, rowing well together and in good style. To do this requires great practice, and attention to a few essential points, which we will here endeavor to describe.

MANAGEMENT OF THE OAR.

The rower should, as far as possible, take some good oarsman for his model, and endeavor to imitate him in every respect, which is the only mode of acquiring a good style. Description is useful in putting the learner in the way of acquiring what is to be taught, but it is not all-sufficient for the purpose. In the first place, the learner should place himself square on the seat, with his feet straight before him, and the toes slightly turned out. The knees may either be kept together, or separated considerably, the latter being in our opinion the better mode, as it allows the body to come more forward over the knees. The feet are to be placed firmly against the stretcher, which is to be let out or shortened, to suit the length of the individual; and one foot may be placed in the strap which is generally attached to the stretcher in modern boats. The oar is then taken in hand, raising it by the handle, and then either at once placing it in the rowlock, or else first dropping it flat on the water, and then raising the handle it may gently be lowered to its place. The outside hand is placed upon the handle at a, *with the thumb as well as the fingers above it*, while the other hand firmly grasps it lower down at *b*, keeping the nut toward the person. The arms are now quickly thrust forward until they are quite straight at the elbows, *after which* the back follows them by bending forward at the hips, carefully avoiding any roundness of the shoulders. When the hands have reached their full stretch they are

COMMENCEMENT OF THE PULL.

raised, and the blade quietly and neatly dropped into the water; immediately after which, and with the water just covering the blade, the body is brought back with a graceful yet powerful action, till it reaches a part a little behind the perpendicular of the back of the seat, when the hands are brought back to

MIDDLE OF THE PULL.

the ribs, the elbows gliding close by the hips; and at the last moment, as the hand touches the rib, the wrist of the inside hand is depressed, the knuckles being at the same time brought against the chest, and the oar is made to

END OF THE PULL.

rotate in the rowlock, which is called "feathering" it, and by which it is brought cleanly out of the water. The next action is to push the oar rapidly forward again, first however restoring it to its original position in the rowlock, which is effected by raising the wrist, and then darting the arms forward till the elbows are quite straight, which brings the rower to where we started from in the description. In "backing water," the reverse of

RETURN OF THE SCULLS.

these actions takes place. The oar is first reversed in the rowlock, and then it is *pushed* through the water with as much power as is needed, and *pulled* through the air. When the oars on one side are pulled, and those on the other are backed, the boat is made to turn on its own water. "Holding water" is effected by the oars being held in the position of backing without moving them.

THE ESSENTIAL POINTS IN ROWING.

1st, To straighten the arms before bending the body forward; 2d, to drop the oar cleanly into the water; 3d, to draw it straight through at the same depth; 4th, to feather neatly, and without bringing the oar out before doing so; 5th, to use the back and shoulders freely, keeping the arms as straight as possible; and 6th, to keep the eyes fixed upon the rower before them, avoiding looking out of the boat, by which means the body is almost sure to swing backward and forward in a straight line.

MANAGEMENT OF THE BOAT.

Every boat without a rudder is manœuvred in the water, either by pulling both sides alike, in which case it progresses in a straight line, or by reversing the action of the oars, equally on both sides, pushing them through the water instead of pulling them, and called backing water, when the boat recedes; or by pulling one side only, on which the boat describes a segment of a circle, which is made smaller by pulling one oar, and backing the other. By means of a rudder the boat is made to take a certain course, independent of the rowers, called "steering," the chief art in which consists in keeping the rudder as still as possible, by holding the lines "taut," and avoiding pulling them from one side to the other more than is absolutely necessary. Some steersmen think it necessary to swing backward and forward with a great effort, but this is quite useless, and the more still they keep the better. Every cockswain should know the course of the stream or tide; and when meeting other boats, he should, if he is going down stream, give them the side nearest the shore, so as to allow them the advantage of the slack water, which is quite prejudicial to him. When a crew are steered by a competent cockswain, they ought to be perfectly obedient to his commands, rowing exactly as he tells them. His orders are communicated by the following words, viz. : when desiring his crew to row he says, "Pull all;" or if wishing any one oar to be pulled, he says, "Pull bow," or "Pull No. 3," or 4, etc., as the case may be. If they are to stop rowing, he says "Easy all," or for any one oar, "Easy bow," or No. 2. The same kind of order is conveyed when "backing" or "holding water" is desired; the only variation, as before, being between confining his order to any one or more oars, or extending it to all. In this way all the evolutions practicable on the water are managed, and the cockswain has complete control over the boat, being able to cause her to be rowed slowly or quickly, or to be stopped, backed, or turned on her own centre.

LANDING.

If the tide be in your favor, bring the boat in a rather slanting direction toward the place of landing, so that as you reach the place the tide may take the stern down, as it is always best to land stern to tide. When you got to the landing-place, unship the sculls as before directed: but instead of letting them lie alongside, lay them in the boat, with the looms aft and the blades forward; then take hold of the headfast, jump ashore, and fasten the boat safely. This applies to river rowing; but in landing on the sea-shore when there is a swell, a little more care must be used; your boat, however, will be larger and stronger manned. In this case you must watch for a smooth; as soon as you have it, "give way" with all your power to the shore. The bowman must be ready to jump ashore with the painter in his hand, and pull the boat up out of the reach of the surf; all hands must jump out, after having first laid in their oars as before directed, and help him if he is not strong enough.

Launching a boat from the beach is sometimes a more difficult affair. When there is a considerable swell, and the boat is large (it will of course be strongly manned), the two bowmen get into the boat, with their oars ready to act; the other men equally divided lay hold of each side of her gunwale, entering the water with her and forcing her head into the sea. They must not, however, all jump in until she is fairly afloat, for if she were to ground and ship a sea, the probability is that her head would be turned, and that the next sea would capsize her before they could prevent it. In such cases, loss of life is by no means uncommon. But when the boat is afloat her head is sometimes turned for want of readiness on the part of the rowers; in such case, let two bowmen with oars or boat-hooks go to the bow on the lee of the boat, and by forcing them into the strand push the head of the boat seaward. Lying broadside to a sea is very dangerous, but if care and decision are used the boat can generally be kept head to sea; in fact, it is much more easy to keep it so than to return it, when the surf has once thrown it toward the shore.

A FEW IMPORTANT REMARKS ON CUTTER ROWING.

Each oarsman must be particular to take his time from the strokesman.

While rowing he must be strictly under the orders of the cockswain.

Let it be ever kept in view, that keeping time and keeping stroke are the two great points for an oarsman's attention.

When there is any swell on the water, caused either by the paddles of steamboats or rough weather, care should be taken always to keep the boat's head well facing it.

FAULTS TO BE AVOIDED.

Catching Crabs.—This term implies the act of falling backward from the seat, through not taking hold of the water in the attempt to pull.

Not Keeping Time.—Independent of the awkwardness of the appearance, this habit will be an effectual bar to your rowing in concert with any master of the art. Not keeping time, recollect, is not putting your oar into the water at the same time as the stroke oar.

Not Keeping Stroke.—This, be it observed, is totally different from the preceding fault. It is not doing work at the same time as the stroke oar; and this may be neglected even when you have kept time by putting your oar in the water at the same moment as the strokesman did his. Though not so unseemly, it is yet the most destructive fault that can be committed; for it must be evident that the speed of the boat must depend upon the simultaneous and equal effort of its whole crew. Recollect, therefore, that the pull should commence the moment the blade is properly immersed in the water.

Doubling the Body over the Oar at the end of the Stroke.—This prevents the shooting of the arms and body simultaneously forward, which is a most important feature in good rowing.

Jerking is a fault to which men who are powerful in the arms are particularly liable; as, instead of throwing the body gradually back, and thus partially pulling by their weight, they depend solely upon the muscles of their arms. They, therefore, give a violent muscular effort, which not being continued by falling back, the stroke ends, as it were, too soon, producing a jerk, which destroys the uniform swing throughout the boat, and thus decreases the propulsive power, and ultimately tires out the man. It is very annoying to the other part of the crew.

Rowing Round.—This fault arises from not entering the water deep enough at the first. The rower feels that he has not sufficient resistance (and is in danger of catching a crab), he consequently deepens his water with the blade of an oar, forming a portion of a circle, and brings the flat part of the blade perpendicularly to the water, thereby tending to drag the boat down by its pressure; this is a great fault, and must be avoided.

Slacking the Arms Too Soon.—This not only decreases the power of the stroke, but generally causes a positive impediment to the boat's rapid progress; for the habit is generally accompanied by one or two additional errors, viz., either feathering the scull before it is out of the water; or allowing the boat to carry it along. In the first, you add to your own labor; in the second, you, to a certain extent, stop the boat. Very light boats are apt to cause these faults. The remedy in such a case is, to dip the scull deeper at the commencement of the stroke; but the learner must recollect that the same faults are committed in ordinary boats.

Throwing up water in rowing must be carefully avoided. It is excessively annoying to those on the same side of the boat.

Capping the end of the oar with the hand has a very awkward appearance, and conduces greatly to other faults.

Rowing with a round back is another very common fault, and must be avoided, because considerable loss of power is the consequence.

We have now recapitulated most of the faults to which rowers or oarsmen are subjected, and, taken in conjunction with the preceding directions, our hints cannot fail to make any person theoretically acquainted with the art, if he will take care thoroughly to comprehend what we have written. Practice, however, must be had to make a good oarsman. A good theory in the hands of a practical person may lead to perfection; neither theory nor practice alone will do so. The learner must not be disheartened by the difficulties he will be sure to meet with during his first attempts with the oar or scull, not the least unpleasant of which will be his habit of catching crabs.

SAILING.

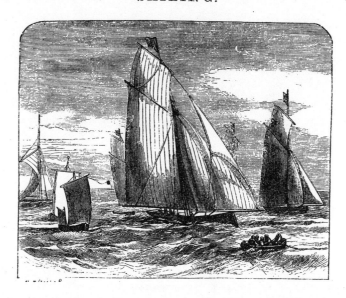

Although the sailing exercise of boys will necessarily be confined to a small boat, it is proper that they should be made acquainted with the distinction between larger vessels, and be furnished with a vocabulary of terms belonging to the art of sailing.

All sailing vessels are set down under the term ships, but, strictly speaking, a *Ship* is a vessel with three masts that are square-rigged; that is, the yards which support the square-sails are rigged at right angles to the masts. But all the sails are not square, the jib being triangular, and the spanker bow-sided, but not square. The *hull* or body of the vessel is divided into the *forecastle*, before the foremast, the *waist*, between the foremast and mainmast, and the *quarter-deck*, which is *abaft* or behind the mizzen-mast. These masts whose names you have had given you, are fitted with other masts, slipping into each other, and securely connected for the purpose of bearing its appropriate sail. Thus, the foremast or forward one is the *foremast*, and bears the *foresail;* the mast above that is the *foretopmast,* and bears the *foretopsail;* the one above that the *foretop-gallant-mast,* and bears the *foretop-gallant-sail.* The mainmast is divided in the same way into mainmast, maintopmast and maintop-gallant-mast, which bear severally the mainsail, maintopsail and maintop-gallant-sail. The mizzen-mast is furnished with a sail rigged on the plane of the vessel's length, or "fore and aft;" and the bowsprit or jib-boom, which projects from the front at more or less of an angle, supports with the foremast a triangular sail called the *jib*, also rigged fore and aft; and has another mast attached to it, called

BRIG.

the flying-jib-boom, which supports the flying-jib. There are usually square sails above the top-gallant-sails, that are called "royals," and distinguished

SCHOONER.

by the names of the masts to which they are attached. Then there are additional sails, projecting on either side of the square-sails, that are used in light winds, called *studding-sails*, and the *booms*, which support them, are attached to the extremities of the several yards. Between the masts are also triangular sails, called *stay-sails*.

SLOOP.

A *Brig* is rigged on the same principle as the ship, but has only two masts; being a ship, as it were, with the mainmast taken out.

DUTCH GALIOT.

A *Schooner* is a vessel with two masts, rigged fore and aft. She may carry gaff-topsails, which are triangular sails, set above the main and fore-

FELUCCA.

sails, or one or two square topsails before. In the last case she is usually called a "topsail schooner." A schooner has sometimes three masts, and is known as a *three-masted schooner*, or as a *ship-rigged fore and aft.*

A *Brigantine* is a schooner, with square sails on the foremast, foretop-mast, and foretop-gallant-masts; being a topsail schooner, with the addition of a foresail.

An *Hermaphrodite Brig*, vulgarly called a "*morfydite*," is brig-rigged fore, and schooner-rigged aft. It is almost peculiar to this country.

CHINESE JUNK.

A *Sloop* is a vessel with one mast, and the sails, which consist of a mainsail, jib, and gaff-topsail, rigged in the plane of its length. The North River sloops are celebrated for their fast sailing.

A *Dutch Galiot* is rigged like a schooner, but of a broader and more Chinese build, her bottom being nearly flat.

A *Billy-boy* is rigged sometimes like a sloop, and sometimes like a schooner; but her bottom is nearly flat, and she draws but little water.

A *Smack* is a small vessel with one mast, like a cutter, used principally for fishing.

A *Felucca* has two triangular sails, is used in the Mediterranean, and is particularly swift. It can also use oars in calm weather.

A *Junk* is a Chinese vessel, used either for war or merchandise. It is built very heavily.

A *Lugger* has two or three masts, with sails hoisted on yards, something like a cutter's gaff-topsail, and some of them carry a jib.

A *Proa* is used by the natives of the Ladrone Islands, and is remarkable for its swiftness and sailing close to the wind. The lee-side is quite straight, and the weather-side is convex, like a common boat. Both head and stern are equally sharp; and in working her there is no necessity to tack or turn

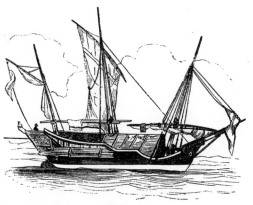

PROA.

at any time. Besides this peculiarity of construction, the proa has on her lee-side what is called an " out-rigger," which is made of two poles, extending about ten feet from her side, having at their extremity a piece of solid wood. This prevents her from having any leeway. She will sail with a good wind twenty miles an hour.

We will now speak of the vessels we have most to do with—viz., yachts.

CHARACTERS OF A YACHT.

Speed, safety, and accommodation are the three first qualities of a yacht. She ought to be pleasing to the eye when afloat, of such a breadth as to carry her canvas with ease, and at the same time so sharp in her bow and

well shaped astern as to displace her weight of water smoothly and gradually, while she leaves it in the same way.

VARIOUS KINDS OF YACHTS.

Yachts are of various kinds, according to their size. If more than eighty
tons burden, the schooner is most suitable; for, as the spars are more
numerous, they are proportionably lighter. The schooner, as has been
before observed, has two masts—the foremast and mainmast; the one
bearing the sail called the boom-foresail, and the other a mainsail. She
has two or more head-sails, called stay-sail, forestay-sail, and jib. Her topsails are either square or fore and aft.

The *Cutter* has one mast and four sails—viz.: mainsail, maintopsail,
foresail, and jib. Some smaller craft have larger jibs, and no foresail.

The *Dandy-rigged Yacht* differs from a cutter, in having no boom for her
mainsail, which can consequently be brailed up by a rope passing round it.

She has a mizzen-mast standing in the stern, which sets a sail called a mizzen,
and which is stretched on a horizontal spar, projecting over the stern. This
style of rig is more safe for a yacht, as the boom in ordinary cutters is
liable to sweep persons overboard; and the sail can be taken in quicker by
brailing it up than by lowering it down.

The *Hatteener* has only two sails, a fore and mainsail, of a triangular
shape. Each has a spar standing from the deck to the peak of the sail, and
a boom at the bottom, like a cutter. This rig, from setting more canvas
abaft, is well adapted for narrow waters.

DESCRIPTION OF THE CUTTER-YACHT.

But the vessel with which we have most to do in our directions for sailing is the Cutter-Yacht, which stands closer to the wind than any other

kind of boat; and of which we propose, in the first instance, to give a general description.

CONSTRUCTION OF THE HULL.

The first step in the construction of the hull is laying down the keel or backbone of the vessel; which is done by fixing a strong piece of wood, generally oak, upon blocks, that the rest of the timber may be securely added; the stem is then joined to the fore-post, nearly at right angles, slanting a little forward as it ascends; and the stern-post to its after or hinder part, sloping upward and backward. The timbers and ribs are next cut out of solid wood, and placed transversely on the keel, their width varying according to the lines of a plan previously drawn out—being, of course, farthest apart at the beam; these, as well as the planks of larger craft, are

THE AMERICA.

made to bend into the required shape by being steamed and bolted in while hot. The skeleton being completed, her planks are then secured by copper or iron nails to the timbers, and riveted. The deck is made of narrow planks, running fore and aft. From the level of the deck, her sides are raised by upright timbers, called "stancheons," cased over by the bulwarks, and surmounted by a rail called the "gunwale." Some yachts are only half-decked, the after-part being left open and fitted with seats; but, in order to prevent the water from getting in, a portion of deck, called water-ways, is left at each side; which opposes a further barrier by its terminating on the inner edge in a high crest or combing. The stepping the mast requires great care, since the good or bad sailing of the boat depends very greatly upon it. The model of the celebrated yacht, "The America," after all the study and ingenuity that have been applied to yacht-building, seems to resemble the simple yet beautiful model which nature has given us in the duck. The bow of this vessel rises very gradually for some distance along the keel, like the breast of the duck; and, further imitating the same model, her beam or widest part is abaft, or further back than the centre. This superior vessel will sail nearly four points off the wind. We have now glanced at all the principal parts of the hull, except that all-important part, the rudder; which swings by a hinge from the stern-post, and is moved by a handle fixed to its upper part, bearing the name of "a tiller," and which is used to steer the boat. Before proceeding with our instructions for sailing a yacht, it will be necessary to describe the action of the rudder; as the art of steering is the nicest and most important branch of seamanship.

The rudder is a flat board, with a pole rising up on the side, which is fastened to the vessel; on the top of which is fixed the tiller. In large vessels there are two ropes fastened to the tiller, which are carried through

blocks on each side of the vessel; then brought back through blocks fastened on the mizzen-mast, and passed round a wheel, by which means a greater command is obtained over the rudder. When the tiller is moved to the right (starboard), the rudder, of course, is forced in the water to the left (port). As the vessel moves on, the water presses against the rudder on the port side, and thus forces her stern to the starboard side, and her bow to the port. When the tiller is moved to the left, it of course produces a contrary effect. If the ship is moving backward, then, by moving the tiller to the right, the bow is also turned to the right; for the water presses against the rudder behind it on the left side, and thus pushes the stern to the left. In steering, care must be taken not to steer too much— that is, not to move the rudder too violently, or more than is necessary—as this materially stops her way.

We here present the young yachtsman with a cutter at anchor, with her ropes and spars numbered; and which ought to be thoroughly known, as well as the uses to which they are applied in sailing a yacht:

1. Stem.	11. Vane and Spindle.	21. Forestay.
2. Stern.	12. Cross-trees.	22. Topping Lift.
3. Tiller.	13. Trussle-trees.	23. Lift Blocks.
4. Anchor.	14. Gaff.	24. Mainsheet.
5. Cable.	15. Boom.	25. Peak Halliards.
6. Bowsprit.	16. Topmast-shroud.	28. Foresheet.
7. Bobstay.	17. Topmast-backstay.	29. Signal Halliards.
8. Mast.	18. Topmast-stay.	30. Companion.
9. Topmast.	19. Runner and Tackle.	31. Forecastle.
10. Truck.	20. Traveller for Jib.	32. Rudder.

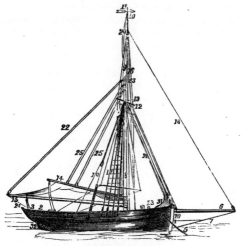

CUTTER AT ANCHOR.

SOMETHING ABOUT THE MASTS, SPARS, ROPES, ETC.

The *Mast* (8) is a spar set nearly upright, inclining a little aft, to support yards and sails.   In a yacht, it is kept in its place by two shrouds on each side, made of strong rope, and fastened to the sides of the vessel.

CUTTER BEFORE THE WIND. .

The *Bowsprit* (6) is a spar carried out from the forepart of a yacht, secured at its inner end between two strong posts piercing the deck, called "the bitts." It is kept in its place by the bobstay (7), which is fastened to the stem, and by a shroud on each side secured to the bow.

The *Boom* (15) is that spar which sets out the mainsail below, and is attached at one end to the mast by a swivel cable, called the "goose-neck," and is eased off or hauled in at the other by the main-sheet (24), which is a rope passing from the end of the boom through a block on the side of the vessel.

The *Gaff* (14) sets out the mainsail above, and slides up and down the mast by means of a crescent end, which embraces it. The sides of this curve are called "horns."

The *Topmast* (9) stands above the mast, and is made to slide up and down. On it a topsail (*i. e.,* a gaff-topsail) is set in light winds; but both sail and mast are generally lowered in squally weather. It is kept steady by a backstay (17) on each side of the foretopmast stay. The latter is brought down to the bowsprit.

Ropes.—There are various ropes to hoist and lower sails, called halliards. There are also other ropes of great importance, especially those called the sheets, which are to haul in the sails, and make them

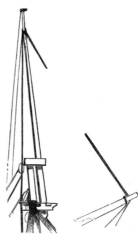

stand to the wind. In a yacht, the mainsail has sometimes a sheet on each side; and sometimes only one sheet reeved through double blocks, which travel on an iron rod, called a "horse," from side to side. The jib has two sheets, the starboard and port (right and left). The foresail has the same, except in some instances, when it has but one sheet working on a traveller, like the mainsail. The topsail has only one, which is rove through a sheave at the end of the gaff, and a block at the throat of the gaff, and then down to a cleat or fastening place on the deck. Signal halliards are for hauling up the colors, and pass through a small sheave in the truck (10), at the end of the topmast. The ensign halliards are reeved through a small block at the peak end, and lead down to

TOPMAST AND FORETOPMAST STAY. the boom. The other ropes on board a yacht are for the support of the spars, and are called "standing-rigging," while those used for the sails are called "running-rigging."

We trust we have given our young readers a tolerable idea of a cutter-yacht. We will now proceed to describe the common sail-boat, a little craft, not so complicated in construction, and one which our juvenile friends will learn how to manage more readily.

THE SAIL-BOAT.

The sail-boat is sloop-rigged, with or without a jib; but differs in the fact that she has no main boom nor gaff, the sail being kept up by a *sprit*. Her rig may be described as follows: She has one mast, with a *mainsail,* A, and a *foresail,* B; one mast, a *sprit,* 1, and a short *bowsprit,* 2. The mast will

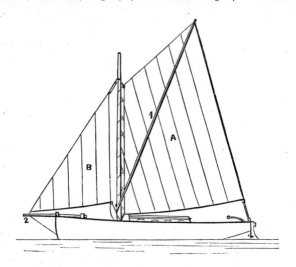

have one *shroud* on each side, and a *forestay* to the stem, each set up by *lanyards.* The mainsail will be hoisted by a *main halliard* passing through a hole, or over a *sheave* in the mast, and it is a very good plan to have this hole or sheave *above* the shrouds, as also the hole for the fore-halliards, one hole being above the other. The *sprit* fits into an *eye* at the peak of the mainsail, and into a *becket* or *snotter* round the mast; and large boats have a rope to hoist and keep up the snotter. In small boats, the snotter, when wetted, sticks tight enough to the mast. The *mainsheet* works on a *horse* at the stern. The *fore-halliards* pass through a hole in the mast-head, and the foresail is *laced* to the forestay. The *foresheets* lead through holes in the knees. To set the sails, hoist the mainsail by the main-halliards *chock up,* or as far as it will go, and then *belay* the main-halliards to one of the *cleats;* then catch hold of the peak of the mainsail, and double the mainsail round forward of the mast; then put the upper end of the sprit into the eye, and shove the sprit up. To do this properly requires practice; in large boats there is a lashing to keep the eye from blowing off the end of the sprit, and the beginner may put a lashing if he likes. Then put the lower end of the sprit into the snotter, and hoist the snotter up the mast till the mainsail begins to wrinkle from the tack to the peak; then haul the mainsheet taut, and belay it till you are ready to start. The foresail is usually wrapped around the forestay; *untoggle* the sheets and unwrap the foresail, then toggle on the sheets again, ship the *tiller*, and the boat will be ready.

The usual small sail-boat, however, is rigged without a foresail or jib, and the mast, in order to balance it, is set somewhat forward of the spot where it stands in the cut. It has no shroud or forestay, being merely shipped into a thwart running across the boat, and secured in a step below. It is set, too, with more of a *rake*, or pitch backward, than in the cut. Such a boat, which can be safely and easily managed by one, is the best for the young yachtsman.

Getting into his little boat, the beginner, who should have a skilled grown person with him as companion, will soon learn the principles on which a boat *tacks* or is *put about*, how to *jibe* safely, how to *reef* the mainsail and the foresail and how to fit a *reefed snotter*, how to *stow the sail* and *moor the boat*, and how to *pick up moorings* and to *come alongside*. Sailing boats are usually made fast by a chain to a stone under water; when the boat gets *under way*, the chain is let go, and is picked up again by a rope, one end of which is made fast to the chain, the other to a piece of wood or small cask called a *buoy*. To pick up this buoy again, sometimes the sails are lowered and the boat runs at it, but usually the boat is taken to leeward, and at the proper distance is *luffed up*, so as to come head to wind, and stop as nearly as may be over the buoy; and to do this with certainty requires much practice. The beginner should go where he has plenty of room, taking out a buoy or piece of wood, and practise picking that up till he can measure his distance pretty accurately. To do this, however, and in fact to sail a boat at all, a clear understanding of the principles of sailing is of great assistance.

TO SAIL A BOAT.

Everybody can understand how a boat can sail *before the wind*—a box for a boat, with a coat or umbrella for a sail, can do that, but to sail with the wind on the side, or to make way against the wind, is far more difficult; in fact, persons not accustomed to it often doubt the possibility of doing so. In explaining this, we will consider the sails as quite flat, for the nearer they can be brought to flatness the better, and wherever they are not flat there is a loss. Supposing the sails, then, to be flat, and the wind to strike them, part of the force is lost (as will be understood on mechanical principles), part of it presses against the flat surface of the sail, and perpendicularly to it. This tends partly to drive the boat *ahead*, partly to drive the boat bodily to *leeward*, and if the boat was a box or tub, she would go in a direction between the two; but as boats are usually constructed, they are sharp at the fore-end, and the surface opposed in that direction is not more than one-seventh of the surface which the nearly flat side opposes—hence the boat is driven easily ahead, but only a little or not at all to leeward; and boats are constructed so as to oppose as little resistance ahead and as much on the side as possible. Any boat will sail with the wind astern, and most boats will sail with the wind *on the quarter*—*i. e.*, blowing in any direction between the stern and the broadside; but only good boats will sail with the wind *on the bow* or *before the beam*, and then not when the wind is more than *four points* before the beam, reckoning by the thirty-two points of the compass, and to do that, the sails must be well set, and the boat pretty good. To explain how this is effected, let us suppose a boat with her head pointing exactly toward the wind, then her sails will only flap about and tend to drive her astern. Now suppose her bow gradually turned away from the wind; if the sails are hauled pretty flat, after a time, usually when her bow is four points or the eighth of a circle off from the wind, the sails will fill with wind, and, on the principles already explained, she will move ahead. And it is obvious that, after having gone some distance in this direction, she may be put about and go at a similar angle to the wind in the other direction, and will thus have advanced against the wind, or towards the quarter from which the wind is blowing. This is called *tacking* or *turning to windward*, and to do this well is the greatest proof of a good boat or of good sailing. In *sailing to windward*, the sails are trimmed or hauled aft to an angle which varies for each boat, and must be found by experience; they should be kept just full of wind—if empty they are doing no good, or even harm; if too full, the boat is *off her course*, and not doing her best to windward. A rough rule is to keep the flag or vane just over the mainsail. Boats ought always to carry a *weather helm*—*i. e.*, the bow should have a tendency to turn toward the wind. Putting weight in the bow makes the weather-helm stronger, putting it in the stern or increasing the head sails has the reverse effect. When the wind is on the *starboard* or right hand side of the vessel, she is said to be on the *starboard tack;* when the wind is on the *port, larboard*, or left side, she is said to be on the *port tack;* and when vessels meet, that which is on the starboard tack either keeps straight or luffs, that which is on the port tack gives way and passes to leeward.

To sail with the wind on the bows the boat must have a keel. In a sail-boat this is generally made movable, sliding up and down, within a well in the centre, and is sometimes called the *sliding-keel*, but more generally the *centre-board*. A skiff may be made to tack by holding the flat blade of a scull deep in the water, against the side of the boat, on the leeward side; but this is inconvenient.

While engaged in learning how to manage a boat it is as well to get an old sailor to teach you how to make the various knots, splices, and hitches for which you will have constant occasion.

Having informed the young sailor of what is necessary to be done on board, we will now impress on his mind a few useful nautical terms and maxims, which may lead to the preservation of life and limb.

OF THE MARINER'S COMPASS.

The ancients, whose only guides over the trackless waters were the heavenly bodies, so often obscured by clouds, could not venture far from shore. It is the compass which has enabled us to steer boldly across the deep. The directive power of the loadstone has been long known to the Chinese, and it was brought over to Europe about the year 1260. The communication of the magnetic power to steel and suspending it on a pivot, is undoubtedly a European invention. The compass is composed of a magnetic

needle suspended freely on a pivot, and supporting a card marked with the thirty-two points of direction into which the horizon is divided, and which are thence called the points of the compass. The needle always points nearly north, and the direction of the boat may be easily seen by looking at the card. The whole apparatus on board a ship is enclosed in a box with a glass cover, to allow the card to be seen without being disturbed by the wind. This box is also sometimes suspended, to prevent the needle being affected by the motion of the vessel. The whole is then placed at the binnacle, in sight of the helmsman. In the inside of that part of the compass-box which is directly in a line with the bow, is a clear black stroke, called the lubber line, which the helmsman uses to keep his course; that is, he must always keep the point of the card which indicates her course pointing at the lubber line. Every young yachtsman must learn to box the compass: that is, to repeat all its points in order.

CAUTIONS AND DIRECTIONS.

1. Never leave any thing in the gangway, and keep the decks clear.

2. Coil up all ropes; and have a place for every thing, and every thing in its place.

3. Take care that in tacking or jibing the boom does not knock you overboard.

4. Stand clear of ropes' ends and blocks flying about, when you are tacking, and the sails shaking.

5. Keep a good look-out ahead, and also for squalls, which may generally be observed to windward.

● 6. Always obey the orders of the steersman promptly.

7. Keep all your standing rigging taut.

8. When the boat is on the wind, sit on the weather side.

9. Should the boat capsize, keep yourself clear of the rigging and swim ashore.

The young yachtsman should on no account attempt to take command of a boat till he is thoroughly experienced, and should never go in one without having at least one experienced hand on board; he should always have his eyes open to what is going on, and be ever ready to lend assistance with the greatest promptitude.

NAUTICAL TERMS.

We shall now give a few of the most common nautical terms, by which the gear and different parts of a vessel are known. For the most part, we shall speak generally, but when we speak particularly of a rope or sail, and the vessel is not named, the reader must apply our remarks to the cutter, as the vessel best adapted for a yacht.

Haul, to pull.

Taut, tight.

Starboard, to the right.

Larboard, to the left.

Close-hauled; or, on the wind; or, flying to windward, steering close to the wind. Cutters have good way within five points of the wind; square-rigged vessels not within six.

Wind on the beam; or, *sailing free*, sailing with the wind across the waist of the vessel; her head is then eight points from the wind.

Before the wind, sailing with the wind right aft, or behind you, that is, with the head sixteen points from the wind.

Sailing with the wind abaft the beam, sailing with the head of the vessel more than eight points from the wind, but not sixteen.

Sailing with the wind before the beam, with the vessel's head less than eight points from the wind, but not close-hauled.

Luff, keep nearer the wind; keep your luff, means, keep close to the wind.

Belay, make fast.

Steady, keep the helm amidships.

Haul aft, more towards the stern.

Put the helm down, put the helm to leeward.

Put the helm up, bring it to windward.

Leeward, the point *to* which the wind blows.

Windward, the point *from* which the wind blows.

Ship the tiller, fix it in the rudder head.

Unship, means, of course, exactly the reverse of the above.

Jibe, the act of bringing over the sail from one side of the vessel to the other.

Bend the sail, fix it in its proper place.

Bowse the sail well up, pull it strongly into its place.

The throat of the mainsail (*a fore and aft sail*), that part of the sail which is fixed to the peak close to the mast.

The Peak, the stick which is at the top of a fore and aft sail.

The Boom, the stick which is at the bottom of a fore and aft sail.

Head-sails, any sails at the head of a vessel; in cutters, foresail, fore-staysail, jib, and any others she may carry before the mast, except a square-sail, which is sometimes used for running before the wind.

Fore and aft sails, such sails as the mainsail of a cutter when stretched fore and aft, by its sheets. (See description of cutter and engraving.)

Sheets, the ropes by which the lower sails are made fast in the position desired; we say, for instance, "Haul taut the foresheet," which means, tighten the foresheet. Each sheet is distinguished by the name of the sail to which it is attached; for instance, the mainsheet means the sheet belonging to the mainsail; in like manner, jibsheet, foresheet, &c. The jib, however, has two sheets, one on each side of the forestay, for the convenience of tacking; the foresail has but one, which is made fast to the traveller of the foresheet horse; as the boat tacks, the traveller enables the foresail to pass from one side of the boat to the other.

Foresheet horse, a bar of iron which crosses from one gunwale to the other, to which the foresheet is fastened by means of a traveller; it is an inch or two above the deck.

Traveller, in the case of the foresheet horse, is the ring that passes backward and forward along the foresheet horse, as the foresail is jibed from one side to the other. Speaking generally, the term means an easy ring attached to a sail, and running upon a boom bowsprit or mast, to enable you to haul out or haul up a sail.

Yards, the sticks by which square-sails are set.

Square-sails, such sails as the main-topsail of a brig. (See description of a brig and engraving.)

Tack, to turn a vessel from one side to the other, with her head toward the wind. When a vessel is obliged to tack several times to get to windward, we say she is beating to windward; when she is tacking to get up or down a channel, we say she is beating up or down;—by the by, in rough weather she often gets a beating in the attempt; when tacking to get off a lee shore, we say she is clawing off.

Halliards, the rope by which signals or sails are hoisted. We say, for instance, "haul taut the peak halliards," which is an order to hoist the peak of the sail well up.

Lee runner and tackle, a substitute for a backstay; used in cutters, on account of its being easily removed when going before the wind.

Stays : in tacking, the vessel is said to be in stays from the time the jib-sheet is let fly until the foresail draws.

Bobstay, the rope fixed at the end of the bowsprit, and fastened about half way down the stern. Chains are frequently used for this purpose.

Backstays, forestays, etc., etc. : each of these denote the particular part the rope supports. The former are ropes from the after part of the head of the top-mast of a cutter-rigged vessel to the after part of the chains on each side of the ship; the latter is a rope from the topmast-head to the farther part of the bowsprit; it there passes through a block and comes in by the stern-head, and is then made fast to its cleat.

Cleat, a projecting piece of wood or iron, to which sheets or halliards are made fast.

Shrouds are also supports to the masts. Each shroud is distinguished by the part it is intended to support—for instance, the bowsprit and main-shrouds.

The main-shrouds are the ropes fastened at the end of the bowsprit, and extending to each side of the bows.

Boom-guy, a small tackle, one end of which is hooked to the main-boom, and the other forward, to prevent the boom from swinging.

Topping-lift, strong ropes, which are near the end of the main-boom, and led through blocks on each side of the mast, just under the cross-trees, from whence it descends about half way, and is connected with the gunwale or deck by a tackle.

Bow-line, a rope made fast to the foremost shroud, and passed through a thimble in the after lurch of the fore-sail, then round the shroud again, and round the sheet.

Thimble, a small ring, of iron or brass, inserted into the sails.

Cringles, short loops of rope, with a thimble inside them, and spliced to the lurch of the sail.

Gaskets, ropes made by plaiting rope-yarns.

Slack : take in the slack; draw in the loose rope.

Lanyard, a small rope.

Reef : taking in a reef, is tying in a portion of the sail.

Reef-tackle, a small tackle formed by two hook-blocks, one of which is hooked to the under part of the boom, about one-third of its length from the mast; and the other, farther aft. The fall is belayed to a cleat under the boom.

Earing, a short rope used in reefing, one end of which is made fast to the boom, at the same distance from the mast as the cringle, to which it belongs; it ascends and passes through the cringle, then descends and passes through a sheave on the side of the boom; then it is passed on board and stopped to the boom by means of its lanyard, or small line spliced into its end for the purpose; this lanyard is also to make it fast when the sail is reefed and the tackle removed.

Bowsprit fid, a bolt of iron that passes through the bowsprit bits and the heel of the bowsprit, to keep the bowsprit in its place.

Bowsprit bits, two stout pieces of wood, between which the bowsprit passes. If the reader has noticed the way a carriage-pole is fixed, he will readily conceive how the bowsprit is fastened between the bits.

Channels, the places on the side of the vessel to which the shrouds are fastened.

The quarter of a vessel, is the place on either side at which the side and the stem meet.

Midships, midway between the sides of the vessel.

Abeam, at right angles with the keel of the vessel. The term has risen from the beams of the vessel lying that way.

Cast her : in first making sail, it means placing the head of the vessel in the most advantageous position.

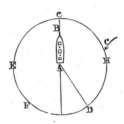

Wear, to ; to come round on the other side of the wind, without backing.

Let A B be the vessel, G the direction of the wind; A B is sailing in the direction B C, and wants to change her course to A D; if she tacks, she traverses the direction C H D; if she wears, she goes off from the wind in the direction C E D.

Helm's-a-lee, the call of the helmsman when his helm is hard down in tacking.

Ready about, a command for all hands to be ready in tacking.

HORSEMANSHIP.

RIDING.

AMONG the possessions which the boyish imagination pictures as treasures of price, a horse or a pony, if it be even the smallest *sheltie* that ever wore a shaggy mane hanging over his brows, will always hold a foremost place. What boy, who has ever been the master of a pony, does not remember the triumphant pleasure he felt on the day when his proprietorship began? How he rejoiced in his new acquisition!

Now, what we want to do in the following pages is, to give our young readers such information about that noble animal, the horse, as shall make them appreciate him more than ever, from a knowledge of his real qualities and usefulness; and we want, moreover, to enable them not merely to admire the horse with an ignorant wonder, because he is beautiful to look at, but *because they all know about him;* besides, no boy who does not know how to manage a horse, and what to do in case of accident or emergency, should ride one. He only who can trust in his own knowledge and resources can really be called independent. Any one of our young readers may at any time be taught, by practical experience, that knowledge is power, and ignorance weakness; and, therefore, before boy of ours was intrusted with a pony, we should take good care that he knew something of the parts, qualities, and character of the horse, and that the new acquisition would not suffer in his hands.

The parts of the horse will be understood by a reference to the cut and explanation on the following page.

TERMS USED BY HORSEMEN.

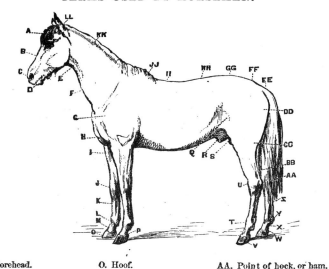

A. Forehead.	O. Hoof.	AA. Point of hock, or ham.
B. Face.	P. Heel.	BB. Hamstring.
C. Muzzle.	Q. Flank.	CC. Thigh, or gaskin.
D. Jowl.	R. Sheath.	DD. Quarter.
E. Gullet.	S. Stifles.	EE. Dock.
F. Windpipe.	T. Coronet.	FF. Croup.
G. Point of the shoulder.	U. Hock.	GG. Hip.
H. Breast, or bosom.	V. Hoof.	HH. Loins.
I. Arm.	W. Small pastern.	II. Back.
J. Knee.	X. Large pastern	JJ. Withers.
K. Cannon.	Y. Fetlock.	KK. Crest.
L. Large pastern.	Z. Cannon.	LL. Poll.
M. Small pastern.		

The left side of a horse is called the "*near side*," and the right, the "*off side*." We now come to

THE MARKS OF AGE IN THE HORSE.

By means of the gradual wearing down of the front teeth, or nippers, the age of the horse may be known. Each of the nippers has a hollow in its upper surface, which is very deep and black when the tooth first rises above the gum, and is gradually effaced by the friction caused by the cropping of the grass, or by biting at the manger, or other kinds of rubbing; but as these vary a great deal according to circumstances, so the precise degree of wearing away will also be liable to fluctuations; and the rules laid down only approximate to the truth, without positive accuracy as to a few months. There are also two sets of teeth; a milk set, which first rise, beginning at once after birth, and a permanent set, which replace the milk teeth as they fall out. The milk teeth come up two at a time, but all are up by the end of the first year. The permanent teeth, also, make their appearance by twos, the first pair showing themselves in the place of the two middle milk teeth in the third year, and being generally level with the other milk teeth by the end of the fourth year, by which time the next pair have fallen out, and the permanent teeth have shown themselves in their places. At five years of age the horse has lost all his nippers, and his corner permanent teeth have nearly completed their growth. The tusks are also above the gums. The centre nippers are now much worn, and the next are becoming slightly so. At six years old the "mark" in the centre nippers is quite gone; at seven years of age this disappears from the next pair, and at eight from the corner nippers; after which, none but a professed judge is likely to make out the age of the horse by an inspection of his mouth; and, indeed, at all times the tyro is liable to be deceived by the frauds of the low horse-dealer, who cuts off the top of the teeth, and then scoops out a hollow with a gouge; after which a hot iron gives the black surface which in the natural state is presented to the eye. This trick is called "bishoping."

THE PACES OF THE HORSE.

The natural paces of the horse are the walk and the gallop; to them are added by man the trot and the canter, and sometimes the amble and the

run. In the walk, each leg is taken up and put down separately, one after the other, the print of the hind foot in good walkers generally extending a

10*

few inches beyond that of the fore foot; but in ponies this is not often seen, and generally the short, quick walk shown in the foregoing sketch, is the pace of that little animal. The order in which the feet touch the ground is as follows: 1st, the right fore foot; 2d, the left hind foot; 3d, the left fore foot; 4th, the right hind foot.

The gallop consists of a succession of leaps, during a great part of which all the feet are off the ground. As the feet come to the ground they strike

it in regular succession; but the exact order will depend upon the lead, which may be either with the left or right fore leg. When the lead is with the right fore leg, the right hind foot comes down first, then the right fore foot and left hind leg, and lastly, the left fore foot. In the trot, two legs of opposite sides are moved exactly together, and touch the ground at the same moment; whilst in the amble the two legs of *each side* move together, and the horse is supported for the instant upon the half of his usual and regular foundation. To counteract this deficiency in the centre of gravity, the body is balanced from side to side in a waddling manner.

VARIETIES OF THE HORSE SUITABLE FOR BOYS.

Besides the several kinds of horses suitable for grown people, those for boys are the galloway, the cob, and the pony. The first of these may be considered either a small horse or a large pony, and is usually about four-

teen hands high; and though strong and capable of carrying weight, yet of a moderately light and active make. He is so called from the district where he was originally bred in large numbers. The cob is a thick and very strong pony, or galloway, frequently made to look still more so by cutting his tail and mane short, called "hogging" them, as in the above cut.

Many ponies are now bred almost of pure Arabian blood, and they are well suited for lads who have mastered the early difficulties connected with keeping the seat under all ordinary circumstances; but as they are generally very high spirited, they are scarcely suited for the beginner, and he had better content himself with an animal of more plebeian pedigree and sluggish temperament.

FORM OF THE HORSE.

It is a common observation of the horseman that the horse can go in all forms; and this is borne out by the fact that he does occasionally do so; but nevertheless, it is well known, that among a large number it will be found that those whose form is most in accordance with the shape considered the best by good judges, will turn out the best movers. In technical language, the horse whose "points" are the best will be the best horse. These points are considered to be: a neat head, well set on a lean, wiry neck, the latter with a very gentle curve, whose convexity looks upward (the opposite form to this makes the "ewe neck"); moderately high withers; a sloping shoulder, wide in the blade, which should be well furnished with muscles; strong, muscular loins; a croup not too straight nor too drooping, with the tail set on with an elegant sweep; ribs well rounded, and carried back near to the hips, so as to make the horse what is called "well ribbed;" circumference or girth of good dimensions, indicating plenty of "bellows' room;" thighs and arms muscular; hocks and knees bony and large, without being diseased; cannon bones large and flat, with the suspensory ligament and tendon large, strong, and clearly defined; fetlock joints strong, but not round and inflamed. The eye should be full, clear, and free from specks; and the ears should be moderately small and erect; the feet should be round, and not contracted at the heels, with a well-formed frog.

THE ACCOUTREMENTS AND AIDS

Required by the young amateur, are either a pad or a saddle, according to his age, together with a bridle and a whip or stick. Spurs are seldom

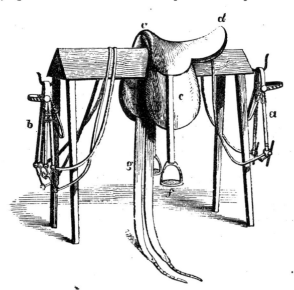

desirable for any but the accomplished rider, as they are apt to irritate the pony if not used with discretion, and it is rather difficult to put an old head upon young shoulders. If the learner is very young, a pad which is made without any tree affords a better hold for the knees than a regular saddle, and will also enable him to ride without stirrups, which feat he will hardly manage on an ordinary smooth saddle. The foregoing illustration will give our young friends a good idea of the saddle and bridle. *a* is a single bridle or snaffle; *b* is a double bridle, or curb and snaffle combined.

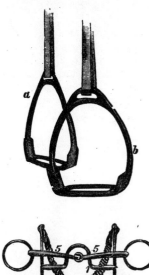

The saddle consists of a pig-skin, strained and stretched over a wooden tree raised in the front at the pommel (*c*); and behind, also, is a long ridge called the cantel (*d*), between which is the seat. The sides are made up by the flaps (*e*). Attached to the tree above, and lying *on* the flap, is the stirrup leather supporting the stirrup (*f*). Underneath the flap is a false and padded flap, on which lie the girths (*g*), which are buckled to leather straps, fastened to the tree above. The stirrups are of the annexed form, but are often, for boys, made much lighter, which, however, is a mistake, as the foot is much more easily thrown out of a light stirrup than from a heavy one. They ought always to be used with strong stirrup leathers, and these should be attached to the saddle by spring-bars, which release the stirrups in case of the leg being entangled in them after a fall. The groom should always remove the leathers after the ride, and replace them on the opposite side of the saddle, by which means their tendency to hang, as shown at *a*, is rectified, and they assume the

position indicated by the one marked *b*, both representing the left or near side.

The bridle is either a single or a double reined one, according to the mouth of the pony ridden. A single-reined bridle is usually a snaffle, it being very improper to allow any one to ride with a curb alone, unless he has very steady and light hands. The snaffle bit is merely a jointed bar of iron (5 5) in the accompanying sketch, but when used alone it has a light cross-bar, as well as the ring there shown, in order to prevent the bit being pulled through the mouth. This, however, in the double-reined bridle is omitted, since it would interfere with the action of the curb. Snaffles are either smooth or twisted, and are made of all sizes, the smallest being only adapted for occasional use, and not for the hands of the learner, who should have a large smooth one. The curb-bit consists of three parts: the mouth-piece (1), which usually has a bend in it called the port, for the purpose of pressing against the roof of the mouth; secondly, of the cheek-piece (2), which has a ring (3) at the lower end for the attachment of the rein, and another at the upper end for the head-piece of the bridle; and thirdly, the curb-chain (4). This chain is pressed against the outside of the lower jaw by the upper arm of the curb used as a lever, and it should be hooked up sufficiently tight to act upon it by pulling the rein, whilst at the same time it should be loose enough to prevent its fretting the jaw. This delicacy of adjustment requires some little practice, and the young rider should always ask his teacher to show him the proper mode of applying the curb-chain. Sometimes a martingale is needed, in order to keep the pony's head down, but generally the young rider is better without it, if he will keep his hands well down, and avoid all jerking of the mouth.

MOUNTING.

The rider, even at the earliest age, should at first examine the girths and the bridle, and see if they are properly adjusted; for though when leaving home he may be able to depend upon a steady and experienced groom, yet after putting up at strange stables, he is liable to be led into an accident by

careless servants, and therefore it is better to get into the habit of always in-specting these essentials to safety and comfort. If there is an attendant groom, he brings the pony up to the place where the expectant rider is standing, and then holds him there, keeping in front of him with a rein in each hand, or, if the animal is fidgety, laying hold of both reins with the left hand, and then pressing him toward the rider by the right. The next thing to be done is for the rider to stand at the shoulder of the pony with his left side toward that part. He then lays hold of the reins with his left hand, drawing them

up so short as to feel the mouth, and at the same time twisting a lock of
the mane in his fingers so as to steady the hand.   Next, the left foot is
placed in the stirrup, when the attitude is presented, exactly as shown in
the preceding page.   At this moment a spring is given from the right foot,
the right hand reaches the cantel of the saddle, and the body is raised till the
right leg is brought up to the level of the left, when the slightest imaginable
pause is made, and then the right leg is thrown over the back of the pony,
while the right hand leaves its hold, and the body falls into its position in
the centre of the saddle; after which, the right foot has only to be placed
in the stirrup to complete the act of mounting.

DISMOUNTING

Is exactly the reverse of the last process, and requires, first, the reins to be
shortened and held in the left hand with a lock of the mane; secondly, the
right leg is taken out of the stirrup, and is thrown over the back of the
horse until it is brought down to the level of the other leg.   After this, if

the pony is of a small size, suitable to that of the rider, the body is gently
lowered to the ground, and the left leg is liberated from the stirrup; but if
the horse is too high for this, the foot is taken out of the stirrup by raising
the body by means of the hands on the pommel and cantel of the saddle, and
then the body is lowered to the ground by their assistance.

THE MANAGEMENT OF THE REINS

Is of great importance to the comfort of the rider, and also to his appearance, for unless they are held properly, the body is sure to be awkwardly
balanced.   When the single rein is used, the best position is to place the
middle, ring, and little fingers between the two reins, and then to turn

both over the fore-finger, where they are tightly held by the thumb. In all cases the thumb ought to point toward the horse's ears, by which the elbow is sure to be kept in its place close to the side, and a good command of the

reins is insured. If a double-reined bridle is employed, the middle finger separates the two snaffle reins, and the little one those attached to the curb, all being turned over the fore-finger, and firmly held by the thumb. In both

cases the ends of the reins are turned over the left, or near side of the pony's shoulder. When it is intended to turn the horse to the left, it is only neces- sary to raise the thumb toward the chest of the rider; and, on the contrary, when the desire is to turn him to the right, the little finger is turned down- ward and backward toward the fork. In many well-broken ponies the mere moving of the whole hand to the right or left is sufficient, which, by pressing the reins against the neck, indicates the wish of the rider, and is promptly responded to by the handy pony. This action, however, is objected to by some good horsemen, though, in our opinion, most erroneously, as it is capa- ble of being made highly effective in practice.

THE SEAT

Should always be square to the front, without either shoulder being in advance ; the loins moderately arched inward, without stiffness ; the elbows close to the side, but held easily ; the knees placed upon the padded part of the flap *in front* of the stirrup leathers ; toes turned *very* slightly outward, and the foot resting on the stirrup, the inside of which should be opposite the ball of the great toe, and the outside corresponding with the little toe. The heel should be well lowered, as far as possible beneath the level of the toe, which gives a firm seat. But the great point is to obtain a good grasp of the saddle by the knees, which should be always ready to lay hold like a vice, without however constantly tiring the muscles by such an effort. The left hand is now to be held very slightly above the pommel of the saddle, and the right easily by the side of it, with the whip held in a slanting position, as at page 225, in which, however, both hands are much too high above the withers. In order to show the effect of an incorrect mode of holding the reins, the rider has only to place his hand with the knuckles in a horizontal position, and the elbow is sure to be turned out in a most awkward manner.

THE CONTROL OF THE HORSE

Is effected by the reins, heels, voice, and whip, variously used according to his disposition and temper. Some require only the most gentle usage, which, in fact, is almost always the most efficacious, especially by young people, for whom the horse and dog seem to have an especial affection, and to be always more ready to obey them than might be expected, when their want of strength to enforce their wishes is considered. The young rider will therefore generally find it to his own interest, as well as that of the noble animal he bestrides, to use his whip and heel as little as possible, and to effect his object solely by his voice and the gentlest pressure of the bit. In this way the most high-couraged horses are kept in order by young lads in the racing stables, and the amateur will do well to follow their example. It is astonishing how fond horses and dogs are of being talked to by their juvenile riders, and it is right to gratify their love of society by so doing on all occasions. The reins serve, as already explained, to turn to the right or left, or by drawing tight to stop the horse, and, on the contrary, by relaxing them to cause him to proceed, aided if necessary by the voice, heel, or whip. When it is desired that the right leg should lead in the canter or gallop, the left rein is pulled, and the left leg pressed against the flank, by which means the body of the pony is made to present the right side obliquely forward, and by consequence the right leg leads off. On the other hand, if it is wished to lead with the left leg, or to change from the right, the right rein is pulled, the right leg pressed to the side, and then the left shoulder looks forward and the left leg leads off.

MANAGEMENT OF THE WALK.

When it is wished to make the pony walk, he must be quieted down, by soothing him with the voice if he has been excited by the gallop or trot; and then by sitting very quietly in the saddle, and loosing the reins as much as will allow the head to nod in unison with the action of the body and legs, the walk is generally at once fallen into, and there is no farther difficulty except to prevent a stumble. A tight rein is not desirable in this pace, since it prevents that liberty of action which is required, and leads to a short walk, or very often a jog-trot; and yet there should be such a gentle hold, or preparation for a hold rather, as will suffice to check the mouth in case of a mistake. This is a very difficult art to acquire, and is only learned by long practice; but as few ponies fall at this pace, great liberty may generally be allowed to their mouths. Beside this, little is necessary, more than to sit steadily, *but not stiffly*, in the saddle, and not to sway about more than is sufficient to avoid the appearance of having swallowed a poker.

THE TROT AND CANTER

Are effected by rather different methods, but both require a very steady hand, and a quiet treatment. In order to cause the pony to trot, the reins are taken rather short in the hand, and the mouth is held somewhat firmly, but taking great care not to jerk it. The animal is then slightly stimulated by the voice, and the body, if necessary, rises from the saddle, as in the trot, so as to indicate what is wanted. This seldom fails to effect the purpose, and the horse at once breaks into a trot; or, if very irritable, he may be compelled to do so by laying hold of an ear and twisting it, to avoid which he drops his head, and trots as a natural consequence. The canter is also an acquired pace, and for its due performance a curb-bridle is required. In order to make the pony begin this pace, the left rein is pulled, and the

rider's left leg pressed against the side, by which the horse's right leg is made to lead off, this being the most usual, and certainly the most comfortable, "lead" for the rider. The hands must make a very gentle and steady pull on the curb-rein, and the body generally must be very quiet in the saddle, whilst, at the same time, a very gentle stimulus is given by the voice, which must be repeated at short intervals, or the canter will be changed to a trot or walk, both of which are preferred to it by most ponies and horses.

THE MANAGEMENT OF THE GALLOP.—LEAPING.

Young riders should avoid cantering long upon one leg, as it leads to inflammation of the joints, and they should either change the lead, or alter the pace to a trot or walk.

THE MANAGEMENT OF THE GALLOP

Requires little instruction, practice being the main agent in effecting a good seat during this pace.   The seat is either close to the saddle, with the body inclining backwards (p. 227), or standing in the stirrups, in which position the knees and calves only touch the saddle, and the body is bent forward over the withers (p. 226). It should be the endeavor of the rider, while he bends his shoulders forward, to throw his loins well back, so as to avoid straining the horse's fore-quarters, by bearing too much weight upon them. This is done by the hold of the knees on the saddle, and by keeping the feet back; also by rounding the loins backward, and thus throwing the centre of gravity as far as possible behind the stirrup leathers.   The object of standing in the stirrups is to save the horse when at his full gallop, as in racing, or in hunting, when he is going over ploughed ground, or up hill. In either of these cases, this attitude allows the horse to exert himself without feeling the weight of the rider to impede his movements more than can be avoided.

LEAPING

Is only an extra exertion added to the ordinary spring of the gallop, the attitude being exactly the same.   It is best learned by beginning with small ditches, which the rider is soon able to clear without difficulty. He may next try very low fences; but the latter, being strong and firmly fixed, are dangerous to the rider, unless the pony is very sure of clearing them.   A leaping-bar, if procurable, should always be adopted in preference to either, as a fall over it is not attended with any bad consequences. The groom should place it at the lowest notch, and the pony then may be suffered to clear it at a moderate gallop; after which, if the young rider is able to sit pretty closely, he may be indulged with a higher notch, and gradually it may be raised, until the limits of the pony's powers are reached. In riding at a bar, the learner should lay hold of a snaffle-rein in each hand, taking care to keep them close together, by the right rein being held also in the left hand. The pony is then to be urged to a smart canter or hand-gallop, and held straight to the bar in this way, so that he is obliged to leap; or, if disliking the act, being urged by the whip down the shoulder, or the spur, or the groom's voice and whip behind. Young riders, however, should never be put upon a bad or reluctant leaper, but should be taught upon one which is fond of the amusement. At the moment of rising into the air for the leap, the reins are relaxed, but should not be left quite loose, and the body of the rider inclines forward; while the pony is in the air, the body becomes again upright, and as he descends it leans well back, until, after a high leap, it almost touches the croup. During this period, the reins should be suffered to remain nearly loose, the hand barely feeling the mouth; but as the pony reaches the ground a stronger hold is taken, in order to guard against a mistake, which might require the aid of the rider to prevent a fall. It is not that he can keep the animal up, but that he checks him, and makes him exert himself in a double degree. There are various kinds of leaping; as the flying leap, the standing leap, the leap in hand, etc. The flying leap is merely one taken at a fast pace, and when the rider can maintain a good seat in the gallop, it is the easiest of all to sit. The standing leap is effected from a state of quiescence, and is much more difficult to sit, because the horse rises and falls more suddenly and abruptly. Between the two is the slow or steady leap, which is only effected safely by the clever hunter or well-broken pony; but when perfect it is almost as smooth as a rocking-horse. This is the mode in which the young rider should be taught to leap. The young rider, when he meets with a gate or other strong fence, which he knows is too much for the powers of his pony, at once gets off and leads him over by the rein; and when well taught, these little creatures will often tilt themselves over high timber, etc., in a marvellously clever manner, so that we have known them in this way obtain a good place in long and severe runs. If, therefore, our readers are allowed to partake in this exciting sport during their summer holidays, they should teach their ponies to leap in hand, or they will be sure to be thrown out.

TREATMENT OF VICES

The chief vices which are met with among ponies are—1st. Obstinate stopping; 2d. Stumbling from carelessness; 3d. Rearing; 4th. Kicking; 5th. Shying; and 6th. Running away.

Obstinate stopping, which in its worst forms is called "jibbing," is a very troublesome vice, and even in the saddle is sometimes attended with danger, while in driving it is so to a dreadful degree.

The rider should never attempt to force his pony forward with the whip or spur, which only aggravates the bad-tempered brute; but should patiently sit quiet in the saddle, and keep his temper, until the pony chooses to move forward again. In this way, sometimes, very vicious animals are cured, when they find that their stable is not the sooner reached by their device; on the other hand, if the whip is used, the pony is very apt to lie down, and roll his rider in the dirt, or even sometimes to bolt into a river, or pond,

and leave him in danger of his life. Our young friends will therefore remember our advice when, being mounted upon an obstinate pony, and having lost their tempers, they have proceeded to use their whips, and are bemired or half drowned in consequence.

Stumbling is more a defect of conformation than a vice; but, nevertheless, it greatly depends upon a want of spirit to keep up a steady action of the fore legs. It often happens that a pony trots along for a mile or two safely enough; but after going that distance he becomes lazy and careless, and trips with one foot and then with the other, a sure prelude to such a fall as the following, which would be a very bad one (page 238), and sufficient to cut both knees to the bone, and to cause serious damage to the rider. The only way to avoid such accidents is to keep the pony at a steady pace, fast enough to keep him alive, but not enough so as to tire him. Loose stones and broken ground should be avoided, and a careful hold should be kept upon the mouth, without being so tight as to gag it. When a stumble actually takes place, the body should be well thrown back and the mouth forcibly jerked, so as to make the pony exert himself to keep his legs. An unsafe

animal of this kind is, however, wholly unfit for young riders, and they
should never be allowed to ride one.

Rearing is a very dangerous vice, and not very common among ponies
after they are once broken in. If the rider should, however, be placed
upon a rearer, he should be careful to avoid hanging upon the bit
when he rises in the air, but on the contrary should loose the reins entirely, and clasp the neck if the pony should rise very high in the air. The

accompanying sketch shows this vice in a very trifling degree, and in such
a case the seat thus represented is sufficiently forward to prevent accidents.

The rider will, however, observe that the reins are quite loose. It often happens that this vice is produced by too tight and severe a curb in a tender mouth, and that upon changing the bit, or letting out the curb-chain, the tendency to rise is entirely gone. Whenever, therefore, the young rider finds his pony inclined to rear, let him look well to his bit, and at once drop the curb rein, if he has one. If, however, he has only a snaffle, he may rest assured that it is a regular habit, and he can make up his mind either to battle with it or to change his pony.

Kicking is much more common among ponies than rearing, and very many of these little animals are given to practise it. It is perhaps partly owing to the teasing of their young masters that it is so common; but whatever the cause, there can be no doubt that it is too prevalent among them. Sometimes it exists as a regular attempt to unhorse the rider, which is a

very troublesome habit, and one very difficult to break, because it so often succeeds that the pony is tempted to try again. When this vice is met with, the rider should do all in his power to keep his pony's head up, by jerking the bit, and at the same time he should sit well back, with his feet well forward. When the habit is a very bad one, a cloth or coat may be rolled up and strapped in front of the saddle, by which the rider is aided in keeping his seat; but unless the trick is very violently carried out, he had better trust to his knees in holding on. When kicking is only the result of high spirits and "freshness," the best remedy is a smart gallop, which soon stops all these pranks, and makes the most riotous animal quiet.

Shying is also very common among ponies, and in them is often the result of cunning, which leads them to pretend a greater degree of shyness than they really possess. The best mode of treatment is to take as little notice as possible of the shying, but carefully to make the pony pass the object at which he is looking, without regarding how this is effected. The whip should seldom be used at all, and never *after* the object is passed.

Bolting, or Running Away, is often the result of want of exercise, but sometimes it is a systematic vice, leading to such scenes as the one here represented. A powerful bit and a steady seat, with good hands, are the best means of grappling with this habit, which is sometimes a very dangerous one. If the pony really runs away, the rider should not pull dead at his mouth, but should relax his hold for a short time, and then take a sharp pull, which is often effectual. A good gallop until he is tired will often cure a runaway for the rest of his life. There are a variety of bits intended expressly to counteract this vice; but nothing is perfectly effectual where there is a determination to run away. A nose-band has lately been invented for the purpose, which answers very well. It consists of a long nose-band which crosses behind the jaw and then hooks on to the bit, in the same way as the ordinary curb-chain. When the rein is pulled hard, this nose-band is drawn tight round the jaw, by which the mouth is closed, and the port is pressed strongly against the roof of the mouth, causing a great degree of pain, sufficient to stop most horses. This powerful remedy, which has been named the Bucephalus nose-band, should not lightly be used; but in the case of a runaway horse, or pony, it is a really efficacious one. A similar arrangement, known as the Mexican bit, is sometimes used, and is even better than the one just mentioned.

DRIVING.

THE usual carriage driven with one horse,—and our young readers should have some experience before they attempt a pair,—is the buggy, or York wagon.   In addition to this there are phaetons, gig-phaetons, rockaways, and others, but all have the same harness, and are managed in the same way, so that the directions for one will answer for all the rest.

The horse is attached to a buggy by means of a set of harness.   By an examination of the engravings, with the letters of reference attached, our readers will learn the names of the component parts of this, and its adjustment.   (See page 242.)

They will see that the harness is divided into, 1st, the driving or guiding part; 2d, the drawing part; and 3d, that for holding up the shafts.   The driving part comprises the bridle and reins.   The bridle is made up of a front piece (U), a head-piece (V), two cheek-pieces and winkers (P and Q), a nose-band (S), and a throat-lash (R).   The cheek-pieces are buckled to the bit, which is generally a strong curb, by means of leather loops, called billets, as also are the driving-reins (W), and the bearing-rein, which is attached to a separate bit, called the bridoon (a plain snaffle), and then is hooked to the pad-hook.   This is now very generally dispensed with, but for young drivers it is often desirable, when they have not strength to check the fall of a horse.   The drawing parts consist of a padded oval ring fitted to the shoulders, and called the collar (A), sometimes replaced by a padded strap across the chest, called the breast-strap (b, Fig.2).   On the collar are fastened two iron bars called hames (C), by means of a strap at the top and bottom

11

(DD), and these hames have a ring in the upper part for the reins to pass through, called the hame teret (E), and nearer the lower part, a strong arm

of iron, covered with a coating of brass, silver, or leather, which receives in its eye the tug of the trace (F).   The trace (G) is a long and strong strap of

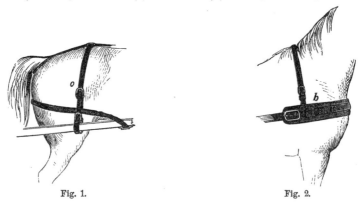

Fig. 1.   Fig. 2.

double leather, stitched, which runs from the collar to the drawing bar, and may be lengthened or shortened by a buckle.   The supporting and backing part consists of the pad or saddle (H), somewhat similar in principle to the riding saddle, but much narrower and lighter. This has two rings for the reins, called the terets (I), and a hook (J), for the bearing rein, all at the top. - It is fastened to the horse by a belly-band (K), and at the back of it there is an eye for the crupper, which is a leather strap from it to the tail, round the root of which it passes, and thus holds the pad from pressing forward. Through the middle of the pad passes a strong leather strap, called the back-band (L), which is attached to a buckle and strong loop on each side, called the shaft-tug (M), by which the shaft is supported and also kept back from pressing upon the horse's quarters, in which latter office it is sometimes assisted by a leather strap passing round these parts, and buckled on each side, either to the shaft or to its tug, and called the breeching (N); a kicking-strap is sometimes substituted for the common breeching, or added to it, as shown at *o* (Fig. 1).

PUTTING TO.

Before driving, it is necessary that the horse or pony should be "put to," which is effected as follows: 1st, slip the shafts through the tugs, or, if there are hooks, drop them down into them; 2d, put the traces on to the drawing-bar, either hooking them on, or else slipping them on to the eyes, and being careful to place the leather stops in these to prevent the trace coming off; 3d, buckle the belly-band sufficiently tight; and 4th, buckle the kicking-strap, or breeching, if either is used. After this, the reins are taken from the terets, where they were previously placed, and the horse is ready.

DIRECTIONS FOR DRIVING.

In driving, the reins are held differently from the mode already described as used in riding, the fore-finger being first placed between them, and then both

the reins are grasped by all the other fingers, and the near side rein is also held firmly against the fore-finger by means of the thumb. In this way, on an emergency, the near or left rein may be pulled by itself, by holding it firmly with the thumb, and suffering the other, or off rein, to slip through the fingers, or *vice versa*.

Whilst turning, or when driving a high-couraged horse, and in critical situ-

ations generally, the right hand must be at all times called to the assistance
of the left; thus, the reins being grasped as before stated, you pass the
second and third fingers between them, and loosening your hold on the off
rein a little, let the right hand have complete command of its guidance, still,
however, firmly holding both reins in your left; this position gives you great
power over your horse.

STARTING.

Holding your reins with both hands, start your horse either by your voice
or by the reins, gently feeling his mouth, but neither pulling at it nor jerking the reins. Many high-couraged horses have been made balkers by the
stupidity of a driver. If a young horse's mouth is hurt by the driver check-
ing him every time he starts, he will be sure to incur some vice; the habit
of rearing, or of balking, will most probably be the result. The learner may
say, "Supposing, however, he refuses to start, what then is to be done?"
We reply, have patience; let the groom lead him off, caress him, speak
quietly, and encourage him to proceed, and if he presses on one side, as if
he wanted to go round, turn him round, if there be room, and as soon
as he has his head the right way, give him his liberty, and by the voice
or whip urge him to proceed. Much must here be left to the judgment; a
touch with the whip in such circumstances would make some horses jib,
while it would immediately start others; some it would be advisable to urge
only with the voice, and to have a person to push the buggy on, so that the
collar should scarcely touch the shoulder in starting. Supposing there is not
room for the horse to turn, and he persist in his attempt to do so, we have
always found it best in such a case to desire the groom to let his head alone,
and to go to the side toward which the horse is inclined to turn, and then
push against the extreme end of the shaft; if he does this, speaking quietly
to him all the time, forty-nine horses out of fifty, that are not irreclaimable
balkers, will after a short struggle proceed. The sooner you get rid of a
confirmed jibber the better: no quality such a brute can possess would
repay you for the trouble the vice occasions; which is besides always a dangerous one.

THE ROAD.

Having started your horse, keep your eyes open, looking well before you,
not merely for the purpose of avoiding other carriages, but looking up the
road, and on each side of it, so as to notice if there be any impediment to
your horse's progress; any loose stones which he might tread upon, and
thereby be thrown down; any sudden risings or fallings in the road, or any
object which might frighten him. Always keep your horse well in hand,
that is, feel his mouth; if you do not you are never prepared for emergencies: if he stumbles, you cannot help him to recover his legs; if he
starts, you cannot check him. But in keeping him in hand, as it is called,
you may still fall into error, for if the horse be very light in the mouth there

is a probability that an inexperienced person may so check him, as not only to impede his progress, but to put him out of temper; and as nothing is more difficult for a novice to manage than a very light-mouthed horse, when he once takes it in his head to have his own way, you must be careful merely to feel his mouth so as to have the reins at command, but still not sufficiently tight to check him. This is called driving with a light hand, and indeed is the perfection of driving, when it has become so habitual as to have assumed the character of "a style." Young drivers, in attempting this, will frequently allow their horses to run from one side of the road to the other; or, if their peregrinations do not embrace the whole of the road, they allow their horse (in fact make him) to sidle about in such a manner, that if they were to look at the track of their wheels, they would be astonished at what they had been doing. This must be avoided; as nothing is so ungraceful as to see a carriage yawing from side to side. A little thought will, moreover, convince you how much unnecessary ground you have gone over by this practice. Holding in hand sometimes produces another bad practice, particularly if your horse's mouth is not delicate; it gets him into the habit of hanging in your arms, and boring continually upon the bit, until his mouth becomes so callous, that if he stumbles he must come down, unless you can hold him up by main strength—a feat only to be achieved by a young Hercules. This may be avoided sometimes by keeping the bit moving in his mouth, but more frequently by not unnecessarily pulling at the rein; many a horse has become an arrant bore from this practice. If the reins are held with both hands, as before directed, you will have much more command of them, and a little attention will prevent these inconveniences.

But the tyro may perhaps say, "But if my horse will hang in my arms, what am I to do then?" The best plan to adopt is the following. We will premise, that whenever your horse has a vice or a fault, you should consider what originated it; and this being discovered, a remedy will very frequently be found. In the case in question, the fault is often produced by bad driving, and often from the horse never having been properly bitted; in either case the advice we are about to give will generally be useful, particularly if the horse be properly driven when he is put in harness. When the horse is in his stable, let him, for three or four hours a day, stand with his head fastened to the pillar reins, and with a colt bit in his mouth; with this he will play, by continually rolling it about in his mouth, and straining on the reins; he thus becomes familiarized to the bit, and regards it, if we may so say, as a source of amusement rather than of torture. From being thus accustomed to the bit when he is not in motion, and when boring on it would become painful, he forgets his former habit, and will bear the bit lightly in his mouth when at work. This process is technically termed biting him, and if persevered in, and the horse be *properly driven*, the evil will most probably be remedied thereby. Sometimes, changing the bit will have a good effect; if he has been used to a port bit, try a snaffle; if he be hard mouthed, and an ordinary snaffle is not of sufficient power, a ring snaffle will generally be effective. When a horse bores to one side of the road, let us strongly advise the young driver never to adopt that unphilosophical and senseless plan of whipping him on the neck upon the side to which he is boring. We grant that the lash drives him over for the moment, that is, if he will bear whipping, but this, continually repeated, has a bad effect on both horse and driver. It either irritates or dispirits the horse, and fatigues both parties; and every one knows that when flogging once commences, a man very soon loses his temper, and from a coachman he is apt to forget himself, and become a brute. Whipping will not remedy the evil; the horse gets more and more weary, and even if he does not become restive, he will soon become knocked up. If the plans just referred to will not cure him; or rather, if he be incurable, part with him, for whoever keeps a horse for comfort and pleasure, will find his object defeated by driving such an animal. Such horses may prove useful in business from some good qualities they may possess; but a horse driven for pleasure should never have a vice that will compel his master to work as hard as a blacksmith. We have been speaking of a horse working alone in a buggy or rockaway. When working in double harness, you can prevent much of the inconvenience by having a check-rein fastened to the other horse's teret; the same remedy holds, in this case, to a horse that is always boring to one side of a road, when working in double harness. Observation will, however, show you that in the one case the check-rein had better be fixed to the trace, in the other to the teret. A few words may here be said as to the cause of a horse's boring to one side. It is frequently the result of weakness, and many a horse will do it as he gets weary, who will not when he starts. Sometimes the mouth is harder upon one side than the other, which will make him flinch from the softer side; a light hand will tend to remedy this; but if he be driven with a port bit, placing the rein which is on the soft side of the mouth right up to the cheek, and the other a bar or two below, will probably prevent any unpleasantness or any danger, particularly if the horse be driven with care. But such a horse is by no means to be desired; if he should stumble, or if, from any circumstance, it is necessary to pull him up sharply, an inexperienced hand may make him jump to one side of the road by not having presence of mind to recollect his fault, and forgetting to pull strongest upon the hard side of the mouth. An experienced hand will feel, as it were intuitively, the exact force which each side of the mouth will bear.

DIFFICULT SITUATIONS FOR YOUNG DRIVERS.

We will now proceed to notice what may be accurately classed under the above denomination.

Tusking the bit, and running away.—Some ill-tempered horses will become violent upon being in any manner put out of their way—such, for instance, as being suddenly stopped two or three times within a short distance, or receiving a sudden cut with the whip; but instead of exhibiting this violence by rearing or kicking, they will seize the bit in their mouths, close against the tusk, and run violently to one side of the road, as if with the intention of landing you in a ditch, or giving you a resting-place in a shop window. Your best mode is to stop them at once by a quiet pull, speaking softly, as if nothing were the matter; and then coax them into good temper until you get home, when we will presently explain to you how to prevent the like again. If this cannot be done, give them the head for a moment (a short one it must be), and after bestowing a violent switch across the ears, snatch the reins suddenly toward the side to which the horse is boring, which will probably, from the surprise, disengage the bit, and enable you almost simultaneously either to pull him up, or draw him away from the danger. You will observe we have said on the side *to which he is pressing*, for it would be all but impossible to draw him to the other; for such a brute always seizes the bit by the branch or side which is next to the place he is running to, knowing, or rather thinking, you will pull the other rein, in which case the side of the face would aid him in resisting your efforts. The remedy for this is a ring bit, for it has no branches for the horse to get hold of, and if he merely seizes that part of the bit which is in his mouth, a sudden jerk will instantly disengage it, that is, if it be done with sufficient decision; but our experience teaches us, that in ninety-nine cases out of a hundred the horse will not attempt this; he misses the branches, and is disappointed and abashed at not being able to play the old trick.

Frequently, however, a horse tusks the bit, as it is called, with the view of bolting; it you cannot disengage the bit in the way directed, you have only to stop him as quickly as you can. Recollect, however, that a continual dead pull will never stop a runaway horse, unless indeed you have the strength of Hercules: his mouth soon becomes callous to the action of the sharpest bit. Nor is it proper to keep jerking a horse under such circumstances, as that would rather urge him to increase his speed. The ordinary mode is to take the reins short in your hands, and then, by a sudden, steady movement of the body backward, exerting at the same time all the strength of the arms, endeavor to pull him up; this, repeated two or three times, will generally be effectual. Suppose it not to succeed, adopt the following plan, by which we have stopped many a determined bolter who had bid defiance to more than one reputed whip. Cross the reins in your hands, that is, place the right rein in the left hand, the left in the right hand, take them very short, and then suddenly put all your strength to them with a sudden jerk, but continue the pressure, violently sawing them at the same time; if this will not bring the horse to his haunches at the first attempt, let him partially have his head—that is, sufficiently slacken your pull to give his mouth time to recover its feeling—and then repeat the effort. We never knew a horse that we could not stop by this method, which, though not very graceful, is very effective.

Stumbling and Slipping.—If your horse be kept well in hand, you will generally be able to keep him from absolutely coming down. You will naturally put more force to your pull upon his making the stumble, and this jerk, if succeeded by a strong, continuous aid, generally keeps him on his legs; a smart stroke with the whip should follow, to remind him that his carelessness is not to be repeated. A horse that is apt to stumble, or even one that from his form is likely to stumble, should not only always be kept well in hand, but also be kept alive, by now and then being reminded, without actually punishing him, that his driver has a whip in his hand. A horse with his head set too forward, that is, low in the withers, is almost sure to come down sooner or later, particularly if his fore legs stand at all under him, as it is technically termed, that is, slanting a little inward. Stumbling, however, be it remembered, is totally distinct from slipping; the stone pavement will give the tyro plenty of opportunity to perceive the difference. If a horse slips, a sudden jerk will probably throw him down; in such a case the driver must aid the horse by a strong, steady hold, letting him, as it were, lean on the bit to help himself to stand. It requires some nerve thus to aid the horse, without being induced to jerk him by the suddenness of the slip.

Jibbing, or Balking.—Demosthenes, on being asked what was the soul of oratory, answered, "Action, action, action!" If we are asked what is the best mode to adopt with a jibber, we should say, Patience, patience, patience! This, however, must be qualified by the temper of the horse. Some balkers (*but very few*) may be started by sudden and severe whipping; ninety-nine times out of a hundred it will render a jibber restive, mischievous, or obstinate. Experience only can dictate the management of such animals. Some will start after waiting for a short time, having their head free; coaxing is generally the best means, and, as before said, have patience, and do not be in too great a hurry to start. Some may be started by being turned round, and others by being backed for a short distance. Many think it a good plan to punish a jibber when he is once started; our experience proves the contrary, for, depend upon it, he will recollect this next time, and will not fail further to exercise your patience, for fear of the flogging.

Kicking—An experienced eye can generally tell if a horse is likely to kick, and also when he is about to kick. We, however, always drive with a kicking-strap, and would recommend the practice. When a horse attempts to kick, you must hold him well in hand, and lay the whip well into him about the ears, rating him at the same time with a loud voice; this plan we have generally found effective. We would, however, recommend the young driver first to try the rating without the whipping; the voice frequently has a wonderful effect upon a horse. Be sure, however, to keep him well in hand.

Rearing.—Little can be done in harness with a determined rearer. When he tries to rear, if you have room give him a half turn, this will make him move his hind legs, and will consequently bring him down; you will find a series of turns punish and surprise him more than any thing else. When you have once got him on the move, with his head the right way, you can punish him with the whip, if he is one that you are sure you can manage;

if not, you had better leave well alone. With respect to rearing in double harness, we will here observe, the best way to act is to push the other horse forward, and soothe the restive one, until you have fairly got him on; you can then punish or not, according to your judgment, but not without reference to your ability to manage the horses.

Shying.—Before a horse starts at any thing on the side of, or lying on the road, he usually gives some notice of his intention, by cocking his ears, and bending his head toward the object. As soon as the driver perceives these signs of uneasiness, he should be upon his guard to prevent a sudden turn round, or flying to one side, which would evidently be dangerous; and not only on this account should he be attentive, but because each time the horse violently shies, the habit is in progress of being confirmed. As soon, therefore, as a horse accustomed to shy gives notice of uneasiness, he should be coaxed up to the object of his terror, so that he may perceive its harmlessness; let him deliberately stand and view it, and if he cannot be got to it, let it, if possible, be brought to him, and then replaced in its former position; thus let him be induced to go up to it by care and kindness before it is passed, and you will generally find that a repetition of this practice will greatly improve, if it do not cure him; but by no means flog or force him up to it—let him take his time. We are now, of course, speaking of a horse whose sight is perfect. Some horses shy from having an imperfect vision; in fact, because they are going blind, and the sight is affected; and we would, therefore, advise a young driver to have his horse's eyes examined (if he is unable to examine them himself), whenever this shying is violent after a few lessons of the nature before detailed. We do not mean to say that there are not horses so timid that they cannot be broken of this bad practice; but we do say that most horses may be, if taken in time, and also that nine out of ten of these animals owe their vice to bad breaking, or bad drivers.

11*

ANGLING.

THIS art of the angler is varied by circumstances. To be successful, it must be based on a knowledge of the habits of fish—different fishes having different tastes, and even the same kind of fishes differing in habits, when placed in different localities. It is our intention to give general information on the subject, through which a smart boy, by using his eyes and judgment, may become an accomplished angler.

The implements of the angler are as follows:

THE ROD.

For small fish,—chubs, dace, roach, minnows, sunfish, and small white perch,—a black alder or willow rod, about eight feet in length, will answer; but for catching larger fish, a carefully made rod is necessary. Besides, it is more comfortable to have a nice rod. It can be had at the shops where they sell fishing-tackle, in great variety of shape and price. One with four joints or pieces—the butt and two succeeding pieces of ash, and the last joint, or tip, of lancewood—will be the best for ordinary purposes. It should have two tips, one short and one long. The wood should be straight-grained, and each joint should have eyes, through which the line will run easily. A rod of cane, without joints, is exceedingly good, if it can be kept near the fishing-ground, as it is not very portable. Whatever the material, the rod should be straight, tapering from butt to point, tight in the joints, and have a good spring to it.

THE REEL.

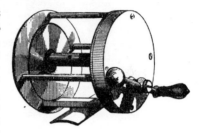

Very good fish have been caught without the reel; but that is a very useful thing, nevertheless, allowing you to let a large fish run out a deal of line, and letting you wind it up at your pleasure, thus affording him play, and making his capture more certain. Without it, you would lose many a large fish, who would snap your taut, short line. The reel is generally made of brass, but sometimes of German silver, and may be either plain or multiplying. The latter is best, but, being complex, is liable to get out of order. The plain imported reel is very good; but if you are able to obtain a multiplying reel, get an American one, as those made in England are very apt to be fitted with brass internal wheels, the cogs of which soon give way. A reel that will hold about fifty yards of line is enough for a boy's purpose.

THE LINE.

Different lines are required for different fish. For catching shiners, a stout piece of homespun thread will answer, and with this, and a No. 11 hook, you can capture a half-pound sunfish, or perch, if need be. Sea-grass is also a good material for a short line of, say, twenty feet. For your main line, a plaited silk, or well-twisted hemp, is best, measuring fifty yards. It should be boiled in linseed oil before being used, which will add to its durability, and render it less liable to kink. To catch large pike or muskelunjeh, where you troll for them, you want a stout cotton or hemp line.

THE HOOK.

Your hook has to be proportioned to the kind of fish you catch, and will vary from the little fly hook, No. 12, up to the salmon, No. 0, which is large enough for any fishing a boy will ever get. As to the style, the Limerick (A B) is decidedly our favorite; although, for some fishing, the Kirby (C) is excellent. The Limerick has a curve extending from the shank to the bottom of the bend, which thence turns up at an angle ; while the Kirby rises up nearly straight, and its barb has a slight turn outwards.

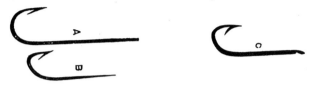

The sizes of both kinds of hooks are the same.

There is also a pattern called the Virginia hook, which is very popular with Southern fishermen. It is shaped like the Kirby, with a Limerick barb, and is longer in the shank than either.

After getting the kind of hook to suit your fancy, test each individual hook, and see that it has a good temper, and that the point is sharp and perfect.

SINKERS, OR DIPSIES.

These are of various sizes, from a small shot, half split, and then closed on the line, to a heavy lead, of a pound or more, used in sea-fishing. A swivel sinker is best, as it prevents the line from being entangled, and, if you troll, aids in spinning the bait.

SWIVELS.

These are very necessary. They are generally made of blued steel, or brass, and should be placed at various parts of the line, one being within a foot or eighteen inches of the bait.

FLOATS.

Floats are usually made of corks or quills— sometimes of red cedar or white pine, and are either egg-shaped, or made like two long, narrow cones, joined at their bases. For small fish, the quill-float is preferable; and for very large fish, the red cedar, hollowed out.

LEADERS.

The leaders, to which the hooks are attached, are made either of twisted horse-hair, sea-grass, or silk-worm gut—the latter being the most elegant material, almost imperceptible in water, and necessary in taking shy fish.

NETS.

The only two nets are the landing and bait. Their uses are expressed in their names. The landing-net is a purse-like net, with a three-eighths of an inch mesh, and is made about sixteen inches in diameter and two feet in length, set on a stout brass wire ring, and attached to a light but strong

hickory handle, five feet long. The bait-net is similar, but somewhat smaller, and has a quarter of an inch mesh.

GAFF-HOOK.

This is a bent hook, about four inches long, with a six-feet handle, by which you get a purchase in the gills of a big fish, and so land him.

THE CLEARING-RING.

This is a ring weighing from a quarter of a pound to six ounces, which is tied to a stout cord, and when the line is caught in some obstacle under water, is placed around the line, and sent down to clear the way.

BAITS.

The ordinary bait in common fishing is the *angle-worm*, as it is called, which may be dug up in any loamy soil, especially in damp situations, or found by rolling over logs, or lifting plank that have lain for some time on the ground. There are other species of worms sometimes used, such as the *brandling*, which you will find about old dung-heaps, and the *marsh-worm*, which has a broader, flatter tail than the angle-worm.

The white grub-worm, which will be found under old decayed logs, stumps, and in freshly-ploughed ground, is much approved by some, but we never found it of much use.

The grasshopper, used without a sinker, so as to float on the surface, is a killing bait for trout, and the large sunfish, red-eyes, or yellow perch. Sunfish will rise readily, too, at the common black cricket, if it be left floating on the surface.

Minnows, gudgeons, shiners, and dace are all used as bait, and chub for large fish. They must be put on alive.

In baiting with a minnow, do not put the hook through the back, fin, or body, as recommended by most writers. Your bait will die sooner, indeed, will inevitably die. By baiting in the proper manner, your bait will live as long as wanted, and if you do not fancy him, may be released carefully, and sent about his business, none the worse for it. A writer on this subject says:

"Your game-fish takes his prey by swallowing it head foremost, not liking the prickles of the dorsal fin to stick in his belly. So I insert my hook carefully in the gill-cover of my bait, which the little fellow hardly feels, and let him play about, until Mr. Gristes, Mr. Lucioperca, or Mr. Salmo call for his breakfast."

Shad-roe is an excellent bait in its season for striped bass, or rock-fish, trout, and white perch.

In salt or brackish water, the soft or shedder crab, the shrimp, the soft and hard clam, are much used.

Dough, or dough and cheese, mixed with cotton, is capital for many ground-fish.

A frog, either whole or in parts, is capital for pike, pickerel, or pike-perch, in some localities.

Spoon-bait consists of the bowl of a spoon, silvered on the convex, and painted red on the concave side, with one or two hooks fastened at the top end, and set on the line. Drawn quietly through the water, the black bass and pickerel dart at it readily.

In addition to these, there is the artificial fly, the most elegant of all baits for trout and salmon, and a great many others, which a smart boy will find in the woods and about the streams, in the shape of flies and beetles. The three main baits are, however, artificial flies, earth-worms, and small fish. In getting the latter, remember that small fish with stiff, prickly back-fins, such as sticklebacks and sunfish, are of little use, no large fish liking to have his throat lacerated with the sharp spines. Even that voracious fellow, the pike, will hardly venture on a young sunfish, however hungry he may be.

MISCELLANEOUS MATTERS.

Besides the foregoing, you will want a disgorger, to aid you in getting out the hook when swallowed very far; and you should have with you always a little leather case, containing, besides your extra hooks, etc., a pair of small pliers, scissors, some shoemaker's wax in a piece of soft leather, and a piece of stout cord, to be waxed and wrapped around your rod, in case it should break, and you would need to splice it. A fish-basket, and conveniences of that sort, should be provided.

GENERAL DIRECTIONS.

Look out for wind and weather. The south wind, and after that the west, is considered the best by all experienced anglers, from Walton down, and a cloudy, though not a cold day, is set down as favorable. Fish are whimsical, however, or it may be have fits of hunger, for we have had fine fishing on a cold day, with an east wind; and have filled our basket when the sun was beaming down scorchingly and not a cloud in the sky. The best time of day is early in the morning, and late in the afternoon.

Be cautious. Fish are shy. Never show yourself near where the fish lie, if you can help it. Fish, like the Irishman's gun, was made to shoot round a corner. Many a big trout, or huge black bass, has been captured while he lay hidden under an overhanging bank, by the skilful angler dropping or casting his bait gently in his vicinity. Never let your shadow fall in the water, and if you cannot fish with your face to the sun, take shelter behind a tree, bush, or rock.

Have on good boots and woollen stockings, the former to keep out the water, and the latter, in case it does get in, to let it do you as little mischief as possible. Have plenty of spare hooks and leaders, with an extra float, sinker, and swivel, to make up any unexpected loss, and always be provided with an abundance of bait.

With these remarks, we come to the various kinds of fish to be met with in different parts of the United States.

THE SALMON.

This, the noblest of all fish, is to be found in but a few places in this country. It is confined to the States of Maine, California, and Oregon, and some of the Western lakes. Occasionally a few make their way up the

Hudson. The time of taking them is from April to July, and they are treated, like the trout, either to the fly, worms, or minnows. You want a heavy rod, with a very large reel, and from three to six hundred feet of line. A swivel sinker and cedar float are to be used, when you fish with live bait, and your hook is a No. 0, 1, 2, or 3, Limerick, with a strong leader of twisted gut, from three to six feet in length. For fly-fishing, you must use a swivel instead of a swivel sinker, and, of course, no float.

For worm-fishing, put on your worm head first, and leave about a half inch of the tail to wriggle; throw it gently in the current, draw it up quietly after it has floated down, keeping the bait continually in motion. Keep a tight line when he bites, but do not strike too soon. Allow him to gorge, then strike suddenly and sharply. If the bite should be only a sudden jerk, pay no attention to it—it is merely a nibble. Wait patiently, and he will call again. If he does, look sharp. Play him gently but firmly. Let him have line enough as he goes from you, but as he returns reel up. Keep him clear of stumps and rocks; be patient, and as cool as you can. At length he will exhaust himself. Draw him gently to shore, put the hook of your gaff in his gills, and land him.

THE LAKE TROUT.

This is found in a few lakes in the Middle and Northern States, and differs from the Mackinaw trout, with which it is often confounded. It is blackish, with many gray spots, body comparatively short; its back-fin has a sinuous margin, and its length is two to four feet. It is taken in the same way as

THE MACKINAW TROUT.

This fish is dark-gray above, of a light ash-gray, or cream-color, on chin, throat, and belly; the back and sides having many lighter gray, brown, or dirty white spots, which do not show themselves on the fins, as in the lake

BROOK TROUT.

trout. The breast and belly-fins are yellowish; teeth, gums, and mouth of a purplish tinge; length two to five feet. It has a finer flavor than the lake trout.

For this fish you want a heavy rod, and spoon-bait or revolver. You troll for him, or you can use the large minnow. Your line must be stout. You manage your fish as in taking any other salmon—for a member of the salmon family he is, and a fine one at that.

COMMON BROOK TROUT.

This fish is too well known to need description. A variety is the

BLACK TROUT,

Which seems to be the same fish, modified by its dwelling-place, which is in muddy streams and ponds principally. Then, there is the

HULBO TROUT,

With a forked tail, dusky back, yellowish belly fin, all the other lines palish purple, and grows from two to four feet long. It is to be taken after the fashion of the lake trout.

The best time for taking the common trout is from April to August, or, if it be mild weather, as early as March. You may capture this fish in one of three ways:—

Top-Angling.—This is done with an artificial or natural fly, grasshopper, cricket, or other small insect to be found near water-courses or ponds. *Middle-Angling* is done with a shiner, minnow, or shrimp; and *Bottom Fishing* with a worm or shad-roe.

Fly fishing is the perfection of fishing, especially with the artificial fly. You use a stout rod, from ten to twelve feet long; your reel has on from thirty to fifty yards of fine silk, grass, or hair line, with a yard long leader, and your fly or flies set on very fine gut. Cast your line with the fly before you, and do it so dexterously that the fly will fall lightly on the water, and as little line with it as possible. This dexterity can only be acquired by practice. Your line should be about half as long again as your rod, though, as you acquire skill, and want to cast at some likely looking hole at a distance, you lengthen it. If you see a fish rise at a natural fly, throw a yard or so above him, so as to let your fly float to him naturally. Fish, when you can, down the stream.

In throwing the fly, a most important point, raise the arm well up, without laboring with the body; send the fly both backward and forward, by a sudden spring of the wrist. Do not draw the fly too near, or you lose your purchase for sending it back, and therefore require an extra sweep in the air before you can get it into play again. If, after sending it back, you make the counterspring too soon, you will crack off your tail-fly; if a moment too late, your line will fall in the water in a heavy and slovenly manner. The knack of catching the proper time is what you want to learn, and that can only be done by a little careful practice. When a skilful fisherman makes his cast, the extreme end of the casting-line reaches the water first, and this is as it should be; and when it is so, the line falls lightly and almost unperceived upon the water.

We should recommend beginners to put their rod together, draw their line through the rings some ten or twelve feet, and practise without casting-line on some grass-plot, until they find that they can obtain the necessary skill without making a crack like a coachman. Throwing the fly should also be practised with the left hand, as it will often be found a great relief. To change hands will also enable you to fish with the one next the river, on whichever side you may be, and whether you go up or down. After the following hints have been studied and you are perfect in them, you may commence the sport. Avoid going too close to the water, if the stream is a small one, and never by any chance permit your shadow to be thrown on its surface, availing yourself of stumps and rocks to hide you whenever available. No fish has keener sight than a trout; and if he should be on a ford feeding, one glimpse of the intruder will send him to the depths of the neighboring pool or under some inaccessible rock, without the slightest desire to renew his disturbed meal. Always fish with the shortest possible line, as you are thereby enabled more certainly to strike your fish when he rises, which is done by an almost simultaneous movement of the wrist, but nothing more—you will at once perceive if the fish is stuck, and your movement will be sufficient to make the hook take hold, but not to tear it from its grip. When a fish is hooked, be particularly cautious that no sudden strain is put on the line, and keep cool and ready for any emergency. If the trout is strong and in prime condition, his first endeavors to free himself will be by throwing himself out of the water, and the angler must be well prepared for this frequently successful plan. Immediately he is above the surface, drop the point of your rod so as to give him a slack line, for if the line should be taut and he strike it in his fall, he will invariably tear himself loose; but at no other time should the line be slack, as the hook, if not borne upon, is apt to work out. The next effort will probably be to run strong up stream : let him go, bearing sufficiently against him to wear him out; as soon as he stops, wind in your spare line as short as possible, almost to the casting-line, but on no account beyond; perhaps he will endeavor to make another run, but each successive one will be more feeble than the previous—always taking carefully in line as soon as he halts; he may now endeavor to go down to the bottom and get amongst rubbish, stones, etc., which must be carefully prevented by giving him the rod, so that all his efforts will come upon its spring. If you have to move from the place where you hooked the fish to land him, always go down stream, and endeavor to keep his head above water, and do not attempt to land him till thoroughly exhausted. Never attempt to lift your fish out by the line, as the dead-weight will frequently break the hold, but use your landing-net, which must be put under and behind, not attempting to raise it from the water till you see that he is in the pouch.

In fishing with the minnow, you use a stouter rod, and shorter top, with a two yard leader, and a Limerick hook, from No. 2 to 5, according to the size of your bait. If you put on the bait in the old way, you must keep it in motion; but, secured as we have before described, the bait will move itself.

In bottom fishing, you may either cast out, and draw gently in, or let it remain stationary, if your worm be lively. Under banks, or near rocks, if the worm be dropped in carefully, and the angler keep himself concealed, he stands a chance of taking the finest trout.

The time to strike, experience will show you better than any thing else. Do not drag him out, even if he be small, as though you wanted to pull the hook from his jaws; and if he be large, give him plenty of line, and play him till he is exhausted, or you may lose both hook and leader.

STRIPED BASS, OR ROCKFISH.

This is a fine game fish, abounding in the rivers, bays, and inlets from the capes and bays of Florida to those of Massachusetts, and in the spring of the year ascending the rivers to spawn. The rod and tackle required is the same as for the salmon, with a hook from No. 0 to 3, according to the game you are likely to find. The bait is minnow, shiner, or shad-roe, and when in the bays or mouths of rivers, shedder crabs, shrimp, and shad-roe in their season. In boat fishing, in still water, you use a cedar or large cork float, but in fishing at the bottom of dams or in swift currents, capital places, you have no float, and no other sinker than a plain swivel.

You manage them, in striking and taking, like the salmon. They can be caught also by trolling, with either squid or spoon-bait, or minnow.

PIKE.

The varieties of this fish are numerous. Besides the true pike, there is the pickerel, and, in the west and southwest, the *Muskelunjeh*. Then there is a fish known on the Ohio and its waters as the salmon, but properly called the

PIKE-PERCH,

Which is taken in the same manner, and is a bold and game fish. They are in time at all seasons, except just after their spawning in April and May, and may be taken even in winter by making a hole in the ice. During the very hot summer months they will not bite freely.

You will want for pike-fishing a similar rod and line to that used in catching salmon; but the hook must be set on catgut, covered with wire, such as is used for the smallest-wired guitar-string, or the teeth of a large pike will saw it through. He fights desperately, and you will need a gaff generally. If you attempt to take him without, grasp him by putting your finger and thumb in his two eyes. If you are not careful, he will snap your finger either off, or wound it fearfully, and that, sometimes, when you think him exhausted.

For bait you can use minnows, large chubs, small suckers, red-horse, or frogs—he is not particular. An extra swivel or two, here and there, in the first three yards of your line, may be useful.

THE PERCH.

In this family you will find the white, yellow, and black or red perch. In the West and Southwest, they call the black bass *black perch*, but he is a

PERCH.

different fish, a *gristes* and not a *perca*. Perch-fishing is very pretty sport. You do not require a very strong line, nor stout pole, and you will rarely, unless with a big fellow, have occasion to use the reel. He is a quick biter, and scarcely ever nibbles. The bait may be small minnows, shrimp, or worms—the latter almost always good in fresh water. Great numbers are taken in rivers, from the first hour before the flood of tide to the hour after, just outside of the channel-grass, with a bow-line, made with a whalebone, which is kept near the bottom by a dipsy. Each end of the bow is furnished with two or three hooks, set on four or five inches of gut, and baited with worms. Sometimes five or six are caught at once. From May to July is their best season, and the hook is a Limerick trout, from 2 to 5 in size.

BLACK BASS.

This fish is peculiar to the Western lakes, and the streams running into the great rivers of the West. It resembles, in general appearance, the sea-bass, but is not black, though it has a blackish appearance above. There are several varieties—some bottle-green on top, some with broad stripes around them, that fade after they are dead—and all game. They harbor in the deep holes in summer, shooting out into the shallows, at times, after small fish. The best bait is the minnow or chub, to be caught in their vicinity, or the brooks round about; and if you want big fish, use tolerably large bait.

You take a medium-sized rod, with about fifty yards of line, and a yard leader. A swivel sinker, large enough to keep your bait from the surface, and a float so large that your bait cannot pull it under, are required. Put your hook through the gill-cover of the chub, set your float from three to six feet deep, according to the depth of the hole, and throw it gently in. Do not strike the first time the float goes under. Wait for the second time, and then strike. Play him well, giving him line in proportion to his size and strength. He plays game for a while, but soon gives up. A landing-net, or your finger in his gills, will secure him.

The above directions, with little variation, will answer for the pike-perch in the Western streams.

THE WHITE LAKE-BASS.

This fish may be treated like the white perch.

THE RED-EYE.

This is a Western fish, looking like a cross between the striped bass and the sunfish, with a red spot in his eye, whence the name. He is a game little fellow, and to be taken after the manner of the white perch. He is good at all seasons. His haunts are principally under the banks, and beneath overhanging bushes.

RED-HORSE.

This is a species of soft-fleshed fish that is not much sought after except in spring, when he swarms in the Western waters. He will not bite well at that time, and they take them by spearing. He may be caught with a worm, by ground-fishing, in the autumn months, but is bony, and not prized. Akin to him is his Eastern relative, the

SUCKER,

Who is to be found in our rivers and streams, and the

MULLET,

Who bites a little better than the preceding at a worm. You must always fish on the bottom for these, with a small hook, and any moderately strong line. They require no skill to secure, and the coarsest and cheapest tackle will answer.

SUNFISH.

Every boy knows him. There are several varieties. An extemporized rod, of length according to the place you fish, a light line, a No. 7, 8, or 9 hook, a lively worm or a grasshopper, and you have him. He loves, like

SUNFISH, OR BREAM.

the red-eye, to lie in holes under the bank, and in tolerably deep water. His spines protect him from the larger fish, and he is quite game and fearless, as well as very handsome.

CARP, OR TENCH.

This is a naturalized fish in the Eastern part of this country; though there is a fine large carp in the Western waters. The mode of taking both is the same. You require strong tackle; for he is a heavy fish sometimes, and strong; a light quill float, a short leader of gut, and a light-colored worm—a brandling being better than an angle-worm. Fish on the bottom, or near it. He is a very shy fish, and you had better bait the spots you mean to fish the day before, by throwing in bread-crumbs, chicken-entrails, or lumps of dough.

EEL.

There is good sport sometimes with this fellow, in bobbing; but he is not much liked on a hook, from his habit of twining the line, and the slime he leaves on your fingers if you handle him. He will be found everywhere, especially in muddy bottoms, and boys need no instruction about catching him. Bobbing for eels is very amusing night sport. You string worms on threads, by running a blunt-pointed long needle through them from head to tail. When you have enough strings threaded, you tie the ends together, and then fold them into a regular hank, like a hank of yarn. This you double and treble, until it is about three inches long. Through the middle

you tie a stout cord, to the bottom of which is a round dipsy. Over this last the two ends of the bunch, which should be about the size of a boy's fist, hang. You anchor your boat on the muddy flats of a river, at high tide, or lean over the bank of a creek or river at a muddy bottom, and drop in your bob and sinker. Presently you feel a sharp pull. Draw up into the boat, or on the bank. Your eel has his teeth entangled in the thread, and cannot generally let go until he is in the boat, or on the bank. Night is the time, and the sport is sometimes very lively.

The way to grasp an eel on the hook, is to place the second finger on one side of him, and the first and third on the other, about an inch and a half from his neck. Then by pressing the fingers together he cannot move, and you may take the hook from his mouth, and throw him in your basket.

GARFISH.

This troublesome fellow, called often the garpike, having a long bony snout, armed with teeth, is a great nuisance to all boys in the West and Southwest, when they fish, by stripping off their bait. No hook will enter his hard snout. The best thing, when garpikes are around, is to go somewhere else. If you want to catch him, however, prepare a bunch of thread and horsehair, which dispose of around your live bait, loosely but firmly.

Pull out suddenly on the bite, and the chances are that the gar's teeth will be so entangled that he will drop on the bank.

CATFISH.

The ordinary mud-cat, bull-head, or bull-trout, is little prized, and may be caught, like a red-horse, by ground-bait, either a worm, piece of beef, or dough-bait. But the blue catfish of the Western waters fights very well; and there is a variety, called the white catfish, which comes from the sea in the east, to spawn yearly, about June and July, that is game, and rather handsome. He is more slender than the others, semi-transparent

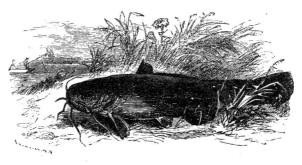

when held to the light, has a forked tail like a herring, and weighs from four ounces up to four pounds. He may be caught like the other. In the Schuylkill River, a number were kept from returning to the sea by the erection of the dam at Fairmount, and they bred in the river in great numbers.

ROACH.

This is a silver-sided, handsome fish, small, and considered poor eating. He may be taken in most of the rivers in the eastern part of the Northern States, in the same manner as the sunfish. He will bite well at small lumps of dough.

GOLDFISH.

These fish, which are a species of carp, originally brought from China, have escaped into many of our rivers, from fish-ponds, and have bred there. Their capture is like that of the sunfish, as is also the

CHUB.

But this is mostly found in small streams, under the bank, or near projecting roots. They, with the dace, shiner, minnow, and gudgeon, are principally used for bait. A willow swivel, a No. 10, 11, or 12 hook, a stout piece of sewing-thread, a worm, and a quill float, if the latter be required, and you can land them very rapidly.

As some of our young readers may happen to live near the shores of the ocean, or some bay, or may be taken there on a visit, we will mention the principal fish caught off the Atlantic coast. The finest of all these, probably, is the

SHEEPSHEAD.

He has a smutty face, banded sides, prominent eyebrows, a grooved dorsal fin, extending entirely down his back, and a queer mouth, not unlike a sheep's, whence the name. To capture him you require a strong cord, a quarter of an inch in diameter, from twenty to fifty yards long, a heavy sinker, and a stout blackfish hook, and either soft shell clam, with the shell on, or small rock-crab, and fish near the bottom.

There is a fresh-water sheepshead, caught at times in the lakes, but he is worthless, his flesh being tough, leathery, and disagreeable.

DRUMFISH.

This is a very large fish, and not likely to be taken by a boy alone, and we only mention it because, when you are fishing for bluefish and bass, you may get one on your hook, and unless you are very expert, and he is very small— say about fifteen pounds only in weight—he will teach you the necessity of always taking extra hooks and leaders when you fish.

WEAKFISH.

This is sometimes called wheatfish, and sometimes squeteague. He has an even tail, speckled back and sides, one or more sharp, long front teeth in the lower jaw, and yellowish ventral fins. He is found chiefly in salt or brackish waters, in New York, Connecticut, and Massachusetts. He bites at shrimp and shedder crab, and is to be caught with the same tackle and in the same manner as the striped bass, with whom he herds. They will be found, however, in rather deeper water, farther from shore, and more in the eddies.

KINGFISH, OR BARB.

This is the most spirited fish in resisting capture that can be found. He is only found in New York bay, and there only as an occasional visitor. He is about sixteen or eighteen inches long, with a pendulous bit hanging from his under lip, light brown color, glossed with blue and silver, and dark blotches and spots. He may be captured with striped bass tackle and bait, but wants about a No. 4 Salmon hook.

BLUEFISH.

This fish is taken by trolling with the artificial squid, a piece of lead, mother-of-pearl, or bone, about four inches long, armed with a No. 0000 Kirby hook, with the bend of the hook at right angles with the flat side of the squid. The line is cotton, stout, and from forty to sixty yards long. When the fish is hooked, haul in steadily and without intermission, or the fish will throw himself off

BLACKFISH.

He is sometimes called the tautog. He may be found in the bays from Cape May to Cape Cod. Striped bass tackle, and soft-shelled clam bait, are wanted for the blackfish; but he will often bite readily at the large salt beach-worm. You must look for him on rocky bottoms; and he will not bite well during a thunder-storm, nor in dull weather.

REDFISH.

This is a fish to be found southward of Cape Hatteras, as far as Pascagoula, and occasionally in Delaware Bay, and on the New Jersey coast. His length is from one to four feet. He is almost like silver in color, but becomes darker after getting out of the water, and dying shows the prismatic colors. Just in front of his tail-fin, near the back of the tail, is a black or brown spot, bordered with white, which has given him the name in some places of the branded drum. His time of biting is from March until January, except very far south, where he is taken all the year. He is caught with a stout hand-line and cod-hook, with shrimp bait or pieces of fish. He may be taken with rod and reel by a patient and dexterous angler.

CODFISH.

Off the coast of Massachusetts these fish are mostly taken. There is no art in catching them. A coarse, strong cord, a large blackfish hook, a piece of mud-clam, or moss-breaker, and a heavy sinker. They bite fiercely.

TOM COD.

This, sometimes called the frostfish, looks like a young codfish, and is caught in all the bays, inlets, and mouths of rivers along the Atlantic coast. It is a little fellow, running from six to fifteen inches in length. He can be taken with the simplest tackle, and with soft clam, hard clam, or shrimp bait, and occasionally will bite freely at worms.

SEA-BASS.

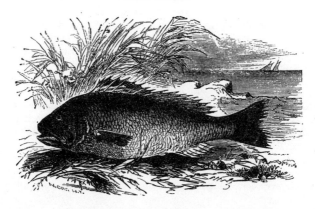

This fish is well known to all who are likely to fish for him. Sometimes boys from New York, or other large cities on the coast, make an excursion in company with older persons, in the steamboats which are chartered for such a purpose during the summer months. All one has to do is to take with him about eighty feet of stout hemp line, with two or three No. 1 Kirby hooks, and a dipsy weighing a pound. This, with hard clams, well salted, for bait, and a pair of old gloves, to keep the hands from being chafed by hauling on the line so much, completes his outfit. He will be apt to catch some porgies at the same time.

The other sea-fish boys are likely to meet with are flounders and smelt.

The former are caught near New York and Boston, and all along the coast of the Middle States, with a small drop-line, No. 8 hook, and soft clam bait. The smelt is taken in the rivers of Massachusetts, New York, and New Jersey, where they run to spawn in March and April, and return again in October and November. They are caught with a small line, a No. 2 or 3 trout hook, a short leader, and pieces of minnow or frog.

In fishing, the angler will often want to tie a secure knot. We can recommend the water-knot, made as follows:

To tie a leader to a line, you use the ordinary loop-knot, although the neatest tie for that purpose is the loop hitch, which we give below.

There are many other fish which our space does not permit us to describe. We have been obliged to content ourselves with a few remarks about the best known specimens, and must trust to our young friends to improve their knowledge, as they may easily do, by personal observation, and by inquiry among the hardy fishermen who are to be found at all our sea-side resorts, and are always ready and willing to gratify the curiosity that springs from a praiseworthy desire to gain knowledge.

And thus we leave our young friends, with the hope that they may not only amuse, but also instruct themselves at the sea-side. The end of all investigation into the nature and habits of living creatures is the same—an uncontrollable wonder and admiration at the wisdom which has adapted the structure of every thing that breathes to its wants and necessities; and a recognition of the goodness of the Creator, on whom the "eyes of all wait," and who, with never-failing bounty, "giveth them their meat in due season."

FENCING.

IT may be that no boy who reads this book will be called on to use either the rapier or broadsword, but the value of the scientific management of these weapons as an exercise,—from the grace it imparts to the movements, the vigor to the system, the keenness of eye it encourages and promotes, is undeniable. The most eminent physicians concur in recommending these exercises, that of the small-sword in particular.

In learning fencing with rapiers, there are required for each one, a strong wire mask to protect the face; foils, or mock swords, with buttons on the tip; a well-padded glove for the hand, and a shield of leather sewn on the front and collar of the jacket. Before proceeding to exercise, the buttons on the tip of each foil should be carefully examined, to see that they are secure.

All being ready, the beginner puts himself in the position called

THE GUARD,

From which all movements, whether offensive or defensive, are made. The beginner must stand with his knees straight, his feet at right angles, heel to heel; the right foot, right side, and face directed to the master. The body must be held upright and firm, the arms hanging down by the side, but easily and without constraint; the left hand holding the foil a few inches beneath its guard. Next let him bring the right hand across the body, and seize the foil-handle; by a second movement, bring the foil above the head, the hands separating as they ascend, until both arms be nearly extended upward and outward. Here pause. This may be called the *first position* of the Guard.

These movements should be frequently practised, as they accustom the arms to move independently of the body, flatten the joints of the shoulders, and give prominence to the chest.

To arrive at the *second position* of the Guard, the right arm, with the foil, is brought down to the front, until the right elbow is a little above and in

advance of the waist; the fore-arm and foil sloping upward; the point of the foil being the height of the upper part of the face; then, by a second movement, the learner must sink down, separating the knees, and stepping forward with the right foot fourteen or sixteen inches; for, of course, the guard of a tall man will be wider than that of a short one. However, his own comfort in the position will direct him as to the distance; and the general rule is, that the knee of the left leg will jut over the toes of the left foot, and the right leg from ankle to knee be perpendicular. It is in this position that he will receive all attacks from an adversary, and from this position will all his own attacks be made. Also in this position will he

ADVANCE

Upon an adversary, when beyond hitting distance. The step in the advance is usually about that of the width of the Guard, although of course this would vary with circumstances. The step is made by advancing the right foot the distance we have named; and on its reaching the ground, the left foot is brought up and takes its place. To

RETREAT,

The reverse of the above movement is made. The left foot takes the lead, stepping to the rear about as far as the right had stepped to the front; the right occupying its place on its taking up its new position. The next movement,

THE LONGE,

Is a very important movement, and is rather difficult to make properly, and fatiguing to practise. Indeed, the first movements in fencing are the most trying to the learner; and he must not be discouraged if he fails to do them correctly at first—practice only will give him this power. The Longe is that extension of body which accompanies every attack, and is thus made:

the right arm is extended straight from the shoulder, the arm and blade being on the same level; by a second movement, the right foot is raised from the ground, and a step made forward, about eighteen inches in length, while the left remains firmly planted in its place. At the instant that this step is made, the left hand is allowed to fall within a few inches of the left thigh, and the left knee is stiffened back until the leg is perfectly straight.

The thigh of the right leg will now be in a position nearly horizontal; from the knee downwards, perpendicular. Having executed the Longe, the next movement to be made is

THE RECOVER;

That is, to return from the position of the Longe to that of the Guard, and is thus effected: the left arm is nimbly thrown up to its place, the right arm drawn in, and the left knee re-bent. These movements must be made at the same time, as it is their *united* action that enables a person to recover from so extended a position as the Longe quick enough to avoid a thrust, if his own attack has failed.

These movements must be frequently practised before any others are attempted—the Guard, the Advance, the Retreat, the Longe, and the Recover; and when the learner has attained some proficiency in them, he may begin the more delicate movements of attack and defence. Of these we will now speak.

THE ENGAGE.

It is customary for adversaries, on coming to the Guard, to *Engage*, or to join blades, on what is called the *inside*, that is, the *right* side; although there are occasions on which it is advisable to engage on the *outside*, or on the left; otherwise called the *Quarte* or *Tierce* sides.

Two men thus opposed to each other will at once perceive that there are two lines of attack open to them, *i. e.*, the line inside and the line outside the blade—these, and no more. But these may be, and in fencing are, subdivided into inside above the hand, and inside under the hand, and the same subdivision for outside. This gives four lines of attack—or, to speak more simply, gives four openings through which an adversary may be assailed. Now, to protect each of these assailable points, are four defensive movements, called

PARADES.

Each opening has its own parade or defence, and each parade will guard its own opening, and, strictly speaking, no other. The opening inside above the hand is defended by two parades.

As its name imports, the first and most natural parade is that of *Prime*. The action of drawing the sword from its sheath is almost exactly the movement made use of in the parade of Prime.

In this parade, the hand is raised as high as the forehead, so that the fencer can see his opponent's face under his wrist. The blade of the foil is almost horizontal, but the point is rather lowered toward the ground. As this parade will throw the right side of the body open to the adversary's sword, it is good play to disengage from left to right, and deliver a rapid thrust at the adversary, in order to anticipate him before he can bring his own sword round for another thrust. His point will be thrown far out of line, so that he is behindhand in point of time.

This is a very useful parade for fencers of short stature, as they can sometimes get in their blade under their adversary's arm, after they have parried his thrust.

The other parade is that of

QUARTE.

It is thus formed. On the approach of the point of an adversary's blade (and how these approaches are made we will presently explain), the right hand is moved a few inches—three or four will be enough—across the body on the inside; the hand being neither depressed nor raised, and the foil being kept on the same slope as in the Guard. This guards the body on the inside above the hand, but (and here comes an important law in fenc-

ing) the very movement which has guarded the body on one side has exposed it on the other; this is the case with all the simple parades.

Suppose, now, that the exposed part *outside above* the hand were assailed, then the defence for it is the parade of

TIERCE.

It is formed by turning the hand with the nails downward, and crossing to the opposite side some six or eight inches; the hand and point at the same elevation as before: this will guard this opening. If, however, the attack had been made *under* instead of over the hand, then the proper parade would have been *Seconde*.

There is another method of parrying called *Quarte*, over the arm, which

12*

is executed by making almost the same parade as in Tierce, with this exception—first, the hand is retained in its original position, with the nails upward; and, secondly, the point is not raised above the eye of the adversary.

It is rather more delicate than Tierce, but wants its power and energy. The Ripostes, or reply thrusts, are made as they would have been had the parade been that of Tierce.

SECONDE

Is formed by turning the hand in the same position in which it was turned for Tierce, but the point of the foil slopes as much downward as in Tierce it did upward; the direction and distance for the hand to traverse being the

same. Again, had the attack been delivered at none of these, but at the *inside under* the hand, then the proper parade would have been

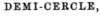

DEMI-CERCLE,

Which, as its name expresses, is a half-circle, described by a sweep of the blade traversing the *under* line. Next comes the parade of

OCTAVE.

In this parade the hand is held as in Quarte; the hilt of the foil is kept lower than that of the opponent; the blade is almost horizontal, the point being only slightly lower than the hilt, and directed toward the body of the adversary.

Octave is extremely useful when the fencer misses his parade of Demi-cercle, as there is but a short distance for the point to traverse, and it generally meets the blade of the adversary before the point can be properly fixed. Moreover, it brings the point so near the adversary's body, that he will not venture to make another thrust until he has removed the foil.

Thus we have enumerated, and partly explained, the forms and uses of these four parades: they are called Simple Parades, to distinguish them from another set of defensive movements, called

CONTRE-PARADES.

We have said and shown that a man standing foil in hand, in the position of the Guard, is exposed in four distinct places to thrusts from an adversary, within longeing distance. We have also shown that he has a defence for each of these exposed places; but if a man has but *one* defence for each assailable part, then his adversary, knowing beforehand what the defence must be, would be prepared beforehand to deceive him. But if he has a reserve—if he has a *second* defence for each part, then the adversary cannot tell what the defence will be, until his attack, false or real, is begun.

To meet this contingency, a second series of defences have been devised, which are of an entirely different nature from the *Simple* Parades.

Again, as each of the simple parades is framed to guard only one opening, it was found desirable that the contre-parades should be of a more comprehensive character. They are therefore devised so that each is capable of protecting the entire front. It is evident that this object could not be attained without the sacrifice of quickness, because a larger space must be traversed, and therefore more time is occupied with a contre than a simple parade.

To know one contre-parade is virtually to know all, as they are all formed on the same plan. They are all full circles in the position of hand and direction of foil of the different simple parades; or, more clearly speaking, each simple parade has a contre-parade; there are, therefore, four simple and four contre-parades, which may be thus arranged:

Quarte .... Contre de Quarte.
Tierce........... .... Contre de Tierce.
Seconde........................ Contre de Seconde.
Demi-cercle .... Contre de Cercle.

We have said that a contre-parade is a full circle in the position of hand and direction of blade of its simple; thus, contre de quarte is made by retaining the hand in the position of quarte, while the foil describes a circle descending on the inside, and returning by the outside to the place of its departure. So with all the others, the foil *following the direction of the simple* parade, of which it is the contre. These complete the entire system of defences.

We now come to movements of an opposite nature, namely, the

ATTACKS,

And shall begin with the most simple of them. We will again suppose two adversaries standing, *en guard*, within longeing distance of each other: now, the most simple movement that the attacking party could make, would be ·

THE STRAIGHT THRUST,

To the outside or inside, according to his line of engagement. We have, in describing the longe, in effect described the straight thrust; it is but a longe in a straight line, taking care, however, to feel firmly the adversary's blade, but taking care also not to press or lean on it during the delivering of the thrust.

Next in character comes

THE DISENGAGEMENT.

This attack is made by dropping the point of the foil beneath the adversary's blade, and raising it on the opposite side, at the same time, rising with the arm fully extended· on the completion of the extension the longe is made and the thrust delivered.

THE ONE-TWO

Is but a double disengagement, the first being but a feint or false attack, to induce the adversary to form a parade to cover the part threatened, for the covering of one part of the body exposes the opposite: the second disengagement is made to take advantage of this exposure. The arm is extended halfway on the first, and then wholly on the second, to be immediately followed by the longe.

The practice of this lesson evinces the advantages of a proper and sufficient extension, and a parade that is not too wide. The quick extension of the left leg and right arm, performed during the disengage, should throw the point towards your adversary's breast with such an emphasis as to resemble a thrust; at once forcing him to a parade, and taking a position much nearer to his body, rendering a second disengage beneath his tierce parade almost certain to hit, if not met with corresponding neatness by the defence. The parades must be precise, coming to sufficient guard, and no more. If the parade of tierce be made too wide, you cannot get back to carte in time.

Let the attacking party have the option of thrusting home in the *one*, as the adversary's knowledge that it is but a *feint* may prevent him from going fully to guard.

ONE, TWO, THREE.

When a facility has been acquired in practising the *one*, *two*, the pupils may commence the *one*, *two*, *three*, making the first disengage by the extension of the arm alone; the *two* by the full extension; and the *three* by the complete longe, to be answered by the parades of *tierce*, *carte*, and *tierce* again.

Let the attack be neat and deliberate, not exhibiting so much anxiety to obtain a hit as to be correct and precise; quickness will follow, of course. The attacked party should stand his ground, with his left foot firm; as nothing gives greater promise of excellence than receiving the hit without flinching the body. Make the parades neat, and keep cool; for any nervous snappishness in your motion is fatal to good fencing. The simple turn of the wrist from carte to tierce, is almost sufficient to cover the body. Take care that your hand is high enough, so that you do not oppose the *foible*, or weak part, of your blade, to the *forte*, or strong, of your adversary's.

APPELS, BEATS ON THE BLADE, AND GLIZADES.

Appels, beats, and glizades, tend to plant you firm upon your guard, to embarrass your adversary, and cause him to give you openings; they may be performed previously to simple thrusts, feints, or counter-disengagements, &c. An appel, or beat with the foot, is performed either on the engagement of carte or tierce, by suddenly raising and letting fall the right foot, with a beat on the same spot; taking care to balance the body, and keep a good position on guard.

The beat on the blade is abruptly touching your adversary's blade so as to startle him, and get openings to thrust. If he resist the beat, instantaneously disengage, and thrust home. If he use a simple parade, mark feint one, two; or, if he use a counter-parade, counter-disengage, or double.

Glizades are slightly gliding your blade along your adversary's, at the same time forming the extension of the arm, or the complete extension, managing and restraining your body, so as to be aware of his thrust, and to make sure of your own. If you be engaged in carte, out of measure, a quick advance, with a glizade, must infallibly give you some openings, either to mark feints or otherwise.

THE BEAT AND THRUST.

This is another variety of attack. Supposing the adversary's blade to be firmly joined to yours, when you wished to deliver a *straight thrust*, there would then be danger of your falling upon his point. This danger is avoided by giving a slight beat on his blade the instant preceding your extension of arm, of course to be followed *en suite* by the longe.

The companion attack to this attack is

THE BEAT AND DISENGAGEMENT.

The *beat* here takes the character of the first disengagement in *one-two*, *i. e.*, becomes a *feint*, and is intended to induce the adversary to return to the place he occupied when the beat was made. You then immediately pass to the opposite side of his blade in the manner described in the *disengagement*.

It will be seen that all these movements pass *under* the adversary's blade. However, there are certain situations in the *assault*, as a fencing bout is called, when an adversary is more assailable *over the point* than under the blade; for this purpose there is what the French call the *coupé sur point*, or

CUT OVER THE POINT.

It is thus made: By the action of the hand, and without drawing it back at all, the foil is raised and brought down on the opposite side of the adversary's blade, the arm being extended during its fall to the horizontal position, on attaining which the longe is delivered.

CUT OVER AND DISENGAGEMENT

Is on the same principle as the *one-two* and the *beat and disengagement.* On the adversary opposing the first movement (the cut) with a parade, the second movement (the disengagement) is made to the opposite side, to be followed of course by the longe; the extension of the arm being divided between the two movements.

These attacks are called simple attacks, because they may be parried by one or more simple parades, according to the number of movements in the attack. In fact, every attack can be parried, and every parade can be deceived: it is the *additional* movement last made which hits or guards.

Thus, you threaten by a disengagement to the outside; your adversary bars your way effectually by the parade of *tierce;* you make a second disengagement to the inside, which is now exposed from the very fact of the outside being guarded (for both lines of attack cannot be guarded at the same time), thus converting your attack into *one-two;* but if your adversary parries quarte on your *second* movement, your attack would be warded off. This can be carried much further, but the above will, we think, be sufficient to explain the nature of simple parades and attacks.

To deceive a *contre*-parade, a separate movement, called a *doublé*, or

DOUBLE,

Has been invented; it is very simple in principle, and admirably answers the purpose. For instance, if you were to threaten your adversary by a disengagement to the outside, and if, instead of tierce, he parried *contre de quarte*, the double is then made by your making a *second* disengagement *to the same side as the first*, for it will be found that his *contre de quarte* has replaced the blades in the positions they occupied previous to your disengagement. You will then have an opening, and may finish the attack by the longe.

As all the contre-parades are on the same plan and principle, so are all the doubles. Of course, it is understood that you will make all the movements of the double *en suite*, and without allowing your adversary's blade to overtake yours.

ALL FEINTS.

The foregoing movements having been well practised in the lesson, the next step is that of *all feints* and *all parades*, and may be practised either with a master or fellow-pupil. The practice consists of one pupil standing on the defensive *entirely*, while another assumes the offensive, and attacks him with *all* the *feints* of which he is master, the other, of course, defending with all his parades. It is excellent practice, as it accustoms the pupil to think for himself gradually, he having thus but one set of movements to think about. He is therefore enabled to make them boldly, without having to encounter unknown movements from his adversary.

It also enables him to see the extent of his resources, both for attack and defence. When he can both attack and defend with some presence of mind he may then begin

THE ASSAULT;

That is, he may encounter an adversary, to attack or defend as occasion presents. He is then left to his own resources entirely. The following

GENERAL ADVICE,

Given by a very eminent fencer and excellent teacher, cannot fail to be of use:

" Do not put yourself on the position of the **guard within** the reach of your adversary's thrust, especially at the time of drawing your sword.

" If you are much inferior, make no long assaults.

" Do nothing that is useless; every movement should tend to your advantage.

" Let your movements be made as much within the line of your adversary's body as possible.

" Endeavor both to discover your adversary's designs, and to conceal your own.

"Two skilful men, acting together, fight more with their heads than their hands.

"The smaller you can make the movements with your foil, the quicker will your point arrive at your adversary's body.

"Do not endeavor to give many thrusts on the longe, thus running the risk of receiving one in the interim.

"If your adversary drops his foil by accident, or in consequence of a smart parade of yours, you should immediately pick it up, and present it to him politely.

"Always join blades (if possible) previously to another attack, after a hit is given."

BROADSWORD.

The principal distinction between the broadsword and the rapier is, that the latter is formed only for thrusting, while the former is adapted for cutting also. Indeed, those who use the broadsword are, in our opinion, too apt to neglect the use of the point, and to give their attention almost exclusively to the cuts.

The first lesson in the sword exercise is necessarily to know how to stand. The learner should be instructed to perform the different movements by word of command, remembering to consider the first parts of the word as a caution, and not to stir until the *last* syllable is uttered. At the last syllable, the movement should be performed smartly. In giving the word, the instructor always makes a slight pause, in order to give his pupils time to remember what they must do. For example, the words Draw Swords, is given thus: Draw . . . . . Swords—the word swords being spoken smartly, in order that the movement may correspond.

POSITIONS.

First Position.—Make the target* about fourteen inches in diameter, and place it on the wall, having its centre about four feet from the ground. Draw a perpendicular line from the spot at the bottom of the target to the ground, and continue it on the floor, in order to insure the proper position of the heels. The learner stands perfectly upright opposite the target, with his right side toward it, his heels close together, his right toe pointing to the target, and his left foot at right angles with the right. His arms must be clasped behind his back, his right palm supporting the left elbow, and his left hand grasping the right arm just above the elbow. In this position, he must bend both knees and sink down as far as possible. This will not be very far at first, but he will soon sink down quite easily. See accompanying figure (1).

* For target, see page 282.

Fig. 1.   Fig. 2.

Second Position.—This is accomplished by placing the right foot smartly in front, about fourteen or sixteen inches before the left. (See Fig. 2.) He must accustom himself to balance himself so perfectly on his left foot, that he can place the right either before or behind it, without losing his balance.

Third Position.—The third position must then be learned. This consists in stepping well forward with the right foot, until the left knee is quite straight, and the right knee exactly perpendicularly placed over the right foot. Great care must be taken to keep the heels exactly in the same line, and the body perfectly upright. (See Fig. 3.)

Fig. 3.

These preliminaries having been settled, the learner stands upright before the target, as in Fig. 1. A sword is then put into his hand, and the target is explained as follows:

TARGET.

The interior lines represent the cuts. Cut one being directed from No. 1 diagonally through the target, coming out at 4. Cut two is the same, only from left to right. Three is made upwards diagonally, and four is the same,

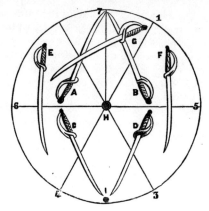

only in the opposite direction. Cut five is horizontally through the target, from right to left, and six from left to right. Cut seven is perpendicularly downward. Care must be taken that the cuts are fairly given with the edge.

The swords drawn on the target represent the guards. The seventh guard ought, however, not to be made directly across, but must have the point directly rather forward and downward, as a cut 7 glides off the blade, and can be instantly answered either by a thrust or by cut 1.

The two dark circles represent the places where the thrusts take effect.

The learner begins by taking the sword in his right hand, having its edge toward the target and its back resting on his shoulder. His right arm is bent at right angles, and the elbow against his side. The left hand must rest upon the hip, the thumb being to the rear. At the word—

CUTS AND GUARDS.

CUTS.

Cut 1.—The young swordsman extends his right arm, and makes the cut clear through the target. When the point has cleared the target, continue the sweep of the sword, and by a turn of the wrist bring it with its back on the left shoulder, its edge toward the left. The arm is then ready for

Cut 2.—Bring the sword from 2 to 3, continue the movement of the sword, and turn the wrist so that the point is below the right hip and the edge toward the ground.

Cut 3.—Cut through the target diagonally, bringing the sword from No. 3 to No. 2, and bring the sword onwards, so that it rests with the edge downwards, and point below the left hip. At

Cut 4.—Cut from 4 to 1, and bring the sword round until its point is over the right shoulder, and its edge well to the right.

Cut 5.—At the word Five, make a horizontal cut from 5 to 6, and sweep the sword round until it rests on the left shoulder, with its edge to the left, and its point well over the shoulder.

Cut 6.—Cut horizontally through the target, from 6 to 5, and bring the sword over the head, with its edge upward, and its point hanging over the back. From this position,—

Cut 7.—Make a downward stroke until the sword reaches the centre of the target. Arrest it there, and remain with the arm extended, waiting for the word

POINTS.

FIRST POINT.   SECOND POINT.

First Point.—Draw back the sword until the right wrist is against the right temple, the edge of the sword being upward. Make a slight pause, and then thrust smartly forward toward the centre of the target, raising the right wrist as high as No. 1, and pressing the left shoulder well back.

THIRD POINT.

Second Point.—Turn the wrist round to the left, so that the edge comes upward, draw the hand back until it rests on the breast, and give the point forward to the centre of the target, raising the hand as before.

Third Point.—Give the handle of the sword a slight twist in the hand to the right, so that the edge again comes uppermost, and the guard rests against the back of the hand. Draw back the hand until it rests against the right hip, and deliver it forward toward the spot at the bottom of the target, raising the wrist as high as the spot in the centre. The object in raising the wrist is to deceive the eye of the opponent, who will be more likely to notice the position of your wrist than of your point. In all the thrusts the left shoulder should be rather brought forward before the point is given, and pressed well back while it is being delivered.

GUARDS.

Wait after the third point has been delivered for the word

Defend.—At this word draw up the hand smartly and form the first guard. Make the other guards in succession as they are named, while the instructor proves their accuracy by giving the corresponding cuts. The guards must be learned from the target, by placing the sword in exactly the same position as those delineated. The guards are these:—

A. First guard.　　　　E. Fifth.
B. Second.　　　　　　F. Sixth.
C. Third.　　　　　　　G. Seventh.
D. Fourth.

The two spots H and I mark the places toward which the points are made, H for the first and second point, I for the third.

PARRY.

The parry or parade of a thrust is executed with the back of the sword. The firmest way of parrying is to hold the sword perpendicular, with its edge to the right and its hilt about the height of and close to the right shoulder; then, by sweeping the sword round from left to right, any thrust within its sweep is thrown wide from the body.

The parry is executed with the wrist and not with the arm, which must not move.

HANGING GUARD.

When the pupil is acquainted with both cuts and guards, he should learn the hanging guard, a most useful position, as it keeps the body well hidden under the sword, and at the same time leaves the sword in a good position to strike or thrust.

It is accomplished in the following way. Step out to the second position, as in Fig. 2, raise the arm until the hand is just over the right foot, and as high as the head. The edge of the sword is upward, and the point is directed downward and toward the left. The left shoulder is pressed rather forward, and the neck and chest drawn inward.

In this position the swordsman is in a position to receive or make an attack, as he may think fit. It is rather fatiguing at first, owing to the unaccustomed position of the

HANGING GUARD.

arm and head, but the fatigue is soon overcome, and then it will be found that there is no attitude which gives equal advantages.

There are two other modes of standing on guard, each possessing its peculiar advantages. These are, the inside and outside guard. The inside guard is made as follows:

INSIDE GUARD.

Stand in the second position, having the wrist of the right hand nearly as low as the waist, the hand being exactly over the right foot. The point of the sword is raised as high as the eyes, and the edge is turned inward, as will be seen from the foregoing engraving.

OUTSIDE GUARD.

The outside guard is formed in the same manner as the inside, with the exception that the edge of the sword is turned well outward.

To get to the hanging guard, the words are given as follows: Inside Guard—Outside Guard—Guard.

ATTACK AND DEFENCE.

The swordsman, having learned thus far, is taught to combine the three movements of striking, thrusting, and guarding, by the following exercise:

1. Inside Guard.
2. Outside Guard.
3. Guard.
4. Cut one.
5. First Guard.
6. Cut two.
7. Second Guard.
8. Cut three.
9. Third Guard.
10. Cut Four.
11. Fourth Guard.
12. Cut Five.
13. Fifth Guard.
14. Cut Six.
15. Sixth Guard.
16. Cut Seven.
17. Seventh Guard.
18. First point. [Prepare for the point in First Position.] Two. [Thrust in Third Position.]
19. Second Point. [Prepare for it in First Position.] Two. [Thrust in Third Position.]
20. Third Point. [Prepare.] Two. [Thrust.]
21. Parry. [Prepare to parry in First Position.] Two. [Parry.]
22. Guard.

Our young friends will find the foregoing a really excellent piece of drill, and sufficiently interesting also to make it a pastime. When the pupil can accomplish all these combinations neatly, accurately, and promptly, he will have made no inconsiderable progress as a broadswordsman or a single-stick player.

The young swordsman must remember that in this, as in all the exercises, the cuts and points must be given in the third position, as in the accompanying illustration, which shows the swordsman just as he has delivered the seventh cut, and is waiting for the next word before he resumes the first position.

SEVENTH CUT.

The guards, on the contrary, are given in the first position, as seen in the accompanying illustration, which illustrates the seventh guard.

These exercises are always learned with the single-stick, or basket-hilted cudgel, in order to avoid the dangers which would be inevitable if the sword were used. But as the single-stick is only an imitation of the sword, we will give the method of getting the sword out of the sheath into any position required.

DRAW SWORDS.

The first word of command is *draw swords*. At the word *draw*, seize the sheath just below the hilt, with the left hand, and raise the hilt as high as the hip, at the same time grasping the hilt with the right hand, turning the edge of the sword to the rear, and drawing it partially from the sheath, to insure its easy removal.

At the word *swords*, draw the blade smartly out of the scabbard, throwing the point upward, at the full extent of the arm, the edge being still to the rear.

SEVENTH GUARD.

RECOVER SWORDS.

The wrist is now smartly lowered until it is level with the chin, the blade upright, and the edge to the left. This is the position of recover swords. The elbow must be kept close to the body, as in the following cut.

RECOVER SWORDS.

CARRY SWORDS.

The wrist is now sharply lowered until the arm hangs at its full length, the wrist being in the line with the hip, the edge of the sword to the front, and its back resting in the hollow of the shoulder, the fingers lightly holding the hilt. The left hand hangs at the side until the word *inside guard*, when it is placed on the left hip.

SLOPE SWORDS.

At the word *swords*, raise the right hand smartly, until it forms a right angle at the elbow.

. RETURN SWORDS.

At the word, raise the blade until it is perpendicular, move the hilt to the hollow of the left shoulder, drop the point of the sword into the scabbard (which has been grasped by the left hand and slightly raised), at the same time turning the edge to the rear. Pause an instant, and send the sword smartly into the sheath, removing both hands as the hilt strikes against the mouth of the scabbard: drop them to the side, with the palms outward, and stand in the first position.

PRACTICES.

There are many exercises with the broadsword, called *Practices*. We have given one of them, which is to be practised alone; but when the pupil has attained some confidence in the use of his weapon, he must be placed opposite another pupil, and they must go through them, each taking the attack and defence in turn.

The young swordsman must be provided with a very stout wire mask, which defends the face and part of the neck, and which should be worked in a kind of helmet above, to guard against the disastrous consequences of receiving the seventh guard. No practices, loose or otherwise, should be permitted without the masks, as neither party would be able to cut or thrust with proper confidence.

SECOND PRACTICE.

This is very useful in teaching the point and parry, as well as giving steadiness on the feet. Two boys are placed opposite each other, at just such a distance, that when perfectly erect they can touch the hilt of their adversary's sword with the point of their own.

The one who gives the first point is called Front Rank (there may be a dozen in each rank, each having tried the distance to his right by extending his sword), and the one who gives first parry is called Rear Rank.

13

WORD OF COMMAND.	FRONT RANK.	REAR RANK.
Guard.	Hanging Guard.	Hanging Guard.
Third Point.	Prepare to give Third Point.	Prepare to Parry.
Point.	Give Third Point, and when parried spring back to First Position, and prepare to parry.	Parry Third Point, and prepare to give Third Point.
Point.	Parry Third Point, and prepare for Third Point.	Give Third Point, and prepare to Parry.
Point, &c., &c.		

This should be continued until both are weary. Both swordsmen should learn to do it more rapidly every time they practise. Next time of going through it, front rank and rear rank change places, as they must do in all the practices.

THIRD PRACTICE.

WORD OF COMMAND.	FRONT RANK.	REAR RANK.
Guard.	Hanging Guard.	Hanging Guard.
Leg.	Cut Four.	Cut Seven.
Inside Guard.	Inside Guard.	Inside Guard.
Leg.	Cut Six [at Leg].	Cut Six [at Neck].
Outside Guard.	Outside Guard.	Outside Guard.
Leg.	Cut Five [at Leg].	Cut Five [at Neck].
Guard.	Hanging Guard.	Hanging Guard.
Slope Sword.	Slope Swords.	Slope Swords.

In this and the other practices, the cuts must be delivered in the third position, and the guards in the first. In the third and fourth practices, the cuts must be given lightly, as many of them are not intended to be guarded, but merely to show the powers of the sword in various positions.

FOURTH PRACTICE.

WORD OF COMMAND.	FRONT RANK.	REAR RANK.
Guard.	Hanging Guard.	Hanging Guard.
Head.	Seventh Cut.	Seventh Guard.
Head.	Seventh Guard.	Cut Seven.
Leg.	Fourth Cut.	Seventh Guard.
Leg.	Seventh Guard.	Fourth Cut.
Head.	Seventh Cut.	Seventh Guard.
Head.	Seventh Guard.	Seventh Cut.
Guard.	Hanging Guard.	Hanging Guard.
Slope Swords.	Slope Swords.	Slope Swords.

In this and the preceding exercise, the power of shifting the leg is shown. If two swordsmen attack each other, and No. 1 strikes at the leg of No. 2, it will be better for No. 2 not to oppose the cut by the third or fourth guard, but to draw back the leg smartly, and cut six or seven at the adversary's head or neck.

In loose play, as it is called, i. e., when two parties engage with swords without following any word of command, but strike and guard as they can, both players stand in the second position, because they can either advance or retreat as they choose, and can longe out to the third position for a thrust or a cut, or spring up to the first position for a guard, with equal ease.

It is often a kind of trap, to put the right leg more forward than usual, in order to induce the adversary to make a cut at it. When he does so, the leg is drawn back, the stroke passes harmless, and the deceived striker gets the stick of his opponent on his head or shoulders.

We now come to a very complicated exercise, called the

FIFTH PRACTICE.

WORD OF COMMAND.	FRONT RANK.	REAR RANK.
Draw Swords.	Draw Swords.	Draw Swords.
Inside Guard.	Inside Guard.	Inside Guard.
Outside Guard.	Outside Guard.	Outside Guard.
Guard.	Hanging Guard.	Hanging Guard.
Head.	Seventh Cut.	Seventh Guard.
Head.	Seventh Guard.	Seventh Cut.
Arm.	Second Cut [at Arm].	Second Guard.
Head.	Seventh Guard.	Seventh Cut.
Head.	Seventh Cut.	Seventh Guard.
Arm.	Second Guard.	Second Cut [at Arm].
Head.	Seventh Cut.	Seventh Guard.
Head.	Seventh Guard.	Seventh Cut.
Right Side.	Sixth Cut.	Sixth Guard.
Head.	Seventh Guard.	Seventh Cut.
Head.	Seventh Cut.	Seventh Guard.
Right Side.	Sixth Guard.	Sixth Cut.
Guard.	Hanging Guard.	Hanging Guard.

This practice is capital exercise, and looks very imposing. All these practices ought to be so familiar, that the words of command are not needed, the only word required being First, Second, or Third Practices, as the case may be.

FORT AND FEEBLE.

The half of the sword-blade next the hilt is called the "fort," because it is the strongest place on which the cut of an adversary can be received. Always parry and guard with the fort of your sword, as, if you try to guard a cut with the "feeble," which is the remaining half of the blade, your guard will be forced, and the cut take effect.

DRAWING CUT.

The drawing cut is made best with a curved sword, and is executed by placing the edge of the sword on the object, and drawing it over it until it is severed. A good large mangel-wurzel is capital practice. Place the root loose on a table, stand at arms' length from it, lay the edge of the sword lightly on it, and slice the root by repeatedly drawing the sword over it. This is very difficult, though it looks easy enough, and is sure to jar the arm from the wrist to the shoulder the first time or two, while the sword glides off as if the root were cased in polished steel. However, a little practice will soon overcome the difficulty. This cut is much in use among the Sikhs.

GENERAL ADVICE.

Never look at your own sword, but watch the eye and sword-wrist of your opponent.

Remember that the great point in this exercise, as in fencing, is to gain time. Endeavor, therefore, to advance your point nearer your adversary than his is to you.

Begin the assault out of distance, so that neither party can complain of being taken by surprise.

If the two parties exchange a cut or a thrust at the same moment, the one who gave his cut or thrust in the third position is victorious.

When a cut or thrust is made, the one who receives it passes his sword, *i. e.*, stick, into his left hand, and his opponent comes to inside guard.

Always spring back to the second position after delivering a cut or thrust.

Keep the line of direction carefully, or you will leave an open space for the adversary to get his sword into.

We cannot be too careful to impress upon our pupils the necessity for always making use of the mask in these exercises. One of the best draughtsmen of the present day, who is also a very fine swordsman, lost the sight of one of his eyes through neglect of this necessary precaution.

In conclusion, we beg our young readers to perform their Fencing Exercises with decorum and gentleness toward each other; endeavoring, at the same time, to execute all their parades, etc., with precision and elegance. Let them then exhibit as little awkwardness as possible, and no loss of temper; for ill-nature always mars the pleasure of any pastime.

PART III.

___

Amusements with Pets:

COMPRISING

SINGING AND TALKING BIRDS, PIGEONS, DOMESTIC AND
AQUATIC FOWLS, RABBITS, SQUIRRELS, MICE,
GUINEA-PIGS, RACCOON AND OPOSSUM,
DOGS, SALT AND FRESH WATER
AQUARIA.

AMUSEMENTS WITH PETS

AMUSEMENTS WITH PETS.

CAGE-BIRDS.

FEW things in creation are more beautiful than birds. Elegance of form, brilliancy or softness of color, gracefulness of motion—all combine to render them agreeable objects to the eye; and when to these gifts is added melodiousness of voice, no wonder that they should be, as they undoubtedly are, favorites with every one who has the slightest appreciation of loveliness in any shape.

Birds are remarkable for the ingenuity with which they construct their nests, and the care and tenderness they show to their young. They have memory, knowledge, gratitude, affection, and even imagination, for they dream; and it will be our business to show with what facility they may be tamed, taught, and trained.

In a state of nature, birds are free denizens of the air and earth. In captivity, they are secured from the vicissitudes of the seasons, and the various accidents to which they are subjected by their own species, for the rapacious birds feed upon the non-rapacious. If caught when they are old and forced into a cage, they often pine and die; but nestlings—those taken from the nest at a very early age, or which, as Cowper defines them, are

> " Strangers to liberty, 'tis true ;
> But that delight they never knew,
> And therefore never missed—"

may be made very happy by kind treatment and assiduous care, which the young bird-fancier is bound to afford them; and which not to afford is very wicked, for it is our bounden duty to be

> " Kind to all that God has made."

Cage-birds are either kept for their song, their powers of mimicry, or their beauty of plumage. The song-birds, with the exception of the mocking-bird, brown thrush, bobolink, and oriole, are mostly natives of other lands, whose ancestors, or themselves, have been imported into this country. As, however, there are many of our native birds who thrive well in captivity, we will give some of the modes of capturing wild birds, which is done either by traps, limed twigs, springles, nets, or dead birds.

TRAPS.

The common brick trap is well known to most youngsters. It consists of four bricks placed as in the drawing, two lengthways, upon their edges or narrow sides, one in front, and the fourth between the two side bricks; this is so placed that it will fall and lie easily upon the front brick. Within the trap a stout peg is driven into the ground, upon which a forked twig is placed horizontally; above this a stick is placed, one end being on the twig

CATCHING BIRDS.   TRAPS.

and the other end supporting the brick in a slanting position. The end of the twig that rests on the peg is cut flat, to give it a better hold. The bait is strewn upon the ground on the inside of the trap. When the bird flies to the trap he generally perches for a moment on the forked twig; this his weight causes to give way, and the sustained brick, falling upon the outer or front brick, encloses and secures the bird. Caution should be used in placing the upper brick, so that it does not fall between the two side bricks unsupported by the front brick, as in such a case the bird would be crushed to death.

The sieve trap, another simple trap, is made by the use of a large sieve, which is propped up in the manner shown in the drawing. To the centre of the stick a fine long line should be tied, and having strewn some bait under the sieve, hide yourself in some place a short distance off, with the end of the string in your hand, and watch. When you observe a bird well under the sieve, give a sharp jerk, and the stick being withdrawn from the sieve, it will fall down over the bird.

THE LIMED TWIG.

The mode of catching birds by the adhesive quality of birdlime,* is one of the most simple methods. The substance is easily made by chewing or macerating wheaten grain till it becomes "sticky," which every boy well knows how to do. When large numbers of birds are to be secured, a large branch or bough of a tree, after being trimmed of the leaves and small shoots, is coated all over with birdlime, which has been prepared on a larger scale than by chewing. The bough is then fixed on a low dead hedge, near a pond, or other place favorable to the resort of small birds. The bird-catcher, concealing himself as near the bough as he can, imitates the notes of the birds he wishes to attract. The birds approach, alight on the bough, and stick fast, when they are easily secured. Sometimes the birds are attracted by a decoy, which may be a bat or an owl, of which the latter is the best. Whenever an owl shows himself by daylight it is sure to be followed by all the small birds that see it; and when it is fastened near the limed bough, the birds will collect around it in great numbers, and will sooner or later settle on the bough, from which they may be easily taken.

THE SPRINGLE.

The springle is a somewhat complicated engine, but very effective as a bird-catcher. It consists of five parts, as follows:

1. The *Stump.*—A small stout stake of wood, about five inches in length, which is fixed firmly in the ground, with its head about an inch above the surface.

---

* This substance is not much known in this country, and is made abroad, from the inner bark of the holly. We believe that the bark of the American holly has been made to answer the purpose. In order that our readers, in those parts where the holly grows, may try it, we give the mode of making the substance in England. In warm weather common shoemaker's wax is as good a birdlime, we fancy, as any.

The bark of the holly, peeled in the month of June, should be boiled with water in a pipkin till the green bark is separated from the gray; the green bark should then be laid upon the stone of some outhouse and covered with rushes; in about a fortnight's time it will turn into a kind of slime: this should be beaten up in a mortar with a few grains of wheat, after which it may be put into an earthen vessel and kept; when required to be used, it should be melted over the fire, with a little goose-grease, in a dry pipkin—the twigs should then be smeared with it.

13*

2. The *Spreader.*—This is a small bent switch, having a notch at its thicker end. It is kept in its bent position by a piece of small cord whipped over its smaller and larger end, which are thus united just above the notch.

3. The *Bender* is also a piece of pliant withe or hazel. It is about eighteen inches long; both ends of it are fixed into the ground so as to form a kind of arch.

4. The *Springer.*—This is a hazel rod of about four feet in length, thick at one end and tapering at the other; to the tapering end is fixed a piece of string.

5. The *Catch*, A, is a small piece of wood fixed at the end of the string of the springer. It is about half an inch long, a quarter broad, and an eighth of an inch thick. It is slightly bevelled off at one end, so as to adapt it to the notch of the spreader.

6. The *Noose* is a slip knot, formed of horsehair, fastened below the catch.

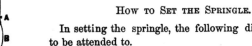

HOW TO SET THE SPRINGLE.

In setting the springle, the following directions are to be attended to.

1. The stump is driven firmly into the ground.

2. The spreader is placed around the stump, so that its bight is in contact with it.

3. The bender is fixed into the ground at about the length of the spreader from the stump.

4. The thick end of the springer is now fixed in the ground, at a little distance from the bender, and the small end of it bent down till one end of the catch is placed upward and on the outside of the bender.

5. The spreader is now raised about an inch from the ground, and the small end of the catch is put into the notch.

6. The horsehair slip knot is now arranged loosely round the bender, and the trap is set.

A little seed is now scattered within and for some distance around the spreader.

The operation of the trap is as follows:

The bird, attracted by the bait, soon perches upon the spreader, which falls, owing to its weight; the catch being thus set at liberty, the springer flies up, and the poor bird is caught either by the legs, wings, or body, by the horsehair noose or slip knot.

The bird-catcher usually watches at a short distance to seize the bird as soon as it is ensnared, or it would in a short time flutter itself to death or be strangled.

There is a curious mode of taking birds which is practised in some parts of France. A frame is constructed of wood, generally of the stripped branches of some of the slender straight-growing poplars, in the centre of which a seat is placed for the bird-catcher to sit upon. The frame so constructed is afterwards covered with boughs and evergreen shrubs, among which are openings for the entrance of the birds, and also for the hands of the bird-catcher to come out, who is seated like a jack-in-the-green within. When the birds alight on or about the sides of the holes, the bird-catcher  nimbly seizes them by the hand, or by means of a small flap trap which he thrusts out at one of the holes, and upon which the birds alight. Modifications of this plan might be successfully adopted by the juvenile bird-catcher.

DISEASES AND MANAGEMENT OF CAGE-BIRDS.

Birds are subject to few diseases, and what some birds are afflicted with, others escape, so also a different treatment is required with different birds; thus it is impossible to give any general remarks or remedies which will be applicable to all occasions, yet the following account of their particular ailments, and the causes and remedies for them, will be very useful for the young bird-fancier.

Almost all the diseases to which birds are subject, arise from improper management. If duly fed, their cages regularly cleaned, and kept in good air, it is seldom that the birds are found in bad health. In a state of nature they are liable to numerous misfortunes, but when confined they are exempt from many of these, and when they are really ill, their complaints can be better attended to; colds are the most general complaints, and they are almost all owing to carelessness. How frequently are birds hung up close to the top corner of a window, with the sash down about one foot, and a draught of air running through or by the cage, fit to turn a windmill. Thus they are frequently exposed for several hours late in the evening, when going to roost, without any consideration, whether the air be damp, cold, or dry. In this manner many a fine bird is endangered, if not killed, by taking cold.

When birds are in good health and lively, their feathers will appear and feel sleek and smooth, adhering close to their bodies; whenever you perceive the contrary to this, and the birds are sitting dull and bunchy, rely on it something is out of order. Therefore, first consider the season or time of year; if moulting is approaching, or if any thing has worried or frightened the bird, if he has been hung up in a draught of air and taken cold; if he is suffering from neither of these causes, see if he can get at his water and seed, and that both are sweet; good seed always appears clear and glossy, and feels dry and hard; if there is no fault here, examine his body, blow up the feathers of his belly, see if his bowels look swelled or inflamed, and if so, it implies that he has a surfeit. If he appears lean and out of condition, look narrowly for vermin about his body, and examine his cage well for little red mites, which attack him at night when he goes to roost, and frequently are the cause of his plucking himself so much by day.

Cleanliness, good seed, and fresh water, frequently renewed, are all that are required for a bird in good health. Green food is to be considered a luxury and not a necessary, except in the breeding season, but this applies chiefly to the seed-birds, such as the canary, etc. Many persons give birds loaf-sugar, but this is a very great error, and we recommend in its place, a small piece of bay-salt, or cuttle-bone, and now and then a drop or two of spirits of nitre in their water. The best green food is chickweed and lettuce. Surfeit is occasioned by improper diet or by cold, and particularly by bad water. There are two symptoms of this disorder, exhibited as arising either from cold or over-feeding. In the first case, if, when blowing up the feathers of the belly, it appears swelled, transparent, and full of little red veins, together with the bowels sinking down to its extreme parts, it may be said that the bird is in a bad state. In this state the bowels should be attended to; generally speaking, when they are not loose, as much magnesia as will lie upon a dime may be put into the bird's water every morning, until the bird is better, or, if it should be very bad indeed, a single drop of castor-oil for small birds, and two or three drops for large birds, may be poured down their throat by a quill. The food at the same time may be bread and milk. If the surfeit arises from cold, put a little saffron and a few drops of port-wine in his water, and let him have to eat a little hempseed (bruised for small birds), and a little dried and powdered sponge-cake, and be always careful that there is gravel at the bottom of the cage, for this is necessary for all birds, as they swallow particles of it which assist their digestion.

The *husk* is another malady of cage-birds, produced by cold; it is similar to a cough among ourselves, and when once caught is seldom cured, constantly troubling them. The only cure is keeping them warm, and giving them the food recommended when they have any other cold, as that of the surfeit cold just mentioned.

Excessive perspiration is another disease which attacks birds, particularly hen birds, which are sitting upon their eggs. Weakness is the principal cause, and to cure it, it must have nourishing food, such as egg and bread, and induced to take exercise; and the bird may be washed every morning in salt and water, applied at a heat about equal to that of milk; the birds must not have it applied cold, lest it should chill them.

The next disease is called the *pip*. This is known by a little bladder of whitish matter which forms near the vent of the bird, and may be seen easily if the feathers are blown up. To cure it, prick the bladder with a fine needle, and put a drop of salad oil to the place.

Dysentery and *diarrhœa* are very common among cage-birds, and should be treated, the former with a drop or two of castor-oil, and the latter with a lump of chalk to peck at, and a rusty nail in the water.

Sometimes the bird loses the feathers of the head and neck, and presents a most ungainly appearance. In such cases, rub the head with almond oil, and feed the bird for a few days on a mixture of lettuce, scalded bread, olive oil, and a sprinkling of maw-seed. Health will soon return, and at the next moult the bird will recover its lost plumage.

Fits.—Many birds are apt to fall down in a fit; if this should occur and there should be no apparent cause for it, you may pull a feather or two out of the tail, which will draw blood, and most likely recover him; or he may be plunged for a moment in cold water. He is then restored to the cage, and induced by every means to drink, and if he can be brought to take a single drop he immediately recovers; after this, a drop of spirits of nitre should be put into his water-glass for two or three mornings. If birds have repeated fits, nothing better can be done than giving frequently a little nitre in the water they drink.

MOULTING OF CAGE-BIRDS.

Moulting, or changing their feathers, is a natural operation with birds, which cannot be prevented, but which must be assisted by care and attention. Cold is the greatest danger to which they are exposed; in passing through this state, therefore, all draughts of air should be carefully guarded against. When the cages are open ones, or have much wire-work, they ought to be partly covered up with a cloth, or with paper, to keep the birds warm, and the cleaning of the cage need not take place more than once a week, though they must be carefully supplied with fresh food and water daily. A little saffron in their water, a little nourishing food, and the extra warmth occasioned by the covering to the cage, will soon restore the birds to a plumage more beautiful than that they cast off. The covering of the cage should not be cast off all at once, but gradually; it should then be cleaned thoroughly, and the birds have their ordinary food. They should, while moulting, be put in the sun for an hour or two, if the weather is fine and warm.

The first moult, which takes place in many birds when they are about three months old, is partial. The birds then throw off all their down and loose feathers, and produce their full plumage. The month of September is the general time for the moulting of old birds.

TO MAKE GERMAN PASTE.

This composition may be made in the following manner, of much better quality than that which is sold in the shops: Take four fresh eggs, boiled very hard, a quarter of a pound of white pease-meal, and about a tablespoonful of good salad oil—if the least rancid it will not do. The eggs must be grated very fine, and mixed with the meal and olive-oil, and the whole then be pressed through a tin cullender, to form it into grains, like small shot; it should next be put into a frying-pan, set over a gentle fire, and gradually stirred with a broad knife, till it be partially roasted and dried, the test of which will be its yellowish-brown color. All insect-eating birds may be kept upon this food throughout the year, except when they appear drooping and unwell, or at moulting-time, when a few meal-worms may be given to them twice or thrice a day.

THE BREEDING-CAGE.

The breeding-cage should be constructed of teak or mahogany, and be about four feet long, eighteen inches wide, and two feet high; and should be made to stand flat on the stand, or it may be hung up against the side-

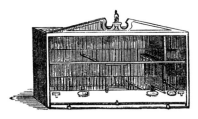

wall of a room. The back of this cage is of wood, and the sides, top, and front, of wire. It should have perches of various heights, for the birds to hop on, and boxes in the further right-hand corner for them to build in. The bottom should be provided with a slide to draw in and out, for the purpose of cleaning; and it should have drawers for food, and glasses for drinking from. At the proper time a net, filled with moss, hair, and other building materials, should be suspended from one of the top bars; and the whole should present a cheerful and comfortable appearance.

THE CANARY.

The **canary**-bird is a well-known captive songster. It is a native of the **Canary** Islands, and in the wild state its prevailing color is brown, mingled, however, with other colors, but never equalling the beautiful yellow exhibited by the captive bird. Dr. Heincken, who describes its character and habits in Madeira, where these birds abound, says it builds its nest in thick bushy, high shrubs and trees, with roots, moss, feathers, hair, &c. It pairs in February, lays from four to six pale blue eggs, and hatches five, and often six times in the season.

LONG AND SHORT BREED.

In pairing the birds, two birds should be matched which are strong and vigorous; this should be done about the middle of April. The cock and hen may at first be put together in a small cage, to pair them; after which they may be turned out into the proper breeding-cage. After the hen has laid, and while she is sitting, both birds may be fed with groundsel, having seed on it, and afterward chickweed with seed on it. When the young are hatched, let the old birds have plenty of soft as well as other food.

The time of sitting is thirteen days, during which the hen is waited on by her mate with the greatest care and attention. After the eggs have been sat upon for seven or eight days, it may be as well to examine them. Take them gently between your finger and thumb, and hold them before the flame of a candle. If they appear quite clear you may as well throw them away, as they will never come to any thing. If the egg be filled with a sort of network of fine red threads, you may rest satisfied that a bird will be hatched from it. Hen canaries will frequently eat their eggs. The only way to prevent this is to replenish the food-box over night, as the first thing the hen does after laying an egg is to see about her breakfast. If she does not find it she may get into a rage, and destroy all the eggs she has laid. If, however, your canary be an incorrigible egg-smasher, you had better purchase half a dozen ivory eggs, and each time she lays, the genuine egg must be removed and a fictitious one substituted. When she has done laying, you must restore to her her eggs and chance all the rest. If you store eggs in this way, it is best to keep them in a warm corner in dry silver sand. If possible, however, it is much the better plan to leave the birds to their own devices; indeed, if you should have a hen that cannot be trusted with her eggs, you had better get rid of her.

At the expiration of the thirteen days, the birth of as many little canaries as there were eggs in the nest will reward your care. Then boil a chicken's egg till it is hard, cut it up fine, and add to it part of a roll that has been soaked for a few minutes in water and then squeezed dry. With this mess, the birds (or rather the cock-bird, for on him the duty of feeding the children devolves) will feed the little ones. Never mix more than a tablespoonful of this food at a time, for if it is allowed to go the least sour, you will certainly have to mourn your young canaries.

If through some accident the little birds should be left orphans, it is possible to bring them up by hand. Keep the nest as warm as possible; grate up a plain biscuit, and pound some hempseed; mix the two together, and, moistened with a little raw yolk of egg and water, drop morsels into their gaping mouths with the end of a quill. This must be done once *every hour*, from six in the morning till six in the evening. The quantity administered to each at a meal should not exceed the third of a teaspoonful.

In a fortnight the young birds will be able to shift without their parents, and to feed themselves. When they are a month old you may take them out of the breeding-cage. Do not, however, entirely discontinue the soft food. It should, for at least five weeks longer, be mixed with the usual food of old birds. A sudden substitution of solid food for the softer sort may occasion constipation and death.

The canary is a justly favored pet among boys, for it is a hardy bird, that requires very little trouble; it is a pleasant, fascinating little being, full of quaint ways and sprightly attitudes, and, better than all, the cage is its native element.

Though an ardent admirer of all birds, and indeed of every thing which draws the breath of life, we can never pass the cage wherein is confined a mocking-bird, a thrush, an oriole, or any other of our indigenous birds, without a feeling of sadness and regret.

They are not cage-birds, and never ought to be confined within the narrow limits of wood and wire. Their attitudes show their uneasiness. The mellow, exultant tone of the mocking-bird sounds as joyously when the bird is imprisoned within a cage as when it soars high in air, its wings quivering in the breeze, its frame rejoicing in the glory of the sunbeams, and its ken surveying the wide panorama which lies spread beneath its gaze. But the gestures of the bird are full of eloquent misery, and speak volumes to him who will stop and listen with his eyes.

So with the generality of our cage-birds. The boy who would imprison the mocking-bird, who would limit to one spot the bird which loves to wander, and who would condemn to solitary confinement the creature which is peculiarly destined for conjugal affection, which finds expression in liquid melody, ought to be imprisoned for a month or two, just to see how he likes it. "I can't get out," is the lament uttered in silent gesture by all birds which ought to roam in wild freedom, and have been imprisoned in a cage.

But with the canary the case is different. The pretty little bird never has known wider freedom than that of the cage, and a humane bird-keeper will endow it with increased freedom by enlarging the size of its cage. The free use of wings has never been known to the bird, nor even to its parents; and the perch is to the canary more familiar than the bough. Release an imprisoned oriole, and after the first few moments of surprise it will speed away, exulting in its freedom. Release a bobolink or a thrush, and it will dart swiftly to the well-known shelter of the woods.

But release a canary, and you have committed an act of positive cruelty. The poor bird knows not where to go, or how to procure its food. Throughout all its little life, it has been accustomed to reside within the narrow limits of its cage, and to find its food and water prepared without any expenditure of labor. Consequently, it has no idea of searching for food, but sits bewildered on the branch of some tree, and would perish with hunger simply because it does not know how to procure food.

Ignorance is ever the parent of fear, and a canary-bird has been known to perish of hunger when removed from a small to a large cage, simply because it dared not fly down from the comparatively lofty perch on which it had settled when first introduced, and to which it clung with the tenacity of fear.

In canary keeping much depends upon the kind of bird. We presume that a good singer will be required, as well as a strong and healthy bird. If you are not learned in canary lore, try to induce an experienced friend to choose a bird for you; but if you are not fortunate enough to possess such assistance, the following concise directions may aid you. Look at the birds for sale, and note those that stand straightest on their perches, and that hop quickly and smartly about the little apologies for cages in which they are mostly confined. Next hear them sing before deciding on your purchase, and select the one that possesses the sweetest and fullest tone. The dealer can always make the bird sing when he likes, and if any bird refuses to sing, do not buy it, however handsome it may look.

When you are satisfied with the song, look the bird well over to see that it has no defects; and if you prefer the variegated breed, take care of three principal points—namely, the top of the head, technically called the "cap;" the markings on the back, called "spangles;" and the number of quill feathers in the wings and tail. The cap must be uniform and rich in color, the spangles bold and well defined, and the quill feathers not less than eighteen in each wing and twelve in the tail. Imperfect or damaged feathers can easily be replaced by pulling them out, for their places will soon be filled with new and perfect feathers.

Some persons prefer the yellow varieties, and many are fond of the crested canaries; others prefer the *long breed.*

The two secrets—if secrets they can be called—in bird-keeping are, a good supply of fresh food and water, and perfect cleanliness.

As to the general management of the canary, it may be summed up by saying that it chiefly consists in judiciously letting alone. Do not meddle with the birds more than is absolutely needed, and do not worry them with medicines whenever they seem to be unwell.

Be careful and protect your birds from insects.

One pest is vigorous throughout the year, and always ready to seize on the birds. We allude to the "red-mite," a parasite known to all bird-keepers.

If you find your birds restless, especially at night, and see them continually pecking among the roots of the feathers, and especially if they lose appetite, and become fretful and ill-tempered to their companions, look out for the red-mite. You can always detect the tiny but formidable foe by placing the bird in a dark room, and, after a few hours, holding a bright lamp close to the cage. If there are any mites about, you will soon see them crawling upon the perches, the wires, and even showing themselves among the feathers. They are not larger than the dot over the letter i, but their numbers are often very considerable, and the injury they inflict is great.

Let not one escape, for it may be the parent of hundreds more. When the red-mites have once obtained possession of a cage, their extirpation is a task of very great difficulty to those who do not understand the constitution of the creatures. So difficult, indeed, is the business, that many fanciers will not even attempt it, but burn the cage and buy another. The metal cages which are now so common, are preferable to those made of wood and wire, inasmuch as they present very few spots wherein the red-mite can find a hiding-place, and for that reason we prefer metal to wood. Even if they have gained admission to an ordinary cage, they can be extirpated without very much trouble. We have succeeded in doing so in several instances, and think that in a fortnight any cage can be freed of its troublesome parasites.

First, place the cage in the sun for a short time, so as to induce the light-hating mites to leave the bird and hide themselves in the crevices of the cage. Remove the bird and transfer it to another cage, or even a box, and let it wait. Take the cage and examine it well, introducing a heated needle or a thin blade of iron into every crevice. Next, take some insect-destroying powder, force it into a hollow paper cylinder, light the paper, put it into the cage, and envelop the whole in a newspaper. Leave it there for an hour, and when you remove it you will see dozens of the red-mites, of all sizes, lying dead on the floor, or clinging half-stupefied by the fumes of the powder. Scrape them all into boiling water, and dust the whole of the cage with the powder. By this time every mite will be dead, but there is a goodly store of eggs which will be hatched in due time, and infest the cage anew. These are destroyed by means of oil. Take a camel's-hair brush and some salad-oil, and with the brush apply the oil to every crevice. If there should be the tiniest scratch on the wood, touch it with the oil. Let oil be applied to every spot where the wires enter the wood, where they cross each other, and where the hinges of the door are fixed. Every egg will thus be destroyed, and the cage freed.

About half an hour before you restore the bird to the cage, hold it in the left hand, and dust it well with the powder, blowing up the feathers so as to get it well to the roots. Scatter some of the powder upon a piece of soft rag, and roll the bird in it, carefully binding down its legs and wings, under each of which a pinch of powder must be sprinkled. You can now attend to the head, which requires rather neat handling, as the powder is very apt to settle upon the eyes and to worry the bird. Let your feathered pet lie for half an hour in this beneficial bondage, and then replace it in the cage, scattering some powder upon the floor. The bird will shake its plumage sharply, and send a cloud of dust flying, and in a minute or two will begin to peck among the feathers and settle the plumage. The different aspect of the bird is then quite remarkable, for it exchanges the fussy, anxious, fretful moments for quiet ease, and even when it does peck among the feathers, it does so gently and deliberately, and seems quite another bird.

Canaries thrive best on a mixture of what is called canary-seed with rape. Take care, however, not to give too much of the latter. A little hemp should also be occasionally given, but not mixed continually with the other seed, as is the practice with some canary fanciers; for hempseed is a hot, stimulating food, and should therefore be cautiously administered when the bird seems to want a nourishing diet. Groundsel or chickweed should always be supplied to the canaries during the warm season of the year. Green meat altogether is not good for them; an occasional sprig of watercress, however, or a young lettuce-leaf, or a little dry sponge-cake, will not hurt them; but do not let them have these—which should be occasional delicacies—as regular articles of diet. A little hard-boiled egg will often set up a moping bird; but, as a general rule, plain food, renewed daily, and not administered in too great quantities, will be found best. Change the drinking water regularly every day, and when the bird is moulting put a sprig of saffron, or a rusty nail into the drinking vessel. Let the birds have a frequent opportunity of bathing, either from a bath fixed at the side of the cage for the purpose, or in a small shallow vessel placed on its floor. The practice of letting canaries out of their cage for an occasional flight must be indulged in with caution. Many a bird has escaped through some unnoticed aperture, and many another has met an untimely death on the bars of the grate; indeed, no bird should be allowed to fly about in a room in which there is a fire.

THE MOCKING-BIRD.

The mocking-bird is peculiar to this continent, and is an ornament of
the forests of the Southern, and some of the Northern States, where it
makes its appearance about the first of June, and begins nesting soon
after. This pet is without doubt one of the most wonderful of feathered wonders. Its imitations are not mere burlesques, and it will render
the melodious notes of the nightingale not less clearly than the bray of the
jackass. The Mexican name for this little creature is "the bird of four hundred tongues." "In extent and variety of vocal powers," says Wilson, "the
mocking-bird stands unrivalled by the whole feathered songsters of this or
perhaps any other country. Its plumage, though none of the homeliest, has
nothing gaudy or brilliant in it, and, had he nothing else to recommend him,
would scarcely entitle him to notice. But his figure is well proportioned,
and even handsome. The ease, elegance, and rapidity of his movements,
the animation of his eye, and the intelligence he displays in listening to and

laying up lessons from almost every species of the feathered creation within his hearing, are really surprising, and mark the peculiarity of his genius. To these qualities we may add that of a voice full, strong, and musical, and capable of almost every modulation, from the clear and mellow tone of the wood-thrush to the savage scream of the bald eagle. In measure and accent he faithfully follows his originals; in force and sweetness of expression he greatly improves upon them. In his native groves, mounted on the top of a tall bush or half-grown tree, in the dawn of the dewy morning, while the woods are already vocal with a multitude of warblers, his admirable song rises pre-eminent over every competitor."

Nothing comes amiss to the mocking-bird—the bark of a dog, the tremulous quavering of the canary, the creak of a wheel-barrow, or the soft cooing of the wood-pigeon. In a domesticated condition, however, the mocking-bird's chief characteristic renders it impossible that he should be regarded as a sober chamber musician. For a while he will be content with his own natural melody, which consists of from two to six short full notes, but the least noise is sufficient to disturb the flow of his natural melody, and one suggestion giving rise to another, you presently hear a Babel of bird music almost impossible to bear. "His imitations of the brown thrush," says a well-known naturalist, "are frequently interrupted by the crowing of cocks; the exquisite warblings of the bluebird are by no means improved by the screaming of swallows or the cackling of hens; the shrill reiterations of the whip-poor-will are introduced into the simple melody of the robin. The uninitiated look around for the original, and then find that what appeared to be the product of a number of performers is really that of the single bird before us."

So jealous is the mocking-bird of its nest, that should it be too closely approached, it will destroy the entire structure, and at once forsake the neighborhood. It is even asserted that if the eggs should be hatched, the hen will, under such circumstances, kill her naked little brood and then decamp. However this may be, it must not be regarded as arising from want of affection, as no bird is more courageous than the mocking-bird in defence of its young. Should a boy attempt the nest, it will attack his face and hands with the ferocity of the hawk; and even its enemy, the black snake, is not always victorious in its burglarious onslaught in a mocking-bird colony; fearless of the reptile's nimble fang, the birds will press about it, and, with the swiftness of an arrow, dart at it with their spear-like beaks.

The eggs of the mocking-bird are four and sometimes five in number, and of a deep blue, blurred with irregular brown patches. Two broods are usually produced each year, though, should the bird be robbed or disturbed during incubation, she will build and lay a third time. It should be stated, however, that Bechstein is of opinion that the parent birds rear only one brood in a season, which would tend to account for the scarcity of this curious bird. In its first plumage the young mocking-bird is of a dull yellowish-gray on the upper portions of the body, while the under portions are yellowish-white, the centre of each feather being streaked with brown. After the first moult, however, the bird's plumage assumes a blending of brown and brilliant yellow, which it wears ever after.

Audubon gives a most interesting account of the loves of these elegant birds, which, though we have not space to quote, we shall embody in our narrative. They often select the vicinity of the planter's house, where, surrounded by the richest scenery, and embowered amidst thousands of beautiful flowers, they build their nest. The female selects the spot, the male the while attending and aiding her in her choice. The golden orange, the beautiful magnolias and bignonias, the fig and the pear trees are inspected, and these quite close to the house; for the birds know that, while man is not a dangerous enemy, his dwelling is usually protected from strong winds, and therefore they fix their abode in its vicinity, perhaps in the nearest tree to his window; and so little suspicious are they of interference, that they often build them so low that you can see into them as you stand.

In a state of freedom, the principal food of the mocking-bird consists of insects, grasshoppers, and worms. Dewberries from the fields, and many kinds of our cultivated fruits, together with insects, supply the young as well as the parents with food. In winter, they chiefly subsist on berries, particularly those of the Virginia juniper (red cedar), wax myrtle, holly, smilax, sumach, sour gum, and a variety of others.

Successful attempts have been made to breed these birds in confinement, by allowing them retirement and a sufficiency of room. Those which have been taken in trap cages are accounted the best singers, as they come from the school of nature, and are taught their own wild-wood notes. The young are easily reared by hand from the nest, from which they ought to be removed at eight or ten days' old. Their food is thickened meal and water, or meal and milk, mixed occasionally with tender fresh meat, minced fine. Animal food, almost alone, finely divided and soaked in milk, is at first the only nutriment suited for raising these tender nurslings. Young and old require berries of various kinds, from time to time, such as cherries, strawberries, whortleberries, etc., and, in short, any kind of wild fruits of which they are fond, if not given too freely, are useful. A few grasshoppers, beetles, or any insects conveniently to be had, as well as gravel, are also necessary; and spiders will often revive them when drooping or sick. But, notwithstanding all the care and management bestowed upon the improvement of this bird, it is painful to reflect that his extraordinary powers of nature, exercised with so much generous freedom in a state of confinement, are not calculated for long endurance; for, after this most wonderful and interesting prisoner has survived six or seven years, blindness often terminates his gay career. Thus shut out from the cheering light of heaven, the solace of his lonely, though active existence, he now, after a time, droops in silent sadness and dies. At times, this bird is so infested with a minute species of louse as to be destroyed by it.

THE BROWN THRUSH, OR THRASHER

The brown thrush, as a songster, ranks next to the mocking-bird, and, like the latter, is a genuine American, being found in almost every part of the United States, from Canada to the shores of the Mexican Gulf, breeding, according to Mr. Nuttall, in all the intermediate space. The brown thrush is more brilliant in plumage than his rival, the mocking-bird: above, he is bright reddish brown; beneath, yellowish white; the legs are black, and the breast and sides are covered with arrow-headed dark-brownish spots.

The habits of this bird are much the same as those of the mocking-bird; but he is more of a Northerner, and occurs as frequently in Northern States as the mocking-bird does in the South. His voice somewhat resembles that of the European thrush, but is far more varied and powerful, rising pre-eminent amidst the forest choir.

On the first appearance of this bird in the spring, he falters in his song, like the nightingale; but when his mate commences the cares and labors incident to breeding and rearing her young, his varied and melodious notes are steadily poured out in all their vigor and strength. In the month of May, while the blooming orchards perfume the air and decorate the landscape, his enchanting voice, in his affectionate lay, seems to give grateful utterance for the bounty and teeming profusion of nature, and falls in pleasing unison with the harmony and beauty of the season; and even the young birds, in a state of solitary domesticity, without the aid of their parent's voice, already whisper forth, in harmonious revery, the pathetic and sweet warble instinctive to the species.

Deprived of other society, in a state of captivity, the brown thrush is exceedingly familiar, cheerful, and capriciously playful. He courts the attention of his keeper, follows his steps, complains when neglected, flies to him when permitted to be at large, and gratefully sings and reposes when perched on his hand. In short, in all his actions, he appears capable of real and affectionate attachment; but, like many other animals, he is jealous of every rival, particularly any other bird, which he drives from his presence with unceasing hatred.

According to Audubon, the natural food of this species consists of insects, worms, berries, and fruits of all sorts, being particularly fond of ripe pears and figs. In winter, they resort to the berries of the sumach, holly, dogwood, and shrivelled wild grapes.

In a state of confinement, these birds may be reared in the same manner, and on the same kind of food as their congener, the mocking-bird. In the autumn of the first season the young begin their musical studies, "repeating passages with as much zeal as ever did Paganini." By the following spring their lessons are complete, and the full powers of their song developed.

THE BALTIMORE ORIOLE.

This beautiful pet is familiar in all the orchards of the United States. The plumage of the male is exceedingly brilliant, the under parts being a bright orange yellow. Head, throat, back, and tail, black; legs and feet lead-colored. Its eggs are bluish white, with pale brown spots and lines, and it raises two broods in a season. Goodrich says: "These birds appear among us from their far Southern home in May; their arrival is hailed by young and old as the harbinger of spring and summer. Full of life and activity, these fairy sylphs are now seen glancing through the boughs of the loftiest trees, appearing and vanishing like living gems. The same curious fact exists in respect to them as in respect to many other birds; in the long migration from the South—often several thousand miles—the sexes have been separate; the males arrive several days before the females, not in flocks, but singly. At this time they fill the air with their notes, which, however, are shrill and plaintive, as if their joy was incomplete. Soon their partners arrive, and after many battles between the lovers, the pairing is completed, and amid frolic and song the nest is begun. This is usually the period when the apple-orchards are in bloom, and nothing can afford a picture of more enchanting and vivid beauty than these brilliant birds, in the midst of perfume and showering blossoms, sporting, singing, and rollicking— nay, sipping the honey and feasting on the insects, as if these bowers were all their own. At this time the notes of the male are often a low whistle, or now and then a full trumpet tone, one following the other in slow or rapid succession; even the female sings, though with less melody. Many of the notes of both are colloquial, and it is not difficult for a listener to fancy he hears questions and answers between the lively couple, with occasional side observations in various keys, indicative of approbation or reproach, admiration or contempt. If a dog or cat chances to approach the neighborhood of the nest, a volley of abuse, in a sharp rapid tone, is sure to be poured out upon the intruder." The nest of the oriole is a pendulous cylindric pouch, of five to seven inches in depth, usually suspended from near the extremities of the high drooping branches of trees, such as the elm, the pear, or apple-tree, wild cherry, weeping-willow, tulip-tree or buttonwood. The food of this little pet consists chiefly of flies, beetles, worms, and caterpillars. When domesticated it can be kept on meal and water with occasionally a piece of sweet fruit. The oriole is easily tamed, and is docile and playful in confinement. It has a turn for mimicry, and can be taught to imitate the notes of other birds.

THE SCARLET TANAGER.

The scarlet tanager is one of our most brilliant birds, and is better known to the woodsman than the frequenter of fields or parks. It arrives among

14

us from the South in April, and extends its migrations to Canada and even farther North. The plumage of the male is a bright scarlet, and the wings and extreme of the tail black. This gaudy sylph, as if conscious of its attractions, seeks to hide them in the thickest woods, where it rears its brood, and during this period the male delivers a highly musical song. The food of the tanager consists of worms, beetles, wasps, and other insects. It departs for the South early in September. This beautiful bird is a gaudy pet, but is difficult to domesticate.

THE BOBOLINK.

"The bobolink" has been called the harlequin of the meadows, and is one of the most garrulous of all the warblers that gladden our Northern springtime, and from the middle of May to the last week in June the meadows are ringing with his merry song. Perched upon the topmost bending branch of some little tree standing alone in the field, he takes his station or music-stand, and pours out his delicious melody, seemingly for the exclusive delectation of himself, and surrounding nature secondarily, as represented in assembled clover-blossoms, buttercups, and wild daisies. Anon, with a sudden start, he flutters skyward with increased volume of song, as if struggling for further inspiration, until his notes are almost lost in the distance. Quickly he sweeps down again upon the tree-top, as if overcome with ecstasy at his own music.

"Of all the birds of our groves and meadows," says Irving, "the Bobolink was the envy of my boyhood. He crossed my path in the sweetest weather and the sweetest season of the year, when all nature called to the fields, and the rural feeling throbbed in every bosom, but when I, luckless urchin! was doomed to be mured up during the live-long day in that purgatory of boyhood, a school-room. It seemed as if the little varlet mocked at me as he flew by in full song, and sought to taunt me with his happier lot. Oh, how I envied him! No lessons, no task, no hateful school; nothing but holiday, frolic, green fields, and fine weather. Further observation and experience have given me a different idea of this little feathered voluptuary, which I will venture to impart for the benefit of my school-boy readers, who may regard him with the same unqualified envy and admiration which I once indulged. I have shown him only as I saw him at first, in what I may call the poetic part of his career, when he in a manner devoted himself to elegant pursuits and enjoyments, and was a bird of music, and song, and taste, and sensibility, and refinement. While this lasted he was sacred from injury; the very school-boy would not fling a stone at him, and the merest rustic would pause to listen to his strain. But mark the difference. As the year advances, as the clover blossoms disappear, and the spring fades into summer, he gradually gives up his elegant tastes and habits, doffs his poetical suit of black, assumes a russet, dusky garb, and sinks to the gross enjoyments of common, vulgar birds. His notes no longer vibrate on the ear; he is stuffing himself with the seeds of the tall weeds, on which he lately swung and chanted so melodiously. He has become a 'bon vivant,' a 'gourmand;' with him now there is nothing like the 'joys of the table.' In a little while he grows tired of plain, homely fare, and is off on a gastronomical tour in quest of foreign luxuries. We next hear of him, with myriads of his kind, banqueting among the reeds of the Delaware, and grown corpulent with good feeding. He has changed his name in travelling: Boblincon no more, he is the *Reed-bird* now, the much sought for tidbit of Pennsylvania epicures; the rival in unlucky fame of the ortolan! Wherever he goes, pop! pop! pop! every rusty firelock in the country is blazing away. He sees his companions falling by thousands around him.

"Does he take warning, and reform? Alas, not he! Incorrigible epicure! again he wings his flight. The rice-swamps of the South invite him. He gorges himself among them almost to bursting; he can scarcely fly for corpulency. He has once more changed his name, and is now the famous *Rice-bird* of the Carolinas.

"Last stage of his career; behold him spitted with dozens of his corpulent companions, and served up a vaunted dish on the table of some Southern gastronome.

"Such is the story of the bobolink; once spiritual, musical, admired, the joy of the meadows, and the favorite bird of spring; finally, a gross little nsualist, who expiates his sensuality in the larder. His story contains a noral worthy the attention of all little birds and little boys, warning them to keep to those refined and intellectual pursuits which raised him to so high a pitch of popularity during the early part of his career; but to eschew all tendency to that gross and dissipated indulgence which brought this mistaken little bird to an untimely end."

The bobolink is black; head and rump white, tinged with yellow. They feed upon crickets, grasshoppers, spiders, and seeds of various kinds.

The young may be easily domesticated, and thrive well upon the seeds for canaries.

He will quickly learn the notes of the canary, and, by breeding together, produce a fine songster.

THE YELLOWBIRD.

The "yellowbird," or "American goldfinch," is one of the few birds we have with us all the year round. It feeds on oily seeds, particularly of the sunflower, lettuce, thistle, &c. His nest is made on small trees or tall bushes. The plumage of the male is quite brilliant. He can be easily domesticated, and takes readily to the food of the canary, and being capable of learning many tricks, is an agreeable pet.

In confinement, the yellowbird soon becomes familiar and reconciled, its song being nearly as animated and sonorous as its transatlantic congener. According to Mr. Audubon, it is extremely hardy, often remaining the whole winter in the Middle States, and, when deprived of liberty, will live to a great age in a room or cage. "I have known two instances," says he, "in which a bird of this species had been confined for upwards of ten years. They were procured in the market of New York, when in mature plumage, and had been caught in trap cages. One of them having undergone the severe training, more frequently inflicted in Europe than America, and known in France by the name of *galérien*, would draw water for its drink from a glass, it having a little chain attached to a narrow belt of soft leather fastened round its body, and another equally light chain fastened to a little bucket, kept by its weight in the water, until the little fellow raised it up with its bill, placed a foot upon it, and pulled again at the chain until it reached the desired fluid and drank, when, on letting go, the bucket immediately fell into the glass below. In the same manner, it was obliged to draw towards its bill a little chariot filled with seeds; and, in this distressing occupation, was doomed to toil through a life of solitary grief, separated from its companions wantoning on the wild flowers, and procuring their food in the manner in which Nature had taught them."

THE BLUEBIRD.

The bluebird, or blue robin, as it is sometimes called, resembles very much in manner the "robin redbreast" of Europe, and is hailed with us as the first harbinger of spring.

They sometimes hibernate in the Northern States, by seeking out some sheltered sunny spot; but this is a very rare occurrence. They make their appearance early in March, and leave late in autumn, going as far as Mexico. The bluebird is very prolific, laying from four to six blue eggs, and raising several broods in the year. They usually select a nesting-place near the house, and in any sheltered crevice. We have often seen them nesting in old rail-holes in fence-posts.

They will also appropriate the little boxes which have been nailed up for the martins, and frequently contest with the wrens for lodgment in them. In summer they feed upon insects, changing in the autumn for cedar-berries, wild cherries, &c. They can be quite easily accustomed to the cage, and become agreeable pets.

THE REDPOLE.

This beautiful little bird is found in both the Old and New Worlds. It is a hardy northern species, inhabiting even Lapland and Greenland, and is a permanent resident of the fur countries. In winter, numbers of them migrate southward, proceeding in the United States as far as Pennsylvania.

Its winter haunts are those spots which abound in alders, on the seeds of which, as well as on those of the fir and the berries of the ash, it delights to feed. Linseed and rape are also a favorite food with it.

It is subject to bad feet, sometimes losing its toes, which drop off one after the other. This is a beautiful bird when in full plumage, the rump, under side of the neck, and breast being a rosy red color, and the vertex a bright crimson; across the wings are two transverse bars of white, clouded with rusty yellow, which is the color of the beak. In the female the tints are paler, and the red on the breast is wanting, as well as on the rump, except in very old birds, which have a slight tinge in these places. The males of the first year also want the red breast, but they may be distinguished from the adult hens by the rusty yellow markings and a darker brown on the back.

In consequence of their docility, they have been taught to perform a great many tricks, to come and go at command, to draw up water, go up a ladder, to fall down as if dead, &c. Their food is rape and canary-seed, and they are fond of groundsel, plantain, and seeded chickweed; they may also be occasionally treated with a few grains of hempseed.

THE EUROPEAN BLACKBIRD.

Being a permanent resident throughout the whole of the Old World, even as far north as Sweden, the European blackbird is sufficiently hardy by nature to withstand the climate of nearly, if not all parts of the United States. Of all the thrushes, with perhaps the exception of the American robin, he is the most capable of instruction. His song is rich in melody, and contains some deep notes like those of the nightingale, varied indeed with some that are disagreeably harsh. At large, he sings only from March to July, especially at night; but in the cage, during the whole year, except at moulting time. A single bird will enliven a whole street, so pure, distinct, and clear is his note. His memory, also, is so good, that he will learn several airs and melodies without mixing them; and sometimes even to imitate words. Neither does he forget what he has once well acquired.

When wild, the blackbird, like other species of thrush, feeds on all kinds of edible berries, such as the elder, cherry, and mountain ash; and when this food is not abundant, it satisfies itself with the tips of the white thorn. At this time it often seeks for insects in the vicinity of warm springs.

In confinement, these birds will eat bread, meat, and most kinds of food that comes to table. The young, which must be taken from the nest when their quills have but just sprung, can be reared upon roll steeped in milk.

The blackbird should be kept in a large cage, for it is not prudent to allow it to associate with other birds, as, either through covetousness or caprice, it will attack the smaller kinds, and even peck them to death. Like all the allied species, this bird is fond of frequent bathing, and consequently should be amply supplied with the means. In captivity, he will live from twelve to fifteen years, especially if his food be varied.

THE BLUE JAY.

The American blue jay is a very handsome bird; on his head he wears a crest of light blue, and the upper portions of his body are of a light bluish purple. The chin, cheeks, and throat are bluish white, while the abdomen is pure white. The wing-coverts are of rich azure, barred with black streaks, and tipped with white. The middle feathers of the tail are light blue, deepening into purple towards the tips, and the remaining feathers are light blue, barred with black and tipped with white.

The blue jay is a great scamp, and robs the nests of other birds, frequently feeding upon their young.

As an imitator of voices and sound, the blue jay is unequalled, and will, with equal fidelity, utter the softest and most musical notes, or the harsh screaming of the hawk. Indeed, in the latter performance it seems to take an especial delight, and, true to the mischievous character of the family, will sometimes break out into the loud scream of the hawk, to be immediately followed by the tiny wailing of a bird in distress, at once putting all the little songsters in the neighborhood into terrible commotion.

The negro slaves in the Southern States regard this bird with singular superstition. They believe the jay is the special agent of the dark gentleman below, and that it carries all manner of slanderous tales to him, especially concerning "niggers," and also supplies the fuel to burn them with. Hence they are regarded with deadly animosity by the blacks.

Says Webber, "When I was a boy, I caught many of them in traps during the snows, and the negro-boys, who generally accompanied me on my rounds to the traps, always begged eagerly for the jay birds we captured to be surrendered to them, and the next instant their necks were wrung, amidst shouts of laughter."

As to diet, the blue jay is not a strict vegetarian, but devours more animal food than any thing else. Still it is very partial to fruit and nuts, as the agriculturist often finds to his cost. It will, if captured young, become very domesticated and attached to its owner, and will readily learn to talk, which acquisition it is very fond of displaying to strangers.

THE CROW.

This is an amusing fellow, who is frequently caught when young, and tamed. He has a great many amusing tricks, and may be taught a few words, with patience. He is a great thief, however, and, like the English magpie, hides many trifles in out-of-the-way places. He is fed on corn and peas, with occasional scraps of raw meat. The crow, jay, mockingbird, and oriole are all mimics, and to some degree talkers, but in the latter respect they will not compare with the parrot tribe, which we will hasten to describe.

MEDITATION.

TALKING-BIRDS.

FOREMOST among Talking-birds are the Parrots—a most numerous, splendid, and highly characteristic family of birds, subdivided into several groups, chiefly according to the form of the bill and tail; as the macaws, cockatoos, lories, paroquets, &c. The greater part are tree-birds, belonging to the order of climbers. The foot of the true parrot is a grasping rather than a walking one, and partakes more of the nature of a hand than of a foot. They all unite great beauty with great docility, and their facility in imitating the human voice is greater than that of any other bird.

Parrots inhabit principally the luxuriant tracts of the torrid zone, but are not exclusively confined to it, and are found in latitudes as far as forty or fifty degrees north and south of the equator. They are almost exclusively vegetable feeders, and the kernels of fruit and the buds and flowers of trees are their principal food.

In the natural state, many of them are social birds, often issuing from the trees in large flocks, and laying the cultivated fields under severe contributions. Social birds are almost always capable of being tamed, nearly in the same ratio as they are sociable; and this is particularly true with regard to parrots, who may be trained to do almost any thing; and they show great attachment to those who feed them and are kind to them. They also suffer less from confinement than most other birds, because their habit of climbing enables them to take a great deal of exercise in a small space. They are long-lived birds, and some have been known to attain the age of eighty years. Both cock and hen birds are equally gifted with the power of speech. As regards beauty, however, the cocks claim the advantage.

14*

MACAWS.

The macaws are not among the best talkers. They have the bill rather short, but of great power. The upper mandible is very much hooked, with the lip descending far over the under one. In a wild state, they nestle in

the holes of trees. They are particularly distinguished by having their cheeks destitute of feathers, and their tail feathers long. They are all natives of the tropical regions of South America, where they perch upon the summit of high trees. The scarlet macaw is one of the most splendid with regard to color, as well as size; for, from the top of the bill to the extremity of the tail, some have been known to measure more than a yard. Its color is, for the most part, of a beautiful scarlet; the quill feathers, externally, of a bright blue, and on their under side of a faint red; the first feathers next the quills are of a bright yellow, some of the feathers being tipped with green. Other parts of the body are of a fine blue, and the longest feathers of the tail are entirely red.

BLUE AND YELLOW MACAW.

The blue macaw, or the blue and yellow macaw, is less common than the red macaw, but little inferior in point of size. The feathers on the head of this bird are green, gradually becoming blue on the neck; the upper side of the neck, the back, and upper sides of the wings and tail, are of an exceedingly fine olive color. All the blue feathers of the back, wings, and tail, are of a reddish yellow on their under sides. The forepart of the neck,

the breast, belly, thighs, and covert feathers under the tail, are of a fine yellow orange color, as are the covert feathers withinside. The legs and feet are nearly black.

THE GRAY PARROT.

This species is remarkable for its loquacity, docility, and distinctness of articulation. It is about the size of a pigeon, and in length about twelve inches. Its color is an elegant ash gray, deeper on the upper parts, and more inclinable to white underneath; the whole of a sober color, having a very elegant appearance. The tail is of the brightest crimson, the temples, or orbits of the eyes, bare and white, the bill black, and the legs cinerous. It is said to live to nearly a hundred years; and the facility with which it can be taught, not only to speak, but to repeat sentences, is scarcely credible.

THE GREEN PARROT.

This beautiful bird is rather larger than the common gray parrot. Its plumage is a fine green, the feathers edged with purplish brown, in the front; all round the base of the bill is bright red, the cheeks deep blue, and the top of the head yellow; the edge of the wings at some distance beyond the shoulders is red; all the quill feathers and wing coverts deep or dusky blue. The outside feather on each side the tail deep blue, tipped with yellow; the next feather red, with a similar yellow tip; and all the remaining ones green, with yellow tips; the bill pale, and the legs and feet dusky.

PAROQUETS, OR PARRAKEETS.

These belong to the parrot tribe, but are much smaller in size, and have longer tails. There are numerous species, the most beautiful of which is the song paroquet, which is not more remarkable for its beauty of form and gracefulness of movement than for its docility and imitative powers. It is about the size of a common pigeon, and its general color an elegant bright green above, paler or yellower beneath. It has a moderately broad black band or stripe round its neck, and a red collar, near half an inch in width, but narrowing as it passes forward, immediately beneath the black one, almost reaching the front of the neck. The bill is of a bright orange color, inclining towards red; the tail feathers often of a bluish tinge; the legs ash-colored. The Ringed Parrakeet is frequently seen domesticated in this country, where its pleasing manners and gentle disposition render it a general favorite. It soon learns to repeat words and short sentences, and to speak with tolerable distinctness.

THE CAROLINA PARRAKEET.

This parrot is peculiar to North America, and is indeed the only bird of the species found there. It is met in the United States as far north as Lake Michigan, but on the east coast does not extend beyond Maryland.

Not the least singular fact connected with the Carolina parrakeet is, that, being of a family otherwise so exclusively confined to the hottest regions of the tropics, it should be discovered at such an immense distance from what has been designated its natural home. That it is not a bird of passage is evident, as it has been seen in great flocks on the shores of the Ohio as late in the season as February. Various attempts have been made to account for the existence of such eminently hot-climate birds in a region where, at certain seasons of the year, ice and snow prevail, but among them all the following seems most feasible. "It is not to be ascribed to a milder climate prevailing in these parts, so much as to the existence of certain peculiar features of country, to which these birds are particularly and strongly attached. These are low, rich, alluvial bottoms, along the borders of creeks, covered with a gigantic growth of sycamore-trees or button-wood; deep and almost impenetrable swamps, where the vast and towering cypresses lift their still more majestic heads; and those singular *salines*, or, as they are called, *licks*, so regularly interspersed over that country, and which are regularly and eagerly visited by the parrakeets."

The Carolina parrakeet averages about fourteen inches in length from the base of its beak to its tail tip. The ground color of the bird is vivid emerald green dashed with purple and blue. The forehead and cheeks are orange red, and the rest of the head and neck gamboge. The body and under parts are a delicate yellowish green. The tail is green, tinged with orange red. The beak of this parrakeet is rounded and very hard and strong, and if it gets a fair chance to bite, you may depend it will not neglect it. ·

In a natural state the parrakeets of Carolina are exceedingly sociable and kind one to another. They fly in large flocks, and roost in companies thirty or forty strong in the inside of a hollow tree, or other convenient shelter.

COCKATOOS.

Cockatoos are distinguished from true parrots, although they belong to the parrot family, by a crest or tuft of elegant feathers on the head, which they can raise or depress at pleasure. They are, in general, natives of Australia and the Indian Islands, inhabiting the woods, and feeding upon seeds and fruits. They make their nests in decayed trees; and, if taken at an early age, are easily tamed. There are several varieties of the cockatoo, of which the broad-crested or great white cockatoo is the most common. It is about the size of a common fowl; the color white, with a faint tinge of rose-color on the head and breast, and of yellow on the inner wing and tail feathers. The head has a very handsome crest of long feathers, which are of a fine scarlet underneath, and cover the whole head. The orbits of the eyes are bare and of a deep ash color; the bill is of a bluish black, and very strong. It is of a mild and docile disposition, but can rarely be taught any other words than its own name.

The Great Sulphur-crested Cockatoo is somewhat larger than the above; its color is white, slightly tinged with yellow on the sides of the tail and about the wing coverts; and it has a longish tail. The small sulphur-crested cockatoo is much smaller, but is much like the above; its crest is sulphur color, and it has in addition a large yellow spot beneath each eye; the bill black, and the legs deep lead color. It is a native of the Molucca Islands.

MANAGEMENT OF PARROTS, ETC.

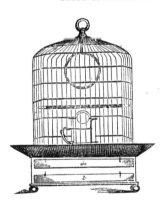

All the varieties of parrots require great care and attention. Their cages should be commodious, strong, and comfortable. The perches should be thick in the middle, and conveniently placed for the bird to exercise himself upon without injuring his feathers. Besides the perches, there should be hung, quite clear of them, at the top of the cage, a ring or hook, freely movable, upon which the bird can take exercise, and roost at night; and the grasping part of this should be of the requisite thickness for the size of his hands or claws. Unlacquered brass wire is frequently used in the construction of parrot cages, but this is an error which has caused many a fine bird's death. It is impossible to avoid the accumulation of verdigris on this metal, and this the bird will peel off. Although the effects of the poison may not be manifest for some time, even for a year, the bird's constitution will be gradually undermined, his body will waste, and he will die. Let the cage be constructed of tin wire. Attached to the perch, one at each extremity, should be the food and drinking vessels. They may be made of glass or porcelain. The floor of the parrot cage should be well covered with coarse red sand, and the cage itself should be cleaned out every day in the summer, and twice a week in the winter. Some prefer to do without the cage altogether, and to attach the bird to an open perch fixed to an ornamental stand. When this is done, care should be taken that a slight metal chain should be used for the purpose, as any less durable material would speedily be bitten through by the parrot's powerful beak. One of the most tiresome maladies from which birds of the parrot family suffer is diseased feet. Not only is it unsightly, causing the poor creature to squat down in an ugly manner, but the pain is sufficient to spoil the temper of the most amiable parrot that ever lived. In nine cases out of ten, the sore feet are occasioned by some fault in the perch. It is not kept clean, or it is merely a straight round stick. This latter shape should be avoided. Let the perch be at least a third  bigger in the middle than at the ends, tapering gradually. This will afford the bird considerable ease, and tempt him to change his footing.

The macaw cage should be cylindrical, and at least three feet and a half in diameter, and six feet high. Unless the blue macaw has at least this space for exercise, he will speedily get diseased feet, and be liable to fits. Its excrement is particularly offensive, and should be removed at least twice a day. He is fond of bathing, and if not indulged with plenty of water for this purpose, his close plumage will soon swarm with parasites. When this is the case, the bird should be well syringed with a solution of white precipitate, and furnished afterward with a tepid bath, as the precipitate is poison, and might be pecked off by the bird if allowed to remain.

TRAINING, FOOD, AND DISEASES.

There can be no doubt that the best way to win the affections either of a reasoning or an unreasoning animal is to treat it with gentleness. This is true as regards all grades, from the Indian savage to the performing canary. Approach them with harsh or threatening gestures, and Nature will immediately prompt them to stand on the defensive ; approach them with a soft word and kind look, and they are, if not at once subdued, ready to listen to any thing you are about to say or do.

This is particularly true of the parrot. You may depend on it, the impression you make during the first three or four interviews will be lasting, whichever way it tends. As a rule, parrots will learn quicker from women than men, and quicker still from children. Vieillot had in his possession a gray parrot which he never dared approach without having his hands covered with leather gloves, and yet the bird was in all respects obedient to Madame Vieillot. He further states that a female of the same species was, on the contrary, peculiarly attached to himself and indifferent to the caresses of his wife.

We believe the very best way to teach all birds to speak is to keep quite out of sight while you are giving a lesson. We know of nearly a dozen birds of various sorts who have been educated on this principle, and who in a miraculously short time have turned out fluent talkers. As we have before observed, too much attention cannot be paid to the "linking together" of words forming any sentence you may wish them to learn. Let each word glide into the next as smoothly as possible. If you find that your bird experiences great difficulty in repeating a particular lesson, you had better not persist in teaching it at that time, as you may make him sullen or irritable.

The staple diet of the gray parrot, and indeed of every other sort, should be bread and milk. Parrot-fanciers cut a stale loaf into slices, lay it in a pan, and cover it with warm water. After it has soaked for a quarter of an hour, it is taken out, and squeezed as dry as possible. Then, enough of scalding milk is poured over it to moisten it without making it pappy. We were inclined to think that the first soaking in water was a mere economic trick to save milk, but it appears that a "mash" thus made will keep sweet much longer than that prepared entirely with milk. This food, however, may be varied very considerably. You may give them any sort of nuts or almonds (except of course the bitter kind), biscuit (without seed), cold boiled Indian corn, and almost any sort of fruit.

We have heard many persons complain that their parrots pluck out their feathers, giving themselves an unsightly appearance. The reason is simply this—they are allowed to eat animal food. Most parrots have a great relish for meat, and we are sorry to say most parrot-keepers are nothing loth to gratify the propensity. After a while the birds acquire so determined an appetite for this sort of food, that they pluck out their own feathers for the sole purpose of sucking the stems. Instances have been known of parrots stripping themselves of every feather within reach of their beaks. Desmarest, the French naturalist, states that he once saw a parrot who had plucked its body as clean as a chicken prepared for the spit. Yet during two very severe winters, this bird never ailed in the least, and always had a capital appetite and good spirits.

It should always be borne in mind that a bird's gizzard is to it what teeth are to us, and further, that the said machine can no more act unless attended to, than a mill can grind without mill-stones. Clean, coarsely sifted dry gravel should be supplied to the bird at least three times a week. Do not be tempted to neglect this replenishing because the parrot "has plenty of gravel" in its cage. It may have plenty, but you must allow him to be the better judge as to whether it is suitable. Do not argue the matter beyond this; brush out his house, and supply him with fresh mill-stones.

Some little care is requisite in the preparation of bread and milk for a parrot. It must not be sloppy. Not the least particle of what is left of the previous day's supply must be allowed to remain in the food-pot. It will indeed be as well, especially during the summer months, to *scald* out the food-vessel each day, and wipe it thoroughly dry. Looseness of the bowels is the commonest and most dangerous ill that parrot flesh is heir to, and nothing causes it sooner than sour food. By the by, avoid zinc food-vessels,—they are poisonous.

Another of the diseases to which parrots are subject, is asthma. This either arises from an undue allowance of heating food, or through cold. This last is a matter that requires special mention. A choice exotic bird should be carefully placed in the sunniest nook, and scrupulously screened from cold draughts; but these unfortunate natives of the hottest countries in the world are too often left hanging before open windows on chill autumn nights.

The symptoms of asthma are shortness of breath and a frequent disposition of the bird to gape. If the attack is but slight, it may be cured by altering the diet, taking care that a good portion of his food is of a moist and warm character. If the bird is very ill, make a stiff paste of boiling milk and wheat flour, and add to every table-spoonful half a dozen grains of cayenne pepper. Give him nothing else for at least three days.

Insufficient attention as regards cleanliness will induce bad feet. The bird's perch should be movable, and scraped and scalded at least once a week. The feet should be frequently cleansed with a piece of flannel and Windsor soap. A covered perch may be substituted for the bare one until the bird's feet heal. They are subject to a disease which seems much the same sort of thing as gout with us. The legs and feet swell, and the bird is unable to grasp its perch properly. Like gout, it is very difficult to cure, and the best remedy we know of is to place the bird in a smaller cage, and stand him up to the thighs in water,—two parts boiling and one part cold. Let him remain in this warm bath fifteen minutes, then take him out, dry his feet before the fire; do this daily. If he has sores on his feet, apply to them a little loaf sugar.

Scouring is caused either by a sudden change of diet or through taking sour fruit, or some other improper food. The symptoms are a drooping tail, a tenacious white excrement adhering to the feathers beneath the tail, and a general uneasiness exhibited by the bird. The hinder parts, which will be found to be much inflamed, should be anointed with palm-oil; rice-biscuit, crumbled with the yolk of hard-boiled eggs, may be given with advantage; also boiled Indian corn, with which a chilly has been cut up.

Diseased eyes may proceed from cold or improper food. When you see the rims red and inflamed, bathe them with a warm decoction of white hellebore. It is deadly poison, so be careful that the bird does not drink it.

Consumption is a disease by no means uncommon with birds of the parrot tribe. The symptoms indicative of this disease are ruffled plumage, hollow eyes, loss of appetite for all sorts of food except green; gouty appearance of the lower extremities, and prominence of the breast-bone. Let him have plenty of the best food proper for him. Two days in each week feed him on nothing but fresh bread and milk, in which there is mixed some hempseed; do not let the quantity of hempseed exceed a tea-spoonful for a day's consumption; along with the hempseed you may throw in a black peppercorn. Bechstein appears to think that water-cresses are a certain cure for consumption. He says, "The birds should be fed with the best description of their appropriate food. In birds which will eat vegetables we have always found this, and especially water-cresses, the surest remedy against consumption and waste." If treated according to the above directions as soon as the symptoms become manifest, the disease may be speedily eradicated.

Some parrots (especially the lories) are subject to fits. They will tumble off their perches, and after a few convulsive struggles lie as if dead. When this happens, squirt the coldest water you can get over its head. If this does not revive the bird, take him by the legs and dip him three or four times into a pan of cold water. If he should still remain insensible, pluck out a tail feather and lay him on the warm stones. If after this he does not recover, you may make up your mind if you will have him buried or stuffed. Parrots subject to fits should occasionally have administered to them a little spirits of nitre. Pour half a dozen drops on to their bread and milk. There is nothing more likely to produce fits than costiveness. You may know when a bird is so afflicted by his constant and useless efforts to relieve himself. A little saffron boiled in their milk will usually cure this, but if it does not, you should give the bird four drops of castor-oil. It is no easy matter to administer castor-oil to a full-grown and strong-beaked parrot unless you know how. The best way is to have a piece of hard wood or bone, about a quarter of an inch thick and three quarters wide: in the centre of this there must be a small hole; open the bird's beak, put in the piece of wood, so as to keep it open, put a quill through the hole in the wood, and pour the castor-oil through the quill.

Sudden changes in the weather, or want of proper care as regards warmth, will sometimes produce inflammation. The symptoms of this disease are melancholy and a disposition to go to roost while it is yet daylight. If you blow up the feathers of the belly, you will find the extreme parts much swollen and a multitude of tiny red veins showing through the skin. This is a dangerous malady, and should be seen to in time. If the bird's bowels are relaxed, give him, until he gets better, as much magnesia as can be piled on a dime. His diet should be bread and milk and maw seed. A little port wine in his water will do him no harm. As the magnesia will sink, you had better put it in a vessel so shallow that the bird will be sure to disturb and partake of it when he goes to drink. Some parrot-keepers cure their birds of relaxation by giving them Indian corn that has been boiled in rice-water.

Impure water, stale food, or want of sand, will produce surfeit. The head, and sometimes the back, becomes covered with angry sores, which discharge a humor of so acrid a character that wherever it runs it removes the feathers.   Dissolve a quarter of a pound of salt or half a pound of loaf sugar in a quart of spring water, and bathe the parts affected twice a day. Dry the sores thoroughly, and anoint them with Florence oil.   Their diet should be as simple as possible.   Rice-bread, scalded with milk, is the best food while the surfeit continues, and nothing else should be given, but keep the bird warm.

As we have already observed, through a foolish indulgence in animal food, parrots pluck themselves quite bald in places, and make themselves look extremely ugly.   The best thing to do is to bathe the bald parts with a strong pickle of salt and spring water, and to diet the bird strictly on bread and milk.   We have heard that if the bird be well syringed with diluted ox-gall it will cure him of this disagreeable habit, but we have never had an opportunity of trying the remedy.

During the moulting period, parrots require great care and attention. Sometimes considerable pain and difficulty attend the operation, and two or even three months will be thus miserably passed by the poor bird.   The only way in which you can aid him is by giving him extra nourishment and keeping him as warm as possible.   It is a good plan to cover the cage entirely with brown paper.   Add saffron to the bird's drinking-water, so that it is the color of pale sherry.   A biscuit (without seeds) soaked in milk, in which a few chilly pods have been boiled, is a good thing to give occasionally.

THE REARING AND MANAGEMENT OF PIGEONS.

THERE is nothing more delightful to the sensitive mind than the sight of a pair of turtle-doves. They are emblematical of enduring affection and constant attachment, and afford lessons of love to brothers and sisters; for this reason, the rearing and management of them is a delightful task to young persons, and the lessons they may learn in these labors are many and important.

Pigeons have been known from the earliest ages. The dove was consecrated to the goddess of beauty, and a pair of turtle-doves, or two young pigeons, were a mother's first offering among the chosen people of God. The use of the carrier-pigeon as a messenger, was celebrated by the poets of Arabia, Greece, and Rome. Ælian mentions that when Taurostheus was victor at the Olympic games, a carrier-pigeon bore the intelligence to his father with great rapidity; and Pliny relates that at the siege of Modena a correspondence was carried on by means of these birds between Decimus Brutus and Hirtius.

Pigeons live together in pairs, and when a cock and hen once form an attachment the union generally lasts, and the instances of faithful and enduring attachment between these birds are very many. The pigeon in a wild state breeds only once a year, but the domestic pigeons of the dove-cot will breed every month or six weeks, and when the weather is severe, and the fields are covered with snow, they must be fed. In fine weather, however, they will provide for themselves, and will amply repay the keeper for his trouble.

Whatever number of broods a pair of pigeons may bring up in a year, the hen never lays but two eggs before she sits. She then sits eighteen days, or twenty-one days from the laying of the first egg. Both the cock and the hen assist in the hatching: the hen usually sits from the afternoon till the following morning; the cock then takes her place, and sits while she goes out to feed and exercise herself, and generally keeps on the nest the greater part of the day. The young ones are usually hatched during the daytime.

When hatched, the young only require warmth for the first three days, a task which the female takes entirely upon herself; and she never leaves them except for a few minutes at a time, to take a little food. After this, they are fed for about ten days with a milky secretion prepared from the glandular coat of the crop, and regurgitated, and afterward with what the old ones have picked up in the fields and kept treasured in their crops.

This way of supplying the young with food from the crop, in birds of the pigeon kind, differs from all others. They have the largest crops for their size of any birds, and they have the power of distending the crop by use in such a manner, that, in one species in particular (see *pouter*), the bird's breast appears larger than its body. The numerous glands, assisted by the air and the heat of the bird's body, are the necessary apparatus for secreting the milky fluid before mentioned, but as the food is macerated, that also swells and becomes considerably diluted.

The dove-cot pigeons, like the rest of their genus, retire to their roost at a very early hour, but they leave it unusually late in the morning; and though they will perch on trees in the daytime, nothing will induce them to rest there at night. They are greatly attached to the cot of their choice; so much so that they are scarcely to be driven from it but by fire-arms.

THE DOVE-COT.

This may be made of any size and of various shapes.

In erecting a dove-cot, care should be taken to fix it in some quiet, secure spot; and a small one is very often formed from a wine-cask which has holes cut in its sides, and a small platform being made of woodwork before each in front, forms a resting-place for the birds to alight upon. The interior is apportioned into chambers by the carpenter, or any boy of common car-pentering ingenuity may readily do this. The cask is then elevated on a stout thick scaffolding pole, or what is better, the trunk of a straight tree, and being made perfectly secure, is very eligible for the live-stock to be therein congregated. In  arranging the internal chambers for the birds, these should be large enough for the birds to turn round in with ease; and if two holes can be allowed for each compartment for the egress and ingress of the birds, it will be of great advantage and comfort to them. The cot should be fixed in a warmish spot, out of the "blow" of cold east and northeast or northwest winds, and the pole upon which it is elevated should have a circular platering half-way up, to keep the cats and vermin from ascending. The top of the cask may be thatched or boarded, and should come well over the holes and sides of the cot.

Should the young fancier not be ingenious enough to construct such a dove-cot, which is one of the best we can recommend, he may content him-

self with one after the following fashion, which, with its compartments, may be fixed up against the south or southwest side of a stable, barn, or out-house. Here the birds generally do very well, but the outside should be well secured, and painted several times over with black paint, and the foot, or alighting places, slightly slanted, so that the water or rain may not lodge in them, but run off to the ground outside. This inclination of the footboards must, however, be very slight, or it will be disagreeable to the birds. The whole must be approached by a ladder, which ought not to be permanently attached to the cot, or it will be a means for the depredation of cats and vermin.

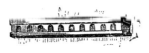

It sometimes happens that a spare loft or room presents itself to the young pigeon-fancier, which may be made use of for a pigeon-house. When this is the case, it can easily be filled up with long pigeon-boxes, which may be arranged round the sides. The means for exit and re-entrance must be first thought of, and if no window is in the loft, two holes must be made in the wall, at about five feet from the floor, each sufficiently large to admit a pigeon through easily. A shelf must also be fastened both inside and outside of these openings, and on the outside shelf a trap or aërie should be affixed, the intent and purpose of which we shall presently explain.

Perches may also be placed across the roof of the building, upon which

the birds may rest to preen themselves, as at A. The boxes may be arranged at the gable end and at the sides of the building, at the height of about eight feet from the ground, b, b, and a short ladder should be kept in the building, for the purpose of getting at them. The cells should be at least a foot square. In this arrangement, water may be constantly kept in a large clean pan, which should have some large stones put in it, to prevent the birds from splashing it about.

As to the compartments, or nests, every one must be furnished with a pan, box, or straw basket, of a size adapted to the pigeons for which they are intended; a small tile or flat piece of wood should be placed in front of the pan or basket, to assist the birds in getting out of their nests, and the pan should have a little clean straw or hay cut short within it. Sand or gravel should be sprinkled over the shelves and about the spot, as the small stones with which it abounds are useful to the birds in helping them to digest their food. Every thing about the birds should be kept very clean, and once a year the whole apparatus, of whatever kind it may be, should undergo a thorough purification, and the nest-pans or boxes should be well cleaned for every succeeding hatching. Care should also be taken to prevent other birds from visiting their nests, as they will suck or destroy their eggs.

PIGEON-TRAPS.

Pigeon-traps are necessary when persons are particularly solicitous regarding the admixture, and consequently the sporting of particular breeds. Stray birds will very frequently visit pigeon-houses, and, by associating with the birds, do them much injury. To se-cure such intruders, traps are necessary. One of the simplest is merely a square box of lath, the top part of which hangs nicely suspended by a hinge at its side, from which is carried a  projection called the lever, upon the end of which is fastened a piece of lead. The bird alights on the dark spot, which part of the trap falls, and conveys him into the interior of the cage in which the bait is placed. The balance weight of the lever immediately shuts the cage, and the bird is secured.

There is another contrivance of great use, which is employed for letting in those birds who may not happen to come home before the aëries are closed for the night. The object of this door, which ought to be called the "late door," is to let the *out* birds in without letting the in birds out. It is made by placing before a square aperture cut in the pigeon-house a couple of wires, about three inches apart from each other (as seen in the drawing), upon a piece of wood, having a swivel-hinge (A) above, and letting their lower ends come over the lower ledge or sill (B) on the inside of the dove-house. By this arrangement, when the late bird presses against the bars, and tries to get in, the whole opens  inward, and he easily enters; but if a bird from within tries to get out, the wires press against the side of the sill at the bottom, and effectually prevent his egress. The call, by which pigeons are enticed into their trap or house after they have been indulged with a flight, is a very shrill, loud, and prolonged whistle. They should be trained to come at this call invariably before they are fed.

The aërie before mentioned, which is fastened on the shelf outside the loft, is a trap made of laths; it has two sides and a front only, the wall of the loft forming the back; the front and sides act upon hinges, so that they may be thrown open and laid flat on the platform, as in the annexed figure A B C (Fig. 1), and on the upper parts of these flap-strings are fastened,

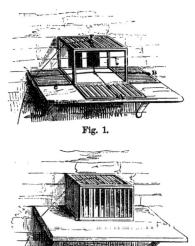

Fig. 1.

Fig. 2.

which are united to a single string in the middle of the trap; the string is carried over the swivel E, at the top of the machine, and thence to a hiding-place, from whence the owner can see all that passes; and when a bird alights within the aërie, he jerks the string, the flaps are elevated, and the bird is immediately a prisoner. (Fig. 2.) This kind of trap is used not only by fanciers, but by amateurs, and is an important appendage to the loft, both as a means of self-defence to secure strays, and to shut in their own birds; among amateur fanciers, the first-mentioned purpose is to secure valuable and favorite breeds from being deteriorated through stray birds of no value pairing with them.

Within the pigeon-house should be placed also two or three boxes for the grain, pulse, and beans to feed the birds upon. These should be made so

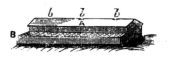

that the birds may be able to pick the seeds from them without scattering them about. This is easily prevented by placing over the tops of the boxes a covering of wire, the meshes of which are about half an inch square. The upper part (A) is a hinge top (b b b), which opens for the food to be placed in. The partition (B) is the feeding part of the apparatus, having the wire top, which prevents the seed being spilled about.

FEEDING.

Whenever pigeons are fed, they should be accustomed to come to their food at one particular call, and the best is that of a common pea whistle, which may be heard at a very great distance. By always using this when birds are brought to their food, they will come at your will, whenever you wish to bring them home, which is a very great advantage.

Pigeons are great devourers of food, and will eat any kind of grain, such as wheat, barley, oats, peas, beans, vetches, tares, buckwheat, hempseed. Small beans, called pigeon's beans, are the best general food for all pigeons, but this may be varied occasionally by mixing with it tares, gray peas, and buckwheat. The tares should, however, be very old and good, and the buckwheat should be sparingly given. Hempseed is very stimulating, and although pigeons are very fond of it, it should be sparingly given, except in very cold weather, when they may have an extra supply.

Pigeons are very fond of lime and salt, and sometimes do a great deal of mischief to houses, by pecking out the mortar from between the bricks. To prevent this, it is best to make them what is called a "cat," which will be exceedingly grateful to them, as it will tend to keep them in good health. This is made in the following manner:

Take sifted gravel, brickmaker's earth, and the rubbish of an old wall, half a peck of each; add to these a pound and a half of cummin-seed, a quarter of a pound of saltpetre; let these be mixed with as much natural animal brine as will make a stiff mass. Portions of this mixture may be put into strawberry pottles, or into old canvas bags, with holes in them, and hung about the grounds, where the birds can alight and peck at them; or some portions may be placed in flower-pots, and stationed in various situations where the birds can get at them easily.

DISEASES OF PIGEONS.

The diseases of pigeons are many. The principal, however, are the megrims, the wet and dry roup, and the canker. The megrims is a kind of nervous madness, in which the bird seems to have lost all control over itself, and flutters about wildly, with its head turned towards its back. The wet roup is attended with a discharge from the beak and nostrils, and may be treated by giving the affected bird a few pepper-corns daily, and a handful of green rue. The dry roup is a dry, husky cough, which may generally be cured by a few cloves of garlic every day. The canker is mostly caused by wounds made by the cock birds when fighting with each other, and is generally cured by rubbing the part affected with burnt alum and honey.

VERMIN.

Pigeons are often sadly annoyed by vermin, such as tick, lice, etc.; when once they get ahead, the whole brood will soon perish. The birds must frequently be looked at, and every thing of the kind taken from them. If they should be increasing, the best way is to fumigate their feathers by puffing tobacco-smoke into them. To prevent vermin, the most scrupulous attention should be paid to cleanliness, both in the birds themselves, and in every part of their houses, nests, and places of resort.

15

MATING.

Sometimes there is a little trouble attending the mating of pigeons, and it is of as great importance that they should be comfortably matched, as it is, that men and women should be properly married. To produce this desirable state of things, the coops should have only a thin lattice-work partition between them, so that the birds may make "acquaintance" with each other; they should also be allowed to feed out of the same vessel, and in a short time the young observer will find the birds selecting for themselves the bird of their choice, when they may be placed together in one pen. If they agree, of course they will be continued together, but if they should disagree and fight, a deed of separation must be drawn up. When the "loving couple" are properly mated, they may be left at liberty to arrange their own domestic affairs, and to build their nests, which they will do very readily.

MOULTING.

Sometimes the birds will suffer a good deal in moulting, and when they do not throw off their feathers freely, at the proper time of moulting, it is a sign that the birds are not in vigorous health. Such birds should be removed to a warm place; hempseed should be mixed with their food for a few days, and a little saffron should be placed in their water. Their tail-feathers may be also gently removed, and any other little office performed for them which the necessity of their case seems to call for.

COMMON PIGEONS.

BLUE ROCK-DOVE.

THE DOVEHOUSE PIGEON.

There are two very distinct varieties of the common pigeon, which are kept in large flocks for the supply of the table. Some naturalists regard them as separate species. The first is the blue rock-dove; the second is the dovehouse pigeon. Both are found wild, breeding independently in a state of nature; but the former affects caverns, cliffs, and rocks as its resting-place (whence its name); while the latter seems to prefer the inaccessible parts of public buildings, ruins, and ecclesiastical edifices—such a home, in short, as the jackdaw would choose. A very permanent difference between the two is, that the rock-dove has the rump, or lower part of the back, just above the tail, decidedly whitish, while the dovehouse pigeon has it of a light slate-color. This feature is particularly noticeable when the birds are flying, especially if they are in a flock of any considerable number, when it imparts quite a character to them as they are wheeling about. A reference to our engravings will help the reader to recognize the two varieties much better than any description could do. The general coloring of the dovehouse pigeon is considerably darker than that of the rock-dove. The distinction between them has long been known to dealers, less so to fanciers (who are apt to despise both these species, notwithstanding the exquisite beauty of the latter), and is scarcely acknowledged by ornithologists. The dovehouse pigeon is much the more common inhabitant of dove-cots, is less capricious in its sojourn therein, and, when it betakes itself to a state of complete independence, exhibits much less dislike to the neighborhood of man than is shown by the rock dove, under similar circumstances.

It is to be remarked that these two species are the only kinds of domestic pigeon which ever desert the homes provided for them, and betake themselves to the wilderness. The fancy pigeons, the truly tame pigeons, do not reassume, or rather adopt, wild habits, as has been asserted; when they lose their way, or escape from a new, and therefore a distasteful home, they do not betake themselves to the rocks, or to the ruins, but enter some trap or loft, or join some other flock of tame pigeons. The pigeons which do choose to return to a wild condition are always either blue rocks or dove-house pigeons, and not pouters, fantails, or runts; whereas the blue rocks do not voluntarily take up their home in an ordinary pigeon-loft, but, on the

DOVEHOUSE PIGEON.

contrary, will escape from one that is not to their liking, or is too much interfered with, even if hatched and brought up there by parents of a tamer breed.

The common pigeon requires very little care, and is exceedingly prolific, breeding seven or eight times a year. The female pigeon lays two eggs, which produce generally a male and a female. It is pleasing to see how eager the male is to sit upon the eggs, in order that his mate may rest and feed herself. The young ones, when hatched, require no food for the first three days, warmth being their only nourishment; they are then fed from the crop of their mother, who has the power of forcing up the half-digested peas which she has swallowed, to give them to her young. The young ones, open-mouthed, receive this tribute of affection, and are thus fed three times a day. The varieties of the domestic pigeon which follow have been produced by various crossings, etc., with different and parent stocks, some of which we shall now describe.

FANCY PIGEONS.

THE CARRIER.

The carrier-pigeon has been known from a very remote period, and has been employed as a messenger from the earliest ages. It is a larger bird than the common pigeon, measures about fifteen inches in length, and weighs about a pound and a quarter. The neck is long, and the pectoral muscles very large, denoting a power of vigorous and long-continued flight. An appendage of naked skin hangs across its bill, and continues down on each side of the lower mandible. According to its size and shape, the amateurs of carrier-pigeons estimate the value of the bird. They consider those pigeons the best that have the appendage rising high on the head, and of considerable width across the bill, and that are also distinguished by a wide circlet round the eyes, destitute of feathers. The sellers of these birds sometimes employ artificial means to produce these appearances, and torture the pigeons by introducing a small piece of cork, fastened by a bit of wire beneath the skin, to enlarge its apparent width.

The instinct which renders this bird so valuable is founded upon a very high degree of the *love of home* which it possesses. The mode of training them in Turkey, and which is the best mode to be followed generally, is this: The person who has the charge of rearing and training them watches for the arrival of the young pigeons at the full strength of wing, and then takes them in a covered basket to a distance of about half a mile from their home.   They are then set at liberty, and if any of them fail in returning home from this short distance, they are considered stupid, and are rejected as value-less.   Those that return home are then taken to greater distances, progres-sively increased from two to a thousand miles, and they will then return with certainty from the farthest part of the kingdom.   It is usual to keep these birds in a dark place for about six hours before they are used; they are then spar-ingly fed, but have as much water given them as they will drink.   The paper upon which the message is written should be carefully tied round the upper part of the bird's leg, but so as in no way to impede its flight.   When loosed, the bird usually soars high in the air, and after flying round in circles for a few times in succession suddenly darts in the direction of "home."

The usual speed of the carrier is about thirty miles an hour, or one thou-sand a day.

THE TUMBLER.

This pigeon derives its name from its habit of turning over, or "tumbling" in the air.   They rise to an immense height in the air, and generally, when commencing their upward flight, make a series of somersaults in the air, like the clown in a pantomime.   When in the blue empyrean, they will re-main on the wing for several hours in succession; and, when soaring in the air on a fine summer's day, the flight, tumblings, and antics of a flock of these pigeons is very amusing.

The finest variety of this pigeon is the *bald-pated tumbler*, from its having a snow-white head and pearl-like eyes; another is called the *ermine*, or *almond tumbler*, and is a very elegant and beautiful bird, and is distin-guished by the colors and marking of its feathers, in which it varies very considerably.

THE ERMINE, OR ALMOND TUMBLER.

The almond tumbler is said to be the result of cross-breeding between the various kites, such as blacks, whites, and cinnamons, and the various splashes, as myrtle-splash and cinnamon-splash.   Their form is the same as in other good tumblers, but their coloring must be a combination of at least three tints on each feather, if possible, so as to give the idea of the petal of a well-broken tulip, or a rich and polished fragment of breccia marble.

The most curious point about almond tumblers is the form which some of them have been brought to attain ; the whole thing, however, is very simple. The common well-bred tumbler, in its ordinary state, has a compact little body, with a round head, short beak, and neat little feet.   But this did not content some fanciers.   By pairing together birds in which these qualities were the most exaggerated, they got bodies still more compact, heads yet rounder, beaks shorter, and feet neater.

A third variety is the *black-mottled tumbler*, which is generally all black except about a dozen white feathers on the shoulders. A fourth is the *yellow-mottled tumbler*, which has a body mottled with white on a yellow ground, and with a yellow flight and tail; and many other individual varieties are constantly produced.

THE ERMINE, OR ALMOND TUMBLER.

Tumblers should be kept in a loft by themselves, and never suffered to mix with any other sort of pigeon, as they soon lose their peculiar habits of soaring and tumbling; they should be turned loose only once a day to take wing, and never on a very bright or clear day. A gray, clear morning is the best time for them to exercise. They should never be let out on a foggy or misty morning, for they may in such weather be irrecoverably lost; nor should they be out in windy weather. When their hours of liberty are expired, they may be enticed home by a little hempseed scattered round their usual places of feeding. A hen tumbler should never be let out to fly when with egg.

THE POUTER.

The pouter is a fine, handsome bird, distinguished by the peculiar size and form of the crop, which the bird is able to distend by filling with air. He measures, generally, about eighteen inches in length, and ought to have a fine hollow back, sloping gradually to the shoulders, to be prized. When the back is straight, or bows out, the bird is then said to be hog-backed. It ought also to carry its wings close to its body; and its legs, from the toe-nail to the upper joint of the thigh, should be at least seven inches in length, and well covered with downy feathers.

Pouters are difficult birds to rear, and the bringing them up is attended with considerable expense. Being very voracious, like the whole of the pigeon tribe, it requires great care to prevent their over-feeding. Every single bird should be kept in a separate coop, lofty and capacious; and when the young ones are hatched, as the old birds are apt to pay but little attention to them, they should be carefully watched. Some fanciers never suffer pouters to rear their own young, but put their eggs under a hen dragoon, which variety are good nurses.

THE POUTER.

The pouters most esteemed are the black-pied, the blue-pied, the yellow-pied, and the red-pied; but the colors are not of so much importance as the general shape of the bird, the hollow of its back, the roundness of the crop, the length and feathers of its legs, the mode of carrying its wings, etc. The front of the crop, however, should be white, surrounded with a shining green; and the head, neck, back, and tail, should be uniform in tint. Sometimes a pouter is unable to distend his crop handsomely; it is then called loose-winded, and considered a defective bird.

THE RUNT.

This is a short, full-breasted bird, with tail turned up. It has rather a long, thick neck in proportion to its other parts The beak is short, and it has a small wattle over the nostril. The plumage is generally grizzled, and ermine round the neck; but those most esteemed by fanciers are black, white, red, or mottled. The Leghorn variety is the most valued, and is a hardy bird; it breeds tolerably well, but is a bad nurse; hence their eggs are often shifted from the nest, and put under the hen horseman to hatch and bring up.

THE RUNT.

The Friesland runt is larger than the common runt, and it has a very odd appearance, from its feathers sticking out the wrong way. The Spanish runt is a short, thick-legged, ugly-made bird, with a very long body. The feather-footed or Smyrna runt has feathers growing from the outside of its feet. The Roman runt is large, thick, and unwieldy; and, upon the whole, none of these birds are pleasing to the eye, either as regards shape or color.

THE SPOT

Is a modern variety of pigeon. It derives its name from having, with a white head, a small pea-like spot on its forehead, just above the top of the beak, which is rather long and hooked.

THE BARB,

Or Barbary pigeon, was originally introduced from that part of the African coast; hence its name. It has usually a tuft of feathers sprouting from the back of the head. The plumage is generally dun, dusky, or black—darker on the wings. It has a short, thick beak, to which a small wattle is attached. The insides of its eyes are pearl-colored, and there is a circle of

15*

incrustated flesh round the eyes, of a red color, and the larger and more brilliant this is, the more the bird is prized by the fancier.

THE MAWMET.

The mawmet, or Mahomet, is supposed to be the kind of bird that whispered in the ear of the false prophet. It is a beautiful bird, of a cream color, having bars of black across its wings. The most remarkable thing connected with this bird is, that while the outer face of its feathers is of a pure cream color, the part next the body, its flue feathers, and even the skin, are sooty and black—very much like the Mohammedan religion, fair to look at, but foul underneath. It has a black wattle on its beak, and its eyes are surrounded by a small circle of black flesh.

THE DUTCH CROPPER.

This variety was originally brought from Holland. It has a pouch below its beak, stands wide on its legs, and is gravel-eyed. It seldom stands upright.

THE ARCHANGEL.

The archangel pigeon is both rich and unique in its coloring. The head, neck, and fore part of the back and body, are chestnut, or copper color, with changeable hues in different lights. The tail, wings, and hinder parts of the body are a sort of blue-black; but many of the feathers on the back and shoulders are metallic and iridescent—a peculiarity not usual in other domestic pigeons. The chestnut and blue-black portions of the bird do not terminate abruptly, but are gently shaded into each other. There is a darker bar at the end of the tail. The iris is very bright orange-red; the feet clean and unfeathered, and bright red. Archangel pigeons have a turn of feathers at the back of the head, very similar to that of the trumpeter. It is the coloring, rather than the form, which so specially distinguishes them. Their size is very much that of the rock-dove. They are sufficiently prolific to be kept as stock birds, and a flight of them is a particularly beautiful object; but they are at present too valuable, either as presents or for exchange and sale, to be consigned to the hands of the cook. Still, it is with the higher rather than the lower class of pigeon-fanciers that they are in much request, in spite of the bright and glowing hues with which their plumage is adorned. Their name is probably derived from their having been originally brought to us from the Russian port, or *via* Archangel from some other quarter, as Tartary, India, or the Chinese empire.

THE TRUMPETER

Is so called from the sound it utters after playing, which is thought to resemble the sound of a trumpet; which strange propensity in the birds is increased by feeding them with hempseed and other stimulating food. It is something like the Leghorn runt in size and appearance. It has a tuft

of feathers sprouting from the root of the beak, and the larger this is, the greater to the fancier is the value of the bird. The legs and feet are feath-

ered, and it is, in general, pearl-eyed; and, to be a valuable bird in the eyes
of its rearers, it ought to have a hood at the back of its neck.

THE FANTAIL, OR SHAKER.

The fantail is a beautiful variety of the pigeon tribe. It has its name
from its spreading its tail in the shape of a fan, and bending it over the
back, so that the tips of the feathers brush the back part of its head.
There are two sub-varieties of this bird—the broad-tailed and the narrow-
tailed shaker. The former ought to have a tail of at least twenty-four

feathers, a swan-like neck, a full breast, and a quivering motion of its tail,
which gives it the second name of shaker. The plumage of this bird is
generally white, although some are red, blue, or cream-color. The narrow-
tailed shaker is produced by pairing the broad-tailed shaker with the stock
dove. The tail of this bird is not so wide or spreading as its name imports;
while it is also a shorter, thicker, and less graceful bird. It is usually
white, but sometimes it is spotted or ermined, and occasionally displays a
rich variety of colors.

THE CROPPER.

The body of this variety is thick, short, and clumsy; as are also the legs,
which are feathered down to the feet. They have a large pouch, or bag,
hanging under their beak, which they can inflate with wind or depress at
pleasure. Their crop hangs low, but is very large; and they are loose
breeched on their thighs.

THE JACOBIN, OR JACK,

Has a range of inverted feathers on the back part of the head, which turns towards the neck, like the cap or cowl of a monk; thus having a fanciful resemblance to the religious of those orders who wear cowls.

THE TURBIT.

The turbit has a roundish head, and is chiefly remarkable for a tuft of feathers on the breast, called the purl, which opens and spreads like a shirt-frill; and according to the fulness and beauty of this, the bird is prized by fanciers. It has a short beak, and a tuft behind its head. It varies greatly in color, some being reddish, some dun, while others are blue and black. The most valued have their body plumage white, or of one entire color. The blue turbits have black bars across their wings. They are called yellow-shouldered or blue-shouldered, according to the different tints of the shoulders or wings. The original blue turbit has always a blue tail, and the black turbit, a black tail; which are essential accompaniments.

THE RUFF.

This bird is something like the jacobin, but it has many shades of difference, and is a distinct variety. The hood and span are larger, but the feathers do not grow so near to the shoulders, and the hood is not so distinct and compact. It is rather a larger bird than the jacobin.

THE NUN.

The head of this bird is almost covered with a veil of feathers, whence its name. Its body is chiefly white; its head, tail, and the six flight feathers of its wings should be entirely red, yellow, or black; and when its head is red, the tail and flight feathers should be red; and when its head is yellow or black, the tail and flight feathers should invariably correspond with it.

The nun is perhaps the very prettiest and most striking of the toy pigeons. It is smaller in size, but resembles the trumpeter in having a tuft of feathers rising from the back of the head, and bending forward, like a hood thrown a little back. The small bill and pearl eye of this bird also add to the neatness of its appearance.

THE OWL.

This is rather an odd but not an inelegant looking pigeon. Like the turbit, it has a purl on its breast. It has a short beak and a pearly eye. In color it varies considerably, being of various hues, red, blue, yellow, black, and silver; the yellow and red are however the most prized, and specimens of these colors, when the birds are otherwise handsomely formed, are rare and valuable.

THE HELMET.

The helmet is a pretty bird much coveted by fanciers. It is rather smaller than the nun, which it resembles in appearance, but it has no hood on the back part of its neck. It derives its name from the tuft of feathers which overshadow its head, and which is of a white tint. Its head and tail are black.

THE HORSEMAN,

In appearance and qualities, greatly resembles the carrier-pigeon; but he is smaller in size, and can be distinguished by his shorter neck. He may be trained like a carrier-pigeon, to whom he is scarcely inferior.

THE DRAGOON

Is bred between a tumbler and a horseman. It is a good serviceable pigeon and, as has been observed, is sometimes invaluable for its devotedness as a nurse. A good flier, it is yet not so strong as the horseman, and therefore less adapted than that pigeon for long flights, as its strength and courage give way more quickly.

DOMESTIC FOWL.

INTRODUCTORY REMARKS.

THERE is nothing more delightful than the care and charge of domestic poultry. It is the most interesting of sights to behold a hen with her chicks, and to mark her care and tenderness for them; while the little chicks themselves are so pretty to look at, and have so many engaging ways with them, as to claim our love and sympathy. To see them picking and scratching about, basking in the sun, or running hither and thither after their mother hen, or nestling under her wings when a cloud comes over the face of the sky, or on the approach of night, is a sight, to a person of right feeling, very grateful and pleasant; and to young persons, the care and management of poultry engender every hour happy occupation.

VARIOUS KINDS OF POULTRY.

Domestic poultry may be divided into three kinds. First, the gallinaceous kind, as the common and foreign fowl, peacock, &c. Second, the columbine, or pigeon group, or family; and thirdly, the aquatic family, such as the duck, goose, swan, &c.

GALLINACEOUS FOWLS.

The principal varieties of these are, the dunghill, the Dorking, Poland, game, Chittagong, bantam, shakebag, Spanish, Seabright, Persian, Cochin China, &c.

THE COMMON FOWL.

We have no history so ancient as the domestication of the cock and hen. The cock is supposed to be of Persian or Indian origin; but the species, in numerous varieties, has been introduced throughout the whole world. The common barndoor fowl, of which the cock is so brilliant a specimen, is probably derived from some of the wild or jungle fowls of India, and has been no doubt mixed with more than one species. It needs no description; it is of every variety of color, and is to be found in every part of the country.

GAME VARIETY.

Game fowls are also too well known to need any description. Their plumage, particularly the red, is most beautiful and rich; their size somewhat below the common, and their symmetry and delicacy of limbs to be compared with those of the race-horse and the deer. They are, however, a most pugnacious family, and will fight till they die; wicked men and boys, taking advantage of this, have matched cocks to fight under circumstances of great barbarity, but which can now be put a stop to by the strong arm of the law.

THE DORKING VARIETY.

This is so called from the town of Dorking in England. Their genuine color is pure white, and their chief distinctive mark is *five* claws on each foot, the fifth claw being little more than an apology for a claw. They are the largest of our fowls, well shaped and good layers; they also make the finest capons.

THE POLAND VARIETY.

The Poland fowls, as they are generally called, were originally imported from Poland. Their color is shining black, with white tops on the head both of the cock and hen. The head is flat, surmounted by a fleshy protuberance, out of which spring the crown feathers or top, white or black, with the fleshy head in the centre of the crown. The Polanders are not only kept as ornamental, but are one of the most useful varieties, and are sometimes called everlasting layers.

The Poland fowls require more warmth, care, and attention than the common breed, and they are more subject to disease. Their topknots should likewise be occasionally clipped, or they grow into the eyes of the birds and nearly blind them.

THE BANTAM.

This well-known bird is small in size. It came originally from India, and is valued chiefly for its grotesque figure, feathered feet, and delicate flesh. Sir John Seabright was a great amateur of this bird, and obtained a beautiful variegated kind, with smooth legs, which go after his name. There is another variety imported from Brazil, which are very beautiful—partridge spotted and streaked, the eggs of which are colored like those of the pheasant.

THE CHITTAGONG, OR MALAY.

This is another Indian variety, and is probably the largest of the gallinaceous tribe. They are in color streaked yellow and dark brown, long-necked, serpent-headed, and high upon the leg. They are good layers, and, being well fed, produce the largest of hen's eggs.

SPANISH FOWLS.

These fowls are of large size; the hens lay enormous eggs, but do not sit well. The plumage is black, the comb loose, and often pendulous, and the naked skin behind the ears white. Two breeds, remarkable for beauty of plumage, are the gold-spangled and silver-spangled Polands, which are sometimes mixed with the Spanish. Fine fowls of this breed are highly valued.

PERSIAN BREED.

From Persia we have the rumpless or tailless breed, in which not only are the tail feathers wanting, but the tail itself. Fowls of this breed lay well, but are not sightly in appearance. The Friesland breed is also another ugly sort, which has the feathers frizzled or curled up the wrong way.

COCHIN CHINA FOWLS.

The Cochin China fowl was imported from Cochin China, hence its name. From their stupendous size and shape they have attracted great attention; the height of the male bird is from twenty-two to twenty-five, and the female from eighteen to twenty-two inches. There are several varieties, of which the most favorite are the buff and cinnamon colored; and there is a white variety, for which very large sums have been occasionally realized.

From their general introduction into the country they have lately much deteriorated in value.

CHOICE OF STOCK.

It should be a general rule to breed from young stock, a two-year old cock or stag, and pullets in the second year. Hens are in their prime at three years of age, and decline after five. Hens with a large comb, or which crow like a cock, are of no use. Yellow-legged fowls are of tender and delicate constitutions. Healthy fowls are bright and fresh in the eye, and their combs are of a florid red. The most useful cock is a bold, fierce, active bird. The indications of old age are, fulness of the comb and gills, dulness of color, large scales on the legs, and stiffness of the feathers. The spring is the proper time to commence laying your stock, and nine hens to one cock is sufficient.

THE POULTRY-YARD.

We do not expect a boy, keeping a few fowls for his amusement, to establish a regular poultry-yard; but still, he should provide some sort of playground for his feathered favorites. If neglected in this particular, they will trespass on forbidden ground, and cause no end of trouble and damage. In a half-hour's visit to a flower-garden, a few energetic Dorkings will exhibit a modern style of gardening that will astonish, but not gratify the proprietor; and in proportion as the fowls are confined at home, will their propensity to stray be increased. In these days of cheap wire fencing, it is an inexpensive, and at the same time an efficient plan, to enclose a certain space—a corner of a field, if in the country—with this netting, to the height of nine or ten feet; it will effectually prevent the fowls from straying, without cooping them up and keeping the air from them. Part of this enclosure should be gravelled, and part should consist of turf. A good supply of fresh water must always be maintained. In many cases, however, a small paved court-yard is used, and here the fowls will thrive well enough, so long as the yard is sheltered from biting winds. Pure water is the first and the great requisite of health in fowls.

FEEDING POULTRY.

In feeding your poultry, you may practise a wise economy, and prevent waste, by establishing an understanding with the cook, for the reversion of the cold potatoes, and the leavings of the vegetables from the dinner table. Any kind of root, such as carrots, turnips, parsnips, etc., *after being boiled*, is good food for poultry; and if of a watery nature, it may be mixed with bran, bread crumbs, or other farinaceous matter, and the poultry will eat it greedily and thrive upon it. Wheat, Indian corn, oats, rye, and peas are often given to poultry; and the seeds of the sunflower furnish a capital food for them, and one upon which they fatten rapidly. Be very careful to feed them regularly; if they expect a meal at a certain hour, they will be sure to assemble; but disappointment will make them irregular. The best plan is, perhaps, to have a trough with narrow openings, through which the fowls can thrust their heads, and peck a few grains of corn when they choose. Accustomed to find a continual supply, they will not waste your store, but will use it with a moderation and judgment worthy of all praise. If, on the other hand, they are allowed to get ravenously hungry without receiving a supply, they will over-eat themselves, to the detriment of.their health, and to your disadvantage in the long run. A cooped fowl can eat, it is said, about a quarter of a pint of corn in a day.

If fowls are pent up and have no run, worms, beetles, grubs, earwigs, ants' eggs, etc., should be searched for and given them in their houses. They should also always have a plentiful supply of pure and clean water.

LAYING.

Hens begin to lay in the early spring, and go on doing so till the middle of summer, when they cease for a few weeks, and then at its end commence again, again cease toward mid-winter, and commence again. When the period of laying approaches, it is known by the brightening of the red in the combs and wattles of the hen, in the proud archness of her gait, the glistening of her eyes, and her frequent cackling. She then looks out for her nest, and after going in and out of it for some few days, pulling the straw about, and making a kind of hollow in it, she lays; and having performed this wonderful feat, generally proclaims the "fait accompli" to the whole world within hearing.

In domestic birds, artificial nests must be made for the hen, in boxes which we shall describe presently, in which a chalk egg or two should be put. The nests may be made of short straw. In some instances, a hen will make choice of a particular nest to lay in, and when, on desiring to lay, she finds this nest preoccupied by another hen, she will wait until it is vacated. With respect to fecundity, some hens will lay one egg every day, and others one every other day.

The eggs ought to be taken from the nest every afternoon, when no more may be expected to be laid, for if left in the nest, the heat of the hens when laying the next day will tend to corrupt them.

HATCHING.

When the hen has laid her number of eggs, nature has provided for their being hatched by giving the bird an instinct to sit or incubate. This instinct is made known by a particular sort of cluck, which is continued till the chickens are full grown. At the same time, the natural heat of the hen's body is much increased, and she flutters about, bristles up her feathers, searches everywhere for eggs to sit upon, and then is the time to give her eggs.

In selecting the eggs to be sat upon by the hen, choose recently laid, handsome, moderate-sized, but rather large eggs. If you wish to raise hen-birds, examine the eggs by candle light, and if the vacancy at the extremity is a little to one side of the apex, the chicken will be a female; if exactly under the point of the shell, it will be a male.

The number of eggs to be hatched by the hen must in some degree depend upon her size. A moderate sized hen will very nicely cover nine eggs, but many hens bring up eleven or thirteen. An odd number of eggs is always chosen, as they have a centre egg which the others lie round in the nest. Those hens which sit best are generally short-legged, and are well furnished with feathers. The hen having received her eggs may then be left to herself; she may have water placed at a convenient distance, and her food may be given to her near the place of sitting.

The hen sits on her eggs twenty-one days, during which period she seems in a dozy state, and requires but little food or exercise; some hens will feed every day, but others will go for several days without leaving the nest, or taking the least kind of nourishment.

THE BIRTH OF THE CHICKENS.

Now comes a great and wonderful event—in place of a yolk and a white in which nothing can be discerned, we have a living animal and a broken shell. For twenty-one days it has been gradually forming, by the power of the Divine Being, into a lively little thing of beauty. It has been doubled up in its close prison; yet as the time comes for its emergence into a world of life, it has strength given it to set itself at liberty from its shelly confines. It pecks at the inside of the shell till it breaks, and then the impatient chick makes its entrance to the world in which it is to live. The length of time required for this process varies from one hour to six.

Some hens will sit for days together without leaving their eggs; and when this is the case, she should be lifted from the nest once a day, and fed separately in the yard, after the other fowls.

When chickens are thus hatching, it is best to leave them entirely to themselves; but sometimes it will happen that a chick has not sufficient strength to break the egg-shell; a small tap may in such a case be given to it, but never before you are certain that the little inmate of the shell requires it.

As soon as the hen becomes a mother, a great change is seen in her character—all her former feelings and habits give way to maternal solicitude. A good hen attends to her brood with the most persevering fondness; she will attack the fiercest animal who dares to molest her progeny. The cock too enters into her feelings, and commences his work of scratching for the young ones. We had last year a fine brood of chickens, but the parent hen was accidentally killed by the blowing to of the stable-door. The cock, however, took to the chicks, nestled them, fed them, and brought them up with all a mother's care.

REARING OF CHICKENS.

When the chickens are hatched, they require no food till the following day, when they may be fed with crumbs of bread slightly moistened, and egg boiled hard, cut up into small pieces. For the first few days the quantity they require is very small. Their crop will only contain their food, which will not take up more space than a large pea. At the end of a few weeks, the crop is not bigger when distended with food than a cherry, but the food is soon absorbed, and therefore they should be fed often—at least four times a day. On the day after they are hatched, they should be placed with the hen in a nice coop, having a little short-cut straw at the bottom. In a couple of days, the coop and hen should be placed in some nice spot in the lawn or garden, within constant sight of the dwelling-house, and where no cats, rats, or other vermin are likely to prowl about. It should be placed on a dry and warm spot, and the roof of the coop, which should have hinges by which it can be slightly opened, should be partially raised. There should, of course, be cross-bars within the roof, to prevent the hen getting out. Likewise a little pan of water set within reach of the hen, near the bars of the coop, and stones must be placed in it, to prevent the young brood from drowning themselves, and this water should be frequently changed.

As young chickens are generally brought from the egg in March, of course a great deal of rough weather may be expected before they come to years of maturity. The changes of weather should therefore be watched, and when it sets in wet or cold, the young brood should be carefully protected against these dangers by the removal of the coop into some warm sheltered place, such as a stable, coach-house, or outhouse, and so with care continue to be nursed, guarded, watched, and attended to, till they are about seven weeks old, when they will of themselves separate from their parent hen, take to the roost, and act and do as independent creatures ought, get their own living, and set up for themselves as free and enlightened chickens.

DUCKS.

The duck (*amnon*) belongs to a very extensive natural genus of water-birds found in all parts of the world. They feed in great part upon animal matter, such as insects and mollusca, as well as upon vegetables and grain. They are generally seen upon the lakes and rivers of the interior of a country, although they are often found upon the sea-shore. Their principal characteristics are, a body adapted for swimming, feet having membranes or webs between the toes, which they use to propel their bodies along, and bills with rounded points, strong, flat, and depressed, and commonly furnished with a kind of nail at their extremity.

The common wild duck is the original stock of the domesticated duck, and appears to have been reclaimed at a very early period.

The tame duck, that is, the common one, appears in the same livery as the wild one, but is a larger bird, while some vary greatly from them and from each other. Tame ducks are reared more easily than any other domestic fowl, and the best way to get them is to place duck's eggs under a hen, for the tame duck is a careless mother. The hen, on the contrary—who is an

indefatigable nurse—generally hatches a duckling from every egg with which she is intrusted; she does not indeed conduct her young to the

water, and generally exhibits much anxiety when the young brood take to it, but she watches over them, and is ever ready to defend them from danger.

There are many varieties of the tame duck, and many foreign varieties have been brought to this country. That most in request is the dark-colored Rouen, originally from France, which is very prolific in eggs. The English, or Aylesbury white variety is also considered valuable, as large and profitable. The Muscovy duck is a distinct species, and not a mere variety, much larger than the common duck, and distinguished by a sort of compounded membrane of a red color, covering the cheeks, and extending behind the eyes. This kind is easily fattened, and is a profitable breeder. There are also several other foreign species and varieties, which are sometimes kept rather for ornament than use.

The tame duck will lay from eleven to fifteen eggs, and she sits for thirty days. They begin to lay in February, and when not watched will lay abroad, and conceal their eggs. They generally lay at night or early in the morning. When she is about to lay, she looks very large behind, and should then be kept within the stable-yard or duck-house. While sitting,

MUSCOVY DUCK.

the duck requires a secluded and soft place. On hatching she should be taken with her brood and put under a coop; a shallow pan of water should be placed near her for her drink and for that of her young ones, but it should be very shallow. In about ten days she may be let loose, when, with her brood, she will immediately take to the water.

Young ducks should be fed upon corn-meal or curds, and kept in a warm place at night-time, and not let out early in the morning. They should, if possible, be kept from water to swim in, as it always does them harm. When the ducks grow large they may be fed upon oats, which should be bruised; to which may be added peameal, some broth, chopped vegetables, such as carrots, turnips, potatoes, and particularly lettuce, of which they are very fond. They may be fattened on the same food, with the addition of corn-meal made into doughy lumps; but all offal and filth should be particularly avoided.

16

THE SWAN.

This well-known ornament to the lakes at our Central Park was introduced here from Eastern Europe. All are familiar with the graceful deportment of this bird while sailing on the surface of the water. Unfortunately, its progress on land by no means corresponds with its aquatic grace, being confined to an awkward waddle.

The female swan makes its nest of a great mass of dry reeds placed among osiers or rushes near the water, and lays six or eight large white eggs. During the time of incubation, and while the young are still small, the parent birds defend them with great assiduity and courage.

THE TURKEY.

Turkeys are too well known to need much description. Their appellation is a misnomer; for they come not from Turkey, but from this country, and were quite unknown in Europe till after the discovery of the New World. In the great forests of the Western States, the turkey is found wild in flocks. It is esteemed a stupid animal in its wild state, and indeed does not seem to belie that character when tamed. Often threatening, but very seldom fighting, it is looked upon with merited contempt by courageous cocks, and in the poultry-yard occupies the equivocal position of a bird known as a bully and a coward. The poultry-yard in which turkeys are kept should be large and roomy. Their food is principally corn, of which they will eat a large quantity.

While the turkey chicks are very young, they may be fed with a mess made of bread, milk, and hard-boiled eggs chopped small; afterwards with a mash of boiled potatoes, or other vegetables, and bran; then a little soft barley; gradually giving them stronger food, until they are able to take the

same diet as their full-grown companions. As to breeding or fattening turkeys on a large scale, that is quite beyond the province of our young friends, and must be left to those who make the poultry-yard a source of income and profit rather than amusement.

THE PEA-FOWL.

The peacock and hen are two of the most beautiful of our domesticated birds. Though long naturalized in America, it is of Eastern origin, occurring in the greatest profusion in the neighborhood of the Ganges, and in the extensive plains of India. They were brought from India into Greece, about the time of Alexander. They are too well known to need description, but occasionally the peacock has the whole of the plumage of a green white color, the eyes of the train not excepted. There is also a variety or mixed breed between the common and the white variety, in which every different proportion of color between the two is minutely observed.

Peacocks are granivorous like other birds, and they may be fed in the same manner as common fowls. Their age extends to twenty years, and at three the tail of the cock is quite complete.

THE PINTADO, OR GUINEA-FOWL.

This has been said to unite the character and properties of the pheasant and the turkey. It is an active, restless, and courageous bird, and will even attack the turkey, although so much above its size. Guinea-fowls assimilate perfectly with the common species in habits and in kind of food; but they have this peculiarity, that the cocks and hens are so nearly alike that it is difficult to distinguish them.   They have also a peculiar gait and cry.   The head is covered with a kind of casque, with wattles under its bill,

and the whole plumage is either black or dark gray, sprinkled with regular and uniform white spots.   The pintado is a native of Guinea and South America, and in the wild state makes its nest in the holes of the palm-tree. It is gregarious, and is often found in large flocks.

These birds lay abundance of eggs, rather smaller than those of the common hen, and speckled.   They may be reared by placing the eggs under a hen; but the chicks are extremely tender, and very often a sudden change of the wind in March will sweep off a whole brood in a few hours.

DISEASES OF FOWLS.

One of the first diseases of domestic fowls is what is called the pip, a white scale or skin growing upon the tip of the tongue.   To cure this, scrape off the skin with your nail, and rub the tongue with salt.   An imposthume, or boil, on the rump, is called the roup; this should be opened with a large needle, and the part afterward washed with salt and water.   Another disease is the flux, or looseness of the bowels, which is generally cured by good solid food, and a few coriander seeds.   Another disease is called the chip, in which the poor little creatures, about six weeks after they are hatched, sit chirping and moping in corners.   It is a kind of consumption, and when so affected the chickens should be put into flannel, and placed in a basket near the fire, which will occasionally restore them.   The gapes is another disease, or rather a similar disease with different symptoms.   The sun or fire warmth, generous diet, and a small quantity of black pepper, are the best remedies.

Sometimes it happens that a fowl will overfeed itself, and be unable to dispose of the great quantity of grain lodged in the crop, which will puff out almost as large as a base-ball; the bird then sickens, and will speedily perish unless some relief is afforded, and the only remedy is to open the crop and take out the obstructing grain; for this purpose the sharp end of a small pair of scissors should be used to pierce the crop a little on one side, and when an opening is thus made, a slit should be cut in it about an inch long. The grain may then be taken out, and the hole being sewn up with a fine needle and thread, the bird will soon be well. It should, however, be kept by itself, and fed on soft food for a day or two.

THE PEACOCK.

RABBITS.

COMMON AND FANCY RABBITS.

Rabbits have long been favorite pets with boys, and they deserve to
be so, for they are brisk, merry, bright-eyed little creatures; and being,
moreover, easy to rear, will richly repay the care and attention lavished
upon them.   The color of the wild rabbit is a brownish gray; the tail black
above and white beneath.   In its domestic state it is of various colors—
white, black, and piebald.   Over all the temperate and warm parts of
America the rabbit is diffused; and in its wild state it thrives admirably in
the United States.

The extraordinary prolific nature of the rabbit has often been remarked
upon, and it has been calculated that a single pair, whose progeny were left
undisturbed and unmolested by the many enemies that prey upon poor
bunny, would, in four years, produce the amazing number of 1,274,840
descendants.   They attain an age of eight or nine years, under favorable
circumstances.   A gentleman who devoted a good deal of time to rearing
rabbits, and observing their manners and customs, noticed that the off-
spring paid great deference to their first father.   Upon a call which they
were accustomed to obey, he always puts himself at their head, marching
first, and stationing himself at the entrance of their burrow, where he re-
mained until they had all passed in before him.   The males are, however,
frequently cruel to their young, whom they sometimes kill and devour.   It
is a pretty sight, in a rabbit warren, to see them coming out of an evening

to feed, sitting at the entrance of their holes, cleaning their faces with their fore-paws, and darting into their burrows on the slightest alarm.

COMMON WILD RABBIT.

Rabbit-keeping is in general a sufficiently simple affair. As with all pet animals, *regularity* in attending to the little creatures' wants, and care of them during sickness, are most necessary to insure success.

FANCY RABBITS.

The fancy rabbits bear various names, of which the most common are the smut, the double smut, the lop, the dew-lop, the oar-lop, the horn-lop, and some others. These occasionally fetch very high prices among fanciers; but we would warn our young friends against expensive habits of every kind, and especially against expensive rabbit-keeping. Animals kept for amusement, and also for instruction—for much is to be learned of the instinct and habits of animals from familiar acquaintance with them—should be such as incur little expense beyond what a lad can spare from his own pocket-money; and the habit of seeking assistance from parents for foolish fancies is pregnant with the greatest mischief. We should, therefore, strenuously advise our young friends not to waste their time and money upon those ugly, overgrown creatures which fanciers choose to designate as beautiful, but to confine their attention to the rearing of the finest, most perfect, and purest stock of rabbits that can be produced, and therewith to be content.

According to fanciers, when one ear grows up straight and the other lops over the shoulder, it is a great thing, and when the two ears grow over the nose, so that the poor creature cannot see (as in the horn-lop), or when both ears stick out of each side horizontally (as in the oar-lop), or when the hollows of the ears are turned out so completely that the covered part appears in front (as in the perfect-lop), these peculiarities are considered as marks of varied degrees of perfection, but to unsophisticated minds they present nothing but monstrosities; we can see no beauty in such enormities, and shall no further describe or allude to them. (See Engraving at the head of this article.)

CHOICE OF STOCK.

With regard to color, rabbits nearest in color to the wild ones are, in general, the most hardy; after the black or black and white, then the white

then the sandy, and lastly, the gray and white. The young fancier may
either purchase a doe with young, or he may obtain four or five young ones.

If the former, he should be guided in his selection
by some experienced person; if the latter, he
should take especial care that the young ones are
in good health, and have no signs of pot-belly, and
that they are of full size and strong build. The
rule is, to "take the largest of the rabbits where
there are the fewest in the litter." He should
take them when about six weeks old, and when
taken they should be placed in pairs, in separate
hutches, till they are about four months old, when
each may have a separate hutch.

THE RABBIT-HOUSE, HUTCHES, ETC.

The rabbit-house should stand upon a dry foundation, and be well ven-
tilated. Frequently a spare loft, or some such place, will be a very good
place. The huts, or hutches, should be placed on stands about three feet
high, around the sides of the rabbit-house. Each hutch intended for breeding should have two apartments, a bedroom and a dining-room. The floor

of the hutches should be planed smooth, that the wet may run off, and a
common hoe, with a short handle and a short broom, are convenient for
cleaning the hutches. The breeding-hutches should be about two feet
high, two feet six deep, and four feet long; about one-third of this length
should be separated from the other by a panel and arched doorway, separating the dining from the bedroom. Above this there should be a sliding
door, which can at any time be put down, so as to shut the doe into either
of the compartments, as occasion may require. The edges of the doorway
should be cased with tin, as should also the edges of the feeding-trough, and

any other part that the rabbit can get at with its teeth. The front of the hutch has two doors, one of which, belonging to the inner apartment, is made of boards, and the other, belonging to the feeding-room, is open, having wirework in front; both these doors are fastened by buttons in front, but open in a contrary direction. The bottom of the hutch should have a long narrow piece of wood in front, below the wires, at B, which should be movable, and this, upon being removed, will permit an iron rod or scraper to be introduced for cleansing the hutch from time to time of any loose matter collected in it. In placing the hutch on the stand, it should be set a little aslant backward, and there should be a few holes drilled at its back partition, for the purpose of letting all liquid pass off as soon as it is voided.

THE BUCK'S HUTCH.

It is the plan of some persons to make the buck's hutch different in every way from that of the doe, and to place him in a small, inconvenient place, with the back rounded off in the form of a dutch-oven, in which he has little or no room for exercise. This is *bad* in every respect. The buck should have a large roomy hutch, with a partition, and a back room into which he can retire when he pleases; for it is a great comfort to him to be able to hide himself, and to skip in and out of his little chambers. His hutch ought, also, to be higher than that of the doe, and it should have a little trough for his dry victuals, and a little iron-wire rack on one side for his green food, if you wish to make him very comfortable. It is a bad plan to put hutches on the top of each other, and the buck's hutch should always be put out of the sight of the doe.

FEEDING RABBITS.

Rabbits should be fed three times a-day; and the principal thing to be attended to is, always to give a good deal more dry than succulent food. All weeds and the refuse of vegetation should be banished from their diet, except the roots and leaves of dandelion, sow-thistle, and hog-weed. The most nutricious food are the tops of carrots and parsnips, cabbages, parsley, fine grass, clover, tares, coleworts, and the tops of the furze-plant, which should be cut up with their dry food. The grain proper for rabbits are oats, peas, wheat, or buckwheat; to these, as the best kind of dry food, may be added bran, dry clover, pea and bean straw. Rabbits, full grown, which have as much corn as they will eat, can never take much harm from an abundant supply of vegetable food. But young rabbits ought to be very carefully attended to in this respect; and a very little vegetable food is the most proper, and that should be of the best kind, or they will soon depart to that "bourne from which no rabbit e'er returns."

NEGLECT.

One of the most common faults of young rabbit-fanciers is, first to over-feed their pets, and afterward to neglect and half-starve them. Not only

16*

do thoughtless boys forget to feed the objects of their care, but too frequently suffer them to become diseased, for want of attention to cleanliness.
This is a very cruel and wicked thing. Rabbits should have their hutches
cleaned out every morning, and require many little attentions to provide
for their comfort and health; and those who are not disposed to afford
these, ought not to think of rabbit-keeping.

BREEDING.

The doe will commence breeding at the age of six months. You may
know that she is going to have young ones by her biting the straw and hay
about in her mouth, and her general restlessness. She should be supplied
with plenty of warm, dry litter for her bed while breeding. It is not desirable that a doe should have too many litters in the course of the year, or
too many rabbits in each litter. Five or six litters in the year, and five or
six rabbits in each litter, ought to be enough for any reasonable fancier.

DISEASES OF RABBITS.

No animal is less liable to disease than the rabbit, when carefully attended; but neglect and want of cleanliness, or improper food, produce in
them many complaints, among the foremost of which is what is called "pot
belly," and which is very common to young ones. It is generally occasioned
by want of air and exercise, and the use of too large a quantity of green
food. The remedy is dry food, and to let the rabbits run about in an open
dry space every day; but the best of all remedies is a stroke behind the
ears, as few pot-bellied rabbits ever come to any good.

Rabbits are subject to colds and hoarseness, as we are, and have what is
called the "snuffles." While this disease lasts, they should be kept dry and
warm, and be fed with barley-meal, made into a paste with a little milk;
and no water or green food should be given to them till they recover. Rabbits are also afflicted with a complaint of the liver, which generally arises
from damp beds and foul hutches, want of exercise, &c. The only remedy
for this complaint is the blow behind the ears; but it is easily prevented by
nice dry hutches, bedding, and good and wholesome food.

SQUIRRELS.

THE squirrel is one of the prettiest and most engaging animals of all the pets. It is elegant in form and cheerful in disposition, and is completely formed for a "life among the trees." When on the ground, it moves by successive leaps, with the tail extended and undulating; when sitting, the tail is elevated over its back like a plume, in a most elegant manner. The squirrels most common here are the gray and flying squirrels.

The squirrel lives upon nuts, acorns, beech-mast, the bark of trees, leaf-buds, and tender shoots. Like the hare and rabbit, it generally sits upon its hind-legs; and it uses its fore-paws, which are like hands, to convey its food to its mouth. It is most provident in laying up its winter stores, not only in a place of safety, but in several holes of trees in the immediate neighborhood of its own retreat.

The squirrel's nest is constructed with great art in the hollow of some old tree, or in the bark; and is composed of twigs and dry leaves. It breeds generally in May or June, and the young family consists of four or five.

The squirrel never appears in the open fields, but keeps among the tallest trees, and avoids as much as possible the habitations of man. It is so extremely vigilant, that if the tree on which it resides be only touched at the bottom, it instantly takes the alarm, quits its nest, leaps to another and another tree, and then travels on till it finds itself in perfect security. They have been seen, when hard pressed, and when the distance to the next tree has been beyond their most extravagant leaps, to throw themselves off, spreading abroad their limbs, so as to make their bodies as parachute-like as possible, to break their fall; and, on reaching the ground without harm, bound along for the few intervening paces, and ascend the tree with a celerity almost too quick for the eye to follow.

THE GRAY SQUIRREL.

In a domestic state, squirrels are kept in a cage—many persons confine them to a miserably small one. What notions of things such people must have! Think of a free, liberty-loving creature to be

"Cabin'd, cribb'd, confined,"

in a small space of a square foot, in which every motion tends to the brushing off or grinding down of the most beautiful tail in the whole order of mam- miferous creation! Oh, my good young friends, if you do keep a squirrel, let him have elbow-room! Teach him as much as possible to forget his native woods, by the freedom you give him in his prison. Let his cage be at least six feet long, and four high; let it have perches like the branch of a tree; let him have a sleeping-box, opening with a door behind, for the pur- pose of cleaning it; let him have a food-box and water-pan, nicely ad- justed, both of which ought to be of glass; while the edges of his cage should all be covered with tin, or else the love of liberty will soon give him ⹀eans to escape. The movable, or turn-about, cage is a most unnatural affair; it induces the animal to perpetual up-hill running, with the un- pleasant feeling of the hill sliding under him, which is neither good for his health or recreation. It is, in fact, a species of misery. The custom, too, of chaining them by a collar, like a dog, is a very foolish one. Chain a squirrel! Why, it is like chaining the air itself, or "putting manacles upon the wind." No; give him a good large cage, and make his captivity endurable, if you wish your squirrel to be happy.

THE FLYING-SQUIRREL.

The flying-squirrel is a gay pet, and is frequently carried in his young master's pocket. He is fed and treated like others of the squirrel kind. He has an expansion of the skin, by means of which he takes enormous leaps, the extended skin acting both as a parachute to support, and an air-rudder to guide him.

Squirrels may be fed on all kinds of fruits, particularly those of the nut kind, such as filberts, woodnuts, walnuts, almonds, acorns, beechmast, and they are very fond of the cones of the fir-tree. They will also sip milk, and eat bread and milk with avidity. Some squirrels are very difficult to tame; and when this is attempted they must be taken from the nest at a very early age. With care and attention, and *method*, for there is a great deal of method required in taming animals, the squirrel is frequently brought to know, love, and obey his keeper, and will come at his call. Some exhibit excessive fondness for those who keep them, and will come and nestle in their bosoms and play all kinds of engaging tricks.

THE MOUSE.

THE COMMON MOUSE.

The mouse is a lively little animal, and one of the most timid, although he eats in the trap as soon as he is caught. The brown mouse can very rarely be tamed, but white mice are bred and brought up in a state of domestication, and the young fancier can obtain a pair at any of the fanciers. The female has frequently six or eight broods in a year, but at these times she must be separated from the buck, who very frequently destroys the young ones.

The best kind of cage is that like a squirrel's, but on a small scale.

Some boys who have ingenuity will construct pretty little houses for their white mice. We remember seeing one on which there was a mill, by which the white mice, very much like millers in their looks, ground their own corn, by means of a turnabout fixed on a post of the dormitory, and it was very amusing to see the little creatures come out of the chimney and look about, as unlike chimney-sweeps as white is to black.

The principal food for white mice is bread and milk, oatmeal grits, and any other common food, except cheese, which is bad for them. They should be kept particularly clean, and their cages ought to be arranged, and beds made up every day, or they will give out a most disagreeable smell. With care the mouse will live several years.

THE GUINEA-PIG.

GUINEA PIGS AND WHITE MICE.

Guinea-pigs are far less popular now among boys than they used to be; and no wonder, for they are stupid little things, and, as our old gardener was accustomed contemptuously to observe of a specimen on which we lavished much unrequited affection, in our younger days, are "*of no use to nobody.*" All they seem capable of doing is to give a pretty good imitation of a pig, as they run about grunting, from corner to corner. The guinea-pig is a native of Brazil; it feeds on grain and fruits, and may be kept in a domestic state on sopped bread and vegetables, with an occasional slice of apple or a similar fruit. In its wild state the guinea-pig is extraordinarily prolific, and a single pair, it is said, might be multiplied so as to produce a thousand within a year. In their native country they would become absolutely innumerable, were it not for the many enemies against whom they have to contend. Among these may be enumerated dogs, cats, and other animals, which greedily devour their young, and inclement weather and damp, by which vast numbers are annually destroyed. In size they are considerably less than a rabbit; the upper lip is only half divided; they have two cutting teeth in each jaw, and their ears are broad and erect. They are of varied colors, white, black, and fawn; the tortoise-shell (*i. e.*), a mixture of three colors, is generally preferred. Some of the white ones have red eyes, similar to ferrets and white rabbits. Their flesh is said greatly to resemble that of the rabbit in flavor; and it is moreover asserted, that those kept in houses contract the flavor of the wild, or warren rabbit, while the guinea-pigs that run about the garden have the more insipid taste of the domestic rabbit; but we do not think our young friends will make the trial.

THE RACCOON

Is frequently found among pets, especially in the country. If taken young, he can be thoroughly domesticated. He is a very amusing companion; but never gets over his fondness for chickens. He will have to be supplied with green corn and vegetables, but will help himself to tidbits from the poultry-yard, if not watched.

THE OPOSSUM,

Or possum, as he is more commonly called, is sometimes a great pet with country boys, though what they can see to pet in so homely an animal is more than we can comprehend. The possum uses its tail for climbing, and swinging from branch to branch, as the monkeys use theirs. Lawson says: "If a cat has nine lives, this creature surely has nineteen; for if you break every bone in their skin, and mash their skull, leaving them for dead, you may come an hour after and they will be quite gone away, or perhaps you may meet them creeping away." The food of the possum consists of insects, birds, eggs, etc. His length is about twenty-two inches, and his height about that of an ordinary cat.

He is a great scamp, and should be watched, as he is very destructive among the hen-roosts.

DOGS.

DEERHOUNDS.

ALL boys like dogs, and boys' dogs, as a general thing, are well taken care of—the attachment of the young master, as well as motives of humanity, prompting him to guard the interest of his favorite, and see that he is well taken care of. Before giving our young friends some information that may be useful in treating their canine companions, in health and sickness, we will notice the different varieties of dogs known in the United States.

Dogs may be divided into four classes: first, those who find game for man, leaving him to kill it—of which are the setter, pointer, and spaniel; secondly, those who kill it when found, as the greyhound and deerhound; thirdly, those who find and kill it, as the staghound, foxhound, bloodhound, harier, beagle, otterhound, and terrier; fourthly, those who bring in dead or wounded game, as the retriever, water-spaniel, Newfoundland dog, etc.; fifthly, those that guard property, as the shepherd's and drover's dog; sixthly, those that guard the house, as the mastiff, bull-dog, and bull-terrier; and, seventhly, those who are household pets, as the poodle, lap-dog, etc.

The pointer, of which there are the Spanish and English, is so called from his habit of pointing at game when he scents it, and is a desirable dog. It ranges the fields until it scents the bird lying close on the ground. It then remains still, as if carved in stone, every limb fixed, and the tail pointing straight behind it. In this attitude it remains until the gun is discharged, reloaded, and the sportsman has reached the place where the bird sprung. It then eagerly searches for the game, and brings the bird in its mouth.

THE POINTER.

There are many anecdotes of its intelligence, among which the following is not the least interesting:

"In 1829, Mr. J. Webster was out on a shooting party, when a female pointer, having traversed the field which the sportsmen were then in, proceeded to a wall, and, just as she made the leap, got the scent of some partridges on the opposite side of the wall. She hung by her fore-feet until the sportsmen came up; in which situation, while they were at some distance, it appeared to them that she had got her leg fastened among the stones of the wall, and was unable to extricate herself. But on coming up to her, they found that this singular circumstance proceeded from her caution, lest she should flush the birds, and that she had thus purposely suspended herself in place of completing her leap."

The greyhound and deerhound resemble each other with only this difference—the former having a sleek, and the latter a rough coat. They are long, slender, and elegant dogs, of great swiftness and agility; but generally supposed not to be so capable of attachment as other dogs. We believe this to be a slander, especially as regards the deerhound, which, if brought up properly, becomes very much attached to its master.

THE MASTIFF.

The bloodhound is unknown in this country, and scarce even in England—that which is called bloodhound here, being a mixed variety in which the mastiff predominates, and which is bred principally in Cuba. The staghound is little known here; but there are foxhounds, hariers, and beagles in

BLACK AND TAN TERRIER.

abundance, with no end of terriers, from the black and tan English, to the shaggy, wiry, active little Scotch terrier. Either of these are fine dogs for boys to have. They are faithful, affectionate, intelligent, and courageous.

Terriers are extremely attached to their master, and are capable of learning many amusing tricks. An English naturalist says: "I had a terrier, said to be of Irish breed, who had imbibed many of the eccentricities of the Irish character. He was particularly fond of terrifying lapdogs—a species of animal which he held in supreme contempt. On one occasion, he met a very fat lapdog, the property of an equally fat old lady, waddling along the street. Rory looked at it for a short time, and then gave it a pat, which rolled it over on its back. Its mistress immediately snatched it up, and put it on her muff, whereupon Rory erected himself on his hind legs—an art which he possessed in great perfection—and walked along by her side, making occasional snatches at the lapdog. The terrified old lady struck at him with her boa, which Rory immediately caught in his mouth, and carried off down the street in an ecstasy of delight, ever and anon tripping over it, and rolling head over heels."

NEWFOUNDLAND DOG.

The Newfoundland dog is a fine fellow, and the boy who has one of a pure breed is to be envied. He is the prince of water-dogs; but you had better keep him home when you go to swim, unless he is well trained, for he will be apt to think you are drowning, and drag you out, whether or no.

The shepherd's dog and drover's dog are very much alike in character, though not resembling each other in appearance. They are very useful and greatly valued in some parts of England, and in the Highlands of Scotland. They are not much known in the United States.

The spaniels are several. The King Charles, which may be used as a retriever—but he and the Blenheim are usually pets—the springer, cocker, chamber, and water-spaniel. The last is a good one for a boy, being droll, affectionate, and capable of being taught to fetch and carry, bring sticks from the water, etc.

KING CHARLES SPANIEL.

The setter is probably a large species of spaniel. It is taught to set or stand at birds, and is held in great value by sportsmen. He is not always a clean house-dog, and should be confined to his kennel. There are

THE SETTER.

three kinds of setters, the English, Irish, and Russian—the latter more like a poodle.

The poodle is a curly fellow, about the size of a spaniel, and can be taught an infinite variety of tricks and capers, to find lost money, bring articles from a distance, go through the military exercise, &c.

SCOTCH TERRIER.   COMMON ENGLISH TERRIER.

The Scotch terrier is a rough, wiry little dog, with hair hanging over its eyes, so that those organs are hardly visible; and when it is in the water, its wetted hair quite obscures its vision. There is a smaller breed of these dogs, called the "Skye terrier," whose principal beauty seems to consist in their ugliness.

BULL-DOG.

The mastiff is a faithful and valuable dog, especially the Mount St. Bernard breed, and is large and stately. The latter variety is becoming common here—the true, old mastiff is but rarely seen. The bull-dog and bull-terrier are mere fighting-dogs, quarrelsome and disagreeable. Their proper place is, chained up on the premises. They are no companions for boys.

As for the small poodles and lapdogs, a boy who owned one would be laughed at. They are the least useful of any variety of dogs extant.

DISEASES OF DOGS.

Dogs are afflicted with various diseases, some of which you may treat yourselves—others, again, would be beyond your skill.

Mange.—This is a disagreeable disease, the surface of the skin being covered with sores, and the hair coming off, often in patches. It only comes, however, by neglect, or improper food. You mix up train or tanner's oil, one quart, spirits of turpentine, a wine-glass full; sulphur, sufficient to make a thin batter, as though you were about to put it in pancakes; mix well, apply it all over, rubbing it in for an hour or two. Let it stay on about two weeks, then wash it off with soap and water. About three applications, if they are well rubbed into the skin, will answer.

Distemper.—This commences frequently with a white, mucous matter running from the nose, which is rather favorable. If it begin with a dry, hot nose, it is not so good a sign. The dog is restless, has heaviness and disinclination to move about, loss of appetite, looseness of the bowels, a dry cough, general debility, and wasting of the flesh. Some have only part of these symptoms. The first thing is to give the dog an emetic—a tablespoonful of table salt—any quantity that can be got down at once is not too much; for it will be sure to come up again. Let him have beef soup, with rice, and a little meat well cooked, for his diet. The second day give him a teaspoonful to a dessert-spoonful of castor-oil every two hours until it operates, if he be costive. If his bowels be loose, give him a dessert-spoonful of spiced sirup of rhubarb every two hours, until the passages are colored by it. Give him rich soup, little and often. If he still grow weak, you may put a teaspoonful of whiskey in each pint of soup. With patience and care he will be apt to recover. He may require to have tincture of bark, as a stimulus, and opium, or some mild astringent, to check the looseness of the bowels, but about these, which are rather powerful medicines, you had better consult some experienced person. Do not be too quick to take volunteer advice, for no dog can stand the amount of medicine people will recommend you to give him.

Worms.—Dogs occasionally suffer with these, to the injury of health, and you will see the worms ejected now and then in the passages. If the animal starts a deal in his sleep, is troubled with itching at the nose, and does not gain flesh on his fair allowance of food, you may suspect worms. The best remedy is: Cowhage, half a drachm; tin filings (very fine), four drachms. Make up with molasses and flour, into five or six balls, or boluses. You had better get this done by the apothecary, or you may get more of the cowhage than you like on your hands. Give one every day, followed four hours afterward by a purge of salts. Or give the following: Cowhage, a teaspoonful; aloes, forty grains. Make into ten pills, with molasses, and give one every morning.

Colds, Coughs, etc.—A purge of oil, a little less food than usual, and keeping him in a warm place, will generally answer.

Bruises or Sprains.—Rub opodeldoc well into the part frequently through the day.

Fleas.—To kill these, mix a half teaspoonful of snuff in two quarts of gin, and wash him well. If less gin, then less tobacco. If you make it too strong, you will not only kill the fleas, but probably your dog.

To take out Thorns.—Extract them with pliers, if they are to be grasped. If too far in, bind up the place with a plaster of shoemaker's wax, or a bread poultice, and you will soon draw it out.

POINTERS.

THE SALT-WATER AQUARIUM.

ONE of the most delightful amusements of the day, for boys, is the fitting up and stocking an aquarium, or mimic fish-pond. The aquarium is a tank, wherein the fish and water vegetables are placed—the one to consume carbon and give out oxygen, and the other to consume oxygen and give out carbon, in such proportions that the water is always kept pure. In the aquarium, by an imitation of nature, you have a miniature fish-pond, wherein the habits of fish and the growth of sub-aqueous vegetation are laid open to the observer, so as to afford him continual amusement.

THE PRINCIPLE OF THE AQUARIUM.

The salt-water aquarium is a miniature sea, and the fresh-water aquarium a miniature pond. Both, to be real aquaria, must have in themselves the power of keeping vegetable productions fresh and growing, and animals alive, without the necessity of changing the water. The few cubic feet of water enclosed in the glass box must remain pure from month to month, kept so by the animal and plant life therein existing; and so soon as any appearance of decay in the plants, or of unusual mortality among the live inhabitants is observed, it may be taken as a sure sign that something is wrong in the structure or condition of the little world.

The principle upon which the aquarium, either of sea or fresh water, is founded, is the following: A plant immersed in water will, under the influence of light, exhale oxygen gas; and this oxygen it is that all fish and marine and fresh-water animals require to sustain life. When goldfish are kept in a bowl, they would soon die if the water were not continually changed; for they exhaust the oxygen from the small supply of water in the bowl, and there is nothing to revivify the water from which they have extracted what is to them an indispensable element of life. The introduction of plant-growth, however, alters all this; the plants give out the necessary oxygen, while some of the animals, on their part, repay the obligation by feeding on any of the vegetable matter that begins to decay, and cause turbidity in the water. Thus a balance is maintained, the vegetable and animal inhabitants of the little glass world being equally and mutually necessary to each other's well-being. A few sea-snails, or periwinkles, for a salt water, and half a dozen pond-snails for a fresh-water aquarium, are the best scavengers in the world; and the best of it is, they *keep* themselves, without putting their owner to any expense whatever.

THE CASE, OR TANK.

The aquarium is made properly of two materials. The bottom and ends should be made of marble or slate, and the two sides of glass—though for fresh-water aquaria all the sides may be made of glass, set in iron pillars, if the latter be enamelled. We prefer the former method. The end-pieces have grooves cut in them to receive the plate glass, which is then cemented, and made water-tight. There are similar grooves in the bottom. The cement should be such as will not decompose and taint the water. The tank, if you are near a large city, can be bought cheaper than you can make it.

Having bought your tank, see that the cement or putty it may contain is perfectly dry. Cleanse it thoroughly by filling it with successive changes of water. It is useless introducing any specimen until the water in the tank remains perfectly free from any impurity, contracted from the vessel in which it is placed.

WHERE TO PLACE THE AQUARIUM.

This is a very important point, and one which should be very carefully attended to—the object being to imitate, in the artificial pool of water, as closely as possible, the position of a natural pond, or sea. The first thing to remember is, that *light* is necessary for the exhalation of oxygen; but that the light must fall as it would on a real pool of water—*i. e.*, never laterally, or from the side, but always from the top. The aquarium should, therefore, be placed in a position where it may receive plenty of sunlight, tempered, however, by the shade of over-hanging plants, or by a screen during the hottest hours of the day; for should the water become thoroughly warm, a great mortality among the inhabitants is almost certain to ensue. For this reason, many aquaria are made with a slab of slate on the side where the sunlight, if unchecked, would strike sideways through the water; when this is not done, a thick curtain of green baize, or some other impervious material, will answer the purpose. Do not place the aquarium in any place where it is likely to be moved, or shaken, in closing shutters, or similar operations; a grand point towards success is that, once fixed, it should remain entirely undisturbed.

17

HOW TO LAY THE FOUNDATION FOR THE PLANTS, ETC.

The aquarium being thoroughly cleansed and clear, the next thing is to prepare the ground or bottom of the miniature sea. Sand and pebbles, to the depth of about four inches, must first be introduced. Rockwork must now be introduced—either artificial material, such as is used for the borderings of gardens, or pieces of natural rock, collected on the sea-shore. A great deal of the appearance of the aquarium, when finished, will depend upon the manner in which these pieces of rock are distributed and arranged. They should form natural caves, in which the animals may conceal themselves at pleasure, and jutting promontories, one or more extending above the water. These rocks should be firmly fixed, by propping them up with sand and pebbles, scooped away around their bases. No pains should be spared to make the arrangement of rock and water as picturesque as possible, as, once completed, it cannot be again interfered with. In some aquaria, this layer of sand and pebbles is dispensed with, and the pieces of rock are merely fastened with a little cement, or even placed loose on the slate floor of the vessel, on the ground that some of the smaller animals hide themselves among the shingle, and, dying there, infect the water; but, with care, this may be prevented.

HOW TO STOCK THE AQUARIUM—THE PLANTS.

The period of the sea-side visit is the time to procure treasures for the aquarium. There are, indeed, several places in New York and other large cities where specimens of all kinds, both animal and vegetable, may be procured; but no supply thus purchased can make up for the pleasure and profit to be derived from collecting the whole stock for your aquarium yourself, and the specimens thus collected may easily be brought, safe and sound, to the finder's inland home; for this part of the task, moreover, we shall presently give a few directions. At low water, when the sea is retiring from the foot of the cliffs, leaving a large expanse of weed-covered rock uncovered, follow the margin of the retiring waters, armed with a chisel and hammer; for you must, in collecting your specimens, avoid all that are merely lying on the rocks, and which, in nine cases out of ten, are dead. You must chip off a little piece of the rock on which the weeds are growing that you collect, and bring them away adhering to a piece of their native rock—though a very small fragment, just enough for the weeds to cling to, will be sufficient, as sea-weeds have no roots. Take care that there are no decaying weeds or animals on the bits of stone; for if they are suffered to remain, and begin to decay in your vase, they may be the ruin of the whole collection.

In making your selection of sea-weeds, or algæ, choose exclusively the smaller and finer kinds; the large coarse fuci are too strong for the purpose, and cover the aquarium with slime in decaying. The smaller and more delicate specimens are frequently found hidden under the shelter of the larger kinds, or nestling beneath rocky ledges. In every case, remove them gently, taking care that a portion of the rock on which they grow is detached with them.   Endeavor to obtain specimens of as many various colors and forms as possible; for on the judicious arrangement and contrast of colors—crimson, and purple, and green, and olive—the appearance of your aquarium will mainly depend.   The pretty little purple-tinted coralline (*corallina offici-nalis*) is exceedingly well adapted for the purpose; likewise the pinnate-leaved laurencia.

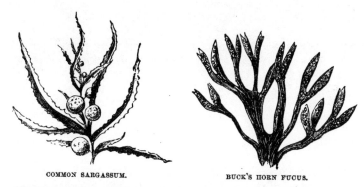

COMMON SARGASSUM.   BUCK'S HORN FUCUS.

The COMMON SARGASSUM is an interesting specimen, found on the American shores of the Atlantic.   The stems are a foot or more in length, alternately pinnated with simple branches.   The plant is dark olive-colored, changing to reddish brown, upon exposure to air.   The small pea-like shells growing upon its stems are *air-vessels*, which float the large stems of the plant in water.

The BUCK'S HORN FUCUS is destitute of air-vessels, but the extremities of the fronds are inflated, forming terminal receptacles.   The fronds are from a few inches to a foot and a half in length, olive-green color, with a tinge of yellow at the extremities.

The DICHOTOMOUS DICTYOLA grows upon rocks, as well as upon the larger algæ.   The fronds are from two to nine inches in height, green in color, forming a beautiful specimen when dried.   There are narrow and broad fronded varieties, of the same species.

The PEACOCK'S TAIL PAVONIA is a curious species, growing chiefly in rocky pools, where the water is still, and exposed at low tide.   The frond is membraneous and spreading, presenting various shades of brown, and yellowish or reddish olive, which, with the numerous darker and concentrical lines, and a white bloom-like powder, spreading over and more or less modifying the multiplied hues, renders this one of the most

DICHOTOMOUS DICTYOLA.

beautiful and remarkable of all our marine vegetables. Several generally
rise from the same base in erect or slightly spreading tufts, seldom more
than two or three inches high, the divisions ·arising apparently not from
growth, but from laceration, or separation after growth, the same concentrical lines being continued in the same curve through all the segments.

PEACOCK'S TAIL PAVONIA.

ARTICULATED CHYLOCLADIA.

The ARTICULATED CHYLOCLADIA may be found either growing upon
rocks, or attached to some larger plants. Its fronds are tubular, looking
like a series of the cells of an orange, united at their extremities; the
branches spring from some of these constructions, and the plant grows in
tufts, from a creeping, fibrous base, and rises in height from one to six
inches; they are of a tender substance, and purplish or pinky red colored.

RED ROCK-LEAVED DELESSARIA.

ESCULENT IRIDÆA.

This plant, and other varieties that are allied to it, are only of annual dura-
tion; but the minute disk, in all of them, is accompanied by fibres, which

creep along the rock or stem of the supporting plant, fixing themselves here and there, and forming the rudiments of future fronds.

The RED ROCK-LEAVED DELESSARIA is one of a beautiful genus, of which there are about a dozen varieties. They are plants of very fragile texture, rarely found entire, unless growing in rocky pools, or drawn up in nets from deep water. The leaves of the Delessaria sanguinea are of a rich red color, and satiny texture, and from three to twelve inches in length; the short-branched stem is fixed by a small red disk.

When this plant is perfect, it is scarcely equalled in brilliancy of hue by any vegetable production, the membraneous part of the frond being of a vivid and glossy rose pink, the midrib and veins of deep carmine. Frequently small zoophytes are found attached to it.

The ESCULENT IRIDÆA consists of a subcartilaginous cuneiform frond, attenuated below into a short stipe. Being an inhabitant of deep water, it is most commonly found near the low-water mark. The fronds are from four to eight inches long, deep blood-red or purple, changing to greenish or yellowish white upon exposure. It is sometimes eaten by fishermen, and other people on the coast, after being fried or roasted, and it is said to taste like roasted oysters. The term *iridæa* has reference to the iridescent hues of the growing frond in some of the species.

FEATHERED PTILOTA.

BLUNT RUSCOUS-LIKE DELESSARIA.

The FEATHERED PTILOTA is of a red color, characterized, with some three or four varieties, by the feathered form of the frond. It is frequent on rocky coasts, grows from three inches to a span in length, and is attached by a small disk. The younger branches are pale crimson or pink; the older, deep purplish red, passing into brown. This is a beautiful object, viewed under a microscope or magnifying-glass of high power; the surface appears dotted with coral-like scales, and the fruit is contained in small involucres at the extremities of the segments.

The BLUNT RUSCOUS-LIKE DELESSARIA is a red-fronded species, growing
upon rocks, and upon the larger marine plants. This is remarkable for the
production of small leaves from the midrib of the fronds.

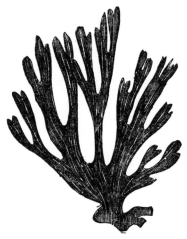

LACERATED NITOPHYLLUM.

The LACERATED NITOPHYLLUM is another of the red group, its fronds
being irregularly divided. It is very frequently met with on rocky coasts,
growing from a minute discoid base, from which it is frequently broken away
by the waves. The whole plant is in general very thin and delicate, of a
pale pinkish red, varying to reddish brown. The lower part of the frond is
always more or less distinctly marked with parallel, interbranching dark
veins, originating at the base, and generally vanishing at the length of two
or three inches, but sometimes extending even into the branches. The species is exceedingly variable in reference to the breadth and lacerations of the
frond. This alga thrives well in a tank.

The feathery bryopsis, leafy laminasia, and curly condrus, also flourish
well; and with the broad-leaved ulva, the purple bagnia, and purse-like cod-
rain, will form a beautiful mixture of colors, that may well rejoice the heart
of the aspiring projector of the aquarium.

There is much difficulty in exhibiting by small engravings the true por-
traits of sea-weeds, because the forms of the most interesting specimens are
minute, and more particularly the *details* are such as can only be observed
by attentive examination, aided, in some cases, by the microscope, or by
magnifying-glasses. To be transported from the sea-side to the collector's
inland home, these specimens must be very carefully packed in damp sea-
weed. The broad oar-weed is the best for the purpose, being at once stout
and smooth, and holding a great amount of moisture. The weeds should be

replaced in their native element, in the tank, as soon as possible, before the least decay has had time to set in.   There are certain periods in each month when the tide recedes lower than usual, leaving a portion of the rocks dry that is usually covered even at low water.   If possible, these times should be chosen for collecting, for a rich harvest of beautiful specimens is sure to reward the collector ; and the plants that grow just below low water-mark are exactly those that thrive best in the narrow precincts of the tank.   Very few of the smaller specimens will fail to flourish if, when obtained, they are quite healthy ; but they must be carefully watched, and any weed that exhibits the least sign of yellowness or decay at once removed, before it can infect the rest.   Avoid brown weeds of the larger kind ; they slough, and make the water turbid and offensive, and thus ruin all your efforts.

THE LIVING SPECIMENS IN THE AQUARIUM.

When the vegetable products of the ocean have been left undisturbed for a few days in the tank—a fortnight is not at all too long—and the water assumes a clear, greenish, crystal appearance, and when minute bubbles are seen adhering to the sides of the leaves, and rising to the surface of the water, the time has come for introducing the zoological specimens to their new abode ; for these minute bubbles are filled with oxygen gas, and their presence is a sign that the water is in a fit state to support animal life with all its acquirements in the way of oxygen.   Now is the time to go out on the sea-shore in search of inhabitants for the newly-organized sea ; and we must give a description of some of the animals that will best thrive in the aquarium, and a few directions as to the method of finding and preserving them.

The SEA-ANEMONE, or ACTINIA, in its different varieties, is one of the first objects for which the young naturalist should search—if, indeed, it can be called a search, when the objects of quest lie scattered at low tide along every coast, and it is rather a matter of selecting than finding ; but on this

SEA-ANEMONE (Fig. 1).

selection the appearance of the aquarium will greatly depend.

These are the curious creatures that were once thought to form the link between the animal and vegetable kingdoms.   Because they were found attached to rocks, it was contended that they derived nourishment by a system of roots ; and because they put forth long and slender arms, it was contended that they had branches analogous to those of a plant ; while, being able to move their arms, and taking and digesting food, they were held to partake also of an animal nature.

Attentive observation has shown, however, that they are not *permanently* fixed to rocks : they have the power of moving from one place to another, and attaching themselves anew, whenever such a removal is desirable.

When the animal is left dry by the tide, or is reposing or feeding, the tentacula are drawn in, and the common orifice closed, Fig. 1; when

covered with water, and searching for food, the tentacula are extended, Fig. 2, and move about with a gentle undulating motion. When the anemone changes its abode, it quits hold of the rock, and, reversing its position, uses the tentacula as legs. When shells, pieces of raw fish,

SEA-ANEMONE (Fig. 2).

or meat are offered to them, if not too large, they will be immediately seized and swallowed; and although the shells of mollusks given to them may be firmly closed, they manage in some extraordinary way to consume the fish and to eject the shells empty.

There are many varieties of the sea-anemone; the handsomest is the carnation-like sea-anemone, tinted in various shades of red. The scientific name for the carnation-anemone is *Actinia mesembryanthemum;* but Americans, who don't in general care for long Latin names, have unceremoniously shortened this into "mes." There are other well-known kinds of anemone, known as the "daisy," the "wheatsheaf," and the "crass," which is an abbreviation of crassicrais.

A little below high-water mark, plenty of specimens of the "mes" anemone may be found. The more they are exposed to the light and the air, the darker is their color. Thus, the beautiful pale pink varieties are to be sought for nearer to low-water mark, and in situations where overhanging weeds or stones shelter them from the sun. Those found half-way between high and low water mark are generally a fine bright red; and the anemones in exposed positions are almost brownish in the darkness of their tints.

The "crass" is generally to be sought for in crevices, behind bunches of overhanging weeds. In your wanderings along the coast, if you stop at any overhanging lump of rock, from which sea-weeds hang down, so as to form a natural screen, if you lift this screen, you will see some stones and shells which seem to be arranged on some gelatinous substance. This substance is a "crass." By touching the base with your finger, you will find whether the crass is fixed on the solid rock, or on the loose sand. If the former is the case, better leave him alone, and search for another specimen; for he holds on so tightly, that you will scarcely succeed in detaching your crass without injuring him in such a way that he won't live in the aquarium. A good many are generally found together, so that there is no need to run the risk of carrying away an injured specimen, as a little further search will almost invariably show you plenty more crasses where you have found one. Choose two or three that have fixed themselves to small bits of stone or rock that you can chip off, and bring them away with the stone. The smaller specimens are best, for they live longest, and look most ornamental.

Small specimens of star-fish are very interesting objects for the aquarium, with their strangely colored rays and extraordinary motions. There aro many varieties of this strange creature. The star-fish has a considerable tendency to locomotion, and is quite a lively object among the sedate occupants of the aquarium. The brittle star-fish is one of the handsomest specimens, displaying, in addition to its curious form, vivid hues, arranged in beautiful patterns. It is called brittle from the curious property

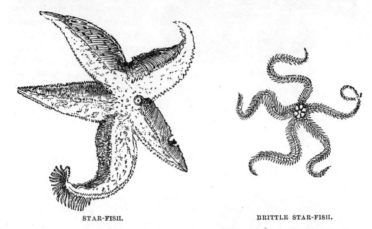

STAR-FISH.   BRITTLE STAR-FISH.

of spontaneously dividing itself, separating into pieces with wonderful quickness and ease. Touch it and it flings away an arm; hold it, and in a moment not an arm remains attached to the body. The star-fish moves by means of a multitude of little suckers on the under side of each ray, which adhere to the surface over which he walks, on the principle of the leathern "suckers" with which boys raise bricks and stones, by exhausting the air between the stone and the sucker. In travelling, the star-fish puts three of his rays out in front, while the remaining two follow behind. They are evidently affected by the presence of light, and in the aquarium will grow lively when a lighted candle is brought near them.

ECHINUS.

The ECHINUS, commonly called the sea hedge-hog, or sea-urchin, is a great treasure for the aquarium, and may be seized as a prize whenever found. They are mostly of a conical or spherical shape, divided into five segments, covered with minute holes, from which project tentacles, serving as organs of locomotion, touch, etc. The surface of the body is covered with shelly spines, of various forms and thicknesses. The mouth is in the centre; they feed upon marine productions.

17*

MUSSELS are bivalve mollusks, living in strong shells of an oblong triangular form, terminating in a point. The head of the animal is situated to-

MUSSELS.

ward the point near the hinge. Mussels abound on rocks, and the piles of piers and quays, to which they attach themselves by bunches of strong fibres. When they move, which they sometimes do, they thrust a tongue-like foot out of the shell, and,

fixing it some way in advance, draw themselves onward. The Mussel should always have a place in the Aquarium. It is a very hardy creature, and although familiar to every one, is by no means an uninteresting object of contemplation. It especially commands our admiration, whenever, by means of its byssus (formed by a number of silk-like threads), it anchors itself to the sides of the tank, becoming so fixed that it would take pretty considerable force to dislodge it.

BARNACLE.

BARNACLES are often to be found upon the sea-shore, drifted thither upon the wood of a wrecked ship, or other floating body. We have seen a ship's mast, which had long driven about at sea, literally covered with them. They are often found clinging in great numbers to the bottoms of ships, greatly retarding their speed. They grow or live in clusters, each barnacle consisting of a membranaceous branch or arm, which is fixed to some body, the animal being invested with compressed shells, attached to the pedicel. The larger barnacles cluster with the smaller in the same group, and form bunches of various sizes. They are furnished with many tentacula, with which they gather their food.

When ships covered with the Barnacle arrive in our ports, the Barnacles are eagerly scraped off by men, who take them for sale as marine curiosities, or who make their delicate white porcelain-like shells into some kinds of fancy shell-work. The Barnacles themselves are eaten on some coasts of Africa, where they are very abundant. The shell of this animal is at the end of a long fleshy stalk, generally of a purplish red, sometimes of a bright orange color, and is of the form called multivalve, being composed of five pieces or valves, two of them on each side of the animal, and a narrow piece down the back. It is a pretty shell, clear and brittle, of a white color, tinged with pale blue.

The COMMON CRAB is too well known to require a description of its peculiarities of form; but there are interesting facts connected with the history of its species which are not commonly understood. Some few species of crabs penetrate to a considerable distance inland, but are compelled to return to the sea at the period of spawning. Among the marine species, the majority do not quit the shores, whilst others are found at great distances in the high seas, where they can rest only on the floating banks of sea-weeds, so abundant in the tropics. Some species again frequent only the

COMMON CRAB.

rocky parts of the coast, while others prefer sandy shoals, in which they bury themselves.

The most remarkable facts in connection with their history, are their periodical moulting, and the recently discovered *metamorphoses* which they undergo in the early stages of their existence. Some very curious creatures, long regarded by naturalists as a distinct genus, *zoea*, have been discovered to be the *larvæ* of *crabs*, into which they ultimately become transformed. These transformations take place when the crabs are of very diminutive size, little larger than a flea; and hence they are not open to ordinary observation, but may be seen with the aid of a microscope, or a powerful magnifying-glass. At first the young crab appears with a curiously helmeted head, surrounded by numerous lengthy processes, and having large sessile eyes, Fig. 1; in the second stage it presents more of the crab-like character, the abdominal organs being more fully developed, Fig. 2. A similar metamorphosis takes place amongst both the highest classes of

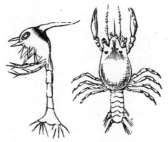

Fig. 1.   Fig. 2.

crustacea; and in their earlier stages of development they very nearly resemble each other, though they may differ very widely when fully developed.

HERMIT CRABS are soft-tailed creatures, and, in the absence of a shell to cover their posterior extremities, they occupy the empty shells of whelks,

HERMIT CRAB.

or other mollusks, as they may happen to find them. As they grow they are occasionally obliged to quit their old tenement, and seek a larger one. Its manner of doing this is thus described by the Rev. J. G. Wood:

"When a hermit desires to change his habitation, he goes through a curious series of performances, which, if he had hands, we should be disposed to call manipulations. A shell lies on the ground, and the hermit seizes it with his claws and feet, twists it about with wonderful dexterity, as if testing its weight; and having examined every portion of its exterior, he proceeds to satisfy himself about the interior. For this purpose he pushes his fore legs as far into the shell as they will reach, and probes, with their assistance, every spot that can be reached. If this examination satisfies him, he whisks himself into the shell with such rapidity, that he appears to have been acted upon by a spring."

Helpless as these poor hermits look, and tossed about as they sometimes are by the waves, when, from a scarcity of shells, they are obliged to occupy tenements too big for them to manage, they are said to be highly pugnacious. The following account of them, given by George Henry Lewes, in his "Sea-Side Studies," is well worth perusal:

"You doubtless know the hermit crab, *pagurus?* Unlike other crabs, who are content to live in their own shells, pagurus lives in the empty shell of some mollusk. He looks fiercely upon the world from out this apparently inconvenient tub, the Diogenes of crustacea, and wears an expression of conscious yet defiant theft, as if he knew the rightful owner of the shell, or its relatives, were coming every moment to recover it, and he, for his part, very much wished they might get it! All the fore part of pagurus, including his claws, is defended by the solid armor of crabs. But his hind parts are soft, covered only by a delicate membrane, in which the anatomist, however, discovers shell-plates in a rudimentary condition. Now a gentleman so extremely pugnacious, troubled with so tender a back and continuation, would fare ill in this combative world, had he not some means of redressing the wrong done to him at birth; accordingly he selects an empty shell, of convenient size, into which he pops his tender tail, fastening on by the hooks on each side of his tail; and having thus secured his rear, he scuttles over the sea-bed, a grotesque but philosophical marauder.

"Very ludicrous was the scene which I witnessed between two of these crabs taken from their shells. Selecting them nearly equal in size, I dropped them, 'naked as their mothers bore them,' into a glass vase of sea-water. They did not seem comfortable, and carefully avoided each other. I then placed one of the empty shells (first breaking off its spiral point) between them, and at once the contest commenced. One made direct for the shell, poked into it an inquiring claw, and having satisfied his cautious mind that all was safe, slipped in his tail with ludicrous agility, and, fastening on by his hooks, scuttled away rejoicing. He was not left long in undisturbed possession. His rival approached with strictly dishonorable intentions; and they both walked round and round the vase, eye'ng each other with settled malignity."

Mr. Lewes then goes on to describe how the hermits contested for the possession of the shell; and again for the better of two shells, when such were presented to them. And in the following manner he showed that hermit crabs do not, as has been hitherto supposed, devour whelks before taking forcible possession of their tenements. Having placed a shell, containing a living whelk, in the vase—

"The hermit crab at once clutched it, and poked in his interrogatory claw, which, touching the operculum of the whelk, made that animal withdraw, and leave an empty space, into which the crab popped his tail. In a few minutes the whelk, tired of this confinement in his own house, and all alarm being over, began to protrude himself, and in doing so gently pushed the hermit before him. In vain did the intruder, feeling himself slipping, cling fiercely to the shell; with slow, but irresistible pressure, the mollusk ejected him   This was repeated several times, till at length the hermit gave up in despair, and contented himself with his former shell."

So, it is consoling to think that the hermit crab takes possession only of empty tenements, legitimately "to be let," and does not eject and devour the rightful owners!

Crabs are very dangerous characters, and are likely to give the keeper of the sea-menagerie a vast amount of trouble. They have a horrible idea of fighting among themselves, and tyrannizing over each other; but worse than this, is their voracity and cruelty towards their weaker fellow-citizens. The large kind, or green crab, should be entirely avoided, for besides their voracity, they are of a terribly restless nature, and, frequently escaping from the "durance vile" of their watery home, introduce themselves unbidden among the visitors in the drawing-room, sitting down on foot-stools and chairs, and in other respects manifesting a disagreeable and intrusive character. The hermit crab, though testy and churlish—a sort of marine Timon of Athens—is generally quiet enough, and will take up his sojourn, with edifying gravity, in an empty whelk-shell. The squinados, or spider-crabs, are very useful as scavengers, being more energetic in that way than even the sea-snails. A successful aquarium-founder relates the following anecdote of the voracity and the churlish disposition of crabs:

"The hermits are very hungry creatures. I put one into a bowl, where I had a few bits of rock and weed, and one or two shell-fish. I laid before him the half of a good-sized mussel, and he instantly darted upon it in a kind of ecstasy, and hugging it to him, disappeared, with a sudden snap, with it into his shell. There he lay for a minute or two, then he slowly came forth again, pushing his food before him, which he turned over and over with an apparent fondness that was very ludicrous to the beholder ; he then handed it to his mouth with his two claws, and bit pieces out of it, just as we do from bread and butter, only that we hold the said bread and butter with one hand. When he had eaten as much as he could, he pushed the remainder under his shell ; and I gave the other half of the mussel to a poor little spider-crab, or squinado, who, while the other ate his meal, was looking on with an air of sheepish meekness. He had no sooner made a movement towards it, than the hermit sidled towards him, gave him a rap with one claw, and with the other seized his dinner, which he dragged away, and turned over a good many times ; while the spider-crab squatted submissively before him, sitting upright, in the droll manner peculiar to his species. When the hermit was tired of playing with his slave's dinner, he tossed it over his own shell, and as it was plain that he did not mean to let it be approached, I took out the poor persecuted little squinado, and put him into another establishment, where there was no inmate but a crab of his own tribe, rather smaller than himself. And now appeared all the mean-ness of his nature. I threw a shrimp to him, which I supposed to be dead, but it no sooner found itself in salt-water than it began to spring. The larger crab, however, soon put an end to that, by stretching out his long claw, and clasping its transparent body ; the poor shrimp was soon killed. That feat accomplished, the crab pulled off each leg in turn, and handed it to his mouth, holding the shrimp's body at a distance; he then pulled off its tail, and ate all the soft flesh it contained, allowing the shell to float away. This was evidently enough for his meal. He now drew the re-mainder to a bit of rock, and pushed it under; sitting near at hand to watch the place. The other crab, who had not yet been fed, looked on with hungry admiration, till at last, when his sated rival moved away altogether, and hid himself behind a large shell, he ventured humbly to the spot, but had no sooner put a claw beneath the rock, in search of the rejected mor-sel, than out darted the enemy, and he was fain to retreat as fast as his legs would carry him ; while his scornful rival took out the shrimp, and played with it in his sight, as a cat does with a mouse, pushing it from him with his claws, tossing it up, and catching it again, tantalizing the other poor fellow, but evidently not able to eat any more himself.

"I then dropped a piece of meat close to the destitute crab; but the other no sooner saw it, than he left his shrimp, and proceeded to the spot; whereupon I took him away to a third receptacle, where there was no one for him to torment with his grudging disposition, and where he walked about disconsolately, finding nothing of the crab kind to fight with. Thus I became practically convinced that it is of no use trying to keep more than one crab in the same aquarium."

LIMPETS are eligible inhabitants to admit to your little salt-water world. They are eminently quiet and self-contained, and sometimes their shells are very prettily marked.   Those should be chosen that are found adhering loosely to the rocks, with the shell raised some little distance from the body; for when they are firmly fixed to rocks and stones, and have to be dislodged with some degree of force, they are likely to become injured and die.   It is best to choose those which have a sea-weed growing from the shell; for then you have a sort of *multum in parvo*—several specimens in one.

LIMPET.

Such animals as the limpet, and others resembling it, belong to a species of mollusks called *gasteropoda*, which are so named from their locomotive organs being attached to the under part of their bodies.   They are, however, to a certain extent, armed against attack or danger by a shelly covering.

There is another class of mollusks that creep about without any such protection, and whose gills, or lungs, instead of being inside, are exposed on the exterior of their bodies.   These are hence called *nudibranches*, or naked-gilled mollusks.   The DORIS and EOLIS are types of this class.   The gills of the former are spread out in an arborescent form, and have a most elegant

THE EOLIS.

effect.   The latter has these organs branching out over its entire body, like semi-transparent quills, giving a most remarkable appearance to the animal, as it glides along.   Both are to be found adherent to the under surface of stones, etc.

The writer had always been led to believe that these animals were very voracious, and, indeed, that "a wolf would be about as appropriate an inmate of a sheep-fold, as one of them in an aquarium, where sea-anemones live." Naturally, in consequence of this sweeping assertion against the beautiful eolis, he watched his specimen with considerable attention for several weeks, and came to the conclusion that he had been shamefully libelled by sundry writers.   But, that this opinion on his part was premature, he one day discovered.   Happening to give my usual peep into the tank before going to bed, I saw plainly that my eolis "was no better than he should be," and that the charge of greed brought against him was perfectly correct.   I was therefore obliged to come to the conclusion that his quiet, sedate manner was merely assumed for my deception. During the dusk of evening, the little fellow had crept to the neighborhood of a sweet purple bellis, that sat flowering on a grassy bank. Upon my first discovering him, he had just reached the object of his attack. The plan of his operation was rather remarkable. It seemed as if he possessed the power of fascinating his victim by a basilisk glance; for if I touched the little daisy, though ever so slightly, it would close its hands quickly over its breast, shrinking, like the sensitive plant, in evident alarm. But now, this dandified mollusk, with his milk-white coat, and purple-tipped streamers waving therefrom, not only touched my pet, but insidiously crawled about, and by slow degrees detached it entire from the disk, the tentacles not being in the slightest degree contracted during the whole of the manœuvre. When this was done, he dragged down the unsuspecting creature, and, serpent-like, crept forward until he reached her pretty golden lips. Then, and then only did she infold her blossom, and,

> "Like a lily drooping,
> Bow her head and die."

Next morning, having dispatched his meal, the eolis appeared highly delighted with himself; and to show that his gormandizing had had no bad effect upon his usual graceful gait, but, on the contrary, had rather exhilarated his spirits, he marched prettily up the sides of the tank. Thereafter, to my great astonishment, he walked on the surface of the water, like a fly upon the ceiling of a room, *head downward!*

Such an occurrence is by no means unusual with this class of animals; but it struck me at the time as being very curious, as I had not had any opportunity of witnessing it before. I have often done so since.

THE SEA-MOUSE belongs to the class *annelida*, or red-blooded worms. Its appearance is much like that of an enormous caterpillar. Its upper sur-

SEA-MOUSE.

face is covered with a double row of broad membranous plates overlapping each other, beneath which are the gills, resembling little fleshy crests. These plates are covered with a sort of hair, which springs from their outer margin, and besides these the upper surface is beset with bundles of iridescent bristles, brilliant as the plumage of the humming-bird, and of which metallic blue, green, and gold are the predominating tints. After a gale of wind, many of them are thrown upon shores, and fishermen frequently dredge them from deep waters.

The FISH-LOUSE, or ROCK-LOUSE, may frequently be seen running over rocks, and particularly quays, where the crevices between the stones afford them a safe retreat. They resemble in appearance the common wood-louse, and are sometimes used as bait for small fishes. When disturbed it rolls itself into a ball.

CORALLINES, or ZOOPHYTES, are compound animals that live upon one general structure, frequently assuming a plant-like form. Those most commonly known are *moss corals*, so called from their moss-like appearance. In some instances they grow upon sea-weeds, completely covering their surfaces with small cells, resembling honeycomb. These possess a higher organization than the simpler *polyps*, many of which so closely resemble delicate sea-weeds, that they have freequently been mistaken for them. Viewed under the microscope these are highly interesting objects; specimens enclosed in vials with a little salt water may be favorably observed, the animals coming forth from their concealment and displaying their beautiful and delicate forms.

CORALLINES, OR ZOOPHYTES.

The tank will sometimes begin to be coated on the inside with green matter; this is a sure sign that you want a few sweepers, or scavengers, among your colony. Sea-snails, or periwinkles, are very useful in this department; they are active devourers of decaying vegetable matter, and will often keep the aquarium perfectly free from confervoid growth. They are likewise very good, quiet, inoffensive citizens, which is more than we can say of all the inhabitants usually introduced into aquaria, some of whom require to be very carefully watched, on account of their pugnacious and voracious habits.

The PERIWINKLE is one of the *gasteropodous* mollusks, so called because of their habit of creeping, using the *belly* as a foot. It is well known to our young friends who have visited the sea-shore, where it is found in great quantities. Its eyes, unlike those of the land-snail, are placed at the base of the tentacula,

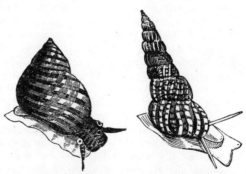

COMMON PERIWINKLE.   SPIRAL PERIWINKLE.

instead of at their extremities. Their tongues are long, and armed with transverse rows of teeth. Members of this group inhabit all regions of the sea, but by far the greater number of them live near the shore, and a very considerable portion of them are found between tide-marks. The shells of some of the species are more spiral and acute than that of the common periwinkle.

A writer, treating of this mollusk, pleasantly observes:

" The pleasures of a sea-side ramble are much increased by an intelligent observation of the various forms of animation that are met with—among which the periwinkles are often prominent, not only for their numbers, but also for their activity. They dot and stud the slimy rocks with their turbinated shells, or creep through the tiny corallines, or slide among the overhanging fuci in search of food—

> 'Part single, or with mate,
> Graze the sea-weed, their pasture;
> And through groves of coral stray.' "

GENERAL DIRECTIONS FOR MANAGEMENT.

Do not over-crowd your aquarium at first. Introduce the animals gradually, and you will be able to see, by careful watching, if any specimen is objectionable, by disagreeing with the rest of the inhabitants, or if the aquarium disagrees with him. Remove decaying weeds and drooping animals at once. Never allow the full glare of the sun to rest for hours together on the aquarium, during a hot day; and particularly take care that the sun does not shine through the side of the tank. When the weather has been dull for some days, or if the water looks turbid, you may stir it slightly with a small stick, taking care, of course, to avoid injuring the plants and animals; this will oxygenize the water, and make up for the deficient generation of oxygen by the plants, in the absence of sunlight. The water must never be allowed to get lukewarm. Avoid introducing voracious animals among the quietly disposed. Dust is another evil to be guarded against, for if it once thoroughly coats the surface of the water, it will hinder the oxygen of the air from mixing with it, and your creatures will pine and die. A plate of glass, as a lid to the aquarium, raised about half an inch above its upper edge, so as to allow a passage to the air, and the occasional stirring of the water, by agitating the dust, will also prevent its accumulation on the surface. Remember that light is the great means by which oxygen is generated from plants; and give your aquarium plenty of it. But, though your tank must stand in a window which admits plenty of light, the blind should be kept down during the heat of the day. Once let the water get warm, and your pets are, in all probability, doomed.

If you find the water-level in your salt water aquarium sinking, you must fill up the deficiency by adding fresh water, a very little at a time. Do not fear that your aquarium will thereby lose its saline properties. Remember that the salt does not evaporate, and that the water drawn by the sun out of your tank has been as fresh as that with which you supply its want.

HOW TO BRING YOUR SPECIMENS TO TOWN.

The vegetable contents of the aquarium are transported easily enough. A good supply of the brown sea-weed, called "wrack" by the fishermen, to wrap them in, and care in seeing that each specimen is attached to its original rock, or stone, will generally insure your treasures arriving in good condition at their inland destination, though it be two days' journey distant from their sea-side home. But with the animals more care must be taken. The best method is to procure two or three glass or earthen jars, about ten inches in height, and six or seven in diameter. Fill this three parts full (*not more*) with good sea-water, as shortly before your departure as you can; have a close-fitting lid, or a bladder, over the mouth of each jar. Any heavy shells, or bits of rock, or stone, which you have to put in the jars, must be suspended from the top with string, that they may not roll about and bruise the more delicate creatures at the bottom. Put the animals into the tank as soon as you get home; for the sooner they are put in, the better chance have they of thriving. As a last direction, we would impress on our young friends to make a point of visiting their aquariums at least once every day, and ascertaining, by a critical glance, if any thing is to be done in the way of removing dead specimens, agitating the water, or even feeding some of the more unruly inhabitants with minute pieces of meat, if they are found especially voracious, and consequently disposed to prey upon their weaker neighbors.

THE FRESH-WATER AQUARIUM.

SOME of our young friends may wish, before engaging in the more difficult task of stocking and maintaining a sea-water aquarium, to try the easier but not less charming experiment of establishing an aquarium in which fresh-water plants and fresh-water animals shall live and grow, and disport themselves, and afford endless delight and instruction to the proprietor, and all who will take the trouble to watch with intelligent interest their ways and habits, and the changes that occur in their short lives. The theory of the fresh-water is exactly the same as that we have just described in explaining the sea-water aquarium. In both it is the oxygen, generated by the plants under the influence of light, that supports the animal life; and the precautions to be taken with regard to heat, the selection of animals, and the removal of all impurities, are likewise, in both cases, exactly identical.

The tank for the fresh-water collection is like the receptacle for marine animals and plants. It may be either cylindrical, standing on a broad foot, or rectangular. The cylindrical form is the cheapest.

Having your tank prepared, you cover it about an inch deep with clear, well-washed white sand, on which you strew fine pebbles, with here and there a few coarse lumps of stone. At or near the centre, place two stones near together, and so arranged as to form a sort of arch, and to support each other. These must be so large that the end of one will project out of water when the tank is seven-eighths full, so as to allow your newts, *et cetera*, to occasionally get into the atmosphere. On the summit you may place a little moss, and a small fern-plant, by way of variety. This arrangement of rocks should have a natural and accidental appearance, as though it had not "come there on purpose." Into the crevices between these pieces the little fish like to hide at times, when they wish to shun observation.

You now pour river or spring water into your tank, and after a few days remove it, and replace it with fresh. After the scum has ceased to rise, and the water seems to be pure, you remove it, and replenish with fresh. Now is the time to stock it.

The first thing is vegetable matter. Go to the nearest brook, pond, or run, and you will soon be able to select small water-plants, with which to commence your water-garden. Of these, you may begin with a single plant of starwort, which you will find in any pond. Then add a plant of *valisneria spiralis*. At the bottom of brooks and runs, you will find, on rocks and stones, small plants of river weed. Add one of these, stone and all. The water weed, a species of *anacharsis* which you will find in ponds and slow-running streams, is a necessary as well as a handsome plant; but it multiplies so fast that you will be obliged occasionally to remove some of it. The tape-grass will be found in some rivers, and you must obtain two plants, one male and the other female. They are to be distinguished by their flowers—the male being borne on short and straight, while the female flowers are on long, spiral foot-stalks. On the projecting rock you may cultivate the forget-me-not. To these you may add one or two others, from time to time, but do not crowd your aquarium. To set them, place a ball of clay around the roots, sink it, and hold it in place with two or three pebbles. It will soon take care of itself.

THE FISH AND INSECTS.

About a week after the plants are in, removing in the mean while dead leaves and scum, or other impurities, you introduce your fish, and one or two fresh-water snails, who will act as scavengers. Of these last, one of the varieties of *planorbis* is best. The crawfish, which every boy knows, will be a very pleasant inhabitant.

Of fish, the first fellow to introduce to confined quarters will be the dace, a lively, graceful little fellow, with a black stripe running lengthwise. You will find him in most small streams, where he may be caught with a hand-net. The stickleback is a fine fish for your purpose. You want a pair of

CRAWFISH.

these, for they will breed in the tank; and as the stickleback builds his nest somewhat like a hanging-bird's—a regular little house, with back door and front door—and is a lively, spirited fellow, he will afford you a deal of amusement. A small eel or two will be nice enough until they grow large. The gudgeon, and the catfish, dace, or rockfish, will answer. So will the sunfish, while very small. As he grows older he is apt to disturb the others. A small goldfish, where you can obtain it, will add variety, and the newt, or water-lizard, to be had in every pond and stream, must not be forgotten. They soon grow tame, and will feed from your finger.

The fish must be fed occasionally with small pieces of worms and shreds of lean beef, cut fine. Occasionally a few dough-pills is a kind of medicine they will take with relish. Do not starve them, but, on the other hand, do not overfeed them. Whatever they do not eat must be removed, as its decomposition will affect the water.

Theoretically, the balance of animal and vegetable life will supply the fish with enough oxygen; but practically not, because you cannot attain the exact proportion between the two. The water must be aerated from time to time, and this is done with a small pair of common bellows, with which you blow air into the water, to the comfort and satisfaction of the inhabitants of your pond.

PART IV.

Play-Room Games, for Rainy Days:

INCLUDING

ROUND GAMES AND FORFEITS, BOARD AND SLATE GAMES,
AND TABLE AND TOY GAMES.

PLAY-ROOM

N. ORR N.Y

GAMES

PLAY-ROOM GAMES.

A RAINY HOLIDAY! what a dampness the very idea flings over many a young heart! A holiday when the rain comes steadily, perseveringly, obstinately down—drip, drip, drip!—without a chance of its holding up until the sun has gone down, and it's time to go back to school; when there's no chance of getting out to stroll or run, and all knowledge of out-door games is, for the time being, utterly useless and unprofitable; when perhaps you have half a dozen youngsters come to spend with you the holiday you have obtained to celebrate your birthday, or Christmas, or some other festive occasion; and each of you, under the necessity of keeping in-doors out of the rain, feels as much like a fish out of water as a catfish in a ball-room. Then is the time when an acquaintance with play-room games becomes really valuable; and the person who can impart such knowledge appears as that most welcome of all benefactors, "a friend in need." In this character we, the editor of the present treatise, mean to appear; for do we not devote the following pages to play-room games, and ought we not thereby to be considered as having established a title to the permanent gratitude of our young readers, one and all? We should rather think so.

BLIND-MAN'S-BUFF

Consists in one persons having a handkerchief bound over his eyes so as to completely blind him, and thus blindfolded trying to chase the other players, either by the sound of their footsteps, or their subdued merriment, as they scramble away in all directions, endeavoring to avoid being caught by him ; when he can manage to catch one, the player caught must in turn be blinded, and the game be begun again. In some places it is customary for one of the players to inquire of Buff (before the game begins), "How many horses has your father got?" to which inquiry he responds, "Three." "What colors are they?" "Black, white, and gray." The questioner then desires Buff to "turn round three times, and catch whom you may," which request he complies with, and then tries to capture one of the players. It is often played by merely turning the blindfolded hero round and round without questioning him, and then beginning. The handkerchief must be tied on fairly, so as to allow no little holes for Buffy to see through. In Europe they have a modified way of playing at blind-man's-buff, which, though less jolly than our American method, may be followed with advantage on birthdays and holidays, when boys and girls are dressed in their best, and careful parents are averse to rough clothes-tearing play. The party are not scattered here and there over the ground, but take hands and form a circle. In the midst stands Mr. Buff, blindfolded, and with a short thin stick in his hand. The players keep running round in a circle, generally singing, while Buff approaches gradually, guided mostly by their voices, till he manages to touch one of the twirling circle with his stick. Then the dance stops, and the dancers become motionless and silent. The player who has been touched must take the end of the stick in her hand, while Buff holds the other; and she must distinctly repeat three times after him, any word he chooses to name—"Good morning" or "Good night," for instance ; of course, disguising his or her voice as much as possible. The blind man tries to guess the name of his captor by the voice. If he succeeds, the person caught becomes blind man ; if not, Buff must try his luck again.

HOW D'YE LIKE YOUR NEIGHBOR?

The company must be seated in a circle round the room, with a clear space in the middle. The chairs are placed close together, and the number of chairs is one less than that of the players ; for instance, if thirteen players, twelve chairs. The chairless person stands in the middle of the room, and addressing one of the company, says, "Master Jones, how do you like your neighbor?" Jones may either answer, "Very well indeed ;" or, singling out two of the company, he may say, "I prefer Master A. to Miss B.," or "Miss A. to Mr. R." If, being of a contented disposition, he likes both his neighbors "very much indeed," all the players must change places ; if, on the contrary, he prefers Master A. to Miss B., the two whom he names must change, the others sitting still ; in either case it is the object of the person in the middle to get into one of the vacant chairs while the changing is going on ; and if he can succeed in doing this, the person thus left seatless must stand in the middle, and ask the players how they like their neighbors ; if not, the first player has to take up his position in the centre again, and the game goes on.

ONE OLD OX OPENING OYSTERS.

This is a capital round game, and will tax the memory and the gravity of the youngsters. The company being seated, the fugleman says, " *One old ox opening oysters,*" which each must repeat in turn with perfect gravity. Any one who indulges in the slightest giggle is mulcted of a forfeit forthwith. When the first round is finished, the fugleman begins again:—" *Two toads, totally tired, trying to trot to Troy ;*" and the others repeat in turn, each separately, " *One old ox opening oysters ; Two toads, totally tired,*" &c. The third round is, " *Three tawny tigers tickling trout,*" and the round recommences:—" *One old ox,* &c.; *Two toads, totally,* &c.; *Three tawny tigers,* &c.*" The fourth round, and up to the twelfth and last, given out by the fugleman successively, and repeated by the other players, are as follows:—" *Four fat friars fanning a fainting fly ; Five fair flirts flying to France for fashions ; Six Scotch salmon selling six sacks of sour-krout ; Seven small soldiers successfully shooting snipes ; Eight elegant elephants embarking for Europe ; Nine nimble noblemen nibbling nonpareils ; Ten tipsy tailors teasing a titmouse ; Eleven early earwigs eagerly eating eggs ; and Twelve twittering tomtits on the top of a tall tottering tree.*" Any mistake in repeating this legend, or any departure from the gravity suitable to the occasion, is to be punished by the infliction of a forfeit ; and the game has seldom been known to fail in producing a rich harvest of those little pledges. Of course, a good deal depends on the serio-comic gravity of the fugleman.

MAGIC MUSIC.

One of the players is sent out of the room, and a handkerchief, a pair of gloves, a brooch, or other small article, is hidden in some cunning nook. The signal is then given for the banished one to return ; and a lady or gentleman acquainted with music takes up a position at the piano. It is for the musician to indicate, by the strains of the piano, when the seeker is approaching the object hidden. As he recedes from it, the music falls to a low tone, and a mournful cadence ; as he approaches it, the notes swell out loud and clear, and bursts into a triumphal strain as he lays his hand on the prize. If properly managed, the magic music may be made to have almost magnetic power in drawing the seeker toward it.

Another way of playing the game, and an improved one, is to set the seeker some task to perform, instead of finding the handkerchief. Say, for instance, he is to take a book from a bookcase, and present it to a lady. As he walks round the room, the music increases in sound as he approaches the bookcase, but falls as he passes it. This tells him in what locality his task is. He takes a book, and the music sounds loudly and joyously. He begins to read—no ! the music falls at once ; he is faltering in his task. He carries the book round the room. As he approaches the lady, the notes burst forth loudly again, concluding with a triumphant flourish as he presents the volume to her with a gallant bow. In case of failure, a forfeit is exacted, and each player must have a task set him, or her, in turn.

TWIRLING THE PLATE.

The players sit or stand around a table covered with cloth, and one of them takes up a wooden or metal plate, which sits on its edge, and gives it a spin. As he does this he names some one of the players, who is obliged to catch it before it has done spinning, or pay a forfeit. The player so called on sets the plate spinning in turn, calling upon some other player to stop it, and so on around.

HOW DO YOU LIKE IT? WHEN DO YOU LIKE IT?
AND WHERE DO YOU LIKE IT?

This is a guessing game. One of the company retires, while the rest fix on some article or object—for instance, light, an apple, money, &c. The person who has gone out is then recalled, and proceeds round the circle, asking each player in succession, "How do you like it?" Supposing the thing thought of to be *money*, the first may answer, "In abundance," the second, "Ready," and so on. The questioner tries to gain from the answers thus given some clue to the nature of the thing thought of. The second question, "When do you like it?" will probably help him. One of the players may reply, "When I have to pay my bills;" another, "When I want a new coat," and so on. The third question is almost certain to help a judicious questioner out of his puzzlement. "Where?" "In my pocket," one of the players will reply; another, "At my banker's," and so on. Some one is almost sure to drop a hint which will set the guesser upon the right track. Three guesses are allowed him. If he succeeds, he must point out the player whose answer gave him the clue, and the latter pays a forfeit and goes out to be puzzled in his turn. Failing to guess in three trials, the first player must try another question. The art of the game consists in choosing words with more meanings than one, such as cord (chord); for then the answers may be varied in a very puzzling manner. One will like a *cord* round his box; another a c(h)ord in a piece of music; another on the piano, &c.; thus key (*quay*), bark, vessel, are good words to choose.

WHAT IS MY THOUGHT LIKE?

The party sitting round as usual, one of them thinks of some person, place, or thing: the Emperor Napoleon (the first or third will do), New York, a coal-scuttle, the Island of Tahiti—any thing, in fact, that first occurs to him; and then he asks each of the company in turn, "What is my thought like?" They, in complete ignorance as to the nature of the said thought, reply at random. One says, for instance, "like a steam-engine;" another, "like a cavern;" a third, "like a tea-kettle." When an opinion has thus been collected from each one, the questioner tells what his thought was, and each player, under penalty of a forfeit, has to give a reason for the answer made to the first question. We will suppose, continuing the instance just begun, that the questioner says to the first in the company, "My thought was Napoleon III. Now, why is Napoleon III. like a steam-engine?" The answer is ready enough: "Because he goes at an uncommonly fast pace." "Why is he like a cavern?" "Because his depth is one of his distinguishing qualities," replies the second. "Why is he like a tea-kettle?" "Of course, because he boils over occasionally," says the third player, triumphantly; and so the game goes merrily on through the circle. There is an anecdote told of the poet Moore, which is worth repeating. Moore was once at Lord Holland's house, among a distinguished circle of guests, and "What is my thought like?" was the game of the evening. When the question came to him, the poet replied, "a pump." The thought happened to be, "Lord Castlereagh," a statesman famous for the absurd speeches he made in Parliament. Among other strange assertions, he had said of an opposition member, "The honorable gentleman came down to the house *like a crocodile, with his hands in his pockets.*" Well, every one thought Tom Moore was posed; but the poet, with a merry smile, gave not only an answer, but a poetical answer to the query; he replied:—

> "Because it is an empty thing of wood,
> Which up and down its awkward arm doth sway,
> And coolly spout, and spout, and spout away,
> In one weak, washy, everlasting flood!"

CUPID'S COMING.

A letter must be taken, and the termination "ing." Say, for instance, that P is chosen. The first player says to the second, "Cupid's coming." "How is he coming?" says the second. "Playing," rejoins the first. The second then says to the third, "Cupid's coming." "How?" "Prancing;" and so the question and reply go round, through all the words beginning with P and ending with ing—piping, pulling, pining, praising, preaching, &c. Those who cannot answer the question on the spur of the moment pay a forfeit.

CROSS QUESTIONS AND CROOKED ANSWERS.

The company sit round, and each one whispers a question to his neighbor on the right, and then each one whispers an answer; so that each answers the question propounded by some other player, and of the purport of which he is, of course, ignorant. Then every player has to recite the question he received from one player and the answer he got from the other, and the ridiculous incongruity of these random cross questions and crooked answers will frequently excite a good deal of sport. One, for instance, may say, "I was asked 'If I considered dancing agreeable?' and the answer was, 'Yesterday fortnight.'" Another may declare, "I was asked 'If I had seen the comet?' and the answer was, 'He was married last year!'" A third, "I was asked 'What I liked best for dinner?' and the answer was, 'The Emperor of China!'"

CONSEQUENCES.

This is a round game, to play at which the company must be seated at a table. Each player has before him, or her, a long, narrow piece of writing-

paper and a pencil. At the top of the paper each writes a quality of a gentleman. "The fickle," for instance, or "the insinuating," or "the handsome," "the ugly," or any epithet, in fact, that may occur to the mind at the
moment. But nobody may see what the neighbors to the right and left
have written. The top of each paper is then folded down, so as to hide
what has been written, and each one passes his paper to his neighbor on the
right, so that every player has now a new paper before him. On this he
writes a gentleman's name; if that of one of the gentlemen in the company,
so much the better. Again the papers are passed to the right after being
folded over; the beauty of the game being that no one may write two consecutive sentences on the same paper. *The quality of a lady* is now written.
Fold, and pass the paper—*The lady's name*—then where *they met*—*what he
said to her*—*what she said to him*—*the consequence*—and *what the world said.*
The papers are now unfolded in succession, and the contents read, and the
queerest cross questions and crooked answers are almost sure to result.
For instance, the following will be a specimen:—"The conceited Mr. Jones
(one of the company) and the accomplished Miss Smith met on the top of an
omnibus. He said to her, ' Will you love me then as now ?' She said to
him, 'How very kind you are;' the consequence was, 'they separated for-
ever,' and the world said 'Serve them right.'" Another strip, on being unfolded, may produce some such legend as this: —"The amiable Artemus
Ward and the objectionable Mrs. Grundy met on the mall at the Central Park.
He said to her, ' How do I look ?' She said to him, ' Do it;' the consequence
was 'a secret marriage,' and the world said, ' We knew how it would be.'"

I LOVE MY LOVE WITH AN A

Is a well-known game, but it must be kept up briskly; for if too much time
be allowed the players for deliberation, the interest flags at once, and the
sport becomes dull. "The very *defect* of the matter," as Launcelot Gobbo
would say, lies in quickly finding epithets beginning with any given letter
of the alphabet, such as A, B, or C, and the penalty for failure is a forfeit.
The company sit round, and each has to love his or her love with a different
letter. The first (we will say a lady) begins—"I love my love with an A,
because he's amiable. I hate him with an A, because he's arrogant; he
took me to the sign of the ' Artichoke,' and treated me with apples and ale."
" I love my love with a B," continues the second, "because she's beautiful.
I hate her with a B, because she's bounceable. I took her to the sign of the
' Brown Bear,' and treated her with bread and butter, and beer." " I love my
love with a C," says a third, " because he's candid. I hate him with a C, because he's captious. He took me to the sign of the ' Cart-horse,' and treated
me to curds and cream." And so the game goes on through all the letters of
the alphabet, with the exception of poor X, for the very good reason that no
English word begins with that unfortunate letter. Instead of going regularly round the circle, it is better that each player should have the power,
after " loving his love," to call upon any one of the rest to continue the game.

This gives an additional interest to the proceedings, from the unexpectedness of the summons.

PROVERBS.

One of the company who is to guess the proverb leaves the room; the remaining players fix upon some proverb, such as "All is not gold that glitters"—"A bird in the hand is worth two in the bush"—"Birds of a feather flock together"—"Train up a child in the way he should go"—"A miss is as good as a mile." A proverb being chosen, the words are distributed in rotation through the company, each player receiving a word which he must bring in in the answer he gives to any question asked by the guesser. We will suppose the proverb, "Train up a child in the way he should go," to have been chosen. The first person will receive the word "train," the second "up," the third "a," the fourth "child," the fifth "in," the sixth "the," and the seventh "way," and so on. The person who has gone out is now called in, and begins his questions with the first player, something in the following manner: *Q.* "Have you been out to day?" *A.* "No, I must *train* myself to like walking better than I do." He turns to the second player. *Q.* "Are you a member of the National Guard?" *A.* "No, I gave it *up* some time ago." The third player has an easy task to bring in the word *a,* but the fourth, with the word *child,* finds his work more difficult. *Q.* "Are you fond of reading?" *A.* "Any *child* might answer that question." Now, the guesser, if he be a sharp reasoner, will see that this answer is evasive, and only given to bring in the word *child;* he will, perhaps, guess the proverb at once; but if he is a cautious personage he will go on, and finish the round of questions before committing himself by a guess, for he is only allowed three. If he succeeds in guessing the proverb, he has to point out the person whose answer first set him on the right track, who must then pay a forfeit, and go out in his turn to have his powers tested.

THE EMPEROR OF MOROCCO.

This is one of those games in which the art consists in preserving an immutable gravity, under every provocation to laugh. In "the Emperor of Morocco," two of the players, generally one of each sex, advance with measured steps into the middle of the room, and ceremoniously salute each other, and the following dialogue takes place, the speakers being compelled to look one another full in the face :—

FIRST PLAYER : The Emperor of Morocco is dead. SECOND PLAYER : I'm very sorry for it. FIRST PLAYER : He died of the gout in his left great toe. SECOND PLAYER : I'm *very* sorry for it. FIRST PLAYER : And all the court are to go into mourning, and wear black rings through their noses. SECOND PLAYER : I'm VERY sorry for it. They then bow again and retire to their places, while another pair comes forward to go through the same impressive dialogue ; and so on, till the game has gone all round the circle, a forfeit being the penalty for the slightest approach to a giggle.

BUFF

Is a similar game to the last. One of the players comes forward armed with a poker, which he taps on the floor—knock, knock, knock. "Whence come you?" asks one of the company. "I come from poor Buff, full of sorrow and care." "And what said Buff to you?" is the next question. The intruder replies—

> "Buff said, 'Baff!'
> And he gave me this staff,
> And he bade me not laugh
> Till I came to Buff's house again."

And with this he delivers the poker to his questioner, and marches out. But in the mean time the spectators have been trying their best, by grimaces and droll remarks, to overset the gravity of the emissary of the respectable Buff. One says, "Just look at him; he is going to laugh!" Another, "He hasn't a staff at all—it's a poker!" "Don't he look as if he wanted his dinner!" and any other facetious remarks that may suggest themselves on the spur of the moment.

Sometimes the formula is changed, and Mr. Buff's allocution is as follows:

> "Buff says Buff to all his men,
> And I say Buff to you again ;
> Buff he neither laughs nor smiles,
> In spite of all your cunning wiles,
> But keeps his face with a very good grace,
> And carries his staff to the very next place."

THE FAMILY COACH.

Each person in company represents something connected with a family coach; one is the harness, another the horses, a third the coachman, a fourth the footman, a fifth, sixth, and seventh, the pole, whip, and drag, and so on, till each player has a representative office. One of the company begins to relate an anecdote, and each time he mentions the "family coach," all the players must rise from their seats and turn round. When he mentions harness, or wheels, or pole, or any other part of the equipage, the persons representing those parts must rise, each at the mention of his name, and turn round. Failing to do this, they pay a forfeit. The story itself will be something in the following way:—

"You must all have heard, at some time or other, of my friend, Mr. Timothy Tapertit. He lived in a capital house at Hackensack, with Mrs. Tapertit, and all the little Tapertits, who all had snub noses and crooked legs, and were considered very like their father. He was a very comfortable sort of man, Mr. Tapertit, and liked to have a good establishment about him, a steady *coachman* (coachman rises and turns round), a tall *footman* (footman does likewise), and every thing comfortable and handsome; but the thing he prided himself on most of all, was his *family coach* (all the players rise and turn round). This *family coach* (all turn round again) was a very complete machine in its way. It had real *wheels* (wheels turn round), and a *pole* (pole turns), and there was a good set of *harness*, and a pair of *horses*, and a *drag*, and every thing complete ; in fact, it was a famous *family coach*." Then he proceeds to describe Timothy Tapertit ordering out this famous vehicle for a drive ; and an accident that takes place, involving endless difficulties with the coachman, footman, harness, horses, and every part of the turn-out, ending with the expression of a fixed determination on the part of Mr. Tapertit to get rid of his equipage as soon as possible, and to be bothered no more with the *family coach*. If well managed, this game cannot fail to produce plenty of fun and forfeits.

EARTH, AIR, AND WATER.

One of the players is furnished with a handkerchief, which he throws suddenly and unexpectedly at another, crying out the name of "earth," "air," or "water," whichever he likes, and then counting ten as rapidly as he can. Before he has come to ten, the person at whom the handkerchief is thrown must name a creature that inhabits the element thus mentioned, or, failing to do this, pays a forfeit. Thus, suppose the thrower of the handkerchief says WATER—one, two, three, four, five, six, seven, eight, nine, TEN, the person challenged must call the name of some fish ; if air, the name of a bird ; or, if earth, that of a quadruped. If the question is put very abruptly, and the number quickly counted, the players will often be unable to get out their reply quickly enough, and the forfeits come in merrily. The best way is, to look at one person, and then unexpectedly throw the handkerchief at another.

ORANGES AND LEMONS.

A good children's game. Two of the players take each other's hands and hold them up in the form of an arch (as in the "Sir Roger de Coverley" dance), and the others, taking hold of each other's coats and dresses, pass under the arch one after the other, while the archway players chant the following ditty :

"Oranges and Lemons, say the bells of St. Clements.
You owe me five farthings, say the bells of St. Martin's.
When will you pay me ? say the bells at the Old Bailey.
When I grow rich, say the bells at Shoreditch.
When will that be ? say the bells at Stepney.
I do not know, says the great bell at Bow.
Here comes a candle to light you to bed,
And here comes a chopper to chop off the last, last, last man's head."

And as the last man comes to the arch, it descends like a portcullis, and cuts him off from his companions. His captors then ask him if he prefers oranges or lemons, and according to his reply he is sent into the right or the left corner of the room ; the chant then recommences, and continues till all the last men's heads have been duly cut off, and the players are divided into two parties on opposite sides. They then take hold of each other round the waist, and the foremost players grasp each other by the hands. The party that can drag the other across the room wins.

18*

PIGEONS FLY.

The players are seated at a table, and each puts his two forefingers on the board before him. The leader cries out, "Pigeons fly!" and suddenly lifts his hands in the air to imitate the action of flying; all the players have to do likewise. The leader raises his hands each time he calls out a name; but the others must only remove their hands from the table at the names of such creatures as really fly. The leader's object is to entrap them into incurring forfeits by lifting their hands at the wrong time, which, under judicious management, some of them are sure to do. Thus, the leader cries in rapid succession: "Crows fly!—Eagles fly!—Gnats fly!—Sparrows fly—*Horses* fly!" In the excitement of the game, some are sure to lift their hands from the table, oblivious of the fact that horses do *not* fly, and they pay forfeits accordingly.

RED-CAP AND BLUE-CAP

Is a good game, and used to be very popular at sea, in the olden times, among the little middies. The penalty of a mistake was cobbing with knotted handkerchiefs; but, of course, in polite society, this part of the ceremony is dispensed with—a forfeit, or something similar, being substituted. The players sit round in a circle, and represent tailors. Each has a name, and one is the master. One man takes the name Blue-cap, another is Red-cap, a third Yellow-cap, a fourth Black-cap, and so on, through as many colors as there are players. The leader then pretends to examine the work, and says: "Here's a false stitch; who made it, Blue-cap?" Blue-cap immediately answers: "Who, sir?—I, sir?" "Yes, you, sir!" "Not I, sir." "Who then, sir?" "Yellow-cap, sir." Yellow-cap must at once take up the word, and the same dialogue is repeated. "Who, sir?—I sir?" &c., another workman being named as the delinquent. Any one who fails to answer to his name pays a forfeit. If briskly kept up, the game is a thoroughly good one.

CONCERT.

The players represent an orchestra, each one taking charge of an imaginary instrument, and going through the motions of playing upon it. Thus, "Fife" too-toos on an imaginary instrument about nine inches long; "Drum" bangs away at an invisible parchment; "Trombone" puts one hand to his mouth, and shifts the other to and fro as he grumbles out an accompaniment; "Cymbals" clashes his two hands together, and each and all are kept in order by a conductor, who stands in the midst, beating time energetically. At a signal from the leader, they all go off simultaneously; but when he holds up his hand, they must stop instantaneously. He then pretends to find fault with one or more of the players, who must instantly answer with some excuse adapted to their instruments; violin pleading that he has no rosin; harp, that a string is broken; and so on. Any hesitation at once entails a forfeit, as does, also, an answer not immediately connected with the instrument of the person challenged.

PRUSSIAN EXERCISE.

This game furnishes a good joke, but must be played circumspectly, that no offence may be given, and no unpleasant consequences arise. The company are drawn up in line, with a sergeant and captain—the former standing at the head of the line, the latter in front of the regiment, to give the word of command. The two officers must be in the secret, and act in concert. The captain gives the order, and puts his men through their drill, they taking the time from the sergeant. After a few ordinary commands, such as "Heads up," "Eyes right," etc., the word is given to "Ground right knees," whereupon all the men kneel down on the right knee. Then comes, "Right hands forward," whereupon the sergeant stretches out his right arm and hand horizontally in front of him, at full length. "Left hands backward," and the left arms are thrust back as nearly horizontal as possible with the shoulders. Now comes the word "Fire!" at which the sergeant gives his neighbor a push; he, taken unawares, tumbles against the next man, and down goes the whole row like a house of cards.

"MY LADY'S TOILET"

Is very like the "family coach." Each person represents some necessary of the toilet—brush, comb, soap, scent, brooch, jewel-case, &c., and the lady's maid stands in the middle of the circle, and calls for any article her lady is supposed to want. The personator of that article must then jump up, or be fined a forfeit for negligence. Every now and then the abigail announces that her lady wants her whole toilet, when the whole circle of players must rise and change places. The lady's maid herself makes a bolt for a chair, and the player who is left chairless in the scuffle becomes lady's maid.

YES AND NO.

One of the players thinks of any person or thing, and the rest sit round and ask him questions about it, which he answers with "yes" or "no," taking care to give no other explanations. From the information thus gained, each gives a guess as to what the thought was. If the questions are ingeniously framed, the solution is generally discovered, unless the "thought" be peculiarly abstruse. The game is a very good one, and we herewith emphatically recommend it, particularly as affording an opportunity of "cooling down" after a romp.

COPENHAGEN.

First procure a long piece of tape or twine, sufficient to go round the whole company, who must stand in a circle, holding in each of their hands a part of the string; the last takes hold of the two ends of the tape. One remains standing in the centre of the circle, who is called "the Dane," and who must endeavor to slap the hands of one of those who are holding the s..ng, before they can be withdrawn. Whoever is not sufficiently alert, and allows the hands to be slapped, must take the place of the Dane, and, in his turn, try to slap the hands of some one else.

THE FAGOTS.

This game consists in forming a double circle, the players placing themselves two by two, so that each boy, by holding a girl in front of him, makes what is called a fagot. It is necessary that the players should be of an even number. The circles being formed, two persons are chosen, the one to catch the other. When the person who is pursued does not wish to be overtaken (which would oblige him to take the place of the pursuer), and at the same time desires to rest, he places himself in front of any one of the fagots he chooses, but within the circle, so that this fagot is then composed of three persons, which is contrary to rule. Then the third one, who is on the outside of the circle, must at once run, to avoid being caught. If he *is caught*, he takes the place of the pursuer, who, in his turn, starts off, or, if he prefers it, enters into the circle, and places himself before one of the fagots, thus obliging a new player to run like the former one; this one himself can at once oblige another player to run, by placing himself, in his turn, before a fagot, and it is this which gives life to the game, provided the players have a fair share of spirit and agility.

HUNT THE HARE.

The company all form a circle, holding each other's hands. One, called the hare, is left out, who runs several times round the ring, and at last stops, tapping one of the players on the shoulder. The one tapped quits the ring and runs after the hare, the circle again joining hands. The hare runs in and out in every direction, passing under the arms of those in the circle, until caught by the pursuer, when he becomes hare himself. Those in the circle must always be friends to the hare, and assist its escape in every way possible.

THUS SAYS THE GRAND MUFTI.

In this game one of the company sits in a chair, and is called the Mufti, or the Grand Mufti. He makes whatever grimace or motion he pleases, such as putting his hand on his heart, winking, sneezing, coughing, stretching out his arm, smiting his forehead, etc. At each movement he says, "Thus says the Grand Mufti," or "So says the Grand Mufti." When he says, "Thus says the Grand Mufti," every one must make just such a motion as he does; but when he says, "So says the Grand Mufti," every one must keep still. .A forfeit for a mistake is exacted.

HUNT THE RING

Is a good substitute for the old game of "hunt the slipper," which has become almost impracticable in these days of crinoline. A long tape, with a ring strung on it, is held by all the players, as they stand in a circle, with one in the middle. They pass the ring rapidly from hand to hand, and it is the business of the player in the midst to hunt the ring, and try to seize the hands that hold it; while the other players, on their part, make his task more difficult by pretending to pass the ring to each other, when it may really be in quite another part of the circle. The person in whose hands the ring is found has to take his turn in the middle.

TRANSPOSITIONS.

A capital game to sharpen the wits, and one from which amusement for many hours may be extracted. The company sit round a table, and each person is provided with a pencil and a scrap of paper. Each one writes on his or her scrap a name of a city, country, river, mountain, or, if preferred, of some historical personage, transposing the letters so as to make the recognition of the word as difficult as possible, and accompanying it with a few written words of explanation; for instance, if a town is selected, the explanation must give some particulars of situation or circumstance, to set the guesser upon the right track; if a personage, the date at which he flourished and the country which gave him birth ought to be given. Then the papers are folded together and deposited in the middle of the table; and when they have been well mixed, a folded paper is drawn by each player, and those who cannot decipher the transposition which has fallen to their share are condemned to pay a forfeit. When all have been read, the game begins anew. The following transpositions of words may serve as hints to those who wish to introduce this very amusing pastime among their friends:

Ann Filkr.—The name shared by two great discoverers, one of whom visited an unexplored region, and the other explored a region he had never visited.

Simon Ficar ran.—A celebrated general of the Revolution, who rarely commanded over fifty men, and yet was more dreaded than those whose followers numbered thousands.

Voosarinlimb.—A soldier who gave his country a government, and died while in arms against the government he created.

Jack Wanders? No.—A man who rose from obscurity to the highest position in the country; who became a soldier, without a military education; and received the highest degree a university could confer, without learning.

Lollcomew River.—A potent sovereign, who ruled a nation with despotic sway and profound wisdom, advancing her glory and consolidating her power, but whose name is not recorded among her kings.

TASKS FOR REDEEMING FORFEITS.

Now that we have shown our friends so many ways of getting rid of their property, under the guise of forfeits, it is but fair that we should give them a few directions concerning the methods by which they may win them back, and therefore we give, for the benefit of all players of games of forfeits, the following selections, from a large variety of tasks to be executed by those players whose gloves, handkerchiefs, and other properties have been laid under embargo for their owners' shortcomings during the game. The usual method of proceeding in redeeming forfeits is this: A lady, who undertakes to cry the forfeits, sits on a chair or sofa, and another player, who is to pronounce the various sentences, sits or kneels on a low stool before her. One of the forfeited articles is held up by the lady on the sofa, over the head of the doomster, who must not see what it is. The following formula is then gone through:

> " Here's a pretty thing, and a very pretty thing;
> What shall the owner do, now, of this very pretty thing?"

"Is it fine (belonging to a gentleman), or superfine (belonging to a lady)?" asks the pronouncer of sentences, and, according to the reply, he selects a task appropriate for a boy or a girl. The task having been selected, the article is held up to be owned.

Among the penalties most frequently inflicted are the following:

To Perform a Grecian Statue.—This is a boy's forfeit, and he achieves his task by mounting on a chair or table, when each one of the company advances, in turn, and puts him in a different attitude, in which he must remain until it is altered by the next person. The fun consists in the ridiculous postures the unfortunate victim is compelled to assume by his tormentors.

To Pay each Person in Company a Compliment, and then Spoil it.—This will exercise the quickness and wit of the performer, and enable him, besides, to take a little harmless revenge on those of his friends who have been harassing him during the evening. To one, for instance, he says, " You have a finer voice than any one in this present company; but," he adds, as the person addressed bows to the compliment, " it's a pity that you never give it any rest." To another, " You have certainly a great amount of wit, *only* you always exercise it at the expense of your friends;" and to a third, " Your eyes are certainly very bright, and is that the reason why they're always searching for their own reflection in the looking-glass?" and so on, until you have finished your round.

To Brush off the Dime.—This is a trick which may be played off on a novice, and will excite much merriment if well managed. The owner of the forfeit is told that he will have to shake off a dime from his forehead, and a coin is shown him. The dime is then enclosed in a damp handkerchief, and pressed hard against the forehead of the victim, who is not allowed to put his hands up to his head. Feeling the impression of the dime on his brow, he will have no doubt that it has been really fastened on, and not suspecting its removal in the handkerchief, he will begin shaking his head from side to side, and even rubbing it against projecting pieces of furniture, to the delight of the spectators, in persevering efforts to get rid of what is not there.

Bow to the Wittiest in the room, kneel to the prettiest, and kiss the one whom you love best.

To Play the Judge.—This consists in sitting on a chair in a conspicuous part of the room, and listening with the most perfect gravity to the complaints brought by the rest of the company, who try, by all kinds of ridiculous reports and artifices, to upset the stolidity of the learned gentleman on the bench.

Compliments under Difficulties.—Pay six compliments to six different persons, avoiding the use of the letter *l* in every one.

Prison Diet.—A glass of water and a teaspoon are brought into the room, and the person who has to undergo "prison diet" is blindfolded, and a teaspoonful of cold water administered to him by any of the others, until he guesses who is feeding him, which seldom happens, unless he be born under a fortunate star, till the glass of water is half empty.

Repeating a Piece of Poetry, or telling an anecdote, is a very favorite way of redeeming a forfeit. Singing a song, either humorous or sentimental, is also admissible.

The Knight of the Rueful Countenance.—The knight whose forfeit is to be redeemed is marched slowly round the circle of company by his squire, who kisses the hand of every young lady (and the cheeks of all under a certain age), wiping the mouth of the knight after each salute. If the knight's countenance relaxes from a rueful expression into a smile, his forfeit is not returned until he has gone through some other task.

Other penalties for forfeits there are in abundance, such as to laugh, cry, cough, and sneeze in the four different corners of the room; to count forty backwards; to kiss your own shadow, without laughing, four separate times; to compose a rhymed verse; to hop on one foot three times round the room; to ask a riddle of each person in company; to repeat, without hesitation or mistake, some such brain-puzzle as the following:—

> "Robert Rowley rolled a round roll round;
> A round roll Robert Rowley rolled round;
> Where rolled the round roll Robert Rowley rolled round?"

Or the still more heart-breaking epic:—

> "There was a man and his name was Cob;
> He had a wife, and her name was Mob;
> He had a dog, and his name was Bob;
> She had a cat, and her name was Chittrybob.
> 'Bob!' says Cob.
> 'Chittrybob!' says Mob.
> Bob was Cob's dog;
> Mob's cat was Chittrybob;
> Cob, Mob, Bob, and Chittrybob!"

And when all these pains and penalties have been gone through, if there should still be some pledges remaining, we recommend that a general amnesty be published, and such pledges returned to their respective owners, the penalties being remitted. Above all things, let these round games, like all others, be pursued in a hearty and generous spirit; and let us, in concluding this chapter, remind our young readers that the real way to enjoy them is to preserve a hearty good-humor in the heat of playing.

THE INTERRUPTED REPLY.

The company place themselves in a circle. The one who commences says in a whisper to his right-hand neighbor, "Of what use is a book?" (or any other article he may select.)

His neighbor must answer, correctly, "It is of use to read," and then ask another question of *his* right-hand neighbor—for instance, "Of what use is a goblet?"

The art in this game consists in so framing one's questions, that they will produce answers altogether unsuited to the preceding question. If the answer is, "It is of use to drink from," a laughable consequence ensues; for, when the round is finished, or, in other words, when the person who has commenced the game has been questioned in his turn, the questions and answers are repeated aloud, by taking the answer of the person on the player's right as a reply to the question of the person on his left; it follows, that to the question, "Of what use is a book?" one of the company has answered, "It is of use to drink from;" and so on with the rest of the questions and answers.

SEEING'S BELIEVING.

BOARD AND SLATE GAMES.

LOTO.

THIS is a good quiet game, and one that will keep the attention alive, and quicken the eyes of the players, if properly conducted.   The cards and numbers used in playing loto may be procured at any toy-shop.   There are twenty-four of these cards in the game.   Each card is divided into three rows, and each row contains nine squares, five numbered, and four blank.   These numbers are arranged in columns down the card, the first column containing the units, the second the tens, the third

LOTO CARDS AND NUMBERS.

the twenties, and so on up to ninety, which is the highest number in the game.   Thus, each card contains fifteen numbers, and each number is contained four times in the set of cards.   Besides these cards, there are two bags; one containing a series of numbers, from one to ninety, on little wooden disks; the other about a couple of hundred round counters of horn, or, better still, of glass; for these counters are used for covering the numbered squares, and the numbers can be read through the circular glasses without uncovering the squares.   One of the players shuffles the loto cards, mixing them well together, and then distributes them in turn to the rest, reserving a share for himself.   If there are twelve people to join in the game, each will receive two cards; if only eight, each may have three, which must be placed one under the other, so that the player can glance his eye rapidly down the series of units, tens, &c.   Sometimes, however, it is agreed that each person shall receive only one card, which proceeding is said to increase the interest of the game by protracting it.   The dealer then puts his hand into the bag of wooden numbers, and draws them out as they come, calling them aloud, and the players cover the numbers on their cards as the names are cried. A pool must previously be made, of nuts, cherries, sweetmeats, ratafia cakes, or any similar agreeable offerings the liberality of the host or hostess has provided; sometimes a collection of marbles, contributed by the players, is made to answer the purpose. The player who first covers five numbers in a row on the same card, takes one-quarter of the pool; he who covers two rows entirely in the same way has the second quarter, and the fortunate wight who has first crowned the whole series of numbered squares on his card or cards with the little disks of glass obtains the remaining half. As each portion of the pool is cleared, the player who claims it has to read out his numbers, which are verified by the wooden marks drawn from the bag, to make sure that there are no mistakes. When the pool is small, it is sometimes better to make no payment for the first row, or even for the first two rows; the whole being adjudged in undivided splendor to the fortunate player who covers his whole card. On the other hand, where the pool consists of a number of small objects, such as nuts, the number of prizes may be increased, a small fee being paid for the first two *consecutive* numbers covered, a larger for the first three, another for the first four and five, and still larger premiums for one, two, and three rows. All this is to be agreed upon before the game is commenced.

TIT-TAT-TO.

This is a game that small boys enjoy, and some big ones who won't own it. A figure is drawn on the slate, as in the cut, and the object of the game is that one shall draw three crosses in a row before the other can draw three naughts in that way; each to mark but one at a time, somewhere between the bars, and the two to mark in turns. Thus A makes a mark + in the centre; B begins with his O on the upper right-hand corner. Then A puts another + on the upper left-hand corner. B discovers his aim, and puts an

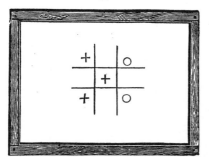

O in the lower right-hand corner which stops A from getting his three crosses in a row diagonally. Now if A, looking to get his three crosses, makes his mark down at the lower left-hand corner, as the cut shows, B will make a naught between his other two, and so get "tit-tat-to, three in a row." If A is smart, he will put his cross between those two naughts, though it end in a draw game, for B will put his naught on the opposite side, and then no one can make it.

THE GAME OF GOOSE.

This is an old-fashioned game, originally brought from Germany, where it is still known under the name of "*Post und Reise-spiel*" (Post and Journey game). To play at "Goose," a large square sheet of paper is used, marked with sixty-two squares, arranged in a spiral line, and numbered successively; the goal of the journey, number 63, being in the centre of the paper. Two dice and a box are provided, and each player has some mark, generally a little figure shaped like a chess-pawn, and painted in some distinguishing color. One after the other, the players throw with the dice, and move their tokens according to the numbers they throw. Thus, he who throws six and four, advances ten squares; while the next player, who may, perhaps, only throw one and two, can only get three stages on his journey. The traveller who arrives first at the goal, 63, wins the pool. But the number, 63, must be thrown *exactly*, neither more nor less; if more are thrown, the player has to count the excess number backwards, which considerably increases the fatigues of the journey. For instance, he may be at 59, and only want four to land him safely in 63. If at this conjuncture he should throw 10, he must count *four forward* to 63, and the remainder backward, which will land his token in square 57, two squares farther from the goal than he was before. The name "game of goose" was given to this pastime, because, in the old-fashioned cards for playing it, every fourth and fifth compartment bore the figure of a goose; and the player whose throw brought him into one of these goose compartments might count his throw double. In the journey game, several obstacles are introduced to test the patience of the adventurous traveller. On one square he finds a bridge, to pass which he must pay a toll of one counter, or one nut to the pool; again, there is an inn, where he must rest two throws, and pay two counters by way of reckoning; further on he meets with a pond, and if the dice cause him to tumble in, he must remain till another player casts the same throw, and thus helps him out. A prison is also introduced, in which the same thing takes place, except that the relieving player has to stay there himself, until he in turn is released by some one else who casts the same number. Other obstacles may be introduced at the player's option.

FOX AND GEESE.

This is another quiet game of skill; and a capital preparation for those who wish to become good draught-players, or even chess-players, some day, is to render themselves thorough masters of the mysteries of "Fox and Geese." The form of the board is shown in the accompanying cut. The geese are represented by white pegs (or by pins, if the players draw their own board on a card), and the fox by a red or black one.

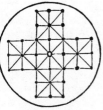

FOX AND GEESE.

The geese are seventeen in number, and are ranged as shown in the diagram; while the fox stands in the centre of the board. The geese may be moved along in the direction of the lines, but only one hole at a time. Their object is to block up the fox in a corner, or to surround him so that he cannot move; while he, on his side, can take any goose which has not another in the hole behind it for protection. If the fox can clear so many geese off the board that not enough are left to block him up, he wins; but if the geese are skilfully worked, they have a decided advantage over Reynard, and must win, by penning him into a corner, from whence he cannot extricate himself—and serve him right too.

There is another method of playing Fox and Geese on a chessboard, namely, with four white men, representing the Geese, and one black one, representing the Fox. The Geese are ranged on the four white squares

nearest one player, and the Fox may be placed where his owner pleases. The best place for him is that marked in the diagram, as he can manœuvre in a very puzzling way. The Geese can only move forward, and the Fox moves either way. The object of the Geese is to pen up the Fox so that he cannot move, and the Fox has to break through. If the game is properly played, the Geese must win, the secret being to keep them all in a line as much as possible. The Fox tries to prevent this plan from being followed up; and if he can succeed in doubling the Geese, or getting one to stand before another, he is nearly sure to pass through them.

NINE MEN'S MORRIS.

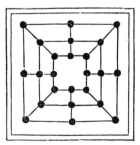

This game, sometimes called Merelles, is a very old one, and is interesting, though little known in this country. It is played upon a morris-board, or table, which is made as follows: Take a piece of wood or cardboard of any shape, and then paint or rule the central part in the manner shown; the black spots at every angle and intersection of the lines being the places for the men to be laid upon.

The men are 18 in number, nine white, and nine black or colored.

The manner of playing is briefly thus: There are two players; each has nine men (either draughts or counters), one set black and the other white. The pieces are to be laid down by the players alternately, the first object of each being to place his pieces, so that there may be three in one line (as on 6, 14, 21—4, 5, 6—10, 11, 12, etc.), and also to prevent his adversary doing so. (The angles, as 18, 21, 24, are not counted as one line.) When one player succeeds in this, he takes that one of his adversary's pieces from the board, which he considers most advantageous to himself. All the pieces being laid down, the game proceeds by moving the pieces along the lines to other spots, each player's object still being to place his men, and to take the forfeit as before described; he must not, however, take either of his adversary's which are already in their desired position, unless the line become broken. The game is decided by the men becoming blockaded, or being removed from the board, as in draughts.

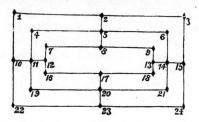

The following game will elucidate the above rules. The figures are placed on the diagram only for convenience of notation.

PLACING THE PIECES.   THE MOVES.

White.	Black.		White.						Black.				
7	16	1.	14 to 15	9.	7 to 12		1.	10 to	1	9.	8 to	7
18	9	2.	11	10	10.	12	16	2.	19	11	10.	11	12
11	10	3.	3	2	11.	10	11	3.	9	3	11.	7	8
4	19	4.	3	2	12.	20	19 × 14	4.	13	9	12.	8	9
5	6	5.	18	13	13.	19	20	5.	16	17	13.	12	7
2	8	6.	7	12	14.	6	14 × 5	6.	6	14	14.	1	10
14	23	7.	5	6	15.	2	5	7.	8	5	15.	7	8
20	22	8.	12	7	16.	14	6 × 9	8.	9	8	*Black resigns.*		
1	24 × 1												

The diagram .or the game may be drawn upon a slate, or upon a piece of stiff paper; and wafers or colored papers may be used where no better materials can be found.

SOLITAIRE.

This game has for the last few years become very fashionable. It is said that it was first invented by a Frenchman, to beguile the wearisome hours attendant on forest life, and for the amusement of the Indians, who pass much of their time alone at the chase, waiting in ambush for their prey for hours together. Be this as it may, the present attractive form and materials that are used to represent the game, *i. e.*, glass balls, of various brilliant colors, was the invention of an English clergyman, who had several made in this form, and, adding a profit to the expense of the materials, had the game sold for the benefit of a charity.

The game is played by a board with a number of holes, into which pegs are placed and removed during the progress of the game. But the balls of pretty colored glass are so universal, we will describe the game here as played with the latter. The board is round, with either thirty three holes, as seen in Diagram No. 1, or thirty-seven holes, as seen in No. 2. A groove

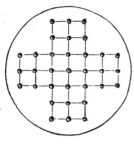

runs all round the board, for the convenience of laying the balls in as they are taken off the holes. In commencing the game, although the board is generally set out with thirty-seven or thirty-three balls, one must be removed at one of the corners, or in the middle. One ball takes another when it can leap over it into a vacant hole, in the same way that men are taken at draughts. The player must so calculate his progress that at the end of the game but *one* ball remains on the board; and the crowning point of success is to make this solitary ball

Fig. 1.

occupy the *centre* hole. Two players may play at this game, though originally intended only for one—alternate moves being made. The player who has fewest balls left when neither are in a position to take any more, is de-

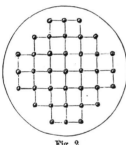

Fig. 2.

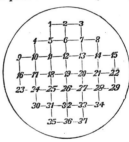

Fig. 3.

clared the winner. We have numbered the diagram (No. 3,) for the convenience of players who follow our method of winning the game, by leaving only one in the centre hole, which is called the "GENERAL."

Remove Ball No. 19	From 11 to 9	From 29 to 27
From 6 to 19	26 " 24	14 " 28
4 " 6	35 " 25	27 " 29
18 " 5	24 " 26	19 " 21
6 " 4	27 " 25	7 " 20
9 " 11	33 " 31	21 " 19
24 " 10	25 " 35	leaving the General alone in his glory.

THE DECIMAL GAME.

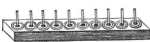

Ten pins are fixed in a mahogany board, with ten rings lying on the pins. The game is to make these ten rings into five pairs, the player passing over two pins every move, and the five pairs being accomplished in five moves only.

AGON, OR THE QUEEN'S GUARDS.

Each player has seven pieces, viz., one queen and six guards. To commence the game, the pieces are to be arranged as follows:

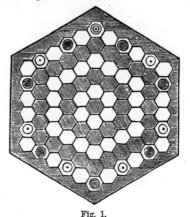

Fig. 1.

READY TO COMMENCE THE GAME.

Put the two queens on two opposite corners, and the guards on each side of the queens, each color alternate, with one hexagon left vacant between each piece (two hexagons will be vacant on each side farthest from the queens.) (See Fig. 1.)

If the players so agree, the game may be commenced by each alternately placing a piece anywhere on the board, and then, when all the pieces are laid down, each alternately moving forward to obtain the middle. Having decided which shall move first, the players alternately move a piece towards the centre, one hexagon at a time, or to the next hexagon of the same color, so that the piece shall remain at the same distance from the centre, it not being allowed to move a piece backward.

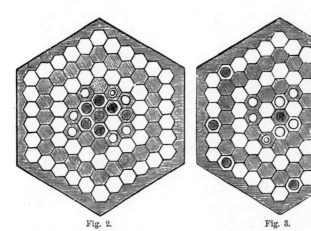

Fig. 2.

THE DARK PIECE BETWEEN THE TWO LIGHT ONES STANDING IN A RIGHT LINE MUST BE PUT BACK.

Fig. 3.

THE DARK QUEEN, BEING IN A RIGHT LINE BETWEEN TWO LIGHT PIECES, MUST RETIRE.

Any piece, except the queen, being in a position between two of the adversary's, so that the three pieces form a straight line, must be taken off the board for the next move, and put down anywhere in the outer row. (See Fig. 2.)

If the queen should be placed in the position between the adversary's, so that the three pieces form a straight line, the queen must be removed for the next move, but may be put in *any place*, being vacant, the player pleases. (See Fig. 3.)

That player who can first put all the pieces in the middle, that is, the queen in the centre, and the six guards around her, wins the game. (See Fig. 4.)

The players, being supposed to be sitting opposite each other, have the board placed with two corners right and left of each, and if the pieces have been placed as in Fig. 1, the color of those pieces the queen of which is on the right hand, is to be taken by each player.

Two experienced players may put the pieces in a particular position, symmetrically or otherwise, and, each taking the colors alternately, endeavor to win the game. The following are the laws of the game.

I. None but the queens are to occupy the centre.

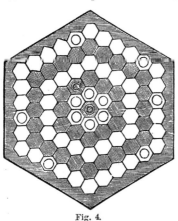

II. No piece must be put between two of the adversary's, standing in a right line.

III. No piece must be moved backward.

IV. Of two or more pieces liable to be put back at one time, the queen must be first moved off; any others at the player's option.

V. Any piece touched must be moved, or the move lost.

VI. Should the player put the six guards in the middle, leaving out the queen, such player loses the game by forfeit, as both are prevented from accomplishing the ultimatum of the game.

Fig. 4.

HINTS TO PLAYERS.—No advantage will be gained, but, on the contrary, frequently a loss, by throwing back one only of the adversary's pieces, as the piece thrown back may be placed so as more readily to obtain a much better position than that thrown back from.

As no piece is allowed to move backward, the queens must not be moved into the centre too hastily, as when there (having no move unless thrown out) their usefulness is impaired.

The player should endeavor to obtain such a position as to be able to throw back several pieces by following moves, and then move on to the middle, before the adversary can overtake or get between the pieces.

The surest mode to win the game, is to crowd the adversary's pieces as quickly as possible toward the middle, at the same time taking up a position to be able to throw back all his pieces in succession, as soon as an opportunity offers.

When a player has the queen in the middle, if not able to win the game, he may often reopen it by bringing a piece against the adversary's, so that, if his queen should be thrown back, he may throw back another piece in return; hence, in throwing back the queens, the greatest caution is always necessary.

The player will generally find it advantageous to have one piece at a greater distance from the centre than any of the adversary's, it must, however, be in a position to get to the middle when the game is drawing to a conclusion.

The position shown in Fig. 2 is certain loss of the game to the dark pieces; the light pieces, having forced the dark queen to move into the centre, will be able to throw back a dark piece every move, and thus win the game; but should the light pieces be moved too early into the middle, it will be impossible to throw back the dark queen without hazarding the reopening of the game.

In this game no advantage will be obtained or lost by having the first move, and it will be impossible for any player to determine which has the advantage until the game may be fairly considered to be won.

In variety of situations, the game will be found almost equal to Chess, and from the mathematical figure of the board (being a combination of hexagons), many symmetrical figures and situations may be devised, and the game played from these particular positions, thus affording an endless variety of amusement.

19

BACKGAMMON.

The origin of this game has long been a vexed question to the antiquary, as well as its present designation. One part of its machinery—the dice—defies chronology, they having been found in Etruscan tombs, and traced in the hieroglyphics of Egypt. Its early name in England is believed to have been "Tables;" when it was played with three dice instead of two, and the men commenced their action from the adversary's table.

The backgammon-board is quadrangular, and on it are depicted twenty-four points, or *flèches*, of two colors, placed alternately. The board is divided into four compartments; two inner and two outer ones; each containing six of the points, alternating in color.

The game is played by two persons, each having their two dice and boxes, as well as fifteen men, or counters, black and white, like draughtsmen. These, at the commencement of the game, are placed on the board as follows.

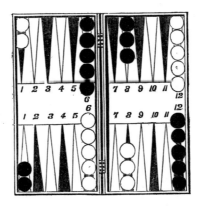

Two of your men—which we shall call, for convenience, the white—are placed on the ace point of your opponent's inner table; five on the sixth point in his outer table; three on the cinque point on your own outer table; and five on the sixth point of your own inner table. The adversary's men are placed in corresponding order in the same positions directly opposite your own. The game consists in moving your men from point to point so as to bring them round into your own inner table (or the table on your left hand), and then moving and taking them off the board. Whoever gets all his men off first, wins.

The dice are thrown to determine the moves of the men; the great object of the game being to bring your own men into your inner table; so all throws that aid this course are advantageous, and the reverse to your adversary. It is therefore very important that you should, as you travel round to your inner table, endeavor to block up and detain your adversary in your own tables, unless all your men have made their progress to your own inner table, and so have the best chance. The two players, on commencing the game, agree which end of the board they will play. Each one plays into one of his tables on his own side; for example, if black plays into his left-hand table, white plays into his right; this being directly opposite to black's left, and *vice versâ*.

For the right of the first move both players throw one die; and the highest number wins. He then throws both his dice, and plays one of his men to the point indicated by one of his dice, and another man to the point indicated by the other die. Or, if he prefer it, instead of moving a second man for the second die, he may give both the moves to the first man. This being done, the adversary does the same, and the other again throws and moves, and so on alternately to the end of the game. When a pair is thrown by the dice, it counts double; for instance, two sixes will enable you to move four men each six points forward, or two men each twelve points, or one man the whole twenty-four points forward, if your adversary has left the position vacant. Your men must move from the adversary's inner table, through the adversary's outer table, into your own outer table, and thence home into your own inner table.

When a single man occurs on a point he is called a "blot," and may be taken by your adversary, who must strive to "hit" the blot by bringing one of his men to this point. In this way he takes, and must place on the bar or division of the table, the "blot," and the player who owns it cannot move until he has made a throw which will enter this single man on the table again. He can only effect this by throwing a number that is vacant, or left a "blot" on his adversary's inner table, playing it as from a point off the board adjoining the adversary's ace point.

When most of the adversary's inner table is covered, that is, the points have two or more men on them, it becomes difficult to enter, and yet you must remain on the bar until your adversary leaves a point vacant to be gained by your throw. "Hitting" a blot always adds interest and excitement to the game.

If, during the game, every point on which a man could be placed is covered by your adversary's men, you must wait till your opponent opens a move by his own play. After bringing all your men home you must begin and "bear them," or take them off the board. Every number thrown allows a man to be borne or taken off, according to the throw. If, however, your adversary is waiting for "blots" to enter his men, you must take care by your moves to avoid as much as possible leaving any. If higher numbers are on the dice than on the points, men may be taken from any lower point to "bear off" the board. If a lower one is thrown, and the point has none on it, a higher one may be played. If one player has not borne off his first man before the other bears off his last, he loses a "gammon," which counts as two games or "hits." If both players have borne off it is a game that counts one. It becomes a "backgammon" if the winner bears off all his men before the loser has carried his out of his adversary's table; and this is equivalent to three hits or games. The following are the laws of the game:

1. If you take a man from any point that man must be played; the same must be done if two men are taken from it.

2. You are not understood to have played any man till you have placed him on a point, and quitted him.

3. If you play with fourteen men only, there is no penalty attending it, because, by playing with a lesser number than you are entitled to, you play at a disadvantage, by not having the additional man to make up your tables.

4. If, after you have commenced bearing your men, you should leave a blot, and one of your men be hit, such man must be entered in your adversary's table and brought home to your own inner table, before you can bear any more men.

5. If you have mistaken your throw, and played, and if your adversary has thrown, it is not in your choice to alter it unless both parties agree.

General Hints and Maxims.—In playing safe at backgammon, your great object will be, in the first place, either to secure your own or your adversary's cinque point, or both, if you can. After doing this, play a pushing game, and strive to gammon your adversary. If only playing for a hit, one or two men taken up of your adversary's will be safer than more, if your tables are made up. Never at the commencement of a set play for a back game, because by doing this you play at a disadvantage, running the risk of a gammon to win a single hit. Be careful, in playing for a gammon, not to crowd your game at any time, if possible. What is meant by crowding a game is placing a number of men either on the trois or deuce points in your own tables, which comes to the same thing as losing those men, since you do not have them in play. By thus crowding a game you become liable to be gammoned, because your adversary has liberty to play as he likes when he finds you crowded in your own tables. If your adversary be much in advance of you, do not play your man from your quatre, trois or deuce points in order to bear that man from the point where you put it, because nothing but high doublets can give you a chance for the hit; therefore always play them on, from your size or highest point, by which you will find, if you throw two fives or two fours, that having cased your size or cinque points will be of service to you; and had, on the contrary, your size point been loaded, you must perhaps have played those fives or fours at length. Never be prevented taking up any of your adversary's men from the fear of his hitting you with double dice, because the highest chance that your adversary has of hitting you is five to one against him.

Supposing also you have five points in your own tables covered, and you have got to take up one of your adversary's men, and are obliged to leave a blot out of your tables, leave it sooner on doublets than any other chance, because doublets are thirty-five to one against his hitting you, and the other chances are only seventeen to one against him.

DRAUGHTS.

This game is far less difficult than the game of chess, consequently it does not require the same amount of skill; but it is nevertheless a scientific game, and next to chess is, perhaps, the best of all the pleasant and innocent pastimes which young people can enjoy.

The game is played on a board precisely similar to a chess-board. Two players engage, and twenty-four pieces are employed, twelve being allotted to each player. The pieces are all of the same kind, and are all equal. There is neither queen nor bishop, knight nor chatelaine; there is not a king until one or other of the players is successful in pushing one of his men to the other side, and winning for that intrepid hero a royal crown. Greatness, in this game, is only to be achieved—it looks as if it were built up on our own republican principles.

The board should be so placed as that a black square should be at the right hand of each player. The pieces are placed on the white squares; the squares occupied being indicated by the following diagram:

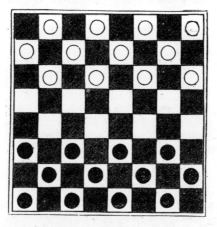

The pieces are moved diagonally to the right or left, one square at a time. They must always move forward until they reach the last line of squares on the opposite side of the board from which they started. If they reach any one of these squares, they are elevated to royal dignity, one piece being placed on the top of the other as a crown. Kings so crowned may move backward as well as forward, either to the right hand or the left.

In capturing a piece, it is necessary that the square beyond that on which the piece to be captured stands should be vacant, as the capture is made by leaping *over* the unfortunate captive, who is immediately removed from the board.

A player can compel his opponent to take a prisoner if the piece be in a position to be taken. If the capture be neglected by the opponent, the piece by which the capture should have been made is forfeited, or, as it is technically called, *huffed*. Instead of *huffing*, however, the player may insist on the capture being made.

When one party huffs the other, in preference to compelling the take, he does not replace the piece his adversary moved, but simply removes the man huffed from off the board, and then plays his own move. Should he, however, insist upon his adversary taking the piece, instead of standing the huff, then the piece improperly moved must first be replaced.

To give an example of huffing. Suppose a black man to be placed at 28 (see following diagram), and three white men at 24, 15, and 6, or 24, 16, and 8, with unoccupied intervals, he would capture all three men, and make a king, or be huffed for omitting to take them all; and it is not uncommon with novices to take one man, and overlook a second or third "*en prise*" (*i. e.*, liable to be taken).

Two or even three pieces may be captured at one move, supposing they are so placed as to have a vacant square beyond each one—a square on which the victorious assailant may alight between the capture of each piece.

The game is brought to a close by one or other of the players losing all his pieces, or being unable to move ; or by their being so equally balanced —as, for example, one king each—that neither can win; in this case it is a *drawn game*.

The game is played out on thirty-two white squares. These squares we may, in order to render our directions plain, be allowed to number 1, 2, 3, and so on, as given in the above diagram.

We will suppose that white occupies the squares 1 to 12 inclusive, and that black occupies the squares 21 to 32 inclusive.

The first move must be arranged by lot—or something like it; let one player, for example, take up a piece, and the opponent be challenged to state whether that piece be white or black: if he guesses correctly, he has the first move; if incorrectly, the first move falls to the lot of his adversary.

Supposing black to begin—

BLACK. Squares.	WHITE. Squares.	BLACK. Squares.	WHITE. Squares.
1. 23 to 18.	1. 10 to 14.	22. 14 to 10.	22. 7 to 14†.
2. 27 to 23.	2. 12 to 16.	23. 18 to 9†. 9 to 2†*.	23. 11 to 18†. 18 to 25†.
3. 24 to 20.	3. 8 to 12.		
4. 28 to 24.	4. 7 to 10.	24. 23 to 19.	24. 25 to 30*.
5. 22 to 17.	5. 9 to 13.	25. 26 to 23.	25. 30 to 26.
6. 18 to 9†.	6. 5 to 14†.	26. 2 to 7.	26. 27 to 31*.
7. 26 to 22.	7. 10 to 15.	27. 7 to 10.	27. 31 to 27.
8. 22 to 18.	8. 15 to 22†.	28. 23 to 18.	28. 27 to 23.
9. 25 to 18† 18 to 9†.	9. 13 to 22†.	29. 18 to 14.	29. 23 to 16†.
		30. 20 to 11†. 11 to 4†*.	30. 26 to 23.
10. 9 to 5.	10. 6 to 10.		
11. 21 to 17.	11. 10 to 15.	31. 14 to 9.	31. 12 to 16.
12. 17 to 14.	12. 15 to 18.	32. 4 to 8.	32. 16 to 19.
13. 32 to 27.	13. 4 to 8.	33. 8 to 11.	33. 19 to 24.
14. 24 to 19.	14. 3 to 7.	34. 11 to 16.	34. 24 to 27.
15. 19 to 15.	15. 2 to 6.	35. 9 to 6.	35. 27 to 31*.
16. 30 to 26.	16. 22 to 25.	36. 6 to 2.*	36. 29 to 25.
17. 29 to 22†.	17. 18 to 25†.	37. 10 to 14.	37. 31 to 26.
18. 23 to 18.	18. 25 to 29*.	38. 16 to 11.	38. 26 to 22.
19. 26 to 22.	19. 16 to 19.	39. 11 to 15.	39. 25 to 21.
20. 31 to 26.	20. 19 to 24.	40. 15 to 10.	40. 22 to 18.
21. 27 to 23.	21. 24 to 27.		

These forty moves, which leave the players pretty equally balanced as to prospect of success, will serve to accustom the young player to the movement of the pieces.

We recommend slightly pencilling the draught-board with the numeral indicated.

The † signifies that a piece is captured; the * that a crown is won.

WHITE.	BLACK.	WHITE.	BLACK.
1. 9 to 13.	1. 23 to 18.	12. 5 to 9.	12. 23 to 18.
2. 12 to 16.	2. 24 to 20.	13. 15 to 19.	13. 18 to 14.
3. 16 to 19.	3. 28 to 24.	14. 9 to 18† 18 to 25†.	14. 31 to 26.
4. 19 to 28†.	4. 20 to 16.		
5. 11 to 20†.	5. 21 to 17.	15. 25 to 29*.	15. 26 to 22.
6. 8 to 11.	6. 25 to 21.	16. 19 to 23.	16. 22 to 18.
7. 10 to 14.	7. 17 to 10†.	17. 20 to 24.	17. 18 to 14.
8. 7 to 14† 14 to 23†.	8. 27 to 18†.	18. 24 to 27.	18. 14 to 9.
		19. 27 to 31*.	19. 9 to 5.
9. 6 to 10.	9. 18 to 15.	20. 4 to 8.	20. 32 to 27.
10. 11 to 18† 18 to 25†.	10. 29 to 22.†	21. 31 to 24†.	21. 30 to 26.
		22. 23 to 30†*.	22. 21 to 17.
11. 10 to 15.	11. 26 to 23.	23. 13 to 22†.	

The above is a good example of a game of draughts. Black is regularly "used up," having but one piece left on the board, and that piece no move.

In particular situations, to have the move on your side is a decisive advantage. This is a matter little understood by ordinary players, but its importance will fully appear by studying particular situations. To have the move, signifies your occupying that position on the board which will eventually enable you to force your adversary into a confined situation, and which, at the end of the game, secures to yourself the last move. It must, however, be observed, that where your men are in a confined state, the move is not only of no use to you, but, for that very reason, may occasion the loss of the game. To know in any particular situation whether you have the move, you must number the men and the squares, and if the men are even and the squares odd, or the squares even and the men odd, you have the move. With even men and even squares, or odd men and odd squares, you have not the move. This will be best explained by an example: We will suppose that white has a king on 26 and a man on 32, and that black has a king on 28 and a man on 19, and white plays first: we see the adverse men are even, two to two; but the white squares, being five in number, are odd. The squares may be thus reckoned—from 26, a white king, to 28, a black king, are three, viz., 31, 27, and 24; the white squares between 32, a white man, and 19, a black man, are two, viz., 27 and 23. You may reckon more ways than one; but reckon which way you will, the squares will still be found odd, and therefore white, so situated, has the move. When you have not the move, you must endeavor to procure it by giving man for man.

There is another mode which will, in less time than reckoning the squares, enable you to see who has the move. For instance, if you wish to know whether any one man of yours has the move of any one man of your adversary's, examine the situation of both, and if you find a black square on the right angle, under his man, you have the move. For example, you are to play first, and your white man is on 30, when your adversary's black man is on 3. In this situation, you will find the right angle in a black square between 31 and 32, immediately under 3, and therefore you have the move. This rule will apply to any number of men, and holds true in every case.

There is a third mode, more ingenious still. Count all the pieces (of both colors) standing on those columns (not diagonals) which have a white square at the bottom, and if the number be odd, and white has to play, he has the move; if the number be even, the move is with black.

It is a mistake to suppose that any advantage is derived from playing first. It is admitted that he who plays first has not the move, the men and squares being both even; but though he who plays second has the move, it can be of no service to him in that stage of the game. The truth is, that when the combatants continue giving man for man, the move will alternately belong to one and the other.

Bear in mind that it is generally better to keep your men in the middle of the board, than to play them to the side squares, as, in the latter case, one half their power is curtailed.

Be careful to look well over the board before making your move; but let not your caution descend to timidity. Resolve the consequences of every move before making it, and never touch a man without moving it.

The above is a curious illustration of what the game of draughts may sometimes become—*a regular fix;* black to move, with nowhere to move to.

THE LOSING GAME.

A very pleasing variety in Draughts is made by playing what is called the Losing Game. He who first *loses* all his men *wins* the game. This losing your men is not so easy as might at first sight appear. The secret of success lies, however, in a very simple series of moves. What you have to do is, to open your game by giving piece for piece for the first three or four moves, and then open your back squares, and leave spaces between them and the advanced pieces, so as to enable you at a favorable opportunity to give two men for one. Having lost a man more than your opponent, be careful to retain that advantage by giving man for man. But you must not be too anxious to crown your men, or to pass the squares protected by your opponent's pieces. If you do, he will presently regain his loss, and perhaps turn the tables upon you. Sometimes it will happen that with a single king you can compel your adversary to give up piece after piece till you find yourself able to offer yourself as a sacrifice and win. In the Losing Game you must take the piece offered, and he who refuses it loses the game, of course. There is no such thing as standing the huff in the Losing Game.

In the Losing Game it is well to gain the side squares; as, when your opponent advances, as he must after a while, you are enabled to offer your men with the certainty of losing them. All pieces that can be taken must be taken. Great care is necessary in order to keep the move, for the player who has it ought always to win.

19*

The following is an illustration of the Losing Game.

White to open.

WHITE.	BLACK.	WHITE.	BLACK.
1. 9 to 14.	1. 23 to 18.	22. 22 to 13†.	22. 27 to 23.
2. 14 to 23†.	2. 27 to 18†.	23. 13 to 17.	23. 11 to 7.
3. 11 to 15.	3. 18 to 11†.	24. 9 to 13.	24. 7 to 3*.
4. 8 to 15†.	4. 22 to 18.	25. 6 to 9.	25. 23 to 19.
5. 15 to 22†.	5. 25 to 18†.	26. 17 to 14.	26. 19 to 16.
6. 10 to 15.	6. 18 to 11†.	27. 13 to 17.	27. 16 to 11.
7. 7 to 16†.	7. 24 to 19.	28. 17 to 22.	28. 11 to 8.
8. 16 to 23†.	8. 26 to 19†.	29. 22 to 26.	29. 8 to 4*.
9. 12 to 16.	9. 19 to 12†.	30. 14 to 18.	30. 4 to 8.
10. 3 to 8.	10. 12 to 3†*.	31. 9 to 14.	31. 3 to 7.
11. 4 to 8.	11. 3 to 12†.	32. 14 to 17.	32. 12 to 16.
12. 6 to 10.	12. 28 to 24.	33. 26 to 31*.	33. 16 to 19.
13. 5 to 9.	13. 31 to 26.	34. 18 to 15.	34. 19 to 10†.
14. 2 to 7.	14. 32 to 27.	35. 31 to 26.	35. 10 to 15.
15. 1 to 6.	15. 26 to 23.	36. 17 to 21.	36. 8 to 11.
16. 7 to 11.	16. 24 to 20.	37. 21 to 25.	37. 11 to 16.
17. 11 to 16.	17. 20 to 11†.	38. 25 to 30*.	38. 16 to 19.
18. 10 to 15.	18. 23 to 18.	39. 26 to 23.	39. 19 to 26†.
19. 15 to 22†.	19. 29 to 25.	40. 30 to 23†.	40. 15 to 19.
20. 22 to 29†*.	20. 30 to 25.	41. 23 to 16†.	41. 7 to 11.
21. 29 to 22†.	21. 21 to 17.	42. 16 to 7†.	

CHESS.

BOYS PLAYING CHESS.

Both Chess and Draughts are very ancient games, so that it is impossible to ascertain with certainty when they first came into play. Chess is known to have been played by the Greeks—perhaps it was played by Nimrod in his leisure moments; who shall say? It was known in India at a very early date, and, according to some authorities, Ravan, king of Ceylon, was its inventor. He was besieged, it is said, in a strong fortress, and amused himself, during his leisure, with devising this game, in which he mimicked the movements of his enemies. Other authorities attribute the invention to the Chinese (Chin-chin-chop, or " any other man"), invented for the diversion of troops disposed for mutiny. Both in India and China it is a favorite game, and so it is in Persia. The resemblance to our chess is very close; the bishops in India are elephants, in France they are fools; we, however, stick to the episcopate. In the Indian game there is sometimes this difference from our own—the king is not permitted to move beyond a certain fortress, and the elephants—answering to our bishops—are not allowed to cross a certain line of squares, known as a river, and which the Pachydermata could not be supposed capable of fording.

From its very nature, Chess has always been a favorite game with warriors and students. We are told that Tamerlane, the great conqueror, was a devoted lover of the game, and that he was playing at it the very moment that Bajazet was brought into his camp a prisoner. Charles the First is said to have been so deeply engaged in a game at Chess that he did not desist from it, even when the news was brought him of the final intention of the Scots to sell him to the English.

But chess, wherever played, or under whatever circumstances, is still chess, and the same principles are taught—moral principles, we mean—

which makes it not only an interesting pastime, but calls into action several very valuable qualities of the mind, useful in the course of human life. Benjamin Franklin points out these valuable lessons in some such words as these:

" First, foresight, which looks a little into futurity, and considers the consequences which may attend an action, as it is continually occurring to the player. 'If I move this piece, what will be the advantage of my new situation? what use can my adversary make of it to annoy me? what other moves can I make to support it, and to defend myself from his attack?' Second, the circumspection which surveys the whole chess-board, or scene of action, and the relation of the several pieces, and considers the dangers they are respectively exposed to, the several possibilities of aiding each other, the probability that the adversary may take this or that move, and take this or the other piece, and what different means can be used to avoid his stroke, or turn its consequences against him. Third, caution not to make our moves too hastily. This habit is best acquired by observing strictly the laws of the game, such as, if you touch a piece you must move it somewhere; if you set it down you must let it stand; and it is therefore best that these rules be observed, as the game thereby becomes so much the more like human life, and particularly of war, in which, if you have incautiously put yourself into a bad or dangerous position, you cannot obtain your enemy's leave to withdraw your troops, and place them in more security, but must abide the consequences of your folly "

Chess is essentially a game of skill. The players, so far as pieces and position are concerned, are equally matched, and the issue depends not on any chance or hazard, but simply on the manner in which the pieces are moved. A great many books have been written, some of them exceedingly heavy, in all senses of that word, and so overladen with examples, that the student would feel inclined to make an example of the author. But practice is better than any book, old or new, and it is only by practice that any one can ever become a skilful player. There are many players so skilful that they can play blindfold; can sustain three or four games at the same time, the moves of their various adversaries being simply mentioned. These men must have a very clear mental vision of the board, and a very excellent memory. Clever players, pretty equally matched, will manage to keep up a game of chess for a very long time. We have heard of a game which lasted through two lifetimes, begun by the fathers and left unfinished by the sons. We do not suppose our readers would care to carry on a game so long as to make it hereditary, but they must bear in mind that the best players are not those who are the most rapid in their movements, but players who take time to think well what they intend doing before they move a piece.

To play the game of chess, it is necessary that the players should provide themselves with the board and pieces. A good set of chess-men, with a capital board, may be had at a very moderate price.

The game of chess is played on a square board, divided into sixty-four squares, black and white alternately. Here is a representation of an ordinary chess-board:

A white square, it will be observed, is at the right hand of each player.

The game is played with thirty-two pieces, each player—no more than two can engage—holding sixteen. These pieces are known to us by the following names:

King, queen, king's bishop, queen's bishop, king's knight, queen's knight, king's castle, or rook; queen's castle, or rook; and eight pawns, or common men, each one supposed to belong to the more exalted pieces; thus: King's pawn, queen's pawn, king's bishop's pawn, queen's bishop's pawn, king's knight's pawn, queen's knight's pawn, king's castle, or rook's pawn; queen's castle, or rook's pawn.

Both players have the same number and quality of pieces; they are distinguished by color—white and red, or white and black; the latter are the most common.

Various forms are used for the pieces. Some of these are very elegant, and designed to represent ancient grandees, lay and clerical, chiefly fighting men; and we know that, in old times, bishops could wield swords as well as crosiers. But the forms of the pieces most commonly in use in books treating on this subject are given below, and we shall use these forms in our illustrations of the game:

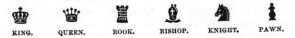

KING.   QUEEN.   ROOK.   BISHOP.   KNIGHT.   PAWN.

The arrangement of these pieces on the board is given in the annexed diagram.

The rule as to the arrangement of the pieces is arbitrary—the kings must always stand on squares the reverse of their own color—black king on a white square; white king on a black square. Attention to this rule settles all difficulties as to the arrangement of the men.

The manner in which the pieces in the game of chess are moved is somewhat intricate; we shall endeavor to make it as plain as possible.

First of all, it must be borne in mind that the king is apparently regarded more as the representative of power than as its active agent. He has not the same latitude allowed to him, as to moves, as that of his queen, his bishops, his knights, and rooks. The king is allowed to move only one square at a time, backward or forward, to the right hand, or to the left hand; or diagonally the king may move, always supposing that by so doing he would not place his royal person in a position which, in any one of a lower grade, would admit of capture, but which, in his exalted position, is simply designated *check*.

BLACK.

WHITE.

For the chess-king, you must know, is never captured. When he is in jeopardy, he is said to be in check. When, let him move where he may, the same danger awaits him, he is said to be *check-mated*, and loses the game.

The king is allowed to approach any other piece, avoiding the position of danger, as closely as he pleases—that is to say, the next square, if he likes; but he must not come next to his royal adversary in person: king must never meet king, otherwise he would be, or both would be, in jeopardy, for, as the king moves one square at a time, so he can only capture that piece which is on the next square to him; and if the king were on the next square, then one king would check the other.

The queen may move in any direction—backward, forward, to her right hand, or the left hand, or diagonally; and in this way she may move over any number of unoccupied squares, and seize upon the piece which occupies the square which terminates her range. The queen may be captured, and well for the adversary if she be captured early, for she is terrible as a Dahomey Amazon.

The bishops, the prelates of both king and queen, move diagonally backward or forward, and pass over any number of squares unoccupied, seizing upon any piece that may chance to occupy a square in his range; but, in taking a piece, they must remain for the time on the square of the piece taken. The bishops, of course, never change their colors (who ever heard of such a thing?)—the bishop who begins the game on a white square dies on a white square; the prelate who entered on his episcopal duties on a black square sticks to the blacks till the last.

The movements of the knight are very eccentric. They consist of a complicated movement of the rook and bishop, forward one square, and diagonally one square; or, sideways—to the right hand or the left hand—one square, and diagonally one square. Consequently, a knight on a black square moves to a white square, two distant sideways and one forward or backward, or one distant sideways and two forward or backward. The knight, by his eccentric movements, is allowed to leap over the heads of other men, even over the head of the queen herself, and he may often do this without rendering himself liable to capture.

The castle, or rook, moves forward, and backward, and sideways, in a straight line. He may move in this way over any number of unoccupied squares, only stopping when he comes upon a piece belonging to his adversary, which he immediately seizes.

The pawns, or common men, at the beginning of the game, are allowed to take two steps forward; after this, they move forward one square at a time, until they reach the opposite side of the board, when they are rewarded for their prowess by being knighted, or elevated to the episcopal bench, or being charged with a castle, and even, sometimes, are permitted to assume the regal coronet, and become queen. Indeed, a pawn who has reached the last row of squares on his adversary's side of the board, may become any thing he pleases, except king.

In capturing prisoners, the pawns move diagonally—either way—but always forward. No pawn is allowed to show his back to the enemy.

In describing the various moves of the pieces, we have followed their positions on the board; in playing chess, however, the rook ranks next to the queen, and the bishops and knights are regarded as minor pieces.

The final object of the game is attained by checkmating the king, that is to say, placing him in a position in which, wherever he moves, he is still exposed to the liability of capture.

The king is often put into check when it is perfectly easy for him to move out of it, or to be screened from the danger by interposing another piece.

448   BOARD AND SLATE GAMES.

When the king is so exposed, it is the duty of the adversary to call attention to it, by saying "*Check*."

We shall now furnish some illustrations of the king in check, exhibiting the most common forms in which this occurs, our readers bearing in mind the various moves permitted to the pieces represented.

In our first diagram, the black king is represented in check from the white

No. 1.—BLACK.

WHITE.

king's bishop; it is incumbent upon his majesty to move out of check; he cannot advance—the white queen's rook ranges the whole of his second row of squares; he cannot move sideways to the left, or queen's square, as that is ranged by the white queen's bishop. "Blackie" is evidently in a fix: his course, however, is plain—he must move sideways to the right, taking up the position once held by his own bishop, and thus, for the time, get out of check.

Sometimes the king in check may be delivered by the heroic behavior of one of his people. We have an example in the diagram No. 2.

Here, it will be seen, the black king is in check from the white king's bishop; the king himself has no chance of moving, but he may readily be protected: the queen may throw herself before her undefended lord, but, if she does, be sure the bishop will have no scruple about seizing her, even though it cost him his life; her bishop may advance and face his brother church dignitary—then, if he be taken, what is it but bishop for bishop, life for life? or the knight, by one of his eccentric leaps, may place himself in the post of danger; or the black queen's bishop's pawn may step forward —one step only—and defend his king's honor with as much success, and far less danger, than the queen herself.

In the following diagram (No. 3) we have an example of check-mate.

Here the white king is in check from the black queen; he cannot seize upon her majesty, seeing that she is well defended by her trusty knight; whither can his highness move? there is but one square for him to move into, and that is equally exposed to his queenly adversary, and no help can he obtain from any of his servants. Alas! for him, with a queen and twelve attendants, he must resign his crown, and submit to check-mate!

No. 2.—BLACK.

WHITE.

No. 3—BLACK.

WHITE.

The object of the game, which is to give the enemy checkmate, can scarcely be effected without some settled plan; the player must look forward through a considerable number of moves, which will be requisite to bring his men into a given position, and also to provide, from time to time, against his antagonist's attempts to frustrate his design, or attack him in turn.

The following diagram (No. 4) illustrates what is known as a stalemate:

No. 4.—BLACK.

WHITE (to move).

Here it will be seen that the white king is not in check; he has to move, but in whatever direction he moves he places himself in check. Of course, if he had any other man to move, it would not be imperatively necessary that he should move himself; he has none. His bishop is blocked up by the king's own majestic person, and of his two pawns, the progress of one is stopped by another pawn, the other by a knight. Wherever the king moves, he moves into check—try it: and this moving into check is a thing not allowable—hence his opponent, by over "cuteness," has lost the game, by making, not a checkmate, but a stalemate. This is usually regarded as a drawn game.

What is called SCHOLAR'S-MATE is played thus: but black must be *very, very green* to allow it to come to pass:

WHITE.	BLACK.
1. P to K 4th.	1. P to K 4th.
2. K B to Q B 4th.	2. K B to Q B 4th.
3. Q to K B 3rd.	3. P to Q 3rd.
4. Q takes K B P and MATES.	

Very similar, but still more simple, is the FOOL'S-MATE, which is accomplished in two moves, in the following manner:

WHITE.	BLACK.
1. K Kt P to K Kt 4th.	1. K P to K 4th.
2. K B P to K B 3rd.	2. Q to K R 5th, checkmate.

Black, poor unsophisticated black looks black enough, depend upon it! This mate cannot possibly be given by the first player.

OPENINGS.

No. 5.—BLACK.

WHITE.

Of the various openings, which are all more or less strongly recommended, and each of which has its warm advocates, we shall offer only three—the king's knight's opening, the king's bishop's opening, and the king's gambit.

KING'S KNIGHT'S OPENING.

WHITE.	BLACK.
1. P to K 4th.	1. P to K 4th.
2. K Kt to B 3d.	2. P to Q 3d.

It will be seen by this that the attack is immediately commenced by white, that black is put upon the defensive, that the black king's pawn being threatened by the white king's knight, a black pawn has to be brought up to the rescue. The position of the pieces is given above. (See Diagram No. 5.)

This opening of the game is common to many of our best players. It has the honor of being that usually adopted by the great chess-player, Philidor. The moves we have given are those which he approved. On continuing the game, black king's pawn being thus defended by the queen's pawn, as shown in the diagram, white moves—

WHITE.	BLACK.
3. P to Q 4th.	3. P takes P.
4. Q takes P.	4. Q Kt to B 3d.

This, it will be seen, endangers the white queen.

5. K B to Q Kt 5th.	5. Q B to Q 2d.

White, by bringing up his king's bishop, prevents the capture of his queen, as the movement of the black knight would leave the king in check; black, in order to relieve his knight, advances his bishop, so as to cover the king from check on the removal of the knight; and it now becomes obvious that white must move his queen, or capture the black knight at the sacrifice of the bishop.

KING'S BISHOP'S OPENING.

This opening is said by Philidor to be the very best; more recent writers, however, recommend the king's knight's opening in preference.

WHITE.	BLACK.
1. P to K 4th.	1. P to K 4th.
2. K B to Q B 4th.	2. K B to Q B 4th.
3. P to Q B 3d.	3. K Kt to B 3d.
4. P to Q 4th.	4. P takes P.
5. P to K 5th.	5. P to Q 4th.
6. B to Q Kt. 3d.	6. K Kt to Q 2d.

Thus both players are obliged to retire, and no advantage is really gained on either side. Of course, in adopting this or any other opening suggested, the player must bear in mind the very obvious fact, that he cannot reckon on his adversary following, as it were, his lead; supposing the adversary to be well acquainted with Philidor's movement, for instance, he will not, in all probability, allow the rival player to make the moves, as he can readily divert it by eccentric moves on his own part. Each player must carefully watch his opponent, and be ready to take advantage of any error.

THE KING'S GAMBIT.

Gambit is derived from a word (Italian) which signifies tripping up in the act of wrestling. In chess it is used when one player sacrifices a pawn in order to facilitate an attack. Here is an example—

WHITE.	BLACK.
1. P to K 4th.	1. P to K 4th.
2. P to K B 4th.	2. P takes P.
3. K Kt to B 3d.	3. P to K Kt 4th.
4. B to Q B 4th.	4. P to K Kt 5th.
5. K Kt to K 5th.	5. Q to K R 5th (check).
6. K to B square.	6. K Kt to R 3d.
7. P to Q 4th.	7. P to K B 6th.

(See Diagram No. 6).

White is in a regular state of siege, and the greatest precaution is neces-sary. Suppose, for example, white proceeds as follows:—

WHITE.	BLACK.
P takes P.	P to Q B 4th.
P takes P.	K B takes P.
P takes P.	Q to K B 2d (mate).

Here the tripping up by gambit goes on throughout the game.

It will be seen from what we have stated that the more usual mode of opening the game is by pawn to king's fourth; but this should not be rigidly adhered to by amateur players. They should practise other moves, and learn from experience the best.

No. 6.—BLACK.

WHITE.

The Relative Value of the Pieces.—The Pawn, as the lowest piece in this case of value, is usually considered as the unit by which to measure the value of the other pieces. It is, however, difficult to measure the pieces by this standard. The King's, Queen's, and Bishop's Pawns are called the *centre Pawns*, and are of more value than the other Pawns, particularly in the beginning and middle of the game. The Rook's Pawns are considered as least in value.

The Bishops and Knights are considered to be equal in value; and are worth rather more than three Pawns.

A Rook is valued at five Pawns, and may be exchanged for a minor piece and two Pawns, and two Rooks may be exchanged for three minor pieces.

The Queen is equal to two Rooks and a Pawn, and is superior in value to any three minor pieces.

The relative value of the King, from the nature of the game, cannot be estimated. His powers of attack, however, from his being able to move both in right lines or diagonally, are very considerable. At the latter end of the game, his strength materially increases, especially when the issue of the struggle is to be determined by Pawn-play.

RULES.

We furnish a few plain rules for beginners:—

I.—The board must be so placed as to give to each player at his right hand a white corner square.

II.—The queen must stand on a square of her own color.

III.—The king must never be left in check.

IV.—No piece ought to be touched without being played; and no move should on any account be recalled.

V.—Every pawn reaching the last square of the chess-board must be exchanged for another piece.

VI.—When your adversary places your king in check, he must say " *Check,*" thereby calling your attention to it; if this is neglected, and the fact of the king being in check remains unknown for several moves, the player whose king is in check must then, and not till then, obviate it.

VII.—A stalemate is a drawn game.

VIII.—Once in the game, the king, under certain conditions, is allowed to move two squares at once. This is called "castling," as it is performed in conjunction with the king or queen's rook. The king, in cases where the castling is made with his own rook, is played to his knight's square, the rook taking up the position of the bishop. In castling with the queen's rook, the king is played to the queen's bishop's square, and the rook to the queen's square. Castling cannot take place if the king or the rook have been moved; if the king be in check; if the king in castling would have to pass over any square attacked by any one of his adversary's pieces; and if there be any pawn between the king and the rook.

IX.—A drawn game occurs when neither party can checkmate the other.

X.—In playing the game, strive to checkmate, not to take pieces.

XI.—NEVER LOSE—IN LOSING THE GAME—YOUR TEMPER!

TABLE AND TOY GAMES.

DOMINOES.

THE authors who have "wasted the midnight oil" in investigating the origin of this popular game, have not yet come to a definite conclusion.

"Grammatici certant, et ad huc sub judice lis est;"

but, by the time the controversy shall have continued for some trifling time longer, say a couple of hundred years or so, there is every reason to suppose the question will be definitely set at rest—a reflection which cannot fail to inspire our young readers with a lively satisfaction. Certain it is, however, that the introduction of dominoes into America is of comparatively recent date, and that the game has enjoyed a large and steadily increasing popularity, being played not only by youngsters, but affording agreeable amusement to many "children of the larger growth."

Every one is familiar with the appearance of the little rectangular objects called dominoes, and made out of bone, ivory, or wood. A game usually consists of twenty-eight dominoes. Each of these is divided into two compartments, and the number of points on each domino varies, from the double-six downward, through six-five, six-four, &c., to double blank.

There are several ways of playing at dominoes. The following method, for two players, is at once the most simple and the one generally pursued. The dominoes are placed on the table, with their faces downward, and each player takes up one at hazard, to settle which of them is to have the *pose*, or right of playing first. The highest number of points decides this. The two dominoes used in the trial are then put back among the rest; the dominoes are well shuffled together, and the two players choose seven dominoes apiece, ranging them upright in a line on the table, with the faces toward them, so that each may see his own hand, but not his adversary's. Thus the players will have taken up fourteen out of the twenty-eight dominoes, of which an ordinary game consists. The other fourteen remain on the table, faces downward, to form a reserve. The winner of the *pose* now puts down on the table, face upward, the domino that it suits him best to play (we shall give some advice on this subject presently). The adversary, in his

turn, places a domino of his own, corresponding in one of its numbers with that placed by his adversary. Thus, suppose the first player to have played double-six; the second may play six-four; the first then puts six-five; the second follows it up with five-four; and the first plays the double-four—the single numbers being placed lengthways, the doubles transversely; and so the game proceeds, till the player who has won the *pose* has expended all his dominoes, his adversary having one domino left—say six-three. In this case, the first player will count nine toward the game, that being the number of points remaining in his adversary's hand. The game itself is won by the player who first scores a hundred. The dominoes are then shuffled again, the second player having the *pose* this time, and the game continues with a fresh deal.

Generally, however, things don't go so smoothly. After two or three dominoes have been placed by the two players, one of them is unable to match any of those in his hand with the numbers at each end of the row on the table. In that case he passes, and his adversary plays instead of him, and continues to do so until the first player can again make use of one of his dominoes. If both players are compelled to pass, neither of them having a domino that will suit, they turn their hands face upward on the table, and the one who has the smallest number of points counts all his adversary's points toward his own game. This is called the *block game*.

. The general rule for the player who has the *pose* is to play out the number which occurs the most frequently in your game. For instance, if the number four occurs four times in your hand, the chances are that your adversary will have only one, or, perhaps, none at all of the same number, and he will thus be compelled to *pass*, and you will gain a turn. It is good policy, too, to get rid of the higher numbers in your hand as soon as possible, for in case of a block, he who has the lowest number of points wins. Get rid of the *doubles* also; for they are the hardest to place.

It will thus be seen that the game of dominoes is one of mingled skill and chance. Of course, nothing can avail against a lucky hand; but the combinations of the game are various enough to give scope for a good deal of ingenuity. Sometimes, with two players, the system of "drawing" is resorted to; that is to say, when one of the players cannot follow suit, he takes a domino at hazard, from the reserve; and if this will not do, a second, and so on, till his purpose is answered. This is called the *draw game*.

Generally the game is confined to two players; but four, five, or even six, may join in it, each playing on his own account, or divided into sides. In the latter case, the partners sit opposite to each other, the players having first drawn for partners, in the same way that they would for the *pose*, and the two highest playing against the two lowest. He who has drawn the highest domino has the pose. The play is from left to right, and the side of the first player who is out wins, counting to its score the number of points still held by the opposite party. In this game there may be drawing or not, according to agreement. If the players don't draw, and, on a block occurring, and the dominoes being turned up, both sides are found to have the same number, the deal counts for nothing.

Another method of playing dominoes is called *Muggins*. Each player in the game draws five pieces. The highest double leads; after that they lead alternately. The count is made by fives. If the one who leads can put down any domino containing spots that amount to five or ten, as the double-five, six-four, five-blank, trey-deuce, &c., he counts that number to his score in the game. In matching, if a piece can be put down so as to make five, ten, fifteen, or twenty, by adding the spots contained on both ends of the row, it counts to the score of the one setting it. Thus a trey being at one end, and a five at the other, the next player in order, putting down a deuce-five, would score five; or if double trey was at one end, and a player was so successful as to get double deuce at the other, it would score ten for him.

A double-six being at one end, and a four at the other, if the next player set down a double-four, he counts twenty — double-six $= 12 +$ double-four $= 8 = 20$.

If a player cannot match he draws from the pool, the same as in the draw game, until he gets the piece required to match either end or exhausts the pool. As in the draw or block game, the one who plays his last piece first, adds to his count the spots his opponents have; and the same if he gains them when the game is blocked, by having the lowest count. But the sum thus added to the score is some multiple of five, nearest the actual amount. Thus, if his opponents have twenty spots, and he has nineteen, he adds twenty to his score. If they have twenty-two he adds twenty, because that is the nearest multiple of five; but if they have twenty-three he would add twenty-five—twenty-three being nearer that than to twenty. The number of the game is two hundred if two play, but one hundred and fifty if there be three or more players.

BAGATELLE.

BAGATELLE is played on a table, smaller than that for billiards, cushioned circular at one end, and, instead of pockets at the sides and corners, it has cups, set flush with the table, into which the ivory balls are driven with the cue.   These pockets are nine in number in the small table, which is about ten feet long, and are set equidistant from each other—one in the centre, and the others arranged around it, at one end of the table.   The playing is done from the other end.   In the larger table, which is from twelve to four-teen feet long, the cups are fifteen in number.   Each of these is num-bered—the centre being the highest; and the number of the cup counts for the player who puts a ball in it.   The balls are nine in number—one red, and eight white.   The red counts double when put into a hole.

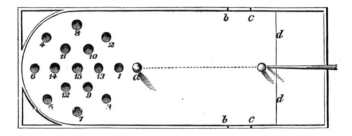

In playing, there are two games generally used, and known as the Eng-lish and French.

The English game is played thus: The red ball is placed on the spot a. A white ball is driven by the cue, from a spot anywhere between the base-line, dd, and an imaginary line drawn from the plates at cc, so as to hit the red ball.   If the red ball is driven into any hole, it counts double the num-ber set down to that hole.   If the white ball, it counts the number it gets. If the red ball is missed at the first go, it counts one to the opposing party. After the first go, it is not necessary to hit the red.   All the balls are now driven up.   This is repeated, and the sum of the cups made in the two "rolls" is scored to the player.   The next player follows, and the one scoring the most wins the game.

The French game is different.   The score is one hundred.   Each player, unless they are divided into sides, and then only one of a side, rolls up for the "break."   The red ball is set on the spot, and the player, grasping the eight white balls in his hand, rolls them up.   The sum of the cups into which the balls enter is ascertained; and the one who has the most in this way, plays first.   The red ball is set on the spot, as in the English game; but to miss it scores five to the opposite party.   Whenever it is not in a cup, the red ball must continue to be hit by the player, under a like penalty in

case of failure. If it be pocketed, he must aim at and hit any white ball
out of cup; and, if he fail in that, the opposite party scores one. Should
both his balls go in, and there is no white ball out of the cups, one is taken
from those not played, and placed on the spot for him to aim at. So long
as the player puts a ball in a cup, he plays on; and what he makes is
counted to his score. When his stroke cups no ball, he gives way to the
next, and so on, in succession. When all the white balls are played up, and
the last one played makes a cup for itself or another ball, provided it hits a
white ball in doing it, the white balls are returned, the red ball replaced on
the spot, and the same player takes the break and plays on. If the last
ball effects nothing, the next player in order takes the break. Whoever
first scores one hundred is out. The highest number to be made by any one
player, by cupping all the balls, would be one hundred and fourteen, the
red ball being in the centre, and counting thirty, and the others in the next
largest numbers, from 14 to 7, inclusive. This is rarely, if ever, done.

If any ball is driven with such force as to return beyond an imaginary
line, drawn from and between the plates *b b*, it is dead, and put on one side
until the next break.

As you may often best succeed by cushioning and carroming, the study
of angles is necessary in this game, as in billiards.

RUSSIAN BAGATELLE.

DESCRIPTION OF THE BOARD.

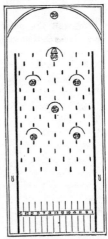

ELEVATED END OF THE BOARD, WHICH IS AN INCLINED PLANE, LOWEST AT THE STRIKING END.

A cavity for the red ball to be placed in, at the
commencement of the game, *only*. It counts double, *i. e.*, 20, as marked inside.

An arch, with a bell suspended within it, which,
if rung by any ball in passing through, counts
double for whatever that ball may score by the
stroke. If it does not pass through, but merely
falls into the cup underneath, it counts only as
marked, *i. e.*, 50.

The remaining arches with cups beneath them,
count respectively as marked, viz.: 20 on the sides,
and 25 in the centre.

The pegs are brass pins standing up, about one
and a half inches in height.

There are slightly indented spots (one on each
side of the board), from which the balls are projected.

Cavities into which the balls run; they count
according to the numbers placed above.

The board, which is generally four feet six inches
in length, and two feet four inches in width, is lined with superfine green cloth.

The game is played as follows:

1. Commence the game by stringing for the lead, as well as for choice of balls and side of board; the player who gets the highest number takes the lead.

2. The leader must place his ball in the cavity, on the side of the board he selects, and play it up, counting the points he may make by the stroke; after which, his opponent plays from the opposite side of the board ; and so on alternately.

3. When a ball lodges on the board without going into a hole, or running down to the bottom, the game must be continued with the other ball, each player using it alternately—whoever removes the ball so lodged, scores the number of points made by both the balls, and the game proceeds as at first. Should both the balls be lodged on the board, that ball which was last stopped must be taken up and used to continue the game.

4. The player continues to lead, as long as he can hole his ball in any of the *cups.*

5. The game to consist of one hundred or more, as may be agreed upon at the commencement.

6. If the player's ball ring the *bell*, that is, passes through the bell-arch, he scores double the number he would otherwise gain by the stroke.

7. Playing into the top hole (marked 20), is the game at once.

8. Should the ball go round to the opponent's side, the striker loses five points and the lead; or, should he play his ball up, and it returns without going on the board, he loses one point and the lead.

9. The winner of the game takes the lead in the next.

AMERICAN BAGATELLE.

Although this game bears the name of Bagatelle, it has scarcely any resemblance to that game, either in the form of the board, or the skill requisite for playing. A strong and quick hand are the most necessary qualifications of the player. The board, which is of the following form, has raised sides like the bagatelle-board, and contains within its circumference nine flat pieces of ivory let into the wood, on which the numbers one to nine are marked, in the same order as in the holes of the bagatelle-board; on each of these spots a small wooden pin, resembling a skittle-pin, is placed, that on the central spot being white. The object of the player is to knock down as many of these pins as possible, that he may count the numbers on which they stood: this he effects by means of the spinner, *a*, Fig. 2, which consists of a piece of wood with a round flat top, from which a peg or foot

Fig. 1

projects: a piece of string is wound tightly round this peg, and passed through the slit in the raised side at one end of the board, *a*, Fig. 1. The spinner is then pressed closely against the side with the left hand, while the player, grasping the handle, *b*, attached to the string in his right, pulls the string forcibly, and with a sudden jerk; the consequence is, the string is unwound from the spinner, and the latter, falling on the board, has acquired the spinning motion a humming-top would have acquired under nearly similar circumstances.

Fig. 2.

Away goes the spinner into the midst of the pins, knocking down some and passing safely between others: in the course of its evolutions it soon reaches the side of the board, and, if it is spinning with tolerable force, the instant it touches the wood it flies off suddenly at a tangent, and again dashes among the pins. The principal amusement consists in watching the progress of the spinner, as it bounces from one side of the board to the other, and when it appears about to expire, it suddenly perhaps starts forward and wins the player the game. The game, as in bagatelle, is counted by adding together the numbers marked on the spots on which the fallen pins stood, and may be decided by one, two, or three spins from each player, to be previously agreed upon.

BROTHER JONATHAN.

This is the name of a modern game which may be played out or in doors; a square board being laid upon the ground, if out of doors, or if in a room, a square being chalked upon the floor. It is divided into sixteen compartments, in each of which a number is marked from one to five hundred. These numbers are not placed regularly, but are contrasted, so that those of the smallest value are nearest to those of the highest, and in some instances the squares for the higher numbers are made much smaller than those for the lower numbers. (See Diagram.) A mark is made, at an optional distance from the square, for the players to stand, who

40	200	10	400
90	5	300	50
1	500	20	80
70	30	100	60

in succession throw up one cent or more, and make their score according to the number assigned to the compartment in which the cent rests, provided it be within the square; for if it lies upon one of the lines that divide it from the others, the cast is forfeited and nothing gained. Two thousand is usually the game, but this depends upon the pleasure of the players.

Brother Jonathan is similar to a simple game known as *crack loo*, which consists in throwing up a copper to see who can come nearest the cracks in the floor.

SHOVEL-BOARD.

The method of playing this game is as follows:—A shovel-board is chalked out on the boarded floor. About nine or ten yards in length will be quite enough, and three feet in breadth. At one end of the shovel-board a line is drawn across, about four inches from the end, and parallel with it. At four feet distance from this line another is drawn across the board. The players stand at the opposite end of the board, with heavy pieces of wood in their hands. Each man has four of these, and each set has a distinguishing number or mark. Then, in rotation, the players each shove one of their pieces of wood along the board. Those that glance off at the side, or go beyond the end of the board, or fall short of the first line, are not counted. Those that lodge between the first, or four-foot line, and the second, count one; those that cross the second line, or lie upon it, without overhanging the extreme edge of the board, count two; and those that overhang the edge, without clearing it, three; this being the most difficult feat to achieve. When two players only are engaged, twelve is generally the game; but when there are more, the number must be increased in proportion, and averages between fifteen and twenty. The board is usually sanded, and sometimes iron weights of about one or two pounds weight are used instead of the wood, as they slide somewhat easier.

DIBS, OR KNUCKLEBONES.

This game is played with five little joint bones from a sheep's leg; hence its name, "knucklebones." It is generally played by two persons.

There may be four, two on each side; but the game should be limited to this number, as only one player is occupied at a time, and the others would find the long interval of looking on till their turn came somewhat tedious. Artificial dibs may be obtained at the ivory-turners, and at many toy-shops. The first player takes the five knucklebones in his hand, and throws them upon the table. Then he has to go through the first figure, or "ones." He takes up one dib from the table, and tosses it into the air; while it is still rising, he takes up one other dib from the table, and then catches the first as it descends. This he repeats until all the four dibs have been picked up, one by one. The next figure, "twos," consists in taking up the knucklebones, two at a time; "threes," in taking up the first three, and then the remaining one; and "fours," in taking them all up in a bunch together. Then come "picka-backs," one, two, three, and four. In these figures the dib is first tossed up, and caught on the back of the hand; and then, it being tossed up again, the four other dibs are taken up successively, as in "ones." Hand-sweeps, elbow-sweeps, and arm-sweeps, consist in putting two dibs at the hand's length, an elbow and wrist length, and the length of an entire arm apart; then another dib is thrown up, and the dibs on the table must be taken up by a sweep of the hand in the interval, before the dib thus thrown up descends and is caught. When the first player misses any of the feats, lets a dib drop, or fails to pick the others up as required, he loses his innings, and the second begins; the first having to recommence, when his turn comes again, at the point at which he left off. There are many other figures, but it would take more space than we can spare to describe them. The player who gets through all the figures first, of course, wins the game.

JACK-STRAWS.

Some people call this game *Spelicens:* it may be played by two, three, or four players separately, or by taking sides. The straws, which are little pieces of wood, bone, or ivory, mostly shaped like lucifer matches, with some made into little battle-axes, halberds, spears, shovels, &c., are thrown in a heap together, either out of the hand, or a very large dice-box. The player, then, with a little stick, having a crooked pin at the end, endeavors to remove each straw, without stirring the heap. If he should stir it, he stops and the next player goes on. When the straws are all picked up, the players count their gains, and

whoever has the most wins the game. The plain straws count one each, the spears five, the hatchets ten, the halberds fifteen, the shovels twenty, and so on—though this is at the pleasure of the players. Some boys may think this poor fun, but it is more exciting than is supposed. A good story is told of a young man, who had a great passion for that terrible and degrading vice, gambling. He had played away his whole estate, and was reduced to want. His wealthy relatives agreed to give him a new fortune, if he would solemnly promise never to play again at the games they enumerated. He agreed, and they wrote out a list of every thing like chance or skill they could think of, down to marbles and dibs. But one game they missed. A fortnight after they had given him his new fortune, one of them dropped in to see him, and found him playing jack-straws with one of his old cronies, at ten pounds (the affair happened in England) for a plain straw, and a hundred pounds each for hatchets and shovels.

THE WATER-CUTTER.

The water-cutter is a toy whose action depends on the same mechanical law as the bandilor. It is formed of a piece of lead, or other metal; the edges, if you prefer it, notched like the teeth of a saw. In this metal disk two holes are pierced, at some distance from each other, and through these a piece of string is passed, the two ends being afterwards tied together. If the two extremities of the doubled string are pulled sharply, and the string instantly slightly relaxed, the "cutter" will make several revolutions, on account of the impetus it has received when the string was pulled: in per-

forming these revolutions it will twist the string, which being again pulled with a jerk will be unwound, and necessarily carry round with it the metal disk; the string is again loosened, and the greater impetus the cutter has now acquired will twist the string to a greater extent than in the first instance: by continuing to pull and relax the string adroitly, the cutter may be made to revolve with great rapidity. The name water-cutter has been applied to this toy, because one mode of playing the game is to make it revolve with one of its edges dipped in water, so that it may sprinkle the bystanders and the player himself, to the amusement or annoyance of one or both, according to circumstances.

CUP AND BALL.

A ball of ivory or hard wood is attached to a stem of the same substance, having a shallow cup at one end, and a point at the other. The player holds the stem in his right hand, as shown in the figure, and, having caused the ball to revolve, by twirling it between the finger and thumb of his left hand, he jerks it up, and catches it either in the cup or upon the spike, to receive which a hole is made in the ball. We need scarcely say, that the latter feat can only be performed by a skilful player. Cup and ball was the favorite pastime at the Court of Henry III., of France.

THE BANDILOR.

The bandilor is a toy made of hard wood, resembling a pulley with a very deep groove; round this groove a piece of string is wound. To set the bandilor in action, the end of the string must be held between the finger and thumb, and the toy allowed to fall; by this means the string is neces- sarily unwound; but if its fall be suddenly checked by a sharp jerk, the motion is instantly changed, and instead of continuing to fall, it will rise towards the hand again, and the more rapidly it is falling, the more readily it can be made to change its course.

JACK-STONES.

This is the same game as "dibs," except that it is played with five smooth, flat, and circular pebbles, instead of the bones. Every boy knows the rhyming jingle attached to the Latin word "Finis," meaning "The End," which used to be placed at the close of every book:

> "F, for figs, and I, for jigs,
> And N, for knuckle-bones,
> And I S, for jack-stones."

N is not a good initial letter for knuckle-bones, but the I, for jigs, and I S, for jack-stones, will do. In old times, and the jingle is very old, I was used for J.

BATTLEDOOR AND SHUTTLECOCK.

The best quality of this really capital old game is, that it can be played by quite young children of both sexes, and is equally adapted to "children of the larger growth." By increasing the size and weight of the shuttlecock, and substituting heavy wooden battledoors for the light, leather-covered frames, with their catgut network, used by the little players in our illustration, the game of shuttlecock may be made to yield considerable exercise, as well as amusement. The simplest form of pursuing it is where there are two players, who strike the shuttlecock alternately, the one who first suffers it to fall to the ground being the loser. But the game may be made more interesting, and at the same time amuse a greater number, when there are five or six players, who divide into sides, each having his number—one side, 1, 3, 5; the other, 2, 4, 6. The shuttlecock, first struck by 1, must then be hit by 2, and then, in turn, by 3, 4, 5, and 6. The player who lets it drop is out; and the side of which one or more men are still in, after all their opponents have lost their position, wins the game.

A good shuttlecock may be made, where there are no toy-shops to supply it, by cutting off the projecting ends of a common cotton-reel, trimming one end with a knife, and drilling holes in the flat surface left at the other, in which holes the feathers of quill pens are to be inserted. As for the battledoors, we should think very little of the boy who could not, on an emergency, cut out a set from a bit of thin board, or the flat lid of a box, with the help of the big blade of his pocket-knife.

The French are great adepts at this game, and light battledoors and shuttlecocks are wielded by them with great perseverance and considerable skill. There is one great advantage about this game, namely, that without requiring any great amount of strength, it thoroughly exercises every muscle of the player, and furnishes real exercise without producing exhaustion.

20*

The Siamese play shuttlecock in a way that would astonish our readers, their battledoors being nothing more nor less than the soles of their exceedingly flat feet.

GRACES.

This is an in-door sport, which answers when a boy is kept in the house on a rainy day, but it is only an amusement to be indulged in when there are girls of the party. Boys never play it with each other, except for a "lark." It is a very graceful exercise, however, and a good training for catching a ball. Each party is armed with a hoop and two light sticks. The hoop is to be thrown by one party toward his opponents, from the crossed ends of his sticks. The young lady throws hers in the same way; and each catches the hoops thrown by the other party—the two hoops being kept going back and forth through the air. Or it may be played with one hoop, which is less difficult.

SCHIMMEL.

To play this amusing game, which is of German origin, it is necessary to be furnished with five cards on which are painted the figures of a white horse, an inn, a bell, a hammer, and a bell and hammer, with eight little ivory cubes marked on one side only; six numbered 1, 2, 3, 4, 5, 6, and the other two marked, one with a bell and the other with a hammer; with a box for throwing the dice, a hammer for disposing of the cards by auction, and a proportionate quantity of counters for the players. The cards, dice-box, and auctioneer's hammer, are shown in the annexed illustration. Any

youth who can draw may easily prepare the cards; the cubes may be procured from an ivory-worker's and may be marked with ink. The game can be played by as many persons as are present. The counters are to be distributed by one of the players who holds the office of cashier, and their value having been previously determined upon by the players. This being done, twelve are to be deposited by each player in the pool. The cashier then disposes of the five cards separately to the highest bidders, the produce of whioh is also to be placed in the pool. The white horse is by far the most valuable card, and therefore fetches the highest price in counters. The inn ranks next, and is usually purchased by the most speculative player, as its value depends upon circumstances. The bell and the hammer generally fetch the same number of counters, these cards being equally valuable, and the card upon which both bell and hammer are painted fetches about half the number that is given for one of the single figures. The bidders are not bound to confine themselves to the number of counters dealt out to them at the beginning of the game; should they exceed it, they may pay the remainder of the debt by instalments out of their receipts in the course of the game.

Each person is at liberty to purchase as many cards as he may think proper.

The dice are then to be thrown by the players alternately, beginning with the holder of the white horse, any one being allowed to dispose of his throw to the highest bidder. When all blanks are thrown, each of the players pays one to the holder of the white horse, and he pays one to the inn. If with the blanks the bell, or hammer, or the bell and hammer together are thrown, the possessor of the card so thrown pays one to the white horse.

When numbers accompany the bell, hammer, or bell and hammer, the cashier is to pay counters, to the amount of numbers thrown, to the holder of such card, from the pool; but if numbers are thrown unaccompanied, the cashier then pays to the thrower.

When the pool is nearly empty there arises an advantage to the inn, for if a player throws a figure greater than the quantity contained in the pool he pays the overplus to the inn; thus: suppose 4 are in the pool, if the player throws 10, he is to pay 6 to the inn; and if 2 are thrown, those 2 are paid to him from the pool, and so on till a figure is thrown which clears the pool, and so concludes the game.

If all blanks are thrown after the inn begins to receive, the players pay nothing, but the owner of the white horse pays one to the inn; and should the bell, &c., be thrown with the blanks, the holder of that card pays one to the inn; and if numbers accompany the bell, &c., the holder of that card must pay to the inn the number thrown above those remaining in the pool.

LE DIABLE.

This is a French game, with a French name, which we do not care to translate into English. The toy-dealers, who include the plaything among their stock, get over the difficulty by calling it a *Les graces cone*, so we will do the same. The pastime consists in balancing a double cone on a string attached to two sticks. The cone can only be prevented from falling by

being kept continually in motion. After the player has learned to balance it on the string, he tosses it up and catches it again, and it may also be made to whirl round the string, and to dance upon it. Two players can also toss it from one to the other, like a *Les graces* hoop, and a good deal of exercise can be got out of this demoniac toy, which we recommend, as somewhat of a novelty, to our young friends.

And now, we hope that we have redeemed our pledge, by enumerating some ways in which even a rainy holiday may be made to pass off pleasantly. One observation we must, however, still make, and then, we hope, our young friends will be able to say as Cicero said to the tailor, in the senate-house, "*Rem acu teligisti*" (Thou hast touched the matter sharply), *i. e.*, WITH A NEEDLE. The secret of the whole matter of passing a dull day happily lies in the one word *good-humor*. Even wet weather may be made indirectly agreeable by becoming the occasion for the exercise of wit and invention in our amuse-ments.

> "There is some touch of goodness in things evil,
> If men observingly distil it out,"

said Shakespeare; and the remark applies just as strongly to boys. But our tempers on a wet day ought not to be influenced by the weather, except, by way of contrast, they appear all the brighter. If a boy is testy and impracticable, let him be first reasoned with, then snubbed; and then, if refractory, banished by his companions in the play-room for a season, for, as one bad egg will spoil the pudding—as one little rift within the lute will spoil all the melody of music—as one falsehood will destroy confidence that has taken months, and perhaps years, to establish—as one wasted opportunity will sometimes destroy the prospects of a whole career, and prevent the success that would have crowned the efforts of a lifetime—so a whole merry party may have a disagreeable flavor imparted to it, merely by the presence of that very objectionable boy, young quarrelsome.

PART V.

___

Evening Amusements:

COMPREHENDING

COMIC DIVERSIONS, PARLOR MAGIC, SCIENTIFIC
RECREATIONS, AND PUZZLES.

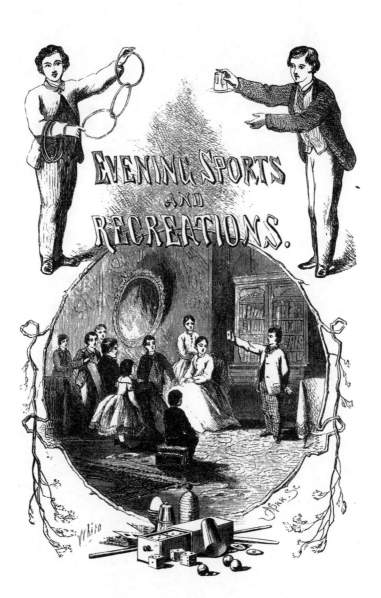

EVENING SPORTS AND RECREATIONS.

EVENING AMUSEMENTS.

THE GERMAN DWARF.

COMIC DIVERSIONS.

As, during the Christmas holidays—happy times, looked forward to with impatience, and ever remembered after they have passed—the long evenings of winter will demand a variety of amusements, we have here put together a few evening sports and recreations; some of them of very recent invention, and others of older date.

All, however, are provocative of mirth, and, whenever possible, they have been so framed that they take the form of competition, and place the unsuccessful in ludicrous positions. We have personally tested every amusement which is here mentioned, as is our usual custom when we make any recommendations, and we can declare, with perfect truth, that every game described will be universally successful, if played with proper spirit.

THE GERMAN DWARF.

This is a most comical entertainment, and one which, if well managed, will deceive the sharpest eyes. Two persons are required to enact the character of dwarf, and they do so after the following manner: A good, deep window is chosen, where the curtains are full and voluminous, and where there is plenty of space for movement. A table is drawn to the window, and the curtains disposed so as to fall over the table, and to conceal the persons behind it. The speaking player, whom we will call, for shortness, the speaker, then proceeds to array himself in as gorgeous a manner as possible, taking care to put on a rather voluminous jacket, with large sleeves. The ladies are capital hands at improvising such costumes. The arms must be dressed to represent legs, and the hands thrust into shoes or boots, the latter being preferable. Of course, the real origin of the pretended legs is concealed by the jacket.

The second player, whom we will call the actor, takes his place behind the speaker, pushes his arms under the sham legs of the speaker, and fits them carefully into the sleeves of the jacket. The speaker puts his hands on the table, and the curtain is then carefully drawn and pinned up, so as to prevent any one from seeing the performers. This part of the business is performed by some one who has been let into the secret.

The doors of the room are then opened, and the spectators admitted.

The dwarf, who is not restricted to Germany, but may assume any other nationality at pleasure, then begins an harangue, interlarding it copiously with foreign words and expressions. While he speaks, the actor performs the gestures, and here lies the fun of the whole thing. (*See illustration.*) The actor always tries to make his gestures wholly inappropriate to the language of the speaker, and indulges in all kinds of practical jokes.

It is a good thing to introduce the national dance. Of course, any thing will do for a dance, and a lady can always be persuaded to play some brisk tune. If well arranged, this is very effective, for the legs have no weight to support, and can be as lively as you please. Here, also, the hands of the actor come in well, and the combined effect is inexpressibly ludicrous.

Once, when the writer was enacting the part of speaker, he made a most ridiculous mistake. Just as he was delivering an eloquent discourse, a fly settled on his nose, and, forgetting the rôle which his arms were then playing, he brushed it away with his right hand, which was at that moment dressed in a silk stocking and Turkish slipper. There was a general shout through the room, and he was told by one of the spectators, that no studied piece of acting could have been half so comical as that unexpected gesture into which he was surprised.

THE KENTUCKY GIANT.

This is a jolly companion to the German Dwarf, and, like it, never fails to produce roars of laughter, when performed at an evening company. It is necessary to have two persons to represent the giant, and the method of enacting the part is best explained by the accompanying engraving. It will be seen that one boy puts on a *long* cloak, and perches himself upon the shoulders of his companion, who arranges the folds of the cloak so that the parts shown by the *dotted* lines in the illustration, are entirely concealed from the eyes of the spectators. The boy who *does* the head and shoulders of the giant should carry a long staff, as a cane, and, if he wear a stove-pipe hat, with a feather in it, it will greatly *heighten* the effect. The giant's wife may also be repre-sented by one person, with the assistance of a cane and piece of lath, the latter eighteen inches long, fastened about four inches from the top or end of the former, thus forming a cross. The person representing the giantess attires himself in an old dress. A long shawl is pinned over the lath, an old bonnet placed on the end of the cane, and the preparations are complete. The giantess usually walks into the room and pretends to look for a nail in the wall (this gives the performer an opportunity of concealing his face), and, after looking at the wall a minute or so, he stoops down as low as he can, at the same time being careful to lower the cane. He then *gradually* rises, until he stands upon the tips of his toes, and *as he does so*, he as *gradually* raises the cane, with the bonnet and shawl upon it, until he appears to touch the ceiling. The lath represents the shoulders of the giantess, the bonnet her head, and the cloak covers the whole deception. The giantess, if well done, is sure to be greeted with shouts of laughter.

THE ELEPHANT.

This is as comical a diversion as either of the foregoing, and never fails to elicit applause. Two boys are required to person-ate the elephant; one represents his fore, and the other his hind legs. The two boys place themselves as shown in the illustration; a quilt doubled over *three* or *four* times is now placed on the backs of the boys, which serves to form the back of the elephant; a large blanket or travelling shawl is then thrown over them, one end of which is twisted to represent the trunk of the animal, the other end serving in a similar manner to represent his tail. Two paper cones enact the tusks, and the elephant is complete. A bright and witty boy should be selected to perform the part of keeper, and he must lecture upon the prodigious strength, wonderful sagacity, and extreme docility of the animal, proving the latter quality by lying down and permitting the elephant to walk over him. It always amuses a company to *show them the elephant.*

THE DECAPITATION.

This is a rather startling *ruse*, and though in the sequel it is very funny, it should not be practised upon those who have very weak nerves.

Fig. 1.

Fig. 2.

The object sought to be represented is a decapitated head, and is done in the following manner:—A large table covered with a cloth, reaching the floor all around, is placed in the centre of the room. A boy with soft silky hair should be selected to represent the *head*, and to do this he must lie on his back under the table, with all his person concealed except a portion of the head, which should be exposed to view from under the table-cloth, as shown in Fig. 1.

Next a companion, in collusion with him, must carefully comb the hair to imitate the whiskers of a man (see Fig. 2). He must also paint false eyebrows on the *under* part of the eyes, and false nose, mustache, and mouth upon the forehead (see Fig. 2). This is easily done with the assistance of a camel's-hair brush, and a little Indian-ink, and when well completed the head appears to be entirely disconnected from the body, and has a very startling effect. The effect may be intensified by powdering the face, to make it appear pale.

THE OLD MAN'S FACE

Is also a very comical amusement, and productive of much merriment. The only requisite for producing it is a person's hand, a handkerchief, and a little Indian-ink. The engraving will show the simplicity of the arrangement, and demonstrates how easy it is to form an old man's face.

HOW TO STRIKE THE KNUCKLES WITHOUT HURTING THEM.

Select a marble mantel or any other hard surface, then tell the spectators that by a certain preparation you use, you have made your knuckles so hard nothing can hurt them, in proof of which you offer to strike them on the marble slab of the mantel. To do this, you raise your fist firmly clinched above the mantel, and as you bring it rapidly down, open your fingers suddenly and strike the marble, then close them again as represented in the engraving, 1, 2, and 3. If this is quickly done, you will seem to have knocked your knuckles violently.

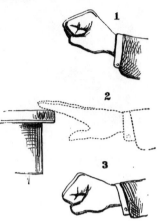

KNOCKING THE HEAD AGAINST A DOOR.

This ruse is very similar to the preceding one, and will surprise a company if well done. The performer should introduce the diversion as follows:—

"Do you desire me, ladies and gentlemen, to teach you my secret for making impromptu verses? It is to rub your forehead well, not with the hand, as Horace did of old, but by giving your head some good sound blows against a wall." Then proceed to knock your head three or four times against a door, and put your hand to your forehead, as if to deaden the pain produced by the violence of the blows. But you must do something more than merely touch the door with your head. At the same moment that you make the movements as if knocking yourself, you ward off the

blow, by the aid of the left hand held to the door, about the spot which you appear to strike, while the closed right hand, concealed from the audience, strikes on the other side of the door.

The correspondence of the movements of the head with the noise of the blows given by the clinched fist, produces a perfect illusion on the minds of the spectators.

HAT MEASUREMENT.

Very few people are aware of the height of the crown of a stove-pipe hat. A good deal of fun may be created by testing it in this way: Ask a person to point out on a wall, about what he supposes to be the height of an ordinary hat, and he will place his finger usually at about a foot from the ground. You then place a hat under it, and to his surprise he finds that the space indicated is more than double the height of the hat. The height of a common flour-barrel is just the length of a horse's face, and much fun may be derived from getting a company to mark the supposed height of a flour-barrel. In nine cases out of ten they will mark many inches too high.

THE IMMOVABLE CARD.

Take an ordinary visiting-card, and bend down the ends as represented in the annexed figure; then ask any person to blow it over. This seems easy enough,  but it may be tried for hours without succeeding. It is, however, to be done by blowing sharply on the table, at some distance from the card.

THE BOTTLE IMP.

This is a feat productive of much amusement, and can be played, or rather  exhibited, by one person at a time, while the others are resting from some game that demands exertion, or after some lively dance.

Nothing is simpler than this feat. The player has to stand a wine-bottle on his head, stoop down, pick a dime from the ground with his lips, and raise himself again to his feet, without letting the bottle fall from his head or touching it with his hands.

To perform this feat correctly, it is necessary to bend the head forward until the chin rests on the breast, and then to lodge the bottle on the crown of the head. Unless this precaution be taken, the bottle is sure to fall off before the lips can be brought near the ground. The best plan is to bend the knees very gently, and come to the ground on one knee. Then lower the hands to the ground, and, thus supported, push the feet gradually back until the face is able to reach the ground.

In order to make the feat more imposing, the following arrangement has a very fine effect. Get two corks, and push one firmly into the neck of the bottle. Into the upper part of the other stick the points of two equal-sized forks, and run a needle perpendicularly through its middle. Then push a tolerably stout pin at right angles with the cork in the bottle, and rest the needle point upon the pin's head. The balance will be found perfect, the forks will rotate easily when touched, and the needle will not slip off the pin unless it meets with a jerk.

This arrangement does not greatly add to the difficulty, though it appears to do so, the forks rocking and revolving in a most alarming manner with every movement of the player. Nor is there any danger of the upper fork falling off, and the point of the needle running into the head, although such a catastrophe seems to be extremely probable. If the experiment of knocking the needle from its hold be tried, it will at once be seen that one fork-handle will be the only object that can strike the head; and although it may give a sharp rap, it will do no further harm.

The principle of the balanced forks will be explained hereafter in " *Scientific Recreations.*"

PARLOR MAGIC.

SLEIGHT OF HAND.

It is our intention, in the following pages, to lay more stress upon those tricks which require no apparatus, than upon those for which special apparatus or the assistance of a confederate is required. No one is so well pleased by a trick whose essence evidently lies in the machinery, while every one feels pleasure at seeing a sleight of hand trick neatly executed. For our own part, we despise all the numerous boxes, bottles, variegated covers, and other gimcracks which are generally seen on a conjurer's table; and we have never been so pleased with any performer as with one who did not even require a table, but pressed into his service articles borrowed from his audience, as he stood before them or walked among them. The spectators should never be able to say, "Ah! the trick lies in the box; he dares not show it to us!"

The following tricks have almost all been successfully performed by the editor, and have caused him some reputation in the magic art. Some are his own invention

THE TRAVELLED BALLS.

This is always a favorite feat, because it needs no apparatus, and is remarkably effective. You take three or four cups, whether of metal or china is of no consequence, provided that they be opaque: breakfast cups answer very well, and silver goblets better. Professional conjurers always have three highly-ornamented conical vessels, but we prefer to use cups and tankards because they can be borrowed in the house and excite no suspicion.

You place three cups upon a table, and exhibit an equal number of balls. Walnuts, potatoes, plums, &c., &c., will answer very well, but the easiest balls for work are made from cork, in the following manner. Take some champagne corks and cut them into spherical form, rubbing them smooth with a file. Then hold them in front of a bright fire, and they will begin to swell rapidly. When they have swollen as much as possible, char the outsides by holding them in the flame of a candle, rub them smooth with a rag, and polish with a little oil upon leather.

You put a cup over each ball, and cover them from sight. You then take each ball separately and fling it in the air. After the third ball has been thus flung away, you take up the cups again, and, to the surprise of the spectators, the three balls have come back again, and each is found under its respective cup. Then you take a ball out of one cup, fling it in the air, and presently find it under another cup; and, lastly, you bring all the three under the same cup.

The secret of this capital trick lies chiefly in the *fourth* ball, the existence of which the audience do not know.

Before you begin, put a fourth ball in some place where you can easily get at it,—in your pocket, for example, or stuck on a little spike fastened to your own side of the table: a broken needle answers well for this purpose. Throw the three balls on the table, and while you are handling the cups with the left hand, and shifting the balls about in them, quietly get the fourth ball into the right hand, and hold it at the roots of the second and third fingers. You will now find that with the tips of those fingers you can pick the ball out of the palm of the hand. Being thus prepared you may commence the trick.

Put a ball under each cup, and be careful to get the balls close to the edge of the cup which is farthest from you. Let them stay there while you talk to the audience in some flourishing style, and, in the mean time, get the fourth ball between the *tips* of your second and third fingers; keep those fingers well doubled into the palm, take the right-hand cup between the thumb and forefinger, keeping the rest of the fingers behind it, lift it off the first ball, and as you set it down, neatly slip the fourth ball under it. As you will now have your hands quite empty, it may be as well to make some gesture, which shows that you have nothing concealed.

Take up the first ball, and say that it is going to Europe. Draw your hand quickly back, as if to throw, and while doing so drop the ball into the palm of the hand and catch it between the roots of the fingers, just as the fourth ball was held. Pretend to throw it away, opening your hand as if you did so, but taking care to hold it tightly in the finger-roots. Take up the second cup, slip the first ball under it as before, and proceed to do so with the third, pretending each time to throw the ball away. Take up the cups, and exhibit the three balls which have now come back again.

Now comes a neat little piece of legerdemain. Replace the cups over the balls, and as you do so slip the ball in your hand under the left-hand cup, so that there will be two balls in it. Take up the right-hand cup, pretend to throw the ball into the middle cup, pick it up and show the two balls there. As you replace the cup, slip the concealed ball into it, so as to bring three under one cup, and proceed as before. When you have finished the performance, by showing the three balls under one cup, get rid of the fourth ball by sticking it on the projecting needle.

PALMING COIN.

This phrase involves an explanation of the first grand principles of the art, without which no feat of mere sleight of hand with coin can be successfully performed, and to accomplish which with ease and rapidity, requires considerable practice and experience. The exhibitor, before commencing, should turn back the sleeves of his coat, to avoid the appearance of passing any thing down the arm, and may then prepare himself for the first illusion in the manner following:—

Place a coin, either a dime or a quarter, on the *tips* of the middle and third fingers, so that it may rest there of its own weight. By now turning the hand with the knuckles uppermost, and quickly closing the fingers into the palm, the coin may be held securely by the contraction of the thumb, and the hand still appear to contain nothing. This is *palming*, and with a little practice nearly every feat of simple legerdemain may be performed by its means. Care, of course, must be taken not to expose the coin by any reversed movement of the hand.

Securing the coin in the right hand, and simultaneously making it appear to pass into the left, the exhibitor may cause it either to disappear altogether, or, by holding a glass in the right hand, bid it fly from the left into the tumbler, where the expansion of the thumb will readily cause it to fall. This feat, when skilfully performed, never fails to elicit surprise and admiration.

The following simple trick may in many cases be employed instead of *palming*.

THE MAGIC COIN.

Although a purely sleight of hand trick, it requires but little practice to perform this recreation with dexterity. Take a quarter of a dollar between the thumb and forefinger of the right hand, as represented in the engraving; then, by a rapid twist of the fingers, twirl the coin, by the same motion  that you would use to spin a teetotum; at the same time rapidly close your hand, and the coin will disappear up your coat-sleeve; you can now open your hand, and, much to the astonishment of your audience, the coin will not be there. This capital trick may be varied in a hundred ways. One good way is to take three dimes, or quarters, and concealing one in the palm of your left hand, place the other two, one each between the thumb and forefinger of each hand; then give the coin in the right hand the twirl, as already described, and, closing both hands quickly, the coin in the right hand will disappear up your sleeve, and the left hand, on being unclosed will be found to contain two quarters, whilst that which *was* in the right hand will have disappeared. Thus you will make the surprised spectators believe that you conjured the coin from the right hand into the left.

TO BRING TWO SEPARATE COINS INTO ONE HAND.

Take two cents, which must be carefully placed in each hand, as thus: The right hand with the coin on the fourth and little finger, as in the illustration. Then place, at a short distance from each other, both hands open on the table, the left palm being level with the fingers of the right. By now suddenly turning the hands over, the cent from the right hand will fly, without being perceived, into the palm of

the left, and make the transit appear most unaccountable to the bewildered eyes of the spectators.. By placing the audience in front, and not at the side of the exhibitor, this illusion, if neatly performed, can never be detected.

THE MAGIC HANDKERCHIEF.

You take any handkerchief and put a quarter or a dime into it. You fold it up, laying the four corners over it so that it is entirely hidden by the last one. You ask the audience to *touch and feel the coin* inside. You then unfold it, and the coin has disappeared without anybody seeing it removed. The method is as follows:

Take a dime, and privately put a piece of wax on one side of it; place it in the centre of the handkerchief, with *the waxed side up;* at the same time bring the corner of the handkerchief marked A (as represented in Fig. 1),and completely hide the coin; this must be carefully done, or the company will discover the wax on the coin.

Fig. 1.

Now press the coin very hard, so that by means of the wax it sticks to the handkerchief; then fold the corners, B, C, and D (see Fig. 1), and it will resemble Fig. 2.

21

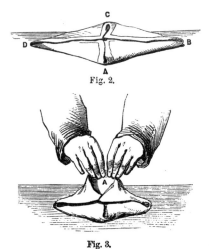

Fig. 2.

Fig. 3.

Then fold the corners, B, C, and D (see Fig 2), leaving A open. Having done this, take hold of the handkerchief with both hands, as represented in Fig. 3 at the opening, A, and sliding along your fingers at the edge of the same, the handkerchief becomes unfolded, the coin adheres to it, coming into your right hand. Detach it, shake the handkerchief out, and the coin will have disappeared. To convince the audience the coin is in the handkerchief, drop it on the table, and it will sound against the wood. This is an easy trick.

THE DOMINO ORACLE.

This trick, to one not familiar with it, is certainly very surprising.

Arrange twelve of the dominoes as shown in the illustration, and inform any one present, that if he will think of one of the dominoes and remember it, you will point it out to him. Now, supposing the double-deuce is the

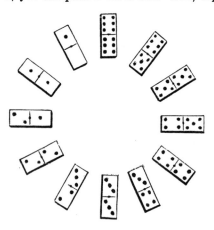

domino selected, you tell the person who has chosen it that you will count around the circle, and when you have counted twenty, *including the number of spots on the selected domino*, he must tell you to stop, and that your finger will then rest on the domino chosen. The secret is simply this,—you count carelessly around, 1, 2, 3, 4, 5, 6, 7, on any of the dominoes ; but at the eighth count you always manage to point to the *double-six*, and after that you continue counting around *regularly to the right;* be sure and remember this, for it is the key of the trick. For example, as we have before said, we will suppose the double-deuce to be the selected domino. We follow the above instructions, and count and point at the dominoes *promiscuously* the first seven counts; but at the eighth count we point at the double-six, and continue to the right on the six-five, double-five, and so on in succession until we arrive at the double-deuce, when we will be told to stop, because by that time we will have counted sixteen, to which if we add the spots on the domino chosen we will have twenty. This rule holds good no matter what domino happens to be selected. It is perhaps useless to inform our reader that he must not count out loud, or appear to count mentally, but let it seem as if he were only pointing at the dominoes by chance. You must let the person who selects the domino appear to do all the counting.

TO GUESS THE TWO ENDS OF A LINE OF DOMINOES.

Cause a set of dominoes to be shuffled together as much as any of the company may desire. You propose to leave the room in which the audience are assembled, and you assert that from your retreat, be it where it may, you can see, and will be able to tell, the two numbers forming the extremes of a line composed of the entire set, according to the rules established for laying one domino after another in the draw game.

All the magic consists in taking up and carrying away, unknown to every one, one domino (not a double) taken at hazard; for the two numbers on it must be the same as those on the ends of the two outer dominoes. This experiment may be renewed, *ad infinitum*, by your taking each time a different domino, which, of course, changes the numbers to be guessed.

DOMINOES SEEN AND COUNTED THROUGH ALL OBSTACLES.

Lay a set of dominoes on their faces, one beside the other, in one black line. Then say to the company, I will go into the next room, with my eyes as closely covered as you may desire. In my absence, you may take from the line the number of dominoes you please, *provided you take them from that end which is now at my right hand*, and place them at the opposite end, so that, except for the change in the places of the pieces, the line is just the same as before.

At my return, without unbandaging my eyes, I will tell you exactly the number transported from one end to the other, for I shall have seen every thing through the wall and the handkerchief which has covered my eyes. I will do more. From the midst of these dominoes, of which you have changed the position, I will draw one which, by the addition of its spots, will tell you exactly the number which you took from right to left.

To perform this trick, arrange the first thirteen dominoes, *beginning at the left*, so that the spots on the first form the number *twelve;* of the second, *eleven;* of the third, *ten;* and so on, up to a double-blank, for the thirteenth and last. You place the other dominoes afterwards, in the order in which they happen to present themselves.

If your eyes are bandaged, count with your fingers the dominoes *from left to right,* as far as the thirteenth. The spots on this thirteenth will invariably represent the number of dominoes whose position has been altered.

In performing this and many other tricks, you will employ any ruse you can think of to puzzle those who may try to fathom them.

THE MAGICAL KNOT,

A very amusing trick, consisting in simply tying one knot with two ends of a handkerchief, and, by apparently pulling the ends, untying them again.

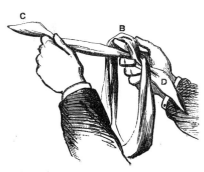

Take two ends of the handkerchief, one in each hand, the ends dropping from the inside of your hands. You simply tie a single knot, when your hands and your handkerchief will be in the position shown in the cut. Instead of pulling the ends C and D, grasp that part marked B with your thumb and forefinger, dropping the end D, and pulling upon the end C and the bend B, when, instead of *really* tying, you unloosen the knot.

All this should be done as quickly as possible, to prevent detection. Examine the engraving closely, and you will more readily understand the explanation.

TO CAUSE A DIME TO APPEAR IN A GLASS.

Having turned up the cuffs of your coat, begin by placing a cent on your elbow and catching it in your hand.

That easy feat performed, allege that you can catch even a smaller coin in a more difficult position.

Then place a dime half-way between elbow and wrist, as in the illustration; suddenly bringing the hand down, the coin drops into your cuff, unseen by any one, and you express the greatest astonishment at its disappearance. Tell the audience to watch, and they will see it drop through the ceiling. Then, taking a tumbler, place it at the side of your arm, and elevating the hand for the purpose, the coin falls jingling into the tumbler, causing great marvel as to how it came there.

A THREADED NEEDLE.

Get a needle, and a piece of cotton about five or six feet long; then thread and draw the cotton through the needle, so that both ends will be even with each other. Lay the doubled cotton over the end of the forefinger, about four inches from the needle, holding the doubled thread firmly between the thumb and middle finger. Now pass the needle through each thread

at point A (as seen in Fig. 1), taking care that in passing the needle through the thread you get it exactly through the fibres, so that the one side will be as strong as the other. Then draw the needle and thread through the part of the thread just mentioned, until it comes out straight,

Fig. 1.

and to all appearance there is no knot or catch in the thread where the needle has passed through. You say, "See, I have threaded it once." Then turning your back to the company, you pull the single thread that goes through the eye of the needle, until it comes to the place where you passed the needle through the eye of the fibres.

Draw the loop through the eye, and you have three threads in it; still continue to pull upon the three threads, and when you have pulled the loop part through the eye again you will have five threads through, and so you can keep on till you have the eye as full as it can hold.

Now with the knife cut the threads off about two inches from the needle, and exhibit it to the audience as in Fig. 2.

Fig. 2.

MAGIC MONEY.

This conjuring trick is performed thus:—Procure two quarters and a half-eagle; conceal one of the quarters in the *right* hand; lay the other quarter and the half-eagle on a table, in full view of the audience; now ask for two handkerchiefs; then take the gold-piece up, and pretend to roll it in one of the handkerchiefs; but, in lieu instead, roll up the quarter, which you had concealed, and retain the gold coin; give the handkerchief to one of the company to hold; now take the quarter off the table, and pretend to roll that up in the second handkerchief; but put up the half-eagle instead; give this handkerchief to another person, and beg him to "hold it tight," while you utter, "Presto! fly!" On opening the handkerchiefs the money will appear to have changed places.

THE STRING AND CORALS.

Take two pieces of white cotton *cord*, precisely alike in length; double each of them separately, so that their ends meet; then tie them together

very neatly, with a bit of fine cotton *thread*, at the part where they double,
i. e., the middle. (See A, Fig. 1.)

This must all be done beforehand. When you are going to exhibit the
trick, hand round two other pieces of cord, exactly similar in length and
appearance to those which you have prepared, but not tied, and desire your
company to examine them. You then return to your table, placing these
cords at the edge, so that they fall (apparently accidentally) to the ground,

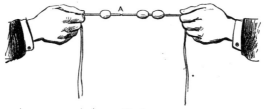

Fig. 1.

behind the table; stoop to pick them up, but take up the prepared ones instead, which you had previously placed there, and lay them on the table.
You then take round for examination three wooden balls, each having a
hole through the centre, sufficiently large to permit the balls to slip on and
off the strings with ease. These balls we will call *corals*. When the corals
have undergone a sufficient scrutiny, pass the prepared double cords through
them, and give the two ends of one cord to one person to hold, and the two
ends of the other to another. (See Fig. 1.) Do not let them pull hard, or

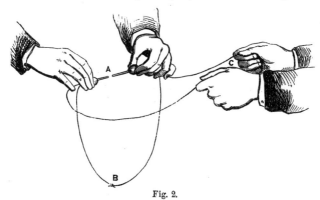

Fig. 2.

the thread will break, and your trick be discovered. Request the two persons to approach each other, and desire each to give you one end of the cord
which he holds, leaving to him the choice.

You then say that, to make all fast, you will tie these two ends together,
which you do. (See B, Fig. 2.) And returning to each person the end of

the cord next to him (see C, Fig. 2), you state that this trick is performed by the rule of contrary, and that when you desire them to pull hard, they are to slacken, and *vice versâ*, which is likely to create much laughter, as they are certain to make many mistakes at first. During this time you are holding the corals on the forefingers of each hand, and with the other fingers preventing your assistants from separating the cords prematurely, during their mistakes (see A, Fig. 2); you at length desire them, in a loud voice, to slack, when they will pull hard, which will break the thread, the corals remaining in your hands, whilst the strings will remain unbroken.

THE MAGNETIZED CANE

Is a very surprising little fancy, and is calculated to create much astonishment in the drawing-room. Take a piece of black silk thread, or horsehair, about two feet long, and fasten to each end of it bent hooks of a similar color. When unobserved, fasten the hooks in the back part of your pantaloon legs, about two inches below the bend of the knees. Then place the cane (it should be a dark one, and not too heavy) within the inner part of the thread, as represented in the engraving, and by a simple movement of the legs, you can make it dance about and perform a great variety of fantastic movements. At night your audience cannot perceive the thread, and apparently the cane will have no support whatever. The performer should inform the company, before commencing this trick, that he intends to magnetize the cane, and by moving his hands as professors of magnetism do, the motion of the legs will not be noticed.

THE OBEDIENT DIME.

Lay a dime between two half-dollars, and place upon the larger coins a glass, as in the diagram. Remove the dime without displacing either of the half-dollars or the glass. After having placed the glass and coins as indicated, simply scratch the table-cloth with the nail of the forefinger in the direction you would have the dime to move, and it will answer immediately. The table-cloth is necessary; for this reason the trick is best suited to the breakfast or dinner table.

THE HAT AND QUARTER TRICK.

Place a hat, tumbler, and quarter, as represented in the cut; then after making several feints, as if you intended to strike the hat upon the *rim*, give the hat a sharp quick blow upon the *inside of the crown*, and the coin will fall into the tumbler. This is a beautiful trick, if skilfully performed.

TO MAKE A DIME PASS THROUGH A TABLE.

To perform this feat you must have a *dime*, or counter, sewn in the corner of a handkerchief. Take it out of your pocket and request one of the company to lend you a dime, which you must appear to wrap carefully up in the middle of the handkerchief; instead of doing this, however, you keep it in the palm of your hand, and in its place wrap up the corner in which the other dime or counter is sewn in the midst of the handkerchief, and bid the person from whom you borrowed the dime feel that it is there. Then lay it under a hat upon the table, take a glass in the hand in which you have concealed the dime, and hold it under the table; then give three knocks upon the table, at the same time crying, "Presto! come quickly!" drop the dime into the glass, bring the glass from under the table, and exhibit the dime. Lastly, take the handkerchief from under the hat and shake it, taking care to hold it by the corner in which the counter or dime is sewn. This is a very good trick if well managed, and the dime *may be marked* previously.

THE ERRATIC EGG.

Transfer the egg from one wine-glass to the other, and back again to its original position, without touching the egg or glasses, or allowing any person or any thing to touch them. To perform this trick, all that you have to do is to blow smartly on one side of the egg, and it will hop into the next glass; repeat this and it will hop back again.

THE MAGIC SPLICE.

Here is a very simple, but not the less effective trick. Take a piece of string or tape, at least six feet in length, and as much longer as can conveniently be obtained, and hold each end with a finger and thumb. In order to render the description more intelligible, we shall call the end which is held in the right hand A, and that which is held in the left B. Measure the distance to the centre of the string, and take it up so as to make a couple of loops, one depending from each hand. Tell the audience that you are going to cut the string in the middle, and to mend it in half a minute so that no one shall be able to see the junction. They will probably think that you are going to cheat them (as indeed you are), and will demand that one of themselves shall cut the string. Yield the point, under protest, and lay the string on the ground, showing that all is fair, and that the centre of the string will really be cut. Now take up the end A in the same manner, and while you are drawing your left hand along the string, hitch, the middle finger of your

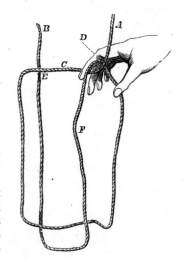

right hand under the loop that hangs from A, and bring B across it, as is seen in the illustration. If this is neatly done, the spectators will imagine that A is a continuation of F, for as the two thumbs come upon the points E and D, the real direction of the strings is concealed. In the illustration, the exact form of the string is given, so that the young conjurer may see whether he is right or wrong.

Offer the string to be cut at C, drop the end B, and the string will appear to be divided into two equal parts. Now throw the string F over the back of the forefinger, and tie the ends A and C in a double knot, rolling the strings well up so as to conceal the true character of the knot. Show the spectators that the knot is tied quite tightly, and place your right hand over it. Give a smart pull, and the knotted portion will come off the main string and fall into your hand, where you must conceal it. Now put your left hand over the same place, and with your right convey the short string to your pocket, or rid yourself of it in any way that your ingenuity may suggest.

Then remove your left hand, and call attention to the perfect manner in which the string has been mended.

THE NEEDLE AND THREAD TRICK.

Considerable amusement, not unmixed with wonder, may be occasioned among a party of ladies, by a clever performance of this trick. It is most frequently performed by a female, but the effect of it is considerably increased when it is displayed by a youth. A piece of calico, muslin, or linen is taken in the left hand, a needle is threaded in the presence of the spectators, and the usual, or even a double or treble knot, made at the

21*

extremity of one of the ends of it. The operator commences his work by drawing the needle and the thread in it quite through the linen, notwithstanding the knot, and continues to make several stitches in like manner successively.

The mode of performing this seeming wonder is as follows: A bit of thread, about a quarter of a yard long, is turned once round the top of the middle finger of the right hand, upon which a thimble is then placed, to keep it secure. (See illustration.) This must be done privately, and the thread

kept concealed, while a needle is threaded with a bit of thread of a similar length. The thread in the needle must have one of its ends drawn up nearly close, and be concealed between the forefinger and thumb; the other should hang down nearly as long as, and by the side of the thread, which is fastened under the thimble, so that these two may appear to be the two ends of the thread.

The end of the thread that is fastened under the thimble is then knotted and the performer begins to sew, by moving his hand quickly after he has taken up the stitch. It will appear as though he actually passed the knotted thread through the cloth.

THE "TWENTY CENT" TRICK.

Borrow twenty cents from the company, which display on a plate, having previously prepared five cents in your *left hand*, which you keep concealed. Then take the cents from the plate in the right hand, and, mixing them with the concealed five, give them to one of the company to hold. Ask the possessor to return five to you, which he will do, supposing he then retains only fifteen, although, in reality, he of course has twenty. Now have another cent palmed in your right hand, so that when giving the five cents to another person to hold, you may mix it with that sum, and place the *six* cents in his hand. You may now ask him, as before, to return *one;* when you take it remind him he has only four, and you must now proceed with the most marvellous part of your illusion. Taking the one cent you have just received in the right hand, *palm* it, and pretend to place it in the left. Then, striking the left hand with a rod, bid it fly into the closed hand of the person holding five, or, as he supposes, the *four* cents. On unclosing the hand the cent will of course appear to have been transferred thither, and great amazement will result. Now, taking the five cents, make a more dexterous pass into the left hand, whence you bid them fly into the closed hand of the person holding the supposed fifteen, and whom you now ask to return you the full sum of twenty cents, much to his own wonder and that of the company. If executed with care and dexterity, no illusion can be more effective.

TRICKS REQUIRING SIMPLE APPARATUS.

WE admit no tricks that are wholly managed by the apparatus, as we think they are unworthy of notice. Therefore, every trick mentioned in the following pages must be carefully practised in private before it is produced in public. The apparatus, of course, cannot be inspected by the audience, and for that reason it is better to mix them with those tricks that have been already mentioned, in order that suspicious persons may be quieted by an occasional permission to inspect the objects used in the performances.

The young conjurer should always vary the mode of performance in the non-essentials, and should study combinations of one trick with another, by which means he will produce more astonishing results than if he restricted himself to the methods mentioned in this work. He should also invariably make a little speech, acknowledging that he is only deceiving the eye and not the mind, and should therefore request the company not to ask any questions, or to demand inspection of any of his apparatus.

THE DIE TRICK.

Get a wooden die about two inches and a half square (1), and a hollow tin die exactly the size of the wooden one, but without one of the sides (2). Then paint them both exactly alike, as in the engraving. It will be better to let an *accidental* flaw appear on the same side of each. Then get a tin cover (4) that exactly fits the dice. Now for the trick itself.

Borrow two hats, and while you turn your back upon the audience as you go to your table, slip into one of them the false die. Place both hats on the table, and send round the real die and cover for inspection. When they are returned say, " Now, ladies and gentlemen, it is my intention to place these hats one above another, thus." You then place the two hats as in No. 3, the hollow die being in the bottom hat. " I shall then cover the die

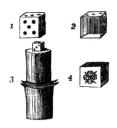

thus," which you do, "and after I have knocked on the cover I shall take it off, and you will find that the die is not under the cover, as it is now," taking it off, "but inside the hat, like this." You then put the real die into the hat. "You do not believe me, ladies and gentlemen, but I will soon convince you." You then take out the false die, and, replacing the upper hat, put the die on the upper hat (of course with the open side downward), and place the cover over it. Pick up your conjuring wand, give it a few flourishes, and bring it down on the cover. Grasp the cover tightly near the bottom, when both cover and false die will come up together; put the end of your wand into them and give them a good rattle. Then knock off the upper hat with a blow of the wand, and push the lower one off the table, so that the die tumbles out of it. Always use plenty of gesture about your tricks.

THE PEPPER-BOX TRICK.

Procure a common pepper-box, and get a tinman to unsolder the bottom, and then fasten on to it a tube of tin that will just fit the inside of the box, like a telescope. At the bottom side of this tube a slit must be cut that will let a quarter slip through. In the lid of the box a duplicate top is to be fastened, leaving inside a piece of tin, that will rattle when shaken. Now for the trick. Take the box in the *left* hand, ask one of the company for a

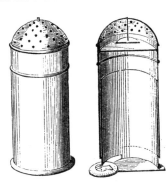

quarter, and to mark it that it may be identified. With the *right* hand draw off the lid, and request that the money be put into the box. It will of course slip through into your left hand. Put on the lid and push up the telescope bottom quickly, and passing the box to the right hand, rattle it, and ask where the money shall fly to. Have a cup at hand (near the left), and, as a feint, say "Here it is!" at the same time letting the money fall into the cup. "Presto! Fly!" It is now again in the box, and by a rattle it appears so. Remember all the while to hold the money fast in the cup, to prevent detection. "Presto! Fly again!" It is now down Willy's throat—is it not so? Place the cup to his ear; out it falls! Well, I never! Is it the same quarter? To be sure it is; there's the mark! This completes the pepper-box trick; but the routine indicated for its performance can be easily varied by any adept at legerdemain.

TO PASS SIX CENTS THROUGH A TABLE.

When this trick is well done it is one of the best "table moves" that can be shown for the amusement of a "small party." It is performed thus:

Get a brazier to cut out all the interior of five cents, only leaving the rims. He must then bore out nearly all the interior of a sixth cent, merely leaving a shell of copper at the top. A long rivet must then be let into the rim, as shown in Fig. 1, B, and a hole must be drilled in each of the five rings, as in C. The rivet is to be passed through the holes in the rings, and fastened below, so that all the rings can play easily upon it. A is a sec-

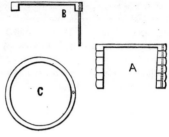

Fig. 1.

tion of the entire apparatus, the dotted lines representing the rivet. They can then be placed as shown in Fig. 2, B, and no one will imagine that they are only shams, as you can rattle them or move them about upon each other. A leathern cover, Fig. 2, C, is then made, which then passes easily over the heap of cents, but, being pliable, is capable of picking up the hollow cents with it, when it is held firmly. To the under surface of the table you fasten a little shelf, Fig. 2, A, which moves on a hinge, and is let fall by placing the foot on the pedal, D, which draws the catch.

To perform this trick, place six real cents on the little shelf, and have the sham cents on the table. Take them up and rattle them, and put them down as in Fig. 2, B. Keep a sixpence in the palm of your hand, pick up the sham cents, and as you put them down slip the sixpence under them. Take the cover, and put it over the sham cents, and make a short speech, and knock the cover with your wand, at the same time press-

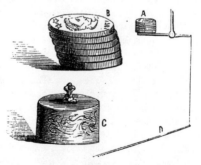

Fig. 2.

ing the pedal with your foot, which will cause all the six real cents to tumble down with a great crash. Take up the cover and false cents together, put the end of your wand into them and hold them up triumphantly, showing the spectators that the six cents have been replaced by a silver sixpence. While you are picking up the cents, slip the sham ones out of the cover into your left hand, and take some opportunity of letting the empty cover roll towards the audience, one of whom you ask to pick it up and bring it to you. This manœuvre generally disarms all suspicion, for the picker-up is sure to examine it very closely.

We have only given mere outlines of this really excellent trick, which may be varied in a hundred ways, and is capable of combination with other tricks to a large extent. For the pedal may be substituted a lever running immediately under the surface of the table, if the performer prefers to have a short cloth on it. There should be always two cloths on the table; the lower one thick and soft, to prevent jingling of objects, and the upper one white, as it displays every thing better than a colored one. The ingenuity of the young conjurer will easily find methods of varying this trick. The following is a capital variation.

THE MYSTERIOUS COIN.

After performing the last trick, you may address the company again, and say: " I will show you the nature of this trick, if you will only look sharp enough to see how it is done. Therefore, watch closely, and if you have *very* penetrating eyes, you may see the money go through this glass and fall upon the plate, and from that through the table into my hand. I will do it deliberately, so that you may have every opportunity of detecting the deception, which will make you as wise as myself."

Now you take a plate and place it on the table ; place upon that a wine-glass upside down, and take the empty leathern case and hold it before the audience, to convince them that nothing is inside. Place it, in a careless manner, over the riveted money, which you had before put a little aside from the view of the spectators. Place a small ball on the bottom of the glass: then take the case with the concealed coins therein, and place them over the ball, which will be secreted therein. Now tell the company to keep a sharp look-out, and they may discover the whole process. Take the loose coins and throw them on the table ; bring them again under the table, and exchange them for a ball previously deposited on the shelf, and lay the same upon the table. Remove the case alone, which, of course, will leave the money exposed on the top of the glass. " Now," says the performer, as he brings his hand from under the table, " I have made the ball go through the wine-glass, plate, and table, into my hand, and I presume that you have discovered the whole mystery; but if not, I will give you another opportunity, and will return the money whence it came." Cover the money with the case, and bring the ball which you previously exposed to the spectator under the table, and exchange it for the money on the shelf, which you again toss upon the table. Remove the case with the coins concealed therein, and the ball will appear on the top of the glass, as at first ; then bring your hand from under the table, and throw the real coins upon the table. Our performer makes the following concluding speech: " Now, as you have, I suppose, discovered the whole mystery, I hope, ladies, that *you* will not set up an opposition line against me; since, if you do, you will very seriously injure my pockets, and, of course, *attract* all the company, and leave me in an empty house with empty pockets."

TO CHANGE A DIME TO A QUARTER.

This is quite a simple parlor trick. In fact, it surprises on account of its very simplicity. Procure two pieces of marbled paper, about seven inches square, and having put the marble backs of the paper together, cut them in the shape

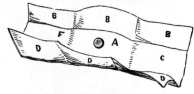

Fig. 1.

of an oblong square. (See Fig. 1.) Be very careful to have them exactly the same size, as the success of the trick depends, in a great measure, upon the regularity of the paper. After cutting the paper in the manner described, place a dime in the centre of one of the pieces, at the place marked A, then fold it carefully over at the crease on the side marked B, and also again at the side marked D. When you have done this, turn down the end marked C upon the centre A, and again fold over on F. When this is accomplished, you will discover that you

Fig. 2.

have formed a small parcel (the same shape as Fig. 2), with a dime in the centre. You then place a quarter of a dollar in the centre of the other piece of paper, and fold it up exactly the same size and shape as the first piece. Next gum the two parcels together at the back of the ends marked F, Fig. 2, and the sides will be so even that the parcels will appear as one. You can then open the side of the paper containing the dime and show it to your audience, informing them that you are going to open a mint on a small plan, and coin a quarter from a dime. Then mutter some cabalistic words and dexterously turn over the side containing the quarter, and upon opening the paper, to the astonishment of the company, instead of a dime they will behold a genuine quarter.

THE MAGIC CUPS.

Procure two tin cups without handles, quite plain, straight sides, with the bottoms sunk a quarter of an inch. On the bottoms spread some glue, and completely cover the glue with some kind of bird-seed, only so as not to be seen when standing in an ordinary position. Have ready a bag filled with the same kind of seed as you used in covering the bottoms. Put the cups on the table; also two hats. Put one cup then into the bag, appear to fill it, and take it out turned bottom upwards, when it will look as if it had been filled. Put it in that position under one hat; in doing so turn it over. Then take the other empty cup, put that under the other hat; and, in doing so, turn that over, which, of course, must be invisible to the audience. Then remove the hat and the cups will appear to have changed places.

TO PASS A QUARTER INTO A BALL OF WORSTED.

Like all the best magical tricks, this is one of the most simple. A marked quarter is borrowed, a large ball of worsted is brought. Presto! the

worsted is unwound, and out falls the money, that a minute before was in its owner's pocket. Here is the solution :—First, procure a few skeins of *thick* worsted, next a piece of tin in the shape of a flat tube, large enough for the quarter to pass through, and about four inches long.

Now wind the worsted on one end of the tube, to a good-sized ball, having a quarter of your own in your *right* hand. (See engraving.) You may now show the trick. Place the worsted anywhere out of sight, borrow a marked quarter, then taking it in your *left* hand, looking at it, and saying, "It is good," place the one in your *right* hand on the end of the table furthest from the company ; then fetch the worsted ; while so doing drop the marked quarter through the tube, pull it out, and wind the worsted a little to conceal the hole ; then put the ball into a tumbler, and taking the quarter you left on the table, show it to the company (who will imagine it to be the borrowed quarter), say, "Presto! fly! pass!" Give the end of the ball to one of the audience, request them to unwind it, which being done, the money will fall out, to the astonishment of all who see this trick of legerdemain.

THE MAGIC CANISTER.

Get a tinman to make a double canister, such as is shown in the engraving, with an opening in each end. This must so slide within a tin tube,

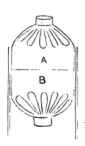

that either end can be concealed within it alternately, as seen in the engraving, where the end A is shown, and B is concealed. In this position it looks like an ordinary canister. The interior is divided into two parts. Into B put a piece of cambric made to look like a handkerchief.

Borrow a cambric handkerchief, and say, "Now, ladies and gentlemen, I shall burn this handkerchief to ashes, place them in this canister (so saying, you put it into A), and when I have uttered a spell, it will be restored perfectly whole. Will the owner say what mark it has?"

While the audience are looking towards the owner, you turn the canister over, and push up the canister until the shoulder of B is on a level with the top of the tube. When the mark has been declared, you open B, take out the cambric, and pretend to verify the mark. You then put it into a candle-flame, and when it has burned entirely to ashes, put the ashes into B, shut it up, and rapidly reverse it as you turn round to your audience, so that A is uppermost again. Then utter any nonsense you like, open A, and take out the handkerchief uninjured. It rather adds to the trick if you drop a little eau de cologne into A before performing the trick. With this simple apparatus many wonderful tricks may be performed.

EATABLE CANDLE-ENDS.

Take a large apple, and cut out a few pieces in the shape of candle-ends, A, round at the bottom and flat at the top, in fact, as much like a piece of candle as possible. Now cut some slips from a sweet almond, B, as near as you can to re- semble a wick, and stick them into the imitation can- dles. Light them for an instant, to make the tops black, blow them out, and they are ready for the trick. One or two should be artfully placed in a snuffer- tray, or candlestick ; you then inform your friends that during your "travels in the Russian Empire," you learned, like the Russians, to be fond of candles ; at the same time lighting your artificial candles (the al- monds will readily take fire, and flame for a few sec- onds), pop them into your mouth, and swallow them, one after the other.

THE MAGIC RINGS.

Get a blacksmith to make a number of rings, about six or seven inches in diameter, as in the cut. A is made with a spring opening on one side, B is a set of two rings forged permanently within each other, C is a set of three rings formed in the same manner, and D D are two simple rings. The rings should be about the thickness of a rather large black-lead pencil.

Lay the rings on one another, and they will all appear to be separate and distinct. D D should be the uppermost rings, then B, then A, and then C. Hand around D for inspection, and if any more are desired, hand round the other D. When returned, hang them over your left arm, or grasp them in your hand, and tell the company that you are going to weave all the rings together. You clash them together, and after going through some complicated movements, bring out B, which the spectators will think you have just fastened together. Hand them round. When they are returned mix them all up, and bring out C. Then take A in your hand, and passing one of the

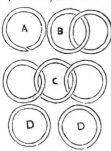

outer rings of C through the opening, you have four rings together. Then

add D and you have five. Take off D and substitute B, which will give you six.
So you go on weaving them into all kinds of fantastic shapes. You must
always conceal the joint in A with your thumb, and contrive as often as you
can to have one at least of the rings D at liberty. This is a capital trick, and
may be diversified to any extent, especially if the number of rings is increased.

THE BURNED HANDKERCHIEF RESTORED.

Get a flat-topped stand, such as is shown at A, and make a neat pasteboard or tin cover, as is seen at C, and be sure to ornament it with various
showy devices. The cover must slip very easily over the stand. Cut a flat

circular plate, B, the least bit wider than the top of A, and
just large enough to slip easily into C. Here is all your
apparatus.

Before you show this trick, place in your pocket a piece
of white rag that looks like a handkerchief. Borrow a
clean white cambric handkerchief from among the audience,
and just before you receive it, conceal in your hand the
white rag. Have the apparatus ready on a side-table, with
the movable plate laid on the stand. Lay the handkerchief on the plate, place the cover over the handkerchief,
and press it down with a smart slap.

Now take off the cover, squeezing it well so as to take
up the plate as you do so; put your hand into it as if about
to pull out the handkerchief, and substitute in its stead the white rag. Lay
the rag on the stand, apply a match to it, and let it burn to ashes. Replace
the cover on the stand, and press it down. Then loosen the grasp of the
hand and the plate will fall on the stand, completely concealing the ashes.
Lift the cover gently, when the handkerchief will fall upon the plate, and
may be restored unhurt to the owner.

THE MULTIPLIED MONEY.

Collect two or three dozen cents, and get a cheap and showy-looking salver
at a hardware store. Take the salver to some intelligent smith, and get him

to make a false bottom to it in the following manner. Give him one of the cents and let him cut
two slips of tin about twice as deep as the coins
are thick. Then let him set them on their edges,
parallel to each other, leaving just room for the
cents to slide easily between them, and solder them on the bottom of the
salver. Then let the plate which forms the false bottom be soldered upon
the slips, and a narrow slip of the same metal run round the edges, with
the exception of the slit shown in the illustration, at A, which corresponds
to the extremity of the space enclosed by the two parallel slips.

It is now evident that if some of the coins are pushed into the open slit, they will lie in a row across the bottom of the salver, the number being regulated by the diameter of the salver. If the inside of the groove in which they lie be lined with soft woollen cloth, the coins will be prevented from rattling, which is a point of some importance.

When you are about to perform this trick, have the salver nicely polished, so as to look as like real silver as possible. Slip into the groove six of the coins, and then stand the salver on a side-table, as if it were one of those which belonged to the house. Call one of the audience, place eighteen coins in the salver, taking care to turn the slit *towards* you; tell him to hold out both his hands, and pour the coins into them. Then tell him to return the coins one by one, counting them aloud, and to make them ring upon the salver, so that every one shall hear them. Pour them back into his hands and make him repeat the process.

While he is doing so, shift the salver quietly round until the slit is turned from you and towards his hands, and take care to hold the salver so low that the projecting rim throws the slit into shadow, and conceals it from his view. Then tell him to cover them up at once, when you put them

into his hand, in order to prevent you from playing any tricks, and pass them smartly into the palms of his hands, making him close them at once. Of course, the six coins that you have placed in the slit will tumble out and mingle with the others in the platter, and in the hurry will not be noticed, so that he will have twenty-four in his hands.

Put the salver down, and take up six of the remaining coins, one by one, ringing them on the salver as you do so. Pick them up, pretend to close the right hand upon them, but pass them really into the left and convey them away. Hold your right hand over the closed hands of the person who has the coins, strike smartly with your left hand in your right, say "Pass!" and open your hand, when it will be seen empty. Offer the salver again for the coins, and when they are counted, twenty-four will be found in his hands. In order to insure the proper position of the salver, it will be as well to have some mark on the upper edge, just over the slit.

THE LOST RING FOUND.

This is a simple and a pretty trick, requiring little apparatus,—a piece of elastic thread and a few rings being all that you need. Go to a jeweller's, or even to a toymaker's, and buy a set of showy rings, all alike. You may get them for a few cents each. Take a piece of elastic thread about three or four inches in length, fasten one end to one of the rings, and the other to the inside of your coat-sleeve, taking care to have it of such a length that it permits the ring to be placed on the finger, and that when the ring is removed it is pulled up the sleeve so as to be concealed from every one.

Before you begin the trick, furnish yourself with a few lemons, and in each of them cut crosswise a little slit in the middle, and push one of the rings into the slit until it lies in the very centre of the lemon. Take care to wear one of the rings during the whole evening, and make it as conspicuous as possible ; and just before commencing this trick quietly remove the ·ring, and slip on your finger the one that is attached to the elastic thread. Ask if there are any lemons in the house, and have your own brought in a basket. Also ask for a piece of tape and a bodkin.

Get the audience to choose a lemon, take it in your hands, and send the rest away. Then take a knife and cut the lemon into slices, nearly, but not quite severing them, and hold it so that if any thing were between the slices it would fall out. Of course you take care that the ring which you have inserted remains in the middle slice. Now slip the end of the tape through the eye of the bodkin, and push it lengthwise through the lemon, so that it passes through the ring. Give both ends of the tape to be held, and tell the holders to stand so as to keep the tape at full stretch.

Now slip the ring off your finger and hold it between the forefinger and thumb, taking care to hold it so that the spectators cannot see the thread. Point your hand towards the lemon, suddenly spread the fingers, and away flies the ring up your sleeve. Look into your hand as if surprised at the disappearance of the ring, show that it is empty, and then go to the lemon. Separate the divisions one by one, and push them apart. Take each outer slice alternately and pull it off the tape, keeping the central slice to the last. When you come to this, the ring will pull against the tape ; you wonder what is the matter with it; you take your knife and cut the slice gradually down, taking care to destroy the slit through which the ring was introduced, and continue to cut until the metal becomes visible. Then let any one disengage the lemon from the imbedded ring, and the audience will think that you have flung it into the lemon and upon the tape.

In this short account of conjuring, we have purposely avoided such tricks as require expensive apparatus. Such apparatus is either entirely beyond a boy's reach, or at all events he ought not to be encouraged in the notion of spending much money on objects of no real use. A boy of any ingenuity will make the greater part of the apparatus himself. We have mentioned no machinery that need cost more than a dollar at the outside, and not that, if a boy is acquainted with the use of tools.

TRICKS WITH CARDS.

ALTHOUGH proficiency in games with cards is, in our opinion, a most pernicious accomplishment for youth, and one which cannot be too severely reprobated, we do not consider SLEIGHT-OF-HAND TRICKS with a pack of cards at all objectionable, but rather a source of much harmless amusement; and, under this impression, we do not hesitate to insert the following series of excellent deceptions and sleight-of-hand tricks.

TO MAKE THE PASS.

This is a necessary beginning for card tricks. "Making the pass" is the technical term for shifting either the top or the bottom card to any place in the pack that you like. It is almost impossible to describe it, and we can only say that it will be learned better, in five minutes, from a friend, than in as many hours from a book. As, however, a friend is not always to be found who can perform the pass, we will endeavor to describe it.

The cards are held in both hands, right hand underneath and left above, as in the engraving, where, as the *bottom* card is to be raised to the top, the little finger is seen between that card and those above it. By a quick movement of the right hand, the bottom card is slipped away towards the left, and is placed upon the top card, under shadow of the left hand, which is raised for the moment to allow of its passage.

This movement must be assiduously practised before it is exhibited in public, as nothing looks more awkward than to see it clumsily performed, in which case two or three cards generally tumble on the floor.

THE NERVE TRICK.

Let one of the company select a card, and when the person who has taken it puts it in the pack, make the pass, and place it at the bottom; cut them in half; give the party that half which contains his card at the bottom, and desire him to hold it between his finger and thumb, just at the corner; bid him pinch them as tight as he can; then strike them sharply, and they will all fall to the ground, except the bottom one, which is the card he has chosen. This is a very curious trick, and, if well done, is really astonishing. It is a great improvement of this trick to put the chosen card at the top of the pack, and turn the cards face upward, so that when you strike, the choosing party's card will remain in his hand, actually staring him in the face.

THE KNAVES AND THE CONSTABLE.

Select the four knaves from a pack of cards, and either of the kings to act as constable. Conceal one of the knaves at the bottom of the pack, and lay the other three with the constable down upon the table. Then say, "Three knaves went to rob a house; one got in at the parlor window" (putting one knave at the bottom of the pack, taking care not to lift the pack so high that the knave already at the bottom can be seen), "one got into the first floor window" (putting another knave into the middle of the pack), "and one got in at the garret window" (putting the third knave in at the top of the pack.) "The constable, being determined to capture them, closely follows the last knave" (putting the king also upon the top of the pack). You then direct as many of the company to cut the cards as please, and you state that you have no doubt the constable has succeeded in catching them, which will be evident upon your spreading out the pack in your hands, as the king and three knaves will be found together. A very little dexterity only is necessary to enable you to convey a knave secretly to the bottom of the pack.

THE TURN-OVER FEAT.

When you have found a card chosen, which you have previously forced, or any card that has been drawn, and which you have discovered by the means before described, in order to finish your trick cleverly, convey the card privately to the top of the pack; get all the other cards even with each other, but let the edge of your top card project a little over the rest; hold them between your finger and thumb, about two feet from the table; let them drop, and the top card (which must be, as we have said, the one drawn) will fall with its face uppermost, and all the rest with their faces towards the table.

TO TELL A CARD THOUGHT OF BLINDFOLD.

Take twenty-one cards, and lay them down in three rows, with their faces upward; i. e., when you have laid out three, begin again at the left hand, and lay one card upon the first, and so on to the right hand; then begin on the left hand again, and so go on until you have laid out the twenty-one cards in three heaps, at the same time requesting any one to think of a card. When you have laid them out, ask him which heap his card is in; then lay that heap in the middle between the other two. This done, lay them out again in three heaps as before, and again request him to notice where his noted card goes, and put that heap in the middle, as before. Then, taking up the cards with their backs toward you, take off the uppermost card, and reckon it one; take off another, which reckon two; and thus proceed till you come to the eleventh, which will invariably prove to be the card thought of. You must never lay out your cards less than three times, but as often above that number as you please. This trick may be done without your seeing the cards at all, if you handle and count them carefully. To diversify the trick, you may use a different number of cards, but the number chosen must be divisible by three, and the middle card, after they have been thrice dealt as directed, will always be the one thought of; for instance, if done with fifteen cards, it must be the eighth, and so on; when the number is even, it must be the exact half; as, if it be twenty-four, the card thought of will be the twelfth, &c.

THE SHUFFLED SEVEN.

Desire a person to remember a card and its place in the pack; then, in a dexterous manner, convey a certain number of the cards from the top to the bottom, and subtract them, in your mind, from the number of the pack; for example, the pack consists of fifty-two cards, and you have conveyed seven to the bottom; tell the person the card he has thought of will be the forty-fifth, reckoning from the number of the card, the place of which he has to name; thus, if he says it is the ninth, you go on counting nine, ten, eleven, &c., and the card he thought of will be exactly the forty-fifth, as you announced.

TO NAME THE POSITION OF A CARD.

You will take a pack, which you will present to some one in the company, desiring him to shuffle the cards well, and to give them to any one else whom he pleases, to shuffle also.   You will then cause it to be cut by several persons: then propose to some one to take the pack, think of a card, and to remember it, and also the position where it is placed, counting one, two, three, four, and so on, from the bottom of the pack as far as, and including, the card thought of. You may offer to go into another room while this is done, or have your eyes bandaged, assuring the company that you will, if they desire it, announce beforehand the number at which the card thought of will be found.

Now, supposing that the person selecting the card stops at 13, and that this thirteenth card from the bottom is the Queen of Hearts, and supposing also, that the number you have put down beforehand be 24; you will return to the room, or remove your handkerchief, as the case may be, and, without putting any question to the person who has thought of the card, you will ask for the pack, on which you will rest your nose, as if you meant to smell out the secret. Then putting your hands behind your back, or under the table, so that they cannot be seen, you will take away from the bottom of the pack *twenty-three* cards—that is, one less than the number you marked down beforehand. You will place them on top of the remainder, taking care not to put one more or less, which would cause a failure. This done, return the pack to the person who thought of a card, requesting him to count the cards from the top, beginning with the number of the card he thought of. Thus, if that card were the thirteenth, he will commence counting fourteen, and so on. When he has called twenty-three, stop him, telling him that the number you marked down was twenty-four; and that the twenty-fourth card, which he is about to take up, is the Queen of Hearts; which he will find to be correct.

Observe and be sure and have the number you name greater than that of the first position of the card in the pack: for instance, twenty-four is greater than thirteen.

THE THREE PACKETS.

Tell a person to choose as he pleases three cards from a euchre pack, informing him that the ace counts for eleven, the picture cards for ten, and the others according to the number of spots. When he has chosen these three, tell him to put them on the table, and to place on each as many cards as

spots are required to make fifteen. That is to say, in the example, eight cards would have to be put on the seven of clubs, four cards on the ace, and five above the ten. Let him return you the rest of the pack, and (while pretending to count something in them) count how many remain. Add sixteen to this number, and you will have the number of spots in the three bottom cards, as may be seen in this example where twelve cards remain, to which number add sixteen, and the amount (twenty-eight) is the number on the three cards.

LIKE WITH LIKE, OR HOW TO KEEP A HOTEL.

Pick out all the aces and picture cards, and then place any ordinary card upon the table. "This card," you say, "we will call a tavern." You commence your story as follows:

"On a dark night there come four farmers to this tavern, and ask for a night's lodging. As none of the landlord's rooms are occupied, and as he has four of them, he shows each of the farmers to one of the rooms, and goes quietly to bed." (Here you place the four knaves around the card which represents the tavern, and proceed.)

"Not long afterwards, four police officers knock at the door, and request also a night's lodging. As the landlord has now no chamber that is unoccupied, he puts an officer in with each of the farmers." (Here you place the four aces upon the four knaves.)

"Presently four fine gentlemen come along, and these want a night's lodging. Our host is now in great embarrassment, but there is nothing left for him to do, but to put a gentleman in each of the four occupied chambers." (Here you lay a king upon each ace.)

"Thus far matters went tolerably well, although not meeting with general approbation; but now come four fine ladies, who also must have a night's lodging. The landlord is now beside himself with perplexity; indeed he fairly loses his senses, for the stupid fellow actually quarters a lady in each of the already occupied chambers." (Here you place the queens upon the four other cards.)

"The ladies are highly indignant. 'Could he not put like and like together?' they ask. That is what he ought to do, but police officers and farmers, gentlemen and ladies—the fellow is out of his wits!

"'Well,' cried the landlord, at last, 'if you are agreed, I will lodge you like with like.' All readily consent, and soon all the farmers are lodged in one chamber, all the officers in another, all the gentlemen in a third, and all the ladies in a fourth."

While you are saying this, you lay the four heaps one upon another and let the company cut them as often as they choose. But notwithstanding all their cutting, if you now tell them off in order from the bottom of the pack, and place them about the tavern, all the knaves will lie in one heap, all the aces in another, and so on.

THE FOUR KNAVES.

Take the four knaves, and upon the lower half of the first knave place the upper half of the second, rectangularly; upon the lower half of the second knave, place the upper half of the third, also rectangularly; then the upper half of the fourth knave upon the under half of the third; and lastly, thrust the under half of the fourth knave under the upper half of the first, and the trick is finished.

THE MYSTIC COURTS OF ZOROASTER.

Sort the twelve court cards from the pack, excluding the aces, and place them in three rows, that is to say, with four in each row. Beginning with the fourth card in the bottom row on the right, take them up longways, that is, from the bottom to the top, one over the other, the jack of diamonds over the king of hearts, and so on, and offer them to persons to

cut. It is a matter of indifference how often they are thus divided; but you
must be particular and have them cut without shuffling. Now deal

them out in four divisions, and, strange as
it may seem, the king, queen, and knave
of each suit will be found together. The
key to this inscrutable mystery consists in
simply observing the following arrangement in disposing the cards at first: place
one of each suit in the upper row, begin
the next row with the same suit that you
closed with in the first, and commence the
third or last row with a court card of the
same suit that terminated the second. By
thus arranging the cards you will not have
two of any one suit in any of the rows, either vertically or horizontally.
The table shows exactly how the cards should be placed in order to perform
the trick successfully.

On now following the above directions in taking up the cards the result
will be as described. Although this illusion is one easily performed, we
never yet saw it practised without it exciting the wonder and amazement
of the spectators; and the principle on which this is achieved, owing to the
apparent consequence of the suits, has successfully baffled the calculations
even of the first investigators of the art.

THE CHOSEN ONE OF FORTY-EIGHT DISCOVERED.

Take forty-eight cards, and beginning at the *left top* corner, deal them out
in six rows of eight each; then, as they lie upon the table, there will be
eight lines of six each the one way, and six of eight each the other way.
The first we will call *lines*, and the other *rows;* and this distinction being
clearly understood, we may now begin "to show the trick." Ask one of
the company to choose a card. This done, ask which line it is in. When
answered, be particular to remember the top card of the line, for this one
card is the key to the whole trick—so "don't forget it." The cards are now
to be taken up exactly in the reverse order to that in which they were laid
down. That is, you begin at the *right* bottom corner, picking the cards up
to the right top corner. This done, the pack must be again distributed in
the same order as before, and the question, "Which line is the chosen card
in?" repeated. Receiving the reply, you can instantly fix on the chosen
card. The explanation is this: Remember the top card of the *line* the card
is stated to be in. Then, when the pack is again laid out, it will be observed that all the cards that previously were in a *line, one under the other,*
are now all in a *row, side by side* of each other. Now, seeing the position of
the key card, that is, the one you had specially to remember, you will know
that all the cards belonging to the *line* of which it was the topmost, now

follow it in a *row;* consequently, the six cards that were in one line, are now distributed or divided into six lines, one of its cards falling into each of the following lines. When the reply is given to the second interrogation, the card thought of can be instantly picked out, because the line now given only contains one that was in the original line; consequently, the card that is now in it, and which also formed part of the original line, must be the one chosen. After a little practice, half-a-dozen people may each choose a card at the same time, and you will be perfectly able to reveal all.

Observe—that (after the cards have been arranged the second time) when the *line* containing the chosen card is on the *right* of the key card, the chosen card will be in the *row above* the key card. But when the chosen card is to the *left* of the key card it will be found in the same row.

TO MAKE ANOTHER PERSON DRAW THE CARDS YOU CALL FOR.

Take the cards, shuffle them, and spread them out, face downwards, upon the table, without entirely separating them. Before doing this, however, you must carefully note the bottom card.

You now say to the person to whom you wish to display your skill, "I will now ask you to give me certain cards, which I will name to you beforehand. The cards which I ask for, you must give me from this heap, the faces of which neither you nor I have seen, and yet in the end I shall have all the cards that I direct you to give me."

The person you address will, of course, be very much astonished at this, and will refuse to believe you. You assume a confident air, however, saying, "Look sharp!"

You then call for the card which you know is the undermost one, say the seven of hearts. Suppose now the person gives you the queen of spades, you boldly call out for your next card, "Queen of spades!" the other not knowing that you have it already in your hand. He gives you, perhaps, the king of hearts, and you at once ask for this as your next card. He now gives you the ace of clubs. In this way you can ask for any number of cards, but these are enough for explanation. Now you say, "The last card that I want is the ace of clubs, but this I will find out for myself, by means of my very nice sense of smell."

Hereupon, with a grave face, you commence shuffling around among the cards, until you reach the bottom one, which is the seven of hearts. This you take from the table, place it first in order among the cards in your hand, and you are now able to display all the cards that you have directed him to give you.

TO CALL FOR ANY CARD IN THE PACK.

This trick, which requires very little practice, or indeed understanding, to perform, is done in the following manner : Having privately seen a card, put it at the bottom of the pack, then shuffle the cards till it comes to the bottom again, then put the cards behind you and say, "Here I call for," naming the botto.n card, which you have seen; and as you hold them behind you, turn the top card with its face upward; then hold forth the cards, and as you hold them you may see what the next card is. Then put the cards behind you again, and take the top card and put it at the bottom, with its face downward; and turn the next card, with its face upward, and whilst you are doing this, say, "Here I call for," naming the card you saw last. Then hold forth the cards again, showing the bottom card, which will be that you call for; then put the cards behind you again, and proceed in the same manner as you did before. You may, by this method, go through them all, and call for all the cards in the pack, to the admiration of the beholders, who will be surprised how you could find them out when you hold them behind you.

TO DISCERN ONE OR MORE DRAWN CARDS.

Turn unperceived the bottom card of a pack face upwards; then let several of the company draw a card. Reverse the pack rapidly, so that the bottom is now the top card, and thus all the other cards are turned face upward, unseen by the spectators.

Hold the pack firmly in your fingers, and request those who have drawn to replace their cards in the pack. Thus all the drawn cards will lie with their faces downward, while the other cards will lie with their faces upward. You now step aside, select the drawn cards, and show them to the company.

TO TELL THROUGH A WINE-GLASS WHAT CARDS HAVE BEEN TURNED.

The picture cards have commonly a narrow stripe for the border. This border is usually narrower at one end of the card than it is at the other. You place the picture cards in such a manner that either all the broader or all the narrower borders are placed uppermost. You now request a spectator to turn one of the cards while you are absent from the room. On your return you examine all the cards through a wine-glass, and easily discover the one which has been turned, as its narrow border now lies on a level with the broader borders of the other cards. If they try to mystify you by turning none of the cards, you will easily see that this is the case.

THE WINDOW TRICK.

Place yourself in the recess of a window, and let any one stand close to you, as near to the window as possible. You now draw a card, hand it to him, and request him to note it. This you must contrive to do in such a manner, that you can catch a glimpse of the image of the card reflected in the window. You now know what the card is as well as he does, and can point it out to him after the cards have been thoroughly shuffled.

SCIENTIFIC RECREATIONS.

CHEMISTRY, optics, pneumatics, mechanics, and mathematics, all contribute their share towards furnishing recreation and sport for the social gathering or the family fireside. The magical combinations and effects of chemistry have furnished an almost infinite variety of pleasant experiments, which may be performed by our youthful friends with great success if a little care be taken; and the other branches of natural science are nearly as replete with interest.

The following *repertoire* of such tricks and illusions will be found exceedingly complete, although pains have been taken to select only the best and most startling of them. A large number are entirely new, but are described with sufficient clearness to enable any person of ordinary intelligence to become expert in them, with a little practice.

CHEMICAL AMUSEMENTS.

Chemistry is one of the most attractive sciences. From the beginning to the end, the student is surprised and delighted with the developments of the exact discrimination, as well as the power and capacity, which are displayed in various forms of chemical action. Dissolve two substances in the same fluid, and then, by evaporation or otherwise, cause them to re-assume a solid form, and each particle will unite with its own kind, to the entire exclusion of all others. Thus, if sulphate of copper and carbonate of soda are dissolved in boiling water, and then the water is evaporated, each salt will be re-formed as before. This phenomenon is the result of one of the first principles of the science, and as such is passed over without thought; but it is a wonderful phenomenon, and made of no account only by the fact that it is so common and so familiar.

It is by the action of this same principle, "chemical affinity," that we produce the curious experiments with

SYMPATHETIC INKS.

By means of these, we may carry on a correspondence which is beyond the discovery of all not in the secret. With one class of these inks, the writing becomes visible only when moistened with a particular solution. Thus, if we write to you with a solution of the sulphate of iron, the letters are invisible. On the receipt of our letter, you rub over the sheet a feather or sponge, wet with a solution of nut-galls, and the letters burst forth into sensible being at once, and are permanent.

2. If we write with a solution of sugar of lead, and you moisten with a sponge or pencil, dipped in water, impregnated with sulphuretted hydrogen, the letters will appear with metallic brilliancy.

3. If we write with a weak solution of sulphate of copper, and you apply ammonia, the letters assume a beautiful blue. When the ammonia evaporates, as it does on exposure to the sun or fire, the writing disappears, but may be revived again as before.

4. If you write with oil of vitriol very much diluted, so as to prevent its destroying the paper, the manuscript will be invisible except when held to the fire, when the letters will appear black.

5. Write with cobalt dissolved in diluted muriatic acid; the letters will be invisible when cold; but, when warmed, they will appear a bluish green.

We are almost sure that our secrets thus written will not be brought to the knowledge of a stranger, because he does not know the solution which was used in writing, and, therefore, knows not what to apply to bring out the letters.

TO LIGHT A CANDLE WITHOUT TOUCHING THE WICK.

Let a candle burn until it has a good long snuff; then blow it out with a sudden puff, a bright wreath of white smoke will curl up from the hot wick. Now, if a flame be applied to this smoke, even at a distance of two or three inches from the candle, the flame will run down the smoke, and rekindle the wick in a very fantastic manner. To perform this experiment nicely, there must be no draught or "banging" doors while the mystic spell is rising.

MAGIC MILK.

Lime-water is quite transparent, and clear as common spring water; but if we breathe or blow into it, the bright liquid becomes opalescent and as white as milk. The best way to try this simple experiment, is to put some powdered quicklime into a wine bottle full of cold water; shake them well together, now and then, for a day; then allow the bottle to remain quiet till the next day, when the clear lime-water may be poured off from the sediment. Now fill a wine-glass or tumbler with the lime-water thus made, and blow through the liquid with a glass tube, a piece of new tobacco-pipe, or a clean straw, and in the course of a minute or so—as the magicians say—"the water will be turned into milk." By means of this *pastime*, "Wise Men" can ascertain which young ladies are in love, and which young gentlemen are not. With a shrewd guess they present, as a test, a glass of lime-water to the one, and of pure water to the other, with unerring effect.

THE MIMIC VESUVIUS.

This experiment is a demonstration of the heat and light which are evolved during chemical combination. The substance phosphorus has a great affinity for oxygen gas, and wherever it can get it from it will, especially when aided by the application of heat. To perform this experiment, put half a drachm of solid phosphorus into a Florence oil-flask, holding the flask slantingly, that the phosphorus may not take fire and break the glass; pour upon it a gill and a half of water, and place the whole over a tea-kettle lamp, or any common lamp filled with spirits of wine; light the wick, which should be about half an inch from the flask; and as soon as the water is boiling hot, streams of fire, resembling sky-rockets, will burst at intervals from  the water; some particles will also adhere to the sides of the glass, immediately display brilliant rays, and thus continue until the water begins to simmer, when a beautiful imitation of the aurora borealis will commence, and gradually ascend until this collects into a pointed cone at the mouth of the flask; when this has continued for half a minute, blow out the flame of the lamp, and the apex of fire that was formed at the mouth of the flask will rush down, forming beautiful illumined clouds of fire, rolling over each other for some time; and when these disappear, a splendid hemisphere of stars will present itself. After waiting a minute or two, light the lamp again, and nearly the same phenomena will be displayed as at the beginning. Let a repetition of lighting and blowing out the lamp be made for three or four times, so that the number of stars may be increased; and after the third or fourth act of blowing out the lamp, the internal surface of the flask will be dry. Many of the stars will shoot with great splendor from side to side, whilst others will appear and burst at the mouth of the flask. What liquid remains in the flask will serve for the same experiment three or four times, without adding any water. Care should be taken, after the operation is over, to put the flask in a cool and secure place.

THE REAL WILL-O'-THE-WISP.

Into a small retort place about an ounce of strong liquor of potash; that is, pure potash dissolved in water, together with about a drachm of phosphorus. Let the neck or beak of the retort dip into a saucer of water, say half an inch deep; now very gently heat the liquid in the retort with a spirit-lamp until it boils. In a few minutes the retort will be filled with a white cloud; then the gas generated will begin to bubble at the end of the saucer; a minute more, each bubble, as it issues from the boiling fluid, will *spontaneously take fire* as it comes into the air, forming at the same time the

philosopher's ring of phosphoric acid. Care is required in handling phosphorus; but our young chemical readers will, we think, not forego this wonderful experiment for the want of due attention; for, without proper care on their part, we must give up showing them wonders even greater than these.

THE PAPER ORACLE.

Some amusement may be obtained among young people by writing, with common ink, a variety of questions, on different bits of paper, and adding a pertinent reply to each, written with nitro-muriate of gold. The collection should be suffered to dry, and put aside, until an opportunity offers for using them. When produced, the answers will be invisible; desire different persons to select such questions as they may fancy, and take them home with them; then promise, that if they are placed near the fire during the night, answers will appear written beneath the questions in the morning; and such will be the fact, if the paper be put in any dry, warm situation.

THE MIMIC GAS-HOUSE.

The next illustration shows a simple way of making illuminating gas, by means of a tobacco-pipe. Bituminous coal contains a number of chemical compounds, nearly all of which can, by distillation, be converted into an

illuminating gas; and with this gas nearly all our cities are now lighted in the dark hours of night. To make it as represented in our engraving, obtain some coal-dust (or walnut or butternut meats will answer), and fill the bowl of a pipe with it; then cement the top over with some clay; place the bowl in the fire, and soon smoke will be seen issuing from the end of the stem; when that has ceased coming, apply a light, and it will burn brilliantly for several minutes; after it has ceased, take the pipe from the fire and let it cool, then remove the clay, and a piece of coke will be found inside; this is the excess of carbon over the hydrogen contained in the coal, for all the hydrogen will combine with carbon at a high temperature, and make what are called hydro-carbons— a series of substances containing both these elemental forms of matter.

THE SILVER TREE.

Put into a decanter four drachms of nitrate of silver, and fill up the decanter with distilled or rain water; then drop in about an ounce of mercury, and place the vessel where it may not be disturbed; in a short time the silver will be precipitated in the most beautiful arborescent form, resembling real vegetation.

The above experiment shows the precipitation of one metal by another, owing to the affinity that exists between them. The metal in solution, having a greater affinity for the pure metal suspended in it, precipitates itself from the solution, and becomes firmly attached thereto. The silver tree, produced as above described, is frequently called Arbor Dianæ, or the Tree of Diana.

22*

ALUM BASKETS.

Make a small basket, about the size of the hand, of iron wire, or split willow; then take some lamp-cotton, untwist it, and wind it round every portion of the basket. Then mix alum, in the proportion of one pound with a quart of water, and boil it until the alum is dissolved. Pour the solution into a deep pan, and in the liquor suspend the basket, so that no part of it touch the vessel, or be exposed to the air. Let the whole remain perfectly at rest for twenty-four hours; when, if you take out the basket, the alum will be found prettily crystallized over all the limbs of the cottoned frame.

In like manner, a cinder, a piece of coke, the sprig of a plant, or any other object, suspended in the solution by a thread, will become covered with beautiful crystals.

If powdered turmeric be added to the hot solution, the crystals will be of a bright yellow; if litmus be used instead, they will be of a bright red; logwood will yield them of a purple, and common writing-ink, of a black tint; or, if sulphate of copper be used instead of alum, the crystals will be of fine blue.

But the colored alum-crystals are much more brittle than those of pure alum, and the colors fly; the best way of preserving them is to place them under a glass shade, with a saucer containing water; this keeps the atmosphere constantly saturated with moisture, the crystals never become too dry, and their texture and color undergo but little change.

THE MAGIC BOTTLE.

This trick, if well managed, is one of the most wonderful that can be performed in a drawing-room without apparatus; but it requires dexterity at the conclusion.

The person performing the trick offers to pour from a common wine-bottle, port-wine, sherry, milk, and champagne, in succession, and in any order.

To accomplish the trick, you must make solution, of the following chemicals, and label the bottles with numbers, thus:

No. 1. A mixture of two parts perchloride of iron, and one part sulphuric acid (vitriol).

No. 2. A strong solution of the sulphocyanate of potash.

No. 3. A strong solution of acetate of lead.

No. 4. A solution of bicarbonate of soda, or potash.

No. 5. A clear solution of gum arabic.

Procure a champagne-bottle, and wash it out well; then pour three teaspoonfuls of No. 1 into it. As the quantity is very small, it will not be observed, especially if you are quick in your movements. Pour some distilled or rain water into a common water-bottle, or jug, and add a tablespoonful of No. 5 to it; then set it aside, ready for use.

Provide some wine-glasses, of four different patterns, and into one pattern put one drop of solution No. 2; into another, three drops of solution No. 2; rinse the third with solution No. 3, and the fourth with solution No. 4. Arrange the glasses on a small tray, remembering the solutions that were poured into each pattern.

Every thing being ready, take the champagne-bottle that you have prepared, from two or three others, and, holding it up, to show the company that it is clear and empty, you must desire some person to hand you the water-bottle, or jug, and then fill up the bottle with the water.

Pour some of the contents of the bottle into an unprepared glass, in order to show that it is water; then say, "Change to champagne," and pour the liquid from the bottle into one of the glasses rinsed with No. 4; then pour into the glass containing *three drops* of No. 2, and it will change to port wine; but if poured into the glass rinsed with No. 3, it will change to milk; and if into the glass with one drop of No. 2, it will produce sherry.

Be careful, in pouring the fluid from the bottle, not to hold it high above the glasses, but to keep the mouth of it close to the edges, otherwise persons will observe that it undergoes change of color after it is poured into them; and, on this account, the glasses should be held rather high.

As all the solutions used in the above trick are deleterious, they must not be left about in the way of children, and, of course, the fluid in the wine-glasses must not even be tasted; but, if any of the company wish to drink the wines you have made, then the tray must be adroitly exchanged for another, with the proper wines placed on it.

THE FADED ROSE RESTORED.

Take a rose that is quite faded, and throw some sulphur on a chafing-dish of hot coals; then hold the rose over the fumes of the sulphur, and it will become quite white; in this state dip it into water, put it into a box, or drawer, for three or four hours, and when taken out it will be quite red again.

THE PROTEAN LIQUID.

A red liquor, which, when poured into different glasses, will become yellow, blue, black, and violet, may be thus made: Infuse a few shavings of logwood in common water, and when the liquor is red, pour it into a bottle; then take three drinking-glasses, rinse one of them with strong vinegar, throw into the second a small quantity of pounded alum, which will not be observed if the glass has been newly washed, and leave the third without any preparation. If the red liquor in the bottle be poured into the first glass, it will assume a straw-color; if into the second, it will pass gradually from bluish-gray to black, provided it be stirred with a bit of iron, which has been privately immersed in good vinegar; in the third glass the red liquor will assume a violet tint.

THE CHANGEABLE RIBBON.[*]

Dip a rose-colored ribbon into nitric acid, diluted with eight or ten parts of water, and as soon as the color disappears, which it will do in a short time, take out the ribbon, and put it into a very weak alkaline solution; when the alkali will quickly neutralize the acid, and the color will reappear.

THE CHEMICAL CHAMELEON.

Put a drachm of powdered nitrate of cobalt into a phial, containing an ounce of the solution of caustic potass, when the decomposition of the salt, and precipitation of a blue oxide of cobalt will take place. Cork the phial and the liquid will assume a blue color, from which it will pass to a lilac, afterward to a peach tint, and, finally, to a light red.

MUSICAL FLAME.

Fit a good cork into a wine-bottle; burn a hole through the cork with a round iron skewer, and into it fix a piece of tobacco-pipe about eight inches long. Put into the botle about two or three ounces of zinc, in slips, such as the waste cuttings from a zinc-worker; now pour water on to the zinc until the bottle is rather more than half full; then add about three parts of

a wineglassful of sulphuric acid (oil of vitriol); this causes a rapid effervescence at first, but which subsides to a moderate and continuous boiling for a lengthened period; as soon as the boiling is regular, the cork with the pipe through it may be inserted into the bottle. If a light be placed to the end of the pipe, a flame will be produced, which will continue to burn so long as there is any visible action in the bottle. This flame is the ignited hydrogen gas (water-gas) resulting from the decomposition of water by the acid and zinc, and as such is an exceedingly interesting experiment. Now, to be musical, procure a glass or metal pipe, about sixteen or eighteen inches long, and from half to three-quarters of an inch in diameter; place the tube over the flame, and allow the pipe to be about three to five inches up the tube, which will act as a kind of high chimney: it must be held perfectly steady and upright, at a particular distance up the tube, which varies according to the size of the flame. A beautiful sound is thus produced, similar to an organ-pipe. This sound, or "musical flame," varies in note according to the diameter of the tube, being deeper or more bass as the tube is increased in size. By using various-sized tubes, different sounds are thus readily produced. The true explanation of this singular experiment remains yet to be solved.

OPTICAL AMUSEMENTS.

THE science of optics affords an infinite variety of amusements, which cannot fail to instruct the mind, as well as delight the eye. By the aid of optical instruments, we are enabled to lessen the distance to our visual organs between the globe we inhabit and "the wonders of the heavens above us;" to watch "the stars in their courses," and survey at leisure the magnificence of "comets importing change of times and states;" to observe the exquisite finish and propriety of construction which are to be found in the most minute productions of the earth;—to trace the path of the planet, in its course round the magnificent orb of day, and to detect the pulsation of the blood, as it flows through the veins of an insect. These are but a few of the powers which this science offers to man; to enumerate them all would require a space equal to the body of our work: neither do we propose to notice, in the following pages, the various instruments and experiments which are devoted to purposes merely scientific; it being our desire only to call the attention of our juvenile readers to such things as combine a vast deal of amusement with much instruction; to inform them as to the construction of the various popular instruments; to show the manner of using them, and to explain some of the most attractive experiments which the science affords. By doing thus much, we hope to offer a sufficient inducement to extend inquiry much further than the information which a work of this nature will enable us to afford.

THE CAMERA OBSCURA.

This is a very pleasing and instructive optical apparatus, and may be purchased for a small sum. But it may be easily made by the young optician. Procure an oblong box, about two feet long, twelve inches wide, and eight high. In one end of this a tube must be fitted containing a lens, and be made to slide backward and forward, so as to suit the focus. Within the box should be a plane mirror, reclining backwards from the tube at an angle of forty-five degrees. At the top of the box is a square of unpolished  glass, upon which from beneath the picture will be thrown, and may be seen by raising the lid A. To use the camera, place the tube with the lens on it opposite to the object, and having adjusted the focus, the image will be thrown upon the ground glass, as above stated, where it may be easily copied by a pencil or in colors.

The form of a camera obscura, used in a public exhibition, is as follows: D D is a large wooden box, stained black in the inside, and capable of con-

taining from one to eight persons. A B is a sliding piece, having a sloping mirror, C, and a double convex lens, which may, with the mirror C, be slid up or down, so as to accommodate the lens to near or distant objects. When the rays proceeding from an object without fall upon the mirror, they are reflected upon the lens F, and brought to fall on the bottom of the box, or upon a table placed horizontally to receive them, which may be seen by the spectator whose eye is at D.

THE MAGIC LANTERN.

The object of this ingenious instrument is to represent, in a dark room, on a white wall or cloth, a succession of enlarged figures of remarkable, natural, or grotesque objects. The figure given below is a representation of one. It consists of a tin box, with a funnel on the top, represented by B, and a door on one side of it. This funnel, by being bent, as shown in the figure, serves the double purpose of letting out the smoke and keeping in the light. In the middle of the bottom of the box is placed a movable tin lamp, A, which must have two or three good lights, at the height of the centre of the polished tin reflector, G. In the front of the box, opposite the

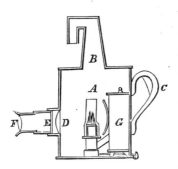

reflector, is fixed a tin tube, in which there slides another tube. The sliding tube has, at its outer extremity, a convex lens F, of about two inches diameter: the stationary tube also has a convex lens, D, fixed in it, of three inches in diameter. The focus of the smaller of these lenses may be about five inches. Between the stationary tube and the lamp, there must be a slit or opening (as at E), to admit of the passage of glass sliders, mounted in paper or wooden frames, such as are represented on the next page; upon which sliders it is that the miniature figures are painted, which are intended to be shown upon the wall. The distinctness of the enlarged figures depends not only upon the goodness of the magnifying glass, but upon the clearness of the light yielded by the lamp A. It may be purchased ready made of any optician.

To paint the glasses.—The slides containing the objects usually shown in a magic lantern, are to be bought of opticians with the lantern, and can be procured cheaper and better in this way, than by any attempt at manufacturing them. Should, however, the young optician wish to make a few slides, of objects of particular interest to himself, he may proceed as follows : Draw on a paper the subject you desire to paint. Lay it on a table or any flat surface, and place the glass over it; then draw the outlines, with a very fine pencil, in varnish mixed with black paint, and, when dry, fill up the other parts in their proper colors. Transparent colors must be used for this purpose, such as carmine, lake, Prussian blue, verdigris, sulphate of iron, tincture of Brazil wood, gamboge, &c.; and these must be tempered with a strong white varnish, to prevent their peeling off. Then shade them with black, or with bistre, mixed with the same varnish.

To exhibit the Magic Lantern.—The room for the exhibition ought to be large, and of an oblong shape. At one end of it suspend a large sheet, so as to cover the whole of the wall. The company being all seated, darken the room, and placing the lantern with its tube in the direction of the sheet, introduce one of the slides into the slit, taking care to invert the figures; then adjust the focus of the glasses in the tube, by drawing it in or out, as required, and a perfect representation of the object will appear.

Effects of the Magic Lantern.—Most extraordinary effects may be produced by means of the magic lantern; one of the most effective of which is a tempest at sea.

This is effected by having two slides painted, one with the tempest as approaching on one side, and continuing in intensity till it reaches the

other. Another slide has ships painted on it, and while the lantern is in use, that containing the ships is dexterously drawn before the other, and represents *ships in the storm*.

The effects of sunrise, moonlight, starlight, &c., may be imitated also, by means of double sliders; and figures may be introduced sometimes of fearful proportions.

Heads may be made to nod, faces to laugh; eyes may be made to roll, teeth to gnash; crocodiles may be made to swallow tigers; combats may be represented; but one of the most instructive uses of the slides is to make them illustrative of astronomy, and to show the rotation of the seasons, the cause of eclipses, the mountains in the moon, spots on the sun, and the various motions of the planetary bodies and their satellites.

THE PHANTASMAGORIA.

Between the phantasmagoria and the magic lantern there is this difference: in common magic lanterns the figures are painted on transparent glass, consequently the image on the screen is a circle of light, having figures upon it; but in the phantasmagoria all the glass is made opaque, except the figures, which being painted in transparent colors, the light shines through them, and no light can come upon the screen except that which passes through the figure, as is here represented.

There is no sheet to receive the picture, but the representation is thrown on a thin screen of silk or muslin, placed between *the spectators and the lantern*. The images are made to appear approaching and receding, by removing the lantern farther from the screen, or bringing it nearer to it. This is a great advantage over the arrangements of the magic lantern, and by it the most astonishing effects are often produced.

DISSOLVING VIEWS.

The dissolving views, by which one landscape or scene appears to pass into the other while the scene is changing, are produced by using two magic lanterns, placed side by side, and that can be a little inclined towards each other when necessary, so as to mix the rays of light, proceeding from the lenses of each, together, which produces that confusion of images, in which one view melts, as it were, into the other, which gradually becomes clear and distinct.

HOW TO RAISE A GHOST.

The magic lantern or phantasmagoria may be used in a number of marvellous ways, but in none more striking than in raising an apparent spectre. Let an open box, A B, about three feet long, a foot and a half broad, and two feet high, be prepared. At one end of this place a small swing dressing-glass, and at the other let a magic lantern be fixed, with its lenses in a direction towards the glass. A glass should now be made to slide up and down in the groove C d, to which a cord and pulley should be attached, the end of the cord coming to the part of the box marked A. On this glass the most hideous spectre that can be imagined may be painted, but in a squat or contracted position, and when all is done, the lid of the box must be prepared, by raising a kind of gable at the end of the box B, and in its lower part at E, an oval hole should be cut sufficiently large to suffer the rays reflected from the glass to pass through them. On the top of the box F, place a chafing-dish, upon which put some burning charcoal. Now light the lamp *g* in the lantern, sprinkle some powdered camphor or white incense on the charcoal, adjust the slide on which the spectre is painted, and the image will be thrown upon the smoke. In performing this feat the room must be darkened, and the box should be placed on a high table, that the hole through which the light comes may not be noticed.

HOW TO SEE THROUGH A PHILADELPHIA BRICK.

Construct a hollow box or case, like the figure in the margin. One side is purposely removed in the engraving, to enable you to see the arrangement of the interior. A, B, C, and D are four small pieces of looking-glass, all placed at an angle of 45°, with respect to those sides of the box on which they are fixed; at E and G two flat pieces of glass are inserted, as in the eye-glass of a telescope. Supposing you look through the opening E, in the direction of an object placed at O, you would see it in the same manner as if there was an uninterrupted view between E and G, which is evidently

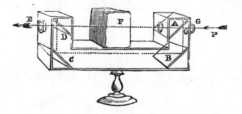

not the case. The cause of this is readily explained. The image of the object at O is received on the looking-glass A, by which it is reflected to B, as it is again from B to C, and afterwards to D; and this last image in D is seen by the eye of the spectator placed at E, in the same direction as if in reality he was looking at the real object itself, in the direction of the dotted line from O to E. From this it is evident that the placing an opaque body at F cannot prevent the object at O being seen. Of course all this arrangement of the instrument is concealed, and you place it in the hands of a companion, that he may look through E or G, it matters not which, at any object placed beyond. You may then safely lay a wager that your instrument is of so magical a nature that it will enable you to see through a brick wall; but as a single brick will be more convenient, and equally wonderful, you are willing to satisfy his doubts at once. Of course the hand or the hat, or any other opaque object, will answer the same purpose.

THE COSMORAMA.

The cosmorama is very simple in construction, and may be formed at very little trouble and expense, while it may be varied to infinity.

It consists merely of a picture seen through a magnifying-glass, exactly in the same manner as in the common shows exhibited in the streets; the difference not being in the construction of the apparatus, but in the quality of the pictures exhibited. For the common shows, coarsely-colored prints are sufficiently good; in the cosmorama, a moderately good oil painting is employed. The contrivance will be readily understood by the following illustration:—

In the hole of a door or partition insert a doubly-convex lens, A, having about three feet focus. At rather less than the focal distance of the lens from it, place, in a vertical position, the picture B, to be represented. The optical

part of the exhibition is now complete; but, as the frame of the picture would be seen, and thus the illusion be destroyed, it is necessary to place between the lens and the view a square wooden frame, formed of four short boards. The frame, which is to be painted black, prevents the rays of light passing beyond a certain line, according to its distance from the eye; the width of it being such, that upon looking through the lens, the picture is seen as if through an opening, which adds very much to the effect; and, if that end of the box, or frame, next the picture have an edge to it, representing the outlet of a cave, a Gothic ruin, or a rocky archway, which might be partially lighted by the top of the box being semi-transparent, the beauty and apparent reality of the picture would be very much enhanced.

Upon the top of the frame is represented a lamp to illuminate the picture; while all extraneous light is carefully excluded, by the lamp being contained in a box, open in the front and at the top.

TO IMITATE A MIRAGE.

Provide a glass tumbler two-thirds full of water, and pour spirit of wine upon it; or pour into a tumbler some sirup, and fill it up with water; when mixed, the object seen through it will be inverted.

THE THAUMATROPE.

Cut out a piece of cardboard of circular form, and affix to it six pieces of string, three on each side.

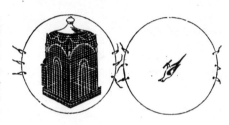

Paint on one side of the card a bird and on the other a cage, taking care to paint the bird upside down, or the desired effect will not be produced. When showing the toy, take hold of the centre strings between the forefinger and thumb, and twirl the card rapidly round, and the bird will appear snugly ensconced in its cage. The principle on which this effect is produced is, that the image of any object received on the retina or optic nerve is retained on the mind about eight seconds after the object causing the impression is withdrawn, being the memory of the object; consequently the impression of the painting on one side of the card is not obliterated ere the painting on the other side is brought before the eye. It is easy to understand from this fact how both are seen at once. Many objects will suit the thaumatrope, such as a juggler throwing up two balls on one side, and two balls on the other; and according to the pairs of strings employed, he will appear to throw up two, three, or four balls; the body and legs of a man on one side, and the arms and head on another; a horse and his rider; a mouse and trap. But we leave it to the ingenuity of our readers to devise for themselves.

TWO-FOLD REFLECTION.

Provide a circular piece of glass, and with a common awl, moistened with spirit of turpentine, pierce the centre of the glass; hold it encircled with the fingers and thumb in the sunshine, or the strong light of a lamp, when these striking effects will be produced. If the glass be *red*, the hole pierced in the middle will be reflected *green;* if the glass be *green*, the spot will be *red;* if *blue, orange;* and if *yellow, indigo.*

PNEUMATIC AMUSEMENTS.

THE branch of the physical sciences which relates to the air and its various phenomena is called Pneumatics. By it we learn many curious particulars. By it we find that the air has weight and pressure, color, density, elasticity, compressibility, and some other properties with which we shall endeavor to make the young reader acquainted by many pleasing experiments, earnestly impressing upon him to lose no opportunity of making physical science his study.

To show that the air has weight and pressure, the common leather sucker by which boys raise stones will show the pressure of the atmosphere. It consists of a piece of soft but firm leather, having a piece of string drawn through its centre. The leather is made quite wet and pliable, and then its under part is placed on the stone and stamped down by the foot. This pressing of the leather excludes the air from between the leather and the stone, and by pulling the string a vacuum is left underneath its centre; consequently the weight of the air about the edges of the leather, not being counterbalanced by any air between it and the stone, enables the boy to lift it.

THE MAGIC TUMBLER.

The air which for about forty miles surrounds our earth has a definite weight; and although we can neither see nor feel it, we are conscious of its presence by the momentary operation of breathing. The weight of a column

of air one inch square, and forty miles high, is about fifteen pounds. The reason why we are not crushed down by this enormous weight is, because we are surrounded on all sides by it, and as the pressure or weight is equal all around, it becomes, as far as we are personally concerned, insensible.

That the air *does* exert a definite pressure, in consequence of its weight, may be easily proved by any one with the above simple apparatus—only a tumbler and a sheet of paper. Fill a tumbler quite full of water, and carefully draw over its top a sheet of clean letter paper, and be careful to see that there are no bubbles of air in the water; place your hand over the paper while inverting it, and when the glass is mouth downward the water will be kept in, until the paper becomes wet through. The air pressing against the mouth of the tumbler is of greater weight than the contained water, and so, until some air can get in to supply the place of the water, it cannot fall out.

THE WEIGHT OF THE AIR PROVED BY A PAIR OF BELLOWS.

Shut the nozzle and valve-hole of a pair of bellows, and after having squeezed the air out of them, if they are perfectly air-tight, we shall find that a very great force, even some hundreds of pounds, is necessary for separating the boards. They are kept together by the weight of the heavy air which surrounds them, in the same manner as if they were surrounded by water.

THE REVOLVING SERPENT.

This illustration represents an amusing and instructive experiment, which proves the ascension of heated air by rendering its effects visible, and it may also be used to test the direction of the currents in our rooms and dwellings. To construct one, a piece of board is taken and cut in the form

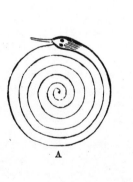

A

B

of a spiral as at A, and to give effect it may be painted to represent a serpent. Then prepare a stand as at B, having a needle in its upper end, and suspend the serpent from its centre on the needle, when it will assume the position shown at B. If this be now placed over a stove, or the tail of the serpent suspended by a bit of thread over a lamp, the heated air ascending through it will cause it to revolve in a very amusing manner. Two serpents may be made to turn in opposite directions, by pulling one out from the one side, and the other in the reverse direction, so that their heads may point toward each other when suspended.

TO PUT A LIGHTED CANDLE UNDER WATER.

Procure a good-sized cork, or bung; upon this place a small lighted taper; then set it afloat in a pail of water. Now, with a steady hand, invert a large drinking-glass over the light, and push it carefully down into the water. The glass being full of air, prevents the water entering it. You

may thus see the candle burn *under* water, and bring it up again to the surface, still alight. This experiment, simple as it is, serves to elucidate that useful contrivance called the diving-bell, being performed on the same principle.

The largest drinking-glass holds but half a pint, so that your diving-light soon goes out for the want of air. As an average, a burning candle consumes as much air as a man, and he requires nearly a gallon of air every minute, so that, according to the size of the glass over the flame, you can calculate how many seconds it will remain alight; of course, a large flame requires more air than a small one. For this, and several other experiments, a quart bell-glass is very useful, but, being expensive, it is not found in every parlor laboratory; one is, however, easily made from a green glass pickle-bottle; get a glazier to cut off the bottom, and you have a bell-glass that Chilton would not reject.

TO PLACE WATER IN A DRINKING-GLASS UPSIDE DOWN.

Procure a plate, a tumbler, and a small piece of tissue or silver paper. Set the plate on a table, and pour water in it up to the first rim. Now very slightly crumple up the paper, and place it in the glass; then set it on fire. When it is burnt out, or rather just as the last flame disappears, turn the glass quickly upside down into the water. Astonishing! the water rushes with great violence into the glass! Now you are satisfied that water can be placed in a drinking-glass upside down. Hold the glass firm, and the plate also. You can now reverse the position of the plate and glass, and thus convince the most sceptical of the truth of your pneumatic experiment. Instead of burning paper, a little brandy or spirits of wine can be ignited in the glass; the result of its combustion being invisible, the experiment is cleaner.

AMUSEMENTS IN MECHANICS.

THERE is no subject of such importance as mechanics, as its principles are founded upon the properties of matter and the laws of motion; and, in knowing something of these, the tyro will lay the foundation of all substantial knowledge.

The properties of matter are the following: Solidity (or impenetrability), divisibility, mobility, elasticity, brittleness, malleability, ductility, and tenacity.

The laws of motion are as follow:

1. Every body continues in a state of rest, or of uniform rectilineal motion, unless affected by some extraneous force.

2. The change of motion is always proportionate to the impelling force. Action and reaction are always equal and contrary.

EXPERIMENT OF THE LAW OF MOTION.

In shooting at "taw," if the marble be struck "plump," as it is called, it moves forward exactly in the same line of direction; but, if struck sideways, it will move in an oblique direction, and its course will be in a line situated between the direction of its former motion and that of the force impressed. This is called the resolution of forces.

BALANCING.

The centre of gravity in a body is that part about which all the other parts equally balance each other. In balancing a stick upon the finger, or upon the chin, it is necessary only to keep the chin or finger exactly under the point which is called the centre of gravity.

THE BALANCED TURK.

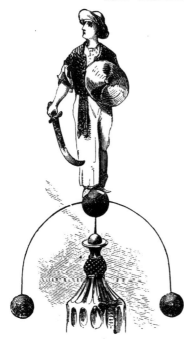

A decanter, or bottle, is first obtained, and in its cork is placed a needle; on this is balanced a ball of wood, having a cork or wooden figure cut out, standing on the top. From the ball project two wires, bent semicircularly, having at their extremities two bullets. Push the bullets, and the whole will turn round on the needle, the figure standing upright all the while; and twist it about from side to side as much as you like, it will always regain its erect position. The two bullets, in this case, cause the centre of gravity to fall below the ball on which the figure is placed, and, in consequence, as the centre of gravity always assumes the lowest position, it cannot do so without making the figure stand erect, or, in other words, until the bullets themselves are equally balanced. Any boy may whittle one of these toys out with a jack-knife.

THE BALANCED PAIL.

To support a pail of water by a stick, only half of which, or less, rests upon the table. Let A B be the top of the table, and C D the stick which is

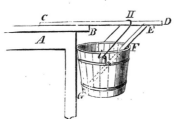

to support the bucket. Place the handle of the bucket on the stick in such a manner that it may rest on it in an inclined position, as H i, and let the middle of the bucket be a little within the edge of the table; to keep this apparatus properly in its situation, place another stick, E F G, with the end resting against the bucket at the bottom, its middle, F, resting on the opposite top edge of the bucket, and its other extremity, E, against the first stick, C D, in which a notch must be cut to retain it. The bucket will thus be kept in its situation, without inclining to either side, and, if not already filled with water, it may be filled with safety.

THE BALANCED COIN.

This engraving represents what seems to be an astounding statement, namely, that a quarter, or other piece of money, can be made to spin on the point of a needle. To perform this experiment, procure a bottle, cork it, and in the cork place a needle. Now take another cork, and cut a slit in it, so that the edge of the coin will fit into the slit; next place two forks in the cork, as seen in the engraving, and, placing the edge of the coin on the needle, it will spin round without falling off. The reason is this: that the weight of the forks, projecting as they do so much below the coin. brings the centre of gravity of the arrangement much below the point of suspension, or the point of the needle, and therefore the coin remains perfectly safe and upright.

THE SPANISH DANCER.

The laws which govern the motion of bodies are capable of many pleasing illustrations, and the example which we now give of causing rotary motion is very interesting and easily performed.

Take a piece of card, and cut out a little figure like that in the engraving, and paste or gum it in an erect position on the inside of a watch-glass, A.

Then procure a black japanned waiter, B, or a clean plate will do, and, holding it in an inclined position, place the figure and watch-glass on it, and they will, of course, slide down. Next let fall a drop of water on the waiter, place the watch-glass on it, and again incline the waiter, and instead of the watch-glass sliding down, it will begin to revolve. It will continue to revolve with increasing velocity, obeying the inclination and position of the plane, as directed by the hand of the experimentalist. The reason of this is, in the first place, in consequence of the cohesion of the water to the two surfaces, a new force is introduced, by which an unequal degree of resistance is imparted to different parts of the

23

watch-glass in contact with the waiter, and, consequently, in its effort to slide down, it revolves. Again, if the drop of water be observed, it will be seen that it undergoes a change of figure; a film of water, by capillary action, is drawn to the foremost portion of the glass, while, by the centrifugal force, a body of water is thrown under the hinder part of it. The effect of both of these actions is to accelerate the motion, or, in other words, to gradually increase the speed.

THE MECHANICAL BUCEPHALUS.

The illustration of the horse furnishes a very good solution of a popular paradox in mechanics: Given, a body having a tendency to fall by its own weight; required, how to prevent it from falling by adding to it a weight

on the same side on which it tends to fall. The engraving shows a horse, the centre of gravity of which is somewhere about the middle of its body. It is evident, therefore, that were it placed on its hinder legs, on a table, *a*, the line of its *direction*, or centre, would fall considerably beyond its base, and the horse would fall on the ground; but, to prevent this, there is a stiff wire attached to a weight, or bullet, connected with the body of the horse, and by this means the horse prances on a table, without falling off; so that the figure which was incapable of supporting itself is actually prevented from falling by adding a weight to its unsupported end. This seems almost impossible; but, when we consider that, in order to have the desired effect, the wire must be bent, and the weight be farther under the table than the horse's feet are on it, the mystery is solved, as it brings the total weight of bullet and horse in such a position that the tendency is rather to make it stand up than to let it fall down.

THE REVOLVING IMAGE.

This little figure may be made to balance itself amusingly. Get a piece of wood, about two inches long; cut one end of it into the form of a man's head and shoulders, and let the other end taper off to a fine point. Next furnish the little gentleman with a pair of wafters, shaped like oars, instead of arms; but they must be more than double the length of his body; stick them in his shoulders, and he is complete. When you place him on the tip of your finger, if you have taken care to make the point exactly in the centre, he will stand upright, as seen in the engraving. By blowing on the wafters, he may be made to turn round very quickly. It is explained by the reasons that were given in the experiment of the "balanced coin."

THE BRIDGE OF KNIVES.

Place three glasses, A A A, in the form of a triangle, and arrange three knives upon them, as shown in the figure, the blade of No. 1 over that of

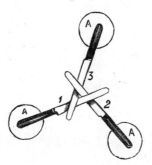

No. 2, and that over No. 3, which rests on No. 1. The bridge so made will be self-supported.

THE PARLOR BOOMERANG.

The boomerang is a weapon used by the savages of Australia. By them it is made of a flat piece of hard wood. The peculiarity of this instrument is, that in whatever direction it is thrown, it will return to the place from whence it started. (See page 51.) The Australian aborigines use it with great dexterity, making it travel round a house and return to their feet, or they can throw it on the ground so that it will fly into the air, form a perfect arc over

Fig. 1.

their heads, and strike them on the back. This curious instrument can be made in miniature, and is a very amusing toy for the parlor.

Get a piece of tolerably stiff card-board, and cut from it a figure resembling Fig. 1, and you will have a boomerang.

The next thing is to propel it through the air so that it will return to your feet; to do this, lay the boomerang on a flat book, allowing one end to project about an inch; then, holding the book at a slight angle, strike the projecting end of the boomerang with a piece of stick, or heavy penholder, as represented in Fig. 2, when it will fly across the room and return to your feet.

Fig. 2.

THE COMPLACENT VIZIER.

Among the novelties which scientific investigation has added to our toys, are several figures which will raise themselves upright when thrown down,

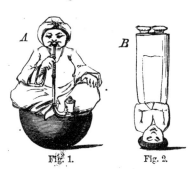

Fig. 1.   Fig. 2.

and regain the erect position, notwithstanding their equilibrium is disturbed. The figures themselves are made of the pith of elder-trees, or any other very light substance. Each is placed on half a bullet, as at Fig. 1, or may be made to stand on its head, as at Fig. 2, by making its cap of lead. Their appearance is very droll when they are moved about, as they seem every moment to be falling over, and yet continually right themselves. The philosophy of this is, that the centre of gravity being in the base, and always trying to assume the lowest position, it keeps the figures upright. However much the equilibrium is disturbed, it will always try to regain its original position.

ARITHMETICAL AMUSEMENTS.

As the principal object of this volume is to enable the young reader to learn something in his sports, and to understand what he is doing, we shall, before proceeding to the curious tricks and feats connected with the science of numbers, present him with some arithmetical aphorisms, upon which most of the following examples are founded.

APHORISMS OF NUMBER.

1. If two even numbers be added together, or subtracted from each other, their sum or difference will be an even number.

2. If two uneven numbers be added or subtracted, their sum or difference will be an even number.

3 The sum or difference of an even and an uneven number added or subtracted will be an uneven number.

4. The product of two even numbers will be an even number, and the product of two uneven numbers will be an uneven number.

5. The product of an even and uneven number will be an even number.

6. If two different numbers be divisible by any one number, their sum and their difference will also be divisible by that number.

7. If several different numbers, divisible by 3, be added or multiplied together, their sum and their product will also be divisible by 3.

8. If two numbers divisible by 9 be added together, the sum of the figures in the amount will be either 9 or a number divisible by 9.

9. If any number be multiplied by 9, or by any other number divisible by 9, the amount of the figures of the product will be either 9 or a number divisible by 9.

10. In every arithmetical progression, if the first and last term be each multiplied by the number of terms, and the sum of the two products be divided by 2, the quotient will be the sum of the series.

11. In every geometric progression, if any two terms be multiplied together, their product will be equal to that term which answers to the sum of these two indices. Thus, in the series,—

1	2	3	4	5
2	4	8	16	32

If the third and fourth terms, 8 and 16, be multiplied together, the product, 128, will be the seventh term of the series. In like manner, if the fifth term be multiplied into itself, the product will be the tenth term; and if that sum be multiplied into itself, the product will be the twentieth term. Therefore, to find the last, or any other term of a geometric series, it is not necessary to continue the series beyond a few of the first terms.

Previous to the numerical recreations, we shall here describe certain mechanical methods of performing arithmetical calculations, such as are not only in themselves entertaining, but will be found more or less useful to the young reader.

TO FIND A NUMBER THOUGHT OF.

FIRST METHOD.

	EXAMPLE.
Let a person think of a number, say......................	6
1. Let him multiply by 3...........................	18
2. Add 1..	19
3. Multiply by 3................................	57
4. Add to this the number thought of..............	63

Let him inform you what is the number produced; it will always end with 3. Strike off the 3, and inform him that he thought of 6.

SECOND METHOD.

	EXAMPLE.
Suppose the number thought of to be....................	6
1. Let him double it..............................	12
2. Add 4..	16
3. Multiply by 5.................................	80
4. Add 12.......................................	92
5. Multiply by 10...............................	920

Let him inform you what is the number produced. You must then, in every case, subtract 320; the remainder is, in this example, 600; strike off the 2 ciphers, and announce 6 as the number thought of.

THIRD METHOD.

Desire a person to think of a number—say 6. He must then proceed—

	EXAMPLE.
1. To multiply this number by itself................	36
2. To take 1 from the number thought of............	5
3. To multiply this by itself.......................	25
4. To tell you the difference between this product and the former........	11
You must then add 1 to it.........................	12
And halve this number...........................	6

Which will be the number he thought of.

FOURTH METHOD.

Desire a person to think of a number—say 6. He must then proceed as follows:

EXAMPLE.

1. Add 1 to it..................................... 7
2. Multiply by 3................................. 21
3. Add 1 again................................... 22
4. Add the number thought of..................... 28

Let him tell you the figures produced (28):

5. You then subtract 4 from it................... 24
6. And divide by 4....... 6

Which you can say is the number he thought of.

FIFTH METHOD.

EXAMPLE.

Suppose the number thought of be..................... 6
1. Let him double it........................... 12
2. Desire him to add to this any number you tell him—
   say 4.. 16
3. To halve it................................... 8

You can then tell him, that if he will subtract from this the number he thought of, the remainder will be, in the case supposed, 2.

Note, the remainder is always half of the number you tell him to add.

TO DISCOVER TWO OR MORE NUMBERS THAT A PERSON HAS THOUGHT OF.

FIRST CASE.

Where each of the numbers is less than 10. Suppose the numbers thought of were 2, 3, 5.

EXAMPLE.

1. Desire him to double the 1st number, making....... 4
2. To add 1 to it................................. 5
3. To multiply by 5.............................. 25
4. To add the 2d number......................... 28

There being a 3d number, repeat this process—

5. To double it................................. 56
6. To add 1 to it................................ 57
7. To multiply by 5............................. 285
8. To add the 3d number......................... 290

And to proceed in the same manner for as many numbers as were thought of. Let him tell you the last sum produced (in this case, 290). Then, if there were two numbers thought of, you must subtract 5; if three, 55; if four, 555. You must here subtract 55, leaving a remainder of 235, which are the numbers thought of, 2, 3, and 5.

SECOND CASE.

Where one or more of the numbers are 10, or more than 10, and where there is an *odd* number of numbers thought of.

Suppose he fixes upon five numbers, viz., 4, 6, 9, 15, 16.

He must add together the numbers as follows, and tell you the various sums :

1. The sum of the 1st and 2d................. 10
2. The sum of the 2d and 3d................. 15
3. The sum of the 3d and 4th................. 24
4. The sum of the 4th and 5th................ 31
5. The sum of the 1st and last............... 20

You must then add together the 1st, 3d, and 5th sums, viz., 10 + 24 + 20 = 54, and the 2d and 4th, 15 + 31 = 46; take one from the other, leaving 8. The half of this is the first number, 4 ; if you take this from the sum of the 1st and 2d you will have the 2d number, 6 : this taken from the sum of the 2d and 3d will give you the 3d, 9 ; and so on for the other numbers.

THIRD CASE.

Where one or more of the numbers are 10, or more than 10, and where an *even* number of numbers has been thought of.

Suppose he fixes on six numbers, viz., 2, 6, 7, 15, 16, 18. He must add together the numbers as follows, and tell you the sum in each case :—

1. The sum of the 1st and 2d................. 8
2. The sum of the 2d and 3d................. 13
3. The sum of the 3d and 4th................. 22
4. The sum of the 4th and 5th............... 31
5. The sum of the 5th and 6th............... 34
6. The sum of the 2d and last................ 24

You must then add together the 2d, 4th, and 6th sums, 13 + 31 + 24 = 68, and the 3d and 5th sums, 22 + 34 = 56. Subtract one from the other, leaving 12 ; the 2d number will be 6, the half of this ; take the 2d from the sum of the 1st and 2d and you will get the 1st ; take the 2d from the sum of the 2d and 3d, and you will have the 3d, and so on.

HOW MANY COUNTERS HAVE I IN MY HANDS?

A person having an equal number of counters in each hand, it is required to find how many he has altogether.

Suppose he has 16 counters, or 8 in each hand. Desire him to transfer from one hand to the other a certain number of them, and to tell you the number so transferred. Suppose it be 4, the hands now contain 4 and 12. Ask him how many times the smaller number is contained in the larger ; in this case it is three times. You must then multiply the number transferred,

4, by the 3, making 12, and add the 4, making 16; then divide 16 by the 3 *minus* 1; this will bring 8, the number in each hand.

In most cases fractions will occur in the process: when 10 counters are in each hand and if 4 be transferred, the hands will contain 6 and 14.

He will divide 14 by 6 and inform you that the quotient is $2\frac{2}{6}$ or $2\frac{1}{3}$.

You multiply 4 by $2\frac{1}{3}$ which is $9\frac{1}{3}$.

Add 4 to this, making $13\frac{1}{3}$ equal to $\frac{40}{3}$.

Subtract 1 from $2\frac{1}{3}$, leaving $1\frac{1}{3}$ or $\frac{4}{3}$.

Divide $\frac{40}{3}$ by $\frac{4}{3}$, giving 10, the number in each hand.

THE THREE TRAVELLERS.

Three men met at a caravansary or inn, in Persia; and two of them brought their provisions along with them, according to the custom of the country; but the third, not having provided any, proposed to the others that they should eat together, and he would pay the value of his proportion. This being agreed to, A produced 5 loaves, and B 3 loaves, all of which the travellers ate together, and C paid 8 pieces of money as the value of his share, with which the others were satisfied, but quarrelled about the division of it. Upon this the matter was referred to the judge, who decided impartially. What was his decision?

At first sight it would seem that the money should be divided according to the bread furnished; but we must consider that, as the 3 ate 8 loaves, each one ate $2\frac{2}{3}$ loaves of the bread he furnished. This from 5 would leave $2\frac{1}{3}$ loaves furnished the stranger by A; and $3-2\frac{2}{3}=\frac{1}{3}$ furnished by B, hence, $2\frac{1}{3}$ to $\frac{1}{3}=7$ to 1, is the ratio in which the money is to be divided. If you imagine A and B to furnish, and C to consume all, then the division will be according to amounts furnished.

THE MONEY GAME.

A person having in one hand a piece of gold, and in the other a piece of silver, you may tell in which hand he has the gold, and in which the silver, by the following method: Some value, represented by an even number, such as 8, must be assigned to the gold; and a value represented by an odd number, such as three, must be assigned to the silver; after which, desire the person to multiply the number in the right hand by any even number whatever, such as 2, and that in the left by an odd number, as 3; then bid him add together the two products, and if the whole sum be odd, the gold will be in the right hand, and the silver in the left; if the sum be even, the contrary will be the case.

To conceal the artifice better, it will be sufficient to ask whether the sum of the two products can be halved without a remainder; for in that case the total will be even, and in the contrary case odd.

It may be readily seen, that the pieces, instead of being in the two hands of the same person, may be supposed to be in the hands of two persons, one

23*

of whom has the even number, or piece of gold, and the other the odd number, or piece of silver. The same operations may then be performed in regard to these two persons, as are performed in regard to the two hands of the same person, calling the one privately the right, and the other the left.

THE PHILOSOPHER'S PUPILS.

To find a number of which the half, fourth, and seventh, added to three, shall be equal to itself.

This was a favorite problem among the ancient Grecian arithmeticians, who stated the question in the following manner: "Tell us, illustrious Pythagoras, how many pupils frequent thy school?" "One-half," replied the philosopher, "study mathematics, one-fourth natural philosophy, one-seventh observe silence, and there are three females besides."

The answer is, $28: 14 + 7 + 4 + 3 = 28.$

THE CERTAIN GAME.

Two persons agree to take, alternately, numbers less than a given number, for example, 11, and to add them together till one of them has reached a certain sum, such as 100. By what means can one of them infallibly attain to that number before the other?

The whole artifice in this consists in immediately making choice of the numbers 1, 12, 23, 34, and so on, or of a series which continually increases by 11, up to 100. Let us suppose that the first person, who knows the game, makes choice of 1; it is evident that his adversary, as he must count less than 11, can at most reach 11, by adding 10 to it. The first will then take 1, which will make 12; and whatever number the second may add the first will certainly win, provided he continually add the number which forms the complement of that of his adversary to 11; that is to say, if the latter take 8, he must take 3; if 9, he must take 2; and so on. By following this method he will infallibly attain to 89, and it will then be impossible for the second to prevent him from getting first to 100; for whatever number the second takes he can attain only to 99; after which the first may say—" and 1 makes 100." If the second take 1 after 89, it would make 90, and his adversary would finish by saying—"and 10 make 100." Between two persons who are equally acquainted with the game, he who begins must necessarily win.

THE DICE GUESSED UNSEEN.

A pair of dice being thrown, to find the number of points on each die without seeing them. Tell the person who cast the dice to double the number of points upon one of them, and add 5 to it; then to multiply the sum produced by 5, and to add to the product the number of points upon the other die. This being done, desire him to tell you the amount, and having thrown out 25, the remainder will be a number consisting of two figures, the first of which, to the left, is the number of points on the first die, and the second figure, to the right, the number on the other. Thus:

Suppose the number of points of the first die which comes up to be 2, and that of the other 3; then, if to 4, the double of the points of the first, there be added 5, and the sum produced, 9, be multiplied by 5, the product will be 45; to which, if 3, the number of points on the other die, be added, 48 will be produced, from which, if 25 be subtracted, 23 will remain; the first figure of which is 2, the number of points on the first die, and the second figure 3, the number on the other.

THE FAMOUS FORTY-FIVE.

How can number 45 be divided into four such parts that, if to the first part you add 2, from the second part you subtract 2, the third part you multiply by 2, and the fourth part you divide by 2, the sum of the addition, the remainder of the subtraction, the product of the multiplication, and the quotient of the division, be all equal?

The first is   8; to which add 2, the sum is   10
The second is 12; subtract   2, the remainder is 10
The third is   5; multiplied by 2, the product is   10
The fourth is 20; divided by   2, the quotient is   10
                 ——
                 45

Required to subtract 45 from 45, and leave 45 as a remainder.

SOLUTION.—$9+8+7+6+5+4+3+2+1=45$
$1+2+3+4+5+6+7+8+9=45$
$8+6+4+1+9+7+5+3+2=45$

THE ASTONISHED FARMER.

A and B took each 30 pigs to market. A sold his at 3 for a dollar, B at 2 for a dollar, and together they received $25. A afterwards took 60 alone, which he sold *as before*, at 5 for $2, and received but $24; what became of the other dollar?

This is rather a catch question, the insinuation that the first lot were sold at the rate of 5 for $2, being only true in part. They commence selling at that rate, but after making ten sales, A's pigs are exhausted, and they have received $20: B still has 10 which he sells at " 2 for a dollar," and of course receives $5; whereas had he sold them at the rate of 5 for $2, he would have received but $4. Hence the difficulty is easily settled.

THE EXPUNGED FIGURE.

In the first place desire a person to write down secretly, in a line, any number of figures he may choose, and add them together as units; having done this, tell him to subtract that sum from the line of figures originally set down; then desire him to strike out any figure he pleases, and add the remaining figures in the line together as units (as in the first instance), and inform you of the result, when you will tell him the figure he has struck out.

```
76542-24
    24
  ------
  76518
```

Suppose, for example, the figures put down are 76542; these added together, as units, make a total of 24; deduct 24 from the first line, and 76518 remain; if 5, the centre figure, be struck out, the total will be 22. If 8, the first figure, be struck out, 19 will be the total.

In order to ascertain which figure has been struck out, you make a mental sum one multiple of 9 higher than the total given. If 22 be given as the total, then 3 times 9 are 27, and 22 from 27 show that 5 was struck out. If 19 be given, that sum deducted from 27 shows 8.

Should the total be equal multiples of 9, as 18, 27, 36, then 9 has been expunged.

With very little practice any person may perform this with rapidity; it is therefore needless to give any further examples. The only way in which a person can fail in solving this riddle is, when either the number 9 or a 0 is struck out, as it then becomes impossible to tell which of the two it is, the sum of the figures in the line being an even number of nines in both cases.

THE MYSTERIOUS ADDITION.

It is required to name the quotient of five or three lines of figures—each line consisting of five or more figures—only seeing the first line before the other lines are even put down. Any person may write down the first line of figures for you. How do you find the quotient?

```
 86,214
 42,680
 57,319
 62,854
 37,145
 -------
286,212

 67,856
 47,218
 52,781
 -------
167,855
```

When the first line of figures is set down, subtract 2 from the last right-hand figure, and place it before the first figure of the line, and that is the quotient for five lines. For example, suppose the figures given are 86,214, the quotient will be 286,212. You may allow any person to put down the two first and the fourth lines, but you must always set down the third and fifth lines, and in doing so always make up 9 with the line above.

Therefore in the annexed diagram you will see that you have made 9 in the third and fifth lines with the lines above them. If the person you request to put down the figures should set down a 1 or 0 for the last figure, you must say, "We will have another figure," and another, and so on until he sets down something above 1 or 2.

In solving the puzzle with 3 lines, you subtract 1 from the last figure, and place it before the first figure, and make up the third line yourself to 9. For example: 67,856 is given, and the quotient will be 167,855, as shown in the above diagram.

THE REMAINDER.

A very pleasing way to arrive at an arithmetical sum, without the use of either slate or pencil, is to ask a person to think of a figure, then to double it, then add a certain figure to it, now halve the whole sum, and finally to subtract from that the figure first thought of. You are then to tell the thinker what is the remainder.

The key to this lock of figures is, that *half* of whatever sum you request to be added during the working of the sum *is the remainder*. In the example given, 5 is the half of 10, the number requested to be added. Any amount may be added, but the operation is simplified by giving only even numbers, as they will divide without fractions.

Think of.. 7
Double it... 14
Add 10 to it 10
                                                      ——
Halve it...................................... 2) 24
                                                      ——
Which will leave 12
Subtract the number thought of 7
                                                      ——
The remainder will be........................... 5

THE THREE JEALOUS HUSBANDS.

Three jealous husbands, A, B, and C, with their wives, being ready to pass by night over a river, find at the water-side a boat which can carry but two at a time, and for want of a waterman they are compelled to row themselves over the river at several times. The question is, how those six persons shall pass, two at a time, so that none of the three wives may be found in the company of one or two men, unless her husband be present?

This may be effected in two or three ways; the following may be as good as any: Let A and wife go over—let A return—let B's and C's wives go over—A's wife returns—B and C go over—B and wife return, A and B go over—C's wife returns, and A's and B's wives go over—then C comes back for his wife. Simple as this question may appear, it is found in the works of Alcuin, who flourished a thousand years ago, hundreds of years before the art of printing was invented.

THE ARITHMETICAL MOUSE-TRAP.

One of the best and most simple mouse-traps in use may be constructed as follows: Get a slip of smooth pine, about the eighth of an inch thick, a quarter of an inch broad, and of sufficient length to cut out the following parts of a trap: First, an upright piece, three or four inches high, which must be square at the bottom, and a small piece to be cut off at the top to fit the notch in No. 2 (see No. 1, in the margin). The second piece must be of the same length as the first, with the notch cut across nearly at the top of it, to fit the top of No. 1, and the other end of it trimmed to catch the notch in No. 3 (see No. 2). The third piece should be twice as long as either of the others; a notch, similar to that in No. 2, must be cut in one

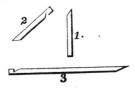

end of it to catch the lower end of No. 2. Having proceeded thus far, you must put the pieces together, in order to finish it, by adding another notch in No. 3, the exact situation of which you will discover as follows: Place No. 1, as it is in the cut, then put the notch of No. 2 in the thinned top of No. 1; keep it in the same inclination as in the cut; then get a flat piece of wood, or a slate, one end of which must rest on the ground, and the centre of the edge of the other on the top of No. 2. You will now find the thinned end of No. 2 elevated by the weight of the flat piece of wood or slate; then put the thinned end of it in the notch of No. 3, and draw No. 2 down by it, until the whole forms a resemblance of a figure 4; at the exact place where No. 3 touches the upright, cut a notch, which, by catching the end of No. 1, will keep the trap together. You may now bait the end of No. 3 with a piece of cheese; a mouse, by nibbling the bait, will pull down No. 3, the other pieces immediately separate, and the slate or board falls upon the mouse. We have seen numbers of mice, rats, and birds, caught by this

FIGURE OF 4 TRAP.

PUZZLES.

To many minds, the pleasure of making a discovery, after long and patient investigation, is greater than any delight that can be offered to the senses. Puzzles may be regarded as an excellent medium for the development of such natural tendencies in youth, combining, as they do, the elements of work and play; necessitating also both application and perseverance, and enabling us to improve the valuable faculty of holding several ideas in the mind at once. In short, the same powers of intellect that will enable a boy to unravel the intricacies of a puzzle, might, later in life, prove, in their fullest development, valuable aids to the investigation of the mysterious problems of Nature, and yield, for their fruits, some fresh contributions to the never-ceasing wonders of Science. For centuries, puzzles, paradoxes, and riddles, have been popular as recreations. Those that we place before our readers in the following pages, have been carefully collected from several sources; the answers we have placed in a separate chapter, so that our young friends may have the chance of deciphering them for themselves, instead of being directly enlightened by the printed solutions.

1.—THE CARD-CHAIN PUZZLE.

The links of which this chain is formed have no joints, neither was any

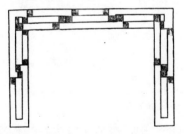

gum, paste, nor adhesive material used in their formation; but they were all fairly cut from a single card. Our young friends will find this one of the most ingenious puzzles in this collection.

2.—THE SQUARE AND CIRCLE PUZZLE.

Get a piece of cardboard, the size and shape of the diagram, and punch in it twelve circles, or holes, in the position shown. The puzzle is, to cut the cardboard into four pieces of equal size, each piece to be of the same shape, and to contain three circles, without cutting into any of them.

3.—THE MAGIC OCTAGON.

Procure a good stiff piece of pasteboard, and draw *four each* of the three

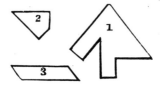

designs represented in the accompanying diagram. If joined together correctly, they will form an octagon.

4.—THE BOARD AND BALL.

Get the cover of a small cigar-box, or any other thin board, about five inches long, and cut it out the shape of the engraving. Then arrange the strings and balls as shown in the same.

The trick is, to get the large ball off the string without untying it, or removing any of the smaller balls.

5.—THE CABINET-MAKER'S PUZZLE.

A cabinet-maker has a circular piece of veneering, with which he has to veneer the tops of two oval stools; but it so happens that the area of the

stools, exclusive of the hand-holes in the centre, and that of the circular piece, are the same. How must he cut his stuff so as to be exactly sufficient for his purpose?

6.—THE PROTEAN PUZZLE.

Cut a piece of stiff cardboard in the shape of Fig. 1.   Let it be about five inches long, by one inch broad.   Cut it then into eleven pieces, and with these eleven pieces form a cross.   After this, by changing the positions of the pieces, form in turn the several shapes in Fig. 2.

Fig. 1.

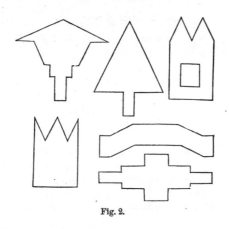

Fig. 2.

7.—THE BUTTON PUZZLE.

In the centre of a piece of leather make two parallel cuts with a pen-knife, and just below a small hole of the same width; then pass a piece of

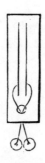

string under the slit and through the hole, as in the figure, and tie two buttons much larger than the hole to the ends of the string.   The puzzle is, to get the string out again without taking off the buttons.

8.—THE HEART AND BALL PUZZLE.

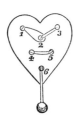

To make this puzzle it is only necessary to cut a thin piece of wood into the shape of a heart, to make six holes in it, as represented in the annexed cut, and provide a thin silken cord, which is to be doubled, and the two ends fastened into a small wooden ball. To play the ball on, pass the loop through the hole 6, from face to back, up to 2, through which bring it, and then through 3, 5, 4, and 1, in succession; then through 2 again, and down the back to 6; bring it through 6 to the face, and pass it over the ball; then draw the loop back again through 6 and 2, and the puzzle (which is to take the ball and string off after being thus fixed) is set.

9.—THE STRING AND BALLS PUZZLE.

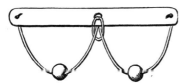

Get an oblong strip of wood or ivory, and bore three holes in it, as shown in the cut. Then take a piece of twine, passing the two ends through the holes at the extremities, fastening them with a knot, and thread upon it two beads or rings, as depicted above. The puzzle is, to get both beads on the same side, without removing the string from the holes, or untying the knots.

10.—PUZZLE PURSE.

With a piece of morocco, or any other suitable material, let a purse be constructed similar to the one given here. The puzzle is, to open the same without removing any of the rings.

11.—THE TWELVE-CORNERED STAR.

The circle represented in the cut, is divided at the twelve points, A,
B, C, D, E, F, G, H, I, K, L, M, by
lines so drawn that they form a
star with twelve points. From the
point A, draw a line to F, from F
to L, to D, to I, to B, to G, to M,
to E, to K, to C, to H, and back
again to A.

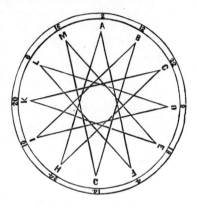

The problem now to be solved, is
how to distribute the twelve numbers of the following arithmetical
progression 2, 4, 6, 8, 10, 12, 14,
16, 18, 20, 22, 24, into the twelve
compartments of the twelve letters
which stand at the twelve points
of the star in such a manner, that
the sum of any two numbers that lie side by side, when added together,
shall be equal to the sum of the two numbers which are at the two opposite
points of the star.

12.—CUTTING OUT A CROSS.

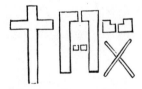

How can be cut out of a single piece of paper, and with one cut of the
scissors, a perfect cross, and all the other forms as shown in the cuts?

13.—THE CIRCLE PUZZLE.

Twenty lines upon paper place,
On every line five circles trace;
These circles should just in amount,
Or number, thirty-seven count;
And every circle, orb, or round,
Upon an angle should be found—
At an equal distance, too, should be
Upon each line—solve this for me.

14.—THE CARD PUZZLE.

One of the best puzzles hitherto made, is represented in the annexed cut. A is a piece of card; *b b,* a narrow slip divided from its bottom edge, the whole breadth of the card, except just sufficient to hold it on at each side; *c c* is another small slip of card, with two large square ends, *e e; d* is a bit of tobacco-pipe, through which *c c* is passed, and which is kept on by the two ends, *e e.* The puzzle consists in getting the pipe off without breaking

it or injuring any other part of the puzzle. This, which appears to be impossible, is done in the most simple manner. On a moment's consideration, it will appear plainly that there must be as much difficulty in getting the pipe in its present situation as there can be in taking it away. The way to put the puzzle to-gether is as follows : The slip *c c e e* is

Fig. 1.

Fig. 2.　Fig. 3.

cut out of a piece of card, in the shape delineated in Fig. 3. The card in the first figure must then be gently bent at A, so as to allow of the slip at the bottom of it being also bent sufficiently to pass double through the pipe, as in Fig. 2. The detached slip with the square ends (Fig. 3) is then to be passed half way through the loop *f,* at the bottom of the pipe; it is next to be doubled in the centre, at *a,* and pulled through the pipe, double, by means of the loop of the slip to the card. Upon unbending the card, the puzzle will be complete, and appear as répresented in Fig. 1.

15.—THREE-SQUARE PUZZLE.

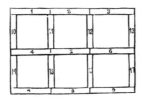

Cut seventeen slips of cardboard, of equal lengths, and place them on a table to form six squares, as in the diagram. It is now required to take away five of the pieces, yet to leave but three perfect squares.

16.—THE CYLINDER PUZZLE.

Cut a piece of cardboard about four inches long, of the shape of the dia-

gram, and make three holes in it, as represented. The puzzle is, to make one piece of wood to pass through, and also exactly to fill, each of the three holes.

17.—THE FLORIST'S PUZZLE.

A florist planted thirty-one varieties of flowers (only one of each kind), so that he had one circle containing eighteen varieties; seven circles with six varieties in each; six straight rows with six varieties in each; and three straight rows with six varieties in each.

18.—ROMAN CROSS-PUZZLE.

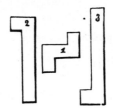

With three pieces of cardboard, of the shape and size of No. 1, and one each of Nos. 2 and 3, to form a cross.

19.—THE FOUNTAIN PUZZLE.

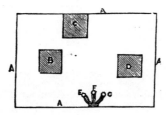

A is a wall, B C D three houses, and E F G three fountains or canals.

It is required to bring the water from E to D, from G to B, and from F to C, without one crossing the other, or passing outside of the wall A.

20.—THE DOUBLE-HEADED PUZZLE.

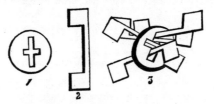

Cut a circular piece of wood, as in the cut No. 1, and four others, like No. 2. The puzzle consists in getting them all into the cross-shaped slit, until they look like Fig. 3.

21.—THE CARDBOARD PUZZLE.

8 inches.

5 inches.

Take a piece of cardboard, or leather, of the shape and measurement indicated by the diagram; cut it in such a manner that you yourself may pass through it, still keeping it in one piece.

22.—THE PERPLEXED CARPENTER.

There is a hole in the barn floor, just two feet in width and twelve in length. How can it be entirely covered with a board three feet wide and eight feet long, by *cutting the board only once in two?*

23.—THE TRIANGLE PUZZLE.

Cut twenty triangles out of ten square pieces of wood; mix them together, and request a person to make an exact square with them.

24.—THE CARPENTER'S PUZZLE.

A plank was to be cut in two; the carpenter cut it half through on each side, and found he had two feet still to cut. How was it?

25.—THE NINE DIGITS.

Place the nine digits (that is, the several figures or numbers under ten) in three rows, in such a way that, adding them together either up or down, across, or from corner to corner, they shall always make fifteen.

26.—THE ACCOMMODATING SQUARE.

Make eight squares of card, then divide four of them from corner to corner, so that you will now have twelve pieces. Form a square with them.

27.—THE THREE RABBITS.

Draw three rabbits, so that each shall appear to have two ears, while, in fact, they have only three ears between them.

ANSWERS TO PUZZLES.

1.—ANSWER TO CARD-CHAIN PUZZLE.

TAKE a card, say four inches long and two and a half inches wide, or of any other size thought fit; but the larger the card the better it is for practice. Draw a light pencil-line from A to B, and another line from C to D, at about a quarter of an inch from the edge of your card. Now lay the card in water for a short time; after which split it down from the edge with a penknife, as far as the pencil-line, and then put the card aside until it is perfectly dry, when you will resume your task as follows: With a sharp penknife cut right through the *straight* lines indicated in the en-

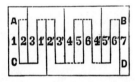

graving, but only half way through the *dotted* lines, as that is the *split* portion of the card. The figures show the bar of each link of the chain. Thus 1 and 1' belong to the same link, and are connected at the top and bottom, the latter by the upper half of the split, and the former by the under half of the split; the links 2 and 2' are also connected in the same way, and so on to the end of the chain, until every link is released, thus forming a cable, which, if not useful for any mechanical purpose, will at least serve to amuse.

2.—ANSWER TO SQUARE AND CIRCLE PUZZLE.

3.—ANSWER TO THE MAGIC OCTAGON.

The pieces are put together in the following manner:

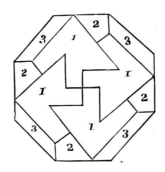

4.—ANSWER TO BOARD AND BALL PUZZLE.

Push the ball close up to the wood, and pull the loop of string down through, as much as it will come; then pass the end of the loop through the hole in the wood and over the pellet, as here shown. The two loops will then separate, and the ball can easily be taken off.

The knots beneath the wood prevent the loops being pulled through by the pellets.

5.—ANSWER TO THE CABINET-MAKER'S PUZZLE.

The cabinet-maker must first find the centre of the circle, and strike another circle, half the diameter of the first, and having the same centre. Then cut the whole into four parts, by means of two lines drawn at right angles to each other; then cut along the inner circle, and put the pieces together as in the above diagram.

6.—ANSWER TO THE PROTEAN PUZZLE.

Cut the cardboard as in Fig. A, and with the pieces the different diagrams may be formed.

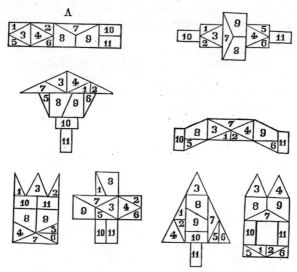

7.—ANSWER TO THE BUTTON PUZZLE.

Draw the narrow slip of the leather through the hole, and the string and buttons may be easily released.

8.—ANSWER TO HEART AND BALL PUZZLE.

To play the ball off, place the heart before you in the position described by the cut; slacken the string by drawing at the back, the ball toward the hole 6; then loosen the rest of the string by pulling it toward you, and draw up the loop as far as you can; then pass the loop through hole 2, down the other side of the heart to 6, through which bring it to the face, and pass it over the ball; then draw the loop back again through the same hole, and the ball and the string will come off. Care should be taken to avoid twisting or entangling the string. The length of the string should be proportioned to the size of the heart; if you make the heart two inches and a half high, the string, when doubled, should be about nine inches long.

24

9.—ANSWER TO THE STRING AND BALLS PUZZLE.

Draw the loop well down, slipping either ball through it. Push it through the hole at the extremities, pass it over the knot, and draw it through again. The same process must be repeated with the other ball; the loop can then be drawn through the hole in the centre, and the ball will slide along the cord until it reaches the other side. The string is then replaced, having both balls on the same side.

There is another and perhaps a neater way of performing this trick. Draw the loop through the central hole, and bring it through far enough to pass one of the balls through. Having done this, draw the string back, and both balls will be found on the same side.

10.—ANSWER TO PURSE PUZZLE.

Pass loop *a* up through ring No. 2, and over No. 1; then pass loop *b* over rings 1 and 2 up through No. 2, and over No. 1, as before; when the same

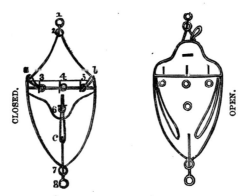

may be easily drawn through rings 3, 4, 5. Again pass loop *c* through ring No. 7 over 8, draw it up through ring 6, and the purse is complete.

11.—ANSWER TO TWELVE-CORNERED STAR.

This singular arrangement of the numbers is effected in the following manner: Place No. 2 over the ring which encloses the letter A, 4 over F, 6 over L, 8 over D, 10 over I, and so on, and the numbers will then be distributed as appears in engraving, page 547.

You may now take any two numbers that lie side by side, and add them together, and their sum will always be equal to the sum of the two numbers found at the opposite points of the star.

For example, the sum of the two Nos. 14 and 4, which cover the letters

G and F, is 18, and so also is the sum of the numbers 16 and 2, which are placed over the opposite letters M and A. The same is the case with every other pair of numbers and their opposites.

12.—ANSWER TO CUTTING OUT A CROSS-PUZZLE.

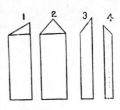

Take a piece of writing-paper, about three times as long as it is broad—say six inches long and two wide. Fold the upper corner down, as shown in Fig. 1; then fold the other upper corner over the first, and it will appear as in Fig. 2; you next fold the paper in half, lengthwise, and it will appear as in Fig. 3. Then the last fold is made lengthwise, also, in the middle of the paper, and it will exhibit the form of Fig. 4, which, when cut through with the scissors, in the direction of the dotted line, will give all the forms mentioned.

13.—ANSWER TO THE CIRCLE PUZZLE.

The lines and circles must be traced as in the following diagram:

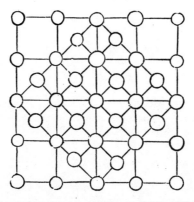

14.—ANSWER TO THE CARD PUZZLE.

In order to take the pipe off, the card must be doubled (as in Fig. 2), the slip passed through it, until there is sufficient of the loop below the pipe to allow one of the square ends of the slip (Fig. 3) being passed through it. Fig. 3 is then to be taken away, and the pipe slipped off. The card for this puzzle must be cut very neatly, the puzzle handled gently, and great care taken that, in doubling the card to put on the pipe, no creases are made in it, as they would, in all probability, spoil your puzzle, by betraying to an acute spectator the mode of operation.

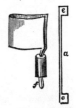

Fig. 2. Fig. 3.

15.—ANSWER TO THE THREE-SQUARE PUZZLE.

Take away the pieces numbered 8, 10, 1, 3, 13, and three squares only will remain.

16.—ANSWER TO THE CYLINDER PUZZLE.

Take a round cylinder of the diameter of the circular hole, and of the height of the square hole. Having drawn a straight line across the end, dividing it into two equal parts, cut an equal section from either side to the edge of the circular base; a figure like that represented by the wood-cut in the margin would then be produced, which would fulfil the required conditions.

17.—ANSWER TO FLORIST'S PUZZLE.

To plant 31 kinds of flowers, one of each kind, so as to have 18 varieties

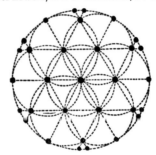

in one circle; 7 circles with 6 varieties in each; 6 straight rows with 6 varieties in each, and 3 straight rows with 5 varieties in each.

This will make a pretty flower-bed if smaller plants are put where they come nearest together.

18.—ANSWER TO ROMAN CROSS PUZZLE.

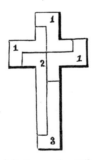

The above diagram will explain to our juvenile friends the puzzling paradox of the Roman Cross.

19.—ANSWER TO FOUNTAIN PUZZLE.

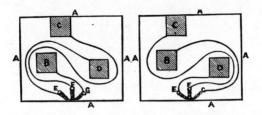

20.—ANSWER TO DOUBLE-HEADED PUZZLE.

Arranging them side by side in the short arms of the cross, draw out the centre-piece, and the rest will follow easily. The reversal of the same process will put them back again.

21.—ANSWER TO CARDBOARD PUZZLE.

Double the cardboard or leather lengthways down the middle, and then cut first to the right, nearly to the end (the narrow way), and then to the left, and so on to the end of the card; then open it, and cut down the middle, except the two ends. The diagram shows the proper cuttings. By opening the card or leather, a person may pass through it. A laurel leaf may be treated in the same manner.

22.—ANSWER TO PERPLEXED CARPENTER

The board was cut after the manner of the annexed diagram:

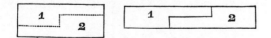

23.—ANSWER TO TRIANGLE PUZZLE.

The solution of this puzzle may be easily acquired by observing the dotted lines in the engraving; by which it will be seen that four triangles are to be placed at the corners, and a small square made in the centre. When this is done, the rest of the square may be quickly formed.

24.—ANSWER TO THE CARPENTER'S PUZZLE.

The plank was to be cut in this way:

25.—ANSWER TO THE NINE DIGITS.

Arrange the figures as explained in the following diagram:

15	6	7	2
15	1	5	9
15	8	3	4
	15	15	15	15

26.—ANSWER TO THE ACCOMMODATING SQUARE.

The square is composed in the following manner:

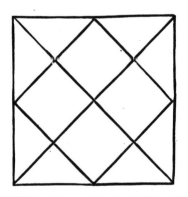

27.—ANSWER TO THE THREE RABBITS.

PART VI.

Mechanical and Miscellaneous Amusements:

INCLUDING

CARPENTRY, PAINTING, GARDENING, POSTAGE-STAMPS,
AND MISCELLANY.

MISCELLANEOUS
AMUSEMENTS

MECHANICAL AMUSEMENTS.

CARPENTRY.

It is not our purpose, by any means, to teach a boy how to be an accomplished carpenter. All we purpose to do is, to give him that acquaintanceship with the essential tools that will enable him to make a box or sled, build a chicken-coop, or even construct a book-case, aided by patience and practice.

THE TOOLS.

We will begin with the *jack-plane*, which is employed for taking the rough parts off a piece of wood. It is about seventeen inches long, and is made with either a single or double iron. For your purpose, working mostly in soft wood, a single-ironed plane is best. You take the handle (*h*)

JACK-PLANE.

FORE-PLANE.

in your right hand, laying your left hand over the top and side, just a little forward of the iron at *s*, and, by shoving steadily forward, the edge of the plane-iron (*k*) takes off the shaving, which rises at *o*, over your hand,

and falls on one side, you assisting its departure with your left hand as you draw the plane back from its stroke. Remember that you give a steady shove the whole length of your stroke, each time, keeping your plane on the plank steadily, so as to take off a clean, continuous shaving.

Fore-plane.—This is longer than the other, being twenty or twenty-two inches, a little broader and higher, and is for the purpose of making the surface level, after the jack-plane has been used, and is used with a longer stroke; for the iron in the jack-plane is ground so as to be rather deeper in the centre, and cut a hollowing shaving, while the iron of the fore-plane is ground square. There is also the jointing-plane and long-plane; but neither of these will be needed in your work. But you will require the

Smoothing-plane (E), which is used with shorter and quicker strokes than the jack-plane, and is employed for smoothing off the work. It is only a few inches long.

SMOOTHING-PLANE.   HAND-SAW.

Hand-saws.—Of these there are several. You will require five, and probably six. These are the

Cross-cut saw, generally called hand-saw, which is used for cutting across the grain of timber, and for general work.

The *mitre-saw.*—There is another useful saw it would be of advantage for the young carpenter to have, namely, the mitre-saw. It is about nine inches long, and contains at least fifteen teeth in the inch. It is used for cutting the dovetails of boxes and mitres. Its plate is very thin, and it requires some care in using. It has a back, for the purpose of strength, formed of a thin piece of brass or iron, let in so as to give the blade the requisite firmness necessary in using it.

MITRE-SAW.   TENON-SAW.

The *ripping-saw,* in which the teeth are larger, and not set so far apart as in the hand-saw. It is used for cutting with the grain of timber, or lengthwise.

The *tenon-saw* is of the same shape as the mitre-saw, but it is somewhat larger, and is made to cut across the grain of the wood so as to leave the ends nicely even, that it may fit to the piece it is joined to, which is called a shoulder, being that part which comes in contact with the fibre of the wood, thus:

To do this it requires that the teeth should be much smaller, and they are therefore placed so close as eight or ten to the inch, according to the length of the blade.

The *circular*, or *compass saw.*—The plate of this kind of saw is very narrow, and not more than one inch wide at the broadest part, gradually diminishing to about a quarter of an inch at the lower end. It is about fifteen inches in length, and is used for cutting a piece of wood into a circular form, and the plate, being narrow, allows it to follow the foot of the compass to a very small diameter.

CIRCULAR, OR COMPASS SAW.   KEYHOLE SAW.

The *keyhole saw.*—The keyhole saw is much smaller than the circular, or compass saw. It is used for cutting short curves, small holes, etc., such as a keyhole. The handle is the same form as that of the chisel, a small slit being cut through from end to end. It has a screw on one side, in order that the blade may be set to any length, according to the circumference of the hole to be cut.

The *spokeshave.*—This is a very useful tool. It is employed for smoothing the edges of round pieces, or other ends requiring to be shaved down. It is a narrow plane, made of box-wood, and has generally a steel blade let

SPOKESHAVE.   BRACE AND BITS.

into it to cut; it is used by taking hold of each end with a hand, and moving it to and fro over the wood to be shaved down.

Brace and Bits.—There are about thirty-six bits to a set, all of different shapes and sizes; but our young friends need not get quite so many; if they provide themselves with a couple of a medium size, this will be sufficient, such as the centre-bit and the auger-bit. The centre-bit will cut holes varying from a quarter of an inch to three-quarters of an inch in diameter, and is used by pressing the knob end against the chest, and twirling the centre part round with the hand. It cuts a hole very clean, leaving it quite smooth inside. The auger-bit is for the same purpose, and is used in the same manner. Another bit, called the taper shell-bit, is used for making holes wider, and is a very useful implement.

The young carpenter should also have the *square*, to lay off work and square the edges; the *compass*, the *brad-awl*, the *hatchet*, the *hammer*—all of whose uses are evident enough—two or three *gimlets*, of assorted sizes, for boring small holes; three *Firmer chisels*, for dressing off the edges of tenons and cleaning out mortises, respectively of one-half inch, three-quarter inch, and inch width; three *mortising-chisels*, of half-inch, three-quarters, and inch and a half in width; you will also want a *chalk-line* for laying out your work; a *two-feet rule* to measure it; and a *mallet* to drive your mortising-chisels.

THE WORKSHOP.

Before proceeding to do any work, you must get some outhouse, or covered shed, for a workshop. In this you must place a workbench. The bench is composed of a platform, or top, supported by four stout legs; A is what is called the bench-hook; this ought to be fitted in tight, so as to

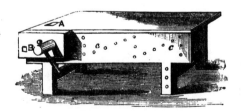

move up and down with a hammer only. The use of it is, to keep any wood steady you may have to plane; B is the bench-screw, used for keeping any wood firm and steady you may have to saw, which is to be put in the grip and screwed tight. Sometimes the edges of wood require to be planed, and then the wood is put in the grip, or cheeks of the bench, and held tight while you plane it. The holes in the side of the bench (*c c*) are for the insertion of a movable pin to support the end of the board you have to plane or saw, which is not in the screw. The height of your bench should be about two feet eight inches. The common length is from ten to twelve feet, and the breadth about three feet six inches.

You will also need a pair of trestles, to hold your plank when you saw it. These you can make yourself, and they should be your first job.

Take a piece of scantling four inches square, and cut off two pieces, each three feet long. Six inches from both ends of each piece make two cuts, two inches apart, slanting at a slight angle. Then cut out those pieces with your large mortising-chisel. Each piece will present the following appearance:

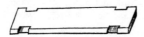

Then get out eight pieces, twenty-four inches long and two inches wide, of inch and a half plank. Insert one end of each of these in one of the

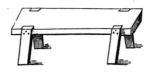

holes cut out in the plank, and nail it there firmly. Serve all the pieces in the same way, and your trestle is complete. On the pair of these you stretch your stuff when you want to saw it.

BOX-MAKING.

We will suppose now that you want to make a box. You may either make it plain or dovetail it. If you wish to make it plain,—say the box is to be fourteen inches wide, fourteen deep, and twenty-four inches long,— you proceed in this way:

Place your plank on the trestles. About an inch from the rough end, scribe a line square across, by means of the square and the points of your compasses. On this line measure fourteen and a half inches. At the point thus made, fasten down one end of your chalk-line with the brad-awl. Carry the other end of the cord to the other end of the plank, chalking it as you go. There lay down another point, fourteen and a half inches from the edge. On that draw the end of your chalk-line, so as to draw the whole line taut by your left hand. Then seize the line with your right hand, as far off as you can reach, and, still holding it tight with your left hand, lift it up and let it suddenly go. You will find the loose chalk deposited all along the line. Remove the brad-awl and the chalk-line, first winding up the latter on a piece of stick. Now take your rip-saw, and begin to saw down the board on that line, sawing with a long, steady stroke, and taking care that the teeth of the saw always bite in the chalk-mark. After you get down a couple of feet, or less, the saw will not work easily. You take a little wedge and drive it in the slit made by the saw, about a foot and a half distant from your saw. You will now find the saw work easily. You remove this wedge and replace it nearer, from time to time, until you have cut the board entirely through.

You now take the plank thus got out and place one end against the catch on your bench, to plane it. You keep it from slipping by driving a thin piece of steel—generally a bit of broken saw-blade—partly into the bottom of the rear end of the board, and partly into the bench. You now jack it off, and then render it truer on the surface with the fore-plane, trying it from time to time with the edge of the square, to see that it is planed even. When it is clean and true, you turn it over and dress the opposite surface. You next draw a line, by means of a piece of straight-edged plank and a pencil, or by the chalk-line—but this should be red chalk—close to the edge, and another opposite, at exactly fourteen inches distant. You place one end of your board in the clamp, and screw it up tight to the side of the bench, supporting the other by a wooden pin thrust in one of the round holes left for that purpose in the bench-side. Plane it, first with the jack and then the foreplane, down to the red line, trying it with the square, so as to get the edge at right angles with the broad side. Then turn it and dress the opposite edge in the same way.

Now take down the board and place it on the trestles. Measure off the following lengths: Four pieces, each twenty-four and an eighth inches, and two pieces, fourteen and an eighth inches, less the thickness of the stuff—that is, if the stuff was originally three-quarters of an inch in thickness, and you have planed it down to five-eighths, your end-pieces must be thirteen inches in length. The extra eighth of an inch is to allow for dressing down the ends smooth, which can be done by planing them down a sixteenth of an inch at each end, with the smoothing or foreplane, securing them for that purpose in the clamp at the side of your bench. As soon as they are all dressed and true on the ends, trying them by your square, the stuff is ready to be put together.

You now take one of the long side-pieces, and, fitting it accurately to the end of one of the short pieces, nail it on with three nails, equidistant, and neither within an inch of the edge. If you are not accustomed to driving truly, you had better first bore holes with your gimlet in those spots in the long piece where you want the nails set. Then serve the other short piece in the same way. Turn over the three pieces thus nailed, and, laying on a long piece on the two uncovered edges, fit it accurately, and nail that on. You have your box now, but without top or bottom. Turn it on either of its edges, apply another of your long boards, and nail it on. There is your box, and the lid is lying beside you.

If you wish to put the four sides of the box together by dovetail, you get out the end-pieces of the full width, allowing an eighth of an inch extra. You then make your dovetail in this manner: Take one of the end-pieces, and place it end up in the clamp of the bench and screw it up. Mark out the dovetails on each end in this way:

Then, with your mitre-saw, cut in into the marks down to the lines squared over on the flat side, like this:

Then, with a chisel, cut out that part of the wood that is crossed, and leave the other part, this being the part which will form the pins or tails. Then take each side of your box and lay it flat on the bench, the inside uppermost; then place the end you have to cut on it, keeping the edges flush, and mark round the shape of the pins, which will leave them after this form:

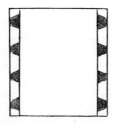

The black pieces represent the mortises, which are to be cut out. In cutting out these you must be careful to cut within side of the stroke, so that the mortises will be a little smaller than the pins, which will admit of their being driven in quite tight, and will allow the glue to adhere to them (for you have to glue these when you fix them). When you have thus put the ends and sides together, let them stand till the glue gets dry; then take your planes and plane  the quarter of an inch off the pins, which you allowed to be a little longer than the length of the box, and you have then made the body of your box. Now nail the bottom on, and "get out" a piece of wood (by cutting and planing in the usual manner) to nail round, so as to form a skirting to it, and at the same time hide the joints of the bottom; "get out" a similar piece of wood to nail round the top, which will form the lid. Then get a pair of box-hinges and put them on.

BOAT-BUILDING.

You cannot so well buy a toy-boat that will really sail. If you want a good one, you must build it yourself, which you can very easily do. To make the hull you will require chisels, a gouge, mallet, saw, plane, and a good knife. Take a piece of white pine, with a straight, fine grain, and mark a line down the middle on two opposite sides and at both ends, then lines equidistant from that to the edge. Then divide it crosswise, first into three and then into six divisions on the top. Then pencil on the top the shape of your boat, as in the illustration. Then draw an inner line, about

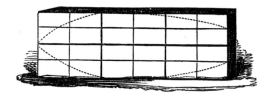

a quarter of an inch, and parallel with the other. Scoop out carefully the inside of this, and fix on it a flush deck, that is, without a raised edge, made of a pine or cypress shingle leaving hatchway holes and a place for the mast. Having done this, cut it on the outside to the shape shown in either of the models given in this article.

The mast should be made of strong light wood, should be tapering, and rather long. The less rigging there is the better; two shrouds and a few stays will be enough. The best models for miniature ships are those vessels that are rigged "fore and aft," such as cutters and schooners; square-rigged ships are unmanageable unless made very large.

Our first illustration shows a model sloop, with her sails set. The principal sail is termed the mainsail; the one above it, the gaff topsail; and the triangular sail attached to the bowsprit, the foresail, or jib.

The blocks used in rigging a model ship are to be made of box-wood or alder. The latter is a softer wood than the former, and can be more readily fashioned into shape with a penknife. The holes for the cords should be bored through the pieces of wood before they are shaped into blocks, as it is not easy to drill the blocks without splitting them. The rudder should be attached to the keel by bent pins. The little staples on the keel, in which the bent pins work, are to be formed of brass wire. The stem of the rudder passes through a hole in the stern of the vessel, and is provided with a tiller. Before launching the ship, the tiller must be fixed so as to keep the rudder at the required angle. Many boys fear to launch their ships in large ponds; but if a ship is properly rigged, and answers to her rudder, there need be no doubt as to her safe arrival in port.

The sail-boat is not so graceful as the sloop, but is a capital sailer. The large sail is called a spritsail, from the spar or sprit which crosses it diagonally from the mast to the upper aftmost corner.

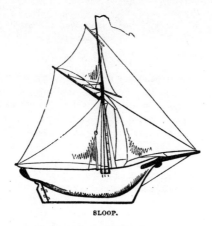

SLOOP.

Model boats, intended for fast sailing, should have but one foresail, as a large balloon jib, rigged with a boom, holds more wind than an ordinary jib and staysail. The ships should be well ballasted, to prevent the wind from capsizing them, and a keel of lead is excellent for this purpose; and their

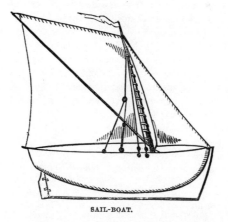

SAIL-BOAT.

topmasts should be made movable, as in rough weather it will be found necessary to "strike" them. Each boat may have two sets of sails—one set large, for light winds, and the other considerably smaller, to be set up when the wind is high. The sails should be made of very light stuff, thin unbleached muslin is best, and should have a line run round them, with loops for hooking them on to the spars. Beware of putting too many blocks and useless ropes about your boats, as the lighter the upper part of a vessel is, the better she will sail. In conclusion, spare no pains in finishing your work neatly, so that your boats may bear witness to your skill and patience.

PAINTING.

A BOY who attempts to paint any thing had better put on a suit of old clothes, otherwise he may ruin his dress, and spoil his temper. Before giving any directions about painting, it will be proper to say something about materials. A boy wants but few of these, as his painting will be mostly confined to his sled, dove-cot, boxes, and flower-pot stands.

BRUSHES.

He will want four brushes:—1. A duster, which should be large, and is used to clear off any particles of dust, before the paint is applied. 2. Two bristle-brushes, one quite small, and the other of moderate size, No. 5, at the shops. 3. A camel's-hair or sable-brush, which he will use for narrow places, where a different color than that on the ground, or main body, has to be employed. Besides this, he will want a long-haired pencil, for drawing lines.

OILS.

Boiled linseed-oil is the only vehicle he should use to thin his colors. A small quantity of drying-oil will be needed, which can be bought of the colorman, and used where quick drying is required.

COLORS.

There are some colors he should avoid, as they are poisonous, and their use attended with danger. These are white-lead, orpiment, and Scheele's green. To be safe, he should obtain only those which we give below, and which can be purchased, ground in oil and ready mixed, at any colorman's:

White, white zinc; *black*, lampblack (this will require a good deal of drying oil, as it is a bad drier); *red*, vermilion, Indian red; *blue*, French ultramarine; *yellow*, chrome yellow, yellow ochre, burnt sienna; *green*, chrome green; *brown*, burnt umber.

With these he can make a variety of shades, by mixing as follows:

Purple	French ultramarine... 2 parts.		Green	French ultramarine... 1 part.
	Vermilion............ 1 "			Yellow ochre......... 1 "
Cream	Yellow ochre.... .... 1 "			Lampblack........... 1 "
	White zinc........... 1 "		Green	French ultramarine... 1 "
Sky-blue	French ultramarine... 1 "			Chrome yellow....... 2 "
	White zinc........... 1 "			French ultramarine... 2 "
Green	French ultramarine... 1 "		Green	Chrome yellow....... 2 "
	Chrome yellow....... 1 "			White zinc........... 1 "

And so on, through puces, drabs, and the whole range of neutral tints—remembering that blue is a cold, and red and yellow warm colors ; and that a delicate tint can be given to white by a slight mixture of one or other of these colors.

HOW TO PAINT.

Having seen that your wood is dry, and dusted it, apply a ground, or first coat of color, rather thin—that is, pretty well diluted with oil. Lay it on thinly and evenly, and work it well into the wood. Then place it, if possible, with its face to the wall, and where no dust will get at it, and let it dry. See that all parts are covered.

When dry lay on the second coat. The paint must be of a thicker consistence, but do not lay it on too thick. Take up the color in the brush, and draw both sides of the brush over the edge of the paint-pot, to remove superfluous color and prevent dripping. Then lay it on evenly, drawing the brush to and fro, till it is properly spread. Let it dry as before.

When you go to draw lines, you charge your pencil with color, removing superfluous color, as you did with the paint-brush, and, guiding yourself by a straight-edge, draw it down the proposed line, which had better be first marked by a soft lead-pencil, or a piece of chalk.

A little practice will soon make you perfect.

When you have done painting, cover up your paint-pots carefully, and clean your brushes.

The best mode of cleaning brushes is by first removing all the color you can with a soft rag, and then wash your brush out in a thick soap-lather, and, afterward, plenty of water to remove the soap. Rubbing them on a piece of soap will do, if you wash the soap well out. Or, after removing the color by a rag, you may let the hair end of the brushes be immersed in water.

Put every thing away in a proper place, and out of reach of the smaller children.

THE RAW MATERIAL.

GARDENING.

THE size of a garden depends on circumstances. In a city it is almost out of the question, and the only chance a boy has there is to cultivate his flowers in pots. In the suburbs, a few yards square can generally be had, and in the country, a great deal more. We will assume that our young readers can get a moderately large space for gardening purposes; and give them the requisite information. If they have less, they must act accordingly.

LAYING OUT THE GARDEN.

A piece of ground for the young gardener should be free from trees, not even fruit-trees being allowed on it, and ought to be about fifty feet by one hundred. It should be divided into twelve parts, as shown in the diagram. The main-path (A A) and cross-path (B B) should cross each other at right

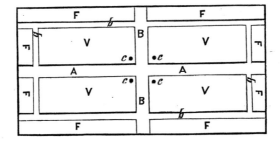

angles, and should each be four feet in width. A two-feet path (*b b b b*) should be laid out at six feet from the outer edge of the parallelogram. This leaves four main vegetable-beds (V V V V), each fifteen feet by forty feet, and a skirting flower-bed (F F F F), two hundred and fifty-two feet by six. If the ground be larger or smaller, it may be laid out on the same plan.

STATIONARY PLANTS.

Perennial plants that bear fruit should have their place in the garden; not fruit-trees, as these take up too much room, but the small fruits, such as currants, gooseberries, raspberries, and blackberries. These should be placed along the edges of the main and cross-paths. At the corners, where the two large paths meet, you may plant four climbing-roses, of different colors—say white, red, crimson, and yellow; to be supported on a light arbor, to be composed of four stout posts set at *c c c c*, and suitable cross-pieces and slats. In planting your currant and other bushes, the ground should be dug out two feet deep, and of dimensions sufficient to allow the longest roots to be laid out at full length. This should be filled in with garden-mould and mixed turf, the latter broken in small pieces, and the whole well mixed with *well-rotted* stable-manure, and a spadeful of wood ashes. The bush should be placed in this so that it sets not quite as deep as it did in its original state, to allow for settling. The earth is to be set carefully around the roots, a little water then sprinkled on, and supported, if need be, by stakes. This planting may be done in fall, after the leaves have dropped, or in spring, before they start. If in autumn, the bushes should be mulched—that is, leaves should be thickly strewn on the freshly-put-in earth.

TOOLS.

The principal tools you will require are—1. The spade. 2. The digging-fork. 3. Hoes. 4. The rake. 5. The planting-trowel. 6. The dibber. 7. The reel and line. 8. The wheelbarrow. 9. The watering-pot.

The *spade* should be steel-pointed, light, and sharp. The *digging-fork* should have four steel tines, or teeth. The *hoes* required are three—the narrow and broad hoe, and the Dutch, or scuffle-hoe, the latter used by thrusting instead of drawing. The *rake*, for your purpose, should be of wrought iron, the new-fashioned malleable iron rakes being almost worthless, and should have about eight teeth, which will do for general use; though one with twelve teeth additional will be useful. The *planting-trowel*, which differs from the ordinary trowel in being curved at the sides, is indispensable for taking up and setting out plants, without disturbing their roots. The *dibble* is nothing but the handle of an old spade, sharpened and shod with iron, and is used for making holes in planting peas or beans, or setting out cabbage and other plants. The *reel* and *line* is useful in marking out lines, although you can get on with a cord and two stakes, if you are not able to get the reel. The *wheelbarrow* should be of the kind used in building railroads, without side-boards. The *watering-pot* should be of medium size, with two roses, or sprinklers, one of which has large and the other fine holes.

PREPARING THE GROUND.

All ground should be dug up one spade-length, and turned over; but, in preparing for root-crops, it should be trenched. To trench a bed, you proceed in this way: You dig the earth out a foot wide and one spade deep, across your bed, and then wheel it down the path to the other end of the bed, disposing it in a long row. You then return, and dig in the same place another spade deep, turning it over and breaking it loosely. You then dig a spade deep a foot farther in the bed, and throw the earth on the place you have just loosened. When that last part is uncovered, you loosen the spade-length below, and then throw the upper spadeful from the next foot back on that, and so you continue until you come to the dirt you have previously deposited at the other end, which you throw in the last vacant space. Thus your earth is loosened about eighteen inches deep, and the roots of your parsnips, carrots, etc., can penetrate downward without trouble. Besides, water descends quicker in rainy, and rises easier in dry weather, in a soil so prepared, especially if it be kept well stirred with the earthfork.

If you apply manure, it may be dug in, or forked in, the latter being preferable. This does not apply to where you trench for root-crops, for fresh manure is not put to roots, as it would make them fork and branch.

Remember, ground must be made loose at the beginning, and kept loose, if you want to have fine flowers and good crops of vegetables.

WEEDING.

The ground must be kept clear of weeds. Attack them when young, especially after a rain. Destroy them in the rows with a hoe, and finish by careful hand-weeding between the plants. Weeds may be thrown on the manure-heap, but not if you have let them go to seed. In that case, they must be left to dry in a corner and be burned.

PLANTING.

After the ground has been thoroughly broken, it must be raked, to make it finer, where small seeds have to be planted. Sow nothing broadcast, as it leads to slovenly cultivation. Plant in drills or hills, as laid down hereafter, under the head of "the plants." Always transplant on a damp or cloudy day, if possible, and toward evening. If it be continued hot weather, shade the newly transplanted plants by a piece of paper fastened to two sticks, or in some other way. In transplanting, if possible, make your hole first, then take the plant from the seed-bed with your trowel, and set it carefully in its place. If the plants cannot be got out with the ball of earth whole, make a hole with the dibber, and, holding your plant in the left hand, set its roots in the hole, fill up with earth, moisten it with a little water, put fresh earth around it, and press it lightly. In transplanting from pots, lay your hand on the top of the pot, with the stem of the plant between the second and third fingers. Invert the pot, letting it rest on the left hand. Tap the bottom of the pot gently with your planting-trowel, and the plant and ball of earth will come into your hand. Remove the pot, and set the plant and ball of earth carefully in the hole prepared to receive it. After transplanting, water your plants moderately in the evening, and slightly early in the morning; but do not keep them too wet. Remember never to water during the middle of the day, unless the weather be cool, and the sun has little power; and sprinkle water, do not pour it.

VARIOUS MODES OF PROPAGATION.

Plants are reproduced or propagated in various ways; some by seeds, some by offsets, as tulips and hyacinths; some by dividing the root, some by layers, some by cuttings. Currant and gooseberry trees, as well as rose-trees, and also the vine, are propagated by cuttings; *i.e.*, pieces of the young last-year branches are cut off about six inches in length, and, the top being taken off, are placed with the thickest end in the ground. Strawberries are reproduced by dividing the root, or by taking the runner which the plant has itself fixed in the ground as the nucleus of a new plant, and putting it in a proper situation. Raspberries give out suckers from the parent root, which may be taken off and replanted, like the lilac, the rose, and many other plants; but in taking them off, which is generally done by a spade, they should be taken pretty near to the parent stem, and should have fibrous roots attached. In taking offsets, such as those of bulbous roots, it is only necessary to take those which nature herself separates from the parent bulb; in tubers, such as the artichoke and potato, the tubers of middle size are to be taken and planted; or in regard to the latter root, the eyes or shoots only are sometimes planted, the root being cut into various portions.

LAYERS.

If we observe the strawberry plant, we find that at a certain season of the year it throws out offsets, and at certain distances a knob or knot arises, from which roots shoot into the earth, while from its upper centre a bud appears, and then a new plant is formed. The process of layering is to artificially produce this, and similar operations of nature. Some plants throw out roots whenever their stump or branches come in contact with the soil, but others require the assistance of art. The art of layering, therefore, consists in taking the shoot of a growing plant as near the root as possible; this is first to be cut half through, and then a slit is made in an upward direction, and, a piece of twig being placed in the divided part, the shoot is pegged down with the joint buried in the ground. After a time this joint begins to throw out roots, and when these are firmly established and begin to draw nutriment from the earth, the shoot may be detached from its parent stem, and it then becomes a new plant. Layers may be made in the spring months, and also in the month of July.

PIPINGS

Are cuttings of carnations, pinks, etc. They are tubular stems, having joints at certain distances, and they are pulled asunder by the fingers at these joints; the lower leaves are then pulled off, and the pipe is placed in some nicely prepared soil, leaving its upper portion, consisting of the sprouting leaf-bud, to grow, while the lower pipe shoots into a root.

GRAFTING.

Grafting, inarching, and budding, are generally performed in the month of March. The operation of inarching is sometimes performed by nature. When two branches of a tree lie in contact, the rough winds of winter often cause them to rub against each other, so that a wound is produced in one or both, and the juices that flow from the wounded parts gradually cause an incorporation of the substances, so that the two branches become united into one. This is not to be wondered at in branches of the same tree, or in those of the same kind, but it is a matter of some surprise to find that a tree bearing small and unpalatable fruit may be cut down, and the remaining part grafted with a scion from a species bearing large and delicious fruit, instead of the small sour fruit of the stalk. Thus it is then that by grafting, we preserve and multiply a favored variety of trees, which could not be propagated from seeds with any certainty of success.

In order to the full success of this operation, grafting must be performed according to the rules that experience has laid down. The first is to graft or unite only such species as have a relationship subsisting between them. The operation never succeeds unless this union of nature is attended to, and the plants belong to the same genus. The next rule requires that the inner bark of the scion, and the inner bark of the stalk, be exactly united together, in order to facilitate the free course of the sap.

The most common method of grafting is whip-grafting, or tongue-grafting. The name of whip-grafting is given from the method of cutting the stock and the scion sloping on one side, so as to fit each other, and then tying them together in the manner of a whip-thong to the shaft or handle. The scion and stock are cut obliquely, and as nearly as possible at corresponding angles. The top of the stock is then cut off nearly horizontally, and a slit is made near the centre of it downwards, and a similar one in the scion upwards. The tongue, or wedge-like process forming the upper part of the sloping face of the scion, is then inserted downwards in the cleft of the stock, the inner barks being brought closely to unite on one side, so as not to be displaced by tying, which ought to be done immediately with a ribbon, or matting, or bass, brought in a neat manner several times round the stock. The next operation is to clay the whole over an inch thick all round, for about half an inch or more below the bottom of the graft to an inch over the top of the stock, finishing the coat of clay in a kind of oval form, closing it effectually, so that no light, wet, nor wind, may penetrate.

TONGUE-GRAFTING.

Tongue-grafting is not very different to whip-grafting, and is performed as follows: The stock being ready, cut it off at three or four inches from the ground, and, with a very sharp, straight, and narrow-bladed knife, cut a thin slip of wood and bark upwards from about two inches below the top of the shortened stock. Make this cut at one pull of the knife, inserting the edge rather horizontally, and when it has gone through the bark and into the wood a little short of the middle, pull straight upwards. Then at less than half-way down this cut a thin tongue, not more than three-eighths of an inch long. Proceed in the same way with the thick part of the scion, making a sloping cut of about the same length as the cut of the stock, and make a tongue to correspond with that in the stock. Bring the four edges of the bark, that is, the two edges of the cut in the top of the stock and the two corresponding edges of the cut in the bottom of the scion, to meet precisely, which can never be the case unless the first cut in the stock and that in the scion is even as a die, and performed with a knife as sharp as a razor.   The two parts thus formed, the tongues and the stock clasping one another, must be bound up as before.

BUDDING.

Budding is the art of taking a bud from one tree and making it grow on another.   A bud can only be planted upon a tree of the same kind as itself, and the operation is generally performed in the month of August.   The bud should be taken from a shoot of the same year's growth, and, in taking it, should be neatly cut out by incisions made above it, below it, and longitudinally on either side, and the piece taken should include the bud, without injury to the bark, and a small piece of wood of an oblong form pointed at its extremity.   A place is now cut to receive the bud in the shoot of a stock, and the best place is near the fork of a branch; the method of cutting is similar to that adopted for taking out the bud, and the bark is open on both sides of the slit, and the piece of bark to which the bud is attached is then filled in, and the bark of the stock closed over it; the two parts are then bound together with strips of fresh matting, tied in bows and ends, for the purpose of being easily loosened as the bud increases in growth. The operation of budding requires the aid of a budding-knife, which may be readily purchased, and the success of the operation depends upon the care and nicety with which it is performed.

INARCHING.

We have already mentioned how nature performs what is called inarching. The gardener's art consists simply in bending a branch partly cut through, and inserting the belt thus formed into a slit made downwards in the stock to receive it.   The parts, being nicely fitted, are bound with matting.   In five or six months the head of the stock may be cut off, and the plant removed.

GRAFTING-CLAY.

Most of the operations of grafting require clay to be put round the parts. This is made of three parts of stiff yellow clay to one of horse-dung, fresh as it falls, with a little cut hay, well mixed together; another kind of clay is made of a pound of pitch and a pound of yellow wax, mixed with two pounds of cow-dung.   The use of them in covering the grafting-posts is to keep them moist and cool till a proper union has taken place.

PRUNING.

The proper time for pruning trees is in December or January, for then the sap is down, and no injury can be done; and the art in pruning consists

25

in cutting away the "water-shoots," or non-bearing wood, "dead wood," and "superfluous wood." The water-shoots, as they are called, appear to be strong growing branches, but generally produce neither flowers nor fruit; the superfluous wood are those shoots which grow in the way of each other, or cross each other, which should always be removed. The great principle in pruning a fruit-tree is to leave all the tree free and open, so that the air and sunshine may pass through it, and to preserve the buds of the bearing wood. The shoots should be cut off as near to the stem or branch as possible, and all growths or suckers which appear below the crown of the tree should be taken off. The present practice of thumb-pruning is very excellent; by this means the superfluous shoots, etc., are removed by the thumb-nail as soon as they appear, and thus the tree does not exhaust itself by the growth of useless wood. The young pruner should be very careful in cutting away, and recollect that what he cuts off he cannot put on again.

TRAINING.

The training of trees applies principally to those that are fastened to wooden trellises, to poles, or to walls. The principle of the art is to extend the bearing branches of a tree or plant, so as to improve its growth, its beauty, and its produce. Peaches, nectarines, apricots, vines, etc., are trained against walls by shreds of cloth being placed round the branches and the two ends nailed to the wall. In doing this, care should be taken to give the branch room to pl... , and yet to confine it, not to hurt the tender fruit-shoots in the operation, and to let all the branches be free of each other. Roses and jasmines are often trained round verandas by their different parts being tied with ropes' end or tarred twine to different parts of the trellis-work. Sometimes flowers are trained by being tied to stakes or long poles, and others are brought to pass through the round of an ornamental ladder, or through the meshes of wirework of different forms. But in every kind of training the principle is the same, namely, that of keeping the branches clear of each other, and of preserving the flowering and bearing shoots. Neatness and taste are also indispensable requisites to the training and management of trees and flowers, whether for use or ornament.

PROTECTION FROM FROST.

The common fruit and rose bushes of the garden require but little care as regards frost, but many plants and shrubs, coming originally from warmer climates, require much attention during winter to keep them alive. It is useless to attempt preserving geraniums, myrtles, and a great many of our common summer plants, without preserving them through the winter in a greenhouse of some kind or other. A small greenhouse may now be cheaply erected, but for the preservation of a small number of plants the greenhouse pit is the cheapest and most convenient substitute. It consists only of a hole, twelve feet by four, dug in the ground to the depth of six feet, having at the top a skylight. It should, if possible, be dug in a sheltered situation, open to the south and well backed behind, and the glass-top, which should merely consist of one frame laid in a slanting position to the south over the top of the hole, the back of which is raised to support it, the front being slightly lowered. The entrance to the pit is at the side, to which a stout wooden door, nailed over with straw bands, should be attached, and two or three steps should lead to the interior of the pit, where a few shelves may be arranged upon which to place the flowers, etc. In this pit flowers, cuttings, bulbs, and a variety of other things, may be preserved through the winter, with very little cost or trouble, and it will be of a great deal of use in many other respects.

A very simple contrivance, which may be used to facilitate the blooming of flowers, and other small plants, is shown in the cut—a common square box, without top or bottom. On the upper edge is fastened a rabbeted frame, the groove of which receives the pane of common glass *a*. The inclination should be such that the rays of the sun will fall perpendicularly upon it at some part of the day. Lay around the bottom of the box, and over the adjoining ground for a few feet, leaves, or litter, to keep it a little warm. Plants thus

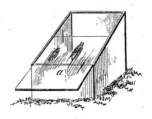

enclosed must receive due ventilation, and some water, as in a hotbed. You can get earlier violets, daisies, etc., by this method than by any other.

HOTBED.

The young gardener near our large cities can generally get a few egg-plants, tomato-plants, or peppers, of the seedsmen, for a trifle, or in the country, of the neighboring market-gardeners; but if he desires to raise them for himself, he will require a hotbed. This is easily made. He will require a sash, differing from a window-sash in having no cross-bars, the different panes of glass being laid edge on edge, like the shingles of a roof; and also a frame to receive it, which should be higher at the back than front, so as to let the rain and snow run off. Hotbeds for vegetables should be prepared and ready for planting early in March.

They are usually made of about the following proportions: Four feet wide, and six feet long; two feet high behind; one foot in front, facing the south. The top should be covered with glass, to be removed in warm weather, and for ventilation.

Choose a sheltered part of the garden, and have a pile of *fresh* stable manure deposited, mixed with some dead leaves. Make a heap three feet high, and wide enough to receive your frame. This may be done about February, in the latitude of New York—earlier if farther south, later if farther north. Let it stand forty-eight hours, then put on your frame, and fill in about three inches of fine light soil, and put on your sash, raising it when necessary to let off steam. When the heat has somewhat subsided, sow your seeds in drills. Water occasionally, so as to keep moist. When the plants show themselves, and as they grow, tilt the sash occasionally on fine days, to give air. You will have to watch them. As the spring opens, give more air, and longer, so as to strengthen the plants. When the time comes you can transplant them into thumb-pots, for greater precaution, or into the open ground. A little practice will soon make you manage a hotbed very well.

FLOWERS.

When flowers flower and die in one season, they are called *Annuals;* when they flower in the second year, *Biennials;* and when they flower year after year, *Perennials.* Annuals are generally sown as soon as the weather opens in spring, and from that to May or June, for a succession. Certain tender flowers must be sown not earlier than May. Some, as the cypress flower, require to be soaked in warm water previous to planting. We give a list of the most preferable flowering plants for the young gardener. The letters of reference are as follows:

Character.—*a.*, annual; *b.*, biennial; *p.*, perennial; *t.*, tender; *h.*, hardy; *hh.*, half-hardy; *c.*, climbing plant.

Color of Flower.—*di.*, diverse; *w.*, white; *b.*, blue; *r.*, red; *ros.*, rose-colored; *d.*, dark; *bl.*, black; *y.*, yellow; *li.*, lilac; *str.*, striped; *var.*, variegated; *tri.*, three-colored; *s.*, scarlet; *cr.*, crimson; *br.*, brown; *v.*, violet; *p.*, purple.

The figures give about the height, in inches, to which the plant attains. The names in italics signify that they should not be transplanted.

The hardy annuals may be sown in the open ground in May, or, if desired for a succession, from that to June; the half-hardy annuals a little later; the tender ones in the same way with the half-hardy, or in pots in the house, and carefully transplanted with the ball of earth entire. The hardy and half-hardy should be sown in fine rich soil, in rich patches, in drills, from an inch down to an eighth of an inch deep. Transplant in cloudy or rainy weather. The tender annuals require light, sandy soil, with rich compost of rotted leaves and manure.

The biennials and perennials are treated like the others, according to their hardiness. Those in the ground may be divided and set out in spring, furnishing new plants. A good plan is to have all plants in beds, giving a mass of bloom; and tall, naked plants should be placed among bushy, low growers, to conceal their naked stems.

LIST OF FLOWERS.

* Those marked with a star particularly recommended.

COMMON NAME.	Duration, etc.	Color.	Average height.	SCIENTIFIC NAME.
Rose Acroclinium..........	*hhA.*	*ros.*	18	Acroclinium roseum.
Adonis Flower..............	*hA.*	*s.*	12	Adonis æstivalis.
Mexican Ageratum.........	*hA.*	*b.*	30	Ageratum Mexicanum.
Rose Campion..............	*hP.*	*ros.*	12	Agrostemma coronaria.
White Campion.............	*hP.*	*w.*	12	*———— ———— alba.
Crimson Campion..........	*hP.*	*cr.*	12	———— ———— kermesina.
Sweet Alyssum.............	*hA.*	*w.*	6	*Alyssum maritimum.
Napoleon Anagallis........	*hhP.*	*d. r.*	12	Anagallis grandiflora Napoleon.
Memorial Anagallis........	*hhP.*	*b.*	12	———— ———— memoria d'Etna.
Triumph Anagallis.........	*hhP.*	*di.*	12	———— trionfo di Firenze.
Shrubby Anagallis.........	*hhP.*	*s.*	12	———— fruticosa.
Blue Hibiscus..............	*hA.*	*b.*	24	Anoda dilleniana.
Scarlet Snapdragon.........	*hP.*	*s.*	24	Antirrhinum coccineum.
Dwarf Crimson Snapdragon.	*hP.*	*cr.*	12	*———— crescium.
Yellow Snapdragon........	*hP.*	*y.*	24	———— flavum.
Striped Columbine.........	*hP.*	*str.*	24	Aquilegia cariophyloides.
Skinner's Columbine.......	*hP.*	*s. & y.*	18	———— Skinneri.
Mexican Poppy............	*hA.*	*w.*	36	Argemone grandiflora.
Mixed German Aster.......	*hhA.*	*di.*	18	Aster fistulosus pleno.
Mixed Globe Aster.........	*hhA.*	*di.*	18	*———— Chinensis globularis.
Mixed Pompon Aster.......	*hhA.*	*di.*	12	———— navissimus.
Double-mixed Balsams.....	*hhA.*	*di.*	24	*Balsamina hortensis flora pleno.
Southern Baptisia.....	*hP.*	*b.*	24	Baptisia australis.
Tassel-Flower	*hA.*	*s.*	12	Cæcalia coccinea.
Marbled Coreopsis..........	*hA.*	*y. & r.*	18	Calliopsis bicolor marmorata.
Crowned Coreopsis.........	*hA.*	*spot.*	18	*———— coronata.
Scarlet Coxcomb............	*tA.*	*s.*	24	Celosia cristata coccinea.
Dwarf Coxcomb.............	*tA.*	*y.*	24	———— lutea.
Rose Centranthus..........	*hA.*	*ros.*	12	*Centranthus macrosiphon.
Great Blue-Bottle...........	*hA.*	*di.*	24	Centaurea cyanus.
Mixed Chrysanthemum.....	*hA.*	*di.*	36	Chrysanthemum album.
Elegant Clarkia......... ..	*hA.*	*li.*	18	Clarkia elegans.
White Collinsia.............	*hA.*	*w.*	6	Collinsia alba.
Scarlet Collomia............	*hA.*	*s. & y.*	12	Collomia coccinea.
Mixed Morning-Glory, c.....	*hA.*	*di.*	120	Convolvulus major.
Bottle Gourd, c.............	*tA.*	*y.*	96	Cucurbita lagenaria.
Wright's Datura........	*hA.*	*w.*	24	*Datura metalloides.
Rocket Larkspur.....	*hA.*	*di.*	12	Delphinium ajacis.
Large-flowered Larkspur....	*hP.*	*d. b.*	24	*———— grandiflorum.
Sweet-William..	*hP.*	*di.*	18	Dianthus barbatus.
Mixed Carnations..........	*hhP.*	*di.*	24	———— carophyllus.
Mixed China Pink..........	*hB.*	*di.*	6	———— Chinensis navus.
Double-clove Pink..........	*hP.*	*di.*	12	———— hybridus corymbosus.
Blue Didiscus..............	*hhA.*	*b.*	24	Didiscus cerulea.
Double Eternal Flower......	*hA.*	*di.*	12	*Elichysum bracteatum amp.
African Hibiscus............	*hA.*	*ro&br*	24	Hibiscus Africanus.

LIST OF FLOWERS.—*Continued.*

* Those marked with a star particularly recommended.

COMMON NAME.	Duration, etc.	Color.	Average height	SCIENTIFIC NAME.
Scarlet Morning-Glory.......	hA.	s.	120	*Ipomea coccinea.
Mixed Cypress Flowers.....	tA.	di.	120	*——— quamoclit.
Blue Kaulfussia.	hA.	b.	12	*Kaulfussia amelloides.
Mixed Sweet Peas.........	hA.	di.	48	*Lathyrus odoratus.
White Leptosiphon..........	hA.	w.	12	Leptosiphon androsaceus alb.
Texan Linhemeria.........	hA.	y.	24	Lindheimeria Texana.
Crimson Flax..............	hA.	cr.	8	*Linum kermesinum.
Scarlet Lychnis.............	hhP.	s.	36	*Lychnis chalcedonica.
White Lychnis...	hP.	w.	36	*——— alba.
Crimson Lychnis............	hP.	cr.	18	*——— flos Jovis.
Bunchy Corymbosa.........	hA.	w.	18	*Madaria corymbosa.
Mixed German Stock........	hhA.	di.	12	*Mathiola annua densifl.
Mixed Nizella.....	hA.	di.	12	Nigella damascena.
Mixed Poppies..............	hA.	di.	36	Papaverum superbum.
Drummond's Phlox.........	hA.	di.	12	*Phlox Drummondii.
Mixed Portulacca...	hA.	di.	6	*Portulacca splendens, var.
Scarlet Scabious.............	hP.	s.	12	*Scabiosa coccinea.
Mourning Bride.............	hP.	p.	24	*——— atropurpurea.
Crimson Scabious	h P	cr	12	*——— kermesina.
Blood-colored Nasturtium...	hA.	d. r.	60	*Tropæolum atrosanguinea.
Large-flowered Whitlavia...	hhA.	b.	12	*Whitlavia grandiflora.
New Dwarf Marigold........	hA.	y.	18	Tagetes signata pumila.

DAHLIAS.

Dig a hole two feet square and eighteen inches deep. Fill up with rich earth, composted with rotten manure. Sprout your dahlia-roots, and set out the sprouts in thumb-pots. About latter part of May or beginning of June set them out, first driving a stake, about four feet long, firmly into the centre of the new-made bed. Mulch during summer with manure. Thin out superfluous branches. Tie up to stake as they grow. Pinch off the first flower-bud. Take up the roots when the frost has killed the tops, and store them in sand, in a dry place. The following varieties are very fine, but new ones are continually appearing:

Jean Caluche.—Pale yellow.

Ariana.—Lilac, globe-shaped; *General Scott*, rosy lilac.

Grand Duke Nicolaiewicz, Julia.—Carmine.

Crepuscula.—Orange-red; *Chairman*, buff.

Duke de Malakoff.—Blood-red; *Beauty*, claret.

Glory of France.—Light purple; *Mrs. Edwards*, rose.

Mad. Guinott, Vesta.—Pure white.

Brilliant, Dr. Bozes.—Scarlet; *Ruby Queen*, crimson.

Othello.—Dark purple; *Miss Caroline*, blush.

Captain Ingram.—Maroon; *Lady Paxton*, red, white-striped.
Monseigneur Silnu.—Peach-lilac.
Polyphemus.—Buff, striped and spotted with crimson.
Gold Vaalle.—Clear yellow.
Lr. Guelly.—Yellow, purple-tipped.
Mutabilis.—Red, lilac-tipped.
Imperatrice Eugenia.—White, crimson-edged.
Lady Cathcart.—White, lilac-tipped.
Le Defi.—Salmon, scarlet-striped.
The Flirt.—Salmon, purple-striped.
Polyphemus.—Buff, crimson-striped and spotted.
Henry Saison.—Violet, white-tipped
Warrior.—Bronze.

BEDDING PLANTS.

These are Verbenas, Petunias, Lantanas, Heliotropes, Gazanias, Pansies, and Salvias, in great variety. You will have to get these from the florist, who will always furnish you directions for their management.

GARDEN VEGETABLES.

You will raise the principal ones of these as follows:

ASPARAGUS.—Make a bed in this way: Dig out three feet, as wide and long as you desire it. Make a layer of bones and stones for a drain. On this lay brushwood and well-broken sod—the whole twelve inches thick. Fill in with sandy loam, stable-manure, and sea or river sand (not earth sand, or sand containing iron), well mixed. On this lay your roots, in foot rows, and eighteen inches apart, and cover with four inches of same compost. Just before winter, cover the bed six inches deep with manure, which you fork-in slightly in spring, after giving it a thick dressing of fine salt.

BEANS—DWARF OR SNAP.—The best varieties are: 1. Early Valentine. 2. Early Mohawk. 3. Early Rachel. 4. Refugee. 5. Large White Kidney—the two latter for main crop. Do not plant until danger from frost is past; and then in drills, eighteen inches in the rows, the beans two inches deep, and two inches apart. Hoe deeply, and draw up earth to plants.

BEANS—POLE.—The best are: 1. White Cranberry. 2. Large White Lima. Plant the first as soon as the night-frosts are past; the latter about 1st of June, in hills three feet by four. Set the poles just before you plant. Watch the weeds well, and cultivate cleanly.

BEET.—1. Early Blood Turnip. 2. Long Blood.—Sow three or four seeds eight inches apart, and eighteen inches between the rows; and when up well and strong, thin out to one in each place. Or sow in drills, in a seed-bed, and transplant the first damp day, after they are two inches high.

BROCCOLI.—Early Purple Cape.—Sow as soon as the ground can be worked in spring, in seed-bed. Set out when plants are four inches high, in hills two feet each way, and cultivate same as cabbages.

CABBAGE.—1. Early York. 2. Early Winning Stadt. 3. Large Late Drumhead.—Sow the early sorts in hotbed, and transplant in May, in two-foot rows, eighteen inches apart. Sow Drumhead in May, and transplant in July, setting them three feet apart. Cultivate deeply, and see that the ground has plenty of manure.

CARROT.—1. Early Horn. 2. Long Orange.—Sow the first as early as the spring opens; the latter, from middle of May to middle of July. The former thin out to five inches in row; the latter, to seven—the rows fourteen inches apart. Dig deep, and plant in ground that has been richly manured the year before.

CELERY—Giant White.—Sow in hotbed, or on warm border, half an inch deep. Thin out plants, when up, to an inch apart, and when they are strong, dig a trench fifteen inches wide, and nine deep. Put three inches of well-rotted manure in the bottom of the trench, pare the sides with the spade, and dig in the parings and dung, with a little of the bottom of the trench. Put the plants in two rows six inches apart, and eight inches between the rows. Water well after planting. As the plants grow, earth them up, and keep the earth loose in the trenches with a fork.

CORN.—Avoid this in a small garden; but if you wish a little early, plant a row of Extra Early Dwarf Sugar, which only grows three feet high, the plants one foot apart. Give it plenty of coarse stable-manure, rank as you choose. It is a gross feeder. Keep it well hoed.

CUCUMBER.—1. Early White Spined. 2. Long Green.—Plant four or five seeds in a sod, which lay, with the turf side down, in your hotbed. When the night-frosts are gone, set the plants, sod and all, in hills, four feet apart. Put a shovelful of wood-ashes, and another of rotted manure, in every hill. Or, plant out as soon as the weather becomes settled, eight or ten seeds in a hill, thinning out the plants to three in a hill. Watch, early in the morning, for the striped yellow bug, which catch and kill. Hoe up, and work well. When the first shoot is well made, pinch off its end, to make it throw out side-shoots.

EGG-PLANT.—Long Purple.—You only want a few plants, which you can buy. If not, sow in hotbed very early in spring, and when two inches high, thin to four inches apart. When the weather becomes perfectly warm, set out two feet apart. Water the plants, if the weather is hot. Draw the earth well up to each plant, and hoe frequently.

LEEK.—Large Flag.—Sow early, in narrow drills, an inch deep. Thin out, when up, to an inch apart. When six or seven inches high, cut an inch or so off the tops, and set the plants out deep, in rows twelve inches apart, and six inches in the row. The soil should be rich.

LETTUCE.—1. Early Silesia. 2. Ice Drumhead. 3. Brown Dutch.—Sow the Silesia as early as possible, in rich ground. Sow Ice Drumhead in April, May, and June, for succession. Set the plants out one foot apart each way. Hoe well and water well, and, if the ground is good, you will have good heads. Sow the Brown Dutch in September.

MUSK-MELON.—1. Early Christina. 2. Green Citron. 3. Allen's Superb.—Plant in hills, six feet apart each way, early in May, with a shovelful of wood-ashes, and one of well-rotted manure, worked in each hill. Put seven or eight seeds in a hill, and treat, as to thinning out, pinching shoots, etc., as directed for cucumbers.

WATER-MELON.—1. Orange. 2. Mountain Sweet. 3. Black Spanish.—Treat the same as musk-melons, but allow the hills eight feet each way.

NASTURTIUM.—Sow in May, in drills an inch deep. Let them have a frame about six feet high, to climb on.

OKRA.—Plant, latter part of May, in drills three feet apart, and nine inches in the row. Put in three or four seeds, and when up thin out to one. Hoe, and draw earth to stems.

ONION.—1. Yellow Dutch. 2. White Portugal.—The soil must be very rich and light. Dig deep, and make fine with the rake. Sow early, in drills twelve inches apart, and one inch deep. Thin out to four inches apart. Or, put the sets *on* the ground, not in it, in drills twelve inches apart, leaving four inches between each set.

PARSLEY.—Soak the seed in warm water for six hours, and sow early in spring, in twelve-inch drills, one inch deep. Thin out, when up, to four inches apart.

PARSNIP.—Hollow Crowned, or Guernsey.—Sow as soon as ground opens, in fifteen-inch drills, an inch deep. Thin out, when well up, to seven inches. Or plant in September, and cover during winter with brush and straw. Hoe well and often.

PEAS.—1. Princess. 2. Warwick. 3. Blue Imperial. 4. Champion of England. 5. White Marrowfat.—We give them in the order of their earliness. The soil must be light, dry, and moderately rich. Plant as early as the ground opens, and thin every two weeks, so as to have a succession during the season. Plant in double drills from three to six feet apart, three inches deep, and an inch apart in the row. When up, stick brushwood for them to climb on. If they are slow in blossoming, run a spade along the row, about eight inches from the plants, and straight down the length of the blade, so as to root prune them.

PEPPER.—1. Mountain Sweet. 2. Long Red Cayenne.—The first for pickles; the second is used dry. Sow in hotbed, or in open ground, about April, and transplant to light ground, in a warm situation. Set them eighteen inches apart each way, and work well.

POTATO.—1. Early Algiers. 2. Garnet Chili. 3. Biscuit.—Plant early in good, rich soil. Give a shovelful of well-rotted manure and ashes, and a handful of plaster to each hill. Hoe well and keep clear of weeds. Before planting, cut your potatoes, so as to allow two eyes to a set. Keep the pieces in a dry place four or five days before planting.

PUMPKIN.—You had better not plant this in your garden at all. It is a field-plant. If you do grow it, the Cashaw is the only fit variety, and you treat it as you do the larger squashes.

25*

RADISH.—1. Long Scarlet Short-top. 2. White Summer Turnip. 3. Scarlet Chinese Winter.—Sow the long scarlet as early as you can work the ground, in rows twelve inches apart, and thin to two inches in the row; and every two weeks for succession, the white summer turnip, in June till August, and thin to three inches; the scarlet Chinese, the first of September, and thin to six inches. Work well and choose a moderately rich soil.

RHUBARB.—Trench and manure your bed in fall, and set the plants in it three feet apart each way. Cover with leaves and coarse manure each winter, and fork in in spring. Six plants will give an abundance of stalks.

SALSIFY.—Sow early in spring, in twelve-inch drills, an inch deep. Thin out to six inches apart, and cultivate the same as carrots.

SKIRRET.—Sow in May, in twelve-inch drills, half an inch deep. Thin out to eight inches, and cultivate the same as carrots or parsnips.

SPINACH.—1. Round-leaved. 2. Prickly.—Sow very early in rich soil, in twelve-inch drills, very lightly. Thin out to eight inches. For winter crop, sow in September; and lay straw thinly over the plants on approach of winter.

SQUASH.—1. Early White-scallop Bush. 2. Honolulu Nectarine. 3. Boston Marrow. 4. Hubbard.—Plant and treat precisely the same as melons—the Bush-squash in hills four feet apart, the others eight feet. They will bear plenty of manure.

TOMATO.—1. Red Cherry. 2. Large Red Smooth. 3. Feejee.—Sow in hotbed and transplant when weather is settled; or in open ground, in May, and transplant when plants are well up and strong. Set them two feet apart, in six-feet rows, with a sloping trellis, about six feet high, to which train the plants. Manure the ground well, and mulch with straw after the first rain in June.

TURNIP.—Early Dutch. For garden use this is the only variety—the later ones being sown in the field. Sow in drills as soon as spring opens, twelve inches apart. Thin to six inches, and hoe occasionally.

VEGETABLE MARROW.—This is treated and cultivated like the squash, the hills being eight feet apart.

TABLE:

Showing the number of plants to be raised on one-tenth of an acre (4,356 square feet) of ground, when planted at the distances annexed:

DISTANCE OF ROWS.	DISTANCE APART.	NO. OF PLANTS.	DISTANCE OF ROWS.	DISTANCE APART.	NO. OF PLANTS.
12 inches.	3 inches.	17,424	18 inches.	18 inches.	1,936
12 "	6 "	8,712	24 "	28 "	1,467
12 "	12 "	4,356	24 "	24 "	1,089
14 "	5 "	9,053	30 "	24 "	880
14 "	6 "	7,544	30 "	30 "	708
14 "	7 "	6,465	36 "	24 "	657
14 "	8 "	5,658	36 "	30 "	586
18 "	6 "	5,868	36 "	36 "	484
18 "	8 "	4,356	48 "	48 "	272
18 "	12 "	2,934	72 "	24* "	363

* See *Tomato.*

POSTAGE-STAMPS.

It has become quite a mania to collect and preserve, in regular geographical or alphabetical order, the postage-stamps of different nations, in little albums made for the purpose. To get a complete set of those issued by every nation is difficult for a boy, but not impossible; and the pursuit, to say the least, is amusing.

It is calculated that over 1,200 different stamps are issued by various governments. Of these, Spain has about 65; the United States, 44; Great Britain and Dependencies, about as many as Spain; Hanover, 34; Prussia, 32; and so on, down to Hamburg, with one.

The way of arranging your stamps is: 1. Geographical—American, European, Asiatic, African, and Oceanic; 2. Numismatical—according to their money value. In each geographical division, each country should have a distinct place.

The engravings in this article will give the young reader an idea of the appearance of a few of the stamps.

NEW GRANADA.

NICARAGUA

In several countries there are stamps issued for special postal purposes. Thus, in New South Wales, Queensland, and Victoria, there are stamps for registered letters only; the latter place has in addition a "too late" stamp.

SPAIN.

SEGNA TASSA.

HONG KONG.

The French have a 10 and 15 centime *à percevoir* label, for affixing on an unpaid letter. The small oval "Segna Tassa," issued for a like reason, is a type of the rest. Wurtemburg has a stamp that is placed on returned letters.

In many stamp catalogues there will be found stamps classed under a separate heading as *Essays*. This is simply a poor translation of the French *Essai*. These stamps are, however, very scarce; in many instances they are proofs taken while the die is in process of engraving. As a good example of this, we give a copy of a Sicilian *essay;* here the lines at the back of the frame are unfinished, and the number of gr. (grano) is not filled in.

SICILIAN ESSAY.

BOYD'S CITY POST.

In the United States we have had several private postal companies, but it is uncertain whether the stamps belonging to them should have a place in our albums. We give above, as a sample, one that formerly existed in New York.

There is in Europe—or there was—only one such company, called the Boten Institute, in Hamburg; the labels are curious, and we think, in this instance, might be allowed to appear as stamps proper, as the Institute was sanctioned by government.

FRAGMENTS.

VEGETABLE SKELETONS.

PROCURE a large earthen open-topped pan, which will hold about a gallon, and put into it some leaves, seed-vessels, etc., of plants; pour over them just so much boiling water as will cover them, and then place the pan upon the tiles of the house, or any other place, exposed to the rays of the sun, or the changes of the weather. Occasionally and carefully stir the leaves, but never change the water. The putrefaction and fermentation will soon ensue, and in about six weeks, or rather more, most of the specimens will be completely macerated, and require no further care than merely to hold them singly under the tap of a water-butt, or a little stream of water, poured from a jug, to wash away all the putrid green pulpy matter. If this matter will not come off easily, when slightly assisted by the thumb and finger, or a small knife, the leaves must be soaked for some short time longer. Such of the leaves as are brittle and liable to break during the rinsing, may be preserved from fracturing by placing them upon a piece of board, and holding them up by the thumb and finger, while the water is running upon them; and if some of the green matter still remain between the veins of the skeleton-leaf, it may speedily be removed by striking the leaf perpendicularly and carefully with a clothes-brush. The maceration and cleansing being finished, the leaves will next require bleaching, which may be done very effectually, by putting them in a band-box, with a small quantity of sulphur burning in a little gallipot by the side of them. The most certain method, however, of bleaching objects of this description, is to immerse them in dilute chloride of lime, or chloride of soda, for a few minutes.

TO TAKE IMPRESSIONS IN PLASTER OR SULPHUR.

The plaster of Paris must be pulverized and sifted through very fine gauze. First rub over the medal or engraved stone very softly with oil, and having wiped it with cotton, surround the edge of it with a slip of thin lead; mix up the sifted plaster with water, stir it gently to prevent it throwing up air-bubbles; then pour it over the medal, or whatever it may be, the impression of which is wanted, and suffer it to harden and dry; it is easily detached, and forms a mould strongly marked. The process by sulphur is the same. Before these are used as moulds, they must be oiled.

TO TAKE IMPRESSIONS FROM SEALS.

Warm the seal a little, rub the end of a wax candle over it, and then sprinkle it with a little Chinese vermilion. Melt the sealing-wax, taking care that it does not catch fire; suffer it to drop upon the paper, press the seal upon it, and a beautiful impression will be the result.

If you wish to produce various colors in the impression, the seal should be powdered with color of one tint, and then impressed upon wax of another; for instance, if the surface of the seal be dusted with lamp-black, the impression will show a red device upon a black ground.

VARNISH FOR ORNAMENTAL PURPOSES.

A beautiful varnish for ornamental purposes may be readily made by the following process. Reduce into powder a stick of superfine sealing-wax, and put it into a phial, together with half a gill of spirit of wine; put it in a warm place to dissolve, which it will do in a few hours, and it will be ready for use. Should it be too thick, it may be reduced by the addition of more spirit of wine till it is of the proper consistency.

The phial should be carefully corked when not in use, by which means the varnish may be preserved for some time.

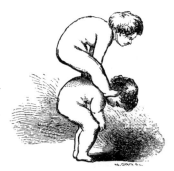

JUMPING AT A CONCLUSION.

INDEX.